STORIES OF AMERICA

LIFE IN PACIFIC GROVE CALIFORNIA

Personal Stories by Residents and Visitors

BUTTERFLY TOWN, U.S.A.

Patricia Hamilton • Illustrations Keith Larson

KEEPERS OF OUR CULTURE
PACIFIC GROVE, CALIFORNIA

Illustrator Keith Larson's grandchildren—the magical Mattias and Kaia Larson

This book is memoir. It reflects each story writer's present recollections of experiences over time.
Some names and characteristics have been changed, some events have been compressed, and some dialogue has been recreated.

All stories submitted for publication appear in this book. Low-res photos were unable to be used. If you submitted a story and you do not find it here, to insure future inclusion, please resend your story as a Word.doc, and any high-res photo, to lifeinpacificgrove@gmail.com

All photographs supplied by individual story writers are used with their permission.
Although the writers and publisher have made every effort to ensure that the information in this book was correct at press time, the writers and publisher do not assume and hereby disclaim any liability to any party for any loss, damage, or disruption caused by errors or omissions, whether such errors or omissions result from negligence, accident, or any other cause.
Please send any corrections with documentation or personal affidavit to the publisher.

All rights reserved. No parts of this book may be reproduced in any form or by any electronic or mechanical means including information storage and retrieval systems without permission in writing from the publisher, except by a reviewer who may quote brief passages in a review.

STORIES OF AMERICA - Building Community One Story at a Time
For all general information contact StoriesofAmerica@gmail.com

LIFE IN PACIFIC GROVE
Softcover: ISBN 978-1-943887-36-1 • FIRST EDITION October 2017; Updated December 2017
Hardcover: ISBN 978-1-943887-54-5
E-book: ISBN 978-1-943887-55-2
Copyright © Patricia Hamilton • Illustrations © Keith Larson
Cover Illustration by Keith Larson
Cover design by Gene Harris and Patricia Hamilton
Book design and production by Patricia Hamilton
Editing by Joyce Krieg, Nina Solomita, Diane Tyrrel, Mimi Sheridan

Published by KEEPERS OF OUR CULTURE, an Imprint of Park Place Publications, P.O. Box 722, Pacific Grove, California 93950
StoriesofAmerica.us • LifeinPacificGrove.com • KeepersofOurCulture.com • ParkPlacePublications.com • Printed in the United States of America

BE HERE NOW

The meeting of two eternities,
the past and future …
is precisely the present moment.
— *Henry David Thoreau*

INTRODUCTION
LIFE IN PACIFIC GROVE

Bill Kampe, Mayor of Pacific Grove

I am so glad that Patricia Hamilton has gathered this collection of stories. Stories of the lives and activities of people who live here, work here, and visit here are the very heart of our heritage.

My wife Cheryl and I have always been fond of this peninsula. We love the coastline, the consistent weather, and human scale of our city, and the charm of cottages in the Retreat area. In my earliest days in Pacific Grove, I heard so much about our heritage as the collection of historic structures. That is the physical part of the city.

Yet our heritage is so much more than the structures from yesterday. It is also the stories of the people who live here, work here, and continue to instill the spirit of what we know of our city today. It's the stories of what real people do, and have done, that connect our memories to the physical structures. The stories make the places special. In the history of Pacific Grove, there are stories of vision and achievement—the grand stories. And equally important, there are the simple everyday stories of humor, the funny things that happen, the whimsical events, and good intentions gone awry, or the special occasions and events that linger in the memory.

When we have visitors, I like to give a quick tour and point out interesting locations. At each of these spots, it's always because someone did something interesting. Or it's something that I have experienced. I urge you as the reader to reflect on your own pattern of how you talk to friends and visitors about our city. I'll venture the guess that you tell them stories like the ones you will find here.

How we ended up in Pacific Grove is part of our story, and I'll offer that, editor willing, to the collection that follows. For me, the stories that I have begun to learn add incredible richness to our appreciation of the city. I hope you will find that the stories here also enrich your appreciation, and add to the lore that makes our city a special place, a place where so many people find relaxation, smile, and enjoy the day.

House Hunting With Cheryl

My wife, Cheryl, had started to ask me, back around 2000, "Where do you want to retire?" Retirement seemed very distant to me. I liked where we were living in the San Jose area and was working at a job I enjoyed. I never had a very good answer, or for that matter, any answer.

Eventually, I noticed that Cheryl changed her approach. She stopped asking where I wanted to retire. Yet as we traveled on vacations and stopped in interesting places, she would ask "how about here?" Over a couple of years, we had a modest list of places that could work. They were small towns, with interesting scenery, and somewhat insulated from the big city feel. We had been to the Monterey Peninsula a few times, and it was on the list. I loved the Pacific Grove golf course.

Then in April of 2003, our company golf club had a tournament at Poppy Hills. Cheryl had taken up painting about a year before, and painted at just about every opportunity. The natural thing was to ask "Cheryl, would you like to go Monterey with me? I can play golf, you can paint, and then you can pick me up afterwards." It was a simple proposal, I thought.

At the end of the day I came into the clubhouse to find Cheryl waiting. She asked how my round of golf was. "Just fine, thank you."

"And how was the painting?"

She answered "Oh, it was too cold and windy and foggy to paint."

So naturally I asked, "So what did you do?"

Cheryl's face broke into an enthusiastic grin and she replied, with a subtle conviction, "I looked at houses!"

There was one house she wanted me to see. The Open House was over, but she said we could peek in the windows … it was not occupied. It was clear we were going to look at that house, that evening.

It was a small two-bedroom cottage near George Washington Park, just renovated. We walked up to a living room window. Cheryl pointed out all the features and described the bedrooms. Then she mentioned a few things that would need to be changed to make them right for us. We walked around to the back yard, a very modest yard. There Cheryl described exactly what could be done with the landscaping to make it more useable and attractive. Then back in the front yard, I asked a question about some feature and she described what would be done there. Oh, my goodness! Cheryl already had the complete end-to-end redo worked out.

Cheryl asked when I'd like to come back to see the house with a realtor. "Tomorrow" would have been a good answer. But we agreed on the next weekend, if the house was still available. The market was very hot, and listings were disappearing quickly. I thought I had a pretty good strategy.

We then went to enjoy a dinner in downtown Pacific Grove, and I realized that I had never actually seen the center of town. We ran into one of my golf teammates at the restaurant and enjoyed our dinner and brief time on Lighthouse Ave.

That house didn't last until the next weekend. Still, Cheryl decided she would go back to Pacific Grove and look some more. She found a new candidate, and again we agreed to go look the next weekend. It was a small cottage on 17th street, a "tent house" near the fire station.

There were a couple of things she wanted to check with me. How often would we hear the sirens as the firetrucks responded to emergencies? And oh, by the way, the back of the kitchen is only 5' 6" high, and would that be OK?

The house was still on the market, and the back of the kitchen was still only 5' 6" high, which wasn't going to work. The even bigger problem was that every door jamb was about 3 inches shorter than I. During my time in the Navy, I had grown tired of ducking to get through doorways. The cottage also had a giant Monterey pine growing against the front of the house. When I asked about it I heard the first of many references to the tree ordinance: "They will never let you take that down." It was the Sword of Damocles hanging over the house.

Still, while we were in town, we had the chance to walk around a bit. That included a stroll down 17th Street to Lovers Point. It was a perfect day—sunshine, modest temperature, and of course, the spectacular coastline. We sat on one of the benches for a while, soaking in the beauty around us. The cares of the world just ebbed away. We also noticed that everyone we encountered was in great spirits. The whole experience felt very good.

Cheryl continued to scout for houses, and when she had a list of prospects, I would go with her to check them out. We saw houses all over town. I heard more tree restrictions, and about historic houses with all the things one couldn't do to change them.

Our original plan was to find a small starter house, and eventually a place that would be a better long term fit. We weren't having much luck, and I'll admit I was still not sure about needing to do something just yet. It seemed a few years too early.

Then driving along Lighthouse Avenue one day in early August, our realtor pointed out a modest Spanish style house and mentioned it had been on the market for a year. It was over our intended price range. Still, it was important that a house feels good to come home to in the evening, and so far, we hadn't quite found it. We said "Sure, let's look."

As we walked in the front door, we immediately felt comfort. There were some complexities in the situation, and that's why it had been on the market for a year. On our drive back to the San Jose area, Cheryl and I decided it was worth a try. So, we made an offer, and set out to resolve the modest issues. I was already starting to connect to folks in City Hall for advice and guidance.

By the end of August, we received the keys, and spent our first weekend here over Labor Day. It was another picture book weekend and a perfect start to our time in Pacific Grove. It was also the beginning of our landscaping and remodel projects, and a gradually expanding engagement in City affairs. And that's another story.

FOREWORD
THE GIFT OF NOW

California State Senator Bill Monning

What a gift! *Life in Pacific Grove* captures the many stories of people who are fortunate enough to visit or to call Pacific Grove "home," people who were inspired to take the time to reflect on their unique histories and capture the present to share the "gift of now."

Author, philosopher, organizer, teacher and publisher Patricia Hamilton has created a gift that will not only connect residents of Pacific Grove in the present but will also capture the connections of experience and humanity that is Pacific Grove to share with generations yet unborn.

My connection to Pacific Grove dates back to childhood visits to the beaches, trails and tide pools to the more recent history of my mother, Betty Monning, living as a member of the Canterbury Woods' community. Our children grew up visiting Grandma Betty in Pacific Grove and enjoying all that included: days spent at the beach at Lovers Point, exploration of tide pools at Asilomar Beach at low tide, standing perfectly still to watch deer graze in a neighbor's garden, butterfly migrations, visits to the Pacific Grove Library and Natural History Museum, and listening to Grandma Betty tell stories of her childhood on the Monterey Peninsula.

Today, I enjoy the honor and privilege of representing Pacific Grove in the California State Senate. So much of our work in Sacramento has a direct impact on Pacific Grove. From school and public safety budgets to environmental protection and tourism issues, we are regularly informed by the needs of the communities we represent. Pacific Grove stands out as a community that is engaged, that cares, and whose denizens do not refrain from speaking their minds and fighting to protect our nation's "Last Hometown."

Life in Pacific Grove presents an amazing collection of the lives and experiences of more than 400 people. People who take pride in their Pacific Grove lives and who were inspired to share a brief insight into what is important at this moment in time.

Patricia Hamilton has shared her mastery of storytelling and has taught and inspired others how to capture the moment with reflection, deliberation, and by answering the call to share.

Patricia's answer to that call can be found in her family's history as pioneering Methodist Ministers and members of the Chautauqua Movement, the 19th century Methodist movement based on a commitment to community building, education, and service to others. With a career dedicated to book writing and publishing, Patricia Hamilton has catalyzed and empowered a discovery process among many in Pacific Grove. They have learned that they have something important to share and that by sharing what is important to them in the moment, they can find new lines of communication with friends, neighbors, and family members. This path of discovery and sharing has even lead writers to find new meaning in life!

In the following pages, you will read a vast array of personal vignettes written from a broad range of life experiences, from 92-year-old Nancy Ricketts, daughter of Dr. Edward Ricketts, to Patricia's 14-year-old granddaughter, Grace McCoy and a young poet in the first grade. What a gift to current family members and future generations!

These contributions cover a range of observations and experiences from music to nature, education to film, science to sports, business owners to community leaders and all with a single common denominator that is Pacific Grove.

Prepare yourself for a collection of adventures that will introduce you to some whom you have never met and probably to some you have known for years. Create and protect the time to savor and absorb as you will be inspired to reflect upon and hopefully capture your own moment in time and the "gift of now."

Writing this foreword has allowed me to reflect on that part of my family's history shaped by Pacific Grove and the gift of my present representation of this beautiful and dynamic community in the California State Senate.

Thank you, Patricia Hamilton, and volunteers who have created this one-of-a-kind compilation that will likely serve as a model to bring other communities together as it fortifies the strong human connections in Pacific Grove. And, thank you for the many contributions of time and resources and for your commitment to share proceeds after costs with the Friends of the Pacific Grove Library, earmarked for the procurement and preservation of historical documents and artifacts. Thank you for the gift of now!

*Senator Bill Monning represents California's 17th Senate District and serves as the Senate Majority Leader. He represents parts of Monterey and Santa Clara counties and all of Santa Cruz and San Luis Obispo counties.

AN INTIMATE VISIT TO BUTTERFLY TOWN, U.S.A.

Introduction by Mayor of Pacific Grove Bill Kampe   vii
Foreword by California State Senator Bill Monning   xi
Preface by Phyllis Edwards   xvii

SECTION 1 – MORE THAN MEMORIES   1

    More Than Memories – Randall A. Reinstedt   3
    A North American Cultural Renaissance   9
    Methodist Minister 1890 – *Semper Progredientes*   10
    In Memoriam   12
    The Heritage Society of Pacific Grove   22
        John Steinbeck   24
        Edward "Doc" Ricketts   30
        12 Outstanding Women Then and Now   32
    Ghostly Goings On   41
    El Carmelo Cemetery   45

SECTION 2 – THE MANY CHARMS OF PACIFIC GROVE   49

    A Unique, Delightful Place to Live   51
    Visitor Information Centers   57
    Our Weather Suits Us Fine   59
    Politicians and Appreciations   64

SECTION 3 – COMING HOME TO PACIFIC GROVE   69

    What Brings You Here?   71
    Finding a House and Making a Home   83
        Writing Canterbury Tales   93
    A Leisurely Stroll Through Neighborhoods   101

SECTION 4 – ANIMALS WITHIN AND WITHOUT   113

    Wildlife, Feral and Pet Animal Friends   115
    Animal Rescue and Adoption   127
        Benefit Shops   129

SECTION 5 - THE GOOD OLD DAYS — 135

    Growing Up in Butterfly Town   137
    Pacific Grove Responds to World War II   162
    Holman's Department Store—Shopping Mecca, Landmark   173
    Friendly Southern Pacific and Del Monte Express Trains   181

SECTION 6 – THE SUPERNATURAL — 185

    Miracles, Magic and Fairy Tales   187

SECTION 7 – A CREATIVE AND LITERATE COMMUNITY — 195

    Artists and Artisans of All Persuasions   197
    Centers for the Visual and Performing Arts   210
    Bookworks and Local Writers   216
    Central Coast/California Writers Club   222
        A Message from the California State President   222
    P.G. Adult Education   241
        A Message from the ESL Program Specialist   242
        Monarch Awards for Exceptional Students   255
        International Recipes from Students   256
    Welcome to the Pacific Grove Public Library   261
        A Message from the Director   262
        Listening to My Elders   263
        Library Staff and Patrons   269

SECTION 8 – DOWNTOWN AND ITS MANY PLEASURES — 279

    Socialize, Dine and Shop 'Til You Drop!   281
    Bike, Hike and Walk About   310
    Movie Stars!   314

SECTION 9 – BUILDING COMMUNITY SPIRIT 319

    Volunteering and the Joys of Getting Together   321
    The Gift of our Community Garden   333
    Sally Griffin Active Living Center   336
    Active Women   338
        Combined Destinies
        Girl's Night Out
    CITY EVENTS—Something For Everyone   345
        Special Feast of Lanterns History   355
            First Person Remembrances   359
        More Memories of Feast of Lanterns   365

SECTION 10 – NATURAL WORLD WONDERS 369

    Pacific Ocean and Monterey Bay Sanctuary   371
    Natural Forests, Parks and Beaches   390
    Monarch Transformations   399
    Pacific Grove Golf Links – All FORE One   407
    Welcome to the Pacific Grove Museum of Natural History   415
        A Message from the Director   415
        "Treasure Trove in the Basement"   422

SECTION 11 – WALKING TOUR OF OUR LITTLE FREE LIBRARIES 427

    "Take One – Leave One"   429
    Downtown Retreat, and Second Addition Areas   431
    Up the Hill from Town to the Third and Fifth Additions   438
    Pacific Grove Acres   442
    First, Third, and Fourth Additions toward New Monterey   445
    Sunset Drive and Forest Hill Areas   450

SECTION 12 – ACKNOWLEDGMENTS 453

    Community Participation   455
        Hero/ine's Journey Memoir Worksheet   462
    Name Index to Profiles and Personal Stories   464-468

IN MEMORIAM—SHARON BLAZIEK, PHOTOGRAPHER

"THE BUTTERFLY EFFECT"

Phyllis Edwards

The Inspiration

The scene is a small, yet airy room located in Jewell Park, Pacific Grove on a pleasant afternoon. The occupants, a rather motley group of adults, have entered the room, seated themselves in chairs around long classroom-type tables, and responded warmly to the cheerful greetings of the group's facilitator, Patricia Hamilton.

Patricia has designed the next nine monthly classes around the theme of present-day experiences, to ground writers in the present and to fully appreciate their life in Pacific Grove today. While students are busy writing their stories, Patricia is completing her own memoir for her grandchildren with her stories of life in Pacific Grove.

These intrepid folks, originally attracted to the offering of "Guided Autobiography Memoir Class" in the abstract, now face the reality that actual writing must soon begin and, as Patricia introduces Theme 1: "How I Came to Live in the Grove," some rather pinched facial expressions appear as writing implements begin to commit thought to print.

The assignment is easy and not a bit beyond the ability or ken of any writer in the room, and thoughts and memories of each participant flow from the internal realm to paper or laptop in a sometimes steady, sometimes intermittent stream.

At the end of the writing period, Patricia invites the participants to read their writings aloud to the group to foster a feeling of community. At this surely not unexpected invitation, discouraging thoughts invade the minds of some. Fears of shame or inadequacy raise their worrying heads and take form as introductory commentary to virtually every courageous writer's offering: "Well, I don't really write very well …" "I don't know, I just …," belittling their story before even daring to share with the group.

Then the magic begins. Spontaneous, authentic reactions emanate from the listeners and each writer's eyes open wide. With each listener's response, thoughts of "Oh, this IS worth writing about …" and, "My little life IS worth something …" begin to replace the writer's former fears. New perceptions emerge in both writers and listeners as they awaken to the realization that what deeply matters to all of them is people and their relationships, here and now.

Sharing personal tales reinforces the sense of connectedness with comments such as, "I can identify with what she said …," "He felt just like I did when …." The power of story has been born: The reticent faces have transformed into those of eager community contributors.

This overwhelming metamorphosis of facial expressions in response to shared autobiographical writing started the amazing process that led to the book you hold in your hands today. Those original classes, based on Dr. James Birren's Guided Autobiography method "to foster the belief that each life is meaningful and something of which to be proud" have initiated a sequence of events previously unforeseen by the writers who contribute, nor even originally by the facilitator who ended up shepherding the project to its conclusion.

Those opened faces of people who love their lives in Pacific Grove brought forth inside Patricia a renewed awareness of how much she, too, loves it here. A reminder that we so often fail to acknowledge the bounty in our lives. The power of just telling and sharing our stories can bring to our consciousness a sense of worth and meaning too frequently allowed to pass us by in the bustle of our daily lives, a sense that we live too fast, turning our attention to the next task/event/moment once the current task is completed instead of savoring the current gift.

The immediate positive response, so overwhelming at the end of that first class, revealed the far-reaching potential. The participants were learning about themselves, seeing themselves in the light of community spirit. The stories people were sharing about their lives in Pacific Grove were so poignant and powerful that Patricia knew immediately that with her extensive background in the publishing industry, she could make a valuable book for the community out of them. But, she also knew how daunting, how time-consuming, such a project would be, and initially attempted to resist.

Fate intervened when Keith Larson, the visual artist in the first writing group, said, "I'll do the illustrations." Patricia knew then that a sacred commission was calling to her. Almost simultaneously came the recognition that she had accomplished big things before and that guidance would come once she committed fully to the project. The book would be a testament to her well-practiced counsel from Johann Wolfgang von Goethe: "Whatever you can do, or dream you can do, begin it. Boldness has genius, power, and magic in it."

While preparing materials for future classes at the "Little House" in Jewell Park, Patricia began to perceive connections with Joseph Campbell's *Hero's Journey* and decided to develop it as a theme for the final class meeting. This theme would remind each of the writers that every day offers a constant, daily opportunity to regard anything that happens to each of us, everything we do, as part of a hero's journey. We can learn to look at our lives as being our own heroes' journeys. To get through each day we face our demons, big or small; we reach defining moments when we figure out what we need to learn; we gain new states of attentiveness and emerge as stronger people—heroes in our own lives—to share our successes with others.

The Process

Thus the project began and its mechanics commenced. Inspired by Napoleon Hill's philosophy of "Conceive, Believe, Achieve," Patricia started with "OK. What do I need to do NOW?" Since *Life in Pacific Grove* would be the sixth collection of people's stories Patricia had completed *pro bono*, she knew the basic steps required to publish a book of this kind.

At first, asking friends and acquaintances in town to write stories was quite easy and straightforward, but it became clear that the challenge would be in convincing people to write their stories about present-day life in Pacific Grove.

Most people she approached responded with, "Oh, sure. I'll tell my grandmother's stories about …" or "Go see my friend; he's lived here for 30 years!" The difficult part was clarifying the purpose of the book: to capture the immediacy of memories. The book would be about the NOW of living in Pacific Grove, what is important to us at the moment, that the lives we live today will be the "good old days" of tomorrow.

Patricia wanted the book to highlight Pacific Grove's diverse faces: all kinds of people in all walks of life. This type of outreach would require a whole team of assistants. She recruited helpers who could gather stories from business owners, public relations specialists, employers and employees, and teachers and students. She always emphasized the opportunity to benefit the community as a whole, as the proceeds from the sale of this book will benefit the Pacific Grove Public Library.

The *Life in Pacific Grove* team became the "P.G. book people," carrying all over town bags and purses full of

bookmarks, business cards, pictures, checklists, writing guides, and contact information (email, website, and phone). Patricia met with members of the Chamber of Commerce, tour guides, local magazine publishers, members of service clubs and special interest groups, and residents of retirement communities.

Soon, the progress of the book became the new topic of discussion all over town, in coffee shops, bookstores, cafés, restaurants, offices, salons, bakeries, shops and, of course, the library. No resident, visitor, or student could escape the excitement about the stories soon to be preserved within the covers of a book, available to all to enjoy now and in the future.

The Butterfly Effect

The publication of *Life in Pacific Grove* brings to life the truth that storytelling is universal, touching every culture in all corners of the globe. It provides evidence that stories have power to build bridges of understanding among individuals and groups that may otherwise appear to have little in common, yet are part of a community's shared culture. An understanding that stories have power—to enchant, to inspire, to entertain, to define our lives, to bring us together as a community—will become apparent as you peruse the pages of this book.

The butterfly effect posits that small changes in the physical world can have unpredictable, larger effects for the entire planet. Similarly, writing our stories and sharing them with others can affect people and their worlds in unexpected ways. While the action of putting our life story on paper may seem like a somewhat futile task at times, the power of the butterfly effect resides within it nonetheless. Even if you sense no specific lesson or purpose can come from writing about a particular episode in your life, you may find that calmness arises inside you, a peace that lingers as you view your life with greater clarity, wisdom and compassion.

The joy you experience reliving moments as a writer changes from one story to the next so that a different person continuously abides in the world in new ways. A sense of "be here now" reframes your view of life; instead of focusing on what happened yesterday or what could happen tomorrow, simply being involved in self-expression is enough. Writing just for yourself causes a greater self-worth to arise, and evokes a new way of being in your sphere.

Even if no one else reads your memoir, the butterfly effect of your personal transformation is at work. The seemingly insignificant exercise of recording personal stories has effects far beyond your immediate perception. Like ocean waves, your new sense of value and significance flows, with or without your understanding, from your way of being in the world to everyone you encounter from that point onward.

The book you hold in your hands offers an opportunity to realize ever more fully the community spirit of Pacific Grove. As you read the individual offerings in this book, allow yourself to experience an awareness that you are a participant in the butterfly effect of life in this special place, to share the awakenings those writers in the first class experienced, and to know that the people and our relationships here do indeed transform our town and, ultimately, our nation and our world.

PACIFIC GROVE
CALIFORNIA

This book is memoir.
It reflects each story writer's present recollections of experiences over time.
Some names and characteristics have been changed,
some events have been compressed, and some dialogue has been recreated.

Your memories may be different ones.
You are welcome to write and submit your own story,
for inclusion in subsequent editions of **Life in Pacific Grove**.
Details at www.lifeinpacificgrove.com

SECTION I
MORE THAN MEMORIES

Randy Reinstedt, *More Than Memories: History of Happenings of the Monterey Peninsula*
Ghost Town Publications, Pacific Grove, California, © 1995, reprints 2001, 2012.
Text for Pacific Grove pages 270–283 reprinted and used with permission of Randy and Debbie Reinstedt, 2017.

Other resources for Pacific Grove history:

Lucy Neely McLane, *A Piney Paradise by Monterey Bay*, 2nd ed. Fresno, Calif.: Academic Literary Guild, 1958.

Kent Seavey and the Heritage Society of Pacific Grove, *Pacific Grove (CA), (Images of America)*, Arcada Publishing, San Francisco, CA, 2005.

Patrick Whitehurst, *Pacific Grove Museum of Natural History (CA), (Images of America),* Arcada Publishing, San Francisco, CA, 2018.

Heritage Society of Pacific Grove, *Board and Batten,* newsletter mailed free to members of the Heritage Society of Pacific Grove, http://www.pacificgroveheritage.org/

Louise V. Jaques, *Story of Wilford Rensselaer Holman,* published by Louise V. Jaques, August 1979.

MORE THAN MEMORIES—RANDALL A. REINSTEDT, historian

"God's Kingdom by the Sea"

The Monterey Peninsula's second oldest city is Pacific Grove. This charming community is known for many things, including its beautiful shoreline, monarch butterflies and Victorian houses. In terms of history, its Point of Pines (Point Pinos) is the site of the West Coast's oldest continuously operating lighthouse. Built in 1855, the lighthouse is still in use. (Incidentally, many people think that Point Pinos was one of the landfalls described by the explorer Juan Rodriguez Cabrillo on his 1542 voyage up the California coast.)

The Point Pinos Lighthouse actually is older than the town itself. Pacific Grove began a little more than a century ago as a seaside retreat. It was a piney paradise that its residents knew as "God's Kingdom by the Sea."

To understand the events leading up to Pacific Grove's founding, we must look back to the year 1873. At that time, much of the property that was to become Pacific Grove was owned by David Jacks, one of Monterey County's largest landholders. In the summer of 1873, Jacks gave Reverend Ross, a Methodist minister, permission to build a small house on his holdings. That house was to become the start of Pacific Grove.

Reverend Ross and his wife both were in poor health. Various medicines didn't seem to cure their ailments. Finally they were advised to seek out a place to live where the climate remained much the same throughout the year. After much research, they chose the Monterey Peninsula.

After only a short time living "amongst the pines," the Rosses experienced a remarkable improvement in their health. Meanwhile, back in the East, Reverend Ross's brother and his wife were also suffering from poor health. During a visit to his former home, Reverend Ross convinced the couple to return with him to his peaceful pine grove.

The move to the shores of Monterey Bay proved to be just what the doctor ordered. The two couples spent much of their time out of doors and lived mostly on fish and game. Soon the happy foursome were all feeling fit. It seemed to them that their cures were almost a miracle.

Many visitors found their way to the Rosses' woodsy residence. It was not long before the reverend's words of praise and feelings of love for the Monterey Peninsula spread to outlying areas.

One of the many guests who visited the Ross house was a Methodist bishop, Jesse Truesdale Peck. Bishop Peck was a member of a group of ministers and church officials who were looking for a site on which to build a church summer camp and seaside retreat. After visiting Reverend Ross in 1874, Peck became convinced that the area around the Ross home was ideal for such a project.

Bishop Peck shared his discovery with his fellow committee members. Soon an agreement was reached. On June 1, 1875, the Pacific Grove Retreat Association was born at a meeting in San Francisco. This historic meeting marked the beginning of a new and colorful chapter in the history of the Monterey Peninsula.

Upon learning of the plans, David Jacks generously contributed both land and money toward the project. Part of downtown Pacific Grove is located on a portion of this property.

During the early years of the Christian Retreat, many of the activities took place during the summer season. Most of the meetings were held out of doors and under the shelter of a huge tent. It was in tents, too, that many of the people stayed while attending these first gatherings.

As the Pacific Grove Retreat became better known, a number of the tent lots were sold. Before long, small houses were being built on the tiny lots and a number of stores were being added to the seaside community.

Early days description

Another 1879 arrival on the Monterey Peninsula was the young Scottish writer Robert Louis Stevenson (as described in Chapter 15, "A Pair of Scots"). During his brief stay on the Peninsula, Stevenson went to visit the Point Pinos lighthouse. In so doing, he stumbled upon the Pacific Grove Retreat. It was the off-season for the seaside resort, and Stevenson found the place nearly deserted. His description of the Methodist campground is one of the best that we have.

One day—I shall never forget it—I had taken a trail that was new to me. After a while the woods began to open, the sea to sound nearer at hand. I came upon a road.... A step or two farther, and, without leaving the woods, I found myself among trim houses. I walked through street after street.... The houses were all tightly shuttered; there was no smoke, no sound but of the waves, no moving thing. I have never been in any place that seemed so dreamlike.... This town had plainly not been built above a year or two, and perhaps had been deserted overnight. Indeed, it was not so much like a deserted town as like a scene upon the stage by daylight, and with no one on the boards. The barking of a dog led me at last to the only house still occupied, where a Scotch pastor and his wife pass the winter alone in this empty theater. The place was "The Pacific Camp Grounds, the Christian Seaside Resort."

Stevenson's description paints a delightful picture of the resort's peaceful setting and charming surroundings. Soon these qualities began attracting people with interests other than religion. The arrival of these people caused the leaders of the Christian Retreat to adopt a set of very strict laws.

The Chautauqua Society

Reverend Ross's "paradise by the sea" soon became home to a number of conventions and get-togethers, including gatherings of the popular Chautauqua Society. This organization began in 1874 at Lake Chautauqua, New York. At first it was a summer training camp for Methodist Sunday School teachers. However, in time, the Chautauqua Society became better known for bringing education, culture, and social entertainment to communities throughout the nation.

The Chautauqua Society arrived at the Pacific Grove Retreat in 1879. Early gatherings were held in a variety of temporary quarters, including a large tent. In 1881, the meetings were moved to a new and rambling wood structure. This building remains a Pacific Grove landmark to this day and is known as Chautauqua Hall.

A number of these laws were meant to help control activities around the resort's popular beach. One law even described in detail the type of bathing suits that could and could not be worn. Other laws prohibited swimming, fishing, or boating on Sundays.

Many other activities were not allowed on Sunday. Among them was the sale of all objects other than medicine. One druggist broke this law by selling a toothbrush to a visitor who had lost his. The druggist is reported to have paid for his mistake with a fine!

A variety of **curfew laws** were also enforced in the early days. One of them required all residents to keep their shades up until 10 p.m. At that hour the shades had to come down, and all lights had to be put out. Other curfew laws were aimed at young people. At certain times of the year, people under the age of eighteen were forbidden to be on the streets between 8 p.m. and daylight.

Gambling of all kinds was also prohibited. Swearing was strictly forbidden. Rude behavior and even boisterous talking were to be immediately discontinued, as they were considered to be not "in harmony" with good order.

Alcoholic beverages, or liquor, could not be bought, sold, or even given away. In fact, the sale of liquor was not allowed in Pacific Grove until as recently as 1969. For many years, this law gave the Grove the distinction of being the only "dry town" in California.

More than laws protected the special character of Pacific Grove. The retreat area was surrounded by a fence with locked gates. The fence was built for a number of reasons. In part, it was meant to protect the peacefulness of the area and to keep out peddlers, wagon merchants, and others.

However, the fence created problems of its own. Before people could drive their wagons and carriages into or out of the area, they had to get a key from the Retreat office. A California state senator, Benjamin J. Langford, has left us an account of how complicated this procedure was.

Langford owned a large house near the waterfront and frequently visited the Grove during weekends. In her book, *A Piney Paradise*, Pacific Grove historian Lucy Neely McLane paraphrases the senator's description of the scene at the gate:

Every time that I pulled up to the padlocked gate with my family, I would have to dismount, go over the stile, hike about a mile to the Retreat office to get the key to unlock the gate, walk back to the gate, drive to the office to return the key in order that others might use it, unload my family and baggage, drive again to the office for the key, drive to the gate, unlock it, drive through, tie my horses, walk back again on foot to the office to leave the key; then, no matter how late the hour or how fatigued I felt, I would have to walk back to my carriage, drive to Monterey to be stabled, hire some equipage to return me to the fence, climb over the stile and limp to my house.* (*Lucy Neely McLane, *A Piney Paradise by Monterey Bay*, 2nd ed. Fresno, Calif.: Academic Literary Guild, 1958), p. 145.).)

St. Mary's Episcopal Church. Pat Hathaway Collection CAViews

A city of churches

In July, 1889, the Pacific Grove Retreat was incorporated as the City of Pacific Grove. Several other events of interest took place around this same time, among them the building of two popular and beautiful churches.

Since Pacific Grove got its start as a Methodist retreat, you might expect that a Methodist church would be the first to be built in the town. However, it was actually the Episcopalians who built the first large church building.

Organized locally in 1886, the Grove's hard-working Episcopalians wasted little time in starting the construction of their church. The impressive structure was dedicated in July, 1887. Modeled after a building of similar design in Bath, England, the Episcopal church became known as St. Mary's-by-the-Sea. This grand old building is in use to this day. A favorite among both visitors and residents, it has become one of Pacific Grove's most prized structures.

Walking in the P.G. Retreat area, you will see small houses, such as this one, built over the original retreat tents, which remain in place under the house siding.

The following year, the twin steeples of a Methodist church rose toward the heavens. This structure was larger and perhaps even more imposing that St. Mary's. Besides being a place of worship, it served as an assembly hall and as a meeting place for summer Chautauqua gatherings. Many noted lecturers spoke there. Among its distinguished guests was United States President William McKinley, who visited the church in 1901.

This historic church became an important building to Methodists up and down the state. For thirty-one years, the impressive structure hosted the California Conference of the Methodist Church. After more than seventy-five years of service this early Pacific Grove landmark was torn down in 1964.

First Christian Church

Members of several other churches were eventually attracted to the seaside resort of Pacific Grove. Over the years, the community has frequently been referred to as "the City of Churches." Two other houses of worship that were constructed before the turn of the century were the Congregational Church (1892) and the First Christian Church of Pacific Grove (1895).

Another important event that took place before 1900 was the purchase of unsold Retreat property by the Pacific Improvement Company. Officials of the company agreed to honor the Retreat Association's goals. With the company's participation, success was ensured for the young community, and important improvements began to be made.

These improvements included the building of numerous new homes. Many of these dwellings were of Victorian design. They can be found in various locations about the community to this day.

In addition to houses, construction began on hotels and other places to stay. Some of these facilities still serve visitors to the Grove. Among them are the Centrella Hotel and the Gosby (originally Gosbey) House Inn, which started out as a boarding house. Both of these Pacific Grove landmarks were built before the turn of the century.

Riding The Rails

Another early improvement was the appearance of the Monterey and Pacific Grove Street Railway. The railway began operation in 1891. Its brightly colored horse-drawn coaches were an immediate success.

The railway's run from Monterey to Pacific Grove was described as "among the grandest scenic roads on the Pacific Coast." This claim may stretch the truth a little, but the trip certainly was interesting. The route led from the magnificent Hotel Del Monte, through California's first capital city, along Monterey's shoreline, and into the pine-forested grounds of Pacific Grove. Along the way, passengers could view many historic sites and interesting scenes.

In 1893, the railway line became known as the Monterey and Pacific Grove Street Railway and Electric Power Company. Ten years later, the two Peninsula communities boasted a "modern" link in the form of an electric streetcar line.

The streetcar line continued to be popular among visitors and residents through the early 1900s. However, as automobiles became more and more common, the Monterey and Pacific Grove Streetcar was used less and less. In 1923, the tracks were torn up, and the line became history.

There were other tracks that led from Monterey to Pacific Grove in the late 1800s. These tracks belonged to the Southern Pacific Railroad. As the Grove attracted more and more people from faraway places, the Pacific Improvement Company and Southern Pacific agreed that the Monterey rail line should be extended to Pacific Grove.

The extension was built, along with a depot and turntable. Soon the Grove became a busy stopping and starting point for the trains that served the Hotel Del Monte. The route was even more scenic than that of the Monterey and Pacific Grove streetcar line, The Southern Pacific's tracks hugged the Grove's shoreline and passed many interesting sights, including the popular Lovers Point area.

Colorful Lovers Point

Lovers Point and its beach have played a colorful part in the history of Pacific Grove. The protected waters and white sands of "Main Beach" (Lovers Point Beach) have made the spot a favorite gathering place for more than a century. From early days the beach and the surrounding area have been the site of such things as prayer meetings, band concerts, and Feast of Lanterns festivals. In the early days, the area also boasted community bathhouses, a Japanese Tea Garden, an ice cream parlor, and a skating rink.

Among the most popular early attractions of Lovers Point were the glass-bottom boat rides. Passengers on these rides could see the remarkable underwater gardens found in the Lovers Point area, as well as many varieties of marine life.

Also quite popular was the beautiful Japanese Tea Garden. The tea garden featured a building of oriental design where delicious cakes and teas were served by women dressed in Japanese costumes.

Hopkins Marine Station

Lovers Point was also the original site of a fine research facility, the Hopkins Seaside Laboratory. The laboratory was established in 1891 by Timothy Hopkins, the adopted son of Mark Hopkins (of San Francisco and Big Four railroad fame). Timothy had visited Dr. Anton Dohrn's famous Zoological Station in Naples, Italy. He returned to America with dreams of a marine research facility that would be operated by Stanford University.

The young Hopkins's plan was greeted with interest and approval. Meetings were held with a number of Stanford University professors. Eventually it was decided that Pacific Grove's shoreline environment and marine life made it an excellent site for the proposed facility.

The Pacific Improvement Company helped things along with a gift of Lovers Point land. Stanford's first president, David Starr Jordan (a noted expert in the study of fishes), became involved in the project. University professors O. P. Jenkins and C. H. Gilbert also helped the station get off to a promising start.

A sizable two-story wood structure was built on the Lovers Point site. A new location was found at Point Cabrillo, near the border of Monterey and Pacific Grove. This site was in the area where Monterey Bay's historic Chinese fishing village once stood. After the move to this location, the facility became known as the Hopkins Marine Station of Stanford University.

This well-known research laboratory has continued to expand through the years, bringing honor and fame to the city of Pacific Grove. Known to scientists throughout the world, the station has gained the respect of all who are interested in the fascinating study of life in the sea.

Asilomar

A second facility that has brought considerable fame to Pacific Grove is the Asilomar Conference Grounds. Tucked into a corner of the Grove, the Asilomar grounds overlook the beautiful blue Pacific. Nearby, rolling sand dunes and twisted pine trees make the setting even more dramatic and appealing. Care has been taken to preserve the forest environment and natural beauty of the site. Even Asilomar's buildings of natural wood and local stone blend with the outline of the land. For these reasons, the Asilomar grounds have won praise from people from throughout the world. They are often pointed to as an example of how we humans can protect our surroundings while providing our needs.

Asilomar's history as a conference site began in 1913 with a gathering of girls from the Young Women's Christian Association (YWCA). The well-known architect Julia Morgan developed the early plans for the Asilomar grounds, as well as for its original structures. (Morgan is probably best remembered as the architect for the fabulous William Randolph Hearst Castle of San Simeon, California.) To this day, the Morgan-designed buildings remain the center of attention and house the majority of Asilomar's activities.

Asilomar's original 30-acre site was a gift of the Pacific Improvement Company. Over the years, the grounds have expanded to more than three times their original size. Following the pattern set by Julia Morgan, later buildings have been designed with the sea, sand, and pines in mind. These structures have won several architectural awards.

Today the Asilomar Conference Grounds are busier than ever. Approximately 200,000 people and nearly 1,000 organizations use the center each year. For residents and out-of-towners alike, the area has truly become—as the word *Asilomar* is frequently defined—a "Refuge by the Sea."

Butterfly Town, U.S.A.

Many other attractions bring people to Pacific Grove. Especially well known are the Grove's many community activities. Three of the most popular are the Good Old Days celebration, the Historic Home Tour, and the colorful Feast of Lanterns Festival, which dates all the way back to 1905. Surfing and scuba diving are also popular Pacific Grove pastimes.

However, most old-timers agree that Pacific Grove is best known for its annual Butterfly Parade. The parade got its start because of the crowds of butterflies that visit the Grove each year. The Monarchs travel from distant places and usually arrive in Pacific Grove during the months of October and November.

During the winter, these orange and black insects make a small section of Pacific Grove their home. On warm sunny days, they fly about the Peninsula, delighting all who see them. When the days turn cold and the fog rolls in, the butterflies can be seen in large clusters as they cling to the branches and leaves of the Grove's "butterfly trees."

Because of the Monarchs' annual appearance, Pacific Grove has become known as "Butterfly Town, U.S.A." To celebrate the arrival of the butterflies, the city's schoolchildren stage a parade each fall. Down the streets they march in a variety of colorful costumes, many of them boasting wings of orange and black. Proud parents and throngs of residents and visitors gather to watch and to help celebrate the homecoming of the Monarch as only the people of a small town can.

With the millions of visitors who come to the Monterey Peninsula, more and more people are discovering Pacific Grove. Some local residents look upon this "invasion" with alarm. They prize the small-town feeling of their community, the beauty of the area, and the friendliness of the people. Today these same attractions are bringing new arrivals to the Grove. Old-timers can only hope that the newcomers will remember what brought them to thisfriendly village by the bay. Then they, too, will help to keep Pacific Grove what it started out to be—a peaceful paradise by the sea..

Randall A. Reinstedt
R. Wright Campbell
Edgar Award Winner

There are two things a writer should possess before sitting down to write about nearly any subject. He should know it and he should love it.

The writer of this book was born right here on the Monterey Peninsula. He played among the same dunes and tidepools, cycled along the same trails that you enjoy. Well, not exactly the same—winds have blown and rains have fallen—but they really haven't changed all that much.

When he grew up, he taught fourth grade for approximately fifteen years. Sometimes he went away to see foreign lands, east, west and all around the world. He always came back with a deeper affection for this wondrous place we share. He came back to teach some more about local history to grownups as well as children. And to write many books, some about ghosts, some about history, and some about legends remembered only by old men and women. He's written down a lot of their memories and published them here and there. In this book he's collected many of them and added many more. And there are lots of other things. This book is more than memories.

A NORTH AMERICAN CULTURAL RENAISSANCE

The Chautauqua Movement sought to bring learning, culture and, later, entertainment to the small towns and villages of America during the late 19th and early 20th centuries. Pre-Civil War roots of the effort existed in the lyceum movement, which paid prominent personalities handsomely to give speeches on religious, political and scientific topics to gatherings in the hinterlands. This was an approach to adult education that underscored the values of an era in which common people were expected to stay close to job and family. Enlightenment, if any, had to be taken to them. Travel and vacations were the preserves of the wealthy. Social changes occurring in post-war America included the emerging democratization of education. On the shores of Lake Chautauqua in western New York, an assembly was held between August 4 and 18, 1874. The organizers were John H. Vincent, secretary of the Methodist Sunday School and later bishop of the Methodist Episcopal Church, and Lewis Miller, an Akron, Ohio businessman. The original intent was to provide a pleasant setting in which to train Sunday school teachers in all Protestant denominations. Eight-week sessions were staged each summer and were later opened to the general public. Within a few years, the idea had been extended to include lectures, discussions, home readings, which recalled the Lyceum movement. Headliners such as Mark Twain and William Jennings Bryan attracted huge throngs, and all of the presidents from Grant through McKinley made appearances. (http://www.u-s-history.com)

Chautauqua Ideals

Jane Flury

Pacific Grove was not born as a summer camp to attract tourists.

It was not a place to party.

It was an out-of-the-way summer retreat for young Sunday School teachers to study and learn about science, nature, other cultures, and the arts. It was quiet and gated. So it would stay quiet.

It was radical in its day.

Pacific Grove was born as the eldest daughter of the ideals of Chautauqua. Pacific Grove was way ahead of its time in study, thought, and ideas. The original creators of Chautauqua (based in Chautauqua, New York) wanted a West Coast annex. Marine biologists from Woods Hole were involved, as were all the entities needed to create a summer program of learning and growth.

What Woodstock was to Baby Boomers, Pacific Grove was to the Chautauqua Movement in 1875.

Chautauqua invented book groups and adult education.

Teddy Roosevelt said about the Chautauqua movement, "Chautauqua is the most American thing about America."

Its efforts to educate a young adult population who couldn't afford college did not go unnoticed by the American public. Chautauqua's height came in the early 1900s when it was reported 10,000 lanterns were sold in Pacific Grove for Feast of Lanterns, also a Chautauqua invention.

Please don't think we were born as a tourist community. We were born as a radical idea to cheaply educate young adults. Hopkins Marine Station lives on as a testament to what the Chautauqua movement created.

Ode to the Chautauqua Hall Tree

Patricia A. Davis

Whatever happened to the grand old oak
The one which graced Chautauqua Hall
Once a grand tree, known for its shade
Watching women with their parasol umbrellas
Men in their top hats
Children scurrying by, laughing, playing, running by
With that twinkle in their eye
But now we will never know the stories it could tell
Such a sad day, when they took it away
We will never be the same, some people say
As more and more grand oaks are taken the same way
Dear fellow Pagrovians
Please hear my plea
For our Grove and for its trees

Shooting Hoops in Chautauqua Hall

Bob Crispin

In high school (1959-1963), a buddy who had been a Scout, had a key to this building. When it was not in use, five of us would just go in and play basketball for hours. It was our private gym. If another group arrived, we would say we were Scouts and leave. We did no damage, just made use of a nice space. We used it for three years, never a bigger group than the five, thus keeping it secret and not letting things get out of control. Good fun memories.

Semper Progredientes
1890 – 2017
Patricia Hamilton

Brief memoir excerpts of the seven generations of my P.G. family lineage, from the Reverends Sylvanus Gale Gale and his wife, Jane Elizabeth Cloyd, to my grandchildren, Zachary and Grace McCoy.

1. Reverend Sylvanus G. Gale/Jane Elizabeth Cloyd

The Reverend Sylvanus G. Gale is descended from the Gales who came in 1640 from Yorkshire, England and settled first in New York, where he was born in 1838. He fought in the Civil War after graduating from Wesleyan University.

In 1862 he married Jane "Jennie" Elizabeth Cloyd, who was born in NY in 1840. Cloyds emigrated to the Colonies from Ireland (originally Scotland) in 1730.

Gales and Cloyds are two of our 23 lines that were here before the American Revolution. Brave immigrants, crossing dangerous seas in small boats to a New World.

For many years the couple served as itinerant Methodist ministers in Minnesota, accepting the appointment as ministers to the Retreat of Pacific Grove 1890–1893.

The photo of the Reverend was supplied by Wesleyan University, where he graduated as a minister and returned later to became a professor.

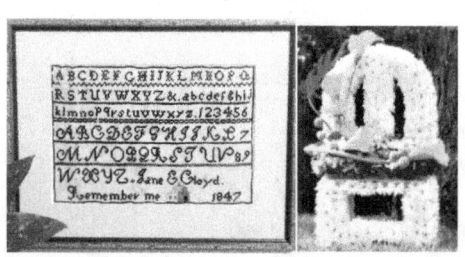

I do not have a photo of Jane Cloyd. Griswold Cousin Evelyn Burris, gave me Jane's Sampler, stitched in 1847 when Jane was seven years old. As she lived in a small western NY village, possibly with no school, this would be how she learned to read and write. Mrs. Trotter recommended Gobel's Framing to preserve my heirloom and Glenn did a beautiful job.

Her obituary in the P.G. local paper reported that at her funeral all the town turned out and there was an "Empty Chair" floral arrangement, signifying the absence of a well loved person who would be missed.

"Jennie" ministered to the physical needs of the congregation as Sylvanus ministered to their spiritual needs. Leading the women's auxillary, she nursed the sick, delivered food to newborn mothers, and headed fundraisers, such as bake sales, for the poor.

Ministers and their families were housed with a family of each congregation to which they were transferred every two years. I believe Rev. Gale and his sons built the first parsonage for the Methodist Church in P.G., and that would have been their first home.

Theirs was a happy family, with respect for each other, always lots of books, music and laughter.

Jane died of a simple nose infection in 1892 (today antibiotics would have cured it). The Reverend was called to minister at "The Oaks" in Santa Clara in 1893. That was his last ministry. He died in 1915 and was buried here in El Carmelo Cemetery beside Jane. Two other Gale children, Mabel and William, are also buried here.

2. Charlotte Cloyd Gale/Charles H. Griswold

Their eldest child, Charlotte "Lottie" Cloyd Gale, attended college at Hamline University where the Reverend was a professor of History and Higher English. In 1882-3 she won a $5 third prize in Greek and a $15 first prize for Latin. She was a founding member of the Browning Literary Society, a sorority at Hamline, whose motto was *Semper Progredientes* (*At All Times Advancing*). At the first public entertainment at Hamline, April 25, 1885, Lottie played a piano duet, "La Baladine," Op. 51, with Anna M. Davis. She also read her essay, "A Hero." In 1884 she was awarded a scholarship and graduated with an A.B. in 1885.

In 1887 Lottie married Dr. Charles H. Griswold, whom she met when they were students at Hamline U.. They became a pioneering family in Modesto, California before the heyday after the dams and irrigation came. I have several fiction and non-fiction books they gifted to my aunts and my mother for birthdays and at Christmas.

Charles' obituary: 1911 – March 22 "C.H. GRISWOLD, M.D. C. H. Griswold, one of the city's leading medical practitioners, is a native of Minnesota, having been born August 16, 1861. He received the degree of A.H. from Hammond (Hamline) University at St. Paul and later too a complete medical course at the Chicago Homeopathic Medical College, graduating with the class of 1887. Following his graduation Dr. Griswold came to Modesto, where he practiced two years before returning to St. Paul, where for thirteen years he was a successful practitioner, before returning to Modesto in 1903. In 1907, Dr. Griswold made an extended trip abroad, spending a year in Germany and devoting his time to medical and surgical research and clinical work at the University of

Berlin and the famous German hospitals and clinics. In 1908 he returned to Modesto and was at once accorded the recognition which his experience and professional attainments entitled him to."

Charlotte was an outspoken Modesto socialite, once urged by many to run for Mayor of Modesto; she declined. She left a recipe for Donotella to be prepared for her funeral gathering. My mother served something similar and we called it goulash.

3. Alice Elizabeth Griswold/Harry Johnson Murray

Their daughter, Alice Elizabeth, surprised her family and married Harry Murray, a peach farmer of nearby Hughson. They visited Pacific Grove to escape the summer heat of the San Joaquin Valley. Alice's wedding dress is on display in the Hughson Historical Museum.

In 1909 Alice gave birth to triplets, one boy and two girls: my mother, Charline, an identical sister, Charlotte, and a brother, Charles. Dr. Griswold delivered the babies, who weighed less than eight pounds altogether. He instructed Harry to fashion a makeshift incubator out of a peach box by making three beds lined with cotton, putting in fruit jars filled with hot water and a thermometer, covering the box over with a glass window pane atop the crate's corner supports, where air was able to enter.

Mrs. Lowry in Hughson invited mother and infants to move into her house for care. For six weeks surrounding neighbors and friends volunteered to come in to refill the jars around the clock to keep the babies warm. It was a point of honor for each woman to say at local gatherings for 60+ years after that: "I helped with the triplets."

Dr. Griswold had been practicing family medicine and after delivering the triplets, he made babies his specialty and became known throughout the county as "the baby doctor." Aunt Charlotte said that's how he got rich—before the triplets he was paid in produce and after they were born with real money.

Alice played the piano and organ at church and at home, where the whole family sang along. Grandpa said she used to care for her siblings and so one hip was higher than the other due to carrying a child on that hip during her own growing up years.

Early photos of Charlotte, Alice, Charline, me, Melanie and Grace all look similar. You can see that we're related.

4. Charline Edith Murray/Claude Fisher Hamilton

Charline and Claude were married in Charlotte and Charles' Victorian home on McHenry Street in Modesto. Aunt Florence, Charlotte's sister, made Charline's wedding dress. My father was a twin, pictured at left with his siblings, Leo, Gladys, Clyde (on the left) and baby Ted, who had polio and wore a brace. Claude worked for his brother Leo for many years, driving teams of horses to level land, and milking cows. Charline was a housewife with seven children—I was the middle child.

1946: Left to right, Shirley, seated on my father Claude's lap, Alice Lorraine, Patricia, seated on my mother Charline's lap, and Richard. Three more boys would be born: Edward, Michael and Robert.

5. Patricia Ann Hamilton/Larry Dean Sawyer

6. Daughter: Melanie Marie Sawyer/Jack Ross McCoy

7. Grandchildren: Zachary Andrew/Grace Erin McCoy

2017: Left to right, Grace McCoy, Patricia Hamilton, Eagle Scout Zachary McCoy, Melanie (Sawyer) McCoy and Jack McCoy.

My grandfather retired in the 1950s from his Hughson ranch to his house on Park Place in Pacific Grove, where I visited often during my childhood. I arrived in 1990 to care for my Aunt Charlotte—the remaining triplet—thereby completing the circle of helping with the triplets.

My grandchildren, Zack and Grace, have grown up visiting me in Pacific Grove, which has been the perfect place to be a grandmother. Maybe they'll live here someday too.

IN MEMORIAM

Gary Kildall
"The Father of PC Software"
David A. Laws

As a technology historian and the semiconductor curator at the Computer History Museum in Mountain View, I was aware that something important to the industry transpired in Pacific Grove in the 1970s. So when I moved to town several years ago, I decided to research the details. Following is a brief history of the development of the first commercially successful personal computer operating system (OS) and the Grecian-like tragedy of the rise and fall of its inventor.

Gary Arlen Kildall was born in Seattle, Washington, in 1942. On graduating from the University of Washington with a PhD in computer science, he taught at the Naval Postgraduate School in Monterey. While living with his wife Dorothy and their two children, Scott and Kristin, at 781 Bayview Avenue, Pacific Grove, he also did consulting work in an office in his backyard workshop for microprocessor manufacturer Intel Corporation. To speed this work, in 1974 he wrote a program called CP/M (Control Program for Microcomputers) that served as one of the fundamental enabling technologies of the personal computer (PC) revolution.

With Dorothy as co-founder, Gary established Digital Research Inc. (DRI) to develop commercial opportunities for CP/M. They opened their first office on the upper floor of 716 Lighthouse Avenue and their software quickly found application in a new, fast-growing market for small business computers. By the late 1970s, DRI had become the leading supplier of operating systems to these users and transformed a staid Victorian residence they purchased at 801 Lighthouse Avenue into a bustling high-tech corporate headquarters.

In 1980 another former residence at 734 Lighthouse was acquired to house the growing engineering staff. Pacific Grove resident and first employee of DRI, Tom Rolander, likes to tell the story of how Gary met with the engineers one Friday afternoon and announced that he was going to give them a raise over the weekend. When they arrived at work on Monday morning the building had been raised on jacks to accommodate a new large computer in the basement. Today the structure serves as offices for the Carmel Pine Cone newspaper.

IBM, the world's largest computer manufacturer, wanted CP/M to power its new PC but demanded a price and other concessions that were unacceptable to Gary. Bill Gates, who had once discussed the possibility of merging with DRI and moving Microsoft to Pacific Grove, acquired an unauthorized clone of CP/M from another vendor and bundled it together with other software to secure the IBM business.

DRI employees at 801 Lighthouse

With its clout in the market, IBM emerged as the dominant PC supplier and MS-DOS as the standard operating system. DRI responded with multi-user, networking, and other enhancements to CP/M years before Microsoft, but by the mid-1980s had lost the OS battle. Novell purchased a shrunken DRI in 1991 and moved the operation to Utah.

When a reporter from the *Times* of London asked how Microsoft had won the IBM business, Gates told him that, "Gary was out flying when IBM came to visit and that's why they did not get the contract." That myth has been debunked by DRI employees who were present, but it stuck. Although Gary contributed many other software innovations, including the first CD-ROM encyclopedia and early code for Pixar, he was forever haunted by the label "The man who could have been Bill Gates." He descended into alcoholism and died in 1994.

My role in this story began when, on recognizing the importance of CP/M, I wrote a proposal to the IEEE (Institute of Electrical and Electronic Engineering) to install a Milestone plaque outside the former DRI headquarters at 801 Lighthouse Avenue. The IEEE Milestone program honors important events in electrical engineering and computing. Achievements, such as Thomas Edison's electric light bulb, Marconi's wireless communications, and Bell Labs' first transistor are recognized with plaques in appropriate locations.

With IEEE encouragement, I approached the city manager about mounting a plaque in the sidewalk. As I had been warned by long-term residents that the process could take years, I was surprised at the positive reception and fast approval of the project. On April 25, 2014, more than 100 former DRI employees, representatives from the Navy, and computer industry pioneers joined Kildall family members and the president of the IEEE to dedicate the plaque that reads:

> "Dr. Gary A. Kildall demonstrated the first working prototype of CP/M (Control Program for Microcomputers) in Pacific Grove in 1974. Together with his invention of the BIOS (Basic Input Output System), Kildall's operating system allowed a microprocessor-based computer to communicate with a disk drive storage unit and provided an important foundation for the personal computer revolution."

Those who are interested in more of the story are recommended to read *They Made America: Two Centuries of Innovators from the Steam Engine to the Search Engine* by Harold Evans. The chapter on Kildall is subtitled "He saw the future and made it work. He was the true founder of the personal computer revolution and the father of PC software." The library has a copy.

In April 2017, the Naval Postgraduate School honored its former faculty member by dedicating the Dr. Gary A. Kildall Memorial Conference Room that included a replica of the IEEE plaque in the university's Glasgow Hall. At the ceremony his daughter Kristin Kildall said, "From the beginning of his career in technology, he valued sharing ideas, moving technology forward and bettering his community. His passion for innovation and ideas was seen throughout his career as a primary force. I am really touched by having the conference room named in his honor. It tells me that his legacy is longstanding, and that he contributed in a powerful way."

More information: "Gary Kildall and the 40th Anniversary of the Birth of the PC Operating System" [http://www.computerhistory.org/atchm/gary-kildall-40th-anniversary-of-the-birth-of-the-pc-operating-system/]

"Groundbreaking Operating System Is Named an IEEE Milestone" [http://theinstitute.ieee.org/tech-history/technology-history/groundbreaking-operating-system-is-named-an-ieee-milestone]

"In his own words" Blog and downloadable version of Gary Kildall's autobiography [http://www.computerhistory.org/atchm/in-his-own-words-gary-kildall/]

"Former NPS Professor and Personal Computing Pioneer Memorialized on Campus" [https://my.nps.edu/-/former-nps-professor-and-personal-computing-pioneer-memorialized-on-campus]

"Three Tenors" and Tibor Rudas
Phillips Wylly
producer, director

It is unlikely that many Pagrovians know that the large building at the northwest corner of 16th and Lighthouse was for many years owned by Tibor Rudas.

And fewer still know anything about Tibor Rudas. He is the man who created and presented in concerts all over the world, "The Three Tenors," Luciano Pavarotti, Placido Domingo and Jose Carreras. A remarkable achievement for a truly remarkable man.

Tibor was born into a humble Jewish family in Vienna, Austria. His talents began to manifest themselves when, as a five-year-old, he began singing and dancing on street corners for the Austrian version of nickels and dimes. In those pre-war and pre-Nazi days, the Vienna Opera Company maintained a school for talented youngsters. Someone from the school discovered Tibor. But then the Nazi regime came to Austria and teenage Tibor was sent to a concentration camp. On a train bound for one of the death camps Tibor and the other prisoners were set free when the train was overtaken by Allied soldiers. How he got from that point in his life to "The Three Tenors" and Pacific Grove would fill a book. A book his daughter Kimberly is, I believe, writing.

Tibor, his beautiful wife Lee and their two children, Kimberly and Dean, lived here on the peninsula for many years and became close friends of ours. There are few people for whom I have more respect and admiration than Tibor Rudas.

Living in the Moment
Stan Maliszewski

As her best friend for 53 years, and her husband for 48 years, I didn't think it was in Judy's best interest to navigate in a wheelchair through two international airports from our home in Tucson, Arizona, to Pacific Grove, California. Judy's cancer was rapidly spreading, resulting in the decreased ability to use her dominant hand and arm, and her walking was limited due to low energy and stamina.

Three months prior to her last visit to Pacific Grove, during a gathering of family and friends in our home, Judy thanked all for their support during the past seven years, and announced that she was refusing to agree to a more aggressive form of chemotherapy. As part of her comments, she said, "We don't get to choose how we die, but we can choose how we live, and I choose to live in the moment."

A couple of days following this gathering, we started to plan for a trip to Pacific Grove. Although we traveled to numerous states, and a few international locales, we agreed that Pacific Grove was our favorite destination. During our numerous visits, we always wanted to stay at the Seven Gables Inn. However, our travel budget didn't allow for us to stay there in past years. This trip was different from our former visits, and we made reservations for four nights in their best available room. Indeed, it almost seemed like our room was on top of the ocean.

Judy's stamina was quite low and leaving our room was difficult for her; however, we were able to dine out a couple of nights, and especially enjoyed the view from the Lovers Point Beach House. Each evening we drove south on Ocean View Boulevard and stopped to watch the sun go down. While viewing the beauty of the bay, in a more quiet moment, I said, "Jude, your cancer is spreading. Would you like to talk?" Her response was one that will never be forgotten. She said, "If you want to talk, I will listen, but look, the sun is going down, such a beautiful sky, look at the waves, seagulls everywhere, and people walking on the beach. I want to live in the moment and enjoy it all."

It was necessary for Judy to rest in bed the majority of the days of our stay at the Seven Gables Inn. One afternoon, she sat up in bed, gazed out the window facing the ocean, and said, "I feel like I am living a dream. It may not seem like it, but I am having a great time." After four days of what we both declared to be the best visit we ever had to Pacific Grove, we left to fly back to Tucson. Judy died ten days after returning from Pacific Grove in our bedroom with a framed print of BookWorks, the book, tea and coffee shop on Lighthouse Avenue, hanging on the wall. I seriously doubt that any Pacific Grove resident or visitor could have lived more "in the moment" than Judy did during her last visit to feel the magic of Pacific Grove.

In March 2017, I made another visit to Pacific Grove, the first time since Judy died. My visit was simply delightful, and I felt Judy's spirit so strongly. While strolling on Fountain Avenue, I met Steve Hauk working in his Hauk Fine Arts Gallery located directly behind one of my favorite restaurants, Aliotti's Victorian Corner. I appreciated meeting this talented writer, Steinbeck scholar, and compassionate individual. Our open conversation about the recent loss of his beloved wife, Nancy Hauk, resulted in my feeling an immediate bond with Steve. Nancy's many legacies to historical and architectural preservation, and quality of life in P.G., as well as her artistic talent, coupled with Judy's spirit of living in the moment, capture the essence of why I will continue to return to Pacific Grove.

Big Kid David Kuwatani
Alex Hulanicki
consultant, adjunct English/Journalism instructor

There's a kid in all of us. But David Kuwatani's "kid" was a Big Kid, and he was always playing football, especially the 49ers and the Breakers. He always knew the odds, sat in the stands, read the sports pages, watched the games on TV and talked about his teams.

Eight-ball and ping-pong. Whatever the game, he played it at the Rec Club.

Golf, he was always part of the Nisei tournaments and swinging his broom like a golf club. He knew Rancho Cañada like the back of his hand. Of course, when you've been all over that golf course, like David and his buddies were, you get to know the entire course.

And you get to know the players. All the players. Let's call them "kids"—whether they were five or 45 or 75. David knew them all and they knew him as they shared their childness, not childishness but childlikeness. The kid in all of us.

How many thousands of times has David been there— at the ball park, basketball court, swimming pool, tennis courts? How many balls, strikes, physical errors made by kids, mental errors made by grown men who thought they were kids again, has David seen, laughed at or groaned at? And how many million rocks did he pick up from the quarry they call a softball park in Pacific Grove? Where do those rocks come from? Grading the infield for all those years, David must be in China by now. And, of course, those rocks skinned up a million knees and caused a million kids to shed tears and cry for help. Of course, David always came to the rescue.

Those rocks were boulders to the nine-year-old kids David took care of in Peanut League every summer. Now, the ballpark has grass for an outfield—it's not the same.

But David was always the same—a nine-year-old kid. With a playful grin, even when he tried to be serious.

I can't remember David being stern. John Miller, longtime Recreation Director who is now with the American Softball Association, knew David, too, for he knew him as a mentor, friend and employee. Donald Mothershead carries on the tradition of David and John. And their mentors, Topper Arnett and Ruby Nodilo.

As teenagers, John and the rest of us went to Rec Club (now the Teen Center), and sometimes we played Friday night socko in Monterey. David drove us to Jacks Park in the "Green Goose," an old-fashioned SUV, which somehow only David could kick into first gear.

David always had a knack to fix things, to calmly go about his job, to ignore the frenzy around him. It was that inner calm that a kid has inside of him or her, while outwardly a temper tantrum may erupt. But David's calmness always overcame the tantrums of the kids of all ages around him, even when they were trying to protest what they thought was an unjust call by the refs or umpires. David always backed up his staff. He wasn't going to let the "kids" get their way.

For that, we must remember David and thank him now for always bringing that inner kid to the surface in all of us. He was not only a Big Kid, he was a Big Brother to all of us, at a time when what was called the Greatest Generation was hard at work, and the Baby Boomers were unleashed and put in the care of Pacific Grove's Recreation Department. Where is the next David if there is no city recreation program to care for the city's future generation? Will that make Pacific Grove truly the last hometown?

With great appreciation, let's give thanks to the Kuwatani Family for its donation of $10,000 to the Lovers Point swimming pool in memory of David Kuwatani.

David Kuwatani died at age 57 on April 15, 2000.

Memories of Mom in Pacific Grove
Ann Doerr

It often seems that the very best things in life are those experienced and shared with others ... so it seems with some of my fondest, most enjoyable memories of our more than 35 years living in Pacific Grove. To know Pacific Grove is to love Pacific Grove ... we feel so fortunate to have been able to make this our home and have always appreciated the unique charm, quality of life and sense of community that makes Pacific Grove so special.

Here are a few of those memories of the days shared with my mom in Pacific Grove, from her very first visit when she walked in the door to be greeted by our very big, very loveable, shaggy dog bounding across the room to welcome her ... through several years of her visits. One of my sisters and her family were living here ... great for all of us!

But those visits for Mom included some especially memorable days—unique to see the "world" through the eyes of four of her beautiful grandchildren ... exploring in the creek, and "plays" performed especially for Grandma with originality of content and costumes unique to the creative minds of bright children ... storytelling and sharing favorite books from the library. Of course there was often a tea party that included not just dolls, but Grandma in a place of honor.

So many evenings by the fire ... and so many walks by the bay. Sometimes in the calm we would be charmed by playful sea otters, or humbled and awed by the crashing waves so typical to winter days. A thermos of hot coffee and homemade biscuits, fresh out of the oven, were a special treat during our walks, a day on the bay with a picnic to enjoy. Mom was always an eager and fearless crew member.

Masquerading as "Trit Trot the Clown" when Rainbow Studio had its debut, and the honor of her presence when we opened our gallery in the La Porte Building with a champagne reception enjoyed and attended by friends in our Pacific Grove business community ... attending St Mary's on Sunday mornings ... a full house for Thanksgiving weekend with all the "deliciousness" of a holiday shared. So many lovely lunches and dinners to celebrate a special occasion at our favorite, Fandango!

On weekends when we were working, Mom was left on her own to explore and enjoy her favorite haunts: Pacific Grove Florist, Bittersweet, The Bookworks, her beloved library, and of course St. Mary's Thrift Shop. She often came home from St. Mary's with a precious treasure to gift us with. She would enthusiastically regale us with her exploits during a cozy happy hour by the fire. Mom never once complained about the cold, foggy summer days, just bundled up and embraced them.

It was always our hope and plan that one day she would be with us in Pacific Grove. She imagined herself an active member of St Mary's Parish, a docent at the Aquarium where she was so proud to be a charter member, and a volunteer at St. Mary's Thrift Shop. Sadly, that day will never come but we all had the fun of looking forward to it.

No matter what happens in this life, we will always

have our memories, so precious, so dear. It is one thing no one can take away from us.

This contribution is in remembrance of my mother and all the wonderful memories we hold dear from her visits, and her love for Pacific Grove and so many memories shared.

Forever in our hearts, A loving daughter

Mrs. Phillips: A Special Teacher
Gone But Not Forgotten
Keith Larson

It was the first day of school at Forest Grove Elementary, second grade for me. I had run home crying because I thought Mrs. Phillips wasn't going to be my teacher. My mom came back with me to make sure everything was OK. I can remember the three of us talking outside room B-4, Mrs. Phillips looking down and assuring me that I was to be in her class. That's how special this teacher was to her students. She always showed an undivided interest in you beyond any requirements; this was Jacquelyn Phillips' reputation throughout her career.

I was one of those students who needed extra attention, I felt cared about and I tried to respond with the best behavior that I could, although many times I could not meet my best intentions. I was one of the afternoon kids, as we were called. Starting school later in the morning, we went home later in the afternoon. The morning kids started earlier and got to go home earlier; this way both groups would get some hours of more individual attention.

Mrs. Phillips gave me a set of Hardy Boys books that her family wanted to give away. It was very special for me to receive this as I loved reading these mysteries. At story time she would read books to us like *Charlotte's Web*, or sometimes we'd get to have an informal time of playing with clay and just talking with each other. Mrs. Phillips gave each of us a small cypress tree when we graduated, a symbol of this area and for the growth she hoped for each of us. Some of the kids, including myself, imagined that we would be building tree forts in them soon.

Every year through sixth grade I would get a graduation card from Mrs. Phillips, a memory that has never left me and in some ways becomes more important as I get older and count those in my life that gave to me without condition. Through high school I worked as a custodian in the summer times, and I remember Mrs. Phillips coming into the cafeteria where the custodians were having lunch. She wanted to make sure to give them a little end-of-the-year present before leaving for the summer.

I had come back to town after being away for a number of years, and was talking to my friend Hal Hodges, who had also been with me that year in Mrs. Phillips' class. He mentioned that she had passed away only a few weeks before I got back to Pacific Grove. I decided to go over to the school and stand in line once more for the last time outside of B-4. I had made a small watercolor that I slipped under the door.

A book with stories about Pacific Grove wouldn't be complete without mentioning this teacher, and if you are reading this and knew her, I can see in my mind's eye a faraway look as you recall the kindness and interest that you couldn't help but feel from her. In writing this piece I am hoping I can give something back and that she will receive all our collective grateful good wishes and thanks for being the one to step into the pages of our life stories just when we needed her most.

Linda A. Jacobs 1950-2013

published in the *Monterey County Herald* on January 27, 2013; currently on display at Alpha Stationers

Linda Arlene Jacobs was the only child of Roy and Audrey Jacobs and was born at Fort Dix, New Jersey. Her father, a highly decorated veteran of WWII and the Korean Conflict, moved his family to Pacific Grove in 1954. Linda attended P.G. High and MPC before going on to UC Davis for her BA in English Literature and UC Berkeley for her graduate degree in Library Science. Linda's intellectual prowess was evidenced by her 4.0 GPA in college. As her college friend and roommate put it, "Linda wouldn't recognize a B if she saw one."

Among the many extraordinary qualities Linda exhibited were her giant intellect, dry wit, photographic memory, eclectic reading and music interests, accomplished knitting skills, gourmet cooking and master of the spoken word.

Linda went to work for what was to become the present-day Alpha Stationers in 1974. As store manager and buyer, she cultivated many long-term friendships and acquaintances among her beloved customers. Alpha Stationers was the focus of her life, and she flourished there.

Linda would want to acknowledge the love and caring of her many friends, especially in the last months of her life: Cynthia Siebe, Richard Flaig, Barbara and Ashley Streetman, Peggy Schmidt, Marilyn Brown, Deborah Taylor, Judy Fede, Laurel and Teresa Costen, Linda Beaudin, Leslie Lathrup, Connie Pearlstein, Dr. John Hausdorff, Dr. Karen Tierney, Dr. Brad Tarnier, Lilly Wolfgamm, Hospice of the Central Coast, and her beloved Sierra Sisterhood buddies: Barbara Simmons, Ann Stephenson, and Beverly Allen. The world will be a lesser place without Linda.

Dick and Becky Iverson
Jane Roland

I have been a student of people most of my life and thought it was an interesting way to pass time or waste it, depending on one's viewpoint. Then I met Maxine Shore, who was a writing instructor extraordinaire at The Carmel Foundation. She taught us that people-watching and random thoughts are the fodder for journalists. The spider takes a fragile strand and weaves a web. The writer has a glance at someone or hears a few words and weaves a story. But the story is fiction. And, as we know, the truth is more compelling than the made-up speculation. The following is an example of this:

In 1999, when we opened the annex to the SPCA Benefit Shop two doors down from 216, I put out a call for volunteers. Along came Dick Iverson, a long-time customer/acquaintance. When we spoke of Dick, it is "Dick and Becky," because it is rare that one was seen without the other. They were scheduled for Wednesday afternoons, and for seven years, with few exceptions (including surgery for each), they were at their post. When I left, they did as well, but we kept in touch via email.

Dick's life could be the basis of a movie starring Tom Hanks. Here is a man who grew up in Salinas. He worked in a produce packing plant after school and during the "big war," joined the Air Force. He was a flying radio operator on C47s. They hauled everything everywhere and while it was not the best of times, it opened the world for a man whose exposure outside of California was limited. His group helped evacuate Omaha Beach, a time, he says he has never forgotten: traumatic, tragic and rewarding.

Returning to Salinas after the war to a job which was too limiting in scope, he started corresponding with a cousin who had moved to Alaska. That was all Dick needed, the call of the wild, the song of the sirens that lured sailors to their death, but Dick not being a seaman was lured to adventure.

He bought a used VW van and took off. His short visit to our 49th state lasted for nine years. His first base was Anchorage where he looked, unsuccessfully, for work, doing odd jobs as they came along. Venturing forth, our young explorer came to Fish Creek on Kenai Peninsula, which is highly touted now as a site for holiday fishing. Stopping for a night at the Silver King Lodge, he was able to barter services for supper and a bunk. As it happened, the owner, hard-headed and single-minded, had dismissed her handyman, jack-of-all-trades, and Dick was there. Need I say more? For room, board and a little change to rattle in his pockets, he remained for seven years. But again, Madam Wanderlust intervened and he was off hoping to make a killing in the commercial fishing industry. The venture was not as lucrative as he had hoped, leading to another career, driving a bus. The time was not wasted, as he built a house from scratch, and from scraps of wood he created a sled. Now, if you build a dog sled, what do you do? You look for dogs. From seven teams he was given seven dogs; he had hoped for the best, but got the worst. It didn't matter to Dick; he loved them, they loved him, and they raced. He was president of the Sled Dog Racing Association in that area. He kept a red lantern because his team came in an hour after the event was finished.

Adventures have a way of ending—a time to grow up and face the world, or at least, that is the anticipation. I am not sure Dick ever grew up, much to the delight of all of his friends. His mother was ill, so he returned to California and the packing plant. During his shift at night, he filled the time making silver jewelry. Again, when you have a sled, you get some dogs; when you have jewelry, you rent a shop on Fishermans Wharf. It was called The Yellow Door and was located where the Wharf Theater now stands. It was the "Age of Aquarius" and Dick went with the tide. He created peace symbols out of silver, leather items, and sold posters, which were in demand. Once when a customer asked him if he had any roach clips, Dick learned a new skill which sold like … well, like roach clips would at that time.

Time marches on and that end of the wharf was demolished to make room for the new. Once again he was out of a job and what does one do when one is out of a job? He buys a balloon business and becomes a clown. Dick created animals from balloons, and did balloon displays in Pebble Beach, once using 5000 balloons at an event at the Beach Club. His favorite was at the Aquarium where guests were greeted with thousands of blue and green spheres waving gently to the sky. Dick, the clown, was entertaining at parties, special events and the Monterey

County Fair. He became so successful at creating balloon figures, once designing a 100-foot dragon, that he sold the clown part of the business and concentrated on balloon art. He lived in Pacific Grove for 35 years.

There were always dogs. We remember Becky specifically because she was one of our team; she had her own name tag, and she came to work, attracting customers from all over. Generally man adopts beast; in this case beast adopts man. Becky lived across the street from Dick but loved him so much that the neighbors, who had gotten her and her brother from the SPCA, felt she should be his for real, so he went from "Uncle Dick" to "Dad." He was a baker, a humorist, a kind soul with infinite wisdom, loyal and true, and his own man. They volunteered briefly at AFRP, but infirmities did them in, and Becky became Phil Crivillo's watchdog at Casper's when she was up to it. Dick sat outside holding court. They made the world a better place.

Becky and then Dick left us in 2008. Mr. Balloon Man and his girl are floating around heaven, entertaining the angels.

Honoring Honor
Sarah Weber
resident, teacher

I find it hard to think of living anywhere other than Pacific Grove, not just for the beauty and mild climate, but also for the support of this loving community. We moved to Pacific Grove in 1999. My sister, Honor, and her family also lived in town.

In October 2010, our families' lives changed forever. My lovely, vibrant, bright sister was diagnosed with an inoperable brain tumor. This was as devastating as one would imagine; she had a busy life, a busy husband, and two kids then ages 11 and 13. Once diagnosed, it took that insidious disease three years to claim her life, and the story to tell is in how our community rallied around my sister and her family.

Honor was one who gathered friends and kept them forever. She was also one who contributed in quiet ways to helping others, without judgment, without fear and without expectation of reciprocation. When her tumor took over her life, our community organized and filled in gaps and helped in ways one cannot imagine.

After a very invasive biopsy, an aggressive regimen of radiation was ordered, which meant that from December well into January, a rotating group of three people each day converged on the house early in the morning. Kids were sent to school, husband off to work, Honor up and dressed, Monday through Friday. "The Posse" made the 170-mile round trip five days a week from Pacific Grove to UC San Francisco. At the return, all was put back into place. The "Sienna of Silence" was filled with gossip and laughter, and, of course, her cancer. Some friends set up schedules; an account was set up to help with dinners and a donation account was established to help with finances.

Schedules were set so that in the early days, she was rarely alone and near the end, she was never alone. Neighbors came several times a week; every week, family came out from all over the country. The endless parade of friends and family that came to see her over those three years still astounds me! They filled the house with laughter and joy. This helped balance the three years of watching her challenges and ultimate decline.

When Honor's time here was done, we threw her a party. I have to say, it was the best send-off I have ever seen. About 300 people came and celebrated her life. It was a true testament to just how special she was to so many. I miss her every day, but love and appreciate the loving community of Pacific Grove that came together and helped us on this journey for her.

Virginia Stone
Friendship – The Staff of Life
Jane Roland

My friend, Virginia Stone, died a few days ago. She was a beloved teacher in Pacific Grove when she was Virginia Hummel. I dreamed about her last night and have been thinking about our long history. We were very close for many years. However, our connection commenced long before I knew her. I was in Pebble Beach visiting with my mother; it was 1952, and I had a friend, Freddy Mills, who was a recent Harvard graduate. One night at the Mission Ranch I met his roommate, Don Woodward. I saw a good bit of him over the next few weeks. He was Ginny's brother.

Years later I met her mother, Lillian. Some of you will remember "Moss Landing Footnotes," the column Lillian wrote in the *Monterey County Herald*. Lillian was her own person, strong, with a divine sense of humor. She was one of my mother's best friends. She lived in Moss Landing during the week, where her son, Richard, ran the office and Lillian wrote her weekly column and pumped gas for the fishing boats when needed. She spent the weekends in the guest house of her daughter, Virginia. Every Sunday, Frannie Doud would drive her blue Rolls Royce chariot to The Church of Religious Science in Monterey. Along the way she would pick up Marge Allen, Lillian (across the street from Marge on Trevis Way in Carmel), Nell Calder and my mother. These ladies would attend the services and often have lunch. The aforementioned Marge Allen loved to entertain and had garden parties if there was any occasion she could dream up. Lillian was always a guest, as was my mother and I (if I was in town). When John and I married in 1972 we were always included in these gatherings; we seemed to be favored by these older folk and enjoyed many parties at their homes. Very often Lillian and I would sit together on a sofa; neither one of us mingled if we could avoid it. I never met her daughter.

In 1984 our friend, Mildred Lancaster, wanted to put together a bridge game once a week during her husband Harry's poker night. She found a fourth, the husband of her former neighbor, Virginia Hummel, to whom Ben Stone was married. Ben was a jewel and a happy little bridge foursome was started and lasted for years (another connection, Ben was from Walla Walla and knew my cousin Harry Morse). When we met Virginia (who generally used those nights to attend concerts), there was an instant click. Before long she and I realized that we had much in common, not the least of which was the love of reading. She had been an outstanding history teacher at Pacific Grove High School and is still cited with praise and adoration. A Steinbeck scholar, she filled her students with a thirst to learn more.

I invited her to join my book club, and we took many day and often weekend trips with the Foundation or Shirley Jones. There are few people with whom I was closer; we shared our joys and sorrows. There was nothing that was forbidden in our discourse. I have had only a couple of friends like that, and one lives in North Carolina. So, most of my emotions remain in my mind. Ben and John liked each other enormously and the two couples spent many happy weekends in San Francisco, more often than not attending plays. We had a small group of friends with whom we celebrated birthdays at dinner at the respective homes, went to football games, and had parties. While she was still living we saw a lot of Lillian, and also Don, who was a newspaperman and for a time had the publication *In Pacific Grove*, I think when Neill Gardner gave it up.

We also had a mutual love of animals. Until Ben left us there was no dog in the ménage, but always a cat. The two I remember are Lupine and Casey. Casey was the errant feline who got trapped in a tree for several days, a traumatic period for all. The same kitty would spend dinner parties at their home draped around Ben's neck. However, he adored dogs and our pups were most excited when they came to visit. We watched the Super Bowl with them and Ann and Andy Simpson. If there were more people, we didn't see the game, which we enjoyed. Holidays were often enjoyed together.

Virginia was with us the moment Ben died. He had been at Westland House and our friend, Terry Durney, was in *State Fair* at Western Stage. The three of us and Rod and Sue Dewar drove over to see him. The doctors had assured Ginny that there was no reason she shouldn't take a break from her constant vigil. What did they know? She called the facility during intermission and was told that her husband had died. It was July 16, 2006.

They had been such a close couple that Virginia suffered deeply, but she had her children, Chris and Chip, and Ben's son, Ben Jr., who had become as close to his stepmother as if there were no "step" in the phrase. There were her brothers, Richard and Don, both of whom have since departed and, of course, many friends. She soldiered on and soon resumed many activities that had been on hold. She joined our little movie group, and attended parties and the book club. She adopted a little dog and two cats. Life was becoming good again. Sadly, the last couple of years have not been kind. She had a number of falls and other physical problems and, despite the support of her family, her body could not survive the various trauma and she died in her sleep a couple of days ago. I can only think that she is enjoying another life with those she loved who had left. Those who are left behind can only be joyful that she was in their lives.

I regret that I was not a better friend at the end. We talked of setting up a play date with our pups, but it never happened. My excuse is that five days a week I am occupied and on the weekends am either too tired or too busy with household things that I postpone visits. If I had it to do over I would find the strength and the time. I am sure she knows that I will miss and always cherish her.

Jane Roland lives in Monterey and is the former manager of the AFRP Treasure Shop. She is a proud member of the Rotary Club of Pacific Grove which underwrote the cost of the frolicking whales in Berwick Park. Gcr770@aol.com

An Inspiring Teacher–Virginia Stone

My name is Chungte Cheng, a 1984 graduate of Pacific Grove High School. I'm writing to thank you for the heartfelt reminiscence that you wrote on Virginia Stone in a late 2016 issue of *Cedar Street Times*. I was fortunate to have "Ms. Hummel" as my English teacher for three semesters during my first two years at PGHS. She was an inspiring teacher who made literature come alive and I was sad when she told us that she would not be able to continue to teach the spring semester of my sophomore honors English class—that was to be her last semester before retirement, and she had asked the school to reduce her workload. After her retirement I had wondered from time to time what had happened to her—your piece provided a much-appreciated glimpse of her later years.

Regards, Chungte

S.F.B. Morse and Pacific Grove
Charles Osborne

I am just finishing a book on Morse, my grandfather and Jane Roland's uncle. In my research on his life I found out quite a bit about his work in Pacific Grove.

Many people rightly associate Sam Morse with Pebble Beach, but his first developments on the Monterey Peninsula were in Pacific Grove. His history with Pacific Grove had its ups and downs, but his final impressions on the town were very positive.

Sam Morse came to Monterey in 1915 as the manager of the Pacific Improvement Company, the holding company for the Big Four's non-rail assets. His job was to prepare the properties for eventual sale. These properties included most of the Monterey Peninsula and vast acreage in Carmel Valley.

The P.I.C. had bought David Jacks' land holdings in the late 1870s, which included most all of Pacific Grove. Jacks had started selling small lots to the summertime Chautauqua families to pitch their tents. By the time Morse had arrived on the scene the town had developed considerably. He decided to sell all the remaining lots in the town proper and focus on the area near the Lighthouse he called Pacific Grove Acres. That project began in the 1920s.

The P.I.C. owned a large hotel in P.G. called the El Carmelo. It was built in the 1880s to handle guests while the luxurious Hotel Del Monte was being rebuilt after a fire. Once the Del Monte was rebuilt, the El Carmelo provided a less expensive alternative for vacationers to the area. By 1917 the El Carmelo was losing money and Sam decided to sell it or tear it down. He went first to the city council and offered to sell it to them for the value of the land. They declined, thinking that he would continue the operation. This was a mistake. Morse immediately had the hotel carefully deconstructed and used the lumber for the new lodge in Pebble Beach. He sold the lot to W.R. Holman, a gentleman who at times was at odds with Morse, but they remained good friends for life. W.R. was one year older than Morse.

By 1923 Holman had built his department store, but he was worried about traffic if the Presidio decided to eliminate access through New Monterey in the event of war. Holman started a drive to connect Pacific Grove with Highway 1, cutting through Pebble Beach. This was not in Sam Morse's vision for the forest. As the county's biggest employer he held considerable sway and was able to convince the chair of the Board of Supervisors to block the construction. Holman went on the offensive and organized the city behind the highway plan. A compromise route was developed and Morse backed down.

In the 1920s Morse, after he had bought out the P.I.C., started the development of Pacific Grove Acres. He built a nine-hole golf course and laid out plans for larger lots on streets that contoured around the terrain. He offered the golf course to the city for an unusual price, a $10 gold piece and a promise. The promise was that the city had to maintain and water the course for five years. The city accepted.

There was a railroad line that ran around the waterfront into Pebble Beach where a sand plant existed. The sand would be refined at the plant, then shipped by rail to factories making fine glass and other products. Eventually Morse decided to close the strip mining operation down and eliminate the rail line. Southern Pacific had stopped running the Del Monte Express, and the connecting line from Pebble Beach was no longer viable. That was in the late 1950s. I remember as a ten-year-old riding with the engineer on the last train to P.G. Morse gave the land the railroad ran on, and the right of way associated with it, to the city, again conditionally. The condition this time was that they would not allow any construction on the ocean side of the line.

Over time Morse continued to be involved with P.G.. His final act was to help start Beacon House with "significant early financial support" per that organization's website. Beacon House was founded by Mary Clark Ross as one of the first alcoholic treatment programs.

Morse had firm opinions on most everything, but he was clearly negative about New Monterey. When the canneries were operating the whole area smelled like dead fish, and the planning department neglected their job, in Morse's opinion. When asked about a solution he suggested a bonfire.

Morse went on to spend most all his time in Pebble Beach and the country club area, but we have him to thank for keeping our coastline free of development.

The first story about the El Carmelo comes from Morse's Memorabilia, an unpublished autobiography. The Holman story comes partly from a 12/31/81 MPH article. The P.G. golf story comes from the golf course website regarding its history, and the comments about burning down New Monterey is another quote from the *Herald* on 5/22/1989.

Mildred "Millie" Gehringer, organizing the children prior to the parade. Circa 1952

Remembering Millie
Helen Gehringer

In 1939 the Pacific Grove PTA ladies decided to plan a parade for children, followed by a bazaar to raise funds for their organization. As recreation chairman, Millie Gehringer was appointed to organize and direct the first Butterfly Parade, and she continued in that capacity for the next 27 years!

Before it became a school project, the children marched from the post office to the ball park and some were so small, Millie had to recruit the Boy Scouts to help them up the hill. On arrival at the ball park the bazaar was set up and a beautiful pageant was performed in the afternoon and evening.

The parade wasn't Millie's only accomplishment. She served on the City Recreation Board for eleven years, taught first grade at Pine Avenue School, became the first Principal at Lighthouse School, and a few years later, the first Principal at Forest Grove, where she remained until her retirement due to failing health.

Millie led the 50th parade in a vintage fire engine and at that time commented she didn't think she would be around for the 75th.

Those who knew Millie were saddened by her passing in 1991, but she left us with the enduring legend of our autumn parade.

"Here's Lookin' at Ewe"

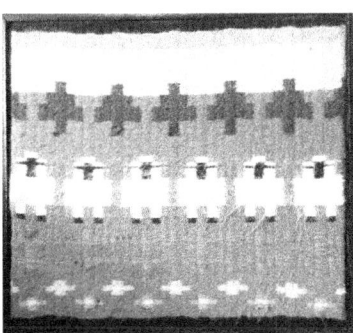

Sally Higgins, Berta Jones, Nadine Annand
Patricia Hamilton

Sally Higgins was my outspoken, quirky, artsy and funny friend—and a friend to many. My grandchildren loved her too. Sally comes from a long line of creative, strong women. Berta Jones was Sally's mother. An inveterate weaver, her house was stacked with weaving machines and books about weaving. She wore many of her colorful creations out on the town and you couldn't miss her, with her multi-colored woven coat, skirt, beret, and the carved wooden cane with a woven tassle tied to the handle. Her brightly colored weaving above is labeled on the back: *A tribute reminder of all the wool produced by all the sheep. Bound weave sample II. "Here's Lookin' at Ewe," Berta Dec 1986.* Nadine Annand was Berta's sister. The Nadine Annand Gallery in the P.G. Art Center is a fitting tribute to this caring, compassionate woman. Our precious Sally was a member and active in the Center for decades as well.

THE HERITAGE SOCIETY OF PACIFIC GROVE—JEAN ANTON, historian

Historic Home Plaques

You have probably seen many of the green plaques that are on the older homes in Pacific Grove. They contain the first owner's name and the year the home was built, or, more accurately, the year it was first assessed.

Since 1978 the Heritage Society of Pacific Grove has given away, free of charge, over 700 of these plaques to homes built before 1926. Such homes must retain their original character and architectural style. An old wooden cottage covered with stucco would not be eligible. A house torn down and rebuilt exactly the same way would not be eligible. But a house remodeled or added on to over the years is eligible as long as it's in harmony with the original structure, and the original characteristics are retained and apparent.

The most common reason for refusing a plaque is the mistaken belief that it somehow limits what you can or cannot do to your house. This is not true. There are numerous examples of homes in Pacific Grove with plaques that have additions and alterations. Some consider plaques the finishing touch to a renovation or rehabilitation.

The plaques are made through a team effort. One Heritage Society volunteer gets the redwood and cuts it to size. Another volunteer does the lettering, and then the plaque is taken to a third volunteer who does the routing. The plaques are painted by a local professional (paid for by the Heritage Society), and then they are returned to a volunteer who puts on the finishing material.

We want the plaques proudly displayed as a reminder of our heritage in Pacific Grove. It gives recognition to the age of the structure and the first registered owner. It is considered an honor to have a plaque on your house.

Plaques must be requested by the property owner. After the request is made, the property is researched, and, if it qualifies (meets the age requirement and retains its original character as determined by the board of directors), a plaque will be crafted with the year that the building was erected and the name of the owner at the time the property was first assessed for improvements.

Ketcham's Barn

The Barn at Laurel and 17th in Pacific Grove, fondly known as "Ketcham's Barn," was built in 1891 by H. C. Ketcham who used it to house animals. Hay and other provisions were brought inside to the loft. A rope and pulley mechanism is still in place. In 1903, Ketcham sold the barn to E. Cooke Smith, who was a banker and real estate agent. Cooke owned a horse and buggy that he used to transport potential customers to Pacific Grove. He used the barn to house the horse and store the vehicle.

The barn was used as a cabinet shop for a short while, and a 1914 Sanborn map reveals that the barn was used as a garage for automobiles. For many years the barn went unused and vacant, and become a sort of refuge for "lost souls."

The property was purchased by the City of Pacific Grove in 1979 and is now leased to the Heritage Society for $1.00 per year. Reconstruction of the barn was completed in 1981, and it now houses a number of local museum articles. It is also used as a meeting place for the Heritage Society Board of Directors.

The Heritage Society also maintains the adjacent lot and has added a wishing well, benches, and plantings that provide a pleasant park area for the community.

The barn is open to the public from 1:00 to 4:00 p.m. every Saturday and by appointment.

Heritage House Awards

Each year in May the Heritage Society of Pacific Grove presents awards to houses and buildings that have been remodeled and upgraded during the year. We also honor new construction and commercial buildings that are exemplary and that fit in with the styles of Pacific Grove.

We seek nominations from the community, and then a panel of judges visits each building nominated. The highest award given is a bronze plaque, carefully crafted with an image of the Heritage Society Barn and letters that designate the house as a Heritage House. Only a few bronzes are given each year, but other houses may receive a certificate of commendation.

In a special ceremony at Chautauqua Hall we acknowledge the owners, contractors, and designers with a community event featuring photos of and stories about each project.

I think I was destined to live in Pacific Grove. When I was growing up my mother had a scrapbook with photos of her family posing along the P.G. shoreline. My grandfather rented a house here each summer to get his family out of the hot Sacramento Valley. My grandmother's journal, which I still have, is full of entries about the Feast of Lanterns and picnics at Lovers Point.

I spent my first eighteen years near the shores of Clear Lake, where the temperature can rise to 105-plus on a July or August day. I hated the hot weather even though I worked summers as a swimming instructor and we water skied in the evenings. My brother and I raised sheep and had horses. But the best weekends were when Dad decided we needed to cool off and spend a few days in Fort Bragg. I cherished the feel of a new sweatshirt as we approached the coast, and I welcomed the look of the fog approaching, knowing it would bring us a few days of comfortable weather.

Next I headed to UC Davis, where the weather was even hotter in the summer. So, how lucky was I to land my first teaching job in Pacific Grove ... where I taught for 39 years!

I'll never forget the day I signed my contract. It was sunny and the "Magic Carpet" was in full bloom. In a family photo I am posed near the "$500 fine for molesting the butterflies" sign, wearing a green dress, and I'm completely surrounded by purple ice plant. It was a happy day. My adult life was about to begin. Over the years I taught history, English, PE and Home Ec, and coached the tennis team, all at Pacific Grove Middle School.

In 1974 I was able to purchase a 1906 beach cottage in the Retreat area, which got me interested in the history and architecture of Pacific Grove. This cottage has served me well over the years and has been remodeled and added on to several times. I'm very proud of the Heritage House bronze plaque that was awarded in 1989 for the remodel to the house. A second award from the Heritage Society came in 2013 for another remodel and addition.

Now retired, I am giving back to this wonderful community by volunteering in many ways, including chairing the Beautification and Natural Resources Commission (BNRC), participating on various city committees, being on the Heritage Society board, singing with Monterey Peninsula Voices, and helping at the Tourist Information Center. I attend Jazzercise at Chautauqua Hall frequently; Tuesdays are kept open for golf. I love walking on the Rec Trail and working in my garden. And I love running into former students who still live here and who are carrying on many local traditions with their families. I love to travel, most recently to Nepal, Antarctica, Brazil, and Australia, but I'm always happy and proud to come home to Pacific Grove.

11th Street Cottage

JOHN STEINBECK IN PACIFIC GROVE—DIXIE LAYNE, historian

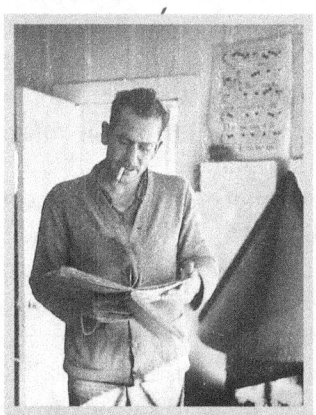

John Steinbeck in the 11th Street cottage living room reading a manuscript c1934

Pacific Grove Was John Steinbeck's Muse

It is where he both celebrated life's successes and mourned its losses

John Steinbeck was born in Salinas but Pacific Grove was his muse.

John was only six when, with his parents and siblings, he made his first trip to the small 11th Street vacation cottage in Pacific Grove that his father built. Growing up, John spent many weekends and holidays at this cottage near the bay where, with his youngest sister Mary, he explored the rocks along the shoreline with their tide pools filled with creatures, was fascinated by the ruins of the Chinese settlement at China Point (Cabrillo Point), and watched the fishing boats cross the bay empty and return to the canneries laden with fish. From these experiences, John developed a love of the natural world and diverse cultures that later figured so prominently in his works.

By the time John was 12, his maternal grandmother had moved from her King City ranch to Pacific Grove. For the next five years she lived on Central Avenue, just down the road from the Steinbeck family cottage. Thus began the family's migration from the valley to the shore. It was here John's resolve developed to become the "best writer in the world" when he was in high school, and where he began filling notebooks with his early efforts. John graduated from Salinas High at 17 and entered

Stanford University that same year as an English major. For seven years he only attended school sporadically, often not registering for classes, and taking only classes that piqued his interest.

During his Stanford years, John repeatedly left school to travel the country, taking jobs where he could at whatever fascinated him. His sister Mary later joined him at Stanford, and in 1923 they both enrolled in a three-month course of general zoology at Hopkins Marine Station in Pacific Grove. Coincidentally, this was the same year Ed Ricketts moved from Chicago to join his business partner in Pacific Grove, where they opened Pacific Biological Laboratories on Fountain Avenue.

In 1926, John left for New York City to become a writer—an experience he often described as disappointing. He soon made his way home, working as a deck hand on a freighter, traveling via the Panama Canal.

Carol Henning Steinbeck c1940

Four years later he married Carol Henning, a hard-drinking, salty-tongued, early feminist he met in Lake Tahoe, and shortly thereafter moved to Pacific Grove, where his father provided them with the 11th Street cottage and a $25 monthly allowance. This arrangement enabled John to pursue his craft, and although it started as a period of rejection, he kept at it with Carol's support and his father's encouragement. Later that year, John met Ed Ricketts, who lived up the road, and their close friendship developed. It was during this six-year period that John would usually write until late afternoon, then walk the two blocks down the hill toward the bay and along Ocean View Boulevard to Ed's marine supply lab. Carol worked days as Ed's secretary in support of John's literary efforts. Her nights were spent typing his manuscripts, correcting punctuation and very bad spelling, and warding off the "Irish in his writing" with her strong editorial hand. For six years John and Carol lived in the little cottage, most of that time spent in abject bohemian poverty.

Steinbeck family cottage on 11th Street c1940

John and Carol spent much of their time on the bay in a launch fishing and sailing—the fish were a valuable addition to their diet. It was here on 11th Street where their circle of friends gathered for evenings of talk, potluck and cheap wine, and where the young author mastered his craft. He published four books, beginning with *The Pastures of Heaven* in 1932, followed by *To a God Unknown* (1933), *Tortilla Flat* (1935), and *In Dubious Battle* (1936), and began work on *Of Mice and Men, Grapes of Wrath* and *The Red Pony*. He also wrote many of his short stories during this time that were published in *The Long Valley (1938)*.

Unwanted attention to his celebrity precipitated John and Carol's leaving Pacific Grove in 1936 for Los Gatos, where he finished *Grapes of Wrath* with Carol's encouragement and strong editorial hand—plus, she gave the book its title. John won the Pulitzer Prize and the National Book Award in 1940 for the *Grapes of Wrath*. Over the next three decades, John would return to Pacific Grove often. In 1941, shortly before he and Carol separated, he purchased a cottage on Eardley Avenue and it was here he wrote *The Forgotten Village* and parts of *The Sea of Cortez*. During this period he found refuge in his sister Esther and her husband Carroll's cottage in the woods on Asilomar Boulevard, where he continued to work on *The Sea of Cortez* with Ed Ricketts. John and Carol divorced in 1942, and he married Gwendolyn Conger in 1943. John and Gwen also lived in the Eardley Avenue cottage for a short time before leaving for New York City. While in New York, John wrote an essay published in the *Monterey Peninsula Herald* in July 1946, where he remembered the Peninsula and taunted the latecomers to California for romanticizing it.

"There was a great Feast of Lanterns—a hundred decorated boats, said the posters. Actually seven boats turned up and four of them forgot to light their lanterns. On the first turn three of the boats wandered away; on the second three more got lost, but the remaining boat went around and around for two hours completely oblivious to the hysterical cheers of the spectators. It is to be prayerfully hoped that this spirit continue—that no city planning—no show business overturn this magnificent attitude. The pledge that it will be kept should be made on the graves of the Elks who were late for the parade and the Eagles who never got there at all, and the fishermen that went around and around."

John Steinbeck, Gwendolyn and their infant son Thom c1944

For the next six years John lived in New York and traveled abroad. John was preparing to leave for Pacific Grove in May 1948, when he received devastating news—his friend Ed Ricketts had been hit by a train. Although Ricketts lived for three days after the accident, Steinbeck arrived "home" the day after his friend died. He had made the trip without Gwendolyn; his second marriage was ending. He moved into the 11th Street cottage and worked extensively on it and its gardens, painting the cottage a color he called "stud red" to celebrate his return to single life. In a letter to his friend and publisher, John described the cottage on 11th Street as "a good way stopping place and a good one to come back to—often." While in Pacific Grove he worked on the screen play "Zapata," met Elaine Scott, returned to New York in 1949, and married Elaine the next year. He began to spend summers in Sag Harbor, in a cottage that was an East Coast version of the 11th Street cottage in Pacific Grove. In 1956 he gave the 11th Street cottage to his sister Elizabeth, who lived there until 1989. After her death in 1992, Elaine Steinbeck gifted the cottage to Elizabeth's heirs. In 1962, Steinbeck received the Nobel Prize for his body of work. In 1964 he received the U.S. Medal of Freedom.

John and Elaine Steinbeck c1962

For nearly two decades John lived in New York and wrote. His affection for his time in Pacific Grove gave him place and characters for some of his work: *Cannery Row, Sweet Thursday, How Edith McGillcuddy Met RLS*. In 1961, John returned briefly to California for the filming of *Flight* in Big Sur—a place his mother had taught school.

John died December 20, 1968, in Sag Harbor, New York. Recognizing his enduring affection for Pacific Grove, his family placed a box with his ashes in the garden of the 11th Street cottage for two nights before its burial in the family plot in Salinas. John Steinbeck loved living near the ocean—Pacific Grove was his home.

©2016 Dixie Layne All Rights Reserved

Steinbeck: The Untold Stories
Steve Hauk
author, gallery owner

It seems I wrote *Steinbeck: The Untold Stories* almost by accident. It just kind of happened.

It began with, I guess, being a reporter for the *Monterey County Herald*—in my travels for the newspaper, or on drives with my late wife Nancy throughout the county, meeting people who had first or second hand stories on the author.

Some stories were harrowing—among them, a young couple hiding Steinbeck in the back seat of their car so he could visit his dying mother in Salinas unseen, or a casual reunion of high school classmates several years later that almost turned violently tragic for the writer with the arrival of a gunman.

I think I approached Steinbeck in reverse, becoming interested in his life before his writing, which I had also done with another great writer, Anton Chekhov. But in Steinbeck's case, I was living in the region where he had lived and created.

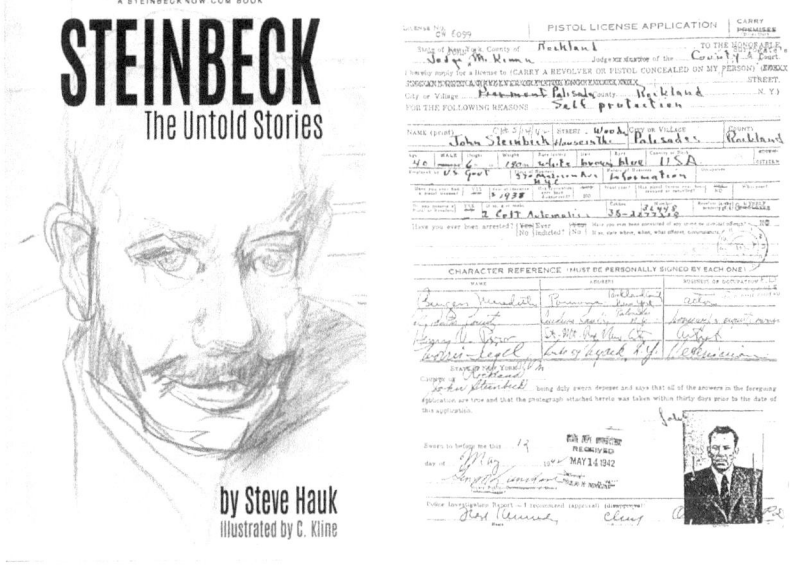

Then in 1998 I was asked to co-curate the inaugural art exhibition at the National Steinbeck Center in Salinas with Patricia Leach, and that settled it: people began bringing me art, letters and documents that related to the writer, including the previously unknown or forgotten New York gun license application that appears on this page.

Suddenly some of those stories I'd heard of threats and danger sounded less like paranoia and more like reality. So I wrote pieces about it for a now-defunct writer's site, then the *Steinbeck Review* and SteinbeckNow.com, the publisher of my book.

While I enjoyed writing those essays, they were not fully satisfying. I wanted to write how it might feel to be endangered for what one believed and wrote. And how it affected those artists, actors and friends who were part of Steinbeck's world.

That's when I began fictionalizing *Steinbeck: The Untold Stories*, and Monterey artist C. Kline began illustrating it. Things happen.

Nancy and I Chose PG

Where you choose to live can have a profound influence on your life.

Around 1970, Nancy and I decided that with two young daughters, it was time to buy. We looked and looked. It came down to a decision between two houses, one in Pacific Grove, the other in Carmel Woods.

We were torn. Both had their positives and negatives; both were smallish (tight budget). We finally opted for the Pacific Grove house, on Lighthouse in the vicinity of St. Angela Merici Catholic Church, known to most as simply St. Angela's.

So the years pass. Nancy serves on the city's Architectural Review Board and Planning Commission while breaking down standardized test biases for McGraw-Hill's California Testing Bureau, venturing into inner cities to make sure kids get a fair break. Once she bravely takes a subway into Brooklyn to witness testing at an elementary school even though the *New York Times* warns that "Violence Escalates on Brooklyn Subways."

Back home, when she finds the time, she paints, capturing in watercolor Pacific Grove and the Peninsula. The missions, the adobes, and Point Pinos Lighthouse intrigue her as well as, when traveling, the French countryside and village life.

For a time we are friends with Pacific Grove residents Gary and Dorothy Kildall. Gary is a genius, eventually creates CP/M, a computer software program that, as Sir Harold Evans writes in his landmark book *They Made America*, underlies every desktop or laptop system in use today. Think of that, coming from our town.

As a journalist I get interested in former Pacific Grove residents John Steinbeck and Ed Ricketts. One day photography historian Pat Hathaway comes up our walkway and says, "Did you know Ed Ricketts and his family lived in your house in the 1920s?"

I tell Nancy, "Oh my God, we'll never leave now." She laughs.

While holding our jobs and raising our daughters, we open a gallery in Pacific Grove. Intriguing people frequently come through the door, including a man who claims to be a Mossad agent. Of course I have to write about him, and do—a play.

Gary Kildall dies tragically. I write a play generally inspired by what he went through, call it "A Mild Concussion." It doesn't get performed, but now, finally, it appears it might.

I co-curate the inaugural art exhibition at the National Steinbeck Center, "This Side of Eden—Images of Steinbeck's California," and write pieces on Steinbeck for the *Steinbeck Review* and the website SteinbeckNow.com, then a book about him, *Steinbeck—the Untold Stories*.

Earlier I wrote a play, *Fortune's Way*, about the great Impressionist E. Charlton Fortune, who did her first liturgical commission at St. Angela's—just down the street from our house. This play does get performed.

Nancy, meanwhile, serves on the Library Board and becomes a founding member of the Heritage Society of Pacific Grove. She continues to produce beautiful paintings and the library does an exhibit of her work, "Loving Watercolor—Paintings by Nancy Hauk." Then, thanks to a generous donor, the library names that gallery for us.

Now and then I reflect how amazing it is that these nationally and internationally prominent people—Steinbeck, Ricketts, Fortune and Kildall, and some others of considerable note—all created, if at different times, in the small town of Pacific Grove.

The town has become part of us, we part of the town. And I can't help wonder, if we had chosen the Carmel Woods' house, what path would we have taken? Would it have been as fulfilling? I hope so, because it was a near thing. It could hardly have been richer.

Steinbeck's Sister Beth
Marion Petersen
as recounted to Jane Foley, May 2017

They met at the emergency room of the university hospital in San Francisco as their children were being treated in critical care. Some time after that, when Lois realized Salinas was not too far from where Beth lived, Lois began to visit Beth Ainsworth in Pacific Grove. Lois would invite my friend Marion along from time-to-time. They had become fast friends while working in an elementary school in Monterey. "We just hit it off!" Marion proclaims. So this is how Marion Petersen came to know John Steinbeck's sister.

Beth lived in the Steinbeck summer home on Ricketts Row in P.G. "When you walked in, the smell was musty, reminiscent of the tenement houses I grew up in," she remembers. There was an old-fashioned drain board and sink, "like a granny house." The mildew conjured pleasant memories of Marion's childhood with her mother in Boston. "Lois was always delivering hand-me-downs to Beth," recalls Marion. She was a prolific reader so when she had amassed enough of them, Lois would take books over to Beth, along with sweaters and other articles of clothing.

"I really liked her," Marion comments. "You could see John in her features—which is not exactly a compliment for a woman!" Beth was not happy that her brother's fame brought the family such notoriety. "The Steinbeck name was everywhere, like the theater on Cannery Row and other buildings in town," according to Marion. She felt her privacy was unfairly invaded. "After all, Beth was a Steinbeck *too*!" Then she adds, "John Steinbeck was not well liked by the people in the Salinas area at the time. Books like *The Grapes of Wrath* put them down, put them in an unfavorable light. Beth didn't exactly care for him either. Dare I say that?"

When they'd arrive, Beth would invite them in and offer them "drinkies." "Beth liked her G and Ts!" You'd have to meet Marion. This former school secretary does not strike you as the type for drinks in the afternoon, nor for that matter drinks at any time—but that is the fun of it! Beth would hand them a tumbler full of gin-and-tonic and the ladies would chat until they were done. When it was time to go, Beth would insist they have a second "drinkie." "Beth would go driving that Lincoln of hers buzzed on the *first* one," according to Lois.

Marion and her husband regularly attended annual Christmas dinners for members of the Monterey Bay Aquarium. Local authors would sign their books for the guests in the lobby of the Pasadera Country Club. Thom Steinbeck was there one time. "It was quite an experience to see him. He looked just like his father." It was a long line but when she got to the front, Marion handed him several copies of *Down to a Soundless Sea* to inscribe for herself and her children. "There are times you have only one shot at things," said Marion, "so I decided to go for it!" She approached him, "Mr. Steinbeck, I knew your Aunt Beth," uncertain how he would respond.

"Oh?" he looked up at her. "Did you ride with her?" he asked. "She was a terrible driver!"

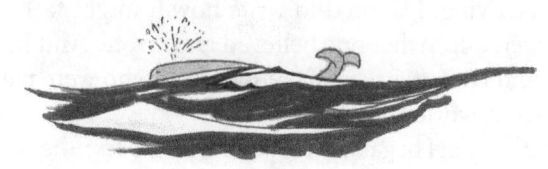

Feeling at Home
A Tale of Two Sister Cities
Madeleine Griffith

Set on the green and pleasant coast of California, where granite outcrops meet the sea at Lovers of Jesus Christ Point, our town of Pacific Grove stretches a bit on its flats and then climbs its way up to Huckleberry Hill. There it shares a street with New Monterey, then ambles along a coastline carpeted with blooming, purply-pink colored succulents to Spanish Bay, where Sunset Drive traces a southern boundary into the piney woods of Pebble Beach.

In all, you could say Pacific Grove faces northwest, a direction which Taoists believe points to the Gates of Heaven.

In 1988, Glastonbury, set in the county of Somerset, England, was decreed Pacific Grove's civic sibling. Glastonbury Tor, a rock and clay hill built near the town in the Iron Age, once stood partially submerged by a tidal estuary that ebbed in and flowed out each day. Rumor has it that Joseph of Arimathea docked his boat to load tin onto this great, grass-covered landmark. Other stories regarding a cup he was carrying and lost on site inspired later generations of knights to look here, there and everywhere for it. It is yet to be found…but I digress.

As we read the plastic placard at the foot of the Tor, it says that we now stand at the entrance to the Underworld. Fear not. Subsequent monks topped the Tor with the magnificent St. Michaels Spire. Whether it was to keep shady souls contained below or to keep us out is still a matter for conjecture.

Back in Pacific Grove, our founding fathers and mothers kept the heathens out and locked its citizens in with a different strategy: roll the sidewalks up at six o'clock then swing closed a gate at Eardley and Pine at nine; once secured and shut, it stayed shut till dawn.

By the time my family arrived in 1958, the only gated street was a student-operated traffic sign which we could swing forwards and back to stop cars at Lighthouse and 17 Mile Drive. When the bell rang at three o'clock, I was one of the belted and capped Lighthouse Elementary School safety monitors chosen to run out to the street to pull and swing the traffic gate. It was a coveted assignment.

Once done, my cap and belt turned in, it was time for a pickup game of baseball with the other 6th graders. Our diamond was drawn on a tree-shaded patch of ground across from our 5th and 6th grade classrooms. How good it felt to feel the ball connect with my bat, to watch it go up and up into the trees, even if I didn't score.

After our game, I cut out down a path where the Butterfly Sanctuary is now located. I pushed through weeds onto the train tracks behind Crocker Avenue, which was my preferred route for my after-school walk home. I would alternately skip over railway ties or balance on the rails as I approached the end of the line, the sand dunes by Asilomar Beach.

On other days, nestled into these dunes, I read *The Grapes of Wrath, Look Homeward Angel* and *The Adventures of Huckleberry Finn.*

Not far from where I now live is the cottage Steinbeck's father built for his family at the turn of the century as a summer place to escape the heat of the Salinas Valley. Steinbeck once said that of all the places he'd ever lived, he felt "most at home" in Pacific Grove. Later in the 30s, he wrote *The Grapes of Wrath* and *East of Eden* here.

His hometown of Salinas, twenty miles due east of here, is a city on the plain between the Gabilan and Santa Lucia Mountains. In some ways it shares features not unlike what you might find in the great Somerset plain where Glastonbury sits in England's green and pleasant land.

Whether called Avalon or Camelot, Arthur's kingdom was thought to be close to Glastonbury, and bears a bright likeness to the locale in *Pastures of Heaven,* a collection Steinbeck wrote early in his life. Here he and his boyhood friends would play amidst chalky cliffs, imagining themselves to be knights of the round table.

After *East of Eden* was published in 1952, Steinbeck moved back east to New York, never returning to Pacific Grove or Salinas. The truth he told in this new novel was too disturbing and accurate for some of its readers in his hometown. They "invited" him to leave for "other parts."

What he wrote in *East of Eden* it is still true today. I find most of his books to be that way. Seems the people who give out the Nobel Prize for literature agree.

As he lay dying, Steinbeck told his wife Elaine that the happiest year he spent with her was when they lived in Somerset. At first glance, this might seem to contradict his telling another that he felt most at home in Pacific Grove. Yet I can understand this. One can feel "lost, unhappy and at home" all at the same time and still be okay. In baseball, if you hit one out of three it is still way better than batting zero.

To lose one's place in a setting, or the sense of being at home, is another matter entirely. So, in order to remain "at home" here in Pacific Grove, I will hold off on my tell-all book about Elmarie Dyke.

Cheers!

DOC RICKETTS IN PACIFIC GROVE

Ricketts Family Pacific Grove Years
Nancy Ricketts
daughter to Ed Ricketts, submitted by Jan Straley

I was born at the new Lying-in Hospital in Pacific Grove on November 28, 1924. We lived in three P.G. houses before moving, in about 1928, to my favorite P.G. house at 221 4th St, and stayed there from three to five years. A note among my papers says that the Depression ousted us, as we paid $85 a month rent and about $40 for electricity.

221 4th Street house. Used by permission of N. Ricketts

It was a lovely house, beautifully laid out, at the top of a steep hill looking out to the distance of Monterey Bay. It was here that I had many fond memories—rolling down 4th Street tucked inside of automobile tires (and luckily not struck by cars at the intersection of upper Lighthouse Avenue) but rolling to a stop on the flat before the next big drop to lower Lighthouse Avenue.

The original black Baptist Church.
Pat Hathaway Collection CAViews

There was a black Baptist church at the upper corner of 4th Street that I just loved to visit, especially during choir practice, until it was gently suggested by one of the adults (not my friend Gertrude—or Geraldine) that I not continue to visit. I had heard and learned "My Lord, What a Morning," "There's No Hiding Place Down There," and "Weepin' Mary."

At one time Dad and Mother took us to the train station at Del Monte and put us on the train, then raced the train to Pacific Grove where they took us off. Cornelia Frances was born in 1927. Dad gave her the name of Bitabee when she was pretty young. It happened when she was stung by a bee and ran to Dad for solace, saying that a bee had bit her. He told her, apparently when older brother Ed and I were there, that she should bite him back—hence Bitabee.

Dad gave Ed and I nicknames, all three of us really. I was "Tata," Ed and I were Sheik and Sheba, Ed was "boy," then "Junior," then Edward, and later would answer to nothing but "Ed." There was "Wormy" and "Peaches" and "Mugwumps" and "Nancy Jane, Butterfly Name."

The voyages of Odysseus (read in an almost archaic version—middle English) were explored at evening bedtime-story sessions, with Ed on one knee, me on the other. We were very young, but enjoyed every bit of it. Just a little bit every night with that lovely-sounding voice going over the lovely-sounding words and phrases, needing much explanation of the story line, none at all of the beauty of the words. Sometimes we got tales that Dad made up, often of baby wild animals in the jungle, usually twins, usually up to no good. Montgomery and Montmorency were the twin giraffes. I don't remember the monkeys' names.

And we thought Dad REALLY was with General Pershing in Europe during WWI—he told us fantastic stories about their exploits; of course we told it all over school—until we found out that Dad was "peeling potatoes in Dixie" during most of WWI. Dad also played "elevator" with us, which I hear I called "alligator," and allowed me to braid his hair sometimes. He taught me to play chess when I was very young and had, I think, pneumonia.

Sunday afternoons were pretty special in our young years, during the story-reading and story-telling days. Mother spent a good deal of time in the kitchen; she was a good cook and enjoyed cooking for company. We often had company for dinner on Sundays, and at other times when Dad invited fellow scientists to our house. We heard beautiful music and lots of quiet interesting conversations, accompanied by cigar and pipe smoke drifting through the air.

Ed and I hated "naps," and were known to chant "we wanna get up" endlessly.

Bee went through some drunken antics when she got into Dad's home lab (just off the kitchen and always kept locked—well, almost always), and drank something poisonous, after which Dad had to give her some antidote that made her drunk at a very tender age; they had to watch her for a while to make sure she didn't run into the stove.

We heard a few words of Serbo-Croatian when we were young—brother was BRAT!, SVIET was world (the name of a magazine Mother used to get in Serbo-Croatian, with lots of beautiful pictures of children, like a beauty contest), and BOZIC (pronounced Bozich) was Christmas.

Dad used to take us over to Monterey when we were very young to participate in Chinese New Year with Chin Yip and his family. We ate Chinese soup in Chinese bowls and spoons (we were once given them to take home), set off firecrackers, and Dad drank something called N qua pi (phonetic spelling).

I loved music from as far back as I can remember, listening at every opportunity to the Atwater Kent radio in the living room and Dad's phonograph. I sure I was in my first year or two of school when we sang:

"Little children of Japan wear mittens on their feet; they carry paper parasols while walking in the street," and, "Baby's boat's the silver moon, sailing in the sky; sailing o'er the sea of dreams while the moon sails by. Sail, baby, sail, out across that sea; only don't forget to sail home again to me." I still remember both tunes.

I appreciated Gregorian chant at a tender age. And, for my twelfth birthday, Dad gave me the records of the Pius X Girls' Choir singing some chant in New York, the records of which I lost track of somewhere along the way. Years later brother Ed gave me a tape of chants which included this music! Oh, thrill! By the time we were living at 9th and Junipero in Carmel, I was listening to the Metropolitan Opera radio broadcast on Saturday afternoon, even, on one occasion I vividly remember, missing a family outing to one of the nearby spots like Corral de Tierra.

My first letter (the first one anyone kept, anyhow) was to Aunto (Aunt Frances, Dad's sister) from 221 4th St. in Pacific Grove: I must have been under eight years old. Bee and I were both baptized at St. Mary's Episcopal Church in Pacific Grove on December 28, 1930.

Apparently we made our first trip to Puget Sound for collecting in 1930, when I would have been five. We made yearly trips for some years after 1930, but this was the first. I hear that we had a Dodge car at that time, but I don't remember it.

12 OUTSTANDING WOMEN THEN AND NOW—DIXIE LAYNE, historian

March is the 30th anniversary of National Women's History Month but this year, this time, it caused me to reflect upon the women in my hometown—past and present. Pacific Grove has always had a reputation as a welcoming place for independent, smart, strong women, women who have made meaningful contributions to the world, the country and to Pacific Grove. This year, the celebration of National Women's History Month prompted me to ask myself, who are some of the women who have had a positive effect on the fabric of Pacific Grove—not because it was their job or an assigned responsibility, but because their call to action came from someplace inside themselves?

I thought, what if I were Mayor of Pacific Grove for this one moment—who would I honor with a tribute this March, this National Women's History Month? It took me about two minutes to come up with 12 women—a deliberate dozen. I posted their photos on Facebook. The result of this simple gesture was welcoming, but there were questions. Some asked me to identify the women in the photos while others asked why I had selected these particular women; there were obviously so many other deserving Pacific Grove women. As simple as that, a Facebook post was the genesis for this feature piece that was originally published in the *Cedar Street Times*.

To answer the first question—who are the women in the photographs?—is quite simple. They are, in no particular order: Ruth McClung, Nancy Hauk, Helen Shropshire, Jayne Gasperson, Zena Holman, Emily Dish, Carmelita Garcia, Carol Henning Steinbeck, Dorothy Fowler, Elmarie Hurlbert Hyler Dyke, Marge Ann Jameson, and Julia Platt.

As to the second question—why these 12 women?—well, I can only say it was personal. I didn't go through some long, complicated selection process. I didn't select them on the basis of their personality, politics, or popularity. I recognized each woman based on how I thought she had made a difference in my hometown and for the example she set for the young women of her time. I did not select any one of them because they were or were not a friend or because someone had suggested I should select one over the other. I selected them because they were the women who came immediately to mind when I asked myself—who would I like to honor? I think of these 12 women as leaders, civic spirited, and strong women of example.

So, this is my list of 12 women of Pacific Grove who have made a difference, but as to the details I have included in each lady's story, well, the stories have been written as I remember them—so if I slipped on a couple of points, well, these are my impressions of 12 incredible women who I believe have made a positive contribution to Pacific Grove. I simply wanted to say thank you to all of them for representing the women of Pacific Grove so well.

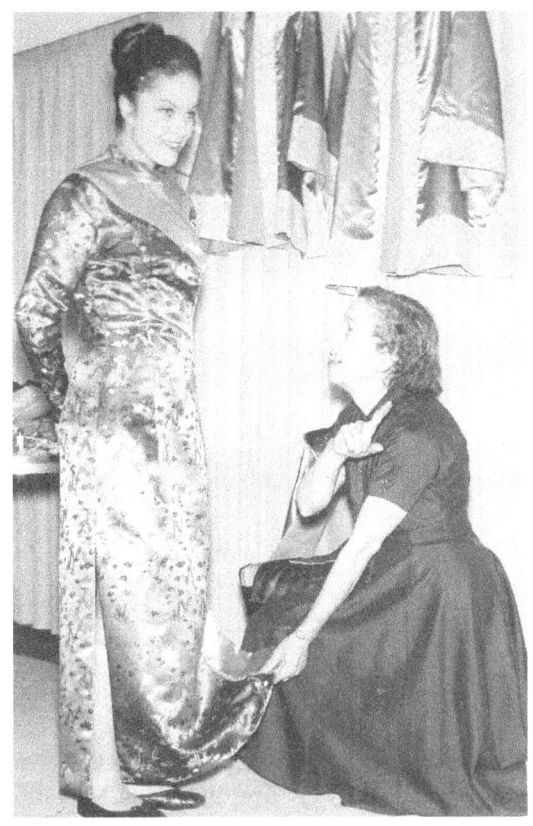

Ruth McClung was a MGM costume designer who moved to Pacific Grove when she retired from show biz. Why she moved to Pacific Grove from Southern California I have no idea, but Pacific Grove does have a long history of welcoming single, talented women into the Grove and Ruth experienced that traditional warm welcome from the Grove—particularly from Elmarie Dyke.

She was the "dressmaker" the Grove asked to create the first costumes for the Feast of Lanterns Royal Court. There would be five young coeds in the first Royal Court who would fill the roles of queen and princesses in the production of "The Legend of the Blue Willow"—now an iconic part of the Feast of Lanterns.

Ruth lent her considerable professional talents to the first Feast of Lanterns committee—from her authentic costume design and detail and story line interpretation to her color and fabric selection of Chinese brocades, silks, and satins and couture work. She approached her work to design and create the first and most elegant Feast of Lanterns costumes with the same deference she gave any of her MGM movie assignments. Her talents and professionalism set the stage for the elegance of the Royal Court. I hesitate to think what an amateur designer might have created … and the legacy such homespun costumes would have left for us. With her needle and thread, Ruth forever became part of the Feast of Lanterns lore.

Nancy Hauk left her mark on Pacific Grove in any number of ways—using her art history education to help establish Hauk Fine Arts in Pacific Grove to her avid belief in education that manifested itself in her support of our library, which made her an integral part of Pacific Grove's fabric. However, it was her work with a small group of residents who were speaking out against the destruction of Pacific Grove's historical architecture at a time when it wasn't popular to do so that put Nancy on my tribute list of admired women.

For over a decade, the character and appearance of Pacific Grove had been changing. Its historical architecture was disappearing at a rapid rate in the 1960s and 1970s—the magnificent Methodist Church was gone, distinctive homes along Ocean View Boulevard were transformed, and many of the small Retreat homes had been remodeled beyond recognition. A small group of residents started meeting to figure out what might be done to change the current course in order that the town's charm and hometown feel might be preserved. Ultimately they worked out a plan with the City, and Pacific Grove put in place an architectural preservation process.

Now assured that their coastal hometown would remain a city flavored with distinctive Victorian, Craftsman, and board and batten homes that gave it its charm and character, these civic minded residents formed a nonprofit organization, The Heritage Society of Pacific Grove, of which Nancy was a founding member. Today Nancy's legacy continues as the Society works to continue to preserve, document, and share our town's history and culture.

Helen Shropshire was someone who got things done and experienced wonderful adventures along the way—I think of her as the Katherine Hepburn of Pacific Grove.

It was Helen who instigated the Crosby Golf Tournament move from the Rancho Santa Fe Golf Club she managed during World War II to Pacific Grove, albeit it ended up next door in Pebble Beach. Think—Pebble Beach without the AT&T. Without Helen, the Crosby may have stayed in Southern California. Helen was the executive director of the Miss Monterey County Pageant when she introduced and managed the idea of adding a Royal Court to the Feast of Lanterns. The Feast of Lanterns just wouldn't be the same without its queen and princesses.

What I most admire about Helen is her gutsy and adventurous style. It was the adventurous Helen, who, during the second half of her life, obtained her private pilot's license and formed the Monterey Chapter of the Ninety-Nines. It was the gutsy Helen who was the aerial photographer whose photographic specialty was the interior of volcanoes. While in Guatemala, she had the opportunity to photograph the inside of a volcano from a bomber—and did it with the bomb bay doors open, not strapped in, while lying on her stomach, just to get the perfect shot. Her fascination for the inside of volcanoes brought her into the Crater of the Sun (Haleakala) in Hawaii for aerial photographs. I get the feeling she would have tried anything, and she didn't let being a "girl" get in her way.

Jayne Gasperson has been part of all things Pacific Grove from the time she was a teenager, when she performed in the 1947 Butterfly Pageant, to the present day when you can find Jayne quietly supporting any number of Pacific Grove's activities, all the while spreading her sunshine.

I think of Jayne as a woman who has always known what she wanted—from the first time she spotted Don on the other end of Pacific Grove's Cove Beach to her desire and will to keep Pacific Grove inviting to all comers. I admire Jayne for her sunny and giving spirit—always there to help a friend, support her alma mater (PGHS), and give a hand to Pacific Grove anywhere, anytime.

It's the little things Jayne does that make a big difference to Pacific Grove—like how she consistently uses her green thumb to tend some of the city's public spaces, especially Elmarie Dyke Park. This place holds a special place in Jayne's heart and on her Sunday morning rounds—you see, it was set to become part of another tall, modern building save for the efforts of a couple of active residents, among them Don Gasperson. Jayne contributed to the park's landscape design and heritage when she donated a bonsai tree given to her by the wife of the Carmel Fire Department's chief on the occasion of Jayne's husband becoming Pacific Grove Fire Chief. To this day, Jayne keeps the park tidy and the flora and fauna trimmed. If there ever was a "Mrs. Pacific Grove" to follow Elmarie, Jayne would be it.

Zena Holman has received so many awards and citations for the many things she has contributed to Pacific Grove and California you may question why she is on my list.

Well, there are three reasons I admire her—the first is a bit tongue-in-cheek. It was about 1912 when Zena brought women's ready-to-wear to Pacific Grove. She installed an entire department dedicated to women's fashion in Holman's Department Store and hired women to serve women. I say ready-to-wear "freed" women to march for women's rights and voting rights—more comfortably.

However, it is the work she did with others to preserve Asilomar through the State Park system that put Zena on my list. As Zena explained in a 1970s interview, the YWCA wanted to sell Asilomar and Zena thought if it sold, it would become a honky-tonk development. So, with the earnest work of a few ladies, the 91 acres known as Asilomar became part of the California State Park system in 1956. Zena was instrumental in making this happen.

Zena then followed up this work by donating her incredible collection of books to Asilomar—first editions all and most signed by their authors. With this collection, The Zena Holman Library of California and Americana was established.

To recap; she gave the ladies of Pacific Grove ready-to-wear, helped save Asilomar from a honky-tonk development, and shared her book collection with the people of California in an effort to use Asilomar to build a better society.

Emily Fish was a remarkable woman, regardless of what one male biographer wrote about Emily "not doing one heroic thing." So, let's talk heroic: Emily went to China when she was 16 years old (1859) to visit her older sister and husband, and upon her arrival her sister's pregnancy was announced to Emily. Her sister died in childbirth and Emily was left to raise her niece. At the age of 17, she married her sister's widower, a medical doctor. To make a long story short, she followed her husband around Europe while he served in a number of government posts before returning to the States so he could fight for the Union in the American Civil War. He died in 1891, when Emily was 48—and she thought, now what?

It was Emily's son-in-law who told her that the Point Pinos light-keeper position was vacant and she applied for it—an unnecessary course for this woman of education and means. I mean, why not? —her husband had recently died and her daughter was married. Emily won the position, and at the age of 50 moved into the Point Pinos Lighthouse with her Chinese servant and luxurious furnishings.

During her 21 years as keeper, Emily brought rich soil to the lighthouse grounds so she could plant grass, hedges, and trees around the lighthouse. She also kept French poodles, Holstein cows, thoroughbred horses, and chickens on the grounds, along with always receiving the highest marks for keeping the station tidy. She was known for hosting Sunday afternoon teas with naval officers and dinners with local artists and writers. It's been said that she hired some 30 men in the 21 years she was light=keeper and fired most of them for incompetence. Emily was known as the socialite light-keeper—I think she was the Ginger Rogers of light-keepers.

Carmelita Garcia graduated from Pacific Grove High School and since has been part of Pacific Grove's social and civic fabric. In public Carmelita presents as a quiet, serious woman but beneath her sober public persona there exists a strong woman of warmth and compassion with a sense of humor. Let's just say, anyone who dresses their rescue dog named "Scruffy" in a Christmas clown collar must enjoy a good laugh.

When Carmelita was a new city councilmember she was named city liaison to the Feast of Lanterns—the record does not show if she raised her hand or drew the short straw, but I can tell you the Feast of Lanterns was the winner with this appointment. For the first time in decades, the city liaison attended board meetings, which made it so much easier for me—I mean the Feast of Lanterns. She was ever-present and helped immensely when it came time to work with the city to coordinate a week-long festival that brought 10,000-plus people onto Lovers Point and the cove for the festival's finale.

It was on the 100th anniversary of the Point Alones/Point Almejas Chinese Fishing Village fire when descendants of the village gathered to remember and pay respects to their ancestors—and Carmelita was there. She said a few words, "A community that reflects upon its past and recognizes historical mistakes is less likely to be forced to repeat them." In 2010, Carmelita worked with the Fishing Village descendants to found the annual Walk of Remembrance to honor their ancestors. Carmelita participates in that walk every year.

Five years ago, Carmelita attended a NAACP banquet held in Monterey that so happened to have national NAACP president and CEO Benjamin Todd Jealous in attendance, and as it happened both grew up in Pacific Grove—a generation apart; Todd was born the year after Carmelita graduated from PGHS. That evening Carmelita personally delivered a letter she wrote of apology for the decades of discriminatory housing practices that occurred in Pacific Grove and across the country. Carmelita read from her letter, "The City of Pacific Grove recognizes the wrongs of the past and the discrimination that occurred …."

Obviously there is much more to these stories but the point is—Carmelita is a strong woman filled with warmth and compassion who recognizes the power of an apology.

Carol and John Steinbeck early 1930s
Photo: San Jose State University

Carol Henning Steinbeck was a hard-drinking, salty-tongued, early feminist who met John Steinbeck in Tahoe, married him in Eagle Rock, and lived with him in Pacific Grove and Los Gatos before divorcing in 1942. Some have said she was the woman behind the great man but arguably she was the woman who made the man great. Carol was his intellectual and creative equal with great editorial instincts.

Soon after John and Carol married in 1930, they moved to Pacific Grove where John could pursue his craft. It started as a period of rejection for him but he kept at it with Carol's encouragement and support. Over the next six years John wrote until late afternoon before wondering off to meet up with his now famous compatriots. Carol worked days as a secretary and spent her nights typing his manuscripts, correcting his punctuation and very bad spelling, and supplying a strong editorial hand all the while warding off the Irish in his writing. Carol set the work schedule with her established routine and John felt obligated to write during the day. If Carol could work all day and be his typist and editor at night, the least he could do was to write every day.

It was during this six-year period in Pacific Grove when the young author mastered his craft. During this time he published four books, including *Tortilla Flat* and began working on *Of Mice and Men*, *Grapes of Wrath* and parts of The *Red Pony*. Unwanted attention precipitated John and Carol leaving Pacific Grove in 1936 for Los Gatos, where he finished *Grapes of Wrath* with Carol's inspiration and strong editorial hand—plus she gave the book its title. John won the Pulitzer Prize and The National Book Award in 1940 for the *Grapes of Wrath*.

They returned to Pacific Grove to join Ed Ricketts on his marine specimen collecting trip to the Sea of Cortez aboard the *Western Flyer*. While they were back in Pacific Grove John wrote *The Forgotten Village* and *The Sea of Cortez* with Ricketts before she and John separated.

The story of an intelligent, talented, creative woman who envelops her life and aspirations into her husband's is a familiar one. In this case, it is possible, even probable, that the world would not have the great works of John Steinbeck if it were not for Carol Henning Steinbeck. In concert, they gave us some of the most lasting stories of modern time.

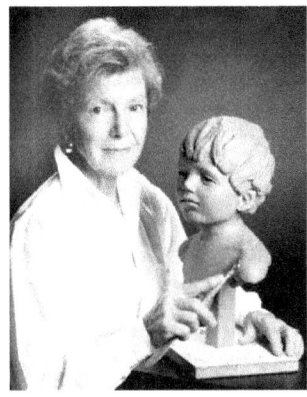

Dorothy Fowler is a woman who lived her life in three acts—and who doesn't marvel at a woman who can reinvent herself as her energy and life circumstances change?

Act I: Dorothy Fowler's high school years were overshadowed by WWII; she graduated from Pacific Grove High School in 1944, a year before the war was over—something that had a profound effect on her generation.

Dorothy was a traditional high school girl who organized the Mothers Tea and Big and Little Sisters Banquet, sang in the Glee Club and acted in the Christmas play. She went on to college to study art at San Jose State University. She married her first husband and moved to Spokane where they had three children and she worked as a medical secretary and homemaker.

Act II: Dorothy met Jack Fowler and his three children; they married and became a real-life Brady Bunch. Jack, a dentist, was an aviation enthusiast, a pilot and builder of planes and ski resorts. The year after she married Jack, Dorothy became a licensed pilot who landed a plane on the Alaskan glaciers and in the Guatemalan jungle, and a member and officer of The Ninety-Nines, the International Women's Pilots Organization founded by Amelia Earhart.

Act III: It was 1979 when Dorothy first became interested in working with clay. "It was like I waited all my life for something to happen to me. I always knew I would be able to do something creative." After studying with local Spokane, Colorado, and Arizona artists, and she went to Europe to develop her craft, but the turning point for her as a sculptor was when her work sold in galleries.

Dorothy set goals for herself. She wanted to be an example for her daughters and granddaughters, "that when you are older, life can still be meaningful and special if you are willing to work for it. I set my mind to become a nationally known female artist." Dorothy exceeded her goal—she became an internationally known female artist, whose bronze statues and striking cathedral doors can be found around the globe from Thailand and Israel to Pacific Grove.

Dorothy returned to Pacific Grove in 1989 to join her classmates to offer the gift of a life-size bronze statue to the city. Dorothy told the City Council about her inspiration for the sculpture. The idea arouse from her memories of growing up in Pacific Grove, sitting on the rocks at Lovers Point and looking out over the bay, and about how much she loved her hometown. In the spring of 1990, her bronze statue was placed on a rock in Lovers Point Park to honor her classmates who fought for freedom in WWII.

Dorothy lost her husband in 2009 and she left us in 2015.

Elmarie Hurlbert Hyler Dyke was and will always be Mrs. Pacific Grove. Legend paints her as a figure bigger than life but history records her legacy as someone grander than the stories told. Her accomplishments were so much more than the Feast of Lanterns.

Elmarie—I tremble as I refer to Mrs. Dyke so informally but I do that only for consistency purposes—was born before the turn of the century; she attended Chautauqua Assemblies with her family before they moved to Pacific Gove when she was 14. She graduated from Pacific Grove High School in 1915, enrolled in San Jose State Normal School (San Jose State University) that same year, received her teaching credential in 1918, taught elementary school in Sutter Creek, and married Nelson William Hyler, Mayor of Sutter Creek, in 1919—she accomplished all this before women had the right to vote.

Summarizing the first 23 years of Elmarie's life was done only to illustrate the breakneck speed at which she lived life.

My personal memories of Elmarie are many, but in general I can honestly say she made us all better people, better citizens; she brought the arts in all forms to all people, was an early civil rights leader, worked to bring the best educational system to Monterey County, and tirelessly fought to protect the true fabric, culture and history of Pacific Grove—and then there were the funny bits: her attempt to keep PG dry—damn the 21st Amendment—but she managed to do it anyway, at least until 1968; then there was the decorum she successfully demanded of residents—she scared me into propriety; let us not forget her fight to save the old Methodist Church, too bad she left town for a couple of weeks.

What Elmarie accomplished for the State of California, the County of Monterey, and the City of Pacific Grove is without parallel and, at best, difficult to summarize, but then-Assemblyman Sam Farr did it so eloquently on the occasion of her death, January 17, 1981—36 years ago. In a rare action, the California State Assembly adjourned January 22 in honor of Mrs. Dyke at the request of Assemblyman Farr. A letter outlining Mrs. Dyke's accomplishments was also published in the Journal of the Assembly. Elmarie Hurlbert Hyler Dyke was something else—and there will never be another like her.

Marge Ann Jameson returned to Pacific Grove over a decade ago. She went to work at the *Pacific Grove Hometown Bulletin* for newspaper founder Lee Yarborough. Shortly thereafter, Lee had a stroke. She managed the paper until Lee ultimately sold it, and Marge Ann was out of a job. Marge Ann is a newspaperwoman through and through, so she didn't let this one event deter her—she founded the *Cedar Street Times* in 2008, and as they say, the rest is history.

However, being a newspaperwoman—even those like Marge Ann with printer's ink running through their veins—did not get her on the Women of Pacific Grove list. It is what she does outside the seven days a week she works to publish a weekly newspaper, and for Marge Ann that list is long. She has served on the Feast of Lanterns board, she was part of the small band of poetry lovers who selected poets and took care of the Poet's Perch, she assisted in the founding of First Friday, and she and Neal opened the Motorcycle Museum and coordinate riding and other events for motorcycle enthusiasts, but what I find most amazing is her support of the youth and aspiring journalists.

For the young newspaper kids, she provides them with routes and pays them to deliver newspapers. She teaches them responsibility and reliability. Marge Ann gives these young elementary and middle schoolers an invaluable experience—a paper route, a job, responsibility. There isn't another paper on the Peninsula that provides this opportunity for kids. Today, she has a high school student managing the newspaper kids who deliver the papers. He organizes the routes and coordinates with the kids and their parents. For just about every kid on her "payroll," this is their very first job. What a gift.

Over the years, Marge Ann has provided high school and college students who are aspiring journalists the opportunity for internships. She works with these interns to develop their writing skills, and teaches them how to track down a story and conduct an interview. She has photo journalists who are honing their skills, looking for "the shot." These opportunities have given students real life work experience—very different from working for their school paper.

I find it amazing how many of them come back after college and apply for a job as a journalist or photojournalist. What a gift Marge Ann is to the youth of Pacific Grove. More businesses should take her lead.

Julia Platt attacking the beach gate

Julia Platt at the age of 42 arrived in Pacific Grove at the turn of the century with a Ph.D. in zoology and no prospects. There is no definitive explanation why she selected Pacific Grove as her home. Perhaps it was her inability to find a position at a university or as a marine biologist —even at Hopkins Marine Station, which only opened a few years prior to her arrival—but whatever the reason, she was not the first nor would she be the last well-educated, single woman of means to move into town.

Julia had studied at Harvard University, then obtained her doctorate at the University of Freiberg in Germany at the age of 41—universities in the United States were not accepting female doctoral candidates at the time. So, armed with her Ph.D. and without a position in her field, it is reported that Julia simply said, "If I cannot obtain the work I wish, then I must take up with the next best." Was she thinking civic duty, politics or saving our shoreline?

There are so many ways Julia had an effect on Pacific Grove, from her serious civic minded achievements to the legendary stories of her "vigorous" behavior. By all accounts she was an intelligent, civic minded, dynamic maiden lady who was known as a "grand old gal," and regardless how radical her behavior, it typically led to a good result. This includes her confrontation with her neighbor's chickens; exasperated with the chickens who continued to trespass onto her property, well, she shot the offenders. This action and the brouhaha that followed resulted in a city ordinance passed that zoned certain areas within the city limits to be chicken- and livestock-free.

Julia single-handedly landscaped Lovers Point. She cleared the land, pushed wheelbarrows filled with plants and gardening tools from home to the Point where she planted and tended them regularly. Imagine the effect Julia had on the conservative ladies and gentlemen of the Grove as she passed them at a brisk pace, pushing her wheelbarrow full of flora and fauna, with a mannish hat sitting on her head of white, short, bushy hair while on her way to do hard labor. Then there is the oft-told story of Julia forcing the gate open that had been erected around the beach because, she proclaimed, the public had the right to beach access. She won that argument, too.

The stories of Julia attending City Council meetings are legendary. The meetings were packed in those days—everyone came to hear what Julia had to say. After 20 years of publishing paid advertisements and combating City Council vocally for what she considered an inefficient government, she penned in her own hand a City Charter, circulated the petition, and it was adopted. The Council got so tired of her telling them off, they told her she should run for office. So she did, and won. In 1931, at the age of 74 Julia was elected Mayor of Pacific Grove. What a grand old gal.

GHOSTLY GOINGS ON

The Witchy Houses of P.G.

concerned in Carmel Valley

My first memory of Pacific Grove was when I was eight. A classmate's birthday party was there. I lived in Carmel Valley but for some reason this girl lived in PG.

Carmel Valley is wide open spaces, with ranches and stuff ... horses and pastures and a river. Before that where we lived was also pretty rural, not too far from Yosemite National Park. There were bigger properties back in Oakhurst. We rented out our corral for people to put their horses in. When you went into town there was one drugstore, one bank.

But PG looked like a city ... a little witch city. The houses all looked old and creaky and too close together. I didn't know they were Victorians at the time, they just looked like they each probably had at least one caldron inside and no electricity. I didn't even want to *go* to this party, my mom made me. She wanted me to make friends, but I didn't want to make any witch friends.

The streets seemed like they were only big enough for one car to go down, so I thought the people probably had to fly their brooms around with a black hat hanging off the end. And it was real foggy. There was this whole ominous layer all around, hanging over you. That town frightened me.

I wasn't in the best frame of mind, anyway, because we'd just moved here. I was intimidated going to a new school and meeting new people. I was very much a tomboy and didn't know if I was going to meet anyone else like me. I had just been told I had to stop running around without a shirt on a year before.

But inside this girl's house was as bad as I feared, with a big carved staircase going up. I could just imagine going up those old stairs and opening a door with bats flying out…or finding her old, locked-up grandma who was a witch.

I was always told I had a very active imagination

The antique mall in the Holman Building also freaked me out when I was about ten. My aunt and my cousin would come visit every summer and this one day my aunt wanted to go pick something up there. She was a big antique shopper. We pulled up in front of the Holman Building with all the witchy Victorian furniture in the windows. I took one look and said, "I'll wait in the car." My mom said, "Don't be ridiculous, we're all going in."

I walked into that building and…it just felt like Holman's House of Horrors. There was a giant stone lion statue, velvet Dracula sofas, evil old jewelry, a huge old mirror. I thought for sure Bloody Mary from the slumber party game was in that gilt mirror. (She *had* to be! Where *else* would she live?) The whole place was just musty and old, like it could collapse on us at any moment and we would be trapped there underneath all that weird old stuff, and the ghosts would come flying out of the rubble.

I couldn't stand it for more than ten minutes.

I've never told anyone about this unease I have in Pacific Grove because they'd think I was psychologically maladjusted! It's just foreboding to me. You have to go on Holman Highway to get there, with all the shadowy trees and the winding road that passes the HOSPITAL. It's scary! And Forest Hill Manor still looks like something out of *Flowers in the Attic*.

If someone gave me a house in PG, I'm sorry, but I would have to sell it. I just couldn't lay my head down there, in the dark.

The Ghostly Spell
A True Story by Anonymous

This piece is written in the third person, to place distance between its author and this long ago, otherworldly experience!

Nolan and Stella were friends who met in Pacific Grove. He'd recently returned to the area after traveling the world, and she had lived there for eleven years.

They had an experience with a ghost who inhabits a Victorian home where Stella was pet sitting. This ghost would make his presence known by various methods; usually subtle, always without malice. On one occasion, he stopped Stella's watch even though it had a recently-replaced battery. On another, he knocked over a container of dog treats from the counter onto the kitchen floor. The ghost pulled out chairs in the dining room that had been pushed under the table, and he stopped the small bedside clock Stella traveled with … which of course started to run again once it was back in Stella's home. When she at last mentioned all this, the pet owner shared that she felt a definite presence in the old house, as well.

When the pet sitting job was over, Stella had a feeling the ghost may have followed her back to her own house. A manta ray model bought at the Aquarium went missing.

Even worse, one morning Stella went to a jewelry store in town to pick up a pair of handmade earrings she'd dropped off to be repaired. She'd owned them for years and they were very sentimental as well as fairly expensive.

The repaired earrings were carefully wrapped in gold tissue by the lovely lady at the counter and then placed in a small box in front of Stella, who noted that they were both there. Off to work with the earrings safely in their box in her tote bag Stella went.

The following morning Stella looked forward to wearing these earrings, as they had been at the jewelers for several weeks. And yet opening the box, she felt shock and dismay when she found only ONE of them amongst the gold tissue!

Stella returned to the jeweler at once, asking the lady at the counter if the missing earring had somehow been left behind at the store. But of course, it was obvious to both of them that two earrings had been placed in that box the previous day. This lead to a hopeless search of Stella's tote bag, purse and car.

When told of all this, Nolan felt that the ghost had played a little trick on Stella, something to get her attention. "What else will he try?" he wondered, and became worried. Nolan asked Stella to take him through everything that had happened, step by step, and she mentioned discussing the ghost's behavior with the home owner. It occurred to him they were now talking about the ghost behind his back, *again!* Could the ghost perhaps be upset it was being gossiped about? Maybe some amends were in order.

Nolan came up with a possible remedy. After dark, he and Stella placed offerings of fruit and candy in the yard of the haunted Victorian, along with a few flowers. They had written tiny apologies to the ghost for gossiping about him, including wishes for his safe travels. These notes they burned in a votive candle so the smoke could reach the ghost on the Other Side. (The candle was extinguished afterwards, of course.)

Since making this peace offering, it appears the ghost has returned to his own home, as there were no further mysterious incidents at Stella's. The missing earring was eventually recreated by the artist who had made the original pair. Luckily, this silversmith didn't charge for the new earring, as there was no way to bill the ghost.

My Favorite Ghosts of P.G.
Elizabeth Fisher
author and women's rights advocate

Lavinia Waterhouse

The past is not an academic study for me in Pacific Grove. Each day here I feel the specter of so many unique ancestors and their special contributions that enrich my sense of this place. Here are highlights about two former residents I have come to value. Thanks to Don Beals and the Heritage Society for introducing them to me.

Social concerns central to me include women's equality and world peace. Pacific Grove has a legacy in both. When visiting the Pacific Grove Heritage Society, I was greeted by a self-portrait painted in oil by Lavinia Waterhouse, who lived from 1809 to 1890. She was a midwife, physician and fiery suffragette. In the portrait, she is dressed in an exotic robe and flamboyant hat. I learned she was well known for her work in the California and national women's rights movement and was very active in the California State Spiritualists Association.

A regular Pacific Grove summer visitor, she moved here in the early 1880s. At the time of her death in 1891, Lavinia Waterhouse owned 57 properties in this area. One, marked by a placard saying it was built in 1894, is still standing on 13th Street, reminding me of her presence.

At the time of her death, Lavinia wanted to set up a retirement home for women, modeled after one she had established in Sacramento. She died before she was able to do so. Still, it's an admirable goal. She is also the first person buried in El Carmelo Cemetery, resting among the cypress trees and nearby dunes. My husband and I found the grave markers of Lavinia and her family completely concealed with soil. We carefully uncovered them and revisit to tend them. Her spirit seems to be pleased.

Edward Berwick

Edward Berwick, who lived from 1843 to 1934, was a World Federalist and mayor. Berwick Park in Pacific Grove, a park he designed and laid out, honors his memory. The plaque in the park says, "This tree was planted to honor Edward Berwick, our splendid pioneer citizen, by the Neighbor Club, May 1, 1930."

He delivered a lecture on "World Federation" before the Chautauqua Literary and Scientific Circle in Pacific Grove, July 2, 1885, which I helped to transcribe for the Heritage Society. He was an ardent pacifist, spoke often to high school classes and developed voluminous writings of his endeavor "to rid the world of that idiocy called war." He was seldom seen without a book of philosophy or poetry. Several of his pamphlets are available in his effects at the Heritage Society. We visit the park regularly and feel the beauty of the site Mr. Berwick loved so well, and reaffirm his vision of a world without war.

I believe, then, it's possible to live in the company of the dead as honored members of our present day community. These two powerful souls, like so many others, have enriched my connections to Pacific Grove, deepening my own soul and making me feel at home.

A Victorian Rental
Gayle Lubeck
non-fiction writer

In 2003, I rented one of the downstairs apartments in a Victorian on Pacific Avenue in Pacific Grove. With its Doric columns, arched windows, and expansive porch, the building had been one glorious marvel in the heyday of the 19th century, filled with the delightful resonances of entertainment and laughter. As a conversion, its purpose serves a variety of lifestyles and tastes, rather than those of a single family. I had just turned 40. This was the year my mother died, as well as the ending of a topsy-turvy romantic relationship. I needed a safe place to mourn and re-group. When I first walked in, I asked myself if I could live there for a year, and began to picture my antiques throughout, along with any suitable additions.

I located a Lane cherry wood carved hutch from a consignment store that was going out of business in Monterey and set it in the dining area, so that I could display my grandmother's Minton Marlow china and vases. I set up the living room as a tribute to my mother. I positioned the marble-topped oak table with the horse

Lavinia Waterhouse self-portrait in full color, on display at Ketcham's Barn, Laurel and 16th, open Saturdays 1:00 to 4:00 p.m.

feet along the side entrance, the carved multi-tiered wooden shelf from the 1950s in the front window, and the coffee table with the hooved feet in front of the sofa. I gathered all of my china cups and arranged them on the shelf so that passersby could see them. After my gracious next door neighbors saw how I had decorated my living room they said, "You added class to the neighborhood." I was touched.

I would sit and linger, reminiscing about the past and all that had recently transpired in my life. This refuge provided the solitude I required for this intense reflection. I experienced every emotion as people in mourning often do. After a couple of weeks, I began to notice something about the space. There was a presence. It was not my mother. I believed that it was one of the former owners of the house, a woman.

I felt energy whirl by me in the dining area, as I was sitting at my computer. I called out, "I know you are here, please show yourself." No response. I just went back to what I was doing and thought that this specter would appear if it so desired.

One late night, while watching a movie in the bedroom, I saw a delicate white female head, dressed in a headscarf, appear out of the wall. Her grimacing grin and piercing eyes briefly captured my attention. I said thank you, I knew you were here. Silently, she melted back from whence she came.

EL CARMELO CEMETERY

The Ghost of El Carmelo
Jane Parks-McKay

We've had burial plots at El Carmelo Cemetery for some time now. Apparently so have many others far and wide. It's not uncommon to be chatting with a family friend from out of town, only to find out they have bought their final resting places in El Carmelo, too.

I've heard that people go to cemeteries for various reasons. For me, in the first few years after Mom died, I found that I did my best writing in the car at El Carmelo. Away from distractions and interruptions I could finally, whew … finish a sentence.

The last time I went to write there, though, I rolled up behind an old beat-up looking VW whose driver was sitting there doing "his thing," listening to music. Loud. Very loud.

I left. I found another way to write amidst the distractions and interruptions of a busy household on top of the demolishing and rebuilding of homes going on around our home on a regular basis. Apparently we live in the "in" place and mega homes are taking the place of once small vintage bungalows.

I can't say I get much writing done as before but Patricia has put out the call for memories of Pacific Grove, and El Carmelo. I have a story that I'd love to share; it's called "The Ghost of El Carmelo."

For a long time when I visited Mom and Dad's graves, I would see a very mysterious-looking man walk the cemetery paths. Coming from the golf course, up the road and around the bend, I would lose sight of him. It's as if he disappeared into thin air before my eyes. He looked like a man from another era, almost like a sea captain. Scratchy-looking beard, a sea hat propped on his windblown hair, he never looked up or engaged with the scenery. He just "was."

I haven't seen him for some time and while I really don't think he's a ghost, I have to say that there were times I wondered ….

Little Chapel by-the-Sea and the History of Paul Mortuary
Jane Roland

In March of 2017, Paul Mortuary marked the 114th year of service to the community. The 100th anniversary was celebrated on March 16, 2004, with visiting local dignitaries, Pacific Grove Chamber of Commerce members and staff, Councilmember Ron Schenk and many local citizens. It is one of the oldest businesses in continuous operation in Monterey County.

J. K. Paul, who established the mortuary, served on the Pacific Grove City Council, was a deputy county coroner, and was a director of the Bank of Pacific Grove. They had four sons, George W. Paul, Forest E. Paul, Ceil W. Paul and Leland J. Paul. J.K. passed away in 1934.

In the early days, it was combined with a retail furniture store: furniture in the front, caskets in the back.

The location was the site of the present Lopez Liquor Store on Lighthouse Avenue. The two businesses split, the furniture portion moving to the site of The Quill and the mortuary to Grand and Lighthouse (where McDermott's Pharmacy once stood). The Paul Mortuary built the Little Chapel by-the-Sea and Crematory on the grounds of El Carmelo Cemetery opposite the Point Pinos Lighthouse. Leland Paul acquired ownership of the family business in 1942; in the early 1960s Leland took in partner Lowell A. Sawyer. David M. Dormedy and Roland H. Siebe became partners in 1972. In 1998, the mortuary was sold to Keystone California.

On May 2, 1948, Paul Mortuary conducted services at the Little Chapel. After paying their respects many of the mourners left and walked across the dunes to the great tide pools and fittingly contemplated the life of the deceased, marine biologist Ed Ricketts.

It's a Small World ... Forever
Jane Parks-McKay

They say it's a small world. Is it ever! They also say things happen for a reason.

Some years ago, Mom and Dad shopped around for a final resting place. My husband and I eventually embarked upon the same project.

We ended up purchasing a nice double plot in picturesque El Carmelo Cemetery. I have a "thing" about resting under trees. We figured our new plot was perfect as there was one lone tree nearby.

As time went on, the city took out the lone tree. After Dad died, my husband and I inquired about buying plots where we could put a gravestone in the old section of the cemetery. Some plots came available and we "relocated" AND it was underneath trees. Lots of them. On my birthday, we stopped by to look at the sites and purchased ours. What a birthday gift, eh?

Knowing that writer Patricia Hamilton had spoken and written about her search for family, imagine our surprise when we turned around and found Patricia's eventual final resting place near ours. Patricia started calling our area of the cemetery "The 'Hood." During this time, a precious baby passed away and his family buried him near our plots. As I would walk around El Carmelo, I would pay homage to this precious baby, and I would straighten out the sunflowers lovingly placed there. One day I visited the site and the family had put a beautiful headstone on his final resting place: a cherub enclosed sweetly in a shell, the marble structure showing the immense love that his family has for him.

Knowing that we are going to be in a "good 'Hood" that has personal meaning to us means the world to us. We don't think we could ever have planned this better and it's definitely a "God thing." What more could you ask for than for ocean breezes, a peek of the sea, curious deer, trees ... AND a nice "'Hood" for eternity?

Ministers' Gravesite Renovated and Re-consecrated

Cedar Street Times article June 2013

PatricIa Hamilton, owner of Park Place Publications in Pacific Grove, and a P.G. resident since 1990, has helped many of her clients explore their ancestry through memoirs and family histories.

In the course of writing her own memoir, she called upon the Heritage Society of P.G., the Family History Center in Seaside, and on some friendly folks at P.G. City Hall for assistance. As a result, she tracked down her great-great grandfather, Sylvanus Gale, and discovered he headed the Methodist Church in Pacific Grove in the early 1890s. She also learned that he, his wife, Jane, and two of their eight children, Mabel and William, were buried in El Carmelo Cemetery.

Sylvanus Gale was born in the Hudson River Valley in New York in 1838. He was active in the Civil War, forming the first company of volunteers from New York in 1861, mustering in as a Lieutenant in "Perry's Saints" Regiment (led by Colonel James H. Perry and called Saints because most were Methodist ministers from Wesleyan University). For the remainder of his life he served as an itinerant Methodist minister.

In 1890 he and his wife came as pastors of the Pacific Grove Methodist Church, where they served until 1893 (his wife, Jane Cloyd Gale, died in 1892). During his tenure he completed the construction of the first parsonage built for ministers. Pacific Grove occupied a special place in his heart, and he chose to be buried here.

Because the El Carmelo coping and grave markers had suffered the ravages of weather and time, Patricia recently had new ones installed. Fittingly, the Rev. Pamela Cummings of the First United Methodist Church of Pacific Grove re-consecrated the burial sites.

In attendance: left to right, Janet Beals, K. Harlow, Marabee Boone (Methodist Church historian), Patricia Hamilton, great-nephew Leland Slarrow, Don Beals, Rev. Pamela Cummings, and Darlene Billstrom (City Cemetery office).

SECTION 2
THE MANY CHARMS OF PACIFIC GROVE

A UNIQUE, DELIGHTFUL PLACE TO LIVE

The Not-so-Hidden Charms of P.G.
Bob Fisher

Living in this unique town for the last five years has been delightful for me. Prior to moving here, I spent 33 years in the San Francisco/Berkeley area and shorter stints in several other locations. I was born and raised in Michigan.

Wandering around town has brought me in contact with gentle deer, old trees, and creative people. Places I especially love: the library, since so many of the books are ones I'm searching for, the rejuvenated museum for its wealth of knowledge of the natural world, the Post Office for its old-fashioned way of communicating with the outside world and its historic mural, and strolling in Rip Van Winkle Park to remember the area used to be a forest of Monterey pines, cypress and oaks.

I am gratified that the harbor seals feel safe enough on our beaches to birth their pups every spring, and that the endangered monarch butterflies return each year to begin their cycle again. I am honored to participate in the Walk of Remembrance, which commemorates the Chinese fishing village that used to stand proudly on our shores. I look forward to the annual Feast of Lanterns that reminds us of the power of love and the blessings of Kwan Yin.

One of the not-so-hidden pleasures of P.G. are the many yards with flowers, native plants and countless *tchotchke*s, especially the gnomes and fairies representing the ever-present world of the Spirit. The way folks decorate and adorn their abodes at Halloween and Christmas and throughout the year truly gives Pacific Grove that hometown feel. The ubiquitous outdoor chairs and benches, some retained from previous generations, remind me of those who have lived here in the past and invite communication with current neighbors as well. The bookstore and the coffee shops keep alive the attitude of friendliness and philosophical inquiry.

Another hallmark of this special town is the many free and low cost events that stir both my mind and soul. Of special note are the entertaining Farmers Market, the stunning concerts performed by the volunteer P.G. Pops orchestra lead by Barbara Priest, and the tours of the Point Pinos Lighthouse, one of the oldest and most fascinating jewels in town. I am grateful to Don Beals for inspiring anecdotes about the past, and to the members of the Heritage Society for keeping the flame of history alive in their charming barn, as well as leading tours and sponsoring lectures.

Other landmarks I appreciate: El Carmelo Cemetery, a prominent memorial to Pacific Grove's beloved ancestors, the cottage where Carol and John Steinbeck developed their social empathy and commitment to phalanx with Ed Ricketts and Joseph Campbell, the nineteenth century architecture of St. Mary's by-the-Sea and the Christian Church on Central Avenue.

And of course Asilomar, for being a state park open to all to enjoy, a nature refuge and the largest existing collection of Julia Morgan's Arts and Crafts buildings.

All of these and more generate life and culture in Pacific Grove.

Heritage, Renewed
John Sanders
historical storyteller

Pacific Grove in California rests upon an ancient bed of granite along the southern shore of Monterey Bay.

Cypresses grow among the boulders and buildings here. Angular, accentuated and artfully groomed by the sea-wind, the regal cypress blends with stone and the perpetual change of light and shadow to stir the imagination.

Along the rocky shores are the tide pools of Asilomar, to the east—the *esteros* of Monterey, to the north—the sloughs of Moss Landing and Watsonville and the chalk cliffs of Santa Cruz.

South are the Santa Lucia Mountains with sea coves of serpentine, jasper and jade. Inland, along the Salinas River, lie the Gabilan Mountains and the valley of Steinbeck.

John Steinbeck, Henry Miller, Edward Ricketts, Joseph Campbell and Eugen Neuhaus are among the writers, scientists, philosophers and painters of the Grove who have defined this setting of land and sea and the character of people and place. They have given us enduring time markers of Pacific Grove, moments to be reconsidered.

Yet, remember: today also calls. And in the twilight of morn and night, as the Pacific thunders against granite, inspiration lingers in the sea mist here. Drink it in. Let it course through your lungs and your hearts and guide your eyes, hands and minds as, together, we renew this heritage.

A Piece of Paradise
Lori Bennett

I first set eyes on Pacific Grove five years ago. My boyfriend's mother, Lillie Lawrence, had lived on Grand Avenue for 25 years. We went to visit and as we arrived very late, Lillie was already in bed, asleep. There was a bright, full moon shining down on the bay, so we decided we would go for a walk along the sea wall. We ended up walking all the way to Asilomar where the waves were crashing mightily along the shore. I totally fell in love with this magical place.

We went with Lillie on her usual treasure hunts to the plethora of thrift stores where all the volunteers would greet her. Sadly, Lillie was suffering from Alzheimer's and has returned to Lafayette to be cared for on a full time basis.

Steven, her son, has inherited her home and we now are in Pacific Grove on a more regular basis. I flew in two years ago and spent a glorious six weeks there on my own.

I volunteered at the Treasure Shop, run by the AFRP. Jane, the manager, welcomed me with open arms and I soon had new friends among the fantastic volunteers. With them, I would try out many of the fantastic restaurants within walking distance. So much to choose from!

As I am from a very tiny, remote village on Vancouver Island, I became even more enchanted with all the amenities that P.G. has to offer. The Farmers Market every Monday. The close proximity to the library and museum. The movie theatre. All those thrift stores! The Grove Market to buy groceries. The amazing sea wall path. I revel in the wondrous time I get to stay on Grand Avenue where we have an amazing view of the bay. I have watched the surfers, boats and even viewed a humpback whale breach.

If I weren't Canadian, I would gratefully and happily make Pacific Grove my permanent home. As it is, I longingly await the next time I can return and revel in the wonderful, welcoming, friendly place called Pacific Grove, California. Till we meet again!

My Heart Belongs to P.G.
Georgia A. Hubley

I'm certain the heart emoji was meant for the coastal city of Pacific Grove, California. For as long as I can remember my wish was to live on the Monterey Peninsula, because of this seaside gem often referred to as P.G. How elated I was when my wish came true. Even though I was only able to call the Monterey Peninsula home for seven years, I made each day count.

I enjoyed Pacific Grove's unique shops, galleries and eateries. Each year I counted the days until my two favorite seasonal events:

Every winter, the monarch butterflies flock to the Monarch Grove Sanctuary located just off Lighthouse Avenue.

Every spring, myriad ice plants produce a magnificent pink carpet beside the walkways along Ocean View Boulevard on the way to Lovers Point.

During any season, my favorite haunt: The Beach House restaurant at Lovers Point. It's the perfect place to relax and rejuvenate one's senses by taking in the view of the beach and bay, while having a tasty meal and a glass of wine or cocktail.

These days, my wish is to visit Pacific Grove more often, because I believe you can go home again.

Indeed, my heart belongs to P.G.

P.G. is the Best Place to Be!
Zack McCoy

Pacific Grove is where my wonderful grandma lives. Whenever my sister, Grace, and I visit we always have a blast. My favorite thing to do in P.G. is to walk along the bay on the Rec Trail, which is by Grandma's house, follow hermit crabs in the tide pools at our favorite beach at Berwick Park, and pet all the cool dogs on the trail. We always go to the Aquarium too. I love that place. Then we take the trolley to go get fresh clam chowder on Fishermans Wharf. First we try all the samples and always end up buying the same one. Over the years we have found many ways to eat it—in a bread bowl or from a cup, with sourdough rolls. But the best way to eat clam chowder is to eat it with people you love and enjoy spending time with. We sit at a table by the Bocce Courts. One time a man taught us how to play. I will forever love P.G. because I get to enjoy the town and the ocean with the people I love. Next time you visit drive, walk, or take the trolley and go get a big bowl of clam chowder!

My Pacific Grove
The Last Hometown
Sue Arlson

There are so many things one could say
About this last hometown by the bay.
The folks here are friendly, the shops are unique
With architecture both new and antique.

The beautiful monarch butterflies we see
Stop for a spell in their sanctuary.
They hang in clusters in eucalyptus trees
Until their journey south in February.

There is a yearly Butterfly Parade
Where butterflies receive accolades.
Folks come from cities around
To celebrate with this Butterfly Town!

Now butterflies are not all you can see
In this last hometown by the sea,
The seal pups draw many a crowd
With cameras clicking without making a sound.

P.G. is also a culinary delight
With food choices for any appetite.
My personal favorite is the International Cuisine
But First Awakenings is also supreme!

Then an after-dinner drive around the coast
Brings a beautiful sunset of which to boast.
The waves come crashing then roll to shore
Leaving you to stay and wait for more.

I lived there not so long ago
And often to P.G. I chance to go.
Even though I'm not there now
I still consider it my hometown!

P.G. is a Magnet
Hans Lehmann, Carmel

For me Pacific Grove is like a magnet. I don't live there. But I visit all the time. I buy take-out food at Grove Market. I stand in line at Pavel's and talk with strangers. I visit Germain Hatcher at her lovely Imagine Art Supplies. I shop at Pacific Grove Hardware with their outstanding service. I pick up my cleaning at Pacific Grove Cleaners while chatting with Randy. I go to Joe or Laura for my travel needs at Pacific Grove Travel. I watch the musical, Beauty and the Beast, at P.G. High. I walk at Lovers Point. I talk to Dave Laredo at the Good Old Days' Pancake Breakfast. In short I feel I am part of the community. Although I am not. Wherever I go I breathe P.G.'s love and laughter. Children. Adults. Strollers. Dogs. I may not live there. *But someday I might.*

A Blend of Carmel and Pebble Beach
Bill Meyer
Pebble Beach

Tourists to the Monterey Peninsula often say, "You must see Carmel because of its interesting homes, eclectic shops and wonderful beach." They may also say, "You must also see Pebble Beach because of its craggy beach fronts with its exploding waves and wonderful homes."

What they don't say is, "You must see Pacific Grove." They may think of it as an adjacent bedroom community for those who can't afford to live in Carmel or Pebble Beach.

However, they should say, "You must also see Pacific Grove because of its diverse and wonderful shops on Lighthouse Avenue. Pacific Grove includes Victorian homes spaced throughout the community and homes with a wonderful view of the ocean. It is endowed with more historical houses per capita than anywhere else in California. The city is also known as the location of the Point Pinos Lighthouse, the oldest continuously operating lighthouse on the West Coast. It includes an excellent public golf links that costs a fraction of those in Pebble Beach. It includes excellent restaurants housed in historic homes and a mayor who is fully dedicated to serving the citizens of Pacific Grove." In summary, tourists to the area should be saying, "You must also see Pacific Grove."

What I Love About Living in P.G.
Joyce Day Meuse
mother, grandmother, wife, pet lover

Back in the wild days of the early 1970s I happened upon Pacific Grove. Having always lived in the suburbs of the East coast, this small town with its variety of homes and exotic flowers, plants and trees was a great discovery. It seemed like a dream. That feeling returns whenever I take a walk among the Monterey pines or the constantly shifting vistas of Asilomar Beach.

Today, the sun shines brightly from our amazing azure blue sky. A walk in the park is a feast for my eyes, ears and nose. The whole area is alive and vibrant after our much-needed rainy winter.

The wildlife on land and in the ocean is always a delight. The deer are abundant and often seen grazing on the golf courses. Raccoons flourish with their nocturnal visits that always causes neighborhood dogs to bark. I've seen the tail end of a bob cat disappearing into the park one night. I also saw a coyote crossing 17 Mile Drive in nearby Pebble Beach. An opossum set up home in my kitchen in the back of my washing machine for a few days.

Pelicans are a favorite as they fly in formation along the coastline. The white egrets are always a treat on their long graceful legs. I once went to Lovers Point Park and saw a group of people gathered near the Cypress trees. They were all looking up at a Golden Eagle perched above. It soon spread its wings and flew up to the roof of the nearby restaurant. It was so big it was hard to believe it was a bird.

It stayed on the roof briefly before it took to the sky.

The summer of 2015 was amazing as an up-welling of cold-water currents caused a huge gathering of all kinds of sea creatures closer to land than usual. Observing a whale close to land is always inspiring. That late summer was captured in a documentary by the BBC and PBS called Big Blue Live. The highlight of the show was when they filmed a blue whale in the area, the largest mammal on earth. We see the yearly migration of gray whales heading south to their birthing area in Baja. Orca sightings are an occasional treat. Schools of dolphins surfing the waves are a delight. The sea lions are always hanging around with their noisy barking. Spring is pupping season where the moms are protected by fences and people can observe the newborn pups being born.

One of my favorite things here is the beautiful "magic carpet" of bright fuchsia colored flowers. It only blooms in May which makes it my favorite month of the year. Along this coastline with its spiky Aloe Vera plants with reddish orange blossoms, the addition of the sweet-smelling magic carpet reminds me of how lucky I am to have landed in paradise.

The Many Pleasures I See
Jintanan Forinash

Pacific Grove (P.G.) is the "Last Hometown," situated between Monterey and Pebble Beach. Life in P.G. is at a slow pace, that's why there are some vacation homes owned by probably high-strung people who want to live a laid-back lifestyle.

When I walked around P.G., I noticed that the sizes of many homes were very small and most of their yards were small, too. Those houses were built so close to one another. I think it is a good idea that people don't bite off more than they can chew. Anyhow, I found the answer when I asked some friends who live in P.G.; they told me that the town was sectioned off for tents. Furthermore, when I looked closer to all those old houses, I saw the names of the first owners as well as the years the houses were built.

P.G.'s landscape is unique; there are attractive ocean-front properties along the area where the land touches the water. In addition, along the shoreline there is an enchanting "purple carpet" perpetually spread out during the months of April and May. The purple flowers' fragrance of ice plant is there to contribute to its sweet smell. People who come to enjoy this breathtaking waterfront of P.G. love to take pictures to show off that they have visited this slice of paradise.

P.G. possesses the historic lighthouse, which was operated in the past to guide the ships that made port of call in the Monterey Bay. Today, you can visit this lighthouse and exercise your imagination relating to what happened in the earlier years.

Since the Monterey Peninsula is known as a popular golf destination, there are many beautiful green golf courses close to the water's edge. I enjoy watching those deer grazing on the golf courses and the cemetery.

Another example of the best of P.G. is the butterfly sanctuary. The smart monarch butterflies choose P.G. to be their habitat during the winter months. Every year in October, there is the Butterfly Parade, and the monarch butterflies are an integral theme.

Better yet, every summer, PG celebrates the Feast of Lanterns to commemorate the way of life in the Chinese in the fishing village which existed before the heyday of the sardine factories.

Even though P.G. is a very small town, it can still boast its Lighthouse Cinemas as one of the best on the Peninsula. I love their comfy rocking chairs and the location. On Tuesdays all day you get a discount, one dollar off.

P.G. offers the best spot to admire the beauty of the setting sun at Asilomar on a clear day. Visitors or tourists should take this opportunity. While you are there, you will see a lot of pelicans and other kinds of birds flying in line above the water; they head in the direction of Pebble Beach to retire at Bird Rock and Seal Rock. I love to look at the turquoise blue water along the beach between Asilomar and P.G.

Originally, I was from Bangkok, Thailand. I won an assistantship to go get my education in Iowa. When I graduated at the University of Iowa in 1991, I saw an ad in the *Chronicle of Higher Education* for a Thai instructor to teach at the Defense Language Institute (DLI) in Monterey, It was interesting that the ad mentioned how beautiful the location of the Institute was. Looking out the Monterey Bay, you would enjoy the blue water and the pleasant atmosphere around the workplace. Immediately, I applied for the teaching position and moved to the Monterey Peninsula to go to work at the DLI.

Ever since, I have been living around the Peninsula—Marina, Old and New Monterey, Del Rey Oaks, Pebble Beach, and Pacific Grove. Last July, 2016 I moved back to Pacific Grove and found a great roommate to share an apartment on Lighthouse Avenue. I find that I have started a really good life in this town. Living a slow pace life is just going well for me. I feel at home even though I have no family here. I have many friends. Pacific Grove provides many social activities which keep me busy and I never feel lonely. In the springtime, I enjoy walking along the purple carpet. I smell the fragrance of the ice plants. Every Monday afternoon, I meander around Pacific Grove Farmers' Market and visit with a friend and feel relaxed.

I can enjoy international foods at the market, Indian, Mexican, Thai, Japanese, and Middle Eastern. Moreover, Pacific Grove has a good library where I go very often.

This summer I started a writing workshop at the Pacific Grove Adult Education Center. I have learned to write columns, short stories, sonnets, and so on.

The other Sunday, I went for a picnic at Lovers Point with a group of ESL students. We enjoyed a gorgeous day to hang out near the water.

Sally Griffin is one of the best places for senior citizens. You can get a healthy lunch for three dollars. All year round they provide seniors with many different interesting activities, such as exercise classes, bus trips, a creative writing group, and older adult classes sponsored by Monterey Peninsula College.

Finally, I end up living in the Last Hometown. Better yet, as a social butterfly myself, I have returned to Butterfly Town, USA.

Friends are integral parts of my life. Wherever I live, I make friends with many nice people. At the Sally Griffin Center and other community centers in P.G., I find it is easy to look for friends. Most of my daily activities are done with friends. Most Wednesday afternoons, I meet up with a friend from Marina at various coffee shops for a cup of coffee or Chai tea to exchange current information.

As a retiree, I am busier than the time when I was working. Since my husband passed away, I have more free time and freedom. I have time for friends. Even though, I don't really have to work for food, some friends expect me to accept their appreciation. For instance, a German friend wants me to entertain her elderly and sick mother by telling short or funny stories, or simply visit with her; in return, she cooks German food for me. A Russian friend who likes going mushrooming usually shares edible and delicious mushrooms with me. Occasionally, other friends want me to accompany them on day trips, doctor visits or shopping out of town; they treat me to lunch. Among a few Thai friends, I help them with the English language. In addition to interpreting at the courthouses, they need help to fill out some forms, or translating documents and interpreting from English to Thai and Thai to English. They love to treat me to delicious meals. Sometimes, they cook for me at their house as well as eating out.

I belong to a creative writing group that meets at the Sally Griffin Center every Tuesday afternoon. We write about our own life stories and what-not.

Anyhow, I imagine myself as a butterfly. I enjoy skimming and dashing here and there around the Monterey Peninsula. Once in a while, I travel to check out other paradises in order to compare to this paradise where I have been living. So far, I have decided to live in Pacific Grove.

The Rollicking Boulevard
Blanca Shield

I have an eagle's eye view of Ocean View Boulevard, breezy with vivacious animation.

This avenue has a walking path to run, bike or just sit on wooden benches and enjoy the view of sea otters, sailboats and fishing boats.

Jumbo tour coaches flashing primary colors compete, their tourists gasping at the surrounding loveliness.

Life on Ocean View Boulevard is in constant motion:

November has the Big Sur Half Marathon. This scenic coastline is a showcase to those runners. The gently-rolling 13.1 mile course travels through historic Monterey, down Cannery Row, and along Ocean View Boulevard on the way to Asilomar and back.

In Pacific Grove the Holiday Parade of Lights is held each December. It's a community event with marching bands through historic Monterey, down Cannery Row, along Ocean View Boulevard and into downtown Pacific Grove.

The annual Pacific Grove Auto Rally on Lighthouse Avenue popularizes old cars. These antique cars parade in late afternoon on Ocean View Boulevard, escorted by motorcycle police.

Each year the Butterfly Parade features children in costume to welcome the monarchs back to "Butterfly Town USA" for the winter.

The famous aquarium at the far end of the boulevard faces the open sea. The treasures within become a child's revelation. Snow White and the seven dwarfs multiplied by hundreds. Foreign languages surround the Kelp Forest at feeding time of the white and leopard sharks, green sea turtles, green moray eels and tuna as they speed past sardines swarming in huge glittering schools. The Splash Zone penguins at ground level tickle the fancy of the children, raising smiles and laughter. In the background come faint happy sounds from the corners of the aquarium.

Ocean View Boulevard is Pacific Grove's El Camino Real.

VISITOR INFORMATION CENTERS

Central and Forest Avenues—and at Central and Eardley Avenues

Moe Ammar
President of the Chamber of Commerce

I met my wife Trina when I was a freshman at UNLV in 1976 studying Hospitality Management. She was a nursing student. In 1979 when we got married, she decided that we would honeymoon in Pacific Grove, California. I had not heard of P.G. before. She is from Marin and used to come down here with her family. We spent two nights at the Bid-A-Wee motel on Sunset.

I fell in love with the town and great people. It was a dream to work and live here one day. When I graduated college, I worked for Hyatt Hotels, then ITT Sheraton Hotels. In December of 1986, I was transferred to the Monterey Sheraton. Trina loved the area and was not willing to move or transfer anywhere. She got a job at CHOMP as the lactation coordinator. Joe Shammas of P.G. Travel was my agent.

When the Chamber of Commerce job opened up in February of 1993, I connected with him and was hired to run the chamber. It has been a labor of love. One of the first people that I met was Richard Stillwell. Richard told me that there are two ways of doing things in P.G., the wrong way or his way. P.G. was and is still unique.

I recall Nora Flatley, co-owner of the Seven Gables Inn, delivering food to the chamber and was always telling me that I am too skinny and need to gain some weight. Don Martine of the Martine Inn opened his inn and hosted a reception to welcome me.

Over the years, I worked with the great people of P.G. such as Dr. James Hughes, Jan Hanson, Erma Dinkel, Morrie Fisher, Fire Chief Don Gasperson, Steve Gorman, Mayors Jeanne Byrne and Sandy Koffman, and John Miller from the Recreation Department. I enjoyed working with six City Managers, five Police Chiefs, and countless city staff members such as Don Mothershead.

Twenty-three years ago, Terry Davis came to see me at the chamber. He told me that he wanted to start a triathlon. I did not know what it was. I helped Terry get it going. I served as a director for few years. The chamber members were meeting one day at Victorian Corner. Ambassador Diane Johnson wanted to have a snow machine blowing snow on top of Holman's. We all thought it was a crazy idea. Richard Stillwell thought it was a good idea. That started Stillwell's Snow in the Park. Flavors of P.G. was started five years ago to feature P.G. chefs. The event has sold out every year for the past five years. Nothing compares to Good Old Days. With 240 vendors, 60 bands, and five stages, it is P.G.'s largest show.

As I am completing my 25 years on the job, I find it interesting that I am interacting with the kids or the grandkids of the business leaders that I worked with 25 years ago. That is a great feeling … there is continuity. I have lived in six countries and visited 46, and I believe that P.G. is the best. I hope that my three kids will be able to live here and raise their families.

Central & Eardley Tourist Center
Erik Adamson

I'm employed with the Pacific Grove Chamber of Commerce. I've been with the Chamber for over five years and work out of our Tourist Information Center. I have been called the Pacific Grove "Destination Expert." Since I've been here, we've had more than 500,000 guests and visitors from all over the world. It's my job to welcome our guests and provide them with information about Pacific Grove—places to stay the night, to get something to eat, or to do some shopping and sightseeing in our beautiful town.

As for myself, I've been a local all my life. My parents moved here from Jersey City, New Jersey. I am the only California native in my family. After my parents, my grandparents moved here, as well as uncles and aunts. I choose to call Pacific Grove my home because it honestly is one of the most beautiful places in the world.

It is a hidden gem that offers the most surreal experience. My passions are walking along our Pacific Coast Recreation Trail with my girlfriend all year round, especially when the magic pink carpet (ice plants) are in full bloom. With its Victorian homes, seascape and picturesque downtown, it all seems to fit that bill. This is why I call Pacific Grove home—for the beauty, but also for the memories.

Mom and the Picture-Perfect Photo
Summer Montanez

The earliest memory I have as a child was around four years old, sitting within the "Magic Carpet" that blankets a small portion of the Pacific Grove coastline. My mother would push me in my stroller as she walked along the trail looking for the perfect spot. She would help me climb out of the stroller and seat me within the biggest patch of flowers she could find. I remember feeling the cold ice plant on my legs as my mom positioned my dress and hat just right, enough to keep the breeze from lifting them away. Standing with camera in hand Mom would have to coax me into looking at the camera from afar, waiving her arm in the air and calling out to me to get her picture-perfect ocean backdrop. Most of our photos revealed me looking around, eyes wide as can be, mesmerized by the hundreds of neon pink petals that surrounded me.

I look forward every spring to their arrival, making the ocean that much bluer than any other time of the year. It puts a smile on my face seeing locals and visitors from all over snapping their pictures and taking time out to enjoy one of many events that make Pacific Grove so special.

P.G. Favorites
Nina Grannis
retired consultant, volunteer

We arrived in Pacific Grove after looking up and down the coast for a possible place to buy, with retirement in mind. My daughter-in-law's grandfather lived in Carmel and he suggested checking out Pacific Grove. We found our wonderful "home away from home" here in P.G., and now it's my permanent home, which I love.

My favorite person in P.G. was Nadine Anand, who has passed away. I met her at Feast of Lanterns soon after we bought our house and she tried to get me to join every organization in Pacific Grove. She was known as "Mrs. P.G." and is still thought of fondly today.

My favorite place is walking my dog Bella among the "magic carpet" which blooms in May/June. Beautiful sights and great pictures with my camera.

I also enjoy my time at the Point Pinos Lighthouse where I meet so many wonderful tourists and is a wonderful place to hang out.

My favorite event is a toss-up between Good Old Days and Feast of Lanterns. Both are entirely different functions, but Pacific Grove would not be the same without both events.

I was born in Missouri, married at 20 and moved to New Jersey where my husband Gary taught high school and I worked for a consulting firm.

After a couple of years Gary got a teaching assistant job at Texas A&M and also received his doctorate while there. I worked on campus and both of our boys were born in College Station, Texas.

We then moved to Fresno where he taught for 36 years and I owned a travel agency. I moved here permanently in 2009.

I volunteer at the PG Chamber, am a chamber ambassador, manage the Point Pinos Lighthouse gift shop am a member of the Heritage Society board, received the "Volunteer of the Year" award in 2015, and am active with Adobe Questers.

Life in Pacific Grove is GOOD!

OUR WEATHER SUITS US FINE

Weather Talk
Jeffrey Whitmore

There's some question whether it was Mark Twain or his pal Charles Dudley Warner who wrote, "Everybody talks about the weather, but nobody does anything about it." It's also debatable which man wrote, "If you don't like the weather in New England, just wait a few minutes."

In early April of 1967, I had waited through a New England winter and part of the following spring for the weather to change from lousy to not-so-lousy. It hadn't.

If the two aphorists were wrong on one count, I figured they might be wrong on the other. I decided the best thing I could do about New England weather was to leave it behind. I headed for California to visit an ex-army buddy who used to boast about the Golden State's weather.

I left Logan Airport in a snowstorm, landed in SFO in sunshine, and took a cab to my friend's house in Palo Alto. The next morning I went out to his backyard in my underwear and picked an orange from a tree. Case closed.

I soon moved to Berkeley, got a job and a driver's license, and registered to vote. I became an official Californian.

Four years later, my new family—three native-born Californians and I—moved to Pacific Grove. We'd visited it before and found it delightful. In some ways it reminded me of the Cape Cod town where I'd spent most of my youth. Each town had at one time been the last in its state to legalize the sale of liquor. (In 1971, the venerable Last Chance Saloon in handy New Monterey was still a reminder of dry times in Pacific Grove.) Each town had also been home to campgrounds for summer religious retreats. Today the area known as the Retreat section in Pacific Grove and the area in Eastham, Massachusetts, called Campground Road hark back to similar Puritanical eras of the past.

Our first house was on Sixth Street near Pine Avenue. We were told it was in "The Sun Belt." We later decided it was a running gag favored by realtors.

One weekend an amateur astronomer friend from Berkeley visited us. The nights were unusually clear. The stars sparkled. How different from the light-polluted nights of Berkeley! Within a month he'd moved to Pacific Grove. Alas, his telescope seldom pierced our persistent fog. He departed in search of a less fogbound clime.

Occasionally I'm asked if I miss the changing seasons.

I try to look wise. I grip my chin, look off into the middle distance, etc.

And I say, "No."

If there's anything weather-wise I miss about New England, it's the warm summer nights. They're rare in Pacific Grove. When they occur, they're a blessing, and we locals stroll the streets. Though the shops downtown may be closed for the night, happy wanderers are still afoot there.

Unless—as some maintain—global warming is a "Chinese hoax," those nights may soon become less rarified. Till then our weather suits me just fine.

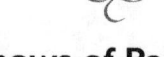

The Snows of Pacific Grove
Barbara Rose Shuler

We arrived in Pacific Grove in a blue Chevy station wagon on January 22, 1962, the day it snowed here for the first time in forty years. I had just turned eleven, and my brother Mark was nine. Stunned by the snowfall, the townsfolk and visiting Crosby Tournament golfers displayed what seemed to us as odd agitation, as if a crimson elephant had just charged down tree-lined Lighthouse Avenue.

"Snow! Snow! Oh my!"

"I know I had some drinks last night, but how did I end up in Squaw Valley?" a veteran Crosby player famously quipped of the snowy landscape.

People stared in disbelief at our car, with the large ice deposits still clinging to it from the freezing winter journey we had just made across the country. We stared back, puzzled at how snow and ice could create such a fuss.

Intrigued but detached from this weather uproar, we set about finding a place to live. We received a warm welcome though we knew no one in the region. My mother, Loel, had chosen Pacific Grove for its coastal beauty, for proximity to live music, live theater, diverse intellectual pursuits and its kid-friendly atmosphere - a different setting from our early childhood in southeastern Alaska.

We settled into a forested rental on Grove Acre, not far from the Butterfly Trees. The trees fascinated me, as I had watched monarchs hatch from their cocoons the previous summer at my grandparents' home in Michigan and learned of their westward migration.

The Michigan butterflies brought me here, I would muse to my young self, marveling when the town filled vibrantly with the dazzling creatures.

My mother chose well. If we had to leave Alaska, Pacific Grove seemed an ideal second best. In those days, rents were low, schools were good, and budget-conscious families could live here with ease. Performing arts indeed flourished on the Monterey Peninsula, and soon my mother established herself as a respected theater teacher, performer and director. I picnicked in the parks and at Lovers Point, played on Asilomar Beach and went folk dancing with new friends. I explored old Cannery Row with its colorful characters, like Kalisa of the famed bohemian coffee house, La Ida Cafe.

We moved into a house on 2nd Street near Cannery Row that once belonged to John Steinbeck's aunt, which under my mother's aegis turned into an informal salon for performers, artists, writers and intellectuals. The house was always full of interesting people, among them the poet Ric Masten and James Drury, the star of the TV program *The Virginian*. I remember a dancer named Ishvani from India, who said our sweet dog, Vanilla, had eaten too much of the lotus blossom. And a mysterious man named Kaidee who spoke of the wisdom of the *I Ching*.

Later, we purchased a home up the street, another residence that once belonged to a Steinbeck relative, where I live and write today. Steinbeck's good friend Ed Ricketts spent time in Sitka, Alaska, where I first grew up. His collaborator Jack Calvin was a friend of my parents. (I recently met Ed's daughter Nancy while visiting Sitka, who spoke of her early days growing up in a house on 4th Street near here ... another Cannery Row-Sitka connection.)

Much has changed since that January day when we three bedraggled Alaskans made landfall in The Last Hometown, our car caked with ice and dust of the road. My heart leaps now to see a lone monarch butterfly, when once thousands fluttered over the town during their annual return. Urbanization and environmental stresses have caused a decline of their Pacific Grove habitat.

I remember balance-walking the train-track rails where a bike path now curves along the shore. I did homework perched in cypress trees by the kelp-covered sea, studied tide pools, gazed at the sea floor from glass-bottom boats at Lovers Point, and bought cookies after school at Hector De Smet's Bakery. Once at Lighthouse Elementary School, I won a writing contest that gave my class free ice-cream for a day with a full week for me. I do not remember the topic but it may have had to do with butterflies.

Many memories fade. But I'll never forget the snows of Pacific Grove.

(Since coming to PG in 1962, Barbara and Mark Shuler both lived in the region until their mother, Loel's, death in 2011, when Mark moved to the East Coast. Barbara still lives in PG.)

Coastal Air
Joe Jacobson
website designer for authors

Family reunion in Pacific Grove/Monterey—In July of 2015, I came to know a bit about Pacific Grove. It was time for a family reunion and this year, we selected Monterey as our destination. It had been many years (in fact decades) since I had visited this part of California.

I was born in Southern California, but left that area as soon as I went off to college. I lived in many areas of California, from the Sierra mountains to the northern coastal towns. I also attended UC Santa Cruz and once took a bike ride through P.G. and Monterey as a student. I lived in several states including Washington, Montana, New Mexico and finally Florida, where I presently reside.

So, in July of 2015, I was happy to be leaving the hot and humid climate of Florida for a brief respite in the cool climate of the central California coast. I had scheduled to stay for two weeks to allow some time to enjoy the environs after the family reunion festivities.

Since I had family living in P.G. and Monterey (and Santa Cruz area), I was able to visit all the nearby towns. My mom was living in P.G., so I spent many days tagging along on her routine jaunts in P.G. We visited the library and several shops in the bustling little downtown area, and was also a guest at the Central Coast Writers monthly meeting and a special summer barbecue. I have to say that the CCW group was one of the most organized and successfully run writer's groups I've attended.

After enjoying the cool coastal air for two weeks, it was time to go home. But then I asked myself, "Do I really have to go back now?" After all, I have my own online business and I can work from anywhere.

I checked with my host (my sister) and asked to stay another two weeks. That additional two weeks gave me time to visit more special places in the area, including Carmel Valley, Carmel by-the-Sea, Santa Cruz, and Felton.

I also got to meet with Patricia Hamilton, owner of Park Place Publications. I was able to help her consolidate all her websites from WordPress.com into an organized package of sites on my hosting platform for authors, WordsandWriters.com.

After a month's stay in Monterey and P.G., I was just getting used to the weather. So, what else could I do … change my return airline ticket for one more month! By the end of the two-month visit, I was almost starting to feel like a Californian again. I became a regular at Whole Foods, Trader Joe's, and the Farmers Market. I learned to navigate around the area's byways and neighborhoods.

One day when I retire, I'd like to live in a town like P.G., where you can walk from one end of town to another without hitting too many street lights.

Shark Weather
Lillian Griffiths

My dad, David Griffiths, started working in his dream job as managing superintendent of Pacific Grove Golf Links when I was a sophomore at Pacific Grove High. After the water shortages of the early 70s, my dad was given the Water Miser Award from the City of P.G. for managing to keep the golf course playable while still conserving water.

As those of us who live here know, when it does start to rain here it pours, as it did in the winter of 1976-77. A steady rainfall deposited water everywhere and especially on the 11th green where a lake formed—getting as deep as six feet.

The Welsh are known for their sense of humor and for being one with rain! A truck tire was found and a board soon attached that looked like a shark fin when painted. It was then placed in the "11th green lake" where it sort of floated around with the wind and water. A sign was eventually put up stating "BEWARE OF SHARK." News outlets, even in San Francisco, picked up the story of the stranded shark and people started to flock to Pacific Grove from the town and surrounding areas to observe the amazing sight. One woman was most concerned how the shark would be safely returned to the ocean. The fact that there was the green, the rough, a road, and the shore rocks to cross to accomplish this escaped her notice. Most folks enjoyed the prank but a few never quite got it.

The sign was eventually stolen and is probably hidden in someone's garage to this day. Eventually the lake dried up and the "shark" managed to safely return to its birthplace.

Midwestern Women and Weather
Jeanne Marino

I came to Pacific Grove in 1977 from a little town called Mt. Clemens, MI. It was home to mineral baths, blue ice cones, Miller Brothers Creamery, sledding down neighbor's hills, sailing on Lake St. Clair and catching lightning bugs in the summer. Not bad you might say. Well yes, but then there is snow and ice.

It was the ice storm of '77 that really got to me. I couldn't take "winter" any longer. I decided after working on a congressional campaign, that I would "Go West" in search of adventure. I started in San Francisco, drifted to Palo Alto and then stumbled into Pacific Grove to visit my friend Jane. That very day Jane answered the door to her apartment she rented on 17-Mile Drive and Lighthouse. She grabbed my hand and said, "Great, you're just in time for a party." It was a crazy 70's bash, one I didn't expect to see in quaint and quiet Pacific Grove. At the party I met a gal who sold me her car for $200, and a man who said he could find me a job no problem. I was convinced he was a long-lost cousin because he had the same last name as mine. All the signs pointed to my revelation that I found my new home.

This was the time of the late 70's, which meant a ton of fun for 20-somethings. But it was also the time of serious drought years. I moved in with my friend Jane and two other women. The two-bedroom apartment was not made for the four of us and with water restrictions I decided to look for another place to live. I found a great place in Jacks Peak with a roommate who was from Fort Wayne, Indiana. About 8 months later we moved to a place in Carmel Valley. Neither one of us liked living so far out so we moved back to Pacific Grove. My friend Jane moved in. There we were, three Midwest women all under one roof. We had moved to this small little town each on our own and independent of each other. What I find remarkable was that in a few years, another friend named Jane, who also grew up in Mt. Clemens found out that I lived in town. She lives two blocks away. I wonder, how is it that we 3 ladies from the same Midwest town decided on Pacific Grove?

I've lived in Carmel, Monterey, Carmel Valley and Pebble Beach. I find Pacific Grove offers a great place to be for the long run. With neighborly neighbors, a conveniently located Post Office, Grove Market as well as other grocers are easily accessible, so many good restaurants, shopping and so close to the beaches and the ocean, that we can hear it from our house. I can't imagine living anywhere else. Maybe it just feels as solid as the Midwest. However or whatever it is, this is home.

Nella Nebia ...
My life in Pacific Grove 2012 to present
Sandra Thompson Iman
realtor

Nella Nebia, moving ahead through the fog, so symbolic of my move to the town of Pacific Grove. Mornings of fog over the coastline and myself with sickening fog so dark and ill inside my own heart and mind. Would it ever be lifted? Would I ever see the light? Would the burden ever be laid down so that I may feel hope and freedom once again? My little prayer was "Nella Nebia"—keep moving through the fog, through the night, through the pressing torment of an army of thoughts like bullets shooting holes in my brain where I was fighting for life, love, peace of mind and clarity. Would I ever be at peace? Here is the backlog in silver bullets:

In 2006, my life began to shatter, first with the death of my husband whom I was married to for 30 years. We had met in Big Sur in the early 1970s. I was a hippie hitchhiking around the country with my friend and one day ended up in Big Sur Grange Hall. That is where George and I met; he was very square and had come to Big Sur to visit a friend. All I can say is, "I knew he would keep me safe." When George passed away I was a very successful real estate agent in Salinas, on the top of my game. The second blow came very soon. In April 2007, my 30-year-old daughter passed away and that was nearly the end for me. Things continued to decline, and blow number three was in 2008 when my miniature poodle that my family shared for 17 years had to be put to sleep because of illness.

In 2009, my dad, who lived 3,000 miles away, passed away and left behind my scared and aging lovely mom. I traveled back and forth a few times till things were set for my mother and I knew she would be in good hands. In 2010 I still owned four homes but I was done with life and sold three with no profit because of the real estate climate at that time. As time went on, my personal residence became a prison of sorts to my psyche, just too many memories. I thought it was better to sell and move on.

That I did! I was broken "Why am I myself?" My world became dark and very small. I had lost everything and I did not know me anymore.

All I could see was a tiny light that I will call HOPE but it seemed so far away. Many times I thought God hated me and He was laying divine punishment on me because He and I both knew my past very well. Somehow I knew I deserved all these tragedies. As the story unfolds you will see that is not the case.

Recovery or Despair?

My inherited drama since the death of my daughter Anastacia: As a mom, the torment of my failures, so much grief and voiceless moaning that she is cannot hear when I call her name. I cannot "fix it." Where does the flame go when the candle is blown out? So many questions and many revelations. I cannot go back, I cannot change one little thing; she is gone, I cannot feel her, I cannot hold her, an empty space that could never be filled by another. She was mine, she grew inside me, I took her everywhere I went for nine months, no sleeping or taking a nap without us being together.

We shared every meal, she heard every word I spoke, every song I sang, and she felt everything I did. We were one and then she was birthed and such a wonder, so beautiful and gentle and soft, so needy for everything and my joy was fulfilling all her little needs and desires. Soft warm clothes and cuddly blankets, rocking and nursing and forgetting about all the cares of the world just so I could be with my beautiful baby.

Was it all in vain? I loved my child, my miracle of life … how can it be that she is not with me now? Will I ever recover? Not today!!!!! Swing low sweet chariot, and let me hop aboard and fly away with joy, expectation and the realization that the promises are true and heaven is real and we truly do reunite. I guess memories are the only place the past can gather. It is turmoil in my soul; I want to leave this earth to reunite.

BUT … the beauty of my youngest daughter, who is still here on earth with me, who I can hug and kiss, enjoy her grown-upness and watch her motherly instincts with her own son, my adorable grandson, is my new hope and joy made manifest.

This has truly been a monumental part of my "recovery." Watching the beauty of their relationship brings my soul back in balance and inspires me to live and try again at redeeming my past torments. It is scary. I am not very good at this but I choose to move forward through the fog—the Nella Nebia—and exercise faith and hope. Hope, Hope, Hope! So many things to hope for and I have been blessed to see many blessings in my life. Today I am good. I walk the salty paths beside the sea, I believe in goodness and the vastness of God the Creator. Surely He is the only one who can mend this broken heart. A miracle brought me here and a miracle is healing my heart.

Up to Date in Pacific Grove:

Well, 2016 has supplied me with some inner struggles; holidays are still very sensitive but so far I am on the winning side and sailing into a new year with only a few bumps and bruises. During the week of Christmas to New Years, my tummy was not normal, I thought I may be dying; that is always my first thought if something in my body does not feel right. It was serious in my head and I carried the thought around continually everywhere I went I was very conscious it could be my last day, month or hopefully year in my subconscious. The thought made me ponder and took me to higher and deeper in places in my heart and mind as I thought of my earthly departing …. Okay, I do love a good drama and the reality was magnified and BOOM—I began to sense with my eyes and lots of heart the deeper knowledge of the beauty I am surrounded by, the loving family and friends who are in my life. The things I love became more intense and I found myself opening up areas inside of me to let the wonderful work progress.

One of the great lessons that I have learned is that sometimes "the valley of the shadow of death" cannot be avoided. It's back to my Nella Nebia, keep moving through the fog and follow that dim light till the sun shines on you once again. Be willing to change and master your disappointment, although I would much rather spend my time mastering fulfillment.

POLITICIANS AND APPRECIATIONS

Buying into Pacific Grove
Rudy and Kathleen Fischer
happy residents
Rudy–Councilman and Chair of MRWPCA

When Kathleen and I lived and worked in Silicon Valley, we used to take weekend trips to towns along the coast—Bodega Bay, Healdsburg, Half Moon Bay and Pacific Grove. At one point we talked about buying a house in the town we wanted to eventually retire in. Pacific Grove, of course, ranked quite high on that list.

Kathleen loves bed and breakfast inns, and during our visits we stayed in some great places such as Centrella Inn, Martine Inn, Sea Breeze Lodge, and many others. We also ate at many of the city's restaurants—and always had a lunch at Taste on the way out of town and back to the Bay Area.

I think we were also impressed by the golf course running down the middle of town. Neither one of us are "beach people," so the rocky shores here were just fine with us. Besides, living between Monterey, Pebble Beach and Carmel, we figured we would never run out of good restaurants to go to.

On one such home shopping trip to Pacific Grove, Liz Bratty of Bratty and Bluhm showed us several places. There were some that were old, some that were funky, and several that were quite nice. At one point we went to Liz's office to talk about some of the houses we had looked at.

As we were talking, one of the other agents looked out the window to the middle Lighthouse Avenue and asked if we had parked a car out there. We looked and there was a police officer getting ready to ticket Kathleen's car! She got up and ran into the middle of the street and started talking to the officer. As Liz, the other agent, and I watched, Kathleen spoke to the agent and explained why we had been parked there so long. The officer eventually nodded his head, closed up his ticket book, and walked away.

I turned to Liz and the other agent and simply said, "I think the police just helped you make a sale."

Now as far as those golf links—little did I know then that I would someday be on the Golf Link Advisory Commission, which would lead to being on the City Council, which would lead to those golf links being a headache for me at times … but we still love Pacific Grove!

Pacific Grove is Home
Bill Peake
city council member

I couldn't wait to leave New Jersey behind and live somewhere far away. Not that New Jersey is a bad place; it's just that I needed to see the world. The opportunity came with an invitation to attend graduate school at UC Berkeley. Although I mistakenly thought California was all sun and beaches, this disappointment soon dissipated after exploring the Bay Area and Monterey Peninsula. The wild coast and trees of the Peninsula struck me as a truly fantastic place.

Fast forward a few years; Shirley and I married, lived in Sumatra where our two boys were born, and settled in the San Francisco East Bay. Shirley also found the Peninsula 'very cool,' not thinking that we could manage to purchase a small house in Asilomar in 1990. It continued to be the perfect spot to call home while we followed work for Chevron up and down California and then around the world: Kuwait, Calgary, and Kazakhstan.

Our first P.G. friends were Tim and Cleo McCoy, the couple that sold us the home and who lived behind us. Tim had the last typewriter store in Monterey. He always had Hershey's chocolate bars to give our young boys, Tom and Dave. And we often visited with Cleo, who was bedridden with MS.

Finally unpacking our bags for good in 2010, making new friends came easily. One of the first was Maureen Mason who quickly welcomed us 'into the fold' and began making plans for me. Shirley's creative passion for making beaded jewelry took off and a small business was born. Arts and crafts shows and the P.G. farmers market became regular affairs for us.

I had caught the wonderful volunteer spirit of P.G. and found spots on the Recreation Board, Heritage Society Board and Lighthouse preservation team. Such terrific and encouraging people—Jean, Don, Mary, Ken, Carol, and Maureen—would launch me to City Council a short time later. Folks write and say, "You have a thankless job," but reality is quite different as people are very appreciative. It truly has been an honor and privilege to serve P.G.

Shirley and I can't think of any better place to be than P.G. It has the best people, willing to give of themselves in many different ways.

A Satirical Look at Life In Pacific Grove As a City Changes Over Time

Ken Cuneo
city council member

The ever restless sea. Yes, that is what I think and believe when the subject is the city of Pacific Grove.

When I moved here in 1992, my vision of Pacific Grove was that of an immutable object anchored into its sturdy granite roots of established families, interesting and often quaint homes and a different tune compared to other local cities such as Monterey and Carmel.

Pacific Grove was the collecting point for all sorts of characters, many still here to this day. Its culture was buttressed by a series of annual events that harkened back to its founding many years past. It was a different time.

Yes, this place was on a nostalgia high when operating traditional events such as the Feast of Lanterns. Never mind that this Chinese faux story of the Blue Willow plate was edited by locals for the entertainment of the residents. There was in fact an actual Chinese Fishing Village that burned in a suspicious fire over 100 years ago. It was located on the grounds where today both the Stanford Hopkins Marine Station and Monterey Bay Aquarium sit. The Chinese inhabitants of the Fishing Village after this disastrous fire were not allowed to rebuild. So they left and moved elsewhere.

Now year after year Pacific Grove continues with its Feast of Lanterns, crowning its Royal Court from the most part the same families from yesteryear's pageant. (I volunteer for this event every year.)

But hark, beneath this powerful back-to-the-past defensive shield a slight vapor of change began to settle in. Old ways were suddenly and subtly challenged. As the slow life and the physical beauty of its three mile coastline became known, new people running the rat race in San Jose, Silicon Valley, and San Francisco made a promise to get off the treadmill of heavy traffic, high crime, and neighbors with names that they could not pronounce. They decided that at some point to get out of Dodge and move to Pacific Grove.

Armed with silicon-sized salaries, these new residents purchased homes at very high rates. This had the effect like an Anaconda of slow but inevitable strangulation, making it impossible for many local residents (today I could not buy my current home) to either rent or purchase a home. If this wasn't bad enough, many of the new buyers even decided to leave their Pacific Grove homes empty!

And the final kick came when many of the new buyers had marginal interest about the Feast of Lanterns and all other sacred stories of Pacific Grove. How dare they!!

So as these changes came to pass a trickle became a creek and then an angry swollen river. Voices are suddenly raised.

We are now witnessing a cultural battle that pits residents with 19th century views against those who are in the 21st century. It is an Armageddon with yet no clear victor.

And as the tide rushes in it will bring new things to our shore every day.

Public Official of the Year 2017
Dr. Ralph Porras
by Jane Roland

Dr. Ralph Porras was named "Public Official of the Year" at the Pacific Grove Chamber of Commerce awards presentation. Dr. Porras is superintendent of Pacific Grove Unified School District and was honored for his longstanding dedication to continuously improving the quality of K-12 education since joining Pacific Grove Unified in 2007.

He was born to a Mexican immigrant farming family in Ontario, California, and is the youngest of three siblings, the oldest of whom (a sister) is a 28-year veteran teacher in Ontario. His mother, a first-generation immigrant, recently retired from teaching after 30 years in the same school.

His father is a Korean War veteran who actively farmed green feed for dairy cows for over 65 years in Chino and Corona Valley. Dr. Porras's wife, Maureen, is an ICU nurse at a local hospital. They have one child, an 11-year-old cattle dog named Maggie.

He has lived in the Santa Cruz area since coming to UCSC in 1985, the first in his family to leave home for college. He has a BA in pre-med biology, with three educator credentials.

Among his hobbies is scuba diving, which he has been doing since 1990, and he dives for the Monterey Bay Aquarium. Other favorite hobbies include mountain and road cycling, marathon and trail running, hiking, and underwater photography. He is a lifelong avid reader, a Pittsburgh Steelers fan, and is a member of the Rotary Club of Pacific Grove.

Dr. Porras obtained his Doctorate in Education in 2007. He has also served for two decades in the Association of California School Administrators and is the organization's current president, leading statewide advocacy efforts to address equity issues in schools and provide professional support and resources to California school administrators.

Citizen of the Year 2017
Jeanette Kihs
by Jane Roland

The Pacific Grove Chamber of Commerce 2017 "Citizen of the Year" honoree is Jeanette Kihs, executive director of the Pacific Grove Museum of Natural History. Jeanette has been the executive director of the Pacific Grove Museum of Natural History since November 2014. She previously worked as development director at the museum and for Santa Catalina School as director of development operations for more than seven years.

Since joining the museum, Ms. Kihs has overseen an expansion of the museum's community orientation, coordinated modification to the museum's entrance, and has implemented and is executing a five-year strategic plan to guide the museum's future growth.

Jeanette is a native Californian and the youngest in a family of five girls. She attended Brigham Young University, majoring in communications. She says, "I met my husband when I was ten and we have been married for 32 years. I always joke that I shouldn't have married at the age of 13."

They have two adult children, a 25-year-old daughter who teaches high school English to underserved kids in Denver and a 21-year-old son who is in his third year of college in New Jersey. "My favorite things to do are hang out with my family, knit, hike and enjoy good food and drink with friends," Jeanette says.

"I started a career in banking, and it evolved into fundraising. I love being the executive director of the wonderful Pacific Grove Museum of Natural History," she concludes.

City Waste Guru David Myers

by Mimi Sheridan

David Myers did not intend to become a garbage guru when he moved to the Monterey Peninsula from Chico—he came to manage a menswear store. Before long, however, he took an accounting job with the City of Pacific Grove and proceeded to work his way up. P.G. staff members were always among the leaders in regional waste management efforts and, in 1979, David became manager of the Monterey Regional Waste Management District. He remained for 25 years before retiring in 2004. Under his leadership, the district became a national pacesetter and, in 1998, was honored as the Best Integrated Solid Waste Management System in North America for its pioneering programs and facilities.

Originally, Pacific Grove's garbage was burned and dumped into the ocean west of Lovers Point. Later, it was shipped to a private site in Sand City. However, the increasing health hazard made it clear that a better solution was needed. In 1951, the county created a regional garbage disposal district, which opened a temporary landfill on leased land near Laguna Seca. Seeking a more permanent solution, the district purchased 570 acres north of Marina in 1961. Four years later, a lined "sanitary landfill," which would not leach into the groundwater, opened.

But that was only the first step. To reduce the amount of waste, drop-off centers to recycle glass and aluminum were set up and, with the help of a state grant, curbside recycling began in the early 1980s. Dealing with hazardous waste was the next hurdle and, in 1987, the Marina site added one of the first household hazardous waste collection facilities in the country. It not only takes toxic materials but allows materials such as leftover paint to be reused. A retail store, known as the Last Chance Mercantile, opened so that people could purchase usable items that would otherwise go to the landfill. In 1996, a new 100,000 square foot Materials Recovery Facility opened; salvageable materials such as wood and metal are diverted from the landfill.

The landfill goes well beyond waste disposal. In 1983, an engine generator was installed to use the methane created in the landfill to produce electricity. There are now four generators, producing five megawatts of electricity a year—enough to power 5,000 homes. The energy that is not used on site is sold to PG&E, earning money for the district.

A Political Novice in the 1950s

Ed Cavallini

At the height of the Cold War in 1956, I was working for Firestone's Guided Missile Division in South Gate, a Los Angeles suburb. Wanting to expand their aerospace business, Firestone established the Monterey Engineering Laboratory for two good reasons: to attract engineers who would like to live and work on the Monterey Peninsula, and to have access to the Naval Postgraduate School scientists and professors for consulting on proposals seeking new business. A third reason, per some cynics, is that President Leonard Firestone had a home that overlooked the 17th green at Pebble Beach.

The American Legion Hall in Monterey's Veteran's Memorial Park was rented and about 40 of us gladly transferred to the Monterey Peninsula. About a year later, a group of us were talking about local politics and wondering if a newcomer could be elected to a local city council. Because I had become active in the community, I was selected to run for a seat on the Pacific Grove City Council. None of us had any political experience but we thought we could learn something about local politics and that it would be an interesting challenge.

We had cards printed with the slogan "Balanced Government—Impartial Representation," which, on hindsight, was rather bland, like most campaign slogans. I talked to service clubs, in homes of cannery workers and fishermen, and was interviewed on local deejay radio shows. We obtained voter names and addresses for the five voting precincts and went door-to-door campaigning.

There were three council seats open and five candidates. Sadly, we came in fourth. We had only enough volunteers to cover the three precincts where we came in second or third. We might have won a seat if all five precincts had been canvassed.

We learned a lot, had some fun, and the experience had two very positive outcomes. It proved the importance of old-fashioned door-to-door campaigning. And Bob Quinn, one of my precinct captains, stayed involved in local politics and became a councilman, mayor and respected elder statesman in Pacific Grove.

Preserving and Cataloging Our Memorial Benches & Historical Signs
Frank D. Pierce
by Kimberly Brown

Frank received a City Volunteer Award in 2017. He has undertaken activities for the City of Pacific Grove, conducted under the direction of the Public Works department, which have included the following:

1) Creating an inventory of City Memorial Benches that included Descriptions, Photographs, GPS Coordinates and Condition Analysis.

2) Removal, Refinishing and Replacement of Historic Wood Street Signs. Also a detailed street map was developed that identified locations where no signs were present, where wood signs were located and where black and green metal signs were located. The number of Historic Sign Intersections that were refinished included 216 intersections.

Mr. Pierce is also the appointed City representative for the Monterey Bay Air Resources District, and the Carmel River Advisory Committee. He also attends the Carmel River Task Force meetings. He has been a resident of Pacific Grove since 1978 when he purchased his present residence.

He has over fifty years' experience in agricultural and industrial engineering and holds a number of US and Foreign patents. He has authored a technical paper for the pulp and paper industry. His 1958 Collage Degree is in Latin American History and Political Science from the University of the Americas in Mexico City.

He is certified as: Registered Agricultural Engineer, California #AG138 and Nationally Registered Environmental Property Assessor, NREPA #704375

Professional Organizations include: Member of National Society of Professional Engineers, California Society of Professional Engineers, American Society of Agricultural and Biological Engineers, Refrigeration Engineer & Technicians Association.

Other Local Organizations: Monterey Bay Air Resources District Advisory Committee, Carmel River Advisory Committee, Carmel River Task Force, Monterey County Task Force, County Historical Advisory Committee, Central California Invasive Weed Symposium, and the Salinas River Channel Coalition.

SECTION 3
COMING HOME TO PACIFIC GROVE

WHAT BRINGS YOU HERE?

Henry Miller and the Oranges of Hieronymus Bosch
Heidi Feldman

It was the year 1992 and my husband Sam and I were trying to make a big decision. Sam had retired from his university teaching job and my work as a communications consultant had slowed down. Our daughter was eight years old, an age before she was too attached to her friends and her life in our beautiful home community of Redondo Beach.

Yes, our life was good there ... a comfortable small home near the beach, with a sweeping view of Santa Monica Bay and the city. We had lots of good friends and a good school system for Julia. But there was all that traffic dictating when we could go see our friends or they could visit us, when we could go to the symphony in downtown L.A., or leave for a weekend in San Diego or the mountains. Bad air quality reached us even at the beach, and we had had a curfew during the recent riots in the city.

But how do you decide when to make that big change when you don't have an overly compelling reason? Leave everything behind that we treasured and had built up for our family? Yes, we told ourselves, there was no immediate reason to leave; we could well stay for several more years.

When I went to visit my family in Germany in October 1992, we had started our conversation, listing all the pros and cons we could think of, but not reaching a major conclusion. Before my return trip, I walked around the Frankfurt airport, looking for a book to read during the long flight back. For some unknown reason—Karma, sheer coincidence?—I picked up a German translation of Henry Miller's book, *Big Sur and the Oranges of Hieronymus Bosch*. In this autobiographical work, Miller recounts the years he spent on the Big Sur coast. This was a time for Miller and his friends to enjoy their Bohemian life here—their simple homes with amazing views of the sea, semi-isolated, living at Partington Ridge and other Big Sur neighborhoods, with frequent visits by interesting guests, and regular gatherings at the much simpler Esalen baths of years gone by.

Sam and I had visited the Big Sur coast many times, making the long drive up Highway 1, usually camping at Pfeiffer Big Sur State Park, treating ourselves to a lunch at Nepenthe, continuing to the Monterey area to visit the then-new aquarium with Julia, and staying with good friends who had recently moved there. When we talked about leaving the L.A. area, we thought about Central California, wanting to be near San Francisco and still close to our friends and family down south. But with a retirement check that could be mailed anywhere and no other major ties, we could have gone anywhere in California or the world, and why not?

On that flight home, I had enough time to read all of Henry Miller's interesting recollections about his life in Big Sur. But it was one line that struck me, and that I repeated when Sam picked me up at the airport: "It takes courage to live in paradise." Miller was wondering why more people would not choose to be in this wonderful and unique part of the world?!?

Sam and I decided on that very day that yes!!!—we would indeed have the courage to move to paradise. We put our home on the market the next spring and bought our dream house, one block from the water's edge, in beautiful Pacific Grove. Our new life in this peaceful small town proved to be everything we hoped for. We could reach every destination in 20 minutes or less—even way over the hill in Carmel! We could park in front of every store and all along the amazing beaches. There was lots of culture here, with many interesting people and new friends wherever we turned. Our daughter Julia had a good transition at the local elementary school. And Sam and I eventually found ideal jobs that matched our backgrounds and professional interests.

And when we saw tourist buses driving along the ocean near our home, with people admiring our local views and natural beauty, we gleefully said to each other, "We live here, yeah!"

Yes, it took courage to live in paradise, but the reward was worth it, and continues for me to this day.

Note: Sam Feldman passed away in 2005, after a final act of courage—single-handedly spearheading the refurbishing of the Pacific Grove tennis courts.

The Journey Home
Margaret McHugh

I'd been to the Monterey Peninsula only once when I was fourteen years old, passing through on a short vacation. After seeing a place where the pines met the ocean I announced to my mother as we drove down Highway 1, "I'm going to live here someday!"

I was amazed to see a place like this where the velvet greens of the pines and cypress trees collided up against the aqua and deep blues of the ocean, as if great-minded landscapers had conspired to create this meeting of land and water. Later I found it had inspired the book *East of Eden* written by John Steinbeck, which recreated the area he grew up in.

"Yeah, yeah," my mom said. "We all would like to live in Monterey," as if it were a dream too far away to consider.

But in 1974, just out of college, I got a job by chance on the Peninsula. Both my mother and grandmother had worked for the American Red Cross, so needing work I applied for a job. Of the five sites I could have been sent to on the west coast, they selected Monterey and then called me with the news. I would finally be leaving the hot asphalt and relatively arid and treeless landscape of Los Angeles; it was time and I no longer belonged there.

Even though I secretly hated bars, my girlfriends took me out the night before I left to a sawdust-laden beer and wine bar, where we had stupid conversations with strangers as we tried to be heard over the loud music. We danced some and stayed till after hours, which meant you were locked in the bar and a bouncer at the door would let you out when you had had enough. It was a pointless way to end my time in Los Angeles but it was a traditional way to say farewell and a last chance to see my friends. I got home a 3:00 a.m. and would be leaving at 6:00.

I loaded up my seventeen potted plants into the back of my 1961 Volkswagen with the small, oval shaped window in the back. I brought a few suitcases and my beloved grandmother, who volunteered to come along for the trip and help me drive the three hundred miles north. She had come to this country in the 1940s from El Salvador and had been to many places in the world. She was no stranger to travel and liked adventure.

After three hours of driving I could hardly keep my eyes open, so I put my grandmother in the driver's seat. I told her how to place her foot on the clutch repeatedly until we were safely in 4th gear and moving happily north down the freeway towards Pismo Beach. She did not know how to drive a stick shift so we made an agreement that if she needed to slow down or shift gears she would wake me up and I would once again coach her on how to do this. I slept like a baby while the Volkswagen purred and my grandmother drove, never questioning our plan.

We stayed at the Travelodge Motel downtown, a pleasant place in the misty and cool air of Monterey. It was run by an older southern couple, Marge and Barns, that treated me like a daughter when I got there. Soon the plants were out of the car and happily lined up along the top of the second story balcony in front of my room, announcing my arrival to everyone who passed by. Marge and Barns did not know about the stowaway. I did not want them to know my grandmother was staying with me as we were on a tight budget. We found a fire escape stairway and for three days came and went as we pleased.

Two days after my arrival a young woman nearly my age, who knew some of the people I would be meeting and working with, called and asked if she could come talk with me. Her name was Gayle and she'd already decided that I would be her new housemate. My grandmother liked her immediately and so did I, so the two of us went on to share a space for the next several years, becoming fast friends for the rest of our lives.

I went out to look for a place for us. A realtor had given me the address of a house in Pacific Grove. It would be my first visit to a potential new home.

When I went to the address I found a tiny, red shingled house with white painted trim covered with foliage. I entered through a small wooden gate and knocked on the door, which an elderly woman of small stature answered. She looked to be in her 80s and was wearing a white print dress, her grey hair pulled back and tucked into a bun. She looked surprised, as if not expecting anyone.

When I explained my purpose she got a worried look on her face and said her house was not for rent. I apologized and asked if I could use her telephone to call the realty company that had sent me there.

On a small table just inside the entry she had an old, black rotary phone. I picked it up as she carefully watched me and I noticed a large photograph of a man just above the table. I recognized him immediately. "Oh," I said excitedly. "John Steinbeck!"

A long silence followed as she stood next to me, and I felt like I had said something wrong. Finally she said, "He is my brother and…I do not want to talk about him, if you don't mind. I miss him terribly."

"I'm so sorry," I said, suddenly feeling like even more of an intruder. I finished the phone call, got the correct address and thanked her profusely. She told me her name was Mrs. Ainsworth and was kind to me, realizing my error. Before I left she told me that her brother had done some of his early writing in this house.

I loved the John Steinbeck books I'd read; *Cannery Row, Tortilla Flat, Of Mice and Men*. I did not really know yet that I loved to write, myself. But even if I didn't, this chance meeting with Mrs. Ainsworth seemed like a good omen, and I took it as such, believing that I'd made the right choice to leave Los Angeles, somehow. I was twenty-four years old. I knew no one in this town, but this felt like some kind of welcome to me. I belonged here. Perhaps years before at fourteen, I had recognized my home.

I put my cherished grandmother on the plane a few days later, said a tearful goodbye and looked forward to the new life I would lead in Pacific Grove. I think she might have been grateful she didn't have to drive my Volkswagen again, and that I had found a new home among the pines.

I grew to love the sacred, natural beauty of this place even more, the amazing plants and trees and biodiversity…a place that looked like a constant English garden fed by the fog, inhabited by the deer, red foxes, the occasional mountain lion and a whole contingent of bird species. I lost my L.A. tan, didn't miss the beach scene, and loved the mist as it made its way into my new life while the fog horn blew softly at night, coaxing me to sleep. I never looked back.

When the Wife Says So!
Tony Albano

I had finally realized that I wasn't going to become the next Bob Dylan, and so I had settled into a very comfortable lifestyle, running my N.Y. deli. My future wife, Pat, did all the great cooking.

On an uneventful morning, a man came in and asked if he could buy the deli. I said, "Boy, even if I sold, I don't know what I would do with the money. I've been here all my adult life. I'm very happy."

As he was leaving, Pat came up to me and asked, "Who was that man? He looked as if he was the Lone Ranger."

I said, "Oh, he just asked me if he could buy the deli."

Interested, she asked. "And what did you say?"

"I told him we were happy."

"Well, how much did he want to give you?"

I told her.

She said in a clear voice, "We're not that happy."

"We're not that happy?" I asked.

"No, we've never been that happy."

"I didn't know we weren't happy. Why didn't you tell me?"

She said, "Well, I know you love it. You're out front having fun with customers and I'm in the back cooking. But for that amount of money, I think we should move out of here."

I called the man up and said, "Listen, I just learned I'm not as happy as I thought I was." I told him, "I think you can buy the deli."

The next thing I knew, I no longer had a deli and we were driving across the country. We visited every friend and relative I hadn't seen in all those years that I was all but married to my business. I started saying, "This looks like a nice place to live."

Pat shook her head a lot. "No, no, no, no. You didn't even pass the Mississippi yet. Wait till you get to California."

When we finally did get to Pacific Grove, we were amazed how reasonable prices were, compared to New York! We rented a place on Spruce and one week led to staying a month. I began working in the hospitality business. Funny me, I didn't know I was relocating; I thought I was just on vacation. I learned.

Then Pat and I got married at Lovers Point in Pacific Grove next to the Butterfly statue and, right after the wedding vows were taken, I said to her, "Am I happy now?"

She said, "Now you're happy."

So the moral of the story is, you don't know you're happy till your wife tells you that you are.

I've found I love working at area restaurants—I've been everything from a dishwasher to general manager! P.G. has been right for us—for the past 30 years!

Pacific Grove residents love reading the 28 cute, short stories in Tony Albano's book of smiles, *"Life is a Bumpy Road—Smoothed Out by the People and Dogs You Meet Along the Way."*

Our Long Road Home Started in P.G.
Cynthia Guthrie
Pebble Beach

In the summer of 1974, my husband Dick, an Army major, was assigned to Korea on a "hardship," or unaccompanied, tour. As a rootless Army brat myself, I wasn't sure where I would live the year he was away. An old friend suggested I go to the Monterey area near Ft. Ord. Although I had previously only flown over California, I came here with my daughter Laura, age six, and son Park, age five, to live on the Monterey Peninsula for that year. We moved into a little house in Pebble Beach, but we lived our lives in Pacific Grove. Although their father was gone, it turned out to be the best year it could possibly be. So began the Guthrie family's love affair with "America's Last Hometown."

That first summer, our children attended enrichment classes at Forest Grove Elementary School: "Tide Pool Explorations" and "Map-Making." They discovered starfish and hermit crabs, and they mapped Pacific Grove as they hiked its sidewalks. We found our "picture book" idea of a welcoming library on Central Avenue and we frequented it often. We climbed the steep stairs to the Pacific Grove Art Center for art classes.

We discovered the beautiful "little red church that cares," St. Mary's by-the-Sea. As a single parent for the year, I found solace and inspiration from the words of the beloved Rev. Dwight Edwards. Each Sunday after church, we'd wind our way home along Ocean Avenue. As we admired the blue Pacific, I'd announce loudly, "Listen, kids, we're going to live in lots of different places in the world, but this will always be one of the most beautiful you'll ever see!" Then we'd stop for tea and scones at the teahouse where the Fishwife restaurant is now.

In the fall, Park entered Mrs. Green's kindergarten, while Laura joined Miss Leatham's first grade at Forest Grove. I was a regular volunteer in both classes. In October, Park marched as a butterfly and Laura as a flower in the annual parade that welcomes the return of the monarchs.

Almost every day we'd head to the beach. Swinging huge fleshy "arms" of smelly kelp became a favorite thing to do. We watched seals and otters close in and farther out, we'd see whales.

We attended every event the Peninsula had to offer, including the festivals at Monterey's Custom House Plaza. We had fun at Pacific Grove's Good Old Days where Laura and Park's ill-tempered cat Kiki won a blue ribbon in the very first pet parade.

Mid-tour, Dick came home from Korea for a week. Laura took her dad to her first grade class "show and tell." He went in uniform, a real life GI Joe. Pacific Grove embraced military service members and their families even during the hippie 1970s.

That spring of 1975, Laura and Park helped me take blankets to St. Mary's for the babies who were flown out of South Vietnam during "Operation Baby-Lift." Later, on our black and white TV, I watched the evacuation of Americans from the roof of our embassy as Saigon fell. Tearfully, I sent flowers to the grave of Park's godfather, who was killed in Vietnam two weeks before he was due to come home.

In the summer of 1975, Dick returned to us and we left California to resume our life on the road. But our year there left its enduring mark on Laura, me and especially Park.

After a year at Ft. Leavenworth, Kansas, we moved to Virginia and then Georgia. In 1980 we flew to Paris, where we lived for two years before relocating to the Netherlands and then to Belgium. We ended our European sojourn in occupied Berlin where Laura and Park both graduated from a German-American school, the John F. Kennedy Schule. We were there when President Reagan said, "Mr. Gorbachev, tear down this Wall!"

After nine years living in Europe, Park wanted to get to know his own country, so in 1988 he rode his bicycle alone across the United States before he entered Stanford University. Except for the year he and his wife taught school in Honduras, he's lived in California ever since.

Even after our international nomadic life—or maybe because of it—he found what appears to be his forever home. It seems that by the end of his kindergarten year at Forest Grove Elementary School, we'd already "lost" Park to the Golden State.

In 1997, when Dick and I returned to the USA after almost six years in Peru, we followed Park's lead and found our forever home in California! It all started in Pacific Grove.

Invitation To My Modesto Friends
Karen Forno

I am only going
up and down a few hills
in the direction of the sunset
where the fog lingers
through the summer,
the opposite of the oven-dry Valley.
I am going where sea otters
and harbor seals
hang out by the wharf
and a few miles offshore
whales and dolphins play
where the mule deer tiptoe
not only in the forest
but across golf courses and gardens.
I am going to breathe
the cool salty air
feel the wind whip my hair
and watch the ocean
beat against the rocks
while families on bicycles
wind along the manicured trail
and the sun plays peek-a-boo
with the ebbing and flowing clouds.
You should come visit.
Get a whiff of the briny air
get sand in your shoes
get tired of the barking
of sea lions
feel your troubles become
dwarfed by the crashing waves
and hear the hiss
of the subsiding tide
drown out your anxious thoughts.
I am only going over a few hills.
You should come visit.
6/12/11

Author's notes: I wrote this when I moved from Modesto to live in Pacific Grove and work in Marina as an urgent care physician. After five-and-a-half years I have now retired to Pacific Grove. The invitation still stands.

At Home with an Ocean View
Karin Forno

When I first moved to P.G. I wanted either a home with a view of the ocean or within walking distance of the ocean. I thought everyone wanted these things.

But as it turned out, I got neither of these things. I had only a few weeks to find a place to rent, and the rental market was tight. I moved into an apartment on David Avenue. It had no garden, no view, no architecture, and it was almost a 20 minutes' walk to the ocean.

My father loved the ocean. He took us to Monterey Bay many times. I remember him taking all of us with our Danish relatives to the ocean-side and at a road stop pulling over and spotting a sea otter which we all watched, taking turns with the binoculars. Even after he died I kept visiting here and eventually I found that the quiet grace of Pacific Grove appealed to me more than crowded Cannery Row or ostentatious shoppers in Carmel.

I believed Asilomar and the rocky Pacific Grove coast to be the most beautiful places in the whole world. If I lived here I wanted as much of the ocean as possible. With a view I could enjoy it any hour of the day or night, even when it was raining, from inside my home. If within walking distance I could jump outside and walk whenever the fog cleared. That was my dream.

So after services at St. Mary's by-the-Sea Episcopal church, I would usually walk down one of the streets, 12th or 13th or 11th, down to Ocean View, then back up, looking at the houses. Disregarding the homes on Ocean View as too expensive, I would study the angles of the windows on the small houses, trying not to be too obvious. Is there a view from that living room? From that upstairs window? I could only dream. I knew I probably couldn't even afford one of those small houses.

I am a family practice doctor. I moved here to escape the Central Valley, where I had lived for 19 years. But I didn't have a lot of money. Most of my working life I had worked for county clinics and done some teaching, and the pay wasn't great.

I was caring for my elderly mother every other weekend, alternating with my brother. Her physical health wasn't bad, but she was slowly developing dementia and needing more supervision. When she died at age 97, it was both a release and a deep loss. Her friends, colleagues and family mourned the loss of a great woman.

But I didn't realize that my mother's living trust would enable me to contemplate fulfilling my dream until months later. Then in October 2015 I started feeling a surprising pull to hunt for a house.

I looked on Pine Street and Walnut Street, at nice houses that did not have a view and were not all that close to the ocean. There were occasional houses with a tiny peek, but nothing where you could sit and look out the window at the view.

I decided to look at a home on 10th street. It was a little out of my price range, but they said it had a view. I walked in and stood, transfixed. Opposite the front door, through the 16 panes of the living room window, was the ocean, framed by cypress trees in Berwick Park. I sat on the sofa and kept staring like a woman in a dream. One block away was the Rec Trail.

I bought that house. I love that I can sit on my sofa or at one of the chairs or benches under my window and gaze at the ocean for hours on end. I love that as soon as the sun comes out I can be out the door with my dog and start walking, watching the waves always hitting the rocks a little differently, seeing something new every day. And I love my mother for giving me this gift that she perhaps never knew I really wanted. Because sometimes dreams are too close to our hearts to be spoken, even though they beat there, like the waves of the sea, without ending.

A truly lovely sculptural Monterey Cypress tree, photo by Andy Cardinalli, before it got old and then reborn as the popular whales sculpture in Berwick Park. The sculpture was meant to remain natural wood, but there was too much surface decay and the whales had to be painted to preserve it.

Dreams Do Come True
Joy Ann Fischer

My story takes me back to June of 1965 at the age of ten. Every summer as long as I could remember, my family would take the four-hour drive to my great-grandparent's log cabin nestled in the pines off of Highway 50 by Strawberry Lodge. When I ponder these summer memories in the majestic mountains, I feel a smile upon my face immediately. Visions of brilliant stars against a black night, the ever-chilling rapids of the American River, the taste of freshly caught trout, hiking Horsetail Falls, or the aroma of pancakes simmering on the griddle. These simple childhood memories were not only something I looked forward to each summer but something I'll cherish forever.

This particular summer day in June held both disappointment and joy, as our family's log cabin was invaded by unwanted termites. My suitcase was already packed with a little girl's essentials like a bathing suit and flip flops, hiking boots and blue jeans, and a mix of Barbie dolls and Matchbox cars. I was ready to go and as the John Muir quote states, "The mountains are calling and I must go." When my mom and dad told my brother and me the news, we were so disappointed. They then told us that instead of a mountain vacation, we were going to visit the coast. This is where our disappointment turned into joy and changed my life forever. My parents had booked a week in a cottage by Asilomar Beach in beautiful Pacific Grove by the sea.

I was forever hooked after that summer of sand in our toes, hiking trails, the colorful sunset skies that light up like flames of fire and the nostalgic Lone Cypress on 17-Mile Drive in Pebble Beach. Yes, we did continue our family mountain adventures to the cabin, but we added ocean visits each year to P.G. as well.

In July of 1980, this P.G. tradition continued as my husband and I had our honeymoon here. We had our first picnic as a married couple in Berwick Park by the old cypress tree that is now an artistic sculpture of two beautiful whales. Since the birth of our children in the late 1980s, we've brought them to the mountains and the coast, and they too have a love of the sea in their souls.

We always thought it would be a dream come true to

have a cottage by the sea in Pacific Grove. Living a couple of hours away in Walnut Creek, my parents would enjoy jaunts to P.G. every two to three months into their 80s. In late 2015, after a wonderful and long life filled with adventure and love, my parents passed away three weeks apart from each other. Although sorely missed, their love for each other and for Pacific Grove lives on in my heart and is a part of who I am today.

In July of 2016, with the Feast of Lantern festivities in full swing, we bought our very own cottage by the sea in P.G. We have to pinch ourselves each day when we hear the ocean waves from our patio or gaze at a family of deer gently passing through our yard without fear. We gain strength and peace to be able to view the towering oak trees and everlasting succulents outside our living room window. Our hearts are smiling as we see galloping squirrels on the fence line or graceful butterflies and hummingbirds greeting us as the morning fog appears through the cypress trees.

Our parents would be so happy and proud of us and our new home. Their legacy and love for PG has been handed down through generations. We know that our children's children and beyond will delight in the magic of mermaids, the migration of monarchs and the wonder of the whales and sea otters. When we bought our little piece of heaven, there was a little note tucked away on a shelf under a paint can in the garage. The note was addressed to "Dear Nancy," whom we found out was the previous owner of the home. My heart skipped a beat as it reaffirmed why we got this house. All that I will say is my mother's name was Nancy.

If there was ever a doubt about dreams coming true, I hope this heartfelt story makes you a believer. Now our family saying is, "The beach is calling, I must go."

My Divinely Inspired Life
Diana L. Guerrero

Over the years I've traveled and lived many places, but it wasn't until after a near death experience that I found myself exploring Pacific Grove. A colleague invited me to visit so I could start the New Year on a better note.

The stunning scenery, a bay teeming with wildlife, quirky history, art events, and adventures around the Peninsula all served to lure me back again and again. Getting a behind-the-scenes tour of the Andrew Carnegie Library* during the restoration and renovation highlighted one trip.

Soon, I stayed for weeks instead of days. Friends and acquaintances encouraged me to "just make the move."

Alas, the quest to find a place to live was frustrating. My efforts seemed fruitless—until a barista told me about a temporary boarding situation.

She said, "Just go knock on the door of the blue Victorian house on the corner …."

Imagine my surprise when I discovered that almost every corner seemed to have a blue Victorian on it! When a particular house caught my eye, I stopped. But since it wasn't on the right street, so I continued. Alas, no answer at the final destination. Confident that I would receive a response, I left a note.

Weeks passed. Nothing happened.

Then one day I watched, *The Shift* (a movie filmed at Asilomar). It inspired me to use my cyber-sleuthing skills and then, with a bit of community help, finally connected with the homeowner. And the large residence that had initially caught my eye? Turns out that it was the house!

Settling in consisted of long walks by the sea, getting a mailbox and a Pacific Grove library card. Voted the most beautiful library card in the nation, it features the sparkling blue water of the bay contrasted by the bright pink floral bloom around the recreational trail. Planted by Hayes Perkins in the 1940s, this magic carpet brightens even the foggiest of days.

Other blessings soon followed. For instance, I won a membership to the Pacific Grove Natural History Museum and was invited to attend some of the donor events at the Monterey Bay Aquarium, which I soon joined as a member. It is a great pleasure to know that this world famous facility sits partially in Pacific Grove and not just in Monterey.

Although housing in Pacific Grove can be hard to come by, within a few months, a quaint one bedroom was soon promised to me. I headed south to cut my ties and say farewell to friends and family. On my return, I nestled in and continue the tradition I established on my first day—daily ambles by the sea.

Pacific Grove is the place I am happy to call home. As a Pagrovian, each day starts with new energy and possibilities. "Pacific Grove-by-God," a local historic phrase, validated that my arrival to the town was really part of my new, "Divinely Orchestrated Life."

My first word was "fish," which proved to be prophetic of my future. Known as the ARKlady, I am a traditionally published author.

*In an effort to bring knowledge to people regardless of status or education, the Carnegie Corporation of New York provided funding to build 142 public libraries in California from 1899 to 1917. A grant of $10,000 was awarded for the Pacific Grove library on March 12, 1906, and it officially opened on May 12, 1908.

Fort Ord to Pacific Grove
Bud Biery

My dad and mom (George and Eloise Biery) had lived in Ohio since they wed in 1938. My sister, Janet, was born in 1939 and I (George "Bud" Biery II) was born in 1943. Dad had been in the horse cavalry in the 1930s at the Presidio of Monterey, Ca., and had been discharged. Being married with children, previously in the Army, working in the defense industry, and 34 years old in 1945, he was not eligible for the draft. However, they were running out of warm bodies for the WW II effort, especially for the invasion of Japan. The draft age was raised to 35 and dad was immediately drafted. He went through boot camp and truck driver training at Camp Wolters, Texas. He was then transferred to Fort Ord in preparation for the invasion.

When dad proposed, he asked Mom to marry him and go to California. She said yes, but 7 years later they were still in Ohio. When he was sent to Fort Ord in Monterey, Ca., Mom jumped at the chance to fulfill the dream of going to California.

Since air travel was expensive and not very trustworthy, we came by train to California, 3 days and nights! We arrived safely in Oakland where my dad met us with his father's car. We stayed a couple of days in Oakland and then took the bus to Fort Ord.

When we arrived in Monterey our first priority was housing. We registered with Ft. Ord housing services and they put us in a motel unit with a canvas top and sides. The lower side of the unit was wood. This sounds exactly like the Methodist camp cabins that were originally in Pacific Grove in the late 1800s. This was all that was available. We had cold water, a two-burner gas plate (camp stove), two beds, a pot (honey pot) under the beds, a communal shower in a separate building, and one restroom for all.

We spent several weeks in the tent and then moved across the street to a motel - - the Sea Breeze Motel, which is still there. We had a full bath, small kitchen and two beds. We hung sheets to partition the room so that the kids could go to bed early. Below is a picture of the motel as it is today along with one of the one room cabins like the one in which we stayed. Of course, the motel has been extensively renovated in the last 72 years!

I have some memories as a two-year-old of our life in Pacific Grove. We went everywhere via buses, which were white with maroon trim. Every time we traveled to Monterey from Pacific Grove on Lighthouse Avenue, I would excitedly say, "I see the boats, I see the boats," as the harbor came into view. We were poor (dad was a PFC) and lived frugally. Mom said we primarily ate hamburger because it was inexpensive. She often said she was going to write a cookbook titled *101 Ways to Prepare Hamburger*.

For entertainment, she would take us to Holman's to window shop since we couldn't afford to buy anything. There were no liquor stores in Pacific Grove and, if we had the money, we would have to go to New Monterey or Monterey to buy any. The two liquor stores on the city boundaries still exist (Bottles N' Bins and Cork N' Bottle). Mom related years later how she had to raise the shades at 7 a.m., purportedly to ensure there were no inappropriate happenings during the day in the home while the husband was at work. She then had to lower the shades at 7 p.m. After about three months, men with families were discharged. Dad was in the Army for 11 months and 22 days!

Upon discharge from the Army, our family moved to the San Francisco Bay area where we were raised. However, we continued to vacation on the Monterey Peninsula, particularly in Pacific Grove. We stayed at the 17 Mile Drive Motor Court, which has been demolished and replaced with condos.

I have come full circle twice from a two-year-old first living in Pacific Grove. I returned to the Peninsula as a student at the Naval Postgraduate School in 1970, where I introduced my young Texas wife to the beautiful Peninsula. She immediately fell in love with the area. Once again, I left to complete my Navy career and subsequent civilian employment, often returning to vacation here. Finally, in 2011 we returned to Pacific Grove and have made this our permanent home!!

The Coat that Lead Me Here
Patricia Purwin

Circa 1985 I fell in love with a tall, dark and handsome vintage black velvet, French Empire style coat which hung in an antique store in Santa Monica where a friend of mine worked.

After secretly admiring it for several weeks, I at last worked up the courage to buy it, only to be told it had already been spoken for just the day before. (And for, oddly enough, a mutual friend by their mother who was in town visiting from San Francisco.) I was emotionally devastated but, at the same time, struck by the coincidence.

As is often the case with well-meaning mothers who matchmake for their daughters, the coat had been a mistake and after begrudgingly going out on the town a few times with the coat embarrassingly in tow, the daughter Casey (having heard of my prior interest from our friend at the antique store) called to ask if I would still like to buy it.

Answering in the affirmative and quite besides myself with joy, I found that to be reunited with the elusive garment would require not only the original $200 for the coat, but an arduous drive up the coast to a place I'd never heard of, where it was living in deplorable conditions – abandoned in the darkest corner of an overstuffed closet in a town called Pacific Grove.

Consulting my Triple A guidebook, I immediately made a reservation at the first place listed – the Butterfly Trees Lodge. Curious name, I thought. Perhaps it has some significance . . .

As expected, the drive up was indeed long and exhausting, but for the sake of the vintage black velvet, French Empire style coat I was willing to go to the ends of the earth. And I was richly rewarded for my pains, for upon arrival in Pacific Grove I was instantly enchanted . . . as it was during the holidays, and twinkling fairy lights illuminated my way down Lighthouse Avenue to the Butterfly Trees Lodge. A rendezvous with the coat had been arranged for the following evening at the Chart House on Cannery Row where Casey was pulling a dinner shift as a hostess, leaving me the entire next day to poke around my new surroundings before I had to return south.

I began the next morning by wandering through El Carmelo Cemetery, unexpectedly located right outside the sliding glass door of my room . . . through which I had beheld the pastoral scene of browsing deer earlier that morning and from whence I was struck by the Gothic grandeur of the 19th Century headstones and felt that, perhaps, I had been traveling not just in distance, but in time.

I then maneuvered my way down Lighthouse Avenue through an ethereal assault of monarch butterflies who had filled the air like confetti, dancing in the gently filtered December sunlight. Upon reaching the center of town I was magnetically drawn up the steps of the Gosby House Inn and crossed its threshold into a Victorian time warp worthy of a chapter all its own in Dickens' *A Christmas Carol*. Continuing down Lighthouse I ducked into Holman's Department Store and rode the elevator up to the beckoning mezzanine where I bought pages of old fashioned stickers dripping with cupids and bluebirds and floral baskets printed in what was then West Germany . . . to be saved for making valentines in two months' time.

Early that evening when I met up with the coveted coat, Casey recommended dinner at what she touted as one of the finest new dining establishments in Pacific Grove; Fandango, whose provincial continental charm once again transported me to yet another dream within a dream.

Needless to say, I was captivated by the magic which seemed to pour out of every nook and cranny of this enchanted place called Pacific Grove. Eventually I had the great good fortune to permanently move to PG, and I still bless the day the vintage black velvet, French Empire style coat was purchased out from under my nose by a mutual friend's erring mother. And by the way, I still have it. It's just the thing to wear out at night to a romantic dinner at Fandango.

Enjoying My Bright Kitchen

Lois Rockefeller

As a Special Education teacher, I was teaching temporarily in Marysville, California. It was time for my three children and I to move on and I was offered a similar job in Carmel Unified School District. We arrived in my 1972 maxi-van in the summer of 1974 at a camping area called Seventeen Mile Drive Village. It was in Pacific Grove on the corner of Sinex Avenue and Seventeen Mile Drive. There were tiny cabins and spaces for vehicles like mine and we were right next door to a restaurant called The Fat Cat. Being at this site gave us time to survey our surroundings and to look for a new home.

As soon as I was teaching at Carmelo School on Carmel Valley Road, fellow teachers suggested I find a home in Carmel Valley. I did have a realtor show me a couple of homes there, including a tree house with a long, high ladder, but I decided I was an ocean person rather than a valley person. So I began my search in P.G. and soon after leaving the realtor with whom I kept saying, "Where's the kitchen?", I saw a small For Sale sign in a window on Monterey Avenue. I decided to climb the stairs on Central Avenue to ask about this sale. A pleasant older lady showed me in to her bright kitchen where she and a friend had been sitting at a round table having tea. I soon asked her to find the realtor so that I could make an offer to buy this house. It is a 1902 Victorian with large rooms and a big kitchen. Now in 2017, we have owned and enjoyed this home for 43 years. We all claim to be Pagrovians.

You Can Find Everything Here
Margot Freud

I first fell in love with a kind gentleman who wanted me to come to his home in Pacific Grove. Born in Quebec, Canada, and coming from South Lake Tahoe, after being there for 49 years, I discovered the beauty of Pacific Grove, the small town atmosphere full of friendly people.

I started exploring on my bike on the shoreline trail, from 17 Mile Drive to the Aquarium, admiring the majesty of the ocean and all the variety of marine life in front of my eyes, and the surfers and kayakers at Lovers Point. Walking every day, I enjoyed the beauty and personality of every house, the beautiful gardens, trees and flowers everywhere.

I concluded that in such a small place you find everything on the planet, from the ocean to the carpet of ice plants to the deer and the birds to the butterflies; this is a grandiose spectacle!

I cannot forget the Adult Education School with its wonderful staff where we took Spanish classes.

Now, because of the love of Pacific Grove and the love of Nicolas, we spend six months in South Tahoe Take and six months in Pacific Grove.

A "Good Morning" Wish Every Day
Jim Mullany

My sisters and brother started coming to Pacific Grove in the 1980s for weekend reunions two or three times a year. We all agreed that Pacific Grove was a perfect place to meet. We had been coming down to the Monterey Peninsula since the late 1950s when my brother, Mike, attended Monterey Peninsula College. We were all born and raised in San Francisco, but as we established our own families, our family of five siblings had spread out throughout Northern California and one sister lived in Kansas. We established a routine for our visits—we would rent rooms at the Centrella Inn, and we would hike along the coast and eat our meals at one of the restaurants on Lighthouse Avenue.

We loved staying at the Centrella, as the hospitality of our host and hostess—Mark and Sunny—was exceptional. They treated us as part of their family. We loved the morning cooked-to-order breakfast, the afternoon wine and cheese reception, and best of all, the plate of homemade cookies that was always on a table in the lobby. For a time, we thought it was the best bargain on the Peninsula, as the room rates were determined by the daily temperature. We seldom had to pay much beyond $60.00. Once Mark told us the temperature was in the 80s—and my brother challenged that, saying, "Mark, we want the temperature *here*—not in Miami Beach." Mark relented and said, "The temperature is in the low 70s." We loved those weekend stays in Pacific Grove and we had great memories from those visits.

When it came time for me to retire from my job with the State of California in Sacramento in 2005, my secret dream was to live in Pacific Grove. Because of a combination of family and personal circumstances, I did not think that would be possible. The following year those circumstances changed and I realized living my dream in Pacific Grove would be possible. I happened across a news article in which a movie actor said that when he realized he needed to change and challenge his life, he needed to move to a city where he did not know a soul. He said that move had changed his life for the better. That article provided a message and the motivation I needed to move to Pacific Grove, a place where I, too, did not know a soul.

Within the first two weeks of living in Pacific Grove I knew I had made the right decision. The old saying, "It's a nice place to visit, but I wouldn't want to live there!" did not apply. The first week I settled into my rental unit on Lighthouse Avenue, which was adjacent to the Sea Breeze motel, the place where my brother had lived years ago when he attended MPC—it seemed like a good omen.

I read a news article announcing there would be a town meeting hosted by the Chamber of Commerce to address the financial issues the city was experiencing due to the recession and the lack of a solid tax base. Library hours were being reduced and there was even talk of closing the library, along with the reduction of other city services and employees. I recall the Saturday the meeting was held; the conference room at the Sally Griffin Center was filled to capacity. After some presentations explaining the financial situation, members of the community were asked to speak and offer their suggestions. Unlike any other city where I had resided, I realized Pacific Grove was very unique, as every speaker began or concluded their remarks with "I LOVE PACIFIC GROVE!"

In all the cities where I had lived before, I had seldom heard people say they loved their city. It was not hard to figure out why they loved Pacific Grove, as it is located on a beautiful peninsula with marvelous views of Monterey Bay and all its natural beauty. I also quickly fell in love with the small town feel of Pacific Grove, where people seemed to be perpetually in a good mood. It was dubbed "America's Last Hometown," and I genuinely believed what people said when they greeted me with a "Good morning!" whenever I encountered them on my frequent walks.

The second image or event that convinced me I had made the right choice in moving to Pacific Grove was held the second week I was here. It was the annual Butterfly Parade, which has been held in Pacific Grove for almost a century. The parade celebrates the return of the butterflies to Pacific Grove. How can you not love a place that is called "Butterfly Town USA" and has a parade to celebrate the return of the butterflies? I love to watch the little kids' parade, in which the kindergarten kids traditionally dress as butterflies, the second graders as otters, the third graders as farmers, and the fourth graders as pioneers. The laughter and smiles I saw during my first butterfly parade, both from the kids in the parade and the adults lined up on Lighthouse Avenue, just sealed the deal for me. Pacific Grove was the place where I wanted to live the rest of my life.

It is now ten years later, and I am still convinced that I made the right choice. And about that place where I moved, not knowing a soul? I now feel like I know everyone in town, especially those people who greet me with a "Good morning" wish every morning.

It Took an Act of Congress
Judy Avila

This goes back to when I was nine years old living in the Azores Islands, 950 miles west of Portugal. We were a family of five girls, and my parents had very little means. My father was a carpenter and my mother a homemaker. Even though he was an excellent carpenter, he only made about one dollar a day back in the 1950s. We always had food, but everything else was at the bare minimum.

We had aunts and uncles in California. When they visited, it was like Christmas for us; they would bring some gifts for us and they wore beautiful clothes and smelled so wonderful. It was a treat. In 1958 my Uncle John, my father's brother, wrote a letter asking my father to come to California, as he had bought a lot in Pacific Grove and was ready to start building the house. This lot was on Jewell Avenue.

My father would come for about a year until the house was built and get all his expenses paid and earn some money. After much soul-searching and talking it over with mother, he accepted the offer. She was brave to stay alone with five young daughters.

When my father returned with a few trunks full of clothes and other household goods, we were all in heaven.

One day my father asked if any of us girls would like to go to California for a while to stay with Uncle John and Aunt Mary. Even though I was only ten, I was the first one to raise my hand, or should I say, I was the only one? It took six years before I made it over here at the age of 16. At the time, I didn't speak any English and had not attended high school.

Soon I was registered to start school, but my visitor permit was only for six months. Luckily enough, I got an extension on my visa for another six months. By this time, I was already in love with Pacific Grove, and the idea of going back to the Azores was very depressing.

One day my aunt and uncle and I went to a lawyer, Senator Fred Farr, to see if there was any possibility of my staying in the States. After much searching and lots of money spent, he told us he would introduce a bill in Congress to grant me permission to be in the United States. After much organizing and lots of prayers and lots of support from teachers and good neighbors and friends, I received a letter saying I had been granted a permanent visa and could stay as long as I wished.

I have been here ever since, but have taken lots of trips back home and have since sent for two of my sisters.

The House My Father Built

I found myself living in the house my father had built. It meant a lot to see his initials: H. T. R. 1950–1951, engraved on the cement right outside of my bedroom. He had talked about this house and described it many times, but it was so much nicer than I anticipated. I had my own comfortable bedroom and bathroom, with hot water running in the faucet, a light switch instead of a kerosene lamp, and a gas stove and a fridge in their kitchen. Those were all luxuries which I had never had before. I had to pinch myself many times to make sure I was not in a dream. I could not thank my Lord enough for this gift in my life.

A few years later my husband and I were married, and we moved into a home he had purchased. This house was on 15th Street, right behind where the Lighthouse Theater is now. Soon after, we had to sell the house to the city of P. G. for the current parking lot construction, and this time we moved to Pine Ave across from the fire department to a much nicer home. Four years later we started raising a family and needed a little more space. We moved to Lobos Avenue where we raised our two boys and still live. This has been a wonderful home.

Now, our oldest son owns the house my father built, and whenever our extended family gathers together, it is usually there that we all meet. He and his wife remodeled it years ago and landscaped the yard, and they (and my two grandsons) generously welcome us. For me this house holds a lot of memories and I love the idea of our family enjoying it for generations to come.

Magic Lights Across the Bay
Sandra Moon

My love of Pacific Grove started before I knew it was Pacific Grove that I was in love with. I grew up in Seaside and when I was very young, I would ask my mom to lift me up to the window each night to look across the bay at all the twinkle lights, and to look at the moon.

I wanted to live over there where the magic was. When I grew up, I met and married a man who was from Pacific Grove and we had the opportunity to purchase his childhood home. The house needed work and, being so close to the ocean, still does, but this house, this town, this is where my soul is most alive.

I love the history here for my daughter. Her father went to Pacific Grove schools, as his father before him, as did her aunts. I love that I have old Sea Urchin yearbooks and that the family has been here since 1930 in this same house. I am grateful that I have been able to live here. I love that the roots for my daughter remain solidly planted in this soil.

I myself have a very short history. I know where I was born and then I was adopted, so I do not have vast roots like my daughter does. So I have planted new traditions over the years for us and many of them involve the holiday open houses, the artists and their galleries and tours, Good Old Days and the Feast of Lanterns. These events have given my soul some roots and history of my own.

In this small and quaint town I love being able to walk to the theater or to look at the shops that are unique and have a special feeling to them. The shop owners, the galleries and their workers, are lovely people. There is familiar in the old and new in this town. My heart is happiest when I feel connected and I feel connected here in Pacific Grove.

I love to go to the ocean, and the sunsets we have are spectacular. I love that it's been a constant place of peace for me, a place where I feel the divine spirit, where the sun sets and the moon rises and both the beginning and the end of the day can be released and welcomed. The night sky here has many stars because there is not a lot of light pollution. I can clear the clutter of my own busy mind and focus on the ebb and flow of the universe here. In bigger cities, I have felt lost and out of sync with this rhythm.

I found my way here, and lost it elsewhere and have come back again to replant myself, to reestablish my root system so that I might grow again. This time around, being older, will establish my spiritual life at St. Mary's by-the-Sea and their many ministries, and getting more involved with the city. I have to try to make a difference now. I want to preserve what makes this town so great and still allow it to grow and change without losing sight of what makes it so special.

I am blessed to be here; I'm blessed to be home again. No matter how many days or years, this is where my soul longs to be and I am so grateful to all who have come before me and for all who hold this place dear and say hello as I pass them on the path or on the sidewalk. I am grateful to call this place home.

I Could Live Anywhere in the World I Wanted
Mrs. "Z"
aka Jean Saltsman

My husband and I moved from the East Coast to California more than 40 years ago.

We fell in love with Pacific Grove. He was a goldsmith and we opened Mr. Z's Jewelry Store.

in the American Tin Cannery. After a long illness "Mr. Z" passed on in 1998. Having no family ties here I realized I could live anywhere in the world I wanted. After giving it much thought I realized there is no place else in the world I would want to live. I love the small town of Pacific Grove. Everything is within walking distance from my home. There are great shops, bakeries, churches, restaurants, museums, the ocean (I even like the fog). I chose to stay here, the shop has been open 39 years now. God willing, I will spend the remainder of my life in beautiful and friendly Pacific Grove.

FINDING A HOUSE AND MAKING A HOME

Our Victorian Structures
An exclusive interview with Rick Steres
William Neish

Rick Steres is a local architect whose specialty is renovating historic homes. His work has won 11 awards from the Heritage Society of Pacific Grove and his offices are in the Fountain Mall.

Q: If someone had never seen a Victorian building before, how would you describe it?

A: In building, "Victorian" relates to a group of styles. Our local Victorian homes, also called Carpenter Gothic or Gothic Revival, were part of an American movement starting in the East around 1850. It slowly moved West, and was still popular here in the 1880s and 1890s.

Its essence is verticality more than anything else. John Ruskin was a very influential art and architecture critic of the 1800s and he pointed out that Victorian homes are tall and narrow, and that's true even if they're only one story. They have steeply sloped roofs…literally like arrowheads pointing upward toward God. The buildings are a metaphor in that way, suggesting the upright posture of man, a striving for morality, a heavenly orientation. The interior spaces are tall and narrow, with high ceilings. The windows are tall and narrow, porch posts and balusters are thin, and even the board and batten siding that's sometimes used, though it's not always used, is placed vertically. The Carpenter Gothic detailing is like lace, having a weightless appearance.

The Monterey Peninsula Museum of Art did a book about local building styles in 1976 and in that there's some reference to Victorian architecture appealing to the religiously minded people, the Methodists, who moved here. It was also a reference to English Victorian society; their morals, their rigidity, their respectability… all those things. And partially, I suppose, what Americans *imagined* English society to be.

Q: Why do you think there are so many Victorians here in Pacific Grove?

A: It was the style at the time the town was established, and it appealed to the people who came to the religious retreats that took place here. The tall, narrow forms reflected a clean, moral and upright style of living. Gothic style was never a requirement and the moral and religious implications were probably not consciously employed, but it reflects the tone of the times and the founders' intentions perfectly. Cities of the Industrial Revolution in the East and the mining and cattle towns of the West were rough, lawless and unstable places. There was a craving for places where safety, order, stability, law, peace, morality, education and culture could predominate. Pacific Grove was one of those places.

The style was cheap to build, because we're in a forest… so wood was plentiful. And these buildings required no foundation; they were just set right on the ground on skids. Concrete, brick or stone foundations came later.

Q: What are skids?

A: They are boards about 3" thick and 8" wide, laid directly on the ground. They were redwood, which is resistant to insects and dry rot. A low wall, at least 18" tall, was then built, defining the perimeter of the house. Then a flat platform, the first floor, was placed on top. The first tent frames were built like this and then the early homes. In the early days, homes were often moved from one lot to another. I imagine they lifted them slightly, supported them on beams attached to wheels and hauled them with a team of draft horses. There were no utilities to disconnect. Water was pumped from springs. Bathing was done in a bath house or in sheet metal tubs in the kitchen. Sometimes tubs were recessed into the kitchen floor and capped when not in use. Heat was provided by wood or coal stoves.

A lot of these original Pacific Grove people weren't even professional builders, they were more weekend warriors who needed something that was fast to build. This was a summer resort. They were just here from June to August and then they went back to San Francisco or the East Coast or wherever they lived.

Other things that made this type of building easy

to do was the invention of platform framing and factory-produced wire nails, the new use of power-driven woodworking machinery, mail-order books by Sears, Montgomery Ward and other companies, the economic prosperity of San Francisco after the Gold Rush and the abundance of timber. Wood was inexpensive, easy and fast to work, and, being light weight, easy to ship. Plus, wood structures are resilient and easy to repair in an earthquake-prone area.

Q: Many of our Victorian houses can be chilly inside. Why is this, and what can we do about it?

A: They are! And sometimes moldy, too, if they're not insulated. The originals were single wall construction, and that is only about an inch and a half thick, the width of two boards. It's a tent made out of wood! Sometimes when you push on the walls, they move...they really do. You have to heat these houses. Forced air heat is actually a good solution for them because it not only heats the air, but it moves the air. And of course, insulating them...the floors, walls and ceilings. A lot of times you come back in with additional 2x4 studs on the interior side of the walls, and put insulation material between those, and then a new finish material, like sheetrock, on top. This gives you space for electrical wiring and plumbing and all those things, as well.

Q: Do you have a favorite Victorian in Pacific Grove?

A: There is one in particular on Cedar Street. It was rebuilt recently with help from the city, and it's a terrific little building. The rooms are all very light filled; they're small, intimate spaces. The upstairs has low walls and steep rooflines, so you're in underneath those sloping ceilings. It's just small and functional, maybe 900 square feet, not much at all. The average size house is maybe 2,500 square feet, but personally I would be very happy to take a chainsaw and cut off one bedroom/bathroom suite from all those. I like small homes that are more in scale with the way we live here, and the scale of the city, too. There is a movement in that direction that Sarah Susanka writes about in her *Not So Big House* series. I like that idea of *enough* space, but not *too much* space. Basically, small spaces that are customized to your particular lifestyle.

Early Realtors
John Roland

I arrived on the Monterey Peninsula in late 1960 and was in the mortgage business. This gave me the opportunity to work with a great many of the realtors in the area and a considerable amount of my business was in Pacific Grove. At that time, there were no large companies such as Coldwell Banker and Sotheby's. Most of the real estate companies were quite small and were what you would call "local people." I do not recall my first contact as there were many and I had the privilege of getting friendly with them all. On the corner of Lighthouse Avenue and Forest was Tom Bratty Real Estate. He and his wife, Adelyne, had four or five salespersons working there. Late in 1961 Tom passed away quite suddenly and his wife carried on with the business to great success.

M. W. Crowley Company was headed by Leland Crowley. It was also on Lighthouse Avenue and was the largest office in Pacific Grove. Michael, the founder, had passed away before I arrived and Leland, his brother, became the operating broker. Leland decided to move his offices to Monterey and many of his associates moved to other offices, some to Tom Bratty's office, and others opened their own offices. Gladys Lewis joined with Thiel Hampton and opened on Fremont Street, forming Hampton-Lewis Real Estate.

Across the street, where Juice n' Java is now located, was John Reynolds Real Estate. He also did some developing but had a small contingent that was very active. Ken Bedell had a small office on Forest Avenue. There were several other offices that were very active, such as Chelew & Campbell, headed up by John Campbell and Bill Chelew. Their office still exists and at the same location on Forest Avenue between David and Prescott. It is now run by Rosemary Coleman.

Alan Foulkes moved into an office run by Sue, whose last name I cannot recall, and their office was on Lighthouse at about 14th Street. Sue also ran a business providing pre-prepared dinners one could buy and have a gourmet meal. I believe she turned it in to a full restaurant for several years.

One realtor who was most active in the community was Manly Douglas who had an office on Forest Avenue. He was well known and active in the Monterey Peninsula Chamber of Commerce and became president of Pacific Grove Rotary.

John Roland
Jane Roland

John was born in Inwood, Iowa, the third child in a family of six siblings—two older sisters, two younger brothers and a sister. They grew up on a large farm that produced pigs, cows, chickens, corn and other animals or crops over the years. His father, a successful farmer, was also heavily involved in politics and, needless to say, the Lutheran Church was the center of the social life of the little town, which often topped out at 600.

John excelled in school and when he was 16 graduated from high school and matriculated to the University of Iowa. From 1953 until 1955 he served the mandatory two years in the Army, after which he went to New York City and later to San Francisco for six years in the mortgage banking business.

He moved to the Monterey Peninsula and from 1963 until 1967 lived in a house which we see every time we drive along Ocean View Boulevard. It is near Seven Gables Inn, and at the time John and his brother, Gene, moved in, the house was bright red. The view was spectacular but when the men decided to make curtains for the living room, they chose blue … well, every woman in the world knows about blue and sunshine. Soon those curtains were white.

During that time John had his own mortgage business. On the weekends, he was chief scorer for the Sports Car Club of America and traveled all over the country. During a period of working in Southern California, he met Alan Fordney, who was the voice for many of the races and announced movies such as *The Love Bug* and *Le Mans*. Alan and his wife Winkie, who lived in Oxnard on the beach, subsequently became among our closest friends. John was also a sailor and went out on the bay and ocean for many a sailing stint with Dick Catlin.

As if that were not enough, he was asked by Mary Shaw and Jean Ehrman to create a domino tournament for the Symphony Guild which started in the fall of 1963 and ran for over 20 years as The Golden Domino Tournament, for which John was the director. The first tournament was also a fashion show and was held at the Mark Thomas hotel. Later it moved to the Pebble Beach Lodge and then to the Monterey Peninsula Country Club. He also had domino clinics during the week at Club IXX for many years when Pierre Bain was the maître d'. John is a master fundraiser and a consummate volunteer. He worked at the benefit shops in Pacific Grove for 30 years and was a huge hit with everyone. He is a devoted P.G. Rotarian, serving as treasurer for the past year and editor of the monthly *Butterfly*. He has also been involved in politics and political issues over the years.

He and I married in 1972; we have one child, now in her mid-40s with two little girls, Lydia and Cora. I brought to the union two children from a previous marriage, John (Jay) and Ellen. The former has two boys, Justin and Spencer. Ellen also has two boys, Will and Joe.

John and I have always shared our home with animals, at the moment two, previously as many as six, not counting amphibians and rodents.

The House with the Diamond Window
Alyce Thompson

It was 1951 when Otto and Alyce Thompson arrived on the Monterey Peninsula from Colorado. They were looking for work and a healthy place for their family to live, while Otto regained his health after having survived the Bataan Death March and three and a half years as a P.O.W. in Japan during WWII.

For the past fifteen years, Alyce has enjoyed being a docent at Ketcham's Barn, where she meets the public and conducts tours of the exhibits.

Otto found work with the Pacific Grove School District as a custodian and worked there for 30 years. After three months of looking, the Thompsons found their dream home at 309 17th Street in Pacific Grove. It was an eight room house with two baths. The property consisted of three lots, and it was right next to the P.G. Fire Station. It took a lot of work to fix up the house, as it had been vacant for over two years.

Alyce received a State License to provide day care for five children. It was an ideal location, so their own children, Mike and Sandy, could attend local schools. Conveniently, Alyce was also the local Girl Scout leader for Troop #90, and there was room enough for the troop to be able to enjoy leisure time in her big back yard.

In 1958, Alyce went to work for the P.G. School Food service, baking and serving for all five schools in the area until 1986, when she retired.

In the early sixties, the "City Fathers" decided that the blocks between 16th and 17th Streets would be a good place for the new city hall.

The Thompson's property was smack dab in the middle of the proposed plans. Needless to say, the Thompsons were not pleased with this proposal. In February of 1963, after two years of intense negotiations, the City took possession, using Eminent Domain as an excuse, and the Thompsons were forced to 'resettle' to another house.

The house was then used as a rental for a few years. It was destroyed at the same time as the grand Methodist church, which took up the entire block of 17th and Lighthouse,

The Thompson's former property is now a parking lot.

The painting of the house at 309 17th was done by Louise McCaslin just before the house was destroyed.

Then and Now
Judy Wills

As I was growing up, every other summer my family would come to Pacific Grove from New York to visit my maternal grandparents. Struggling to survive in Nebraska during the depression, grandfather and grandmother made the decision to go west. They packed their five children into the car and headed to California. They settled in the Monterey Peninsula area. My grandfather had many different jobs but the ones that stand out are his partnership in the Cerney and Vachal grocery store in Oak Grove area. He would tell us stories about the Cannery Row winos sitting out back drinking the wine just like in the Steinbeck novels. Grandfather was also the store superintendent of Holman's Department store for many years. I will be forever thankful my grandparents lived here and introduced us to such an idyllic spot.

Every visit here, my sister, my four brothers and I would badger my mom until we got to cross the street and go to the beach. My grandparents lived right across from Hopkins Marine Station Beach which is closed now for research and harbor seal habitat. But back then it was open to the public. We felt it was our own secluded beach because no one else would be there. We would search for shells and hermit crabs— I especially liked the olive shells because we did not see those on the east coast. The water was very cold, but we did not care; we had to go in— it was summer! We all still love the ocean, and my siblings are drawn to Pacific Grove each Thanksgiving for our annual family reunion. Though these days none of us go swimming, we go whale watching, kayaking and birding instead.

As a child walking past the small houses in the retreat area, I told myself that one day I would live in PG and buy one of those houses. Well, I did manage to get back to PG, but not to buy one of the retreat houses. Having owned a two-hundred-year-old home in NY made me realize how much work went into the upkeep of older homes.

After visiting my parents in California, my husband and I both fell in love with Pacific Grove. We decided to move here and it was the best decision of our married life. Now, every day as I walk along the ocean path, I smell the tangy salty ocean breeze and the memories from my childhood come swarming back. It's only half a mile, as well as half a century, to my grandparents' house.

A Homemade P.G. Movie
Keith Larson

I watched as Maggie ran through the gate across the street from my childhood home like she had done many times while we were growing up. She was older now, in her fifties, and I knew I would never see her run through that gate again. Like me, she had recently lost a parent. We were both cleaning up, clearing out and having to make decisions about our properties.

In the weeks to come I would sit in the same pew at Mayflower Church as I had done as a little boy, usually falling asleep on my mother. At home I would look over in the corner of the living room where the TV had been and hear "Melancholy Serenade," the opening to the *Jackie Gleason Show* on Saturday nights, one of my dad's favorite programs. I had taken a workshop once where the presenter said life is just making movies. For me, being in town for more than a short time and living at home seemed like a *Twilight Zone* episode.

Through the generosity of my brother Eric and his wife Heidi I was able to acquire the family home. My mother's goal was to stay in the home as long as possible, an intent that I shared with her. Although it was not easy, she was able to do this with the exception of a few days before her passing. While my mother was living there, I could not do a lot because she liked things the way they were. Now I was looking at decor from the 70s and through the late 1980s, old wallpaper to deal with and a lot of updating to do.

Through the years I had traveled on and off the peninsula from Southern California taking care of my parents' needs. Now, through a series of life changes, I was able to come back home and create a sense of closure by freshening up the place and re-creating it into something new. As I scrubbed an old kitchen ceiling fan I remembered there had been a lot of frying and grease involved with cooking in those days. My friend Jim said I had to save the fan because it was historic.

The house had been built in 1955, an early ranch-style development near Pacific Grove High School, three bedrooms and one bath. I can't remember any problems with bathroom use even though there were five of us in the home, even on Saturdays, which was the big scrub night when everyone took baths, polished shoes, and laid out their clothes for church the next day.

I remember a summer vacation we took when my dad wanted to visit the places that had meant something to him in his youth. In his book *Returning Home*, psychologist Jerry M. Burger has done a number of studies of people who at some point in their lives want to return home to connect with some personal experience and memory from the past before being able to move forward in their life experiences. I was living in two time zones now. Everywhere I turned I found a memory from the past: places I went in town, the forest that my friends and I played in, the train whistle, the fog horn and the whistling buoy, sounds that were always there with regularity and reinforced a sense in me when I was growing up that nothing changed much. But that was then. Now it felt like the past and the present were superimposed on each other and this blending of time zones became my present moment. Reading this, you are probably thinking I was not getting much done with all these mystical experiences.

I gave myself three months for completion. I didn't think it would be as much work as it turned out to be. I thought I'd have time each day to paint some pictures and relax. A few weeks into the project, I realized I would have to start working longer hours. I'm sure anyone who has tackled an old house can relate. It still felt like I was viewing a movie whenever I would meet someone I hadn't seen for many years or step into a memory triggered by running across something at home. While cleaning out the garage, I would remember my dad, who liked to build things, working on a go-cart for me or helping build framework for my train layout. I was able to learn a lot about tools by helping, which was coming in handy presently with the work I had to do on the house.

Not all the memories that came to me were pleasant. For years I had done a lot of inner work, digging and diving deeply into the self with art therapy, each time coming up with greater peace. Now, being at home and making things new felt like a gift I could give to myself, my parents and everyone in my family. As old memories surfaced, I was able to let them go to a greater degree. Thank you Bill at Ace Hardware for all your advice, to my friend from second grade, Hal Hodges, who rented me everything that I needed, and to Helen Bluhm, who lived just down the street from me when we were growing up and knows everything about real estate. And to my best friend Jim, who always seemed to come around when you needed him or was easy to find.

About two days before I had to leave and head back to Southern California, I was shopping at Whole Foods in Monterey when I looked over at the door at a man in a blue suit grabbing a shopping cart. Hmmm … could that be him? Yes, it was Clint Eastwood doing his shopping. I had never seen him before in town, but knew he was a long-time local. Someone was trying to tell me it really is all just a movie.

How I Bought My House for 25-Cents
Jane Flury
Artist and Antiques Shop Owner

Back in the early 1990s I worked for Christopher Grimes who owned Site 311, a wonderful contemporary art gallery on Forest Avenue. I had an old friend, Nick Robertson, who owned Robertson's Antiques next door. I used to come in on my breaks and visit with Nick in his shop. Nick would have to close his shop when he did antique shows so I decided he needed someone to work for him while he was away. Christopher was about to move his business to Los Angeles so I ended up working exclusively for Nick.

I loved the job! It was so fun creating displays in his shop and Nick warned me that I was going to get the antiques bug. True to his prediction I started going to garage and estate sales. One day I went to an estate sale and found a black-and-white photo laying on a table with other artwork in the basement of the estate. Other people had already been there and rifled through but I carefully looked through everything and saw the simple black-and-white image of two calla lilies. I didn't see the signature at first but when I turned it over I saw a label on the back with the artists' name and address. The photo was by Imogen Cunningham and it was priced at 25-cents.

I knew very well who Imogen Cunningham was because of my years working for Christopher Grimes. One of my jobs at his gallery was framing everything for one of his clients, the Weston Gallery, of Carmel. The Weston Gallery specializes in vintage photographs by California artists such as Edward Weston and Ansel Adams. I had also framed many of Imogen Cunningham's works for the Weston Gallery as well.

When I picked up that photo at the estate sale I knew it was valuable, but I thought it was worth about $500. I was just guessing and it was just before the internet was popular so I couldn't look up the value. I happened to go to a party later that day and mentioned my find to Richard Gadd, who was there. Richard is a big vintage photo collector and at the time was the director of the Monterey Museum of Art. Richard said it might be worth around $10,000! It turned out the photo was one of only five known to exist and was from 1929.

When you find something like that people will find you. Several high-end dealers were interested in the photo. I finally decided to sell it through the Weston Gallery. I already had a relationship with them and trusted them to get the best price. In the end Maggie Weston, the owner, sold the photo for $62,000!

At the time I was renting a beautiful little cottage here in Pacific Grove and thought I should at least ask my landlady if she wanted to sell me the house since I had this chunk of money. She agreed! I used the money as a large down payment on my house.

When I bought my house it wasn't long before I applied to the Pacific Grove Heritage Society for an historical plaque. I found out my house was built in 1907 and the original owner was a Dr. Cunningham. As far as I know there is there is no relation to the photographer, but I have never tried to research it.

My story has made national news and has been the subject of three reality TV shows. The first show was the *Oprah Winfrey Show*; the second was TLC's *Accidental Fortune* and the most recent was TLC's *Suddenly Rich!* which hasn't come out yet.

I tell people that it was because I was an artist that I wanted to work for Christopher Grimes and that I took the time to really look at the artwork on the table in that basement at the estate sale. I may not have gotten rich on my own artwork but I have certainly done well in the art world.

Now I own my own art and antique shops at the Cannery Row Antique Mall. I feel I have a great life thanks to Imogen Cunningham, an artist I greatly admired before I found her photo. I love traveling and finding great art and antiques for my shops. I write regularly about my experiences in a blog called Chancing-it.

It was luck that I found that photo, but it was an opportunity that I feel I was preparing for my whole life.

"The" House
Jeanne Olin

The house on 14th Street did not impress me at first. "I like the picture on the Internet so much better, Janine," I told my daughter. "It just looks so dreary. All that gray is depressing."

"You can paint it, Mom. You haven't seen the inside. Give it a chance. It's reasonable for Pacific Grove."

The real estate agent got out of her car and greeted us. "We just had a terrible storm last night," she said, stepping over tree branches that had blown into the yard. "The owners haven't had a chance to clean up. Picture the house without all this debris around. At least this morning it is sunny. We'll go in this entrance on Ricketts Row. The owner does not use the 14th Street entrance. Please remember, this is a short sale so things are a little rough."

We climbed the wet, white tile steps to the Ricketts Row entrance. "Mom, this is really pretty," Janine said, showing that she was impressed by the room that greeted us when we entered. The main room had vaulted ceilings and an attractive fireplace. The sun created a glow through the large windows that lined the stairs and porch.

"May we go out to look at the porch? I understand it has a peek of the ocean." I was getting more interested.

"It is quite wet out there, but we can take a look at it," the realtor replied. "I would not have advertised that it has a peek of the bay, but when the trees over there lose their leaves you can see a tiny bit of the bay."

The porch needed cleaning. A large oak tree hovering over it added to the charm of the porch but it also added acorns, dirt and leaves. The tiles on the porch were white underneath the dirt. In my opinion the choice of white was a big mistake.

"We really have no yard. This is where we would be celebrating the great outdoors when we are home." I really was hesitant, but I had fallen in love with Pacific Grove and wanted to become a part of its unique community.

My husband, Jim, and I decided to make the move. We never regretted our decision. I have fallen in love with my house and the porch. The oak tree looks great with tiny Christmas lights that we use throughout the year. Jim and I watch the fireworks on our porch for the Feast of the Lanterns. The porch saves us when our house is over-run by guests and is my dog Amber's favorite place to challenge squirrels, blue jays, and dogs that outweigh her by 100 pounds.

Our house in Pacific Grove is tiny but I wouldn't change it for the world. It is a special place in a very special town. Pacific Grove is special in so many ways. Its natural beauty is well known. There can be no more beautiful sights than those along Lovers Point and Asilomar Beach. It boasts wonderful festivals including the Butterfly Parade and Feast of Lanterns. Recently I worked in a booth during Good Old Days for Central Coast Writers. My shift began on Saturday at 9:00 a.m. When I arrived for duty, members of the club were already gathered there. The sun was peeking out from behind many clouds. Before long everyone but me left to join the parade which was to start at 10:00. The parade started about the same time that the sun traded places with the rain. I tried to move books and information back from the edge of the booth to keep them dry. The members of the club marching in the rain got drenched. When they returned to the booth I didn't hear one complaint. They wouldn't let the rain spoil their fun. Although the beauty of Pacific Grove cannot be surpassed, it's the people of Pacific Grove that make it the very special place it is.

Why We Live on Cedar Street
Linnet Harlan

In December 1989, my husband, Duane, our toddler son, Lane, and I were house hunting on the Monterey Peninsula. Like many people, I longed to live in Pacific Grove, but as we drove down Highway 101, I knew we might have to wait a little longer. We'd preliminarily checked available housing a couple of weeks earlier, prior to my accepting a new job, and the only workable house was on Forest Hill in Monterey. It was an okay house, sufficient for our needs, and within our budget.

We arrived at our real estate agent's office, Lane on Duane's hip. "We'll probably buy the house on Forest Hill," I told Norma, our agent. "Are there others we should look at?"

"That house sold," Norma said. I was stunned. It had been on the market three months when we viewed it. Who buys a house in December?

"There are lots of other houses we can look at," she said, and proceeded to take us on a tour of … they weren't quite horrors, but I couldn't imagine raising a child in a house so tiny I wouldn't buy it solely for weekend use or a house so cramped there were no interior doors, only curtains between rooms. I'd accepted the job and wanted it. Could we continue to live in Saratoga while I commuted? The Mom instinct, "what happens in an emergency?" kicked in hard.

At the end of an exhausting, day, we re-grouped at Norma's office.

"Keep an eye out for what we want and call us if something comes on the market," I said to Norma as Duane gazed over a real estate brochure.

"I want to see this house," Duane said, nearly puncturing the brochure with his forefinger. It was a house in P.G. that looked like an urban townhouse built right on the edge of the street. No way I was buying that house. I had a son who needed room to roam on a tricycle without worrying about traffic.

I leaned over to read the blurb. What I noticed first was the price, hundreds of thousands of dollars higher than our budget. "Why do you want to see that?"

"It's four bedrooms, and it's in Pacific Grove."

On our way out of town, we stopped by the house. Norma and I went in while Duane stayed in the car with the now-sleeping Lane.

The cottage was tiny though well-designed; a beautiful view of the bay enlarged a small living room. The kitchen and three of the bedrooms were adequate. The master bedroom's picture window framed a view of the bay.

A sliding glass door led to a small deck. As Norma and I leaned on its railing, peering out to the Moss Landing smokestacks, I said, "I only have one decision to make. That's whether to let Duane see the house. If he does, we'll buy it."

I did; he did; we did.

Club Wreck
Jeanne Marino

We bought the least expensive house that sold in 1992. It was the least expensive property for a reason. Quaint? Certainly not. Old and dated? Most definitely. There were postcards, dating back to 1895, found in the old kitchen. There were horseshoes in the yard dating back to who-knows-when. Besides, the lovely worn-out exterior red paint of the board and batten siding was an alarming feature of the bedroom. There in full view was a two-and-a-half to three-foot, round, gaping hole in the floor. Ivy was growing inside the bedroom and was crawling up and along the far-side wall. We felt like we were inside the movie *Little Shop of Horrors.* It was bad enough that the bedroom was painted Pee Wee Herman pink and the closet was actually made up of half a dozen little doors randomly placed up and down and all over one of the walls. Some of the doors were five-and-a-half feet up from the floor. 'Twas a crazy design idea indeed. The kitchen cabinets were obviously hand-built and didn't seem to be used much. Upon opening the cabinets under the sink, we were startled to find them thickly filled with cobwebs. Scary.

My sister came to visit us shortly after we moved in. She arrived well before we had a chance to start making renovations that significantly made the house more appealing and livable. I picked her up at the Monterey airport, drove through Pacific Grove, and showed off some of the quaint details of our town. She said, "Okay, now go to your house."

I drove up, parked in the driveway and she started laughing. "You do NOT live here. Go to your house."

So I backed out of the driveway, drove around a couple of blocks, came back to "Club Wreck" and pulled in the driveway. She laughed even harder this time and said, "Stop it, I am tired. Please just go to your house."

So again, I backed out of the driveway, drove around one block then returned to the scene of her distain. This time after parking, I turned the car off, grabbed the car key, got out and said, "Okay, we are here. Come on inside."

She refused. She sat in the car and said, "NO, I will not go in there." Yes, our place was in pretty bad shape. That is why our newly bought home was lovingly called "Club Wreck."

Why I Bought Such an Old House
Carol Marquart

Back in 1986, I bought this really old house in Pacific Grove. It was one of those 99-year-old "fixers." Referred to in the newspaper ad as "A Pacific Grove Charmer," it had five rooms, with single-wall construction board and batten. The cottage was sitting on one of those 30X60 nonconforming "tent lots." The roof leaked and sagged, the paint peeled, the front steps were covered with Astroturf and felt spongy under my feet. Still, it was a piece of "The Last Hometown."

The day I bought the house, I left my six-year-old daughter at the daycare in Oakland and headed over the Santa Cruz Mountains onto Highway 1, exiting on Highway 68. Going down Forest Avenue, the sky and sea seemed fused into one silver backdrop behind the town below. The air was clean, salty damp with morning fog. The houses were a hodgepodge: broken down cottages, well-tended Victorians, Georgian mansions, Mediterranean stuccos. I noticed that many houses had little painted paper lanterns hanging from front porches. I wondered about the significance of this strange local custom.

I parked my car and picked up a newspaper in front of Grove Market and went straight to the real estate listings in the *Monterey County Herald*. I was horrified at the prices. Nothing within my measly teacher salary price range, except this little listing.

DARLING LITTLE VICTORIAN IN THE HEART OF PACIFIC GROVE. FABULOUS LOCATION, ONLY STEPS FROM SHOPPING, BEACH, POST OFFICE. PERFECT OPPORTUNITY TO OWN A PIECE OF THE LAST HOMETOWN. WINDOW DRESSINGS, APPLIANCES INCLUDED. NEEDS T.L.C.

At the time that I made an offer, which was only 20 minutes later, I can honestly say that I had none of my homework. Actually, I didn't know much about buying houses, especially OLD houses. I didn't ask anything about the roof, the foundation, the plumbing, the electrical, the water damage; I asked instead about the little paper lanterns that I saw hanging from front porches of all the houses.

The sales agent, Charlie, really knew his local history. He told me about the Chautauqua Assembly 100 years ago, how everyone sat around listening to concerts, lectures and sermons. They lived in little canvas tents, and every year, they brought these paper lanterns to light up along the shoreline. These lanterns also signaled the villagers across the Monterey Bay that fresh fish and produce were needed by the campers at the Methodist Retreat in Pacific Grove. The Chautauquans also had a big closing ceremony called the Feast of Lanterns which lit up the entire shoreline of Lovers Point. They even had fireworks.

"So that's what the Feast of Lanterns is all about, and it's happening this weekend. Do you want to see the house?" he asked.

When we opened the front door, it was very dark and there was a bad smell.

"What's that smell?" I asked.

"Oh, it's just a little musty," Charlie said. "Nobody has lived here for years."

I thought it was more than musty. It was mildew. It was mold. It was dry rot. The former owner had died here and nobody removed her body.

The inside was board and batten, painted mustard yellow. Everything was mustard yellow. Doors, refrigerator, window casings, bathtub, toilet. The carpeting was olive green shag, which was all the rage in the 1970s, with splotchy stains and bald spots. The front windows were covered with plywood which made the room seem cavernous and haunted. "We'll get some new windows fitted in," said Charlie cheerfully. "The carpeting, of course, will have to go."

As we passed through the living room, cobwebs floated like phantoms from the ceiling on top of brown, bulging water stains.

A tiny bedroom was off the living room, the floor of which did not appear to be level, but was sloping downward toward the street. One aluminum window overlooked a clapboard wall of the house next door. The kitchen off the living room had some unusual features. Fake pine paneling throughout the kitchen, including the ceiling, mustard yellow appliances—but the crowning touch was indoor/outdoor carpeting on the floor. In the kitchen?

I had a six-year old-daughter, a dog and two cats. "How do you keep this clean?" I asked pensively.

"Oh, you wash it," said Charlie

The other bedroom off the kitchen, that is, the master bedroom, was quite a shock. It was painted flaming metallic pink, probably another popular feature in the 1970s (maybe leftover from the golden age of hippies in Pacific Grove.)

"Is there space for a washer/dryer?" I asked numbly.

"Yes, right here on the back porch," said Charlie briskly. That's also where the bathroom is."

I noted that the indoor/outdoor carpeting and the fake pine paneling extended to the bathroom, even around the bathtub and shower.

"That's what's so charming about these old Pacific Grove cottages. They were built without bathrooms. The outhouse was right there in the backyard. That's where people dumped their garbage, too."

I opened up the back door, but just in time, Charlie caught my arm. "Don't step down!" he blurted out. It was a good thing, too, because there were no stairs. Just a straight six-foot drop to the dirt.

"I don't know what happened to the stairs," said Charlie in astonishment. "The stairs were here just the other day."

I asked him the price and he told me, but Charlie hedged a bit. "But the owner could come down a bit."

And then I did what no person should do under any circumstance. I said those fateful words. "I'll take it."

Was I insane?

I can now look back on this story and laugh. I can also think of a few more questions I should have asked Mr. Charlie before I made an offer on this 1901 house on Park Street where I still live after 27 years. Needless to say, I have had to make a few improvements.

But, looking back, here are some of the questions I should have asked:

1. Should I have asked a licensed contractor to look at the house before I made an offer? Answer: Yes!

2. Where does the sewage go once I empty the washer or flush the toilet? Answer: It goes through corroded pipes and empties into an open cesspool under your neighbor's house.

3. Is it good that the retaining wall in front is listing forward? Answer: No!

4. Are there lots of subterranean termites under the house? Answer: Lots!

5. Are there lots of funny wires under the house, exposed conductors and extension cords all over the place? Answer: Yes.

6. Will I need a new foundation plus some stairs so that I can exit safely through the back door? Answer: Yes.

But anyway, this house is still no gem, but it's mine, and it looks a lot better than it did twenty-seven years ago. Every July, I hang a lantern on the front porch in honor of the Feast of Lanterns. As a matter of fact, I like to keep that lantern up all year.

City Estates
Alex Hulanicki

By the time he had retired from Pacific Bell, otherwise known as The Phone Company, Larry Yount's eyesight was blurry but that didn't stop him from playing golf with the senior men at Pacific Grove Municipal Golf Links.

Early every morning, he trudged down the fairways in the fog. His ball was usually in the middle and had a large circle on it so he could identify it. And, he was pretty good at finding other golfers' lost balls and taking them home. Those golf balls, he thought, would come in handy as he gave a paper sack each month to the paperboy as a tip.

"Don't lose these," he would say to the carrier, "and thanks for flipping the *Herald* up on the banister of the porch."

Mr. Yount's frugality went beyond golf balls, as Pacific Grove city officials discovered when Mr. Yount died in March 1992 at the age of 97.

With his wife Millie, Mr. Yount had amassed an estate of approximately $900,000, including his residence at 125 15th Street and his phone company stock. The proceeds from that estate are used to improve and maintain educational and recreational facilities, according to municipal reports.

The city benefits from two other estates. The Poet-in-Residence program was the result of a bequest by Whitney Latham Lechich, a writer and longtime Pagrovian who died in 2000. Her 1892 cottage on 18th Street was refurbished and the mortgage paid off with her estate. Poets occupy the three-bedroom cottage at a rent of $900 a month and pay the utilities. In exchange, the poets hold readings and conduct lectures on poetry.

The Bertha L. Strong Fund was established in 1956. It helped build a new clubhouse at the golf course in 1962, but that building was demolished in the 1990s when another clubhouse was constructed.

As of 2014, the Strong Fund had a balance of $985,000.

Amazing Heritage House History
Barry and Kim Bedwell

Having been born and raised in the San Joaquin Valley, the Monterey Peninsula has always had a special attraction for me. Like many generations before us who were drawn by the lure of cooler temperatures and stunning scenery, we looked forward to every chance to make the two-and-a-half-hour drive. But for us, there were more than 40-degree temperature swings and crashing waves. We love history. The first time we accidentally wandered into downtown Pacific Grove in the 1970s, we knew that we had discovered a magical place that immediately felt like home.

Life happens and we were not immune to the challenges of raising a family and paying bills. It was not until the last of the four children graduated from college that we decided to seriously contemplate possibly buying a home in P.G. We had learned financial discipline in putting those youngsters through school and we would need it if we were going to find a foothold.

While the Great Recession was a disaster in so many ways, for us it opened up the chance to take advantage of a rare downward trend in property values. So we purchased, via a short sale, a lovely little home on 16th Street that had been built in 1897 by a San Jose prune farmer. The house was on one of the famous 30X60 foot "summer tent" lots without even a hint of parking. My wife loved it but I longed for the time when I could run an errand without the fear of returning and finding a block-and-a-half hike to our home.

I kept my eyes open and a few years ago, I spotted a dilapidated old house, with character, that had come up for sale that day. I convinced my dear wife that I had a vision. Besides, it had parking. After a considerable period of time and innumerable frustrations, the vision became a reality and we are now blissfully content in our surroundings.

Not only are we in the Retreat Tract, which we love, we are in a home that has a wonderful past, going back to 1910 when William Heman Murray and his family moved in after striking a deal with the Pacific Improvement Company. Mr. Murray passed away in 1918 and a gentleman by the name of David D. Davis moved in with his kinfolk. Mr. Davis was a Civil War veteran who had served with both the 34th and 52nd Wisconsin volunteer infantry brigades. He and his family are buried in a beautiful crypt in El Carmelo Cemetery in P.G. But most amazingly, he was part of the honor guard in Chicago in 1865 that watched over President Lincoln's body during the trip back to Springfield. Can you imagine?

Pacific Grove is a very distinctive and exceptional place that we should never take for granted. We thank our lucky stars each and every day that we have the good fortune to be part of "America's Last Hometown."

WRITING CANTERBURY TALES—MARLEY KNOLES

A baker's dozen of Canterbury Woods residents met for a memoir writing workshop led by Patricia Hamilton, who encouraged the group with step-by-step writing prompts to pen their personal contributions to this book, *Life in Pacific Grove*.

After some lively background discussion about the project and ponderous questions about how one gets started—it was time to jump in.

Happily the sheet of writing prompts quite effectively soon had everyone flowing with pen to page. An hour of concentrated writing time quickly flew by and the quiet energy in the room was conveyed by the sound of pens etching across paper.

And with newfound author status, the writers found they wanted to continue, seeking more time to complete their thoughts. So it was decided to take a break from writing, read aloud and share what each had scribed so far—and to reconvene for another session with Patricia.

Quite encouraged by the fact that they had been able to connect so well with the writing process, they then found that reading aloud and hearing each other's work was a particularly rewarding part of the workshop. So much so, that after this project there are plans to continue with a Canterbury Writing Club to meet on a regular basis.

My First Canterbury Tale
Arrival, August 2016
Barbara Mountrey

I decided to move out of my little house because I did not like what my life had become. I could not walk up my driveway anymore, so friendly neighbors brought up my morning paper and my mail. I could drive short distances, but walking tired me out pretty quickly. When someone asked me how I was, I would say, "Not bad for an old lady." My husband had died five years earlier, and I was getting a bit lonely. I sat around playing computer games, watching TV and eating too much. One day I said to myself, "This is not how I envisioned myself at age 76!" So I started looking for a place to live where I would have fewer responsibilities.

I checked out a couple of places which were uninspiring—and quite expensive. Then I came to Canterbury Woods. The schedule of activities was extensive, with concerts and lectures, movies, games nights, and celebrations of several kinds. The food was excellent. People were friendly. So many people told me, "Coming here was the best decision I ever made!" that I was beginning to think that the administration was putting something in the water. I knew only two people here, but there was an apartment available in Building

B, where they both lived! So I took that apartment, even though it faced north and I felt guilty that Andromeda, my rescue cat, would not get direct sun.

There was sun for part of the day until October, so I thought maybe it would reappear in April. It came back starting the first week in March, a couple of weeks before the equinox! I guess I must face slightly northeast. So I will be able to grow something besides violets and cineraria, and the sun may reach as far as my patio (read: strip of cement) in midsummer, which will make Andromeda quite happy.

It turned out that B is the friendliest building on campus. On my first day, other women kept sticking their heads in my door and welcoming me. About 10 days later, they even threw me a welcoming party—and included my brother!

My building is very close to the dining room, lounge and office. Even so, I found that I was walking more in a day than I had been walking in a week at my old home. I used a cane for support and balance, even though I wear a boot-brace. I had to stop halfway up the gentle slope to my building to catch my breath. After about a month, I realized that I was not stopping halfway and I was barely using the cane. About two weeks after that, I stopped using it at all; my legs were strong enough to support me on their own!

I felt 20 years younger than I had before moving here. Not only was I increasingly healthy physically, but my spirits were lifting as well. I met new and interesting people, many of whom were considerably older than I, so I could no longer think of myself as an old lady. In fact, one day I sat at lunch with three women: one about to turn 95, one a month short of 100 and one who was 101. I felt like a kid being allowed to sit at the grownups' table!

Eating Adventures
Betty Powell

My husband David and I arrived in Pacific Grove 32 years ago. He was to be involved in the opening of the new Monterey Bay Aquarium by being in charge of all live exhibits, excluding mammals (sea otters). We found the house that suited us but we still had to sell our house in Marin County. Since he was to start working right away he moved in with a minimum of furniture and did some cooking in our camper. Except for weekends, I stayed in our old house getting it ready for sale and packing for the big move.

We needed to find places to eat. Thus began the big adventure—locating restaurants in Pacific Grove. We found that we didn't have to leave Pacific Grove—all types of restaurants were available right here almost in our backyard.

We started with breakfast—Victorian Corner suited us to a T. It was good food and was fun to get to know the Aliotti family.

We loved Mexican-type food, so we had many choices! One of our favorites was The Fishwife, located on Sunset near Asilomar and the ocean. It was started by Julio Ramirez who was born in Nicaragua and who had started a small seafood restaurant serving Latin American and Caribbean type food in Seaside called The Fishwife Seafood Café with his wife and partner, Marie Perucca-Ramirez. Years later he opened El Cocodrilo on LIighthouse Avenue. He sold that restaurant to the owners of Passionfish, where chefs Ted and Cindy Walter were among the forerunners in serving sustainable seafood from the list put out by the Aquarium.

We also sampled different and mainly vegetarian-type foods from Tilly Gort's Café, handy as it was near the Aquarium.

Also a great place for seafood and also near the Aquarium was Vivolo's Chowder House. The chowder was outstanding and served in French bread bowls.

For some lunch and evening meals we went to Favaloro's Big Night Bistro located on Lighthouse Avenue, run by the Favaloro fishing family. Mama and papa were the cooks and the children, when they weren't fishing, ran the dining room. Years later, after a fire destroyed part of the restaurant and they were rebuilding, they opened a luncheon spot next door called Cafe Ariana, named after their daughter. Both are excellent and now have outdoor seating.

Also on Lighthouse one of my favorites was Chili Great Chili, which served international foods too. It is now called International Cuisine and is open late, seven days a week.

We also enjoyed eating at Fifi's Bistro Café up the hill on Forest Avenue where they are known for their French cooking and great selection of wines. Their onion soup is out-of-this-world.

Breaching Whales of Berwick Park
Jean Justice McNeil

I am 90 years old and a 17-year resident of Pacific Grove and Canterbury Woods retirement community. My son, Dan McNeil, took me out to lunch for my 90th birthday. We took a ride to Berwick Park to enjoy seeing the breaching whales sculpture. It was a beautiful sight to behold. And then we feasted on clam chowder at a local fish shop. My son is a Colorado artist and blacksmith who creates sculptures of all kinds in wrought iron.

Everything Musical
Beth Storey

My earlier life has featured education, nursing, mothering and church activities, as well as music. A major sea change about seven years ago focused my thinking and dreams on music, especially singing.

Guillermo was a part of that transition—a minor part at first, but growing into a major contributor. As we worked together in a group and in a class, I found him to be very knowledgeable about music theory, history, various instruments (several of which he plays—and continues to learn more), composers and performers. He is a fine resource, I think, for all things musical.

He and his wife have become my good friends, valued for their fine minds, generous willingness to help others, and whimsical funny-bones.

Part of the fun of our email correspondence is Guillermo's smattering of varied languages. I keep learning from him day by day. Moving to Canterbury Woods has brought me amazing new opportunities, in music (along with other activities), as well as in precious new friendships and mutually supportive relationships.

Going to College Again
Richard Neutra
retired Public Health physician, architectural history

A year ago my wife Peggy and I decided to move from the San Francisco Bay Area to Canterbury Woods, a continuing care retirement community, here in Pacific Grove. My friends ask: "How can you stand being around so many old people?"

I have learned something about myself. I spent the bulk of my childhood in boarding schools and then four years away in college. So it feels familiarly pleasant for me to walk from where I sleep to a communal dining room filled with friendly people. It is amazing to me that our visiting granddaughter and I are eating a meal with an alert 100-year-old woman who retired as head of Maryland's Children's Protective Agency forty years ago, or with a 95-year-old man who flew missions in a B-27 over the Ploesti Oil Fields in Romania in WWII or with the man who designed all the enormous fish tanks for the Monterey Bay Aquarium.

As an architect's son, I respond to the unpretentious Bay Area modern design and the lovely small gardens and walkways at Canterbury Woods. It is important to me that, when we can no longer drive, we will still be able to walk a few blocks through those quaint Victorian houses down to Lovers Point and Monterey Bay. The charm of what we enjoy here is the fruit of a century of thoughtful effort of city fathers and mothers who came before us.

As a kid my architect father took me along as he and his photographer friend Julius photographed his buildings. They let me get under the black cloth and see the upside-down image they had composed on the ground glass by subtle shiftings, back and forth and up and down, until the parts of the building lined up just so.

For a long time now I have enjoyed taking color photographs of parts of buildings that strike my eye as delightful compositions of line, shadow, texture and color.

Most days my wife Peggy and I walk our golden retriever Maya down to the bay from Canterbury Woods. Soon Maya and Peggy are tiny figures walking steadily a few blocks ahead. Even with Maya's frequent detours to smell the enticing odors from God knows what sources, her progress is far faster than mine. I have been hijacked by the lure of Victorian architectural gingerbread. It's everywhere, luminous and casting shadows in the low morning sun.

Here is flesh pink board-and-batten with an oval stained-glass window of poppies on dark green-blue glass. The white trim on the triangle of the roof ridge contrasts with the royal blue sky and the gray twisting limbs of an oak.

Nearby, a smooth, gray vertical tree trunk stands in front of a Victorian turret clothed in shingles whose staggered pattern leaps out at me, illuminated by the slanting morning sun.

Like Maya's importunate jerk on the leash for an ecstatic sniffing of the urine-soaked grass, I pull up short once more to haul out my iPhone in order to capture yet another image of Pacific Grove gingerbread.

A Foreigner Helps a Foreigner (or) Foreign Aid
Harriet Blume

I didn't know anyone in Pacific Grove when I moved here from Southern California. I felt as if I were in a foreign country, so I was eager to get to know someone. I can't remember how I first met Gisela, only that I wanted to meet her after I heard that she was Austrian and that her deceased husband had been an orchestra conductor. The fact that she was Austrian interested me because my husband was born in Germany. The fact that her husband had been a conductor gave me cause to think she must love music, as I do. So I invited her to share a meal or two with me.

Gisela is tall, with eyes that *see* you. She is humble, not wordy; she's considerate and appreciative of beauty. After making a New Year's resolution to read one of my father-in-law's books, a novel written in German (a language I used to know but had forgotten), I asked Gisela whether she would be willing to help me, which I thought would be a good excuse to see her longer and more often.

To my surprise, she seemed excited at the prospect. She said she had never done anything like that before, though she had taught German at the DLI. So we set up a date to go over what I had read, a few pages at a time, and, again to my surprise, she admired the text and pointed out particularly beautiful passages that I had hardly noticed due to my preoccupation with simply making sense out of the words. Her admiration of the text touched me, for I dearly loved and admired my father-in-law and was grateful to find a fellow admirer, one more qualified than I to be so.

But even before we started reading together, I had felt that I would like this woman more and more the better I got to know her. She was warm toward me, even during our first couple of meetings—which surprised me, for I had initiated them and had no idea how she would respond.

After our first meeting, the way she looked at me was as if we had something in common. And after our second meeting, she embraced me as we parted. This touched me—first, because it implied that we were friends already, and second, because it was such a European gesture, one that I had practiced regularly with French friends when I lived in France, but which I couldn't practice here in Pacific Grove because I didn't yet know anyone well enough to do so.

And then along came this woman from Austria who embraced me and helped me feel at home in the foreign land of Pacific Grove.

Crocheted Afghans
Shirley and Sharon Devol

She makes them for friends and family. Her grandmother taught her how when she was very young. She enjoys it very much. Since 1990, residents of Canterbury Woods (and their friends and relatives) have knitted and crocheted blankets to give to expectant Navy-Marine parents who have completed a "Budget for Baby." workshop. The Navy-Marine Corps Relief Society provides yarn and individuals knit or crochet 36" x 40" blankets.

Sharon Devol, daughter of Canterbury Woods resident Shirley Devol, recently crocheted four beautiful blankets which were displayed at a Canterbury Woods Resident Council meeting prior to being shipped to the Navy-Marine Relief Society in Lemoore, California. There is a constant need for more people to knit or crochet. If you are interested in helping with this project, call Jean Stallings at X194.

I Never Have to Cook Again!
Betty Powell

About 16 years ago I came home (we were living on Short Street) from my part-time job at the Monterey Bay Aquarium. My husband, David, was climbing down the ladder from the roof where he had just finished raking pine needles. (We lived in a pine forest with a lot of trees). He said that he was getting too old to be doing this (every three to four months, depending on the weather, wind, etc.). I didn't know how to take this—I never wanted to move again. We had decided that this house in Pacific Grove was to be our home forever! Could we perhaps hire someone? How much would that cost?

David suggested we look into moving into Canterbury Woods, where our friends, Libby and Lovell Langstroth, lived. In fact, David rode his bike over there a couple of days a week to play table tennis with Lovell. They had moved there about two years earlier and they enjoyed living there. They had invited us to lunch or dinner a few times so we had an idea of what it was like to live there. However, I wasn't convinced because I was not looking forward to moving ever again!

David's reputation as an aquarist, setting up living marine habitats, meant he was in demand all over the world. As result he had worked at Marineland of the Pacific at Palos Verdes, Steinhart Aquarium at the California Academy of Sciences in San Francisco and Sea World, San Diego. In between he was doing consulting work for other aquariums. During his career we had lived at many different places, moving with two growing daughters, plus various plants and animals, etc. I repeat, I never wanted to move again.

Then he said the Magic Words—"You never have to cook again!" I could picture myself never again having to plan or shop for meals, let alone cooking and cleaning up. That did it! I replied, "Yes, let's look into it."

We have been here over 15 years and never regretted the move!

Memories of the Frog Pond of P.G.
David C. Powell

I'm not talking about the wonderful frog pond story in Steinbeck's *Cannery Row* where Mac and the Boys decided they would do Doc a favor and collect frogs for Doc's biological supply business. That is one of the funniest pieces of writing I have ever read! I have a hard time finishing it from laughing so hard I can't breathe! I don't know if anyone knows where that pond is or even if there was a real pond. It could all have been a product of Steinbeck's fertile mind!

I have never read about the pond in my memory but it is, or it was, a real pond. My wife Betty and I discovered it by locating the source of the frogs' love songs.

One of our favorite restaurants in P.G. is the Fishwife on Sunset Drive near where it meets the ocean. One evening we parked our car on Sunset and walked up to the Fishwife for dinner. Later, on the way back to the car, we heard a chorus of frog calls—the soprano of the Pacific tree frogs and the resonant bass note of the mighty bullfrog.

There is a group of high bushes on the strip of land between Sunset and the Spanish Bay golf course. The frog calls were coming from behind the bushes. Intrigued, I pushed my way past the bushes and saw a lovely little pond lined with reeds and cattails. The minute we stepped in, the calls stopped and we heard the plop of frogs landing in the water.

We returned a few weeks later and the routine was the same. The alert frogs instantly stopped calling and quickly sought safety below water. As quiet as we were, the frogs seemed to know we were still there because they didn't resume calling until we were physically gone.

Sometimes on a quiet and very still summer evening we could clearly hear the love songs of the frogs from our house near what is now the Monarch Sanctuary, a distance of one-and-one-tenth miles.

A few years later we moved away. We have returned to the Fishwife but have heard no frog calls. Pushing our way through the bushes we were disappointed to see no water! There was the outline of the former pond but it was solidly choked with plants and not a sign of water!

As a biologist I recognized it as a clear case of eutrophication, the explosive growth followed by die-off of aquatic plants. As they decay they consume oxygen from the water and aquatic animals die. In this case it was probably caused by excess fertilizer from the adjacent heavily watered and fertilized Spanish Bay golf course. My book about my life in the public aquarium world is in the P.G. library and on Amazon.com

A Hero's Journey WWII
Francis Cartier

In the early '40s, I was a radio announcer, newscaster, actor and radio playwright. I was successful in all these roles and looked forward to such a career. This was at KFBK in Sacramento.

One day early in the U.S. engagement in World War II, an Army Air Corps major asked the station manager to broadcast a series of recruiting programs. I got that assignment despite being the youngest employee of the station.

I had no fear about the task and wrote perhaps 10 half-hour radio plays dramatizing air crew training. My source of information was a book that described the training for pilots, navigators, bombardiers, gunners, etc. The major also gave me a book that described each training program in vivid detail.

I deliberately taught myself to observe what happened to me and other people. Often I had to imagine why people did what they did. and then to write down both the facts and fiction. I believe this contributed significantly to my ability to write radio plays as well as poetry.

After I had written the plays, directed the actors (friends I knew who could act), etc., I convinced myself and went to the recruiting station and volunteered to quit my job and enlist in the Air Corps. I entered pilot training but flunked the final exam. I was not devastated. It was clear to me that I was not meant to be a pilot.

I was, however, successful in graduation from training as a bombardier. I flew 35 combat missions over Germany. Shortly thereafter, Hitler committed suicide and Germany surrendered.

I returned home. The Defense Department established scholarships to universities and I went to University of Southern California to study playwriting, acting, etc., under William DeMille (Cecil B. DeMille's older brother). I was very successful at USC and eventually got a Ph.D. in Speech.

What I learned from doing this exercise in Patricia's class: Even at the age of 93, I can still remember much of my youth.

P.G. Where is That?
Alice Englander

Bill was in the Army in the 1960s and trained at Fort Ord. When we met in San Francisco in 1967, he wanted to visit the Monterey area on weekends. We usually stayed at the Travelodge downtown—or the old San Carlos Hotel—and we took long walks everywhere.

One of our regular walks started at Fisherman's Wharf and took us west on Lighthouse Avenue. We walked and walked and suddenly we weren't on Lighthouse Avenue any more, but on Central Avenue. It took us several trips and a lot of walks to realize that the street name changed—and in fact a new Lighthouse Avenue popped up a block away—because we had left Monterey and had entered a town called Pacific Grove. We had no idea that it even existed.

Those walks are our earliest memories of the town that we've lived in on and off since 1983. We discovered so many of the places and views that are quintessentially Pacific Grove—the Butterfly Sanctuary, the Asilomar coastline and the beautiful buildings in the state conference grounds, the otters and other sea life frolicking in the waves, the Victorians and small cottages of the downtown area, stores like Holman's Department Store, the Top Hat Market, Sprouse-Reitz and others, the ice plant blooming in the spring and so many other experiences.

When we actually moved here, we felt we had lived here a long time and we continue to enjoy many of the same walks today.

First Otter Sighting

When Bill and I first got together, I was not a morning person. We met in San Francisco and were both working at Bank of America at the time (in fact, he was my boss), so we had to be up early during the week, but on weekends I was still accustomed to sleeping in. Bill has always been a morning person, so after letting me sleep "late" until 7:30 or so, he'd nudge me and ask if I was planning to sleep all day.

We spent a lot of weekends in the Monterey area back then and when Bill got up early, he'd often go for a walk.

One morning he came crashing into our room, woke me and insisted that I get up right away. He said, "There's a seal down at the water that's grabbing shells and a rock and pounding them on his chest." Right. I figured he was seeing things. But there was no way I was going to get any more sleep.

Shortly we were back at the water. He was worried that the "seal" might be gone. Luckily he was still hanging around and we watched him for a long time. He would dive down and come back with some sort of shelled creature and a rock, pound on the shell and slurp up the insides. One time he brought up a crab and it would walk down his body; he would grab it and bring it back to his "dining" area by his mouth, giving new meaning to the phrase "dinner to go."

Of course we later learned that it was a sea otter (not a seal) and now we frequently watch them off-shore or at the Monterey Bay Aquarium. Sometimes we listen to tourists exclaim about the amazing seals and we sagely nod and explain about sea otters.

Neighbor's Backyard

Our neighbors' backyard is rustic, with wild grass and lots of yellow flowers (oxalis) that are sprouting everywhere this spring. We have a perfect view of their yard from our kitchen windows.

When they first moved in a few years ago, they planted some flowers and fruit trees. They may not have known about the local deer and their voracious appetites. They told us with dismay that the deer had eaten all their plants.

So they put up a short, rustic fence. Perhaps we should have mentioned to them that deer are great jumpers.

You'll often find one of us gazing out the window as several deer munch away on the grass and flowers. They fill up, lie down and nap for a while, then get back to the buffet. They are often joined by a cat from down the street who loves to stare at gopher holes. We saw him catch one once, but most of the time he sits patiently, waiting and watching.

The Little House Grows Up

When we lived in San Francisco in the 1960s, we frequently visited the Monterey area on weekends. When we moved to San Diego in the early 1970s, we were no longer able to come so often because it was so far away. We came when we could, but we were drawn here and always wished we could be here more frequently.

In 1983 we bought a small fisherman's cottage in the Retreat area of Pacific Grove as a vacation getaway. We fixed it up and made it into a very special "retreat" of our own. The 430-square-foot cottage was perfect for a week or two, and everything was so tiny that it felt like a doll's house.

By the early 1990s, we were at a point where we could move here and do our at-home work from our cottage. We did that, but quickly discovered that the cute, small cottage as a getaway was not adequate as a full-time home, especially with an office and accompanying computers, copiers and files filling a huge chunk.

So we built on and ended up with a small house. One of our favorite rooms was the den we added, with a poem we wrote, painted by an artist around the top of the walls.

The Town … Victorian houses, colorful gardens, John's trees tower.
The Forests … green trees, rolling hills, deer graze all around.
The Coast … waves crashing, seals balancing, shorebirds scurry.
The Setting … friendly neighbors, perfect walking, cats abound

The phrase "John's trees tower" refers to the large pine trees we could see from our backyard. They are in the yard of a house on 11th Street that John Steinbeck lived in from 1930 to 1936 and was occupied by the Steinbeck family for many years after that.

Restaurants of the Past

We used to travel a lot. We typically went to Europe twice a year and eventually visited almost every country in Europe, even the Eastern European countries that were then behind the Iron Curtain. We visited Hong Kong and Shanghai, rode the Trans-Siberian railroad, enjoyed a trip to South America to visit Buenos Aires and Santiago, and took a luxurious trip to South Africa for game watching and wine tasting. We took a year-long camping trip and visited all the "lower 48" states of the United States and most of Canada's provinces. We've been to Hawaii and Alaska, too. We've traveled to most of the states of Mexico and enjoyed a cruise through the Panama Canal. And we loved it all.

So it's no surprise that thinking about our history in Pacific Grove includes food memories. When we had a vacation cottage here, we rarely cooked at home, preferring to explore local restaurants. Every morning we would take a long walk and stop for breakfast at a local café. Most evenings we were able to stroll into town to dine at a favorite restaurant or try a new one.

Bill has an incredible memory for things like this, so when I mentioned that maybe a story about "restaurants past" would be fun, he immediately came up with a long list of places that we used to visit, most of which are now gone. Before we head down memory lane, it's only fair to point out that there are some restaurants that are still open, like Toasties, Fandango, The Grill at Lovers Point, Fifi's Bistro Café, Goodies Deli and First Watch (now renamed First Awakenings). Kudos to them!

Here's a list of restaurants we remember fondly, in no particular order.

Edelweiss

Another place with European flair, upstairs in the building on Lighthouse Avenue where State Farm is now.

The Monarch Café

Just down "the row" (Ricketts Row) from our cottage, this was THE place for eggs benedict. We still remember the hollandaise and continue to compare all versions to the one they made here.

Old Europe

A European experience in downtown Pacific Grove. Wonderful deep fried mushroom appetizer and a great implementation of prosciutto with melon. We took a lot of guests to this restaurant. They had a wild boar stew on the menu, which seemed very esoteric to us back then. One of our guests ordered it and I was almost horrified, hoping she knew what she was ordering. It turned out to be delicious!

The Clock Garden Restaurant

OK, this was in Monterey on Abrego Street, but it was so important to us that I have to include it. We always went here the first night we arrived in town. The food was simple American fare, the atmosphere was kind of funky and we always had a good time. Food-wise the highlight was their baked potatoes. We never found out where they got them, but they were the sweetest, best potatoes we've ever had, even since then. To this day we refer to extra yummy baked potatoes as "Clock potatoes."

Taste Café

We often had lunch here when Paulo & Silvia were the owners/chefs, and Laura (Silvia's sister) and Chris were servers and overall helpers. It was a family run, friendly place with fantastic food. When we first moved here full-time we took the Monterey Bay Aquarium's volunteer training program, which met Tuesday evenings for about two months. We had dinner after each class at Taste and started feeling like it was home.

Writing and Reminiscing

Patricia Hamilton came to Canterbury Woods to tell us about a book she is publishing as a benefit for the Pacific Grove Library. She's encouraging people to submit stories about their lives in Pacific Grove.

For some reason, this struck a creative nerve in my mind. I can't stop thinking about all the things Bill and

I have done and shared over the years. We have found ourselves happily reminiscing about things that happened almost 50 years ago, when Bill trained at Fort Ord and we were newly married. Many of our conversations now start with questions like, "Do you remember when we …?" or "What was the name of …?" or "Do you remember where …?" We often find ourselves saying, "Oh, you should write that story!" when we're discussing totally mundane everyday things and something reminds us of a past experience.

Bill and I have been residents of Pacific Grove on and off since 1983 and have lots of history in the area, so the ideas that come to mind vary from simple thoughts of restaurants we used to love to more complex memories of the major remodeling we did to our vacation cottage so we could move here full-time, or the many friends we've made over the years.

Who would have guessed that such a simple project would pique our interest and give us a refreshed perspective on our lives?!

A Musical Life in Pacific Grove
Bill Englander

At the wise old age of 11, I decided I was going to become a professional musician. I played clarinet in my junior high school band and in a regional band. My fondest memories of my youth include playing at Disneyland when it first opened, marching in the Rose Parade and playing in the Los Angeles Coliseum. I also played guitar in a small group when rock and roll was just becoming popular. I remember a party where we played Rock Around the Clock all evening because it was the only rock and roll song we knew.

It's funny how life has a way of taking you down paths you never dreamed of. I ended up at a high school with no sports or music programs, so musical opportunities pretty much disappeared. I took some college classes including a couple of computer classes. Computers were a new discipline that few people were aware of. I loved them! In the early 1960s, I saw a newspaper ad, "Computer Programmers wanted, no experience necessary." I jumped at it! I passed their test and packed up and moved to San Francisco to participate in a bank's training program. I discovered that I loved programming, I was very good at it and, even better, they paid me to do it!

I met my wife Alice over a computer and we ended up with our own 2-person programming company for about 40 years. Another plus in this new industry was that besides being fun and interesting, it paid quite well. We made a good living and we took advantage of that to travel extensively all over the world.

I had trained in the Army at Fort Ord and had become familiar with the Monterey Peninsula. Alice and I came here often for weekends.

In 1983 we bought a vacation cottage in Pacific Grove.

The more time we spent here, the more we dreamed of living here full time. Years later through advancements in computer to computer communication, we were able to move here full time. We worked from home for many years and finally retired once we had gotten our clients through the Year 2000 changeover. I gave a lot of thought to how I could use my programming skills and my love of computers in retirement. We did volunteer systems design and computer programming for the Aquarium for a few years.

I had long ago given up on music as a career, but still played 1-finger melodies on the piano or a few guitar chords once in a while. I had enjoyed my band days in junior high school so much that when a friend told me about the Monterey Community Band, I decided to give it a try. I rented a baritone horn, attempted to teach myself how to play it and showed up for a rehearsal a month later. I almost didn't go inside because I was so afraid of failing or of what they'd say when I asked "Do you take beginners?" But I did and that started the most amazing phase of my life - I finally became a musician!

Pacific Grove has been the perfect venue for my musical adventure.

I have a knack for learning new instruments, so as opportunities arose, I took advantage of it. My new "career" really took off when we moved to Canterbury Woods. I met another musician who had played saxophone seriously in high school and college, but like me he had gone into other endeavors during his working years. With me on piano and guitar and a woman who sings beautifully, we formed a trio. We play many events at Canterbury including a monthly lounge performance. We play at birthday parties, memorial services, open houses, the annual Blessing of the Animals, holiday parties and other events. We also play in downtown Pacific Grove - First Fridays, the Pacific Grove Museum's Butterfly Ball, art openings, a Beacon House fund-raiser, Christmas at the Inns, Sally Griffin - as well as events in Monterey. We even played Sunset Center … well … at an art opening at the Sunset Center art gallery. I'm a member of the Pacific Grove Pops Orchestra, which brings together middle and high school students with adult musicians to play and learn together. I've sung in several choruses and currently play with a couple of recorder groups. Recently, I bought an electronic stand-up bass and am learning to play it so I can accompany a pianist here at Canterbury Woods.

Pacific Grove is blessed to be a place where music thrives.

A LEISURELY STROLL THROUGH NEIGHBORHOODS

Secret Deer Paths
Russell Sunshine
retired international consultant, writer, CCW member

Many visitors to Pacific Grove's Asilomar neighborhood enjoy the Recreation Trail along the abandoned Southern Pacific railway line. Far fewer discover our secret deer paths.

The paths are actually public utility easements reserved for storm drain maintenance. But two- and four-legged neighbors have claimed them for our own. My favorite conduit slips through four residential blocks from Grove Acre to Asilomar Avenue, traversing Evergreen, the Rec Trail, and Crocker along its route. Most adjacent property owners have erected privacy fences to frame this right-of-way. But one gracious couple planted jasmine to enhance the passage with an enchanting scent. Parallel paths poke landward, further north along Asilomar Avenue. Easily missed from a passing car, their understated trailheads are marked by waist-high posts with butter-yellow collars.

Three mini deer herds appear to have divided up the neighborhood, staking out informal territories—the length of Grove Acre, rolling dunes around the Asilomar Conference Center, and the expansive lawns of El Carmelo Cemetery and P.G. Golf Links. The opportunistic ruminants are creatures of habit, favoring familiar routes between grazing and resting spaces. The deer paths give them safe thoroughfares, buffered from unpredictable autos.

Silent and shadowy at dawn and dusk, the gray-beige deer are nearly undetectable when still. Their forward movement is slow-paced and stiff-legged, almost arthritic until vaulting effortlessly over four-foot fences from a standing start. Called mule deer for their prominent ears, they keep these radar antennae in constant rotation. Wary but calm, even when oblivious humans jog or cycle past, the deer can burst into explosive cheetah-like sprints if genuinely alarmed.

Matriarchal bands are normally composed of two or three does chaperoning up to five offspring. In the fall rutting season, antlered bucks mosey into these groups, but testosterone rarely provokes more than ritual sparring. There are evidently sufficient female partners to support non-competitive mating. Yet the herds never grow large enough to require municipal culling. Invisible but efficient apex predators—mountain lions and coyotes—control against overpopulation.

Spring brings tiny speckled fawns. Twins are common, a sign of an abundant food supply. Because our house lay vacant for years before we moved in, the does appropriated the back woodlot as a nursery. Their annual occupation gives us a ringside seat to observe the offspring's instinctive mobilization, first wobbling and collapsing, soon darting and bouncing on pogo-stick legs. The fawns learn to lie motionless for hours in camouflaging bower grass while their mothers forage. The infants' milky reward promotes speedy growth.

Some gardeners resent the deer's relentless browsing,

equally undeterred by futile fencing, guaranteed deer-resistant plants and noxious repellants. Nancy and I agree that the blessings afforded by proximity to these gentle creatures far outweigh the aggravation of munched buds and shoots. We walk by slowly when coming upon grazers, keeping our heads down and eyes averted. After four years of cordial cohabitation, "our deer" seem to accept us as benign neighbors, tolerating our presence with hardly a shrug.

We cherish sharing their lives and their space, including those secret thoroughfares.

Russell Sunshine's memoir, *FAR & AWAY: True Tales from an International Life*, is available in paperback and e-book editions. www.amazon.com/dp/1943887195 .

My Paper Route
Keith Larson

I don't know what the kids in Pacific Grove do for a living now. I've seen a few cookie and lemonade stands, but when I was growing up, quite a few of us had paper routes.

The main qualification seems to have been you couldn't be an aspiring sports star or have any other after-school activities because at that time the *Monterey Herald* was an afternoon paper. We would get home from school around 3:30 to find a bundle of papers in our drive way ready to be rolled up and delivered; if they were not there when we got home, they would be shortly. We might have enough time for Mom to fix us a snack and watch Captain Satellite on Channel 2, KTVU-Oakland (anyone remember?).

Our paper routes gave us aspiring business types a chance to learn some skills. Each route was kind of like its own franchise. We used sales skills to get people to take the paper and also to hire substitutes when we were sick or couldn't deliver our papers. I had about 75 customers and like most of my fellow carriers, could roll up a paper and put a rubber band around it in two or three seconds. We had to learn to carry a lot of weight or balance the bundles on our bikes. I got pretty good at riding one-handed and throwing the paper with the other.

Ah, now the fun part—collecting the money. Around the first of the month, we carriers would go out at night with our green money bags house-to-house and collect the fee. I always had one or two customers who I guess were short on cash and would hide when I knocked on the door to collect the $2.25 monthly subscription for the paper. I had good ears and could hear them whispering behind the door. Eventually I would track them down. Most people gave me a 50 cent tip. The *Herald* would then send me a bill for the papers which I would pay. The cash left over was what I made for the month, usually about $75. Pretty good for a fifth or sixth grader.

We delivered the news of the day rain or shine six days a week. The Sunday edition was delivered on Saturday. Yes, dogs did not like me and I broke one or two windows, most likely the standard experiences of paper carriers the world over. I loved my paper route. People would sometimes stop me and ask what the headlines were. I had a lot of older people in the houses I would deliver to who would just want to talk. Certainly a child delivering your paper in the afternoon and Walter Cronkite in the evening was a gentler way to digest the news of the day.

Walking in Grace
Sally Sirocky

I walk in grace and gratitude. Aware for the first time what my small town must look like to the outside world … maybe something from a Norman Rockwell painting, only with a liberal slant. Gentle breezes come up from the bay a block down the street; citizens with leisure time walk into the library. I pause in the park where a gazebo adds old-fashioned charm. Children play; an old man, sitting on a bench has fallen asleep. It's Monday and the vendors are setting up for the weekly Farmers' Market.

This is the oldest neighborhood with very small lots and homes to match. Although a Victorian flavor permeates, an Arts and Craft design is thrown in here and there. Each is unique and a little eclectic. The yards are neat, yet not manicured. Maybe the wildness of the ocean just steps away has an influence.

The parents of the children are want-to-be hippies, long hair, Birkenstocks and Volvos beat-up just enough as to not have the appearance of being too well-heeled. Yet they are, if they can afford to live in Pacific Grove.

The sound of the waves rolls up the streets. This town exists because of the bay. As a religious retreat the founders as well as today's natives were drawn to the water, to nature, to forces beyond their control. They make us feel alive. We meet on the Recreation Trail daily. We exchange smiles and nods and revel in the fact that we are the privileged to actually live here. For me nothing else will do.

My home is my sanctuary. I stare through the windows towards the bay or curl up with a good book in front of the fireplace, or sink naked into the hot tub in my private backyard as my neighbors do the same.

This is life in 2018.

> "The echoes and silence, patience and grace
> And all of these moments I'll never replace
> Fear of my heart absence of faith
> All I want, is to be home"
> —Foo Fighters, "Home"

Neighbor Clara Torres
Finding Gifts Through Grief
Kimberly Brown

Six months after moving to Pacific Grove in 2004, my beloved aunt died; she lived just 90 minutes away. Mondays were my day to visit prior to her death. When Monday in Pacific Grove rolled around, it was a difficult day of grief. I live close to St. Angela's church. Even though I was raised Catholic, I did not attend on a regular basis. In my grief, I was so relieved to discover that mass took place every day at 8:00 a.m. I took my grief to church not just on Mondays, but every day for several months.

It is at St. Angela's where I met Clara; she attended mass daily for years. She is the same age range as my aunt. We did not even know each other's name when she needed a ride to the doctor and asked if I was available. I was delighted to be of service. I think it was about two weeks before we finally introduced ourselves. It was a hysterical, entertaining circumstance. I still laugh just thinking about it.

I would converse with my husband about this lady I met at church. One day driving around we saw her walking and I told my husband to pull over; we offered her a ride home. She was so appreciative that she referred to us as "angels on wheels." I have since learned about Clara's other angels. Flora would take her shopping whereupon they would have bouts of laughter and eat good food. Other angels took Clara to church, shopping, the doctor, and to have her hair done. Whatever she needed, an angel was there.

I know that my beloved aunt could not be replaced. Spending time with Clara eased the pain. What a wonderful gift.

Clara and Our Shared Stories
Patricia Hamilton
Victorian living on Central Ave

Clara Torres lives in the apartment across the hall from mine in a lovely Victorian house on Central Avenue. We've been neighbors for 20 years.

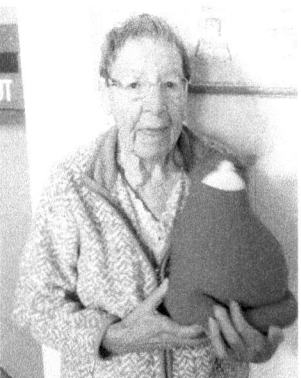

She's always been a social butterfly, up and out early every day walking about town, to St. Angela's or St. Vincent De Paul, or Robert's house. Now at 97 and confined at home, she has visitors stopping by throughout each day.

She loves to tell stories of our times together. Especially when my grandson was born. At 5 a.m. I got the call and rushed to my car for the trip to Folsom. Clara hailed to me from her kitchen window, "What the big hurry?"

"My daughter is having the baby; I've got to get there."

A grumpy neighbor appeared in robe and slippers, waving his arms. "Pipe down; what's so important you woke me up?" To this day neither of us can remember his name when she giggles as she tells it.

Grace McCoy, Patricia Hamilton, Zack McCoy

And the time she stayed at the Borg's Motel when her place was repainted, and I brought a pizza that we ate as we sat on the bed and tried to guess the answers on "Wheel of Fortune."

More stories about summer weekends when she and I took my blue Honda to every garage sale listed in the *Herald*. She collected antique dolls for her great niece in New Mexico, and I picked up a variety of kid stuff, especially after my granddaughter Grace was born.

Clara insisted Grace had to have a doll. When I failed at getting Grace interested in any of the new dolls I bought, Clara presented Grace with what she thought was the perfect doll. Grace didn't even glance at the doll before it slipped through her hands to the floor—I did see Clara's face fall.

Clara is now 97, Zack is 18 and off to college, and Grace, 14, told Clara she loves her. Good stories make good neighbors.

Walter "Wally" Verwold
Clara's Great-nephew and Archangel/Caregiver
Patricia Hamilton

Clara took care of Wally when he was young and now he comes before his day job every day about 5 a.m. to cook Clara breakfast and prepare her food for the rest of the day. He cooks her favorites, even though her tastes vary from his. He checks on her by phone during the day and returns for at least an hour after work to clean, cook, take out the trash and vacuum et al. When she's ill, he sleeps in one of her recliners and stays 24/7 until she can be on her own again. On his days off from his job for St. Vincent de Paul, Wally takes Clara food shopping, on scenic drives around the bay, and out to visit some friendly pigs that live on a farm in Carmel Valley. He takes her to all doctor, dental, and haircutter appointments. He's been following this routine for about 2-3 years, and played a lesser role before but always diligent. Wally is Clara's Archangel and he has promised that he will never leave her.

"Short Street"
Karen Brown

A newcomer to Pacific Grove will instantly recognize Lighthouse Avenue as our "Main Street," but some folks in town will nominate Short Street as the most "hometown" road off all, especially that little block between Granite and Willow. My family lived there from 1990 to 1994, and it remains a golden memory. Our home faced Willow, but the kitchen featured a Dutch door that opened to what I called the alley—Short Street.

My husband placed our baby's seat on a rolling chopping block table we parked on our side of the door, opened the top, and there she spent hours watching the people and dogs walk by and the kids play. Like an alley in New York, Short Street was rarely used by vehicles and served as a playground. In the early 90s, it was a skate park of sorts. Kids on rollerblades and skateboards built their own ramps and even jumped over each other. They threw out light-hearted dares and boasts. They shouted, "Watch this!" and also "You did it!" or "Try it again!" They spent hours day after day after day. And our baby spent the first year-and-a-half of her life watching this show.

The skaters were about a dozen boys ranging from age six to 14, and one little girl who was only four years old. Kayla was David's little sister, and David was a star skater at six. My husband and I admired Kayla's determination to keep trying to skate and even jump. We hoped our daughter would become so brave. Kayla fell, but did not go home crying; she got back up on her feet and tried again. She shouted, "Watch me!" and everyone did.

David didn't seem to grow impatient or embarrassed, as big brothers usually do. Instead he encouraged her, and so did the others. The tone of the playground was set by the oldest, the Foley twins. Whenever the younger ones needed caution, they provided it. When the competition got too heated, they cooled everyone down. They suggested solutions to problems and even monitored language. They made sure everyone was safe when the occasional car came by. When we needed a babysitter, we called on the Foley twins.

For Kateyrae's first birthday "the kids" were all invited. For her present, they put her seat on a skateboard and, working together, they guided her along the alley, her initiation into skating. I held my breath, but no, the Foley twins decided she wasn't ready for a jump. There were other important people in our neighborhood. David's grandma, Adelaide, mother of 13, was known as the "Lady of the Block."

Then there was Don, the event planner! Don held Super Bowl and Feast of Lantern parties, inviting everyone who lived nearby. But it was Halloween that made him famous. There was always a pumpkin-decorating party, and then on Halloween, his house was so scary! Not gross, but filled with delightfully horrible surprises. Hundreds of people enjoyed his house on these holidays. Actually, throughout the year, any time, you could walk by and see trains, boats, teddy bears, and other marvelous stuff he collected and showcased.

Today, Don's house and the Little Free Libraries he (and others) created on the corner make Short Street the best pedestrian path ever. However, the alley isn't a playground anymore. We heard the sad story after we had left the area, how one day the kids were playing basketball when one of the Foley twins fell to the ground. He died from a congenital heart defect, and that important family moved away. And, for the kids, computer screens moved in.

But once, kids played in the alley as the sun was setting and as my family was preparing and eating supper. I remember the sounds of their play were almost always like background music, an old song that we remembered fondly from the 1950s. Now P.G. neighbors can still gather at Don's (as they have for over 40 years now), remembering Short Street as it was in the 1990s, playing golden oldies on his juke box in the sunset, and planning their next neighborhood project.

Walkin' the Dog in Pacific Grove
Duane Edgington
27-year resident

"Eat meat," she commanded. "Eat meat!"

I should set the stage. It had long been my practice to take our two Pembroke Welsh Corgis, Honey and Pip, for a morning walk, following a multi-block route in our Pacific Grove neighborhood, right after their breakfast and my coffee. Usually we encountered few humans, except the occasional morning jogger or fellow dog-walker. Pip, our male Corgi, was especially keen on covering ground, greeting any humans we met, and treeing those pesky squirrels that inhabit the vegetation along Lighthouse Avenue from Cedar Street up to 17 Mile Drive. His sister and littermate Honey was more interested in a leisurely pace, sniffing every inch for new smells, and of course, greeting humans. Squirrels held little interest for Honey. We liked the familiarity of our standard route, seeing people and pets we knew, and visiting old spots with potentially new sights and smells.

On one particular morning, as we climbed the incline from Del Monte Boulevard up Lighthouse Avenue towards 17 Mile Drive, I spied a human, female, middle-aged, walking down the sidewalk towards us from the opposite direction.

As we met, I said "Good morning," my standard greeting, pausing and moving the leashes and Corgis aside so she could pass on the narrow sidewalk. The Corgis waited calmly, in anticipation of a friendly greeting, and maybe a head scratch or pet.

She stopped and demanded, "What do you feed your dogs?"

"Excuse me, what?"

"Dogs need to eat meat. What do you feed your dogs?"

"Kibble. Iams kibble. Our vet says they are very healthy, and their diet is good. And biscuits. They love dog biscuits." I was feeling a bit defensive, although I was not sure why.

"Dogs need to eat meat. Eat meat. You should feed them meat," she admonished us sternly.

"Thanks for the advice. Good morning," I replied as we steered back on our way, now moving briskly.

"Eat meat. Eat meat!" she addressed our backs.

I had never seen the woman before, and I never saw her again. I have often mused whether she was attending a Carnivorous Canine Society symposium at the Monterey Convention Center, and was out for a stroll before catching the bus into Monterey. Or possibly she was visiting a Pacific Grove vegan friend and consequently expressing frustration at the meat-challenged diet of the Pacific Grove mammals that she encountered. Or perhaps, she was a long-time resident just walking a different time or place from her normal habit. In any case, she ought to be a Pagrovian. She has the demeanor to fit right in.

Making Neighborly Waves
Heidi Feldman

It all started last March, when San Jose resident Mike Finn and his wife were scouting around for a home for their retirement years. They'd originally been drawn to Carmel Valley, but when they took a detour through Pacific Grove, it was love at first sight. Next thing they knew, they were purchasing a home on Surf Avenue in P.G.'s Beach Tract.

When Mike wanted to show his new home to family and friends, he directed them to the "street view" feature of Google Maps. And that's when everyone noticed the surfboard hanging above the garage doors. Now, there had been no surfboard attached to the house when the Finns had toured it with the real estate agent, but obviously there once had been such a decoration, proof captured for all time when the Google camera car rolled by. But what had happened to it? And where was it now?

Thus a quest began. Originally, Mike just wanted to locate a surfboard, any surfboard, to decorate the front of his new home on Surf Avenue. He turned to the website Next Door, a private message board for residents of the same neighborhoods, the cyber equivalent of the *kaffee klatsch* and the back fence. He got lots of responses along the lines of "Great idea," but no clues where he could locate a surfboard suitable for decorating the front of a house.

But those initial feelers eventually came to the attention of Heidi Feldman, one of the earlier owners of the Finns' new home. Not only did she have the original surfboard, but she knew the story behind it. She had rescued the surfboard from the Last Chance Mercantile out at the Marina landfill and recycling center, painted it, and gave it a place of honor on the front of her house. When she moved from the Surf Avenue house, she left the surfboard

Albertine Potter—Queen of Granite Street
Kathleen Biersteker

This a story about one of Pacific Grove's well-known citizens, Albertine Theresa Agudo Potter, born October 15, 1929, and raised in Pacific Grove. My words about her life are taken from an oral history she accounted to me and I have incorporated statements about her that others have made to me.

A third generation American of European and Filipino descent, she was raised in one of the town's first Filipino-American families. Her father, Luis Agudo, was a labor activist who founded a weekly newspaper. Her mother, Elizabeth Shiffer Agudo, worked in the canneries.

Once when Albertine was a little girl, her family was at a house located in a local farm field. Suddenly gunfire erupted. Her father put his children into a cast iron tub, telling them to stay down. He was warned: leave the area, or next time, be killed. He left. Her mother and four children stayed.

As a child and a young woman, Albertine suffered greatly from racial discrimination in a mostly white non-inclusive town. The first woman to graduate from Monterey Peninsula College, after graduation she sought a job. It was hard to find. Finally, she applied to the Pacific Grove office of the school superintendent. After all, hadn't she been educated through their system and graduated from MPC? After disparaging remarks, statements that a minority had never before been hired, demeaning qualifying examinations, and being told that she could not fraternize with, talk to anyone, or be seen "up front" because she was "brown," she was fed up. However, her mother told her, "Go back. Never mind, because you are going to make a difference." She went back and was hired.

Albertine married Cecil Potter, a handsome young man of European descent who became a commissioned Army officer. The Asian Exclusion Act prohibited their California marriage, so they married in Nevada. The couple began to have children. Though difficult for interracial couples, housing was found for the family near bases where Cecil was stationed in the U.S. and Europe.

The family returned to Pacific Grove where Cecil and Albertine lived in a house they built next to Albertine's childhood home on Granite Street. They were gifted with 13 beautiful children. As their children grew, Albertine and Cecil became increasingly involved in supporting their activities in community organizations—church, school, and sports. Albertine spent time volunteering, organizing projects, events and fundraising. The hub of a large multigenerational extended family, the Potter home was always a busy place. Albertine did what she could to create an environment of inclusiveness. Her house was always welcoming and open and she made everyone feel special and valuable. With many persons around the dining table, many Pacific Grove youth were nurtured there. She was supportive of her children and their friends. Scores of young people in Pacific Grove will say that they are "the Potter's 14th child."

Of extreme importance was Albertine's service to the Robert Down Elementary School Multicultural Education Advisory Committee, a group of parents, teachers and school administrators charged with implementing the California public school mandate. For the district's first school initiating the program, Albertine contributed her highly developed social consciousness as well as her social skills and very personable attributes, an extremely genuine person, talented in her ability to relate to others. Her wholehearted commitment to and vested interest in this program was intense as she had attended that school herself and had great personal connection to the community, as well as to the resulting influence of the program's successful implementation.

Having suffered repeatedly wounded feelings in her life, Albertine's love of people, her need to relate to their essential being, her great intelligence, creativity, resilience, and tenacity, helped her develop powerful coping skills and strategies to overcome these injuries. She constructed and cultivated a rich rewarding life for herself and her family and contributed greatly to her community.

Albertine was a Naval Postgraduate School administrative assistant, and after she retired, volunteered at the Blind and Visually Impaired Center of Monterey County in Pacific Grove. This incredible organizer was a powerful force for volunteerism who would not take no for an answer. This little tiny woman, with her effervescent personality, who had overcome so much oppression, was a dynamic powerhouse who made things happen. If you met her, your life changed!

After courageously dealing with serious health issues, Albertine, "The Queen of Granite Street," passed away in her Pacific Grove home on March 12, 2017, at the age of 87.

behind. Then she got wind that the then-new owners had removed the surfboard and were about to toss it in a Dumpster. Once again, Heidi came to the rescue, storing the surfboard in her garage … until she learned that her former home once again had new owners, and that they were in the market for a decorative surfboard.

"I never thought I'd get the original back," Mike says. The surfboard is once again on prominent display above the garage on Surf Avenue, and Mike vows that whatever redecorating and renovation he and his wife may have in mind, the surfboard will stay. He calls it a "cool circular story" and "a happy beginning" to the couple's next chapter in their lives in Pacific Grove.

Why My Garage is Set Back So Far From the Street
Richard Stillwell
as told to Linnet Harlan

My wife, Bev, our kids and I were living on Bayview. Bev and I really liked the vacant lot at the corner of Jewell and Cedar. We'd come over and sit on a little bench I put together out of rocks and planks and look out at the bay. We thought the view was really something.

The lot was owned by a couple of Englishwomen who ran a little day care school on Central Avenue. I asked them about buying the lot, but they didn't want to sell. Then, a couple of years later, Bev and I were over at the lot, and there in the weeds was a sign that said it was for sale.

I thought it was worth about $18,000 (this was a long time ago), but when the real estate salesman said the Englishwomen wanted $22,000, I said okay.

I got the permit and was going up to Bass Lake with my family for the summer when the building inspector, Leonard, stopped by and said, "When are you starting work on this?"

"When I get back from the lake," I said.

"The permit's only good for 60 days," he said.

So I had to get something going before I left for the lake. I was putting up some batten boards to show where the corner of the garage would be when Mrs. Campbell, my neighbor just up the hill on Cedar, saw me. "Is that where the garage is going to be?" she asked. Turns out she was worried that if I put the garage close to the street, she wouldn't be able to see the bay from her window or her front porch.

The lot is pretty deep, so I just took those batten boards and moved them to a bunch of different positions until she said yes it was okay, she could still see the bay.

So she ended up with her view of the bay, and I ended up with some good places to park in front of my garage.

The Cook and the Neighbor
Sandra Thompson Iman

What a delightful tale I have to tell. I moved to Pacific Grove five years ago in 2012. My journey was a miracle. Starting in 2006 to 2010 I had five years of tragedy that I never thought could possibly happen to anyone. Here are the silver bullets:

- *2006: My husband of 30 years passed away.*
- *2007: My oldest, 30-year-old, beautiful daughter passed away.*
- *2008: My 17-year-old poodle, my loving companion, had to be put to sleep.*
- *2009: My dad passed away; he lived 3,000 miles away and left my lovely Mom to be settled.*
- *2010: I had all I could take, sold my homes, gave away all my furniture and moved into a small room with friends.*

I decided that I would follow the dim light of hope and walk out this grief and disappointment.

One day at work, I received an email that began to change my life toward recovery. Linda asked me to come for an interview at a real estate office in Carmel. I was working in Salinas at the time. Well, I was hired, still not out of the dark but with a new challenge. I began to think it would be good to move to the Peninsula.

Long story short, I saw an ad for a small place in Pacific Grove. I sat in front of the home very early and hoped to be first, as I had an open house that day. I was interviewed and given the application. They asked for tax returns. Well, mine were somewhere packed away, so I just put my business card from Sotheby's in the envelope and sent it off. Much to my surprise, I was "chosen." Yes, it was the business card.

Linda was a relative and so they called her to inquire about me and it was a thumbs up! I live in Pacific Grove. That was a great start to inner healing, although once I moved into this special little abode, I realized for the first time in my life that I had never lived alone, and I also realized I did not have any close friends near me. I walked the ocean path. I cried and prayed; I was lonely, afraid and missed the life I had built. The fog became my friend, a blanket that hugged me and hid me. I looked forward to meeting her in the mornings.

Well, as the story goes—the next surprise! I had lived in town for a few months and one day turning the corner to walk up my street to home, I ran into an old friend, Kim. We had known each other in Big Sur (her family owns Nepenthe) and Salinas. I knew her children and for the first time I felt close to someone again. Kim grew up in hospitality and service. She is unlike many people I know. Kim is a cook, a listener, and a walking partner.

But the best of Kim's character is her cooking. Her beans are like melted butter. She can heat up bread like no other. She slices it, but not all the way through, and wraps it in tin foil and knows exactly when it is the right temperature. Salads are the best with her homemade seasoned dressings and fresh, crunchy vegetables. She is always cooking something new, and I have had many times of feeling the warmth of her home and the joy of her cooking. She does not realize what a healing she has been. She has stories too, and we have let our hearts become knit together over many a meal. I really do not think that I would be as healthy in mind, body, and soul if I did not have Kim in my life.

Life is good. I have learned to master disappointment. My next goal is to master fulfillment, although I am beginning to realize they walk hand-in-hand.

Morris Grant Fisher
January 8, 1938 ~ March 13, 2017
Maria Villela & Kids

Dear Morrie,
I have just a few things I wanted to share with you….
You were my first friend in P.G.

You carried over enchiladas for my kids and me to eat our first night of living across the street from you. (And you reminded me to return your Tupperware.) Thank you for this welcome.

Remember that one night when I was dragging my trash cans out, and you greeted me from over your fence? You very astutely noticed that I was tearful and you asked me why. I shared with you that I missed my kids, and you started to cry right alongside me. Truly cry. Through your tears you told me that you remember like it was yesterday how sad you were when your girls got back on the plane after visiting with you. You told me that if you could get through it, so could I.

You were also the first P.G. friend to my kids. My young daughter, Eliana, was truly smitten with you, as you well know. She had a specific title for you—she called you "Mr. Morrie, who used to be the mayor." She didn't know what a mayor was, but she told everyone that you were famous.

My wily boys, Benicio and Mateo, also liked to be playful with you—they would decorate your mailbox with stickers, and they would sneak some toys and deflated balloons inside to top off your mail. The next day my kids would race to our mailbox to see if Mr. Morrie had snuck their toys back into our mailbox. Without fail, you always got the toys back in our mailbox before my kids came home from school. You had truly won over my kids.

On Halloween night, our first holiday in our new town, remember how you came over to remind my kids to come to your house to trick or treat? You said that instead of candy you gave out dollar bills to each child. My nine-year-old boy incredulously asked you, "But Mr. Morrie, what if those kids came back a second time?"

You replied, "Well, they would get two dollars, I guess."

A few weeks before Christmas, remember when I was decorating my tree and you came by to say hi, like you did so often? We were talking about our holiday plans and you were looking forward to spending the holiday with your daughters (and your ex-wife and her husband). As we were talking I realized that my ladder was too short to put the star on the top of my tree. You leaned the tree over on its side and simply stuck the star on top.

Then in January, on January 13th to be exact, you walked over and announced to me, "Well, we aren't going to be neighbors for much longer." I stood there in my doorway on that beautiful, crisp, sunny day listening to you tell me how they found a mass in your liver and that you were scheduled for a CAT scan the following week. At that point you knew nothing more, but you sensed that it wasn't good. That conversation, as surreal and unbelievable as it was, was exactly two months to the day when you passed away. Only 60 days.

Now as I write this I imagine that you are sharing your friendship and kindness with new lucky neighbors. You will be known as Mr. Morrie, the famous mayor, who's not afraid to cry with neighbors, hands out dollar bills to kids and will likely place another star on someone's tree.

(written March 14, 2017)

Two Old Guys
Margaret Baldwin
fourth generation in P.G.

Twenty-five years ago, I was a runner. When I rose early in the morning to go for a run, I usually crossed paths with two very old men who obviously shared my taste for Pacific Grove in the early morning. They probably enjoyed the smells of the Scotch Bakery firing up as they ambled down Lighthouse in the half-light. They probably liked the smell of tide pools that blew up into town from Lovers Point. And I'll bet they even liked the fog that swirled around their knees so that sometimes they needed to steady each other as they stepped off the curb. I guessed that they liked those fragments of Pacific Grove life because I liked them too—but I didn't really know. The two old guys were foreign, and I couldn't understand the snatches of conversation I overheard as we passed on the street.

For a long time—maybe a year—we didn't acknowledge each other's comings and goings. I was usually half asleep in those early morning hours, and they had each other to talk to. So it wasn't much of a relationship, even though I often thought about them. I wondered where they were from. And I wondered if they had met here or whether it was a friendship that had its roots many years ago in some other country. Then, after a long time, we began to make eye contact.

Eye contact led gradually to a mutual nodding of heads and a slightly friendlier wave of hands. One morning, thinking they might be Italian, I tried a hesitant "buongiorno," but they looked blank … and the next day I went back to a casual wave.

Then one morning, they smiled shyly as I approached, and each one stepped off the sidewalk so that I had to run between them. They were starting to be silly. By the next morning, they had obviously hatched a plan. They stepped apart like the day before, but this time they applauded as I ran through, like the winner of a marathon. We still couldn't talk to each other, but we had a relationship.

Then one day they simply disappeared. Had one died or moved away, the other refusing to walk without his friend? Or –as I preferred to imagine—had they moved somewhere together, maybe just over the hill in New Monterey? I never knew. But for several years, they had woven themselves into the fabric of my mornings here in Pacific Grove, and the streets seemed emptier without them. Watching these two old gentlemen walk along, heads down and engrossed in conversations I couldn't understand, had given me a daily reminder that human connectedness is what matters most.

We do that here in Pacific Grove. Although these two old men are gone, P.G. is filled with opportunities to connect in small but important ways. Our houses are small, but we get to know our neighbors. We engage in civic life joyously and contentiously because we care about our town. It is our connectedness that draws people here and that makes the rest of us want to stay. All of us have memories that bind us to this community. Two old guys out for a walk is just one of mine.

Love and Pavel's Peasant Bread
Barry Marshall
artist, painter

Fog was setting in as I approached the small cabin in Pacific Grove, my first rental after moving here. My future landlady, Eloise, then in her 80s, interviewed me, her blue eyes flashing. She apparently found me suitable as a tenant for what she described as her "chicken coop out back" and I took the place. This started a friendship that still lasts today, an adopted family, friends for life.

One time, I presented her with a loaf of peasant bread from Pavel's Bakerei, and she loved it so much I decided to make it a tradition. Making my weekly delivery of Pavel's peasant bread to Eloise is something I look forward to. She opens the door, all of 5'3", 92 years of sparkle. She is family to me, a substitute mom for the one that I lost when she was 60. Eloise is still spry as ever and a friend to the end.

 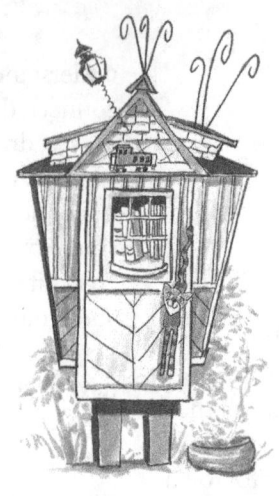 

A City of Neighborhoods
Don Livermore
47-year resident of Pacific Grove

I came to Pacific Grove in 1972. I was a beginning teacher and wanted to buy a home. All I could afford at that time was a small fixer-upper located off Lighthouse Avenue four blocks from downtown. My intent was to clean it up a bit and sell it in five years to get a larger home.

My wonderful neighbors changed that idea. I instead decided to just do a major remodel, for I did not want to leave the area. I had found over those early years just how special and unique Pacific Grove was. Wonderful neighborhoods, neighbors, local businesses, great restaurants and many community events. Even with all the growth and changes over the years on the Peninsula, P.G. still maintains a family-oriented and locals community.

I totally fell in love with my neighborhood and location in Pacific Grove, so much so that I decided to institute local neighborhood parties so we could all get to know each other better. P.G. is known for its unique celebrations. My first attempt was a Feast of Lanterns potluck in 1973. It was successful and has been going on every year since.

After that, one of my neighbors and I started a Pumpkin Carving Contest in 1979. It's still going to this day. I had already been haunting the outside of the house for Halloween since 1973, so the contest was a great prelude to Halloween. On the average, we now get between 300 and 400 trick-or-treaters and we don't even live near Candy Cane Lane. I do, from time-to-time, have to buy extra candy for my neighbors. Now the children of my original tricksters are coming. What fun.

Other neighborhood and friends' parties have also evolved over the years. Christmas Open House, Super Bowl and many retirement parties. Pacific Grove is conducive to all types of neighborly get-togethers. Definitely a special place to live.

I consider it the crown jewel of the Monterey Peninsula.

Short Street ... A P.G. Snapshot

If you want to see wonderful cross-sections of Pacific Grove and its charm, walk down most any street adjacent to the downtown, library or museum.

One street in particular that is a favorite is Short Street. It runs parallel to Lighthouse Avenue and is just one block up. It begins at Park Street across from the Post Office and ends at 17 Mile Drive.

It's only nine-to-ten blocks long (hence the street name). You'll find most every style of P.G. home and garden on your walk, early homes from the late 1800s to present-day buildings. Along the way, you'll meet several friendly dogs and their walkers. It's a question of who owns or walks who in this city.

You will experience our wonderful George Washington Park in addition to a variety of gardens, flowers and free libraries sure to delight. If you want to venture further, continue across 17 Mile Drive to Pico Street, another chapter of Pacific Grove not to be missed. You'll end up at our magnificent ocean's edge and coastal pathway.

Confessional Vignettes of a Mischievous Kid in the Village of Pacific Grove
Peter Krasa
retired School Principal

As a very spoiled only child growing up in the 1950s, I was quite prankish. During one Halloween, dressed as Robin Hood, I began vigorously soaping an unanswered door on Morse Drive, when it suddenly opened, thrusting me inside. I was immediately unmasked, identified, and punished.

There's a stone bench, which still exists, outside David Avenue School's office upon which I spent many, many hours after being kicked out of class. One day on the bench, I looked around, and asked myself, "What's keeping me here?"

When I determined the answer was "nothing," I took off

to the neighborhood store in Del Monte Park and bought some licorice, and felt quite proud of my escapade—until I was identified, caught, and punished yet again.

Across from my house on Divisadero Street, where Hilltop School sits today, there was a field. I prepared a time capsule filled with the most valuable items my parents owned, and buried it. I became frightened when they made such a big deal about the "theft," so I tried to retrieve the box, but I couldn't find it. I was identified, caught, and punished for that caper, too.

My early failure as a criminal forced me to retire from being such an incorrigible kid. "They" say it takes a village to raise a child, and Pacific Grove was such a village for me.

Piecing My Pacific Grove
1967-2017
Kim Ly Bui-Burton

Start with the tumble of rocks at the curve called "Crab Rock" along the coastline before the foghorn. The me-that-was-young hunted beach glass and olive shells in the sand under my mother's loving gaze, sheltered late at night against the stone wall as a reckless teen, studied library science on sunny afternoons as my two children dug sand and tide-pooled for hours. Under the gazebo down the road, with sunlight and waves all around us, stitch a heart for my best love and the two-decades troth we pledged.

Fit the peaked and gently fading Victorians we made our own—one a two-bedroom, claw-foot-tubbed $150/month stone's throw from Lighthouse where one life began, the other a block over and above, with jasmine tendrils in bloom curling through cracked window sills and sweet edible roses twining over the porch. End with our house on the hill, facing hummingbirds in the fountain, sunsets moving along the sky's curve in the evening, trees leafing each window, hawk's flight above, forest below.

Trace the triangle of "sister sails" in the blue of the sea at the end of the street, place the brick bobbing down the full rush of rain water running from sidewalk to sidewalk, press the churn of bicycle wheels as the Butterfly Criterium took over the downtown streets, thread the parades, street fairs, street dances, and spark and dazzle of fireworks (or muffled fog-lit glow). My mother's named bench near Berwick Park, turned to the pups on the beach, making rest for the weary.

Oh the places that were and are gone—the sounds of sifting buttons in muffin tins at Beverly's, toothsome huckleberry muffins from Scotch Bakery, steam of just-right lattes from Wildberries, holiday lights strung across Lighthouse, silken second-hand store treasures, forgotten library books—too faint to be seen. But all the bright threads of friends and neighbors and loved ones woven in, grown up, moved on, still cherished. My Pacific Grove holds them all.

My Lady in the White Uniform
Keith Larson

She had a stark white uniform set against a backdrop of green Monterey pines. Her hair was red and I would see her almost every day walking to the laundry as I was walking or riding my bike to school on Congress Road. Without knowing it then, I was attracted to anchors: those people, situations and sounds that could be depended on to be there with regularity.

Throughout my school years in Pacific Grove, around 3:00 p.m., I would hear the train through town on its way to the sand plant. The fog horn could be heard anytime the fog rolled in and became one of the comforting sounds I could depend on. Looking back, it felt like things did not change much in town during the 1960s and 70s; it was a period that people and places go through like fields that lay fallow for a few years before being planted again.

The freight train came to Pacific Grove one last time in the evening around 1980. The whistle wailing through town seemed to be much louder and it was unusual for it to be heading through town at night because it had always been an afternoon train. The regularly scheduled run and the freight whistle that was so much a part of growing up had become infrequent, and I knew from a feeling I had this would be the last time I would hear it through town.

During the 80s, technology started to replace long-time icons like the fog horn and the whistling buoy, but I would still see her sometimes heading up Congress to work at the laundry. The clean white uniform was gone; now she wore jeans and her red hair was graying. Pacific Grove was coming out of its fallow time; the seasons were changing as the Monterey Bay Aquarium set a dynamic new tone for the area. The tracks were taken up and replaced by the Recreation Trail connecting PG with other cities on the peninsula.

The 60s and 70s, the era I grew up in, to me, was the closest thing to having time stand still. I hope I am becoming more accepting of change, especially the fallow times and the seasons of my own life. And for my friend in the white uniform, I am hoping the seasons have brought a much-deserved retirement rest.

Protector of Bees
LeeAnn Stewart

My husband Tom and I bought a home in Pacific Grove in 2012. I could not help but notice all of the wonderful flowers and the bees in this area.

One of the assignments I had as a volunteer with the California Department of Fish and Wildlife was to monitor 22 wood duck boxes which were placed along Willow Creek in Folsom. My job was to look for signs of nesting and record my findings in each of the boxes. On a routine spring morning I noticed that one of the boxes had been taken over by honey bees who must have swarmed there sometime during the previous week. The boxes were the perfect size and location, providing shelter to build comb and protection at night, as well as being located near a water source.

When the temperatures reach triple digits, which they often do in the summer in Folsom, the forager bees find water nearby, take it into their tiny mouth and fly with it back to the hive. At the entrance of the hive a house bee will take the water from the forager bee, mouth-to-mouth, and place the tiny droplet in an empty comb cell. Dozens of forager bees go back and forth working with the house bees to put water in the hive. Once there is enough, it is communicated to the foragers to stay at the hive entrance and beat their wings, creating an air flow through the hive, having a "swamp cooler" effect, thus cooling the hive.

A few weeks later, I noticed two more wood duck boxes had been commandeered by the honey bees, which were obviously thriving in the area. These particular bees are known as "feral bees" because they have been surviving by natural selection in the wild without any human intervention. They are considered to be very valuable to beekeepers because of their strong genetics.

My supervisor at DFW was in a quandary about what to do, because after all, the wood duck boxes are supposed to be for the wood ducks due to the loss their nesting habitat. At the time, I had no experience as a beekeeper; however, I knew I needed to do something to save those bees. I asked my supervisor for permission to remove the boxes with the help of a beekeeper. We would hive them and return the wood duck boxes empty and intact for the ducks. My supervisor agreed and I was able to assist in the removal of the honey bees.

Alex Young, the beekeeper who helped me also fostered the honey bees for me while I began my beekeeping education. I took several classes through the Sacramento Area Beekeeping Association and I worked alongside an experienced beekeeper for hands-on experience. After about a year of learning and purchasing the necessary equipment, I got my first hive. Not the exact bees that I rescued because they only live six-to-eight weeks (twelve weeks in the winter), but these bees were from the lineage of those strong bees from Willow Creek.

The honey bees that I rescued will make an impact on the declining honey bee population. These pollinators are very important to California and its economy. In addition, they are fascinating creatures, complex in their communication and existence.

I have five hives in my backyard in Sacramento and continue to take classes on apiculture and all things bee-related, and I'm particularly fascinated by the ways in which bees communicate. I sing to my bees whenever I work in their hive, because it seems to calm them.

We're currently in the process of moving to Pacific Grove full time and I look forward to continuing my love affair there with these valuable and remarkable creatures.

SECTION 4
ANIMALS WITHIN AND WITHOUT

WILDLIFE, FERAL AND PET ANIMAL FRIENDS

Dogs, Weather and People
Grace Erin McCoy

The first things I noticed were the dogs. They're everywhere you look. And it's not just the fact that there are so many that captures my attention. No, it's that most of them wear clothes. Unusual, but I guess they've got to stay warm somehow. That's another thing. The weather here is absolutely amazing, nothing like the scorching, 108-degree heat we have in El Dorado Hills. Must be nice living so close to the ocean.

But what makes Pacific Grove so special to me isn't the ocean or the weather. It's not even the sweater-wearing dogs. No, what's made P.G. earn a place in my heart are the people. Everyone I've met in this lovely little town seems to be unique.

Just today my grandmother and I visited Don's house. From seashells to hats to old Coke merchandise, Don collects it all. Each room in his four story house had its own theme. There was an Egyptian room, a movie room, a room full of bears, even a room dedicated to antique or unusual looking perfume bottles, just to name a few—plus there were small scale trains running on tracks high up in every room and outside in and around his garden.

And I met J, the owner of the famous, some say infamous, Butterfly House on 9th Street. Painted in a variety of colors and decorated with butterflies, the house is impossible to miss. J himself is an amazing person. When we stopped the car to get out and take a picture, he came out of the house and greeted us. I asked him how long it'd taken him to cover his garage, house and yard with ceramic, wood, metal and plastic butterflies.

"About 25 years and still counting," he replied, "I don't think I'll ever be done putting butterflies on it."

My grandmother bought a butterfly with my name to go on J's wall and J hung a butterfly with my grandmother's name on it—for doing this book. All butterfly money goes to the Blind and Visually Impaired Center nearvby.

My grandmother introduced me to other P.G. people—Rita, Moe, William, Martha, Jane, Lorna, and others—and they all were the highlights of my 2017 summer visit.

Rambunctious Wildlife
Blanca Shield

The Pacific Ocean is not quiet. Ten foot white waves lick the black rocks, spraying the air. Above, pelicans clip the blue seawater scooping, filling their long bills with anchovies.

On Ocean View Boulevard two life size breaching whales have been beautifully carved from old tree stumps and painted black and white.

Humpback whales are very acrobatic, often breaching high out of the water, up to thirty seconds, to take a look around in a devil-may-care way. They can dive to depths of 500 - 700 feet for up to thirty minutes.

Their flukes (tails) can be eighteen feet wide, serrated and pointed at the top when they "sound" (goes into a long, deep dive) and usually throws them upwards. Their life span is 45 - 50 years. and are not carnivorous, eating one and a half ton of krill daily, unlike the orcas who sometimes eat their babies, willy-nilly.

Deer prowl the Municipal Golf Course in Pacific Grove nearby clipping the grass and my flowers.

Last month my husband went on an errand and left the garage door open. My washer/driver are in this place and when I went to do the laundry I found seven deer sniffing around: two fawns, four does and one buck with light-brown antler. A crown of bone. They saw me and ignored me exploring the garage.

Mountain lions are eternally hungry. Along Ocean View Boulevard they prey on baby otters. Since I live nearby at night I oftentimes imagine a lion softly padding on my front yard on its way to its dinner,

Last year in the daytime a lion was spotted resting on a tree branch in downtown Pacific Grove. "Now, what's for lunch?" he mused.

Coyotes patrol neighborhoods chewing on fawns, cats and puppies. At the equestrian center in Pebble Beach, they chase horses, snapping at their hoofs.

A little boy across the street had a favorite cartoon about a lovable anaconda snake. He was hiking in the wilds of Carmel Valley and saw a rattlesnake lying flat, not coiled. He ran to pet it crying: "Daddy there's Anaconda!"

The Butterfly Town has a wild side.

One Wacky Cat
Denise Turley

They were both looking for someone to love, she having lost her adored cat Serendipity and he having been an abandoned cat on the side of a rural road. They had been brought together to heal each other's hearts—a mutually beneficial friendship grew.

His only concern was the isolation of his mistress. She had lived in a Pacific Grove neighborhood for years near Washington Park and with age saw her friends pass away. What this very social cat did was help reestablish old friendships and create new ones. His name came from a conversation with the woman's caregiver. He would do just about anything for attention. "That's one Wacky cat!" stuck as this kitty's name. Several happy years followed, including his favorite event, Halloween, where he sat on the porch accepting pats as a thank you for candy. Wacky was one of those cats who was of great service to his owner, helping her to feel less isolated until her passing. And through the continued kindness of neighbors Wacky will never have to worry about having a home.

ocelot cat
Inge Kessler

I saw you
not in an Amazon jungle
or on La Gran Sabana in Venezuela
but
right here on
a Pacific Grove lawn
in bright daylight

a tenth the
the size of
your cousin in the wild
your fur spotted
with black dots
brown-yellow undertones
reaching down to
slender legs

sleek and sinuous
preying
and pretending
not to notice me
your admirer

casually you stepped
and watched over a
mole hole
in total concentration
body taut
like a bow
drawn

I resented the collar
as a mark
you
belonged to
someone

I wondered and
pictured you
stealthily
slinking through the dense brush
as the dabbled play of sun and shade
concealed your movement
but here you were

in a foggy part
of a small town
hunting for mice
or moles
instead of a rabbit
a snake or a prairie dog
out from a tuft of high grass
insects chirping
and the sun setting
announcing the coolness of a night
on the savanna

Chu-Chu the Cat
Patricia Hamilton

In 1983 when I found the last home for the thirty cats I had adopted from the RSPCA in Maple Ridge, BC Canada, I just didn't want another cat. That is, until 1991 when I lived with my Aunt Charlotte in Pacific Grove.

"I want another cat," I told my niece Kathy. Next day in the *Monterey Herald* was a free cat who "needed his own lap." She drove me to Seaside to see him. He had showed up one day at a motel and the maintenance man brought him home. He and his wife each had their own special cat on their laps every evening, and the tabby would sit looking from one to the other. They decided to find his forever lap and placed the ad. He took to me right away. I scooped him up, we drove back, I set him down, he scouted the house, and from the rooftop surveyed his new domain, the P.G. Retreat.

We were inseparable, he on my lap every night, nudging aside book and laptop. One night after work he was sitting outside by his cat door. "What are you doing out here?" I asked. Inside I discovered four baby raccoons eating from his dish. I held the cat as they filed out the door, one by one. Our neighbor had visitors with a large, barking dog that was kept chained outside. That night Chu-Chu wasn't waiting for me. It got dark, the cat was nowhere to be found, and I figured the dog had scared him. I walked up and down Grand, Fountain, to Ocean View, Central and back, calling his name and looking about. After a dreadful hour of calling and crying he mewed as I passed a shrub and allowed me to reach in and retrieve him.

He aged and got sick. I held him and cried when the vet euthanized him. "You've been the best cat, Chu-Chu," I sobbed. "Thank you for being a good cat." I mourned him for days.

In a dream I was walking on a sandy beach along Monterey Bay when I saw him sitting under the water looking at me. "You'll drown. No, you can't drown, you're already dead."

He turned then and swam toward the horizon with a stream of thousands identical grey marbled tabby cats, all swimming in unison. Chu-Chu left with an escort to heaven. He had come to say goodbye and ease my suffering. My neighbor wrote this poem and gave me this cat and kitten for the garden outside my window. 2005.

Much More Than a Cat
William Wall

I've heard some say that he was
Just a cat
But he was more
Much, much more
Than that.
He was a smile
When smiles were hard
To be found.
Family
When family
Were nowhere around.
A hug
When hugs were greatly
In need.
He was a
Friend,
A true friend
Indeed.
Yes, I've heard some say that he was
Just a cat.
But he was so much
More than that.
And he'll be missed as much
As missing could ever be
By everyone he loved
Not least of which
By me.
Let everyone
Who loved and was loved by him
For the time he let them
Love
Shall not ever forget him.
For one who loves
Forgets not
Love.
And he lives on in our memories
As in his we, too, immortal be
And as such he is eternal
Much, much more
Than just a cat
You see.

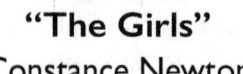

"The Girls"
Constance Newton
general dentistry

What better place than Pacific Grove to tap into your "urban" farmer!

We decided to give raising chickens a try 3 years ago and researched the topic to death before taking the plunge.

We applied for a permit, built a chicken coop that is as well built as our own home, and brought home 4, 3 day old chicks, all of different breeds. Pearl, Maggie, Rosie, and Ethel happily lived in our spare bathroom until the coop was complete (a little longer than planned....) and then were off to their new home. Little did we know the adventure we were embarking upon with the addition of the "girls" to our family!

We had always heard of the "pecking" order of chickens but to watch the social structure has been hilarious. At night the chickens are locked into their coop for protection and we let them out at first light. Pearl was typically the first out the door followed closely by Maggie and Rosie. Ethel usually brought up the rear. Two mornings in a row, however, Ethel came out first! Apparently that was not to be tolerated by the others because on the third morning, Ethel was standing by the open door but waited for her 3 sisters to come out first before she went out. I suspect she had a little talking to behind closed doors and never tried that again.

Then there is Pearl who is fearless and loves to sit on your lap and be petted as though she were a cat. She is the quickest and most curious so by default is #1 in the pecking order. This does not sit well with Maggie who is the largest and would like to be #1 but is just one step slower than Pearl. Pearl became sick and was brought into the house while she was on medication. This ended up being about 3 weeks of her living back in the spare bathroom. When she was healthy and reintroduced to her sisters, we learned that the pecking order had changed and Maggie had taken charge. Apparently she no longer would tolerate Pearl being on the same planet as her and attacked her at every turn. This started a 6 week ordeal of getting Pearl re-established with the flock which was a full time job! Maggie would hide behind a bush and ambush Pearl when she walked by. She would keep her from the food and water. She would stand in the doorway of the coop and not let her in at night. Slowly but surely Pearl would regain some territory while Rosie and Ethel would try and stay out of the fray. It was brutal to watch but all survived and they are a flock again.

So don't mess with the social order! But otherwise they are a complete joy to be around. And the eggs are great!

Legend of Pissy Cat
Anonymous Ceramic Cat Owner

Every day I used to pass the Treasure Shop, a thrift store at the corner of Fountain and Central. As it benefits animal rescue, all the stuffed and porcelain animals that were donated were put in the front window. These items were not for sale, but kept in a locked case of heavy-duty wire (which actually didn't look very pet-friendly, to tell the truth.)

Smack in the middle of this permanent display was a life-size statue of a disgruntled feline I came to think of as Pissy Cat. 'Disgruntled' doesn't quite do justice to his withering, Medusa-like expression. The cat looked utterly affronted…as if you had barged in on him in the bathroom or something.

The question I could never get out of my head was, Had he originally been intended to look so off-putting, or was this only discovered after he was manufactured? Who would make such a chilling object…or worse yet, a hundred thousand copies for mass production? It was a great, unsolved mystery.

Still, I pined for Pissy Cat.

Years passed in which I would regularly leave my name and number at the front desk in the shop. I hoped a new or distracted employee might slip up, forget the store's policy and sell him to me, but it never happened. I posted about Pissy Cat on Facebook and would bring friends to see him in the store window. His weird horribleness had majesty. Filled with cement, I thought he would make the perfect, unwelcoming doorstop. For who amongst us does not have an inner Pissy Cat on certain days?

Then a miracle happened. A friend I had once dragged to the thrift shop to behold my evil idol invited me over for coffee and produced a heavy gift bag. INSIDE WAS PISSY CAT HIMSELF! I was literally struck dumb. How had she done it? How had she, a relative newcomer to town, succeeded where I had failed? As I turned him over wonderingly in my hands, she explained that she had passed the shop and all the locked-up animals had been liberated and put on sale because the store was under new management.

Reverently, we washed him in a warm sinkful of water. He has no maker's mark yet is meticulously detailed, with glass eyes and nylon whiskers. The same slick pink used to color his nose and downturned mouth is eerily traced between his toes. A lot of work went into this ghastly creature!

I do not keep him on the porch, as I originally intended. Surely this local celeb gained other admirers throughout the years, and could be catnapped. I know I would have stolen him long ago, given half a chance! Instead, he is poised under my desk…where he sometimes startles people who catch sight of him.

His freezing cold eyes see and disapprove of all…even me. The Keeper of Pissy Cat.

Ode to the Butterfly Dog
Gary Karnes

Alas, Jordan and Michelle had with them a dog whose name has been lost in the history of the village of long, long ago. Passers-by coming into the city's busy post office hardly notice them anymore. On the dog's bronzed body there is a City of P.G. dog tag, but no name. As is still the Butterfly Town's beloved tradition, these bronzed "Butterfly Kids" wear wings and look just like the little kindergarten children parading annually through the streets. But who was their unnamed dog? I decided to get to the bottom of this mystery. Now, I could try to make the case that the famous Monarchs fly in and fly out, just tourists, if you like, but our dogs stay on, providing companionship year around. I'm pretty sure that Pagrovians of a curious mind would want to know.

P.G. dog people (but NOT cat people) have had to develop some social skills that go along with having a dog. That's good. It's pretty awkward to greet other members of our own species we haven't met before, but it is so much easier if our dog makes the first move for us. The conversation opener is always about our dog, her age, her breed, her temperament and her name. "Is she friendly?" Yet, we human companions usually remain nameless. Heidi and Gary have become quite well-known around town because of our dogs, but not always by our own names.

Our girls who have accompanied us over the years-- Lily, Holly, Daisy and now Annie-- have started so many conversations for us. We dutifully answer all the standard questions, say "thank you" and move on. No one ever asks our age, our breed or our name or whether we bite. We are just Annie's humans, you know, the people rescued from the people shelter. That's OK.

Many visitors to our area who we meet on our daily walks along the Rec Trail or through town confess that they really miss their dog and ask if they can snuggle up with ours. Our dogs have all been up for it, of course, but Daisy especially. Daisy was quite the social butterfly, you might say. We often kidded strangers that she was so forward because she was running for Mayor of P.G., and most people of course proclaimed that she had their vote.

Many times, Daisy would lay down and roll over in front of a crowd of people and they would laugh hilariously. Of course, we would have to explain that we didn't teach her that, but it was always a real crowd pleaser. During our evening walks, Daisy was especially partial to any group of people gathering in front of Passionfish restaurant. She'd walk right into the center of the crowd and make herself known with a friendly little growl and looking straight up into each person's eye.

Many famous people and their dogs have added their stories to our hometown lore. P.G.'s most famous denizen was John Steinbeck, though perhaps to his chagrin, he is more fondly remembered for his companionship with his poodle, Charley, than his marriages to his three wives: Carol, Gwyn and Elaine. Charley and John made the cross-country trip to look for America, like Simon and Garfunkel, firsthand. Charley never lived in P.G. though. The red truck they travelled in can still be seen at the Steinbeck Center in Salinas.

Doris Day had Duffy, and they put Carmel on the map as a well-known "dog-friendly" town. Dog lovers everywhere descend on Carmel in great numbers. These days Carmel rates itself the #1 Dog Friendly Town in America, a world-class pet friendly destination that caters to canine four-legged companions. Water bowls, dog treats and biodegradable bags at most locations are the typical amenities offered, plus high-end services like massages, doggy turn downs, surf lessons and yappy hour locales.

But, never you worry, fellow Pagrovians, I am currently building a case and organizing the campaign and will present it to the City Council, the Chamber of Commerce and the people of P.G. for placement on the next ballot, proclaiming Pacific Grove as the Number One Dog Town, USA. Move over, Carmel.

Butterfly Children and Butterfly Dog
Jane Roland

Perhaps you have wondered about the dog in the statue in front of the Pacific Grove post office. This is a depiction of the Butterfly Children created by the late Christopher Bell, who died much too early, in the prime of his life and career. The life sized statue was created to honor the thousands of children who have marched in the annual parade. He donated it to Pacific Grove in 1996, two years after his contribution of the sea otter at Lovers Point.

We first knew Chris when we participated in the Beacon House Art Auction, a project in which we were involved for over fifteen years. The artists in the community were generous and giving; none more than Christopher Bell. His widow, Nancy, and I became friends when she came into the benefit shop I managed prior to The Treasure Shop.

I learned that their little dog AJ died several years ago. Those of you who love animals know of the grief this can cause. Those who don't, can't possibly understand "it is just an animal" they will say. There is no such thing as just an animal. Our pets are our friends and when they leave it is as wrenching as the departure of a human. The story of AJ is one which many of us are familiar.

The little dog was taken to the SPCA animal Shelter in 1994 by the police; she was about two and a half years old and had been horribly mistreated. She stayed there only one night. The Bells saw her, adopted and loved her without reservation…

Her name was unchanged, as the two boys who became her buddies were Aaron and Jordan. She became devoted to her master, her children and her "mother," Nancy.

The pooch blended into her new family and soon realized that life had turned around. Where there had been abuse there was love, love which was reciprocated with joy.

She was always up for a walk, jumping up and down as if, said, Nancy, "she were spring-loaded." They would set off, AJ tugging at the leash, excited to be seeing old friends and meeting new; sniffing wonderful smells and laughing all the way.

On December 19th, 1997, Christopher Bell died suddenly of a massive heart attack, with no warning, no premonition. It was a terrible time for the family, the boys were teenagers and Nancy, a happy wife, became a grieving widow. Through it all was the little dog who missed her friend and comforted her family. The wounds never completely heal, the departed are missed forever, but life must go on for those who remain…

AJ was attacked by a raccoon, and saved by Nancy. Her face had been slashed.

There was fear that she would die from her wounds and terror of rabies. AJ had a mission to protect and comfort her family, no trauma would deter her, she was determined to survive and survive she did, to rule again, to chase the cats around and go on long walks.

When the neighbors baby sat along with their four big dogs, AJ ruled, she was the Alpha Dog. She was coveted by a friend's little girl who was granted a sleep over with the pup from time to time.

If you wonder why AJ was placed with the children of Butterfly Town, it is because AJ was part Papillion and, you know, of course, that Papillion is French for butterfly. A butterfly dog, with butterfly children in a butterfly town

As you stroll through "America's Last Hometown" and pass Lovers Point, you will see the bronze sculpture of a sea otter "Life at the Top," which Chris and the Pacific Grove Rotary Club presented to the city in 1994. We know that he and AJ are looking down from above and reveling in their gifts. Things may change, hotels discussed, buildings razed but, in perpetuity, the children and the animals will remain as our anchor.

Thank you, Chris and Nancy.

P.G. Cat Ambassadors
Keith Larson

Pacific Grove is full of cats. Where are they, you say? Well, they're less visible, but they are there watching everything that goes on. You can see them in their homes, sitting in the windows or on porches waiting for something interesting to walk or scurry by.

Some of the stores in town have devoted cat owners who help them run their business. Sammy the cat crossed busy Lighthouse Avenue to get to his job at Pier One Imports. He had a favorite chair to sit in and was friendly to the patrons. Sammy would check in, then leave to make his rounds in the business district. Sammy and his family moved away, and only the legend remains.

Up the street on Forest Avenue, Imagine Art Supplies has two kitties in the window, Jordana and Jude, who have their cat toys close by them in case someone comes into the store who is not in a hurry and would like to play. They also like to check out what you are purchasing and often jump up on the counter to supervise a sale.

Over in another part of town you will find Sparkles, an outdoor cat who is so friendly that people will walk out of their way just to visit. Sparkles is surrounded by a number of free Little Library outlets, and there is a bench by one of them that Sparkles likes to sit on and greet people and perhaps help them pick out a book to read.

Freckles
Martha Wilcox
as told to Jane Roland

Martha Wilcox lives on Mora Lane in Pebble Beach. She has her degree in nursing, her husband, Walter, is a Psychologist and worked most recently at Soledad Prison. Martha volunteered for Alliance on Aging and Ombudsman for many years. Eleven years ago, in 2006, she started volunteering at the AFRP Treasure Shop and was there until May of 2017. She and her family has always had a menagerie of dogs, cats and other critters, so it is not surprising that she rescued the pup featured in the following story:

It was an unusually hot day in June 2008 when I received an e-mail from a local animal rescue organization that there was a very nice approximately 6-month-old dog that needed a foster home. She had been picked up by Animal Control in a parking lot in King City—obviously dumped—owner unknown and was untraceable. The dog did not have an identification chip. She did not have any food or water. She was located at the local King City Veterinary Hospital and would be euthanized the next day unless somebody was interested in offering a Foster Home or adopting her. A picture was included in the e-mail that was sent to me. She was a beautiful black lab mix with white freckled paws. I showed the picture to my husband and his remark was "let's go get her." We immediately went to King City where it was 108 degrees and very smoky from a fire in the Lake San Antonio area.

When we arrived at the King City Veterinary Hospital and they brought out this beautiful dog, both of our reaction was "we'll take her." Of course, she was very nervous—strange place—strange people—who knows what happened to her in the previous days—it is speculated that dogs can smell death. I do believe that she knew she was near the grim reaper. We took her home to her forever home, and she immediately did very well with our other dog and our kitties. In fact, she has her own cat as a buddy.

She had some medical problems, but a very good Veterinarian in Castroville helped correct these. Then, she went to Obedience Class where she flunked the course. Much to the trainer's dismay who was rather shocked because she had never had a failure before. Oh well, she is a wonderful friend and pet. I will never regret going to King City on that hot, smoky day 9 years ago. She is very much a part of our family.

Oh, by the way, she is named 'Freckles' because of the freckles on her feet.

A Murder of Crows

C.C. Raven*
"It's a good day
when I wake up vertical
and I ride my convertible
along the Monterey Bay.
It's a Good Day!"

At the pinnacle of the Monterey peninsula lies the quiet, seemingly idyllic village we call Pacific Grove, the last hometown. The seaside village, a town of redwoods and cypress trees and the Monterey Pine, and a charming Victorian town in its own right, is host and home to not only humans, but also clusters of Monarch butterflies, overwintering on the eucalyptus trees, a herd of reindeer (no, plain deer), antlered stags strutting by like so many Donners and Blitzens, families of raccoons, skittering along tall Monterey pine branches in play, red foxes (vixen showing their pups around the local golf course), and a peaceful little cemetery, El Carmelo, with a murder of crows. Not a literal murder, of course, but the equivalent of a gaggle of geese or a scurry of squirrels.

This little murder of crows consists of about twenty birds, particular to Pacific Grove due to white feather stripes on their wings. The leader of the murder has three feather stripes on his wings and was dubbed "Sergeant" by me. The first time I saw him, he was riding on the back of a stag who had roses tangled in its antlers, the residue of a morning's breakfast on the graves of the cemetery.

The rest of the group of crows have single white feather stripes on their wings, like "privates," and all have been fattened by me on a steady diet of raw peanuts, which they have learned to catch quite aerobatically, demonstrating both individual styles and unique athletic abilities in so doing.

They have developed a game I call "Drop the Peanut," similar in some ways to soccer or rugby, where the "referee" flies up high with a peanut and drops it down below. The rest of the murder fly along from one end of the cemetery to the other, cawing in Morse crow and planning their strategy. Thus the game begins. They swoop upside down and sideways, diving like falcons and trying to "catch the peanut."

In another sort of game, the whole flock will take to the air, following my red convertible Mustang, like a bunch of black kites, around the cemetery and along the ocean by our Lighthouse at Point Pinos, catching tossed peanuts all along the way. This can be a little disconcerting to tourists unexpectedly coming upon the sight of twenty crows following a red Mustang. They point. They photograph. And sometimes they duck for cover.

One such day, I was parked by the ocean across from the lighthouse and the whole murder of crows was sitting opposite, along the picket fence by the lighthouse, waiting for peanuts. Sergeant, who literally "keeps the rest in line" along the fence, sat in the #1 spot and let no others pass. He gabbled and squawked at them to keep the proper pecking order.

That particular day, a tourist on his new bike came riding by. Seeing the crowd of crows lined up, he tried to scare them off, waving his arms and shouting loudly, as he passed by.

I decided to make a quick U-turn and follow a bit behind the biker, joined by a large black cloud, hovering ominously above.

Alarmed, the biker began to ride as fast as he could to escape the menacing crows, but we followed him closely for a ways, until the biker took shelter under some cypress trees. But then the crows promptly landed all over the cypresses above, creating somewhat of a Hitchcockian moment of terror for the biker.

We finally took pity and all departed, leaving one puzzled tourist to wonder about the murderous crows of Pacific Grove!

*Steven and Mary Munsie, retired long-time residents

"Mikey the Parakeet"
Jane Foley

Paved in the railroad tracks of the old Del Monte Express, our "Rec Trail" parallels the coast with a world-class bay view, from Pacific Grove to Monterey and beyond. Runners, bicyclists and surrey riders weave in and around the lively parade of dogs and strollers and clusters of meandering tourists. Locals use it but you can hear accents from all over the world. It is the perfect backdrop for my friend and me to take walks, although peculiar things have happened on the way. Like the time we met "Mikey."

A fluttering turquoise parakeet landed on Deborah's shoulder out of nowhere one afternoon, just past Berwick Park. It darted to a cypress branch then flew back. Flitting here and there, it kept returning to her. We were sure it would be dinner for a stripe-tailed hawk who had taken up residence close by. So, she decided to rescue this azure escapee until its owner could be found. We tacked notices along the trail, certain someone would be frantic to find him.

No one called. The week of the Feast of Lanterns, 2006, Mikey moved in. His wire 'suite' was furnished with ambient heating (a pad), a mullet frond and TV for company. The door to his deluxe digs remained open: he was free to come and go as he pleased. Mikey chirped the most joyful songs from his second story windows to other birds and passers-by below. A dog-walking neighbor was inspired to paint his portrait for a fundraiser at the P.G. Art Center. It ended up on the cover of the Monterey County Weekly. Mikey was a star!

A couple years later, Deborah asked me to bird sit. She said she had purchased a new parakeet, "Princess Topaz," to keep him company while she was on vacation. The first morning of my caregiving stint, I found Mikey, his aqua body, lifeless, on the floor of his cage. Oddly, there was no trace of the new bird. My next door neighbor agreed to help give him an honorable send off so, with prayers, sincere accolades, and a flowerpot to mark the site, Mikey was buried in the backyard that afternoon.

While getting ready the morning of vacation, Deborah later explained, she discovered her new bird had died. Not to be late, she quickly wrapped the Princess in foil, then placed her in a zip lock bag in the freezer. She would bury her when she had a chance. No doubt Princess Topaz carried a disease from the pet store breeder, that infected Mikey.

On the back burner, or the back of the freezer, some things we just don't quite get to.

As of last conversation (May 2017) Princess Topaz remains cryogenically preserved. Although it is still 'on the list,' the occasion of interment has not yet presented itself. In the event of my friend's absence, I have promised, if necessary, to "make an early intervention," or provide a plausible explanation—after the body is found!

Adventures of Clementine and Lola
Susan Steele
retired academic

The black Lab, Clementine, has separation anxiety. There may be good reason for her affliction, since she was found as a nine-month-old puppy wandering the streets of Hayward. In any case, when I work on the computer, Clementine is at my feet. When I sit on the patio, Clementine is next to me. When I fix something to eat, Clementine follows me to the kitchen. The three cats and the other dog find her neediness a little silly, but Clementine doesn't care. She can't help it.

The Lab-chow mix, Lola, is independent to a fault. She is also territorial. Again, she may have acquired this trait by necessity when she had to fend for herself in Stanislaus County. Whatever the reason, nobody walks by our house or steps on our porch without Lola letting them know that they are on her turf. She especially dislikes people wearing hats.

One day, I was working in the garden, tracked from the window by a very unhappy pair of brown eyes. After a time, the eyes disappeared and I thought Clementine had adjusted to the distance between us. How much I had misjudged the situation became clear when a neighbor appeared, shouting, 'There's a dog on your roof!' Clementine had climbed through an open dormer window and out onto the roof.

I looked up at Clementine; Clementine looked down at me. Clementine's tongue was hanging out. Her eyes were very big. I ran upstairs to try to coax her back inside, but by the time I got to the offending window, Clementine had jumped from the roof of the house to the slightly lower—and much steeper—roof of an outbuilding. She couldn't go back and as she scrambled to keep from falling, Clementine's eyes got bigger and her tongue hung out even more.

I put a ladder against the shed and climbed up. But I wasn't strong enough to carry 60-lb Clementine down the ladder. The ladder started to shake. Another neighbor, working in his garden, offered his help and I enthusiastically accepted. I forgot about Lola. When this neighbor tried to enter the back yard, Lola was on the job, defending me and her territory.

Finally, in desperation, I grabbed Clementine's collar and lowered her as far as I could. She slipped out of her collar and fell the last few feet to the ground. But she wasn't hurt. She was very happy to be off the roof. I was very happy to be off the ladder. And Lola was very happy that she had done her job.

Mysterious Flying Critters
Gail Skidmore
retired librarian and photo researcher

Wildlife in Pacific Grove is very different from what I experienced growing up in Chicago. The sight of deer on the streets of P.G. was an exotic surprise to this Midwestern transplant. It's unlikely that I would have seen a mountain lion lounging in the neighbor's tree, either. One thing Chicago does have is hordes of voracious mosquitos, which is why everyone there has screens on their windows. Here, not so much.

I left the bedroom window of my attic apartment open a tiny bit one warm Pacific Grove night. Sometime later, in a remote corner of my consciousness, I heard a sound at the window. Good thing it was only open a crack. I rolled back over. Shortly thereafter, I felt and heard something buzzing my head. Ahhh!

I put my arms up to protect myself. Omigod! I was under siege! By the time I scrambled out of bed and turned on the light, it had flown into the next room. The small dark shape darted and swooped without landing. As I turned on additional lights, it became more and more agitated. How was I going to get rid of it? Who could I call at 2:30 a.m.? Nine-one-one? This was an emergency, after all.

As the critter flew around frantically, I started getting the feeling that it didn't want to be inside my apartment any more than I wanted its company. Maybe I could shoo it out with a broom. I opened the door. Off it flew into the night.

Was it a bird? A bat? Superman in miniature? A ginormous housefly?

I'll never know! It's just one of life's mysteries in America's Last Hometown.

Downtown Cats
Jane Roland

Doc Holiday at Home in the Grove

You have seen him all over town. He wanders through or rides his bike, always with the two big dogs, one black one white. He once lived in the building on the corner of Central and Fountain and was the majordomo, the fixer of everything, the builder, the wiring expert. Beloved by all. He grew up on Candy Cane Lane and at one point in his career was a clown. He and his four-legged companions often hang out on the bench in front of the P.G. Library. There is not much that he cannot do with his hands. He fell on hard times and is "homeless," but wherever he parks his bike, his dogs and his mat, is home. He helps when needed and is protected by the police. He is Doc, "Doc Holiday," one of our local treasures.

Missy's Cat Tale

The following is a story I wrote some time ago about an old cat who adopted us when the store was on Seventeenth Street. After we moved to Fountain we kept track of her and visited from time to time. It is the speculation that Missy was close to twenty when she took her final nap. She started visiting the store when it was the Adoption Center and housed cats. The offices moved to Lighthouse and the AFRP Treasure Shop opened. This tale is written from the viewpoint of the cat. We all know what cats think:

My name is Missy. I live at the Plaza, in Pacific Grove, California, and have for many years. In a cat's age it is probably more than 100, but my humans think I am probably about 19. I recall little about my early days. My mother lived in an alley way in this town and was fed by the largesse of the traveling man along the way which resulted in the birth of me and my siblings. We were happy, Mother fed us well, but we all became restless and I found myself wandering the streets, accepting handouts as they were offered. There were times when I was cold, and, often, hungry. I guess the life of a gypsy was really not for me.

One day I saw this big building and I decided to go in and investigate. It was really nice, and I decided to settle down and take a snooze. Suddenly someone reached down and petted me.

"Well, hello there, pretty kitty, what's your name?" I couldn't tell her; I really don't know if I ever had a name, but I liked the attention. I also liked the little bowl of milk and food that became my daily rations. Yes, I had landed in the lap of luxury for a street cat.

Time went on and I became a fixture at the plaza. I learned Heidi, my friend, had cats at home; she really loved them. When one died she decided that I should come to live with her. I didn't like that. Oh, I liked Heidi, a lot, she was wonderful. But she wouldn't let me go outside and I didn't like being trapped. I am an outdoor girl, at least until it is time to go to bed. I enjoy wandering around and smelling the flowers, looking at the birds, and helping people find their way around the building. So, I showed her in ways that are not very ladylike. I gently sprayed around the heating grate, and when it came time to turn on the furnace, Heidi got the message.

She reluctantly took me back to the Plaza where I could meet and greet my friends. We had a brief problem when a little kitten kid came in and wanted to share my digs. That was not acceptable. I was queen of the hill, and I let him know that he was not welcome. So Heidi took him home, and he was happy, she was happy, and most important, I was happy.

It has been 12 years. I have seen all kinds of changes. There was a group that had a couple of rooms not far from the area I call home. There were lots and lots of cats. I didn't really like that too much, but I visited to be polite. Then they went away and people came in with lots of pretty things. They call it a Treasure Shop and they are really nice people. So, now they are part of my daily rounds. I stop by to see them and take naps on warm counters, baskets and even a really pretty bowl. They give me treats and it is usually very nice. Now and then, though, a dog comes in. But there are those dogs who don't like cats … so I just leave. After all, a lady should never stay where she is made to feel uncomfortable. But not when Harly visits; Harly is owned by; one of the ladies. He's old and really nice. We have become friends.

I take a nap on the railing of the stairs, or simply wander around to see that everything is all right. Heidi, Judy and Debbie take good care of me. They feed me, give me a bed and now I even have a collar with my name on it. There are tunes when I spend the night in Roy, the barber's chair, and others on the lap of a man working late in the building. When the people come to live in their time shares, the first thing they ask about is ME. I am famous and loved. What a good life. And, you know what? I can slip through the fence that closes off the barber shop at night and sometimes when Roy comes in he surprises me because he is quiet. But he likes cats so if I spend the night in his chair he doesn't mind.

So, the next time you come to the Pacific Grove Plaza, stop and say hello. I am the one with the green eyes and long black fur. I love to be petted and I will make it worth your while. Well, goodnight! I think I had better go find someplace to nap.

Behind the Thrift Shop Counter
Antoinette Lojkovic

I am at my post at an animal welfare shop on 17th St. It is a day that's been a rarity in this tiny coastal town of Pacific Grove, sunny and warm, with soft clouds lazily hovering overhead.

The little bell on the door jingles and a figure enters as if from a motion picture, dressed in the Cassini creation I remember she recently purchased here. The young woman with copper-colored hair is a true sight to behold. The combination of her hair, pulled back finely, and the radiance of the bright dress is breathtaking. With her is a young man and his smile is as broad as hers.

"Ah," I think. "He now sees how very beautiful she is; does he know how much she pined for this?"

The young lady stands close to the counter, and in a sweet voice, asks, "Can I give you a kiss on the cheek?"

Feeling a little like Dolly Levy, I take her youthful hand and offer my face to her. She pecks my cheek softly. "If you only knew how much this meant to me, you'd cry. Thank you so much."

"But, dear, I did," I say. "That's why I held it for you. I can see that your young acquaintance appreciates fine beauty."

He smiles. She shakes her head, laughs, then says, "Oh, no, it wasn't for him."

"I see," I say. There is an awkward pause, as if these two youngsters are holding something back. Since there's no other customers needing help, I decide it's okay if I ply them for more information.

"May I ask you why it took you so long to buy it, dear?"

The young man looks at her, then to me. He says, "Oh, she's always short of cash."

She laughs at his tolerance, saying, "And your shop doesn't take credit cards."

At once, my feelings mirror my face as I'm somewhat disappointed by the irresponsibility in today's generation. Was it really that hard to come up with the original asking price?

Or maybe these two were con artists, figuring they could dupe an old lady like myself into feeling sorry for them, hoping I'd knock off $10.00 while saving it for her (which, incidentally, I did !) I am approaching the state of being chagrined.

"Well, I hope you don't mind me asking, if it wasn't for your friend," I inquire, "then you just wanted it for yourself?"

The young lady smiles at her companion, who gently puts his arm around her waist.

"Go on," he urges, "tell her."

"It's for my grandmother," the young lady says. "You see, this was the dress she wore when Grandpa proposed. The dress was never supposed to have been donated. But it ended up in the wrong pile, I guess."

"My dear, that happens from time to time at this shop," I say.

"But I guess she won't have to worry from now on," the young man confidingly says. "Grandma made her the sole heiress."

I at once feel bad I passed judgment on her.

"You mean she passed away?"

The young lady's elegance matches her composure. Looking at her young gentleman, I notice a tear well up in the corner of her eye. She brushes it quickly, then leans in over the counter. She smiles so beautifully, then takes my hands in hers. "You see," she says, "Grandmother passed away exactly one year to the day I came in to buy the dress."

The young man hugs her tightly, and as they walk out the front door, the beaded Cassini creation envelops her figure admiringly.

She stops when they reach the curb, turns once more to look at me over his shoulder.

She is not crying, instead she is smiling the smile of grace, of a grandmother who long ago said yes.

ANIMAL RESCUE AND ADOPTION
JANE ROLAND

Society for the Prevention of Cruelty to Animals

SPCA – The Beginning

The Methodist-Episcopal Church on Lighthouse Avenue in Pacific Grove was the location of the first meeting to establish The SPCA on February 18, 1905. The old church was torn down in 1963, but the legacy of that first meeting has lived on. These SPCA founders' core philosophies, their vision to protect animals in Monterey County, and their emphasis on education to bring about a more humane community have endured intact for over 100 years.

In looking at The SPCA's History it's important to note that the goals of the organization have remained on course for more than 100 years. And even though the number of animals and complexities of managing a shelter have grown exponentially, the goals and the spirit of our shelter is much the same as it was all those years ago.

This is how the David Avenue Shelter was described in a *Monterey County Herald* article dated January 15, 1945: "The list of animals handled at the shelter reads like Noah's check list for sailing day on the Ark. Only 'stead of two of each there were odd numbers, including bachelors, old maids, and a few harems. There were 833 dogs, 1050 cats, a horse, 5 cows, a bull, 4 goats, 13 rabbits, 23 chickens, 3 ducks, 5 deer, a pigeon, a coyote, 2 raccoons, an opossum, 3 white rats, a pheasant, a pelican, 2 seagulls, a parrot, a canary, a squirrel and a snake."

Sometime in the middle sixties the shelter moved from Pacific Grove to Highway 68. Although there had been a benefit shop on Forest Avenue since 1974, it was run by volunteers. In February of 1986 a full-time manager was hired and the shop was totally renovated, with a portion of expenses donated by contractor David Stockner and architect Sam Morse III. In 2006 the store moved to Carmel Barnyard, the current site and Animal Friends Rescue Project opened a new store on 17th Street.

Animal Friends Rescue Project
AFRP

"AFRP was founded by Kelly and Dave Lehrian, Monica Rua and a woman named Lee and I cannot remember her last name. She was a volunteer at Marina Animal Shelter at the time. She really didn't do much at all once the org was founded and left the board within a year, I believe. It was founded in 1998. I started volunteering the summer of 1998 and joined the board January 1999." As stated by Carie Broecker.

The Headquarters of AFRP was down on 17th Street below the Time Shares. It had small office space and a large room for cats and cages. The signature color was purple and all trim, and floors were painted a vivid hue. In 2006 the offices and adoption center were moved to the current location on Lighthouse at the corner of Grand. The 17th Street location became a benefit shop which was highly successful, moving three times within that footprint, then to the corner of Fountain and Central and finally to the current location at 160 Fountain. Jane Roland and a loyal group of animal loving volunteers were at the helm. Kelly Lehrian was the Executive Director of the Adoption Center from 2008 until 2017. The current Executive Director is Brian Contreras, Sr. of Salinas.

Monica Rua, the co-founder, served on the board for eleven years, eight of which as President. Monica has devoted over 20 years of her life to animal rescue. She first worked with dog and cat rescue groups in the Bay Area. In 1998, she co-founded AFRP in Pacific Grove, where she served on the board for 11 years, with 8 of those years as Board President. Monica oversaw and actively participated in all aspects of the organization's operations, including educating the public, fundraising, volunteer database management, animal tracking, and fostering many dogs and cats. She was also instrumental in helping foster families with dog behavior issues. Monica has been on the POMDR board since 2009 when she co-founded this organization with Carie Broecker.

Peace of Mind Dog Rescue
POMDR

Executive Director and Co-founder Carie Broecker shares her life with five lucky senior dogs, and is usually fostering multiple POMDR dogs. Carie co-founded POMDR with Monica Rua in 2009. Upon its inception, she worked full time running POMDR as Board President. In 2010 she won the American Red Cross Animal Rescue Hero Award for her role in starting POMDR. In 2012 she was hired as Executive Director, POMDR's first paid staff person.

Prior to co-founding POMDR, Carie was one of the first volunteers for AFRP in Pacific Grove. She joined the AFRP board in 1999, and served for 12 years as Treasurer and unsalaried Executive Director.

Carie and her husband Scott are the publishers of Coastal Canine magazine. Carie's other career achievements include working as a bookkeeper and accountant for several businesses. She also was employed as the Client Services Director for the Monterey County AIDS Project, where her work earned her the 1994 Monterey County Outstanding Woman of the Year award.

Carie graduated from UC Santa Cruz with a Bachelor's degree in Sociology, minoring in Business Economics with a concentration in Accounting.

President and Co-founder Monica Rua currently shares her home with four rescue dogs from POMDR and AFRP (Animal Friends Rescue Project), and is usually fostering one or two POMDR foster dogs also.

Monica has devoted over 20 years of her life to animal rescue. She first worked with dog and cat rescue groups in the Bay Area.

Where Everybody Knows Your Name

It was the shop around the corner, a haven for four and two legged friends. Its mission was to help animals. Indirectly it became the place where everybody knew your name. It started on 17th Street below the Pacific Grove Plaza. Definitely an experiment, the store flourished. It popped its seams and finally out grew the location. To demonstrate the popularity of the site and the people, the Treasure Shop had to be a destination. There was no parking and a very steep hill.

I have some wonderful stories which I will share with you as time goes on. All of our dogs (that were good mannered) came with their two-legged volunteer parents and greeted the public. Pat Stites had Harley and later Annie. Pat had closed a shop and was at loose ends. She donated a wealth of new goods she had left and offered sage advice about operation.

We also had a visiting cat, Missy, who lived in the vacation condo unit in the building. I have written about her many times. She was a lovely, long haired black kitty, beloved by all (except Harley), he sneered when she came in, she avoided him, skirting the desk and wandering into the sales area where she would roost on a counter. Next door was beauty parlor where there was a cocker spaniel.

We all know when Missy was coming as the pup would go insane trying to get THAT CAT. Missy would sleep in the lap of one of our volunteers Art Kessler who had an office upstairs. She would also sneak under the locked barrier at night and go into the shop of Roy the barber, he would often find her in the morning.

One of our group, Olive Griffiths and her husband, David, obtained many of our units, including a sorting counter which we were still using. They would go all over town and generally soft soap people into donating racks and other necessary display units.

Supporters of AFRP donated fantastic goods, Royce and Jim Foster gave vintage Shriner jewelry, Lillian Griffiths, still teaching spent her holiday time helping us and Christmas with the jewels reaped a huge harvest. The years passed, the shop popped its seams friends who passed away left instructions that their estates come to us.

People came to volunteer and, unless their health deteriorated, they never left. Some were still at the shop two weeks ago, giving their all. I cannot name all the volunteers in one column. I simply must say that in all my years working with volunteers I have never known a finer group.

They have become friends, with John and me, and with each other. If we had little in common socially we had the unbreakable bond of a devotion to animals and the mission of AFRP. Many of these pups also volunteered—Annie, Bootsie, Clementine, our ABC girls, all AFRP dogs.

When we simply had to move, to expand, I called on my Rotary group to help. We got some high school students and led by Steve Covell and his trucks, the furniture and larger items were moved over to Central and Fountain. Racks were pushed up the street by other Rotarians and students. Frank Quilantang, the head floral designer at Pebble Beach Company, was a longtime friend. When I told, him we had windows he was very excited. Frank is generous, creative beyond belief, has done award winning windows all over the area, but he has focused all his attention on the Treasure Shop. The new shop had good space but was not ideal as there was virtually no place to work, to process.

At the time, there were two ladies who had assisted me at another shop and moved when I did. Grace Bemis and Irene Harlan were not young but they were dedicated beyond belief and health problems did not deter them. Both remained until infirmities dictated that they leave. I still think of Grace who had Calvin and Hobbs, her kitties and Ursula the Russian Wolf Hound.

As time passed so did the pets, a new kitty joined her ménage and Ursula ll, Ursula always came with her to work, but stayed in the car. One day as she was leaving for the parking lot, Grace fell. The paramedics came and said she should not drive…I told her she must let me take her home, she declined firmly and Gracie was firm…the next day she was back at the shop, bloodied but unbowed until nature simply forced her resignation. Fortunately, Ursula ll had gone to meet her maker.

Shirley and Phillips Wylly, her neighbors, looked in on Grace until she died, and ultimately took her cat. By then Dave Winter had joined us. He was a dog walker for AFRP and started bringing one of his charges in to work with him. Her name was Boots a pup who had been seriously abused and found with broken front legs.

The bonding was so intense that the dog became part of Dave's family and came to work with him up until the shop was closed. Dave had a brother who lived in Hemet, Dave donated all the furniture to us when his sibling died. He continued to bring in valuable items weekly.

He also has a brother who is a famous southwestern artist and many of those paintings came our way. Speaking of paintings, I cannot leave out Terrance Zito. He and Barbara care for the kittens who must be bottle fed. we have been showing and selling his art work for years. Miguel Dominguez, Will Bullas and many members of the Carmel Art Association have been more than generous.

I have barely skimmed the stories of volunteers. These people are so remarkable. They come to work for their shift, but generally stay much longer, they fill in whenever possible. They take items home to repair and clean, items to be donated elsewhere and do all of the cleaning. They collect donated goods and are never too busy to help if possible.

The customers and donors love us. They loved our shop and the fact that the dogs were welcomed. We knew everyone's names. We helped them find what they needed and took info so we could contact them. I have often said that managing a benefit shop is akin to being a bartender. People loved to stop in to chat, tell me their problems and share animal tales.

Second Hand Dreams Come True

We are in Pacific Grove in 1986. The SPCA Benefit Shop had been remodeled and was ready to open but we were very shorthanded. I mentioned some of the stores on Forest Avenue. Joe Shammas reminded me that where Pavel's Bakery is was DeLucas upholstery shop and for those of you who were around the court house had no back patio and the offices were old. I seem to recall, also, that the clock did not work. The one constant is Grove Market which was and is going strong. It was known as The Last Home town. It has grown but still has the atmosphere of the little city we love so much.

I put out the word that we needed help in the shop. It was quite amazing and rewarding. Those who had been on board worked as many shifts as necessary, but it seemed that new folk appeared daily. One was a woman who had just moved here to be with her family after the death of her husband. Her name was Corinne Thomas, her daughter is Karen Calandra, son-in-law, Jim. Corinne signed in and became a staunch volunteer and friend until her death twenty some years later. We became very close. I was enchanted by her sense of humor and devotion. If it was necessary to work late, she stayed with me. One night we were starting to close when a sea gull flew in, he swooped and soared, Corinne chased him with a broom, hoping to shoo him out. He sailed from the front of the shop, through the curtains into the back room and finally turned, zooming into the window area. A gigantic wedding bed filled the area. We couldn't get in.

Birds were no stranger to us. They nested above the sign over the front door. When we heard chirping, we knew that summer was near. However, it was rare that one came inside. In the case of our visitor we really didn't know what to do. I told Corinne to go home, but she would have none of it. It was getting dark, but we dared not leave. For one thing we knew that if trapped inside he (or she?) might "decorate" all of the goods... We were pondering our next step, when a young man walked by. He spotted "Jonathon" (remember the famous story?). "Do you mind if I help?" he asked. Did we mind, we were ecstatic, things couldn't get any worse. He asked for a towel and then inched into the window. It was then we saw a bird whisperer at work. His voice was soft, the bird stopped the frantic wing beating, cocked his head and listened. Our savior (and the bird's) reached in with the towel, gently swaddled the creature and moved him out of the store. Johnathon flew happily away. "Who are you? And where did you come?" from I asked. "Oh, I was just walking by when I saw the bird in the window. I am just up here for a couple of hours from Big Sur. I work at The Ventana Wildlife Society"... We offered him some cookies and he went on his way. I don't recall that I ever saw him again, but I am not sure about the gull, they all look alike. And did you know that they love red cars? Just take a look at mine, doesn't matter where I park, they find me. Do you suppose it is Jonathon seeking revenge for curtailing his activities?

Ten years later I was standing in the shop when Wally Getz, our landlord stopped by. "Jane, why aren't you in Rotary?" "Oh, I don't know, I never thought about it." John had been a member of Monterey Sunrise for years. I was very familiar with the good works done by the organization, but it didn't occur to me that I might become a member. Volunteer work was part of my DNA and I was still very involved with a number of non-profit organizations, Colonial Dames which preserves our history, the Monterey County Symphony and SPCA Auxiliary. My job was full time and while the SPCA encouraged outside activities, I was hesitant about taking on more. None the less, when he invited me to a meeting I accepted. The Rotary Club of Pacific Grove met in Sticks at the Inn at Spanish Bay. They gathered at noon for lunch and a speaker. I was more curious than interested but went with Wally to one of the Tuesday events. There were not many women. The club had been one of the first to accept females as members in 1989 and Pam Norton, one of the first of the "fair sex" members, had been President in 1994. Everyone was warm and friendly. I thought about it over the holidays and realized that if I dropped other involvements I would be able to work it in. In January I was invited to a lunch at Fandango with three members, Bill Schofield, Dick Eldred and Jim Calandra, the son-in-law of Corinne Thomas. They outlined the responsibilities of members. Corinne told me how much Jim enjoyed Rotary. So, I cut back on meetings which took me away from the shop and jumped in with both feet, as it were. I found that Rotary is so beneficial to its members and the community that involvement has been more than positive. This is what happens in our community, the ripples touch. In early 1997 I became a full time member. Members of the club contributed much to the SPCA Benefit Shop and when the SPCA moved its store operation to Carmel, I was asked to assist AFRP, the club assisted whenever asked with manpower, donations and patronage.

Who knew that when I became manager of the shop on Forest Avenue, which I felt would be short term, it would evolve into a career change which has lasted thirty years?

Treasure Shop Volunteers

One might think that this book is all about Holman's Department Store. Think about it. In the old days before Del Monte Shopping Center, there were two stores on the Peninsula as far as the natives were concerned: Putnam and Raggett in Carmel and Holman's in Pacific Grove. The former was more of a dry goods store, the latter a little bit of everything and people happily drove over the hill on what was then always called Holman Highway.

My mother lived in Pebble Beach; she loved the store and its owner, but, as time passed she was no longer able to drive out of the Forest. She had shopped in the Holman's market for years, so she simply started ordering by telephone. When the food was delivered, often the person bringing in the order would stop to visit. It was almost a forerunner to Meals on Wheels, which wasn't started in Pacific Grove until 1972. When she died on Good Friday in 1972, I went down to the store and the market to tell them about her demise. They all cried, even if they had never met her. She affected many people that way, because she was interested in them and their lives.

I also like to learn about people and am a good listener. I would have this happen in college when I was studying late and girls would stop by my room. At the shop I often had customers, donors, and visitors stop by to share their joys and sorrows. As I have said, that kind of job is akin to that of a bartender.

The SPCA Shop moved to Carmel, and at the request of those in charge of AFRP at the time, Carey Broeker and Monica Rua, I started the Treasure Shop from the ground up. Many the volunteers from my previous job joined me and within the year we had tripled our numbers. We moved twice, finally to the Holman's Annex, and more people became involved. We became close knit.

People don't seem to know the difference between "professional" volunteers and board members, and those who offer their souls. The former can give time to a large fundraising activity and do it almost by rote, or serve on a board and rubber-stamp either the edict of the Executive Director or popular consensus. It takes physical and mental acumen for both, but not heart.

The people I have come to know who were

involved at the Treasure Shop gave their hearts to the animals and the organization, but also to me. We have become as close knit as any group with which I have been associated. People such as Doug Lovell (a Pacific Grove product), who went to a paid job early in the morning and once a week, without fail, appeared for a shift at the shop, although he has wounds that won't heal on both bandaged legs and must have therapy once a week. David Winter and Boots were there twice a week, then needed to cut back due to health issues, but still came early Tuesday morning to vacuum and stay through the morning while contributing time to Meals on Wheels. Barry Achtenberg, "my other son," another local treasure, waits on tables at Turn 12, but came very early to the shop twice a week to process goods. Carol Hader first hauled goods to Goodwill for us but then decided she would like to volunteer as well.

I decided I should list these good people who have become my friends. We worked together daily, often socialized; we had lunch, we had cries and happy moments. We tried to remember birthdays and celebrated with little goodies. We brought treats, often homemade. When extra help was needed with few exceptions they were there. Some came from Salinas or San Juan Bautista. Sheila Keifitiz and Sofia Sandoval, who has a big truck, obtained and delivered goods. Donna Houston used her talents to decorate the store and Frank Quilantang was our prize-winning window designer. Alyce diPalma, came on Saturdays; Judy Fehily, after a long debilitating illness, was back sorting greeting cards and Lillian Griffiths spent hours pricing, cleaning and having jewelry appraised. Susan Steele, with Clementine, came week after week to give a few hours, although she has more on her plate than most of us could bear.

There are new volunteers, Dea Moore and Margaret Baldwin, who fit in as if they had been there forever. Karen Sheffer and Ronda Copeland came every Saturday morning to work on clothing and extra times when needed. Lois Sawyer had to be away due to heart problems. She was one who followed me from SPCA, as were Cy Coburn, Gabriele Swanson and Judy and Chase Weaver, stalwarts. Terry Landrey, Patty Bigelow and Barbara Dickinson are relatively new, a couple of years, but they could have been there forever. And what can I say about Michele Tubman, Martha Wilcox, Lorna Randolph, Marcia Napoli, Gillian Hooper and my husband John, without whom we might have needed to close the shop on several occasions and who purchased supplies and hauled things to and from the store. There was little help from the Adoption Center, which was overburdened, but we were able to help them by answering calls and directing potential adoptees to the site.

A benefit shop is not a retail store, it "benefits," in our case, the animals and is very human and friendly. When the weekend manager could not be there or find coverage, those folks jumped in to help, although all were burdened with other responsibilities. I cannot forget Sigrid Stokes who has helped from the beginning; Greg Dexter, there for many years, Jane Bennett and our wonderful appraisers: Steve Hauk at Hauk Fine Arts, Chuck, the owner of Niche in Tyme, and those good folk at the Antique Shop next door who appraised items for us, and, of course, Masiah Johnson, Bob Tintle and, often, Karen Sheffer who made sure we had bread every day which we provided for a small donation. The Pacific Grove Rotary Club had a fundraiser, donated goods and muscle when needed. Thanks also to all of the community people who were our supporters and our friends. It was a happy time and we made over $100,000 for the animals.

So, we became close, sisters and brothers—and critter kids—when the rug was unexpectedly pulled out from under us. We were thrilled when Pacific Repertory Theatre asked us (at once) to open a shop for them. We are looking and ask you for input and, perhaps, convince the City of Pacific Grove to wave its restrictions so we might find a spot in P.G., especially as there is no Treasure Shop at present. Perhaps we can call it The Green Room Treasure Shop. Help us find a spot and you can help name it. In the meantime, if you have goods to donate, give me a call we have a couple of places who will accept and hold items. I miss you, my adopted "family" misses you, and we will be together soon. We thank you for the letters and telephone calls; they mean the world to us. We did our best and are proud of our accomplishments.

SECTION 5
THE GOOD OLD DAYS

GROWING UP IN BUTTERFLY TOWN

Generations Enrich My Life
Joanie Hyler

I grew up in Pacific Grove in the 1950s and 60s, the third daughter of Bill and Olive Hyler. When Dad was asked, "Three girls, Bill?" he replied, "Got three girls because I didn't wear my hat to bed." Some obscure reference that I never learned the meaning of. I grew up in the same house and with the same friends all through school, graduating from P.G. High in 1968.

My mother, Olive Dean Hyler, taught me to be a nice person when I was in the seventh grade sewing class. A girl at school didn't like me and hurt my feelings by saying hurtful things. I told my mother and she said, "Love your enemies, kill them with kindness. Ignore what they say because if you respond with the name-calling, it perpetuates the situation and nothing gets resolved." She was always nice. My friends loved to come over and often my mother would invite them to stay for dinner—after they got an okay from their parents. She was a fabulous cook and there was always room for company. Sometimes we had pajama parties when they stayed overnight. Later they told me my mother was a "classy, nice lady."

My father, Bill Hyler, gave me the confidence and "can do" attitude that grounded me for life. I got my driver's permit in 1965 when I was 15. My father has just bought a new 1965 Thunderbird and I asked to drive the car when we were going to have dinner at the Rocky Point Restaurant in Big Sur. When my mother objected, he told her, "If she doesn't learn now, when's she gonna learn?" After high school he employed me in his plastics manufacturing plant on Cannery Row and I learned I "can do," as well.

My maternal grandmother, Gladys Dean, at one time worked for my paternal grandfather, Clyde Dyke, at Dyke's Grove Pharmacy in the Giles Building. My friends and I would stop in after school and Grandma would give us popcorn and candy—and at Christmas we always received new pajamas and a bathrobe. We often spent the night at their house to sit on Grandfather Ted Dean's lap while he read to us, and Grandma fixed us just what we liked to eat. Grandpa would come to watch us swim down at the Plunge on Lovers Point.

My paternal grandmother, Elmarie Hurlbert Hyler Dyke, didn't want to be called grandmother. My older sister Deanna named her "Ahree," and we all called her that. She was quite an activist and fought for many local and state causes, including trying to keep the old Methodist Church from being demolished. She cried when it was torn down. She tried to keep alcohol from being sold in P.G. Her father, Elgin Hurlbert, had been the president of the P.G. Retreat association, then the first city clerk of P.G. She was instrumental in changing the California state flag from sporting the image of a bear that more resembled a boar, into the current one that looks like a bear.

Ahree introduced me to local culture. She directed and was in charge of the entertainment for the Main Stage at the Monterey County Fair, which led to bringing the same entertainment to the P.G. Feast of Lanterns celebrations. I got to stand by the stage and watch, and later to mingle with the actors backstage. We could see the stage of the Wharf Theatre, which was outside too, with seals barking while a romantic scene played out on-stage. I witnessed Ahree doing her work there and later at the auditorium (now the Performing Arts Center) at the P.G. Middle School. She died when I was 31.

Today I serve on the Feast of Lanterns board, the board of the P.G. High School Alumni Association, and the board of the P.G. Police Citizens Academy. In 1995 my visionary father started the alumni database of all P.G. High School students and graduates dating back to 1898. I take the responsibility for keeping that current, which means endless computer research to record names, dates, and generational connections. Sue Taylor puts out the quarterly newsletter, which Beth Penney edits.

I've been fortunate to have grown up and been surrounded by generations of family in Pacific Grove.

Life in the 50s and My Role Models
Bob Crispin

Raised by a wonderful mom, who did a fine job of being Mom and "Dad" for me, she also went to the schools to see that I had male teachers whenever possible. I present male role models who mentored me in my upbringing:

Calvin Keater: Kindergarten through adulthood, my neighbor, taught me carpentry, use of tools, love of nature.

Mr. Nelson: 6th grade teacher, I learned about art and kindness. He was a gentle soul.

Mr. Barnett: Junior high, ran the after-school ham radio class; I learned math, science and the need to study.

Coach Duke Thayer: Junior high, worked with me solo, after school, as I liked the high jump.

Mr. Savo: Amazing teacher—art, jazz, beatnik lifestyle, civil rights, a practical view of the Constitution.

Coach Chamberlin: Led me to distance running, thus endurance events for a lifetime.

Jim Edwards and Al Melder: Students, mentored me in track and sportsmanship.

Friends: Comradery, fun, moderation, male bonding, adventure. I still meet five of them yearly.

My mom: Sense of equality, racial and gender, a feminist through action more than words.

Special note to the wonderful teacher, George Savo ... teacher in 1963, he wrote in my yearbook, "May you always win the race for love and laughter." I wrote him years later and said that I did. From him I learned about jazz, free expression, modern art, and that teachers could party all weekend at the Monterey Jazz Festival and fall asleep, head on desk, as Vince Guaraldi's jazz played on a record player. I purchased the album that day at Abernaties in Monterey.

Special note to student and mentor, Jim Edwards, class of 1961. He was a junior during my freshman year, a popular kid, but not cliquish. Coach Chamberlin was new to coaching. Jim had studied distance coaching methods from other nations, more off track methods, sand dune running, hill work and trail running. His senior year, he broke the 20-year-old school record in the mile. Soon after, he was injured. The following week, I decided, as a prank, to chase his rival, way over my head, until I burned out. I didn't burn out, and set a new school record. I owe my records and my success in distance running to Jim, along with Coach Chamberlin.

In 1992, my son and a buddy dropped me off in Bellingham, Washington, for an 84-day bicycle ride to Portland, Maine, 72 miles a day for 72 riding days. It was an amazing summer, a goal I had since high school. There were forty of us in the supported group. Here's to junior high PE teacher Duke Thayer, Coach Richard, mentors/students Jim Edwards and Al Melder for being the ones who got me on this path.

My Yard on First and Laurel

In the 1960s, yard work at my house on First and Laurel was a low priority for a mom raising two kids solo. It was a win for us kids, as the 100 x 120, three corner lot became a local, weed-filled playground. We had a tree fort, an underground fort, and later, ham radio antennas and a pole vault pit. I lived from kindergarten through MPC in that house. We had no car till I was in seventh grade. The neighbors were none too impressed, but we had a great time growing up with that yard!

P.G. to Yosemite Bicycle Ride

In the 1950s and early 1960s, bicycling was for kids. When starting junior high school, one best leave the bicycle home, or else it will be vandalized. The car culture demanded, if male, you own a car or walk. There were also zero road runners. Track training was done on a track, no fun runs, no 10k road races at all. P.G. police would ask why I was in such a hurry when I ran the streets of our town. On bicycles, folks threw stuff at us from cars; empty beer cans were common projectiles.

Then came the 10 speeds, a bicycle that could go great distance. A track team buddy of mine, Del Langton, got the first bike in our group. One of our trackster buddies came up with the crazy idea (for the time) of bicycling to Yosemite. Four of us were caught up in the idea, even before we all had bicycles.

Parental permission involved, "You can go if it's okay with your friends parents." In other words, passing responsibility from one set of parents to the next. My mom said, "Bike to Big Sur and back to prove yourselves." Trackster Glen Burwick and I rented bikes, rode to Big Sur, sent my mom a postcard and cycled home. It was done and the parents signed on.

Glen Berwick, Eric Dittmer, Del Langton, all class of 62, and I, class of 63, set out to Yosemite on a foggy summer morning. We went via Hollister and stayed overnight at a fire house. Then it was Merced, and into Yosemite for a one week stay, then home.

The next year was a repeat, adding Lew Decker, Keith Decker and Roland Morgner.

It became a pivotal moment in confidence-building. It also planted in my mind to someday cross the US on a bicycle. I did so at age 48. Eric Dittmer bicycled across the US at age 67.

Those years of track and the advent of the multi-speed bicycle gave us the chance to be lifetime athletes. In the 1950s, one did sports until out of school, then most retired to driving and sedentary lives. Hiking and camping were the main outlets until the 10-speed bicycle and road running came on strong in the 1970s. I feel our little group was on the leading edge of that. I even ran my own marathon, P.G. to Salinas, plus a few miles at Hartnell, as Boston was about it at that time. It was good times in P.G.

Thanks to Coach Duke Thayer, P.G. High School, Coach Chamberlin, P.G. High School, Jim Edwards and Al Melder, class of 61, for inspiring me to distance running, the sport that then led to bicycling.

Golf Carts to School Records

I was born and raised in P.G. and educated here, kindergarten through MPC. I attended P.G. Junior High School. In eighth grade, I was totally into ham radio, a nerd of the day, and above all, nonathletic by the standards of 1959. If skinny, one was not fit. If bad at team sports, not fit. Notwithstanding he fact that I walked and biked everywhere, at six feet, 152 pounds, I worried my PE teacher, Duke Thayer. In the spring, he noted that I liked track, no team to mess up in front of, just me against an event. For me, the event was the high jump. He took me to a track meet; I came in last, but had fun.

Come summer, we got into trouble camping in friend's yards, mine at First and Laurel. Groups of us would meet at Robert Down School and jog into Pebble Beach, where a country club friend had taught us we could "borrow" golf carts. We rode till before dawn, playing in the thick fog, racing, then putting them back on their battery chargers and jogging home, just before sunrise.

We finally got caught!

Freshman year, a sophomore buddy and one of the golf-carters, talked me into going out for track. He was the one who encouraged running on our "tour de golf cart" adventures. In no time, the nerd, attempting to high jump, was put in the mile run by Coach Chamberlain, who may have seen I had a talent for distance running. My first mile was 5:07 at King City in 87-degree heat, after sharing a half gallon of A & W root beer.

I went on to set the school record my sophomore year, and many times throughout my time at P.G. High School. I'm still on the board, number three. I ran in college and crossed the US on a bicycle at age 50. I am still close friends with five of my track teammates, who get together every year to mountain bike, hike, share beers and stories.

The question I pose, would I have been discovered as a "natural" runner had it not been for those many summer workouts, running into the land of golf carts? There were no running programs before high school back then. Running was so rare, P.G. police would stop me, and ask, "What's your hurry, son, do we have a problem?" when I ran the streets of our town. If it had not been for the summer events, I may never have gone that route.

I learned much about court procedure, both criminal and civil court, and above all, the importance of staying out of trouble. My mom had to pay some damages, but the track scholarship far outweighed those costs.

Life is full of pivotal moments. This was one of mine.

Idyllic Time to Grow Up in P.G.
Dixie Layne

Growing up in Pacific Grove in the 1950s was an adventure. This "city of homes" and one-time sanctuary of morality was then a quiet community of cottages and Victorian homes set along the shore in the shade of a piney forest on the tip of the Monterey Peninsula. There seemed to be everything in Pacific Grove a youngster could dream of, all set within their reach—it was idyllic.

All that was Pacific Grove in the 1950s seemed to be there just for us—our playground. We gave little thought to how this seaside paradise of homes filled with children was founded or why its seasons were marked by nature and community events. It seemed all so natural to us—the fall brought monarchs and a Butterfly Parade; winter saw a singing Christmas tree so tall it touched the stars; spring bore nature walks, baby deer, birds, raccoons, and wildflowers; summer was freedom, baseball, new bathing suits, and "be home when the streetlights come on."

A century before we found ourselves exploring the rocky western shores of Pacific Grove, a lighthouse was built on Point Pinos, and thus was the beginning of Pacific Grove. This beacon of light attracted curious kids and any attempt we made to get too close to it, the oldest continuously operating lighthouse, was thwarted by the lighthouse keeper, but it was an unexpected blast from the foghorn that kept us modern-day explorers at a safe distance. Although the lighthouse continues to shine, it is a museum now, open to the public, and the foghorn is no more.

Some 20 years after the lighthouse was built, a large dirt pathway was constructed above the sheltered beaches of the northern shoreline from Monterey to the lighthouse. It was then the Methodists formed the Pacific Grove Retreat Association and initiated a three-week summer encampment on the northern shore of the Grove. They created the first gated community on the Peninsula to keep the devil out, or so went the story. The first Chautauqua Assembly arrived at this summer Retreat just four years later—the same year the Southern Pacific Railroad began service to Pacific Grove. As retreaters began to take up permanent residence and the train brought more visitors to the Grove, businesses began to develop along Lighthouse Road.

Over time, Pacific Grove's appeal moved from religion to recreation, which initiated the advent of hotels and rooming houses, restaurants and souvenir shops. The once rocky shoreline at Lovers Point was blasted to make way for a sandy bathing beach, and a bath house and pier were constructed. Glass bottom swan boats drifted in the cove over the spectacular marine gardens, enabling all to see the wonders beneath the sea. The Retreat was quickly transforming from a city of tents to a city of homes. Pacific Grove now boasted of the first free library in Monterey County and one of the finest natural history museums in the United States. The two-story Pine Street School opened for classes, replacing the small one-room schoolhouse that could no longer accommodate the growing population.

By the 1920s, Pacific Grove was a bustling city of homes with a downtown business district that featured shops and businesses without rival—there were new car dealerships with large showrooms and garages with gas stations to service these gas buggies, and the largest department store between San Francisco and Los Angeles was right here in Pacific GroveThis period of prosperity was followed by the Great Depression and Pacific Grove suffered from the same decline the Depression brought to the rest of the country; however, it benefited a great deal from government relief programs, local philanthropists, and its civic and business leaders' generosity. During this austere time, Pacific Grove gained a Post Office, new museum building, a Carnegie library, new high school, professional ball park, the salt water Plunge (pool), municipal golf links, and the addition of a third story to Holman's Department Store.

With World II came a new set of challenges. Our boys went off to war, Japanese submarines were active off our coast, watch towers were built on the western beaches, curfews and complete blackouts were imposed, and an artillery regiment was stationed at the lighthouse to protect us. After two-and-a-half years, our boys came home. Pacific Grove was the idyllic suburban paradise with bustling businesses and room for expansion that attracted new families.

This paradise, once home to the indigenous Rumsien people and later to the people of a Chinese fishing village, was now home to the children of a new generation, who seemed unaware of what it took to create their idyllic hometown—but oh, how we grew and frolicked and enjoyed this "piney paradise."

There were now horses to ride from End O'Lane Stables along the many forested riding paths that led to the top of the hills above the Presidio or down to the beaches along 17 Mile Drive. The forests are now gone, replaced by a subdivision that stands where once we found adventure. There were once streams that flowed down to the bay, ripe for pirate adventures, and trains that rumbled so slowly along the shoreline that the most adventurous among us could jump the train for a ride west of Lovers Point or lay pennies on the track to be flattened by its wheels. The coastal Recreation Trail has replaced the train tracks.

The cove and Lovers Point offered us endless

entertainment. For two bits we could ride in glass bottom swan boats over the marine gardens or, for those brave enough to climb onto the rocks nestled along the shoreline, there were tide pools filled with critters to explore.

We swam in the frigid waters of the cove and surfed off Lovers Point to the tip of the pier, often without a wetsuit to keep us warm. We instead used the heated salt water of the Plunge to warm our cold bodies—the same Plunge where we learned to swim and dive, and where we watched water ballet performances. There were also enormous cacti on Lovers Point, perfect for crawling through tunnels that were created by the children who played in them.

There were summer baseball leagues for everyone, well, mostly for the boys and men. We watched the teams play in the evenings at the municipal ball park, surrounded by tall pine trees and beneath the fog. There was an announcer to call the games. He sat high above the stands where we sat eating hot dogs and drinking sodas. And in the fall, the trees in George Washington Park were so thick with monarchs, they hid the trees.

Pacific Grove has changed a bit. There aren't as many young families here and the population is less diverse. The Plunge is gone; the train no longer rumbles along the coast, and the butterflies are few. However, Pacific Grove may be one of the last hometowns where love of community is strong, where community is family. There simply was and is no better place to grow up than Pacific Grove.

You Can Go Home Again
Michele DeVaughn Tubman

A fuchsia colored carpet of succulent, covering the rugged coastline, interspersed with bring yellow sour grass, relaxes my senses. I am home!!! Memories return as I hear the fog horn alerting those at sea while assisting them home to safety. Monarch butterflies flutter by reminding you of the cocoon caterpillar transformation. The spindly painted ladies put forth their bright hues. Nature's miracles, indeed.

I look across the street from the Bath House and Pacific Grove Cove. I remember the day Dad decided to open a restaurant on the point and call it Lover's Point Inn. It was a family adventure. My job at four years old was to keep the vases on every table filled with white and yellow Margarita Daisies, which I loved picking from the bushes that lined our driveway.

Dad's starting point for the restaurant was twofold. He wanted a huge used brick fireplace in the middle of the room. But most important GREAT FOOD and SERVICE! Frank Glen was the chef and Curly the potato and onion peeler. I loved them both. They spoke to me as if I were an adult, which I adored. Curly would tell me stories, he was a joyous black man with a bald head. Frank Glen was tall and handsome, I will never forget them.

Dad had some good marketing and opened in 1948. He asked everyone he met, including children, what type of food they preferred. Fried chicken, hamburgers, fries and onion rings, great salads and some fish were the choices. Oldtimers will tell you that the restaurant was known for the abalone sandwiches, a huge hit.

Dessert was a deep-dish cobbler of the fruit that was in season. We, as a family, picked buckets of huckleberries growing out on the 17 Mile drive. Dad had bought a lot out there, hoping to build a home one day, so the berry picking started with our own bushes.
The restaurant's success came readily. Dad was innovative and turned the parking lot into a full service, eat in your car drive-in, unique to Pacific Grove. The locals loved it. It was a hit!

The old fog horn

Life progressed, we were swept up into the community. School began for Ann, Buzz (Neil Jr.) and me. My first school was called Pine Avenue School and is now R.H. Down. There are "two-fold" special memories. One, of course, my first day of school, and it was and is still the starting point for the Butterfly Parade which was my favorite time of the year. We would march down Pine Avenue then along Lighthouse and back. I was dressed as a monarch butterfly and played a drum. Later I progressed to the band and played the saxophone. I attribute that skill to our WONDERFUL music leader, Herb Miller, who was the brother of Glen Miller (many of you will remember the famous band leader). He knew I wanted to march in the parade and that I played the violin in the school orchestra. He said he would teach me the basics of the tenor sax, which he did and I was able to march in the parade. "Where there's a will, there's a way."

Lighthouse Avenue, Forest Avenue and Pine took us wherever we wanted to go and I still think of those days warmly as I frequent those streets today. I think of the post office, doctor's office, police dtation, library, Ray Lugo's

Service Station, Boy Scout building, and the railroad tracks that ushered in Grandma and Grandpa on the Del Monte Express. To say nothing of the P.G. Golf Course.

When I pass the "original" high school, (now the middle school on Forest) I am reminded of the evening Ann played the lead in *Jane Eyre*. Dad showed up with a dozen roses to present to her during the curtain calls when she received a standing ovation.

"Yes, you can go home again," if it is Pacific Grove. America's last home town filled with many generations where traditions mean something and where historical buildings and homes can breathe safely that one day they will not be demolished and replaced with a McMansion.

Dad's success at Lovers Pt. led to the beginning of another well-known successful restaurant. Although he is not credited (but should be) with the first and "really challenging" restaurant on Cannery Row, Neil DeVaughn's Fish and Steak House opened in 1952. I say "challenging" because the ROW was a shabby, desolate, ghost town with hobos and vagrants inhabiting many of the old dilapidated structures. Steinbeck's book which had not been well received by the locals, peaked Dad's interest. He was met by the continuous cry, "Neil, you are crazy, no one will ever go down there to eat." Dad turned a deaf ear. Slowly and at times painfully he introduced his "fine dining" restaurant to the locals.

There were constant fires in the buildings surrounding the restaurant, which was in the old Chinese Hotel, smack dab in the middle of Cannery Row. We would often sit on the top of Prescott Hill, watching the flames as fire hoses tried to extinguish another conflagration. We prayed each time that it wasn't our place. Finally, with the help of the locals who did venture down, more and more each year, plus the Crosby tournament visitors, Neil DeVaughn's Fish and Steak House, like Lovers Pt. Inn became quite famous. QUITE FAMOUS INDEED.

Memories! There are many.

Growing up Local: Monarch at Heart
Allison Haylings Mayorga
wife, dog-mom, monarch-loving, P.G. native

In the summer of 1990, my father and very pregnant mother drove up the coast of California to flee the heat of Phoenix, Arizona, in hopes of landing in the perfect coastal town to raise their child. It was 114 degrees in Arizona on the day they left. My mother was an Air Force brat, never staying in one place for long, and wanted a different type of life for her expected baby. They made their way to Carlsbad, California, where my father was from; frustrated by the insane traffic and city growth, they continued north. Shooting for Carmel, they settled instead in the heart of Pacific Grove, Central Avenue, to be exact. An 800-square-foot quintessential whitewashed beach cottage is where my first memories were formed, our house forever illuminated, either by the gloomy glow of the P.G. fog, or the bright lights of the squid boats at night.

My father had sold his solar business in Arizona and was looking to start fresh and fill a needed niche. While he observed and planned his next move, he picked up a volunteer Meals on Wheels route. Story goes, he even delivered his route on the day my mother went into labor; apparently he mixed up everyone's meals. My mother has continued the volunteer path my father paved to this very day.

I attended the magical David Avenue Kindergarten Center, along with all the other snot-nosed kids in town. The majority of us would grow together through the remainder of our school career. Robert Dixon, better known as "Mr. D," taught PE here. To this day I credit him for getting this VERY attached "Mommy's Girl" through kindergarten. As my teacher would pry me from my mother, I would look at Mr. D through my tears, and he would say consolingly, "She will be back."

Once my father had established his new water purification business, we expanded to a slightly larger home, smack dab in the middle of every school I would attend until graduation. I walked to Robert Down, where I picked up my deep love of the Beatles as Scott Getline directed the Robert Down Chorus and lead tunes like "Let it Be" and "Octopus's Garden," all for the love of music.

I walked to P.G. Middle School, where I met Diana Rookstool, English and art teacher. She fostered my creative side and inspired me to follow in the footsteps of her daughters by joining the Feast of Lanterns Royal Court. To this day we are friends. Her daughter officiated my wedding.

I even walked to Pacific Grove High School until I got my driver's license on my 16th birthday. It was there where photography teacher Matt Kelly sparked a love of photography and planted the seed of a career in journalism. He became our wedding photographer and dear friend. It was also where Mr. Bliss taught students about science, but above all else the power of random kindness. And where Coach Mahaney welcomed me to the girls' softball team, even though I had never held a bat in my life.

I then went on to college to study creative writing and pursued a passion for travel. I met my now husband along the way, and there was no question to where we wanted to settle: Pacific Grove.

I even sported beaded butterflies on my wedding dress. We now live around the corner from the house where I formed my roots and became the woman I am today. I can hear the middle school students frolicking at lunch. I

can hear the P.G. High band on Friday nights in the fall.

And I hope to one day walk my own children Robert Down, where Mr. D will be waiting with a smile and consoling words for a presumably very attached mother, dropping her baby off at school.

Growing up in Pacific Grove meant a lot of things. For me, growing up in P.G. meant life-long friendships and a place to always call home.

A Place Where (Almost) Everybody Knows Your Name
Sharon Randall

Sitting on a bench in front of Forest Grove Elementary, waiting for the end of the school day, I closed my eyes, felt the sun on my face and listened.

Children laughing. Parents talking. Cars passing. Crows cawing.

A perfect soundtrack for a perfect Pacific Grove day.

My children attended Forest Grove years ago. But this time I was waiting for my grandson.

For 35 years, I lived less than a mile from Forest Grove. My kids walked everywhere—to school, to the park, the beach or downtown.

I called it "a little piece of Paradise," and I could not imagine living anywhere else.

But after the kids grew up, we lost their dad to cancer, and I found myself alone in an empty house with five sets of dishes and no one to feed.

Years later, I remarried and moved with my new husband to Las Vegas, of all places. Then our children started having babies. Randy is the oldest of our six grandchildren.

While waiting for Randy's kindergarten class to be dismissed, I shared the bench with a woman who was waiting to do art projects in the afterschool program.

When I told her I was picking up my grandson and that my children had gone to the school, her eyes flashed in recognition.

"Wait," she said, "are you …?"

"Yes," I said, "I am."

We had a lovely visit. Then she hurried off to do art projects and I sat on the bench thinking of how lucky I'd been to live in a place where people remembered your name, even if you moved away.

My children were doing well. My grandchildren were healthy. My husband, the best grandpa ever, was waiting in the car to take Randy and me to the beach. Life was good. I was blessed.

It was a small moment, but I wanted to remember it. I wished I'd had it years ago on darker days, times when I wondered if I would ever smile again.

What a gift it would've been to look into the future and see myself on that bench, older, wiser, happy as happy ever gets.

No one goes through life without a few heartaches. Grief is huge. It hides the sun. The happiest moments can seem small in comparison. But if we do remember them, if we cherish them, they can add just enough light to make the dark times a little brighter. What else is memory for, if not for light?

So I stored that moment in the back of my heart in a place where I keep things I don't want to lose. I hope you're storing some, too. You never know when we'll need a little light.

Then I looked up and saw Randy, looking so much like his dad, with the sun spitting sparks from his curly head, running across the lawn to tackle me.

Family Generations Since 1914
Keith Larson

How we came to live in Pacific Grove is really a family story. At least someone representing our family lineage—the Collins, Bohrmans, Carlsons, Harers, Hemmys, Gillaspies, Larsons, Lindvalls and Skiles—have been continuously living in Pacific Grove dating back to 1914 when a log cabin was purchased across from Washington Park by Albert and Amy Collins, who were interested in a retirement home. When Fred Bohrman married their daughter Ada, they promised him their ranch in Campbell if he would build an addition on the cabin. Both the Collins and Bohrmans spent their retirement years in Pacific Grove and are buried in El Carmelo Cemetery.

At this point I would like to thank and acknowledge Chris and Ken Bohrman, Jeanie Harer De Tomaso, and Karen Lindvall-Larson, also the other family members for their work in recording some of the history that has helped to piece together how we came to call Pacific Grove our home.

To me a place is just a place until you put your own meaning on it, your own story. Given our lengthy family history in the area, I've been pondering our collective family narrative that gets passed down to us from generation to generation and how this is woven into our individual life stories as well. My dad driving the long way around the ocean no matter where he was going, myself as a little boy collecting huckleberries in the forest so my mom could make a pie, or my second grade teacher, Mrs. Phillips, giving each of us a small cypress tree when we graduated. These acts and rituals were recorded in my earliest memories which supported a life-long appreciation of nature in me, especially trees.

Some of my son Wesley's memories of Pacific Grove are of visiting the tide pools along the coast; this interest in marine life later became a career choice. My brother Ned became a tour guide taking people on hiking adventures in Alaska and other parts of the world. My brother Eric was also an avid hiker. The serenity of this area has inspired those in our family line to create art and music, and to become closer to their personal spiritual paths. When we become teachers, we bring to the classroom a love of nature that is so much needed today.

My feeling is that the beauty of Pacific Grove and the Central Coast will continue to have an influence on family generations to come in the form of an appreciation and love of nature. Whether we live in Pacific Grove or come back to visit, we will always keep with us this sacred energy which continually influences our hearts and life stories.

My Own Perfect Day in the 60's

My perfect day was actually three months long, a continuum of experiences created by the long honored tradition of giving kids and teachers a break in the summer. Days were spent in the present moment. As adults, don't we hear a lot about "being in the now?" When I was 10 I didn't worry about the past or the future when it was summer. Time was marked by, "Hey, what do you want to do now?" And so this special time in my life was structured only by what my friends and I could make up.

Perfect days started by lounging in front of the TV with elbows on the carpet and hands under your chin watching a variety of Hanna Barbara cartoon offerings, Wally Gator, Yogi Bear, Quick Draw McGraw and my favorite, Augie Doggie and Doggie Daddy.

I tended to be the one in my neighborhood who wanted to get the day started. Mothers, who were always at home, got the knock on the door quite early. "Can Scott come out and play?"

"He's still watching TV, but you can come in." Parents sometimes were concerned about how much TV to let us watch. I was lucky—I had only one screen to compete with while trying to get my friend's attention. But I had to paint grand visions of tree forts we could build or money-making schemes like Kool-Aid stands to get my buddies away from the cartoons.

Eventually I got at least one friend to put on play clothes so we could start the perfect day. I lived on Marino Pines. There was more forest back then behind the high school and Forest Grove School, which was near to my neighborhood. People dumped their old wood in these places, which was good for us because we could many times recycle the material into a tree house. Nails came from the hardware store in the Forest Hill Shopping Center. At that time they were sold by weight. I remember a friend's dad showing us how to take old nails and bend them straight so they could be reused.

Where did we get our money? A Kool-Aid stand at the corner of 19th and Marino Pines was a pretty good business for us, as was collecting returnable bottles from the forest if we could find a store owner willing to bother with the load we pulled in a red Radio Flyer wagon. Besides money for building projects, there was always a need to finance our comic books, Jolly Rancher candies and bubble gum with cards included.

Heaven for us was the camp store at the corner of 17 Mile Drive and Sinex. The store was adjacent to a collection of rental cabins that is now 17 Mile Drive Village. The camp store was a ways from my neighborhood, but it was worth it because of all the goodies sold there—comic books, candy, ice cream, trading cards.

Well that takes care of the morning. At home, Mom made lunch. I happened to like Campbell's tomato soup with saltines on the side and a tuna sandwich. I don't remember Mom asking me what I was doing all day; she probably assumed that if it was bad stuff she would hear about it later and would let Dad take care of it. The trouble we got into is another story and could fill up this column for weeks.

Summer afternoons were always celebrated with a few spur-of-the-moment baseball games. It seemed like we would always come up short on the number of players needed, so most of the time we used the time-honored ghost runner on first. We could really get into who was winning for awhile but at the end of the game it didn't seem to matter much. Hitting the ball, getting on base and catching some fly balls were all that mattered.

Late afternoons found some of us in front of the tube, tuned in to KTVU out of Oakland, as Captain Satellite blasted off into space with a collection of old Warner Brother cartoons, games, contests, and commercials The captain encouraged us to try a 7-up ice cream float instead of using root beer, which I had while watching the show. Thanks, Mom, for getting the ingredients. We put a lot of trust in the Captain when he made suggestions.

I built my last tree house in 1969 with a friend behind the high school. Childhood came to a close on that Saturday after those few boards had been nailed in place. I recently found an original board that had fallen from the tree. The perfect day made a feeling in me that I have used to measure my other days. There is nothing quite like the freedom to just make it up as you go along.

I'll meet you down at the camp store then maybe we can smash a few pennies on the tracks when the train comes through Asilomar. Just thinking about those times can bring back the feeling of my perfect day in the Grove.

Friends and Motorcycles Forever!

I signed my friends' high school yearbooks, "Motorcycles forever." My buddy Jim, who attended Pacific Grove High in the same graduating class, reminds me of this every so often when he wants to chide me for no longer owning a motorcycle. But it was true: motorcycles were a big focus for me in the 1970s. I noticed recently that my two-year-old grandson, Mattias, always seem to have a little car in his hand and sometimes both hands. There's something about wheels that gets into our blood.

The late Pete Drakos sold me my first motorcycle, a 1967 Yamaha 100 twin. At that time in the 70s there were not many of us who rode our motorcycles to school. Most of my contemporaries were into models like the Suzuki 500 or Kawasaki 900. Hondas were very popular with their four-cylinder models like the 750/4. These were the fast, modern motorcycles of their time.

A typical after-school day would find me riding my motorcycle and thinking to myself, "Well, here's my chance. They're all waiting for the bus out in front of the school. I'll just glide down from the parking lot behind the band room, turn up Sunset and …" inevitably when I was trying to impress the crowd, I would miss the shift from second to third. Not the cool image I wanted to create.

I became fascinated with British bikes and became a fan of the classic look. I thought it would be cool to have something different. I had an after-school job for the Pacific Grove school district, filling in when a night custodian was sick or on leave at Robert Down or the elementary school on Lighthouse Avenue.

When I thought I had saved enough money I started to look through the Monterey Herald classified section where all the motorcycles were listed. Quite a few were being advertised for sale in those days, practically any model you could think of: BSA, Triumph, Norton, Royal Enfield. All the British models were well represented and within my price range. Back then, you could usually pick up a nice one for between $600 and $700. By the way BSA stands for Birmingham Small Arms, a company that made military and sporting guns as well as motorcycles. I decided to purchase a 1967 BSA Lightning that I found in the classifieds. The owner was proud of the candy apple red paint job he had done on the gas tank with just cans of spray paint. It looked really nice along with the standard chrome sides of the tank. The bike was not stock and even was missing the classic BSA starburst emblems, but with the help of Oliver Cycle on Cannery Row and Dave's Motorcycles in Seaside, I figured I could get any part I needed, even though BSA had gone out of business a few years earlier.

If you owned an older machine and wanted that classic look, you sometimes spent a lot of time working on them. My room and garage often had motorcycle parts spread around, but always neatly. My friend Pete liked older cars and had a 57 Chevy that he always seemed to be working on when I came over.

"Hey you look like Fonzie," he said to me once.

I shot back, "What's a Fonzie?" This was 1974, the year Happy Days went on the air, and I hadn't yet seen this guy Fonzie. I tuned in to the show and was not overjoyed, thinking people thought I was trying to copy this guy. I was trying to make my own identity, and was actually attempting to look more like Michael Parks, who starred in Then Came Bronson a short-lived TV series from 1969 about a guy who just travels around on his Harley Sportster from town to town seeing what kind of drama he can get into. One of the episodes was filmed right here.

Sometime around the 1980s I was ready to let go of my last bike, which was a 1973 BMW R-75-5. I mentioned this to my friend Jim, who was always ready to buy my bikes when I was through with them. It seems every few years I have to honor what I wrote in the yearbook and ride again. We keep trading the Beemer back and forth between us, hoping to someday get the bike to 50,000 miles. At present I have not ridden for many years. I did see a blast from the past the other day on Pine Street, a BSA Lightning for sale. Motorcycles forever!

Grandparents, Parents, Uncles, Cousins
Ken Bohrman

When I was growing up in the 1950s and 1960s, I spent every summer at our second home on Chestnut Street in Pacific Grove. My father, Dave Bohrman, was a woodshop teacher in Fresno and purchased that summer home on Chestnut in 1951. My grandparents, Fred and Ada Bohrman, lived around the corner in their log cabin on Alder and Laurel. My brothers and sisters and I loved escaping the summer heat of the San Joaquin Valley for the cool coastal community of Pacific Grove.

We spent our summers playing in the woods of Washington Park building forts, getting into poison oak, and swinging from a rope swing in a large old oak tree across from Grandpa's house, where my father also played as a child in the 1920s. Grandpa Fred would take me for walks in those woods, regaling me with stories of the elk herd that once roamed Washington Park. We would collect yerba buena vines and dry them in his shed, later making mint tea out of the leaves. There were always plenty of cousins around to play with including the Carlsons, Larsons, Skiles, Holders, Harers, Gillespies and Lindvalls. The whole family would don tin quart cans hanging from our belts and go picking huckleberries up on Huckleberry Hill off of Holman Highway. Mom would make the most delicious pies from those berries.

My father and brother, Dave Jr., built a 15-foot plywood boat in his garage. They named it the *Kenny Boy*, and fished in Monterey Bay for over 15 years. Dad eventually bought a larger fiberglass cabin cruiser to fish for another 35 years. My brother Dave caught a 44-pound Chinook salmon in the 1953 season. All of us kids had many adventures fishing in Monterey Bay. We also used to fish off the commercial wharf and drop crab nets in the evening. We caught tommy cod (small bocaccio), jack smelt and sand sabs. Dave actually caught a 50-pound skate, a type of ray, on 12-pound test line off that wharf when he was 14. Dad climbed down a piling ladder to gaff it and bring it up to the wharf.

I remember my favorite Uncle Jack giving me my first fishing pole with a Zebco reel when I was five years old. We went down to the wharf to try it out. He instructed me on how to hold my thumb on the button while casting, then let go when I cast the line. You know what happened next … there went pole, hook, line and sinker off the wharf into 30 feet of water. I was in trouble!

We were allowed to roam Pacific Grove and Monterey freely in those carefree days, riding our bikes everywhere with the exception of Cannery Row. According to Mom, that was off limits because of the hobos and bums who lived in the old boilers around the derelict canneries near Doc Ricketts's Pacific Biological Lab. Of course, some the best fishing spots were under the canneries around the old pilings, so we just had to sneak down there sometimes. The hobos occasionally set the old canneries on fire, creating huge infernos that could be seen from our house in P.G.

When I was around eight years of age, I rode down to Fishermen's Wharf one Sunday afternoon and was visiting the old Customs House Museum. While I was viewing the displays upstairs, the elderly curator locked up the museum for the night without checking upstairs. Fortunately, I was able to get the attention of some tourists outside who got hold of the police to let the crying eight-year-old out. I was in trouble!

My Mother a Prolific Artist

My mother, Janet Bohrman, was somehow a prolific and gifted artist while raising five children. She used to take me on her artistic excursions around the Monterey Peninsula to do *plein air* oil painting. I would take advantage of these outings to fish off the rocks and explore tide pools, etc.

One day she was painting on a bluff overlooking the harbor and Fishermen's Wharf, while I was fishing nearby, below her and out of sight, when I caught a small

Carmel Mission paintings by Carol Bohrman and, right, by Ken Bohrman.

ocean sunfish (mola mola). I didn't think it was any good to eat so I threw it back. I then noticed a protruding fin approaching from offshore, probably attracted by the sunfish I had thrown back. It turned out to be a six-foot blue shark. Excitedly, I summoned the help of another boy I was playing with and together we hoisted a large oblong rock from the beach behind the jetty we were standing on. When the shark swam within a few feet of the jetty, we launched the rock, which landed smack on his head, stunning him long enough to be washed close to the jetty by the next wave. I reached down and grabbed the tail of the small shark and, with the help of the other little boy, hauled it up onto the jetty. I straddled it, holding it down while the other boy ran to find a stick for a club.

About this time my mother came across the bluff to see how I was doing. Much to her horror there was Kenny sitting on a six-foot blue shark that was coming back to life, thrashing around. My mother made me throw it back but I'll always have that memory of catching a shark at the age of eight with my bare hands. I was in trouble!

As kids, we spent many hours in the Museum of Natural History studying the local fauna and flora, as well as at the Pacific Grove Library, reading to our hearts' content. Eventually Dad, with Mom's encouragement, began to purchase small fixer-upper homes in Pacific Grove. Mom had an artistic eye for potential in a prospective house. After that, we spent much of our summers doing renovation, then renting them out. Dad even raised one house on Granite Street with jacks and poured a concrete foundation where there was none. The Bohrman children all learned how to paint, clean and repair old homes and we quickly learned *never* to say, "I'm bored and I don't have anything to do."

Another favorite activity was riding our bikes around the 17 Mile Drive and sometimes stopping for lunch while leaning against the Lone Cypress. One day in July of 1965, my little brother Chris and I were riding our bikes around Point Joe on the 17 Mile Drive when we spotted the stern of a 65-foot yacht, the *Pussycat*, that had washed up between the rocks on the point. The entertainer Jerry Lewis and four friends had run aground on the rocky reef just offshore a few days before and had escaped in a dinghy before the yacht sank. About 30 feet of the stern had broken free and resurfaced, washing ashore.

Armed with screw drivers, crowbar and gunny sacks, Chris and I crawled into the wreckage at low tide and salvaged at least four complete brass port hole assemblies after hours of removing screws. We still have some of those relics, including a large brass 12-inch prop from a 45-foot schooner that went aground just south of Point Joe. That one took me a month of low minus tides to wade out and cut through the one-and-a-half inch stainless steel driveshaft with a hacksaw. A few years later in the 70s, Chris and I were looking for a good place to go abalone hunting down the coast early in the morning when we came across a 55-foot albacore boat run aground and abandoned the night before on the beach near Point Sur. We salvaged that one, too.

My cousins, Michael and Kathy Skiles, and I took an oceanography summer school class in which we had field trips to the great tide pools of Pacific Grove, learning much about the marine life of our wonderful bay. We even cooked squid in class, experiencing fried calamari for the first time.

Favorite P.G. Hangouts

Some of my favorite hangouts in Pacific Grove were Holman's Department Store, which still had the vacuum tube message system to send checks up to the accounting department. Roy Wright Hardware in the present-day Lopez Liquor Store on Lighthouse had a great stash of antique hardware on the upstairs attic floor. My dad would find lots of vintage hardware, like brand-new antique porcelain door knobs and push-button light switches, to repair his old houses around town.

There was Alicia's Ice Cream Parlor across from Grove Market on Forest where Dad took us for ice cream cones after dinner on the way to watch the sunset. Dad made a box that would hold six cones. We saw all the latest movies at the Grove Theater on Lighthouse. My cousin Ritchie Lindvall and I used to wade into the pond on the 17th fairway on the P.G. golf course in our bare feet and collect hundreds of golf balls. He lived down by the railroad tracks off of Pico and we used to wave to the engineer of the sand train as he was hauling away all that beautiful white sand from the 30-foot dunes that used to be around Lake Majella behind The Fishwife restaurant and Spanish Bay.

The family used to go down to the Pacific Grove train station, near present-day Monarch Pines mobile home park at Lovers Point, in the evening to watch the Del Monte Limited turn the engine around on the turntable so it could head back to San Francisco. It provided service to Monterey from 1889 to 1971. The Pacific Grove station closed in 1957. Mom once took me on the glass bottom swan boat operated by Russ and Marge Sprague, who also had the yellow boat rental concession at Lovers Point. It was a splurge for us as it cost 35-cents. I was amazed at the view of the bottom of the ocean and saw a large lingcod down there in the kelp. I learned to swim at the Lovers Point bath house salt water pool when I was five.

I remember when the 1880s Berwick mansion on Ocean View and 9th Street across from Berwick Park was being torn down in the early 1960s. My dad and I salvaged hundreds of 2X4s, 2x10s and an old claw-foot bathtub. My job was to spend hours pulling the antique iron square nails from the old redwood 2X4s.

My brother Chris and I always found time to fish off the rocks below Berwick Park, though. One time Chris and I climbed way out on some rocks there at low tide where the best fishing holes were. After some great fishing, a few hours later the tide was coming in fast and had begun to flood our escape path back to shore. I was able to leap across okay, but seven-year-old Chris couldn't make the leap. I had to run for help as Mom was up at our 9th Street rental house, painting. She grabbed one of those salvaged 2x10 boards and we were able to put a bridge across for Chris to climb to safety. But, I was in trouble again!

When I consider my early life, I realize how fortunate I was to grow up spending summers in the quaint, historic little town of Pacific Grove. My father eventually retired and, like his father before him, moved to the Monterey Peninsula and spent another 30 years enjoying relaxed living in the friendly town that he loved. And, like him, my brother and I have been blessed to also live and retire here. Thank you, Mom and Dad, Grandpa and Grandma, for the legacy that you have left us.

Ken Bohrman is a retired airline pilot and resides in Pebble Beach. Younger brother Chris still lives in the original family home on Chestnut. The old log cabin on Alder is also still in the family, frequented by many cousins. They have family reunions in Washington Park with more than 50 descendants of Fred and Ada Bohrman attending.

Roy Wright's Hardware
Summer 1966 – Going out of Business Sale
Chris Bohrman

I remember the foggy Pacific Grove summer day when I heard from my dad that Roy Wright's Hardware Store was closing its doors and selling off the inventory. I got on my Stingray bike with the sparkly banana seat, butterfly handlebars and super tall "sissy bar" and rode down to see what was what.

My first discovery was that I was going to need to pool all my cash resources and then some for this venture, because the place was filled with all kinds of doo-dads and gadgets that a nine-year-old boy could turn into virtually ANYTHING!

The next thing I discovered was that because this was a GOOB-(going out of business) sale, even the dark and mysterious "upper room" storage attic was now accessible to me. So up the stairs I went and that's where I spent several dusty hours that first afternoon, looking through boxes of hinges and fittings, rods and pipes, my nine-year-old imagination running wild with all the cool things I could concoct back at home with all these parts.

I recall the precariously long trip back up "Short" Street to my house on Chestnut Street, my Stingray laden with all the booty that my young allowance would "allow." One of the items I recall snagging was a box of clear Plexiglas rods that must have been intended as groovy Sixties towel rods—just irresistible to my young inventor's mind.

Before I was able to return to this wonderland, my coffers were going to need a cash influx, so I gathered up my dad's trusty pair of Macabee gopher traps and set off into the neighborhood—"Chris Bohrman, Gopher Bounty Hunter." The bounty was 50-cents per pelt. I didn't actually skin them, but the neighbors were happy to contribute to my Roy Wright's Fund provided I rid their yards of the pests. Several pelts later I was able to return to the store, where today Lopez Liquors sits, and further indulge what is still one of my favorite pastimes, "big boy toy" shopping.

Note: you can enjoy Chris playing his guitar and singing with the children at the P.G. Farmers Market on Mondays.

Architect's Life in Her Family Home
Jeanne and Ray Byrne

My great-grandparents, Isaac and Laura Nuttall, came from Fair Oaks, near Sacramento, and moved to Pacific Grove for the cool climate. They owned the house at 144 Forest, but also purchased two other properties, one on Forest Avenue and one at 141 16th Street.

The 16th Street house was a vacation place for my grandparents, Ashford and Matilda (Nuttall) McCoy. Later it was where my grandmother retired. I came to visit from the time I was little until my grandmother passed away. My grandfather had divided the house into a duplex. The side the family used was a studio with a guest room outside at the back of the garage. It was great fun to come down with a friend when I was in high school to visit my grandmother and stay in the guest room. We used to take the bus from Napa and get off on Lighthouse Avenue in front of the then-theater, where the Rudas building is now.

One of the really fun things my family did when we came down to visit was go to Holman's Department Store. It had a fabulous hardware store in the basement with every part or piece for the turn-of-the-century houses and buildings: hinges, latches, decorative trim, etc. And the upstairs had a cashier on the mezzanine where the money and change were sent back and forth with either spring-loaded containers on cables or the vacuum tubes. We also always made a couple of trips to Fisherman's Wharf, once to buy fish for dinner and once to eat out. At that time there were many fresh fish markets to choose from.

In 1977 Ray and I moved into the house on 16th Street to do some much-needed repairs. In 1979 Ray and I were married at St. Mary's Episcopal Church on Central Avenue. As the repairs continued it became a full project with a complete remodel and addition of a second floor, turning the house back into a single-family house again. At this point 1982, with our son, Loren, on the way, we acquired the property from my dad and my aunt. It genuinely became our long-term residence.

Through the years Ray joined the P.G. Volunteer Fire Department; I became a licensed architect in 1982 and opened my office in the Giles Building, 591 Lighthouse Ave. I have a long list of civic organizations to which I have and/or still belong, including Zonta International, the P.G. Heritage Society, Native Daughters of the Golden West, and Rotary.

I have sat on numerous city commissions/committees including Building Standards Committee, Architectural Review, Historic Resources, and the Planning Commission.

Professionally I have belonged to the American Institute of Architects since 1982 and was advanced to Fellowship in the National AIA organization in 2000. I have been a governor's appointment to the Monterey County Fair Board by two different governors and am currently continuing my second appointment.

I was elected mayor of Pacific Grove from 1992-1994 and am serving my second term of election to the Monterey Peninsula Water Management District Board of Directors.

Following in Grandparents' Footsteps
Kyle A. Krasa
local estate planning attorney

My grandparents purchased their house in Pebble Beach, just inside the Country Club Gate, in the late 1950s. My father was in his early teens when he moved into the house. He attended Pacific Grove Middle School and Pacific Grove High School.

I grew up about two miles from my grandparents' house. I visited them all the time. Their house was like my second home.

I attended Forest Grove Elementary School (the greatest elementary school ever) from kindergarten through fifth grade. My grandparents' house is within walking distance of Forest Grove. For most of my elementary school years, my mother would drop me off at my grandparents' house in the morning. After a short visit, I would walk or ride my bike through the woods of the Rip Van Winkle Open Space to school.

Later, as I progressed to Pacific Grove Middle School, I was able to make a much longer trek to school. I rode my bike from my home near Bird Rock in Pebble Beach, through the Rip Van Winkle Open Space, past Forest Grove, and on to the middle school. I would cut over from Congress to Forest via Hillcrest Avenue in the morning and return in the afternoon via Spazier Avenue and 19th Street on the way home. The Hillcrest Avenue and Spazier Avenue neighborhoods became familiar and comfortable and still hold a special place in my heart. In fact, my office is located just about a block down from the middle school in between Sinex and Gibson.

My wife, young son, and I currently live in my grandparents' old house. Every day, I walk my son, Jonah (who is named in honor of my mom, Joan), to Forest Grove along the same path through the Rip Van Winkle Open Space. It is my favorite time of the day and it feels very special to both of us that I am able to pass this legacy on to another generation. We use the time to talk about school, practice spelling words, and enjoy each other's company.

I imagine that in several years when Jonah graduates from elementary school, his path to middle school will be similar to the one I took. I know that he'll be older then and likely won't want to be around me as much. However, I take comfort in the fact that he won't be too far from me during the day: just a few feet up from my office. A new—but familiar—legacy will be born.

Small Town Girl Forever
Wendy Salisbury Howe

In January of 1970, I sat basking in the winter sunshine in Monterey's Friendly Plaza. My husband Kevin was next door in the old *Monterey Peninsula Herald* building, being interviewed for a job as a reporter. Out he came, with a big smile. Old Colonel Alan Griffin, owner and publisher, had hired him—his first job out of college, which had been interrupted by a stint in Vietnam with the Army. They would pay him $140 a week, a princely sum.

We headed immediately to little Pacific Grove to look for a place to live. Driving along the ocean just past Lovers Point, we spied a sign. "House for Rent." The owner was there and agreed to let us have it for $140. It was tiny, with a bedroom so small that we couldn't both get dressed in it at the same time. The living room, converted from a garage, was dark and damp. But the dining room had a view of the ocean across the neighbor's lawn. We were enchanted! I remember saying to Kevin, "If you can stand to keep working in the same place, I'd like to live in this town forever."

We moved up from smoggy Southern California and began to explore our little piece of paradise. My family had moved often when I was growing up, Kansas, Michigan, back to Kansas. Then suburban Washington, D. C.—the Virginia side, then the Maryland side—and finally to a farm in the "boonies" of northern Maryland. None of them was really home for me.

In Pacific Grove, I'd stroll past Lovers Point, up to one of the little grocery stores on Lighthouse Avenue or to Holman's. I got my first library card. On weekends, Kevin and I sometimes walked to Cannery Row, stopping for a drink at Flora's. Closer to home, we walked up and down the streets of the old Retreat nearby, admiring the old cottages. It wasn't long before I came to realize that I had found my true identity—I was born to be a small town girl! I was home at last!

The years have passed. Our children grew up here, playing in Caledonia Park and eating "face cookies" from Scotch Bakery. We walked them to school at Robert Down, bought one house and then moved to a bigger one, higher up but still overlooking the ocean. I helped found the Heritage Society, joined three other women in the Wild Goose Chase Quilt Shop for a few years, discovered beautiful St. Mary's church and eventually became a priest. Our children love to come back with their children. Now I am happily growing old with Kevin right here in Pacific Grove. I'm still delighted to be a small town girl, a "girl" celebrating her 47th year in my beloved Pacific Grove.

1940's Giggly Girls for Life
Ella Magsalay Corona

Life as a young child in Pacific Grove in the late 1940s was, for me, a very exciting time.

We lived for a short time at the hotel located on Lighthouse Avenue and Forest Avenue, three doors down from Rexall Drugs and above Purity Bakery. Every morning you could smell fresh-caught fish from the ocean and fresh bread from the bakery below. It was a fish sandwich waiting to happen.

It was just heaven!

My brother Ray, sister Alvina and I attended St. Angela's Catholic School. Dad was a chef at the dinner club called The Blue Ox in Monterey. Because Dad didn't drive, he always chose a place in town near the bus stop. So we grew up mainly downtown. Christmas in Pacific Grove was so exciting! We so enjoyed the Christmas displays in Holman's Department Store windows, the electric trains and beautiful Christmas decorations.

What a treat!

Of course, one cannot forget the butterfly parades. My sister Alvina, and I were majorettes; we picked up baton twirling pretty fast and happily marched in the parade.

I met my lifelong friend, Diana Lugone (Diana Dennett Vaughn) at Saint Angela's. We had so much fun growing up. When we weren't laughing, we were eating dill pickles that shriveled up our lips for hours. We were so silly that if a butterfly flew by, we would laugh! We found humor in everything to the point of getting ourselves into trouble with the nuns.

I would not change those memories for anything. Life was good, so serene and safe, and that is perhaps why still today I reside in Pacific Grove.

A Lion, Holman's, Friends The Pool and School
Diana Dennett Vaughn

"History is a cyclic poem written by time upon the memories of man"—Percy Bysshe Shelley

My personal "good ol' days" memories go back to the early 1940s, when I held Grandma Nita Temple's hand as she jerked me back into the doorway of the drugstore on the corner of Lighthouse and Forest Avenue when the air-raid siren went off; it was during WWII, and fortunately just a drill.

I had many walks with Grandma on upper Lighthouse, keeping a watchful eye on that scary, crouching lion overlooking us we walked past 6th Street. Oh, how I wished we were walking faster!

Also from the early '40s, I recall the very happy memory of being able to get a new, sweet, red-flowered dress for Christmas at Holman's Department Store on Lighthouse Avenue. I also received a navy pea coat, size 6 X. I was growing into the last size for "little girls"!

It was fun to go to Holman's. There was the strange and interesting little metal box that took your money on a rail, zooming overhead up to the cashier's office. It would return with your receipt. We would take the elevator with the caged door operated by a uniformed attendant up to the mezzanine. To this day, I miss Holman's.

Much later in the 1940s my uncle Stanley sometimes took me to the beautiful white dunes along the beach at Asilomar. One day, he took one of the very long, bulbous seaweeds and attached it to the back of his panel-van, dragging it behind us as we drove through town. It didn't seem disruptive since there was not much traffic. But then, what did a kid know while eating a large dill pickle, sloshing pickle juice all over herself as well as the interior of the van, all while standing in the back of the van along with the other kids doing the same as we drove around. Obviously, this was not up to today's safety standards! My uncle was a character.

As I grew older, I learned to swim in the old P.G. pool, watch my mom dive off the pier, and I looked forward to every possible beach day and, of course, the hamburger stand—precious memories of Lovers Point.

Going to school at St. Angela's grade school on 8th Street, (now a pre-school), and attending the original St. Angela's Church on Central and 8th, allowed me to make a close P.G. friend, Ella Magsalay Corona, friends for nearly 70 years! We are still laughing despite being in trouble for our behavior back in our school days. We walked in the Butterfly Parade with St. Angela's when it was held on Lighthouse Avenue.

It was over half a century later when I walked in the Parade of Lights on Lighthouse Avenue wearing a replica of my great-great-grandmother's dress from the early California days, along with my friend from school days, Ella. We walked with the Monterey Civic Club.

For many, many years I used to see Warren Claunch, the disabled son of my grandmother's friend, who lived on Pine Avenue, selling newspapers from his motorized, custom wheelchair on the southwest corner of Forest and Lighthouse. As a young person, I thought he was like a fixture and would always be there.

While a teenager in the '50s, it was a fun game deciding last minute if I would drive to town on upper or lower Lighthouse. Everyone I knew did this. It was legal to drive both directions on either road and there wasn't much traffic. Now, those really were the "good ol' days"!

John Courtney and Carol Anne Matranga, My Parents
Laura Courtney Headley

John Courtney was a valley boy, raised in Visalia, California. When he was 15 (in 1960), he enrolled in a summer exchange program run by California high schools and was placed in Pacific Grove for a summer of marine biology coursework. He stayed with the Graham family in a large, gracious home on the corner of Junipero and Fountain. (The Grahams ran a print shop downtown.) John greatly enjoyed his time here that summer. He learned to love the ocean and would later become an avid surfer.

Carol Anne Matranga was a valley girl, raised in Gilroy, California. Her family came to the seaside whenever they could, and she always loved Pacific Grove.

When John was only 18 years of age, he was involved in a near fatal car accident on Pacheco Pass. He was taken by ambulance to Wheeler Hospital in Gilroy. He was in terrible shape on arrival, and his family—who had driven from Visalia—asked that a priest be called to give him last rights. This being done, John's parents sat at his bedside, waiting and hoping for the best. Carol was a "Candy Striper" (volunteer) at the hospital, and she came into John's room in the ICU to bring supplies and check on the patient. John happened to open his eyes as she entered the room, and when she left, he spoke for the first time since the accident, saying, *"Who was that?!"*

During the four year courtship that followed, while John took classes at Cabrillo College and Carol completed her nurse's training in Carmel and at Fort Ord, they often met for a picnic at Berwick Park in Pacific Grove. They would lie on their backs on a blanket in the park, looking up at the sky and the trees and imagining that one day, if they could manage it, they'd settle down here.

But John's work took the young family to Santa Cruz first, and he built a successful Physical Therapy practice there, raising three children as Carol worked at his side in the Dominican Hospital office.

Finally, nearing their retirement, John and Carol found a home in Pacific Grove and moved here permanently in 1998. John volunteered at the Pacific Grove Natural History Museum and Carol, a sculptor, moved into a studio at the Pacific Grove Art Center. We lost John to cancer in 2010, but there were many happy years together in their beloved Pacific Grove before his passing. Now Carol is here—along with her daughter and family—enjoying visits from her sons and their families. They all love Pacific Grove and can easily see why "Grammie and Pop" just had to come back here to stay.

Love Affair Decades in the Making
Tim and Marie David
Tim-retired Public Safety, Marie-Educator

I can't point to a specific time when our love affair with Pacific Grove began. I do recall my first trip to Monterey as an elementary school student. It involved a long bus ride from the Central Valley to Fisherman's Wharf some 20 years before the existence of the Monterey Bay Aquarium. If that 1960s field trip served an educational purpose, it was lost on this "average" student, yet something magical about Monterey and the wharf remained.

My parents were not travelers, resulting in a void lasting until the mid-70s, when a teenage right-of-passage provided the freedom to rediscover the coastal paradise on my own.

By the late 1970s, the Monterey Peninsula served as a "date" destination, eventually leading to a 1978 Carmel Highlands Inn nuptial. The Monterey Peninsula became our respite from the Central Valley, particularly during unbearably hot summers. During those early years we suffered from a geographical ignorance shared by many visitors, thinking Monterey was somewhat inclusive. Departing Cannery Row, driving past Lovers Point, along Sunset Avenue and ultimately back to Highway 1, we mistakenly thought we had never left Monterey.

It was sometime during the following decade we discovered the quaint little town west of Monterey. The 1980s also led to parenthood and the introduction of our children to the Monterey Peninsula. Our son shares

Where My Mother Walked—Jacquelin LaVine Jones

I have always loved Pacific Grove. Ninth Street and Lighthouse, where the statue of the Virgin Mary now stands, was the site of our first home I remember. It was wonderful.

One night the garage next door caught fire. My mother was frightened because her bedroom was on the first floor and all five of us children had the three bedrooms upstairs. So when I was five, we moved across town to 210 Granite St. That is where I grew up. It was a perfect location up Pacific Street from the beach, near Caledonia Park and the ballpark—close to everything we wanted and needed.

I lived in Pacific Grove until I got married and we had our first daughter, Anna. Then my husband's job took us to Watsonville.

Pacific Grove was still my home and my husband always said the car could get here without a driver, we were here so much.

A few years after my husband, Glenn, retired, we came home for good. I always knew I would return to the place I loved most on earth, to walk on the same sidewalks where my beloved mother walked.

the Monterey Bay Aquarium's birth year of 1984. Our daughter followed in 1987 and her childhood dream was to someday work with sea otters at the Aquarium.

Pacific Grove and occasionally Carmel became our go-to destination during the late 1980s, 1990s and into the new millennium. We patronized inns on Asilomar Boulevard, the Conference Grounds and years later our favorite bed and breakfast, the Old St. Angela's Inn.

During these decades we formed memories of biking 17 Mile Drive, walking on Asilomar Beach, swimming in the Conference Ground's heated pool and banana pancakes at the dining hall. Add Good Old Days, Feast of Lanterns, a host of other events, a spectacular land/seascape and who can resist the dream of someday living in Pacific Grove?

That undeniable dream became increasingly irresistible fueled by intolerance for Central Valley summers. To leave the oppressive heat and arrive to a cool bay breeze is literally breathtaking.

In 2008 we were fortunate to have the opportunity to fulfill our dream. Our P.G. cottage has served as our summer/weekend retreat and we absolutely love it here. Our presence on the Peninsula provided an opportunity for our daughter's wedding at the Carmel Mission as well as our son's Monterey wedding. The Monterey Peninsula and specifically Pacific Grove are such a special place that our children are now following us. Our daughter, son-in-law and grandson moved to the Peninsula in 2016. Speaking of our daughter, she volunteers at the Aquarium, working with sea otters.

We are truly living the dream in Pacific Grove.

My submission is dedicated to my wife of 38 years ... thank you for your patience and support.

The Robert J. Downeys
We Put the Fun Back into Hospice
Yolanda Zena Corby

My father, Robert J. Downey, lives in his home on Grand Avenue behind the massive Monterey Cypress that he planted in the 1970's. About five months ago, my father suffered a profound stroke. He also has some dementia. We never planned to move him into a nursing home. Though we never discussed it as a family, I see now that that is just not our style. He would be frightened and we would be worried.

Because he is unable to walk, he spends his days and nights either in a hospital bed or a recliner in the living room. The recliner is best because he can be out in the middle of all the activities in the household. Not long ago, my sweet brother and sister in law moved their family into the house so that my mother could receive more support. We also got Hospice services started for him. I travel from Santa Cruz for three days each week to nurse my father as my brother goes to work as a Paramedic. In our family there are also two children and a dog, so the household can be fairly chaotic.

Now that five months have gone by, we have gotten into a fine rhythm together. My mother and my sister in law do the majority of the cooking. My brother takes care of my dad, lifts him into and out of the wheelchair, takes him uptown for coffee, does all the home and yard maintenance, and parents his two children. I also care for my dad, I do endless cascades of laundry and dishes, and I hang out with the children.

The children just act their ages, and they are very sweet with their Oompa. They bring him flowers and gifts, they hug and kiss him, they stroke his hair. One evening I noticed that our 7-year-old girl was dancing for Oompa. Recently I photographed our 9-year-old boy climbing into the hospital bed for a cuddle. We eat dinners together, we chat and plan constantly, we laugh and cry. We somehow manage to do this very grim work with love and humor. This possibility was not immediately evident in previous years.

My mother is nine years younger than my father. She is beautiful and resilient. She never stops cooking, and she never refrains from voicing her opinion on anything, including us. Even though we are fully grown adults.

I could never say enough about the Hospice staff. Aides, nurses, doctors, movers, a physical therapist and delivery workers have all come to our house to help us look after our father. Without exception they have been gentle sand compassionate. They spend a great deal of time teaching us family caregivers how to do things for dad. Even though I am a Nurse-Midwife, and my brother is a Paramedic, we have learned so much about how to care for someone with limited mobility.

I was never drawn to elder care as a younger student. I have very bad memories or watching my grandmother's 70year decline at Beverly Manor, and as a young child it was very off- putting. The place smelled bad, the residents sat tied into their wheelchairs, there was always someone yelling in the background. It was terrible. I never thought I would have the strength to do home care for a loved one.

But this pulling together of the family to make it happen, and the generally humorous and lighthearted atmosphere which pervades the home really makes it all possible. Don't worry. We also scream and fight and cry. We are just a normal family.

We have always loved living in Pacific Grove. It used to be somewhat rough around the edges when I was a kid, and now look at it! The people are universally kind, the city is very walkable, and no matter where you cast your gaze you see something beautiful. I am more than delighted to see my niece and nephew grow up here.

I will really miss my father when he is gone. I am very grateful to be able to take care of him like this before he leaves us. Take care.

"Tiny Angels with Stained Glass Wings"
Jan Austin
living with gratitude and joy

As a fourth-generation Monterey County resident, my roots run deep in Salinas Valley loam. My great-grandmother Filomena Bontadelli Jacop emigrated from Ticino, Switzerland, to settle, with many other Swiss immigrants, in South County where they often found work on local dairy farms.

Spending more than twenty years as a house- and pet-sitter in Pebble Beach, Carmel, Monterey, Pacific Grove, Carmel Highlands and Carmel Valley gave me the opportunity to experience "living" in various communities on the Monterey Peninsula.

In the mid-1990's when I first met Wrigley, a black Labrador who lived on Spruce Avenue in Pacific Grove, I fell in love . . . both with Wrigley and with Pacific Grove. Because his parents traveled a lot (they once went to China for a weekend), Wrigley and I spent many days meandering around this charming town. I knew I would one day make my home here.

I felt like Alice in Wonderland the first time I saw the magic carpet of pink ice plant in bloom along the coastline. I've been enchanted by this magical wonderland ever since.

My first visit to the Butterfly Sanctuary inspired me to compose some poetry. Some of my words from 1995 were: "In Pacific Grove, California, in a cathedral of trees . . . heaven has opened its portals . . . spilling tiny angels with stained-glass wings."

In 2014 I was blessed to find my perfect little home near Lovers Point in Pacific Grove. After literally walking just ten feet into the living room, I knew with every fiber of my being that this was to be my home. The clarity and certainty I experienced is similar to what you feel when you know you're adopting the puppy that is absolutely the perfect match for you.

Living car-free is easy here since it's only a half mile walk up to town. The weekly farmers market, Grove Market, the library, post office, bank, Back Porch Fabrics and the best thrift shops around are all an easy stroll from my home, sweet Pacific Grove, home.

Saturday night ballroom dancing at historic Chautauqua Hall has been a weekly highlight since I took my first lessons there in 2000. My life wouldn't be the same without this cherished dance community.

Thursday mornings find me walking with The Elderberries, a local ladies' walking group. Together we discover and explore trails and paths around our beautiful area.

I'm blessed to spend my days doing the writing and photography that feed my creative soul, walking my doggies, Joy and Star, along the Rec Trail, and now working on a new project of collaborating on a Field Guide to Monterey County Butterflies. My life is blessed and I am grateful every day.

History Then and Tweets Now
Alex Hulanicki

@alexhulanicki
#PacificGroveMemorialDay2017 *Just saw a fawn running across 13th St into the waist-high grass of Greenwood. Where's mama deer?*

@alexhulanicki
#MissingMamaDeer *Is on Monterey Avenue, below Central, passing a deck party --looks like tourists with Coronas and chardonnay in hand. Boats rock on the shimmering bay. Where are the children?*

@alexhulanicki
#MIA Children *No children in the hood, only in the hands of the rest of the world's mamas on the rec trail of the last hometown. Playgrounds empty and locked.* ☹

Oh, how The Last Hometown has changed yet retained its image since 60 years ago, when the children of parents who came here from around the world in the post-WWII era and at the height of the Cold War to teach Russian, Polish, German and Chinese at the Army Language School (now the Defense Language Institute), following instructions in their parents' native languages at home and learning to be American on the streets and alleys of Pacific Grove. Goals on the streets: speak English without an accent, try not to pick a fight when other kids tease you with the Polish nickname (Aleshka) they hear Mama call at dinner time, and try not to cry when the fight happens anyway.

We were kids of the streets—not flower children—of the 1960s. Our "Rec Trail" was the bayside railroad track on which the freight train chugged twice a day to and from the sand plants in Del Monte Forest (now the Inn and Links at Spanish Bay), and sometimes we put a shiny penny on the rail to be flattened for our amusement. The rocky shoreline was our walkway to Lovers Point. In the

The Chrysler Seat Cover Factory on Cannery Row.

summer, every weekday at the Plunge we had swimming lessons led by the indefatigable Mrs. Baker (her daughters Larise and Laverne also became swim teachers) in saltwater pumped in from the cove; eventually, the pump house pipes disintegrated and the huge pool was filled with sand to become today's volleyball court.

We begged to get rides on the glass-bottom boats, then spent nickels for squid, a hook, line and sinker to try to catch what we had seen under the swan boat's curtain—no luck.

But I was lucky enough to get a nickel now and then from Mrs. Bruno on Carmel Avenue. She was Nana of Raymond and Rosie Ramirez who visited on weekends, and the only woman who worked fulltime in the neighborhood. How did a seven-year-old know she worked hard at the NAFTI plant, making seat covers for cars and boats in the building now called American Tin Cannery? The nickel she handed me was covered in the cheap hand cream she slathered on her chafed hands. My assignment was to walk the six blocks up the alley, past Holman's (okay, I stopped for a few minutes to check out the toys on the mezzanine) to Marrone's Top Hat Market for "*mortadella* and a pack of Marlboro's" and Hector DeSmet's Purity Bakery for French bread. A note for the cigarettes and money to purchase the items were unnecessary because she had an account at each store. By the time I came back after 5:00 p.m., I knew it was close to dinner time. I could smell Mrs. Bruno's meat sauce from two blocks away on High Street (now Ed Ricketts Lane). Mrs. Pires's sweet bread was ready to pop out of the oven. Mrs. Locke's fried chicken was attracting all the friends of her five children. It was time for my sister Helen and I to go home. Mama was about to shout "obyat gutova" because the boiled Polish meatballs, potatoes and vegetables were on the table. My father was about to be dropped off by Mr. Kovalenko, who chauffeured daily in his drab olive Ford.

Fords ruled our street. Mr. Locke, who worked shifts at the Del Monte Sand Plant, had a Ford truck and station wagon, and a trailer. So, summer weekend vacations were a treat for the "neighbor" kids—Leni (Eileen), Raymond and Rosie, and my sister and me.

Mr. Locke could fix our bikes, pitch in our three-person baseball games—pitcher's hand was an out, so was the home run into Mrs. Harris's yard because we were forbidden to climb the fence to get the tennis ball back. In our football games, we drew plays—"cut left at the fender of Mr. Avila's car"—and celebrated touchdowns. Mr. Locke was a good golfer so we made a putting green in his front yard under the "monkey tail tree." Double or nothing was the bet until we kids, particularly oldest son Roger, finally sunk a putt to clear our debt. More than a half-century later we still owe a debt of gratitude to Ray and Lorana Locke for welcoming all of us into their Italian-Irish American home—the Rec Club of Carmel Avenue.

Pacific Grove back then had a Recreation Department of sorts—Rec Club run by Ruby Nodilo, Peanut League run by her son Rob Johnson, and various senior activities overseen by Topper Arnett. This was all before organized youth leagues arrived in Pacific Grove. It wasn't until we turned 12 in 1965 that Pacific Grove Little League was organized. It was prescient that the first homerun hit in that league was by John Sidney Miller at the Municipal Ball Park. He went on to become a coach at Pacific Grove High and Recreation Director of Pacific Grove for 27 years, organizing activities for boys and girls, and men and women of all ages.

We were too young for the Summer of Love, but we were old enough to wander the streets, play in the abandoned canneries of New Monterey, venture farther across the Peninsula on our bikes to Seaside and stare at Hell's Angels and their Harleys outside a bar where In-n-Out Burger now resides. We didn't tarry, fearing that we would catch hell from the Angels.

We didn't have play dates. "Go out and play and be home for dinner at five-thirty" was the only contact we had with our moms after school. We learned how to block errant throws on our makeshift baseball diamond bounded by the gutters on hilly Carmel Avenue so we wouldn't have to chase the ball across Central. The oak tree-filled "empty lot" on Lighthouse was our construction site—forts made with cardboard boxes we salvaged from nearby McMahan's Furniture (now Hambook's Auction Center)—until modernity came to our Retreat 'hood with the construction of two apartment houses.

Sometimes we even ventured under the streets with flashlights in hand and visions of netherworld creatures in mind. Our adventure started at the storm outfall at

Greenwood Park and ended under the football field of the middle school at Sinex Avenue. Looking back at that now, maybe that wasn't such a good idea. But what did we know?! We were fearless, on the loose, at least as far as the Bay Rapid Transit (now MST) buses and our bikes would take us. What our moms didn't know wasn't going to hurt us. Not getting home by dinnertime would.

As we got old enough for afternoon paper routes, delivering *The Herald*, we had a little more spending money: the Bus Depot at Lighthouse and 16th, next to the Grove Theater, for penny jawbreakers and Topps baseball card packs (including the godawful pink gum) for a nickel. That nickel gave us a chance to collect our favorite Giants—the Willies, Mays and McCovey, Juan Marichal, and, god forbid, Dodger Sandy Koufax, who was not such good trade bait. The Saturday afternoon double-bill matinees were only 35-cents, well worth the admission to keep up with Zorro, Jack Armstrong and Palladin.

Nobody dropped us off at the theater, the ball park, and school. We walked, we rode, and by high school, got rides from friends. By that time, Roger had a Bultaco motorcycle and I hung onto his back. Sadly, Roger died at 22 in a solo motorcycle accident. Sadly, other high school classmates died in the Vietnam War.

Sadly, as I walk through the old neighborhood, no children argue over fair or foul balls; the small Victorian cottages have been renovated and expanded into multimillion-dollar mansions, but some families linger. Mrs. Cabral is tending to her junipers. Her son lives next door. Her daughter has moved on, as have most of us, to make our homes in other towns. But first and, in our hearts, Pacific Grove is our last hometown.

@alexhulanicki Will Mama deer make it home in time for dinner? #MissingMamaDeer

(Alex Hulanicki was a news reporter and editor for the *Monterey County Herald* for 22 years. A graduate of Pacific Grove High School, Monterey Peninsula College and Stanford University, he is an adjunct instructor in English and Journalism at Monterey Peninsula College, and he is a public information consultant in politics and election campaigns. He makes his home in Salinas with his wife Joan Weiner, also a former *Herald* editor and now retired from public information and news at California State University-Monterey Bay.)

What a Wonderful Place to Grow Up!
Sheri Stillwell Hauswirth

My mom and my dad were high school sweethearts and got married on July 4, 1951. By 1955 all three of us kids were born—my older sister Suzy, me—Sheri—in the middle, then my little brother Tommy. We all marched every year, K through 6th grade, in the Butterfly Parade. I remember when my sister was in kindergarten in the bungalow at Robert Down School (where the co-op preschool is today) and she didn't want to go by herself. We were exactly a year apart and the teacher told my mom I could walk with her if she made my costume. I was four. I think I hold the record of the most times marching in the parade (14 years), since I also played the flute in the junior high and high school bands.

Christmas in Pacific Grove was a wonderful time of the year for kids. Our parents drove us around when it got dark to look at the lights and yard decorations in Candy Cane Lane and on Egan Avenue. We rode the Santa Express Train from the old train depot in Monterey to P.G. and Santa handed out candy canes to all the children. I remember my mom taking us to see Santa Claus at Holman's Department Store. We had to go up the front stairs to the mezzanine where the toys were. Santa sat in a big chair and my brother, sister and I waited in line to see him. We were so excited to tell him what we wanted for Christmas. For many years we would walk from our house up to the corner of Pine and Grand to listen to the Singing Christmas Tree. This was very popular and a lot of people came to hear the Christmas carols.

We loved going for rides in our 1958 wood-paneled Country Squire station wagon with our parents. We often drove along Ocean View Boulevard to look at the waves and the beautiful pink ice plant. Sometimes we would see Frank's orange food truck parked along Asilomar and we would stop for hot dogs and ice cream. Everybody seemed to know Frank.

We loved going to the old Lovers Point drive-in for

burgers, shakes and onion rings. On cold days we would stop by for hot chocolates topped with lots of whipped cream. Another favorite was driving up to the A & W at the top of Forest Hill for dinner. The girls would skate out to your car to take your order. They would hook a metal tray onto your window to put your food and drinks on. They served the best root beer floats in ice cold, frosty glass mugs. What a treat!

We would spend many hours at the P.G. Library as kids and later as teenagers doing research for school papers. My daughter loves to read and she pointed out that it is an old Carnegie Library. Many of these have been torn down and replaced with more modern ones, which is a shame. Pacific Grove is lucky to still have it. Before we could really read, my mom would take us down for story time in the big room with all the murals on the wall. There was always a very nice librarian who read stories to us. The kids all sat on the floor in front of her and our moms sat behind us in the little chairs. We always enjoyed this quiet time in this very special room.

My dad was a fireman in Pacific Grove and we lived just down the street from the fire department and next door to the Rec Club on 16th Street. This is where all the high school kids hung out. Ruby and Topper ruled the roost and you had better follow their rules or you'd get kicked out. Friday nights were hoppin' after the football games. We would climb up on the roof, lie on our stomachs and watch through the big glass skylights at the teenagers dancing. We never got caught.

A couple of years later we moved a few blocks over to 18th Street. There was a great playground for kids in the neighborhood. We all played outside after school and on the weekends. We lived on a hill and it was "take your life in your own hands" as my sister and I put on our skates (with a key that we wore around our necks) and try to make the turn at the bottom of our block onto Laurel Avenue. My brother had his trusty skateboard that my dad made him out of a 2x4 just long enough for his two feet to stand on. There were four wheels nailed to it. Sometimes Suzy and I would sit on it and go down the sidewalk. When Tommy rode it, he just jumped off when he got to the corner.

Back in those days we were allowed to skate at the fire station on the "smooth cement" in front of the doors where the fire trucks were parked inside. If they got a call, we knew to move out of the way fast! The loud whistle would blow several times and we could tell by the sequence where the fire was. My mom would look on the list that my dad had posted by the phone.

We belonged to the wonderful P.G. Fire Deptartment family for many years growing up, playing with all the kids whose dads my father worked with. The Comptons, Browns, Consiglios, Cowens, Kirkmans and Rosses were some that I recall. We always looked forward to the firemen's picnic that was held every year at George Washington Park. There were barbecued hot dogs, salads and Harold Compton's famous home cooked beans—a huge pot full! We played relay games and had rides on Old Engine #1 which was a LaFrance fire truck built around 1910. It is still at the P.G. Fire Deptartment and you can see it in the Good Old Days Parade. In the afternoon there was always a big family softball game. These were great times with friendships that lasted well beyond high school.

My dad designed and built the mechanical Santa's Workshop that was displayed for many years on the roof of the Fire Department. He cut out all the wood pieces; Bob Ross painted them and Denny Gardner did all the electrical work so the toys could move along on the conveyor belt as the elves made them. Many of the firemen helped work on this and people came from all over to see it. Joe Pagnella, a volunteer fireman, puts this display up at his home every year now in Candy Cane Lane. Howard Cowen built the tall mechanical fireman which stood for years in front of the Fire Department every Christmas. It's now a metal robot and stands in front of his home, also in Candy Cane Lane.

In the evenings back in the early 1960s we would gather up the neighborhood kids and play kick-the-can under the street lamp in the middle of the intersection at 18th Street and Laurel Avenue. It was kind of like hide and seek. If someone saw headlights coming they  would just yell out "CAR" and we cleared the streets. Nobody ever got hurt and we always felt safe. Sometimes Mrs. Bowhay, who lived in the big, two-story Victorian home on the corner, would invite us in for a glass of cold lemonade.

Her son, Phil Bowhay, currently writes a column called "Flashback" for the *Monterey County Herald*. Some of his articles include stories of growing up in Pacific Grove. Besides hop scotch, jump rope, marbles and board games that we all took turns hosting in front of our houses, another favorite was roof tag. There were small, one-story homes on 18th Street that were built very close together and you had to chase each other around without touching the ground. Looking back now it seems a little dangerous to me, but I only remember one friend getting a broken arm.

On weekends our mom would tell us what time to be home for meals, lunch and dinner; otherwise we had all of Pacific Grove to explore. We would play heads or tails, which was involved standing on a corner close to your

house and flipping a penny onto the ground. If it was heads you went right and tails you turned left. Sometimes we did this for hours and ended up many blocks from home and often we just went in circles. It was a fun way to pass the time.

Tetherball was popular at our elementary school, so when the school day was over we would rush home and grab the ball and rope that we probably got for Christmas or our birthday and rush back to Robert H. Down School with it. If you didn't have a yard with a tetherball pole, you could just clip your ball onto the poles at the school, only a few blocks from our house. We would play until it was time to come home for dinner.

Saturdays were always a treat if something good was playing at the Grove Theater. It cost 50-cents and my mom would give my brother, sister and me a dime for candy. The candy in the theater behind the glass counter cost a lot and we had the cartoons, newsreel and movie to get through, so we would go next door to the "penny store" to buy our candy. It was the Greyhound bus stop, owned by two sisters who sold tickets, newspapers, magazines and candy … rows and rows of candy! There were red wax lips (a favorite), cola pop bottles that you bit off the top, drank them, then chewed the wax, candy cigarettes if you wanted to be cool, black and red licorice whips, gold mine nugget bubble gum, twist-up candy lipstick, and much, much more. Almost everything in this section was only a penny. You could pick out 10 pieces of candy, which would fill your little brown bag and it would last most of the Saturday matinee.

We often went to Holman's Department Store to shop for things for my mom for Mother's Day and her birthday. It was almost always Shalimar perfume and dusting powder. They gave receipts that you could take downstairs and redeem for S & H Green Stamps. Wow, we thought, because you could paste them in books and pick out neat things at the store down at the end of the block! We would ride the elevator up and down to all the floors in Holman's and look for these receipts in the trash cans in front of the elevator doors. People would just throw them away. It was something fun to do and we eventually filled up our books and traded them in for free stuff. We would also find glass soda pop bottles and turn them in at the Purity Grocery Store (now Grove Market) for a nickel apiece. It was a good way to earn some spending money.

We spent many hours at the Museum of Natural History … it was free and still is! We never tired of walking around looking at all the interesting displays. Our favorite was the booth with the dark velour curtains. You pushed a button and a light came on that turned all the rocks and minerals kind of a purple color. Eventually we learned it was a black light that did the magic.

We moved again over to Bayview Avenue in the mid-1960s. We all had bikes. My sister and I had matching Schwinn Stingray bicycles with banana seats that still hang in my dad's garage today. We rode them everywhere. We lived close to the beach and would ride down to the beach stand for Mrs. Mothershead's famous cheeseburgers. They also sold pink popcorn and soft, frosty ice cream cones. The whole family worked there.

We swam in the cold water, jumped off the small pier, built sandcastles, went for rides in the glass bottom boats and explored over at the "second" beach. I think we would have been in big trouble if my parents had known that we loved to climb on the rocks at the end of Lovers Point where Devil's Slide was located.

My mom would take us kids to the beach quite often when we were younger and I remember her giving all of us each a dime to buy a treat at the beach stand. One time my sister, Suzy, dropped hers in the sand and it was like looking for a needle in a haystack! She didn't find it so my mom gave her another dime and she held it tight in her fist. That was a lot of money back then. When we were little we had swim lessons for a few summers in the cold fog with Mrs. Baker, who was the swim instructor for many years. We shivered and dreaded Saturday mornings at 9:00. We would have rather stayed home in our pajamas watching cartoons. Once you passed your test in the big side of the pool you didn't need lessons anymore. That did require jumping off the high dive board, which seemed like 50 feet above the water!

For some reason it always seemed like the fog would roll into Pacific Grove the day after school got out in June, then disappear just after Labor Day weekend, when school would start up again! We swam for many years at the Plunge, as it was called. You would pay to rent a wire basket to put all your stuff in and wear the safety pin with a number on it pinned to your bathing suit. You had to walk through two shallow water troughs to make sure you didn't have any sand on your feet from the beach before you could jump in the salt water pool. There was the big pool and the baby pool which was divided by a short, wide concrete wall. The pool never felt like it was heated so when we got out of the water we always looked forward to the hot showers inside the locker room. This was underneath the old Slats Rooftop Restaurant where the Beach House Restaurant is today.

We loved riding our bikes uptown to the Scotch Bakery on Lighthouse Avenue across from Holman's Department Store. For some reason I was the only one who ever had money to spend (I got good grades on my report cards!), so I would treat my sister and brother to many treats over the years. I think our favorite was the chocolate éclairs with real whipped cream.

There were quite a lot of kids who lived on Bayview Avenue and Pacific Street, so we often would all meet down at Caledonia Park for a pick-up game of baseball on the old dirt-and-dead-grass diamond. Sometimes we stayed down there for hours. Kids would come and go, but we always had enough for two teams. It reminded me of the movie *The Sandlot*.

I have such fond memories of that park. My dad built a basketball court there and named it after my brother Tommy, who we lost in a snorkeling accident in 1983. For many years, it has been the site of Stillwell's Snow in the Park (now called Stillwell's Fun in the Park), when Santa arrives. Many benches border the court—my sister and I donated one that reads "What a wonderful place to grow up—Suzy, Sheri & Tommy."

We were all born on the Monterey Peninsula and raised in Pacific Grove. My sister and her husband Bill own Pacific Grove Hardware, which my dad built and started. Their son, Willie, works there also. I stayed for 35 years before starting a family and moving to Toro Park Estates. My husband, Bobby, and I are lucky to have parents who remained in Pacific Grove, four blocks from each other for many years. To this day it is always a treat for us and our two sons, Chris and Aaron, to come in for a visit and drive along the path on Ocean View Boulevard enjoying the beautiful Monterey Bay and remembering the wonderful memories of growing up here. My mom, Beverly, passed away on July 2, 2015, two days short of their 64th wedding anniversary. My dad, Richard, has many, many friends in Pacific Grove who are very special to him. It's a close-knit community that is like a big family. He is lovingly known as "Mr. P.G." around town. My daughter, Lauren, now lives in Pacific Grove, very close to all three of her grandparents, and is making her own life-long memories!

Memories and Rituals
Gary R. Williams

I grew up in Pacific Grove in the 1960s. We lived up the street from the stone mountain lion that perches on the corner of Lighthouse and 6th Street. I can remember looking up at the menacing mountain lion and thinking to myself, "I know it's not real," but just in case, I ran as fast as I could up the hill. Some other things etched in my memory include the soothing sound of the foghorn going off, which sounded like white noise as I snuggled in my bed. Or hearing the loudspeaker at Lovers Point periodically repeating, "All aboard for the glass bottom boats, going right out again." I remember that the Mothershead family ran both the concession stand and glass bottom boats. I also remember watching the freight train go along what is now the bike path by the waterfront on its way to Spanish Bay to get the sand, and kids showing their flattened pennies after the train had run over those pennies.

My fondest memory is a Saturday ritual that I engaged in with three of my friends. The day started with crime, as I stole change from my mother's coat pocket. My friends and I would then go down to watch the matinée at the Grove Theater. I remember the theater owner (I think) frowning at us as we entered. He had the whitest hair I had ever seen, which was accented by the black suit that he always wore. I don't think he liked kids, though I'm sure he liked our money.

Following the movie, we would go next door to the Greyhound bus depot and buy candy (they had a pretty good variety). After this purchase, we would walk to the Sprouts-Reitz (five and dime) store and play with the toys. When we got tired of that, we would go to the toy department on the second floor of Holman's Department store to play with the toys and ride the elevator.

To cap off the day, we went across the street to Scotch Bakery and bought donuts. I still remember our surprise when we saw the enormous donut (the equivalent of three regular donuts) that sold for a quarter. The regular donuts were only six cents.

For me, this time in Pacific Grove was a largely innocent time, though I did not remain unaffected by all that was going on in the larger world around me. Nevertheless, I really appreciate growing up in P.G., with the freedom I had to roam the city, unsupervised by adults, engaging in sometimes only marginally safe activities.

My son has likened Pacific Grove to the Shire (from Tolkien's *The Hobbit*), and in many ways I think he's right.

Life Was Simple Back Then
Pamela Furman Chrislock

I was born in January of 1948. My parents brought me home from the old Carmel Hospital to a small bungalow on Foam Street in New Monterey. Foam Street and its parallel neighbor, Cannery Row, were serene back then, except for the ongoing din associated with the active and prosperous canneries that lined "The Row." The smell of the sardines, the rumbling of fish trucks and the barking of the sea lions gave this "New" Monterey community a humble richness. Pacific Grove seemed like some faraway destination where Doc Ricketts spent time collecting his specimens and you could watch the train hug the rails as it passed Asilomar on its way to the old Del Monte Sand Plant at Moss Beach in Pebble Beach.

Change came slowly back in those days. My earliest memories of New Monterey's quieter neighbor, Pacific Grove, are of the original Saint Angela's Church on Central Avenue, Holman's Department Store, rides around the Pacific Grove coastline, picnics on the beach located behind Hopkins Marine Station and eating at our favorite restaurants.

Life was simple back then. I used to walk to St. Angela's with my mother for Sunday mass and attended summer catechism instruction there as well. My reward for participating in catechism was to spend the afternoon swimming in the salt water pool called "The Plunge," located at Lovers Point. (The Plunge was opened in 1939 as part of the Feast of Lanterns celebration.)

Other fond memories include eating in the car at Langston's Lovers Point Inn across from the Old Bath House. You could eat inside or you could order at the take-out window and they would bring your food to your car. Fish and chips or chicken in a basket were my favorites. We also enjoyed family dinners at Slats Roof Garden Restaurant. There was so much to do in an around Lovers Point.

As kids we also loved to go to the Grove Theater for a Sunday matinee. A few quarters would gain you admittance and a dime would buy your favorite candy. I can still remember the theme song from the movie *A Summer Place* that I saw there in my teens. Portions of the movie were filmed at the La Porte Mansion (the Pine Island Inn in the movie) which still stands at the corner of 17 Mile Drive and Lighthouse.

The Holman's were a prominent family and Holman's Department Store was a popular shopping destination. If you needed something, they would most likely carry it. They had a department for all your needs. You could purchase millinery, jewelry, cosmetics and fragrances, clothing, furniture, appliances, toys, etc., and later on you could even buy your groceries there. Additionally, Holman's restaurant, located at the top of the Holman's building, always served up a wonderful variety of luncheon specials. As a kid and an adult, the ride up in the elevator was as exciting as the views.

As a young adult, I moved away but I always found myself returning to the "Last Hometown." Rents were cheap, housing was abundant, and I loved the sleepy ambiance of the town. So, in the early 70s, I joined the ranks of homeowner.

Pacific Grove was still a quiet, friendly place to live. If you rolled into town after 9:00 p.m., you would find her downtown already fast asleep. However, if you wanted to find a place to "wet your whistle," you would have to go elsewhere, as Pacific Grove remained the last "dry town" until 1969.

By the end of the 80s, I had become a mother and my hometown became the place where I would raise my own child. Soon my days were filled with Sunday mass at the new St. Angela's Church, shopping at Ford's Department Store (originally Holman's), movies at the new movie theater in Pacific Grove (Lighthouse Cinema) swim lessons at the Lovers Point kiddie pool, cookies from Scotch Bakery, and school days at Robert Down Elementary School. With that came the many celebrations for which Pacific Grove is known, such as the Feast of Lanterns and the Butterfly Parade. We carried lanterns and huddled at the beach for the Feast of Lanterns and grew from monarchs to miners in the Butterfly Parade.

Pacific Grove has changed more than I like to think, but it remains a place of comfort to each of us who made a "full circle" in America's Last Hometown. It is interesting to me, that in reflection, our memories are like a roaring fire in an old hearth; they warm our hearts and bring comfort to our soul.

Playing Outside in 1965
Denise Mellinger Slate

I was eight when my family moved to Pacific Grove, California. My mother and my four siblings drove from Southern California to start a new life. We settled on Pine Circle, at the top of Ransford by the quarry. We enrolled at David Avenue Elementary School, all five of us. My brothers were DeLane, ten, Dickie, seven and Dana, four. My sister Dawn was five.

The school sat on the edge of the Del Monte forest. The playground equipment was sparse so we were allowed to play in the woods. Our imaginations ran wild as we created our sectioned-off houses. We used acorns as tender to buy things from each other. After school, we would walk up the hill to the neighborhood store to buy candy with our soda bottle nickels. Then we would beat it over to the quarry to scramble across the boulders.

Our mother was a visiting nurse to Mrs. Gann in Pebble Beach. She was the widow of Ernest K. Gann, author of many fine works, including "The High and the Mighty."

When Mom wanted some peace, she would drop us off at the Dennis the Menace Park. We had a grand time on the train, crossing the rope bridge and actually sticking our heads into a lions' mouth to get a drink of water! What fun we had together.

In the fall, we spent afternoons cutting up newspaper and making confetti for the Friday night football game at Pacific Grove High School. We walked through the woods, in the dark, clutching our candy bars and our grocery bags full of confetti. What a mess we made.

On Saturdays, mom dropped us off at the State Theatre on Alvarado Street. For fifty cents you could spend all day there. At Christmas, Santa was on stage in between the movies. Everyone cheered! After the show, Santa handed everyone a big candy cane as he stood by the ticket booth. That night we cruised Candy Cane Lane. The wonderful excitement of it still exists in me.

Preparing for the Butterfly Parade was thrilling, knowing that every kid in town was going to march. We spent days planning our costumes. Hundreds of people lined the streets and cheered us on.

I had become the marble queen of the neighborhood, winning everyone's marbles. One day, when the forest was still at the bottom of Ransford, I lined up all the kids at the top of the hill and filled their fists with marbles. We let them go at the same time. They raced down the street, crossed David Avenue and bounced into the woods.

From playing in the quarry to searching the beaches of Asilomar and Lovers Point for beach glass, the kids of Pacific Grove had full reign in town. We spent most of our time playing outside and exploring a fantastic wonderland of adventure.

Today, I work at Trader Joe's on Forest Avenue, just over the fence where I went to the moon in a cardboard box!

"The Last Hometown" is Who I Am
Kelly Lesch-Gonzalez

I was fortunate to have been born and raised in Pacific Grove. Even though I no longer live in Pacific Grove the "Last Hometown" is and always will be a part of who I am. I have the fondest memories of growing up in Pacific Grove. I attended preschool at Robert Down Preschool; kindergarten through sixth grade were spent at Lighthouse Elementary School. Then it was on to P.G. Junior High and P.G. High School.

I am proud to say I marched in the Butterfly Parade for 14 years. First as Fire Prevention Officers in preschool, earning my butterfly wings in kindergarten, and then marching in the parade as part of the junior high and high school marching bands. Now that I look back on those years it was a simpler time of growing up.

Many of the businesses I knew as a kid no longer exist, such as the old movie theater, Sprouse Reitz five-and-dime store, Top Hat Market, Holman's Department Store and my favorite bakery—Scotch Bakery. On Saturday mornings, I remember my dad coming home with an almond coffee ring from Scotch Bakery. For our birthdays, it was always such a special treat to get a birthday cake from Scotch Bakery. And of course, there were the frosted blue whale cookies and the yellow smiley face cookies.

While in elementary school we lived on Ripple Avenue in what I would call the "beach track" area. As soon as school ended for the day we would run down to the railroad tracks and put our pennies on the track before the afternoon train came through to flatten the pennies. After a rainy period, we would catch tad poles from the puddles that were left in-between the tracks. I chuckle when I remember how we would run across the golf course into the clubhouse to buy candy from the vending machine and then run back out as fast as we could because, as kids, we were not supposed to be on or near the golf course or clubhouse.

As we got older we would find our way to the Camp Store next to the Fat Cat Café on 17 Mile Drive. I am always proud to share how I grew up in Pacific Grove and to see the amazement on people's faces when I tell them that. Even though businesses have changed, I was still able to share a little bit of my childhood with my own children when they were young.

On Sundays on our way home from church (First United Methodist Church) or any time we would be in Pacific Grove, we always had time to stop by Scotch Bakery to treat ourselves to a frosted blue whale cookie and a yellow smiley face cookie. They are now college students, but still remember the special cookies from Scotch Bakery.

PACIFIC GROVE RESPONDS TO WORLD WAR II

Pioneer Family Wartime Efforts
Jean Hurlbert Jorgensen
homemaker, friend, nature lover, adventurer

Elgin Clifford Hurlbert and Mary "Mamie" Reeves met as teenagers when their families were homesteading in Blunt, South Dakota in the early 1880s. Hurlberts had come from Nova Scotia and Blaines from Illinois, evidently to have "a better life."

Elgin became a printer, publishing a newspaper while in Blunt. Mary's father was a teacher and carpenter. Life on the prairie proved to be difficult and isolated. Years later Mamie reminisced about taking a picnic out to "the tree": the one tree that was visible in the distance from where they lived. Within a few years the two families had had enough of the challenges of life as homesteaders and moved on to the Santa Clara Valley in California where John Blaine's brother had a fruit orchard.

Elgin had a printing business in Campbell. He and Mamie married in 1893 and moved to Pacific Grove in 1909 with their teenage daughter Elmarie and their 5-year-old son Elgin Blaine. They became very involved with the Methodist Church where Mamie was an organist who accompanied the church choir.

Elgin had a print shop in P.G. and published a weekly paper, "The Argus." Mamie sometimes wrote articles for the paper.

Elgin became the P.G. Postmaster in 1913, a position he held for 9 years. He served as the P.G. City Clerk for many years until his retirement in the 1940s. He also "dabbled" in real estate.

Their daughter, Elmarie Hurlbert Hyler Dyke, became a well-known educator and civic leader and was known as "Mrs. Pacific Grove." An accomplishment of which she was proud was to have helped keep Pacific Grove a "dry town" until the mid 1960s. She had two sons, Bill and Bob Hyler, and many grandchildren and "greats." Her husband Clyde Dyke had Dykes Pharmacy at the corner of Lighthouse and Forest Avenues for many years.

Elgin and Mamie's son Elgin Blaine "Oxy" Hurlbert had various jobs, including being paymaster at Hovden's Cannery, later the site of the Monterey Bay Aquarium. He also served as a county probation officer. As an officer in the Naval Reserve he was on active duty during WW II. Following the war he opted to make the Navy his career, retiring to P.G. in 1960. During retirement he was an active conservationist and leader of the local Audubon Society chapter. His wife, Winifred "Wini" Rugh, came to P.G. as a teacher in the late 1920s. During The War she put in hundreds of hours as a volunteer watching for enemy aircraft at the Air Watching Tower near Asilomar and volunteering with the Red Cross. They had two children, Jerry and Jean, and multiple grandkids and "greats" as well.

As members of this well-known family my brother Jerry and I were aware that if we misbehaved the word would reach home before we did! It was fine to grow up in the Hurlbert family, but it wasn't without its challenges!

I was brought up in P.G., my maiden name is Hurlbert, Elmarie Dyke was my aunt. My grandfather Elgin C. Hurlbert was P.G. postmaster for a time and later City Clerk. My dad, Elgin B. ("Oxy") Hurlbert grew up there, became a career Naval Officer after WWII. etc. etc.

I haven't lived there since the 60s, but spent quite a bit of time there as my parents aged at their home on Mermaid Ave. Mom ("Wini") was the last to go in early 2001. I've lived half of my life in Jackson, Wyoming and am now spending winters in Arizona.

How did "The War" affect our family?

Daddy was in the Naval Reserve for some years prior to World War II and was serving on the aircraft carrier USS Yorktown at the time of Pearl Harbor.

A month later we drove with family members to San Diego where we met Daddy and two cousins who were all in the Navy. The Yorktown was there, soon to leave for the Pacific. We were able to go on board to visit, eat some meals, and see how very big it was—especially huge for me since I was only five at the time.

Daddy going away confused me. Sometimes we'd see a military man in uniform and I'd ask Mother, "Is that Daddy?" That had to have been hard on her. Once I found her sitting crying in the kitchen and tried to comfort her with a hug. Mostly she was very strong. She supported the war effort in many ways.

An Air Watch Tower was on a sand dune near Asilomar. Mother trained there as a volunteer who scanned the skies with binoculars watching for enemy aircraft. Jerry and I stayed with family or friends while she was on duty. We visited her there many times, climbed endless steps to the top. Model planes of U.S., Japanese and German aircraft hung from the ceiling so the observers would know what to watch for. By the end of the war Mother had put in more than 1000 hours there. Fortunately the enemy never came near. She also volunteered at the Red Cross and knit many wool hats for service men fighting in cold places.

Word came eventually that Daddy was okay but that the Yorktown had been sunk in the Battle of Midway. We were a lucky family.

Since Daddy decided to stay in the Navy when the war was over we were in P.G. when he was on ships, and we got to go with him to shore duty stations in Massachusetts, Rhode Island, and New York. I loved to travel and we always drove a different route across the country, visiting national parks along the way. I didn't much like going to new schools. It's not always easy being "the new kid." I took a break from college to be with them in Japan for two years, 1956-58. We studied the language, and Mother and I took many different kinds of art classes. I was pleased and proud of my dad that he was very kind and respectful to these people who had been "the enemy." We loved our time there.

He retired to P.G. in 1960. Having been intrigued by various migrating birds that landed on his ships, he and Mother became active Audubon Society members. They had a camper and went to National Audubon conventions, enjoying visits with friends from Navy days who lived around the country.

Yes, war had been difficult, but it led to our living full lives.

How did "The War" affect P.G. kids?

Our dad was in the Naval Reserve off somewhere on December 7, 1941. Mother, Jerry and I were with friends near Big Sur when one of the boys came running from the store with a paper bag on which the store owner had written "Turn On Your Car Radio. We're at War!" That was how we learned what was happening.

We soon settled into wartime behavior in P.G., getting used to rationing, recycling, hearing sirens that announced air raid drills. At school we'd do "Duck and Cover," getting under our desks, covering our heads with our arms in case a bomb dropped near the school. It felt scary. Every week we'd take some coins to school to buy stamps for War Bonds to help pay for the war.

Since we were on the coast it was feared that we might be bombed by Japanese planes so black curtains covered all our windows at night. That was kind of spooky. Porch lights and car headlights were painted black on the top half so the lights might not be seen from enemy airplanes.

Bacon, butter, and sugar were among the foods only available with coupons or tokens. When we ate meat the melted fat was saved in tin cans, taken to the butcher shop and traded for coupons to buy butter. The fat was used by the military to make bombs.

Gasoline, tires, and shoes were also rationed. Different sized families were assigned different numbers of coupons. Boy Scouts collected and recycled newspapers and tin cans for the war effort. We had a Victory Garden in our back yard to grow some of our own vegetables.

The train station was right behind our house with the passenger train leaving from there to go to San Francisco. Mother would send Jerry and me out to drop letters to Daddy in the mail slot on the side of the baggage car. Soldiers stationed at Fort Ord were brought in buses to get on the train there when they were shipping out. Once a little white dog with black spots was seen there after the train left. Probably some soldier couldn't take his pet along. Mother saw the dog by the post office later and brought him home. That's how we got our dear dog Spotty.

We missed Daddy but there was no choice. Jerry's best friend Jack lived close by and his dad didn't have to go to War because he had an important engineering job at Fort Ord. He became like a dad to my brother. Lucky Jerry.

Eventually the war was over, but our lives were still impacted: Daddy had decided to stay in the Navy as a career so Mother, Jerry and I would be in P.G. when he was on ships but would get to go with him when he had shore duty. We got to experience a wider world.

Before and After the War
High School Class of 1950
Virginia Fox Abplanalp

"The most beautiful place on the face of the earth" is how my grandparents described the Monterey Peninsula when they first discovered it in the mid-1930s. Who could argue? Those of us lucky enough to grow up in Pacific Grove in those early years enjoyed an idyllic setting. The beaches, sand dunes, and forests were our playgrounds. Carmel Valley and Big Sur were a short drive away with their own special beauty to offer. It was a child's paradise. I'm sure none of us can forget the gloomy sounds of the foghorn at night, the sardine cannery whistle summoning the workers to their smelly tasks, or the unmistakable, unavoidable stench of a dead whale or sea lion washed up on the beach. We took for granted the return of the monarch butterflies each fall. They would later put our little town on the map—Butterfly Town, U.S.A. It was in this setting in 1937 that our original class members left the security of their family homes to enter the mysterious portals of Pacific Grove Grammar School for the first time. Miss Oliver awaited, Mr. Down hovered, and their lives would never be the same. The rest is history, which follows.

Fourth Grade 1941-1942

World War II changed things forever. Suddenly there were many new faces as classes became larger due to the population explosion the war brought to us. Camp Ord became Fort Ord almost overnight. The Presidio of Monterey was soon buzzing with activity as was the Del Monte Hotel, appropriated by the Navy. (Or should I say confiscated?) It has never been returned. Bay Rapid Transit buses were overcrowded, the sidewalks in Monterey teemed with servicemen, and military vehicles rumbled down our streets and highways.

Fathers who were not called back into service volunteered to be block wardens to make sure everyone was observing the blackouts. This entailed covering windows and glass doors with dark curtains and painting headlights and porch lights black on top to prevent the light from revealing our positions to the enemy.

Rationing became the norm. Coupon books and cardboard tokens were needed to buy such basic items as meat, sugar, butter, shoes, tires, and coffee. White sheets and silk stockings were scarce as hen's teeth. Gasoline was allocated according to priority to the war effort by some mysterious board in Salinas. Stickers were given out to put on windshields to designate one's allotted quota.

At school we helped by buying War Stamps once a week instead of bringing our savings to be deposited in the bank and entered into a passbook. There was a contest to see which student could save the most stamps. Don Wright still has a certificate honoring him for his contributions.

All during the "duration," as our parents called it, our music classes in the auditorium were devoted to singing the anthem of each branch of the armed services as well as every patriotic song written up to that time. "God Bless America," and He did.

Fifth Grade 1942-1943

By this time, the war effort was in full swing. Recycling became the norm for most households. We collected tin cans and flattened them, created aluminum foil balls, and donated newspapers to the Boy Scout drives. Another way we kids could help was to knead plastic bags of snow-white margarine until the little packets of orange food color broke. We kneaded some more until the whole mass had the color (but never the flavor) of butter. Parents drank "ersatz" coffee, which was apparently a poor substitute for the real thing. My mother improvised by making an imitation apple pie with soda crackers and honey. In retrospect, these were very small sacrifices compared to what was going on overseas.

At school some of us in Miss Bailey's class appeared in a little play promoting the purchase of War Bonds and Stamps. Our costumes consisted of large cardboard coins representing all the denominations. Doug Zug, good sport that he was, portrayed a roll of bills. After presenting it for our student body, we were asked to perform it at the high school, for many civic groups, and eventually at a huge rally at the intersection of Franklin and Alvarado in Monterey. I have no idea how much money we raised, but we were very flattered by all the attention and had lots of fun.

Eighth Grade 1945-1946

The supreme injustice occurred! After eight long years of being underclassmen, just as we were about to assume our rightful roles as school rulers and VIPs, we were herded off to Pacific Grove High School's *basement*! Our status was suddenly lower than a snake's belly. In other words, we were now below the despised freshmen in the pecking order.

We were neither fish nor fowl, being required to walk all the way back to the grammar school for assemblies and other special events. The seventh graders had taken over and we were stared at with idle curiosity.

To make matters worse, some of the more brazen high school boys leaned in the windows of our dungeon-like classrooms to leer at our young, cute, sexy social studies teacher, Mrs. Lawler. She obviously hated every minute of it. We girls could tell by the way she wore those short skirts, bare legs, and spike heel shoes. Her favorite pose was sitting on her desk, legs crossed, in front of every boy who could find a seat. (You know who you were!)

The whole experience of being sent off to the high school was extremely disappointing, to say the least. This was another side effect of the war … a small price to pay when others were doing so much and losing so many.

The wonderful news was that the war ended as our school year began. Such euphoria prevailed that we girls were able to convince the teachers to allow us to wear formals at graduation (a minor miracle!). Our tiny class of approximately 50 kindergartners had mushroomed to 97 by this time.

Freshman Year 1946-1947

We had finally arrived! No longer lowly "boarders" at P.G.HS, we belonged. It may have been the bottom rung, but at least we were on the ladder. After the initial jitters wore off we plunged into the many academic and extra-curricular activities offered by our tiny high school. There was something for everyone—art, music, science, sports, and drama to name a few. For such a small school there was a lot going on.

A.B. Ingham and Gertie Ernst were institutions by the time we got there. Gertie knew us all and all about us and our families. We had few secrets from her.

Unfortunately, the excitement of becoming full-fledged high school students was soon dampened by a devastating event—a mysterious fire destroyed a major part of our school. This loss was felt by everyone connected with it. The blaze, which broke out on a Saturday night during Christmas vacation, demolished the administration building, library and several classrooms. I'm sure that all of us who stood across the street watching it burn remember the empty, helpless feelings we shared. We didn't know until then how much it meant to us.

Miraculously, classes resumed on January 6th, but the repercussions of this disaster were long-lasting. We returned to our lockers to discover that our books were soggy, charred masses and unusable. The acrid smell of smoke was everywhere. Classes were held in very strange places. The typing teacher held forth on the stage of the auditorium while history classes were going on in the balcony. Portables were erected on the tennis courts so we were sent down to play on the city courts a few blocks away. "Teach" put us on the honor system. Some of us took sunbaths instead.

The inconveniences were countless. The glee club and chorus practices were held at 8:00 a.m. in the tower of City Hall. But, as the saying goes, "School keeps," and ours did.

Excerpts from Fox Family History, 1930s

My mother's brother, Blair, was a very exciting uncle to have because we never knew when we went to visit him in Pacific Grove after the war what the evening would hold. Some nights he would put up a big sheet between the living room and dining room. Behind that, he and Curtis, or anyone else he enlisted, would put on pantomimes. They were hysterical because he would pretend to be a doctor performing an operation to remove a whole bunch of stomach parts that were really connected hot dogs!

Other nights he would decide that we should go down to Bixby Creek or Carmel Valley and have a wienie roast. This would be way after dark; the adults would gather up a lot of food and drink and we would drive there, then make a fire, sing songs, roast wienies, and then marshmallows. For a little kid under the age of nine, this was heaven!

Once, before we moved to Del Monte Park, we were living across from a pine forest. I organized a group of kids and decided we should pretend it was a deserted island that we should explore. I also decided we should start a fire and have a wienie roast. We put the fire out carefully but created torches to use as we explored. Just as we started our search, Jim called out my name in horror. I turned to look at him and discovered he had set one of the trees on fire. We all rushed home to tell our parents and to start bringing water. Unfortunately for me, the bucket I grabbed had a hole in it so there wasn't much water left on each trip. Two or three fire trucks turned up because the fire was out of control. Needless to say, we had no support and each of us was soundly spanked. We were afraid to go to town after that because they told us the police were after us.

Around the same time as the fire, we were living at 420 Bennett Street when Grandma Munner decided to dress Dave, Jim and me as characters from *The Wizard of Oz* for the annual Halloween parade at the softball park. Jim was to be the tin woodman. They made a cute outfit for him out of cardboard and spray painted it silver. I was Dorothy, and Dave was the scarecrow. When the crowd saw us, they fell in love with Jim and starting chanting, "We want the woodman, we want the woodman!" He won and I was insanely jealous because we were a team, and I thought all three of us should have won.

Despite all the chores that were expected of me by being the oldest child, living next door to the Del Monte Forest made up for it. All we had to do was go under the barbed wire fence and we were in paradise. There were no other children who ever went there so we had it all to ourselves. We could climb trees, make forts out of branches, and play make-believe by the hour. The pine cones were my subjects and I was Queen of the World. It was always disappointing when we would hear the whistle my mother blew calling us home for dinner.

At night we played hide-and-go-seek and kick-the-can with other neighborhood kids who lived nearby. I even played touch football with the boys—a real tomboy.

Jim and I walked two miles to school and two miles home. Nobody ever worried about kidnappers or child molesters. We were on our own and liked it that way. I even walked to the Baptist Church in New Monterey by myself just because I loved to hear Mrs. Bentley's choir solos. I was only 10 and 11 years old at the time.

One of the funniest things happened at about that time. Bumpy and Munner lived right across the street, as I have mentioned before. All the animals and the clotheslines were behind the house, but we had no back door. My mom kept begging my father to make one and add some steps. He kept putting if off. One day when we got home from school, there was an opening in the back wall of the house the size of a door. My mother had convinced her father to cut an opening so that my dad would then have to make a door. He did. People learned not to mess with my mother.

I guess I decided there was no hope for me as far as family duties once my third brother was born. I mustered all my courage and went down to Holman's Department Store and applied for a job. I was all of 13 years old and in the eighth grade. Much to my surprise, I was hired even after I confronted the manager in the elevator! He put me to work in the advertising department for 35 cents an hour. I did odd jobs to help my boss and saved my salary so that I could make a hair appointment and have my braids cut off. When my dad came to pick me up, he was furious. He said, "I hope you're satisfied. Now you look just like everyone else." I told him that was the whole idea. He didn't speak to me for days.

Pioneers in Del Monte Park

My parents paid $100 for an acre of land in Del Monte Park. Impossible, you say? The year was 1940 and the county was selling quarter-acre parcels for $25 each. After 10 years of being renters, moving from pillar to post all over Southern California, they were anxious to settle down as landowners. They had been lured to Pacific Grove by my mother's parents who had found it accidentally. They wired my parents: "Come up immediately. Have found the most beautiful place on the face of the earth." All of them had grown up in the Midwest and this spot must have looked like heaven to them.

So they did and we lived in various rented homes all over P.G. I was enrolled in Pacific Grove Grammar School in first grade. My dad got a job as a bus driver for the Bay Rapid Transit Company and my mother became the bookkeeper for a grocery store on Lighthouse Avenue called the Top Hat, if I remember correctly. That job only lasted until she arrived for work one day to find that the owner had left town with all the money and his secretary. The front door was locked.

It was while we were living at 420 Bennett Street (it has a new name now) that they must have hatched their plans for buying the property. My younger brother Jim should have suspected that something was up—they spent every evening at the kitchen table and paid absolutely no attention to us as we trashed the living room and their bedroom. We couldn't believe we could get away with what we were doing, but soon all that came to an end as their plan went into motion.

Somehow, they scraped together the funds necessary to buy four of the plots so we could live on a whole acre. There was only one catch … there was no way to reach the plots they had selected.

This is when we became pioneers, as they informed us. Montecito Street stopped at the Alsop's so there was at least one block to clear on that street and then one block to reach our land. Every weekend we found ourselves removing manzanita bushes and whatever else was in the way of our goal of reaching the Promised Land. We did it and then the real work began.

The first item on the agenda for my dad was digging the outhouse. (I could never figure out at the time why he built it with two seats. I couldn't imagine two people using it at the same time!) Somewhere they found an old cast iron stove and set it up in what would be the front yard so my mom could cook meals for when he took a break.

My dad had met an old retired carpenter to help him construct the one-room house that would be our home. He spent another $100 on building materials that consisted of knotty pine boards. There wasn't enough money to provide a foundation. Once the project was finished, they moved the stove into the house and what little furniture we had. Jim and I slept in bunk beds, my parents had a double bed and there was a couch, easy chair, and a kitchen table. That is all I remember.

The site they had chosen was right next to Del Monte Forest and a saw mill, separated by a barbed wire fence. We had no electricity or running water so light was provided by a kerosene lamp. My parents had to take turns climbing under the barbed wire fence to reach a water supply in the mill yard. The mill was no longer active at this time. Just like in the Ma and Pa Kettle movies, when the knots fell out of the wooden wall, my dad nailed a tin can lid over the opening.

It wasn't fancy but it was theirs after 10 years of what seemed like endless moving. They had plans, of course, to add the needed utilities and to expand the home to provide for their growing family. Jim and I didn't realize it, but a baby brother was on the way. He was born November 15, 1941. Three weeks later their plans were put on hold.

December 7 changed life for everyone. My dad was frozen on his bus driving job making only 88 cents an hour. All building supplies were also frozen so we were stuck as we were until after the war. They had managed to get the utilities, including phone service, before the war started. We had chickens, rabbits, and a vegetable garden so we could be fairly self-sufficient.

It would be a long time before the road was paved so we had some interesting times during rainy weather. Our automobile was an old Model A Ford my mother had to crank to get started when she took us to school. We were frequently late.

So there you have it … the story of a home that was certainly humble but meant the world to a young couple who wanted desperately to put down roots.

Memories of World War II
Helen Gehringer

The attack on Pearl Harbor caused some big changes in my family. Much to my mother's distress, Dad (who was 39 and beyond draft age), enlisted in the U.S. Navy Seabees. Off he went to Rhode Island for boot camp where it was so cold his long underwear froze on the clothes line. No dryers in those days. His battalion eventually returned to the West Coast, so we were able to see him briefly before he shipped out to the South Pacific, where he remained for four years.

Here in Pacific Grove we looked forward to Dad's letters, and we kept busy with Mother teaching school and I, age six, attending school and taking dancing lessons as well. Our dance group performed weekly at the USO and, occasionally, at the Army Hospital at Ford Ord. I doubt that the GIs were too excited about seeing little kids dance, but there were some teenage girls in our group that I'm sure were appreciated.

We got used to doing without things. Oleo instead of butter, meatless Tuesday, etc. I always wore a silver pendant with my name, address and phone number on it in case we were invaded and I was separated from my family. Of course, there was no internet or TV in those days and when special news occurred, a newsboy would walk up the streets yelling, "Extra, Extra," and we would run out and buy a newspaper.

Finally, it was all over and Dad returned. We drove up to Camp Parks to pick him up and, since we hadn't seen him for four years, Mother and Dad were obviously looking forward to some time alone. Unfortunately, when we arrived at our home, my gregarious grandmother (who lived across the street) had filled it with friends and neighbors to greet Dad, and they stayed until wee hours of the morning!

Pearl Harbor News Changes Our Town
Phil Bowhay

Remember what? I could show you exactly where I was standing that Sunday morning when I first heard of Pearl Harbor. Just ten feet from where, three years later, I broke my arm. Eleven years old and didn't know Pearl Harbor from Cabo San Lucas, but from that moment on, well, you know the story. The date is now elusive, but I think in the previous year we sat in the P.G. Grammar School auditorium with a big radio on the stage and listened to President Roosevelt tell us about all the planes, ships, and tanks we were going to build. We then knew the Germans and Japanese were all bad guys and we had heard about war, England, China, and all that, but here we were, really *in* one, and boy, was that exciting! Maybe you don't remember Eagle Squadron and Yanks in the RAF, but that was *us!*

The gravity of it all hit us slowly, but it was still exciting, with Monterey Peninsula right in the thick of things. Fort Ord was alive with soldiers, coming and going, the boom of artillery night and day, and the rifle ranges, right there, across the train tracks! Caissons went rolling along, part of convoys of trucks and armored vehicles, soldiers waving, bands playing, flags and banners flying, all part of the thrill of it all. And the Presidio crackling with activity, with draftees and recruits being processed for war. Cavalry still had horses and mules, and machine gun practice was up on the hill behind P.G.

The Old Del Monte Hotel became Navy Pre-Flight with three or four football fields on the Polo Grounds, and some of the best teams in the country. Serious stuff, as the boys left Pre-Flight for Pensacola and elsewhere, and came back as pilots flying torpedo planes, dive bombers and fighters over the bay. True or not, we thrilled at the story of Buzz Sawyer flying his Hell Cat *under* Bixby Bridge. And then that tragic crash of a torpedo plane out on Lighthouse, just missing that mansion that later was featured in *A Summer Place*. We had seen the plane flying low, then heard the crash. We ran all the way from the high school and watched as the Navy and our fire crews cleaned up. The crew was killed, and the war didn't seem quite so much fun after that.

Early in the war, we went through blackouts and air raid drills, marching out of the grammar school to the safety of the trees fifty yards away. If we ever got complacent—not likely—there were plenty of rumors to whip us up! KDON one night reported the possibility, actually the *likelihood,* that the Japanese were landing on the Santa Cruz Pier! That's right! Next to the Boardwalk! Silly now, but serious then. And if this was confirmed, we were to crack the blocks on our automobile engines, thereby denying the invaders access to the hinterland. Not taking any chances, some patriots with sledge hammers in hand cracked the blocks prematurely, thereby denying themselves transportation until after the war! Lucky we still had the Del Monte Express.

Speaking of transportation, gasoline was rationed along with tires, and other automobile parts were very hard to get. Not to be denied the joy of driving, some of the guys in auto shop built a sort-of car out of old, salvaged parts. To accommodate the four sizes of worn and salvaged tires, each wheel was a different size. Quite a sight to see the "shopmobile" hopping down the street with three or four grinning mechanics enjoying the ride. And once tasted, friends, you will never siphon gasoline again, $3.50 a gallon or not.

We were stunned when our Japanese classmates were moved away, and this even happened to some families of Italian descent, albeit for a brief period of time. And then, of course, the story of the German typewriter repairman discovered under the Salinas River bridge transmitting "classified information" to God knows who.

One moonlit night, deep into blackout, we stood outside wondering if this was a drill or the real thing. One of our neighbors didn't bother wondering, and having made a good dent in a fifth of Four Roses, aimed and fired his .22, suspecting the moon was the enemy. Missed the moon, but hit the clock on City Hall. Cracked the glass, but time marched on, and the glass was replaced after the war.

Families came and went, stationed here briefly, then away to some distant shore. Just about the time we developed a crush, they left, but promised to write. We bought Savings Bond stamps with our paper route money and grew great Victory Gardens. Boy Scout Troop 46, under the direction of Master Gardener Wilfred Mack, raised bushels and bushels of Idaho potatoes on the corner of Del Monte and Bayview. Picture in the paper and all that. We learned first aid and collected cans of fat, aluminum pots and pans, paper, and tires. We collected Army and Air Force shoulder insignia, and any other military souvenir we could lay our hands on. (If you have forgotten what they looked like, log on to World War II military insignia, and get a lump in your throat.) Our moms cooked around the shortages and rations, and I think we ate a lot of fish. I don't remember thinking about it, but the Depression was over.

You may have seen that article in *Reader's Digest*, late 1945 or so, after the shooting was over. "Nostalgia for War" said people were longing again for national unity with all of us on the same mission, same page, devoted to the same purpose, saving our country and the rest of the world. All well and good, but don't miss the movie (and book) *Flags of Our Fathers*. And haven't you noticed? Our current war isn't quite the same.

Pearl Harbor ... December 7, 1941

Engaging in casual conversation, I am amazed at how many people don't "Remember Pearl Harbor." Then I realize that that happened a long time ago and, unless you are on the north side of eighty, you've only read about it, or heard about, or seen the graphic films. A shame if you can't remember ... changed our lives and country forever. Well, maybe.

My mom and I had just come home from church and the neighbor, almost out of breath, said, "The Japanese have bombed Pearl Harbor!" (These many years later I find I must say "Japanese.") I didn't know Pearl Harbor from New Orleans, but very quickly learned where it was and why it was very serious. I was eleven at the time.

A few months before, Kate Smith had given us something to hang on to, and even today the song "God Bless America" hangs on "a solemn prayer." I refer you once again to the internet and there are several sites that show Kate singing it for the first time. In one clip, a young man says to his mother, "We're going to be in this yet, Mom!" She knows, and looks away. And in it, we were.

If you don't remember Pearl Harbor, you might not remember the Monterey Peninsula at war. You won't remember the black-outs, which never worked, the Civil Defense wardens, the airplane spotters along the coast, or the Coast Guard patrolling Asilomar Beach with Dobermans! Nor the roar of artillery at Fort Ord, the machine gun practice at the Presidio, and the bugle calls or the roar of Hell Cats and torpedo bombers over the bay. Or the tragic crash out Lighthouse Avenue, just missing the La Porte Mansion.

You might have missed the rationing of gas, tires, sugar

and shoes, and a shortage of cigarettes. Fearing air raids—always possible—we were marched out of our classrooms at P.G. Grammar School (now Robert Down) into a vacant lot with a grove of trees maybe 75 yards from the building. Safe! Just in case.

We were stunned and shocked when our Japanese friends were uprooted and shipped away to internment camps. (Won't even start now on the current immigration nuttiness—that's another story.)

We needed heroes, and we got lots of them, quickly. Look up Medal of Honor heroes and be proud, one more time. Remember our pilot who dove his plane down the stack of a Japanese battle ship. There was even a song about him—Colin P. Kelly, Jr!

Our mothers were used to saving things through the Depression, so they knew how to collect bacon grease and deliver it to the butcher for ultimate use in ... explosives?

You won't remember the little banners in windows with stars, declaring that from that home somebody had gone to war. And then, in some windows, the stars were changed to gold.

A story in *Readers Digest* a few months after the shooting stopped was called "Nostalgia for War." Its point was that after Pearl Harbor and during the war we were all involved to different degrees, and we were all on the same side. We had a common cause, and something was expected from each of us, all pulling together. I'm sure there was some dissent, but I can't remember any. Very little agreement on subsequent wars.

Well, even if you don't remember Pearl Harbor (as we did the Alamo), the next time you're in Hawaii, stop by Pearl and spend a few minutes on the *Arizona*. Then later, visit the Punch Bowl. Yes, if you haven't already, visit Normandy.

And next season, even though it's just the seventh inning stretch, sing loud and clear, as a solemn prayer, "God Bless America!"

After the War: Golf and PG Dreams
Dawn Armstrong

After WWII Dad left the Navy and tried to be a civilian. Every morning Mom held my baby brother and we waved goodbye as Dad drove the green Chevy from Larkspur to the JC Penney office in San Rafael. One day he came home and said we were going to be in the Army.

Just out of first grade, I remember that Mom was upset. She wanted to keep what we had: a home with a garden and nice neighbors and a school I could walk to just down the block. She did not want to be a military gypsy moving every 18 months or a split up family.

Dad said his time in the Navy would count toward retirement and we would stay together as a family. He wouldn't be shipping out without us. He would be stationed stateside, on land. It was 1949 and his initial assignment was Fort Ord. I don't recall the exact order of things, but the first time I heard "PG" my mom and her friends were laughing. "PG" was code for "pregnant." Dad had gone ahead and found an apartment in Pacific Grove.

For Dad, PG was heaven on earth. A dedicated golfer, he could walk down to the P.G. Clubhouse (now the Senior Center) from the Ocean View Boulevard apartment. My mother had only a small strip of cement for tomatoes in pots. I don't think the Monterey Bay view ever made up for that. I learned to dive at the P.G. Plunge. My brother and I played on the railroad tracks across Mermaid Avenue. On the way to the Lovers Point beach, mom sometimes walked us to the engine turnaround, replaced by Monarch Pines Mobile Home Park.

I was enrolled in Mrs. Worrall's second grade class at Lighthouse Elementary School. (On our return to the Monterey Peninsula in 1954, my younger brother went to school in the same room with the same teacher.)

When Dad was transferred from Fort Ord in 1951, the owner of the duplex offered to sell. Dad looked forward to coming back to a dream retirement in P.G. one day. In the meantime, he could rent the apartments to help pay for it.

Dad's second assignment after Fort Ord was Korea. He promised when he returned that we would have a house and yard and dog and cat and permanent friends. We did not want to live in an apartment ever again. In 1954, it seemed there were few jobs for again civilian dad. Finally he was offered one by a friend who owned a furniture store on Lighthouse Avenue.

Before joining him in P.G., mom gave orders to find a house with all the promised attributes. He did. For a time, we reveled in our family life on Dennett Street, a full acre with vegetable and flower gardens for Mom at last. For my brother and me, a bonus was that the sand train ran right in front of the house.

From Alaska to P.G. in 1925
Richard W. Gamble
husband, dad, grandpa, o'papa

My family moved to Pacific Grove in 1925 from a gold mining camp in Chichagoff, Alaska when I was three years old. Shortly afterward my brother Tom was born. I have always been thankful for the opportunity to be raised here with the beach, surf, sand dunes, pine forest, huckleberries and fog. Dad first worked for the sand mine belonging to Del Monte Properties Co. and then for The American Can Company. We enjoyed visiting him at work but the machine noise was pretty scary at both places. We lived on Bentley Street, out near Washington Park and this was part of our playground. How I loved to throw pine cones at the clusters of butterflies that hung on the pine trees there. (I hope the statute of limitations has run out on this crime.)

California had a school system that was ranked high in those days and we attended Pacific Grove Grammar School and Pacific Grove High School, under the watchful eyes of Robert Down and Mr. Ingham, respectively.

I belonged to Boy Scout Troop 92, sponsored by the Methodist Church. We met in Chautauqua Hall alongside Troop 90, still in existence. Our summer camp was in the redwoods of Big Sur State Park in the area presently used by the camp grounds. I can still smell the bay leaves that grew everywhere. We attended the Mayflower Congregational Church on Central, which is now the Presbyterian Church. Rev. Hunter was the minister and Mr. Mack was in charge of Sunday School. I learned to shoot a .22 rifle in the basement rifle range there, as part of the youth program.

With my faithful Columbia bike, I delivered papers, first the *Oakland Tribune*, and then the *Monterey Peninsula Herald*. My route covered part of the Seventeen Mile Drive and covered 11 miles and 22 customers. I was handsomely rewarded with $5 per month. Not much but enough to buy my bike.

Following high school, I headed for Indiana and Purdue University where I was enrolled in the school of engineering. In my sophomore year I met the only love of my life, my future wife, Barbara, from Indianapolis. We decided to get married but my parents vetoed that since I was not 21 so we postponed the great event.

Things got confused after Pearl Harbor and I quit school and returned to Pacific Grove for the summer of 1942. To beat the draft, I walked to the Presidio and enlisted in the Army in September and was promptly sent to Camp Roberts for basic training in Field Artillery. While there I turned 21 and marriage became a reality. Barbara

left Indiana in a blizzard and we planned the event for Saturday, Dec 1942 at a minister's house in Salinas. I was a bit late due to a forgotten suitcase, leaving the train in Bradley, catching a southbound train, retrieving suitcase, and hitchhiking on to Salinas. We bussed to Pacific Grove and headed for the best hotel in town, the Forest Hill Hotel where we spent our honeymoon and were charged the exorbitant fee of $4.00 per night. Had an abalone dinner at Mike's on the wharf for $1.25 each.

The war years were hectic with many changes in duty station and locations but included my getting my commission and the birth of our first child, Carolyn. Following my stint overseas we returned to Purdue to finish up my degree and have our second child, Kathy.

After graduation we moved to Washington State for work and ended up working for the Navy Dept. in Seattle. In 1970 the Navy moved us to San Bruno and we lived in Belmont for eight years. Upon retirement, having bought a house in Pacific Grove four years earlier, we settled in to our dream home on Bayview Ave. The house had been built the year after I graduated from high school. While in Seattle our family had grown with the addition of three more children but they were all grown up now so we were happy to be alone in my Last Hometown.

Retirement in Pacific Grove has been great. After doing a bit of remodeling on our home we branched into volunteering, first with the Hospice of the Central Coast and then Meals on Wheels, for some 35 years. We have both recently retired from all that to settle into some quiet time. We are fortunate to be supported by our large loving family and many friends. At 94 for Barbara and 95 for me and both looking forward to our 75th wedding Anniversary we can truly say we are blessed to have spent most of our lives here in good old Pacific Grove.

Has it changed? It sure has, but what hasn't and who would want to be any place else?

10 Survive and Thrive In a Tent House
Dennis R. Bryan
P. G. native

It was 1937 at Ord, Nebraska that my mother and father Arlo and Evelyn Bryan decided that there was no way to find work or buy food and clothing as the depression was in full swing.

They, with my sister, Colleen, my grandparents, Ray and Maude Bryan, and Andrew and Helen Jacobsen, headed west. Lucky for me they arrived in Pacific Grove.

I was born in August 1938 at the Pine Grove Sanatorium on Grove Acres, delivered by Dr. Schilling. I was bundled up and taken to the home on Locust St.

The house was on a typical tent lot. Maybe 500 sq. ft at best. With my grandparents, parents, aunts and uncles we were ten altogether. Somehow we all survived. The adult women worked the canneries, the men found jobs around the peninsula. My grandfather Bryan couldn't find work so he fished off the rocks to put food on the table.

I am so proud to say that I was the first of the cousins to be born in California. I can't imagine a more wonderful town to grow up in.

Wartime in Manila to P.G. Retirement
Katy McDonald

My P.G. story starts in the Philippines during WWII, before I was even born.

There, three ex-pat families from distinct backgrounds and parts of the world became the best of friends.

Their names were McDonald, Simmons and Wentholt. They met under unusual circumstances. In their 30s, with young children, they had all been living and working in Manila when WWII broke out. All being citizens of Allied nations, they were interned in a Japanese prison of war camp. It was in this camp that they met for the first time, and for three years lived side-by-side in neighboring huts. Their children were the same age and played together. My husband, Douglas McDonald, was one of those children. Born in 1941, he was six months old when they entered the camp, and three years old when they were released.

After being rescued from the camp in 1944 and returned to good health, they all decided to continue their respective lives in the Philippines. Their shared experience bonded them for life. Twenty years later, when the kids were all grown up and it was time for retirement, Ernie Simmons invested in some property on the Monterey Peninsula, in a little place called Pacific Grove. There he developed and built three homes on property at the corner of Jewell Avenue and Sunset Drive. He convinced his two old friends, Dolf Wentholt and Doug McDonald Sr., to relocate from the Philippines into the other two homes. So, in 1966, a lifelong friendship that started under tough and unusual circumstances culminated in a beautiful life facing the Pacific Ocean. Many family gatherings took place over the years; and the grandchildren ran back and forth among the three houses to visit their "aunties" and "uncles." These grandchildren, now adults, are still friends today and live all over the world.

The original patriarchs and matriarchs of these three clans passed away during the 1990s. The Wentholt and the Simmons homes were sold shortly thereafter. My husband, Douglas, inherited the McDonald home. Unfortunately, he passed away before he ever had the pleasure of living in it. The house was sinking into the sand dune when it came to me. Over the years I finished the restorations that Douglas had begun. My current husband, Fernando, and I moved in upon our retirement in 2014.

Doug's two daughters have started their own families and live on the East Coast. This home will be theirs one day, as their father always wanted. In the meantime, I feel blessed to be able to live here and am honored that I have been able to preserve a tiny portion of P.G. history.

HOLMAN'S DEPARTMENT STORE—SHOPPING MECCA, LANDMARK

My Father, Rensselaer L. Holman
W. R. Holman
Excerpted from *Story of Wilford Rensselaer Holman*

Rensselaer L. Holman, a handsome forty-five years old man, left Sacramento, his residence for over a decade, to make his home in Pacific Grove with his three children, Clarence at eight, Minnie age six and I, Wilford, age four. His elder sister, my aunt Minorra, who came to us from Vermont after mother died when I was two, and Lee Chong, our Chinese housekeeper and cook for years, went with us.

These two wonderful people raised me to boyhood. Aunt Minorra devoted her whole life to me, day and night. When she was in the parlor reading, she would sit at her feet with my head on her lap for her to rub and scratch, then put her hand down my back and do the same thing. She kept me quiet by the hour. At night she'd hear my prayers then tuck me into bed.

Lee Chong called me "Wilf" my nickname. He made especially large pancakes for me at breakfast, and deep-fried bowls of crispy golden potato chips for us to munch on, He also took me with him to Chinatown to eat the sweetmeats his friends gave us.

Father had definite reasons for making our home in Pacific Grove. The climate there was wonderful! No mosquitos. He suffered severely from malaria in Sacramento. He said, "Pacific Grove will one day be a prosperous city."

He sold his well run hardware business in Sacramento after he ruptured himself while unloading a keg of nails from the wagon. He invested his money into land in Pacific Grove from Lighthouse Avenue to Short Street, between Wood and Granite Streets, buying an extra small house on Lobos Street, with its backyard running through to Wood Street, for us to live in while two fine builders, a Mr. Justin, an architect carpenter from Vermont, and Clefm Buffum, an outstanding carpenter, brother of an outstanding butcher, both of Pacific Grove.

These two men worked from sunrise to sunset to complete our three story, redwood house with three gable roofs at 750 Lighthouse Avenue. I remember toddling over there through our backyard to watch them build our new home from the start of excavation. I went there every day until the house was built.

Father's heavy truck, drawn by horses, loaded with an inventory of hardware to be stored on his land in Pacific Grove. He planned to operate his hardware business from his home. However, he had to abandon this thought when Pacific Improvement Company refused to sell him a business permit. He had to sell the truck and its cargo immediately.

Holman's Department Store

How father managed to establish a new life in Pacific Grove is difficult to imagine. I knew he worried a lot. Yet my optimistic and tireless father soon found a way out, he joined a Mr. Towle in business. It was his first business venture on Lighthouse Avenue. The store was advertised as follows: TOWLE AND HOLMAN, THE POPULAR Dealers of Dry Goods, Boots, Shoes, Clothing, Hats, Caps, Notions, etc.

Soon the gold in the Klondikes tempted Towle. One night he, his brother and father emptied the cash box in the store and went their way. Father renamed the store R. L HOLMAN! I grew up with R. L. HOLMAN. Every few years as it prospered, it was moved, about four or five times on Lighthouse Avenue for one reason or another. Every day, my father just let me "loose" in the store. I did what I had to do. Sweep the floors, wash the windows, straighten out the shelves, attend to customers, deliver orders, receive shipments of merchandise, mark them for sale, and so on, and so on. I dreamed then of having the finest department store in Pacific Grove, just like the Emporium building in San Francisco. This dream, after many years of hard hard work, became a reality.

Fires in Pacific Grove

Upon my return from the Pacific Coast Business College in San Jose, I volunteered at the local fire department. I was at every fire that happened.

All Pacific Grove turned out when there was a fire on 19 and Lighthouse. My father stood with other fathers of boys my age running in and out of the burning house, to save the owners furniture and things When the fire was under control, my father said to me, "I am very proud of you for the way you handled the furniture and the way you put it down outside. Very proud of you."

What father said, made me feel good.

Then there was a paper drive to save the trees. Folks collected newspapers and packed it down in the basement of the Congressional Church. One day the paper caught fire and bvurned the Church to the ground.

Another fire broke out in the closet of the second or third floor of Hotel El Carmelo. We soon put that out.

The loft of the Mammoth Stables where hay and feed was kept, burst into flames. The horses were led to the corral in the back of the building. The fire was put out before it did any great damage. When the automobile era began, the Stables were dismantled.

In 1906 the earthquake struck San Francisco. We felt it in Pacific Grove. However the fire that burnt Chinatown here occurred on May 15, 1906.

During spring and summer, the Chinese went with lit boats into the sea to attract squid. Tons of squid was brought to shore, spread out on land to dry out. The stench was terrible. It drove the tourists away. Property Owners in Pacific Grove and Monterey wanted the City to do something about this.

Chinatown was build in four sections of two room cottages backed up to a narrow alley to the beach. Pacific Improvement Company supplied Chinatown with water, a fire hydrant in the center of town, with a 4" wise fire house within reach of all the houses.

A fire started that spread to three sections of Chinatown. Every China Man deserted his home and belongings and went to China Point. Not one of them fought the fire. I tried to save some of the things for them. I ran into the biggest store there, jumped on the counter to save the merchandise, handing it to the folks there, telling them to save it for the Chinese, instead, they just looted Chinatown. When the blaze was over, I was on the railway track by the section of Chinatown that did not burn. There I saw a young man throwing a lit torch into a building, then threw a can of fuel after it. It went off with a bang. With an ax in his hand, he ran to the fire hose to cut it. I recognized him as a City employee. Soon after he left town with his wife and two children.

That was the end of old Chinatown.

I Will Always Remember Lee Chong

Lee Chong came with us from Sacramento to be our cook-housekeeper. He was the finest dressed China Man in all of California. The tassle of his handsome silk hat stemmed from an Imperial Yellow braiden button. He rose early in the mornings to sweep the garden paths, then he did everything else in the house to make us comfortable. Every afternoon he sat by Aunt Minorra to learn to read, a talent, I fear, he never mastered.

He was the most admired man in Chinatown. When he visited his friends he dressed in his very best. He took me with him. In the afternoons he cycled in the woods, wearing soft shoes. One day he lost control of his bike. It crashed into the Lighthouse gate post at the end of the bicycle path. The handle bar went into him, exposing his gut. A pharmacist and a nose, ear and throat doctor attended to him, who left Clarence, sixteen, and I "Whiff", twelve, to nurse him with wet towels. He suffered a lot for three days, then died in the house father especially built for him to live in.

His friends prepared him for his funeral. They also took away all his fine silk embroidered clothes, shoes and belongings. He was the only man from China here to ever be taken to his burial place at China Point in a horse drawn hearst father ordered for him. All his friends followed it on foot as it wound its way through Chinatown.

Early Memories

Number 218 Lobos Street is a two story, well-built redwood building with an outhouse. When we arrived, we found no bathroom there. My father was told that when people came to Pacific Grove, a resort town, to live, they were not to put in a bathroom, but to use the bathtubs at the bathhouse on the beach, with running salt water, hot and cold.

Every morning we were up early, dressed and noisily ran down the back stairs. Father scolded, "You sound like Norman horses!" But we had chores to do before going to school. My job was to look after our productive cow, to clean out her stall, feed and milk her. Then I'd deliver the milk in pints, half quarts, and quarts in an open-mouth pitcher to my father's customers; after, I'd take the cow out to pasture in the field. When school was over, I brought the cow back to her stall for the night.

In the summertime we went to the bathhouse on the beach. After, we sat on the porch of the outhouse to listen to the band playing on the bandstand on the beach. We looked at the rocks on the coastline, the water in the bay, the waves splashing and the hundreds of tourists on the beach.

To me, Pacific Grove was a lovely large field of trees, wild flowers, birds, butterflies, chickens, cats, dogs, cows, horses, mountains, beaches and the beautiful Bay of Monterey.

I learned to know every mile of this lovely territory and its nearby towns of Moss Beach, Seaside, Carmel and Carmel Valley.

All Holman stories are excerpted from *Story of Wilford Rensselaer Holman, Reminiscences on His Ninety Fifth Birthday*, August 28, 1979, as told to his caregiver—and published by—Louise V. Jaques, Pacific Grove 1979.

Saving The Holman Building in 1994
Alice Englander
Canterbury Woods writer

When we were furnishing our new vacation cottage in Pacific Grove in 1983, we were delighted to find Holman's Department Store just up the road. I spent hours there and found just about everything I could ask for—towels, bathroom rugs, décor items, curtains, kitchen accessories, brooms, mops—all the mundane things you need to set up a household. We continued to shop there for years, and could often be seen strolling home along Ricketts Row carrying a small TV or a microwave. One time during a heat wave we bought a fan. Our neighbors thought it was pretty funny since we were new to the area and thought it would continue to be hot, but they knew the heat wouldn't last! As it turns out, we still use that fan when the rare hot day hits Pacific Grove.

Combining Holman's depth of merchandise with the homey service made it a fun shopping experience. Even Bill, the inveterate non-shopper, was willing to come along and help shop and carry our goods home.

Holman's had been a fixture in Pacific Grove since the early 1900s and we thought it would be there forever. But times change. It eventually sold in 1985 to a regional chain called Ford's, but their flagship store in Watsonville was irreparably damaged by the Loma Prieta earthquake in 1989. They never recovered economically so they closed in 1993.

Since then, the building itself has had a colorful history. Occupying a full block and three-plus stories tall, it is an integral part of the downtown landscape. It has been fixed up and used as an antiques mall for a number of years. Today it is being renovated for residential use. It's pretty sad to look at the empty holes where windows were and to see it in such disrepair, but we're hopeful it will eventually become the icon it once was.

In 1994, a developer offered to make it into a hotel, but local laws didn't allow for that use. Measure E was put on the ballot to change the uses allowed and it passed. That development didn't work out, but we thought the "Save the Holman's Building" poster that had been distributed for the election was beautiful, and was a neat way to memorialize the building in case it ended up being torn down. It had been on display in most of the businesses downtown so one day we decided to see if we could obtain one. It was actually pretty hard to do. Some businesses didn't have it anymore. Some had it, but didn't want to give it to us. We got the feeling that since we were asking for it, perhaps they thought it had some value!

Finally, we found one at Pacific Grove Travel on Lighthouse Avenue. We had it framed and it now resides on a wall we have devoted to posters of personal importance to us.

Note: There is a detailed history of Holman's Department Store in an issue of the Pacific Grove Heritage Society journal, The Board and Batten, *that can be found at http://www.pacificgroveheritage.org/pgdev/wp-content/uploads/2016/03/BB-winter-2015.pdf. The Heritage Society is a treasure trove of historical information about Pacific Grove (www.pacificgroveheritage.org).*

The Christmas Train, the Santa Claus Special, photo courtesy of Benjamin and Zachary Lazare.

The Girl on the (Christmas) Train
Heather Lazare

A few years ago, my mother-in-law began to bring up crates from the neglected cupboards downstairs. These were dusty things: boxes labeled "Holman's Misc.," letters in thin *par avion* envelopes, a container marked "Theme Hosiery" (which in fact housed nearly fifty tiny abalone shells), a bottle of arrowheads her mother had collected, and an unfinished manuscript of her grandmother's on onionskin paper.

There, gathered around her parents' old dining room table, amongst our Marianne's ice cream sandwich wrappers, my husband, my mother-in-law, and I pieced through these memories.

A particularly large format photo album caught my attention and as I turned the pages, I found photos of my husband's great-grandparents, W.R. and Zena Holman, their life outside of their famed Holman's Department Store. The photos were pasted on black cardstock pages, but as I turned a page in the back, a loose photo fell out, one that was thicker and larger than the others, the kind that could have been produced as a keepsake. It was a photo from the Santa Claus Special.

A man always keen on unique promotion, W.R. Holman would offer a train ride for children every December. Their parents could drop them at the train depot in Monterey and pick them up at Holman's in Pacific Grove. I knew about this train from my mom, who grew up with her sister and two brothers in Carmel. She looked forward to the ride and to picking out her Christmas dress at Holman's—always matching but in a different color than her sister's. To her, Holman's was etiquette class with Mrs. Del Fino (plus a fashion show!), an ever-growing collection of Green Stamps to be exchanged for items in the store, and the excitement of watching the series of pneumatic tubing that ran throughout the floors. She enjoyed grilled cheese sandwiches and milkshakes with my aunt and grandma at the top-floor Solarium Restaurant, a day's worth of shopping bags at their feet, the view of Monterey Bay laid out before them.

I thought of her as I held the thick photo in my hands, looking at the happy faces of the two parallel rows of children on the Santa Claus Special. They're laughing and watching as Santa and someone in a polar bear costume walk down the center aisle. One boy is petting the polar bear, who holds a basket likely containing candy. I count more than 40 children on this car, and there's clearly another behind it; a conductor stands between the cars.

I looked around the dinner table, my husband and his mom both smiling at a photo from his childhood (Vashon Island, Low Gap, Berkeley?). I stood up and brought the thick photo to them, pointing to the girl with a ponytail in the foreground, left hand held softly to her mouth. "That's my mom," I say. And it's true. There she is, more than 50 years ago, on a train ride organized by my husband's great-grandfather, in a photo slipped into the back of an album, waiting for me to find her.

Zena Holman, Patricia "Genie" Santini, and W.R. Holman on Genie's wedding day to Michael Lazare, photo courtesy of Benjamin and Zachary Lazare.

A Simple Rhyme
Zena G. Holman

It is the good we do today,
Not the tears we shed tomorrow
That helps the heartache of the present
And alleviates the sorrow.

For every moment of the day,
There is something we can do
If only the tiny, tiny thing
Or just believing what is true.

Knowing what is real and eternal
Is a task of no small mien,
"God <u>is</u> Love," the Bible tells us,
Love each other is His theme.

Growing up at Holman's
Dawn Armstrong

An incident the summer of 1955 threatened to end my tomboy life. Mom announced it was time for me to get fitted for a bra. She told me to get into the car; we were going to Holman's. I protested fruitlessly. I liked my undershirt. My figure had yet to blossom. My wardrobe consisted of a green uniform jumper with matching long sleeve heavy knit sweater and white nylon blouse for school plus a red baseball cap, a t-shirt or two, a plaid flannel shirt, jeans and a pair of Capri pants, blouses and a couple of skirts for dress up. I did not need a bra, let alone the embarrassment of being fitted for one.

Off we went to Holman's, upstairs where lingerie was on display. I have blocked the session out of memory for the most part. I still feel that the sales lady agreed with my view that it was early for a first bra. Nonetheless, we came home with a size 32AA.

As soon as Mom pulled up to the front door, I ran to the back yard and climbed to my tree house. It was three planks nailed to two limbs. From there I could see my immediate world below me: Mom's front yard with smelly blood meal around the roses both she and the deer loved, a variety of other flowers and a large cactus; Dad's backyard with natural vegetation that needed raking and burning in the incinerator before he could go golfing; the chicken coup where the duck that had won at the Carmel Valley Fair got eaten by raccoons just a couple of days after Mom healed its leg; the dog house, where one of the Bantam hens got killed by the dog because she kept laying her eggs there; the lemon trees, back door arbor with grape vines, tomato plants, the shed where Mom parked her prized little car—the first Renault on the Monterey Peninsula, purchased at a Monterey County Fair display— and the thick, tall bushes in the back, home to various critters. It wasn't until recently that I figured out "Grove Acres" was named because everyone had an acre along the railroad tracks. Apparently, I was a late bloomer mentally as well as physically.

High school summers, Holman's was my workplace. Assigned to Housewares, I hated selling though I was a hard worker. When customers arrived, I hid behind pillars, rag and glass cleaner in hand. The regular staff steered people to me so I would get enough sales credit to keep the job. My last summer at Holman's I spent lunchtime across the street at a coffee shop. In my mind, I had to learn to drink coffee because sophisticated college students drank coffee while they socialized in a student union. I ordered it black and by summer's end I could get a full cup down without grimacing.

Holman's
Jacquelin La Vine Jones

For many years, Holman's Department Store was the main source of employment for many on the Monterey Peninsula. It certainly was for my family. Since we lived across the street from Mr. and Mrs. Holman and knew them well, it was inevitable that all five of us siblings would work at the store. My mother worked there also, in the alteration room. I can still see her at the sewing machine with a measuring tape draped over her like a necklace.

My brothers Sheldon and Dave worked in the electrical department. We three sisters, Patsy, Jacquelin and Sally, started at age 14 in the stock room. Soon, Sally went to the garden department and I went to the elevator.

I would park the elevator on the mezzanine until the buzzer sounded and someone needed a lift. From that point there was a perfect view of the entire first floor. It was almost like a movie, watching people coming and going, laughing, talking, and of course working.

One day, someone came in the elevator and said Bing Crosby was in the store with his sons. I parked my trusty vehicle on the mezzanine, knowing I could see them from there.

The shoe department was on the first floor and there they were—Bing Crosby and, as I remember, four boys. They were waiting for the shoe salesman. As the waited, Mr. Crosby walked behind the seated boys with a comb and fixed each boy's hair. That is a sweet memory.

Since Holman's was the only department store in the area, celebrities were often seen there. One of them I did not care for was Greer Garson. She seemed very rude to the man she was with.

Several times, I took John Steinbeck to the furniture department on the third floor, although he could have been going to the solarium, from which you could see for miles in every direction. He was a very polite man and was usually accompanied by a houseboy. I wish I had not been so shy or I would have told him my brother Dave mowed his lawn.

My sister Patsy had the most interesting elevator passengers. Flora Wood, the notorious madam from Cannery Row, would bring her girls in to be outfitted. Patsy said they were all lovely, polite and just seemed to be like any other girls with their mother.

I wouldn't exchange my days working at Holman's for anything. The most interesting people worked there. I wish they had all taken a writing class like ours so I could have known more about them. As a kid, I did not realize the gold mine of people I was privileged to be among.

I Bought My Wedding Dress at Holman's
Linda Pagnella

One of my best experiences at Holman's was shopping for my wedding dress in 1976. Each year Holman's had a bridal fashion show. In 1976 everyone was having July weddings with a red, white and blue Bicentennial theme.

I was not a follower. Jim and I had decided on a May wedding with a spring theme.

Growing up, I had shopped at Holman's a lot. It were the only store around that carried Girl Scout uniforms and badges. You could go to Holman's and find anything you needed, from groceries to underwear, from crafts to books, from jewelry to BBs! Prom dresses, tuxedo rentals, socks and toys. You could get your hair done in the salon and eat lunch at the restaurant on top!

I dreamed of the day I would be choosing my wedding dress. In the Bridal Salon there was a large pedestal that you would step on to get the effect of heels. The effect was amazing! Your personal stage.

I went on to try on dozens of dresses at Holman's and elsewhere.

But I came back to the very first one. $175.00 and it was perfect!

My First Job During Christmas Season
Nina Gough
Carmel

It was December of 1956 and Christmas vacation was soon approaching. I was sixteen and could get a work permit for my first job. Holman's Department Store was hiring for the Christmas season and my mom believed everyone should be employed as soon as possible. She drove me to Pacific Grove for my interview with the sales manager.

Evidently, he thought I could handle the job and he offered me the job as a sales girl in the toy department, the busiest place in the store. I was given my own red leather sales book where all sales were written in triplicate. One copy for the customer, one copy put in the small vacuum tube and whisked up to somewhere high above us with the cash payment (no credit cards in those days) and one we kept in our sales book. At the end of the shift I held a mass of paper that defied any order.

When the Christmas season was over I was summarily called into the manager's office, He thanked me for my service and in a very kind way, fired me.

All-in-all it was a great experience. Holman's Department Store will always be a special place to me.

Pacific Grove in the 70s
Mary Joanna Neish

Whenever I travel to Pacific Grove to see my son William, "there is a memory on every corner" as he would say. There is the memory of how we fixed up his sister Kate with whiskers, cat's ears and a tail and William pulled her in a red wagon down Lighthouse Ave. in the Pet Parade. There is the memory of when William was locked in the library and the newspaper called him "Bill." There's the memory of when John Paul came home from school one day and announced, "My friends call me John." (We reluctantly complied, but continued to speak of him as "J.P." amongst ourselves.)

The children and I lived in a cottage at the Asilomar end of Pacific Grove. The fog would roll in and the foghorn would moan. We had two reliable techniques to lift our spirits as we ventured out in the mist. One was to ride the Mini Monarch Bus. The other was to visit Holman's Department Store.

The Mini Monarch was a jolly little bus with huge orange butterfly wings painted on the side. As I remember, for a quarter you could get on and travel around the town. It was great fun to look at all the houses and their gardens. You could get off at a friend's house or a playground. Even a round trip without disembarking was an event.

Let me tell you about Holman's Department Store, made famous by John Steinbeck who recorded watching a lone figure skating round and round and round on the roof. The china department was on the lowest floor. It provided me with many of the fragrance bottles in my collection, and a white china teapot in a bamboo design. It was also a source of crockery for many Mother's Days, though one year I purchased her a tureen in Carmel in which she kept her mail.

On the mezzanine I bought yarn for my many projects, inclusive of enough for a many colored blanket, and pillow cases, another collection of mine. But our "favorite most" celebration was lunch at Holman's.

Entering through the front door we made our way to the perfume counter, where we sprayed ourselves liberally en route to the elevator. Our destination was the restaurant on the top floor. On one wall was a wallpaper mural of French Poodles. We would sit at a table by a wall of windows and look down the streets to the Monterey Bay. I always felt like I was on an ocean liner. Egg salad sandwiches on whole wheat and glasses of milk were affordable. Sometimes we would splurge on pudding or ice cream.

The children grew up and I grew gray. Since Holman's died, I have relinquished all dreams of a return. I have been told that the foghorn is no more. Maybe this is not true. How strange a silent fog must be. As silent as my memories are, looking out the window down the streets to the Monterey Bay.

The Youngest Employee Ever
Virginia Abplanalp

After reading all the items posted on Facebook about the demise of that beloved store, it brought to mind my experience there as what had to be the youngest employee ever. I was hired in 1945 at the age of 13 and put to work in the advertising department for the lofty sum of 35-cents an hour.

What on earth prompted me to even apply for a job at that age, you may be wondering? Let me explain. The war was still going on and my dad was a driver for the local bus company, his pay frozen at 88-cents an hour. My mother was expecting their fourth child. Not only that, my grandmother, who had made all my clothes until then, had moved away. I was facing a school year in eighth grade with no ability to obtain the wardrobe my changing body required. My income from babysitting was woefully inadequate.

At the urging of my mother, who was well acquainted with the executives at Holman's and other movers and shakers in the community, I mustered up the courage to apply for a job. Why my dad was dead set against it, I had no clue.

So, wearing the braids of girlhood and the body of young womanhood, I marched in to the store in search of Vernon Hurd, the general manager. I planned to find his office and ask for an appointment. Much to my surprise, I ran into him in the elevator on my way up to the mezzanine where the offices were located. Being just a kid of 13 and with no knowledge of appropriate behavior, I blurted out my request. I will never forget the kindly smile and his handsome face as he said, "Let's go into my office." Whereupon he heard my reason for applying and, to my utter shock, hired me.

My mother was delighted and my father was horrified. I thought he was only concerned for my physical safety when he made me promise never to accept a ride from a boy. I was so naive I thought he was afraid I would become involved in an accident. Little did I know what kind of accident he had in mind. I used my first paycheck to go to the nearest beauty parlor and have my braids cut off and a stylish, short hairdo created.

After learning the ropes of my new job, the elevator operator, who was a pretty young woman, offered to teach me how to run it. She wanted someone to take over when she took lunch and coffee breaks. I was extremely flattered and only too happy to oblige. I have no idea why she chose me since there were older teenagers of both sexes working there.

I was enjoying the work and all was going well until one fateful day when I found myself alone on the elevator with three high school boys who were having fun sexually harassing me! They made obscene remarks about their intentions and scared me to death. Since there was no way to escape them, I did the next best thing. I stopped the car between floors and turned off the light. They freaked out completely and literally begged me to turn on the light and let them out. I made them promise to leave me alone from then on. No problem.

I continued working at Holman's for two-and-a-half years before moving on to Johansen's Dairyland. I have many happy memories of that store and am sad to learn its fate.

Pass the Cream, Please
Jane Roland

I remember vividly the tea/lunch room on the top floor at Holman's Department store. It was a real treat to sit in the room and look at Monterey Bay. I vaguely enjoy egg salad sandwiches. It harkens me back to when I was a girl visiting during the summer in Indiana. It was a small town, Shelbyville, claiming fame to Booth Tarkington (but I think that is an erroneous). However, Tarkington was a devoted Midwesterner from Indianapolis and I am sure spent some time in the little town with the covered bridge. My godmother, who we were visiting, my mother and I would go to L.S. Ayers in Indianapolis to shop but, more importantly, have lunch or tea. I shall never forget their banana cream pie. I didn't have another such experience until dining in the delightful room above our Peninsula's only department store.

In 1931 the third and fourth floors were added to Holman's. The fourth was for furniture, the third divided into two rooms for the comfort of employees and customers. When it was suggested that one of the rooms become a tea room, Mr. Holman declined, saying he wanted the space for his customers. Later, of course, a tea/lunchroom was established. I don't know when it closed but I remember a wedding reception for one of our son's good friends, Wendy Godfrey (Wendy Milligan, one of P.G.'s favorite teachers). What goes around, comes around, right?

FACEBOOK REMINISCENCES

Sample Compilation of Facebook posts by Margie McCurry

The closing of Holman's Department Store and the 2017 beginning of its conversion to condos prompted these memories from Pacific Grove residents.

I remember standing in a long line outside of Holman's during the Second World War I was with my mother who was hoping to purchase the priceless, rationed stockings with a seam up the back of the leg. Those were the days.

With both my parents working there for over 30 years, Holman's was a big part of my life. Sure do miss it.

I got my first "professional bra fitting" there. This ancient woman who was probably 50! Did my fitting. Felt like dying, some stranger handling me. Ha-ha. Also, every fall geared up for school there. St. Angela's uniform and such.

In 1953 or so I used to deliver the Herald to all the offices there in the Holman building.

Wow, I remember riding our bikes through the enclosure looking at all the displays, screaming at the top of our lungs. Singing Christmas carols with the junior high class there and buying my Levi's jeans. Sorry to see it change. Real icon of P.G.

I remember going there and sitting in the sound booths in the music department listening to records. It was so awesome they let us do that.

Giving it a functional new life is better than some of the alternatives.

Used to go there just to ride the elevator when I was a kid—and I remember walking up those rickety stairs. Felt like they would sway as you walk up. Just like the spiral staircase at the professional building.

I believe that at one time Holman's was the largest department store in the county. I used to shop there all the time. I remember my mom giving me $5 to go buy myself a pair of Levi's. They had well-made furniture on the third floor and we bought the first furniture for our home therStill have some of it.

I remember going to Charm School there, posture, manners, etc., and the graduation fashion show. Proper girls did not wear pants in public back then.

If I behaved all week, lunches at the top with a view of the bay. Wish they could have stayed a viable business. Loved Holman's, hanging out in the fishing department pestering the salesman for the best lure or fly for fishing the Big Sur River. Choosing a great sweater vest and button down shirt for the sock hop at the Junior High, etc., etc.

Loved riding up and down the elevators with my friends as a kid and later, eating at the Solarium with my high school posse after walking back from buying records at Recycled Records in New Monterey. I also remember loving the "fancy" lounge connected to the ladies' room.

I'll always remember that store as it was the first time I ever walked in and explored each floor and display back in 1970. Small town glamour.

Change is good. Accept it or move on. Wish I had one of the upper apartments. Bought my first Boy Scout uniform there. Shopped the closeout of the antique gallery. Loved the milkshakes at the cafe upstairs all my youth. Greatest structure in P.G.

I bought my wedding dress there, such a great memory—the bridal department.

Visiting my dad at the furniture department. Having him watch me go by from the Fountain Avenue corner of Holman's when I was in the Butterfly Parade each year.

My aunt took me shopping there in '66. Matching skirts, sweaters and tennies, LOL.

My wife bought her wedding dress there.Breakfast on the rooftop (molded salads, meaning Jell-O and goodies!), Mom getting her hair done weekly by Angeline in the salon, shopping for all the wonderful things, buying my first mattress set for my first apartment. So many memories ….

This is embarrassing, but I have to share. I started my womanhood in the ladies' room. A very sweet lady handed me the biggest pad I had ever seen. I ran crying all the way home. Love that store.

I remember laying in the fabric bolt holders off the cutting tables because I was so bored waiting for my mother, who was looking through the pattern books! If my sister and I were good, we got to visit our grandmother on the third floor in the furniture department.

And Girl Scout uniforms! My sister and I purchased our Girl Scout items there, including my Girl Scout sleeping bag!

FRIENDLY SOUTHERN PACIFIC AND DEL MONTE EXPRESS TRAINS

Riding the rails, which now lie beneath our Recreation Trail

Growing up With Trains
Keith Larson

I've always loved trains. My dad helped me build an HO scale model train set in the back room of our house on Marino Pines. Mr. Anderson was the owner of Space Age Hobbies in town. I remember him mostly sitting behind the counter of his store. He usually wore a tie and sweater, a man in his 60s who liked riding his Honda 750-4 and seemed to know everything about the hobbies we kids were interested in. The hobby shop was located at the Forest Hill shopping center; it was a great place to hang out and race our slot cars, buy model cars and airplanes to build, and talk with Mr. Anderson when we needed advice about our interests. I bought most of my trains there and my dad liked painting model soldiers. Looking back, it is hard to believe so much could be packed into that small space below Cork and Bottle Liquors. Mr. Anderson came over to our house once after closing the shop so he could see the train layout we had been working on.

Actual railroad operations on the Peninsula was a big interest for me, as I secretly hoped to work as a railroad brakeman someday. Later in life, as a volunteer on the San Diego Arizona and Eastern Railway, I was able to realize this dream.

"The friendly Southern Pacific" was the nickname of the railroad that ran though The Last Hometown. It was part of a big road with about 15,000 miles of track in operation here in California and other states. My dad would often take me out to the Watsonville train yard Sundays after church. The guys were friendly out there and Dad would always start off the conversation with the fact that my grandfather, who unfortunately I had never met, worked for the Santa Fe railroad in Richmond, California. This would get us in the door, and once the yard master let us go up in the tower to watch the trains bound for other cities being made up. I remember the tower man complaining to my dad that someone who had much less time on the railroad and didn't really know anything about railroading was his new boss.

Back in town, if I was heading off to middle school around 8:00 a.m., I could sometimes hear the blast of the air horns as the Del Monte Express left for its run to San Francisco. It would return at 8:00 p.m. if all went well. The glory days when the Del Monte Express carried rich tourists from San Francisco to the Del Monte Hotel, now the Naval Postgraduate School in Monterey, had long since passed.

During the 1960s, Southern Pacific tried to scrap the two-car train but was not able to until Amtrak took over operations for the nation's passenger trains in 1971. The new government agency axed our service, which was the oldest continuously scheduled passenger train on the Southern Pacific. I remember taking this once proud train with my mother to look after our auntie Peg in San Jose; there were still a lot of farms and orchards adjacent to the right-of-way as we headed north to San Jose.

Another time on the train was the first trip I made by myself, taking it to visit a friend who had moved away. My dad asked the conductor to make sure I got off the train okay. I think I might have been nine or ten at the time. When my station arrived, the conductor came though calling, "Menlo Park, this stop is Menlo Park."

As I was leaving I wanted to make sure and asked the conductor if it was Menlo Park. He said, "Yes," and seemed a bit agitated. "Didn't you hear me?"

Here's an easy quiz: where is the best place to ride on a train? All of you who answered, "Inside a locomotive cab," can now stop trying to get in touch with your inner child. You're there! I was down by the tracks near Asilomar, watching the train crew switching cars around with two of my friends, when we got an invitation from the engineer to come up in the cab, a dream come true for me. Motive power for the sand plant run that day was two SW-1500 back-to-back switch engines. I can remember asking one of the men how much crew they had that day. "Two brakemen, an engineer and a conductor," he said.

It seemed like they were all wearing the standard type of work shoes and bib overalls that were blue, not striped. The engineer seemed really old to me but was probably just in his late 60s. Now that I am approaching my 60th year, I have to be careful with that term "old."

I was a pretty aware and observant when it came to railroads and I had done a lot of reading, so I asked the engineer about layoffs on the railroad. He nodded and said there had been quite a number. This was around 1970 or 71. As he was running the engines slowly up the track, occasionally glancing at his *San Francisco Chronicle*, I took note of the operating controls and learned where the throttle was, air brake and reverse lever,. as well as the all-important air horn which, could be heard wailing though town five days a week in the late afternoons.

The reason for the tracks was a spooky old sand plant, a collection of buildings which could be made even more mysterious by the incoming fog. Top quality sand was shipped to various places to make glass. The Spanish Bay complex now sits on the former site, the sand plant having ceased operations around 1979.

It was time for the engineer and crew to go up to the lead engine. My friend Joe and I are instructed to stay where we are. We're looking out at the beach at Asilomar and my friend Joe says reflectively that it would be nice to work for the railroad, that it seems like an easy life. I said that I didn't think it would be so easy, yet I thought I would trade middle school for this right now. As I looked out the cab window I thought these guys were really good, hopping on and off cars, tightening brakes, coupling the cars, throwing switches and signaling to each other.

Finally it was time to hook the caboose on the end and, with the freight cars having been assembled, head for home. The engineer slowed down but didn't stop as we hung on the grab railings and stepped of backwards, the way you should if a train is moving. It was late afternoon as the caboose rolled by; the conductor used a lamp as he looked down at some paper work. I continued to watch as the Tuscan-colored caboose crossed the street at Sinex and headed into the shadows caused by the tall Monterey Pines along the right-of-way. That day the train crew of the Southern Pacific gave me something I have remembered my whole life. A big thank you to all the engineers, brakemen, switchmen, conductors and yard personnel of "the friendly Southern Pacific."

Last Train Through P.G.

Any history of our area will most likely have a chapter or a few pages about the coming of the railroad, stories of rich San Francisco tourists staying at the Hotel Del Monte and other information about the Southern Pacific and what the railroad meant for the community.

Endings are sometimes less spectacular and unrecorded. In 1971, Amtrak took over the nation's passenger trains. Our own Del Monte Express was not included in Amtrak's roster. The last train out of Monterey in 1971 was well covered in the news, and had many passengers and coaches for its last run. But it was not the last train to roll down the tracks though our communities. The Southern Pacific had a regularly scheduled freight train that served light industries on the Peninsula, but its biggest customer was the sand plant in Pebble Beach where Spanish Bay is now.

I had always been interested in trains as a boy growing up here in town, and you couldn't help but note the trains' comings and goings every day as the locomotive whistle could be heard all over Pacific Grove. The freight had always been an afternoon train and during the late 1970s the throbbing, clanking diesel engines with their load of sometimes 20 to 30 cars of sand became an infrequent visitor to the Grove.

I was working as a night custodian at David Avenue School; the year was around 1979 or 80. I was surprised to hear in the distance the air horns of a diesel engine. Judging from the sound, I thought the train might be near Cannery Row. Soon the whistle become louder as it blew the horn at every crossing in town like in years past. I had this feeling inside that this was the last time I would hear the familiar train though Pacific Grove. The mobile home park in town had put a gate over the tracks. Perhaps those in this community living next to the tracks thought the train was not coming any longer. Either the engineer didn't see the gate or did not care. Instant splinters as the engines crashed through it. This event did not make the news and there was nothing mentioned about the last train through town. Except for the gate incident, this was a quiet ending to the colorful railroad history on the Peninsula.

Some years later, the tracks were taken up and the Recreation Trail put in its place. I still can picture playing at the main beach in the summers and waving to the engineer as the train approached the crossing at Ocean View Boulevard. The crossing at this street was the only one in town that had an electrified signal. So long, "Friendly SP."

Kids and Trains
Jean Hurlbert Jorgensen
homemaker, friend, nature lover, adventurer

"Hurry up. You'll be late!" Mother shooed me out the back door after Jerry, running to the train station.

We lived on Mermaid Avenue, between the ocean and the railroad tracks. Out the front door was the lure of rocks, tide pools, the wharf and swimming pool, places where we spent most of our waking hours with Mother saying, "Be home by dark!"

Out back were the train tracks, another magnet.

One of our greatest rituals, several times a week, was joining other kids on our street to jump onto the turntable to ride when the engine got turned around.

The Southern Pacific Railroad rented a neighborhood house for the train crews to stay overnight. Two crews alternated making the run from San Francisco to Pacific Grove. One crew in particular got to know the families on the street and encouraged us kids to learn about the trains so we wouldn't do stupid things and get hurt.

We'd climb onto the turntable before it started up, hanging on to a slanted post at an angle near the outer edge. Turning around the engine took only a few minutes, but they were exciting ones. Sometimes we were invited into the steam engine to learn how it worked. It was hot and dirty in there from the furnace.

The water tower was down the tracks a ways. Beyond was the flat roof of the covered well. We'd climb through an opening into the dark, damp place about the size of our living room. We'd hold onto boards or pipes, trying not to fall into the murky, greenish water, while trying to grab one of the resident frogs that would leap into the water when we got too close. I caught one once. Wanting to take it home to show to Mother, I wondered how to carry the slippery thing. I stuck it inside my shirt and held it against the skin of my chest while I ran home. It was slimy and yucky, but worth it. Mother was impressed. We examined the poor thing thoroughly. Then she encouraged me to take it back to its home since its family that would be missing it.

We raced on the tracks often. To this day when I walk near railroad tracks I can't resist hopping on to one. How far and fast can I walk before I lose my balance and fall off?

One ritual was to leave a penny on the track to be flattened by the next train. I sometimes run across a thin copper oval in a box of odds and ends, triggering memories once again.

Today the site of these adventures looks so different. "Where did all of that happen?"

Where the tracks were is a paved path from Pacific Grove to Monterey enjoyed by bikers, skaters and pedestrians. They obviously have fun where the tracks once were, but I question whether their experiences could possibly top our adventures of long ago!

What I Remember
Simone Hollander

I was born at CHOMP. When I was little, in the early eighties, Pacific Grove was nicknamed Pacific Grave. My neighbors were retired, two were multi-war veterans, one alcoholic, one rageful. The widow next door razed her lawn and installed AstroTurf as a low maintenance solution. I climbed onto the roof of our rented house with my cat and watched a buck pause under the street lamp. I adventured through my neighborhood alone at night with my dog, tried to follow the raccoons out of our walls (where they periodically had their babies) and into the streets. My alcoholic neighbor adopted a kitten, named her Tomato Head, and when she crossed his backyard the couple on the other side wouldn't return her. On our ocean trail between two points my friend and I invented stories about mermaids, about dark chambers in the giant aloe, and later, about the boys we had crushes on. Shopkeepers followed us in the stores, waiters endured orders of water and French fries. We wore the clothes of our neighbors as they died, purchased from The Church Mouse: silk floral cocktail dresses, argyle sweater vests, wide-lapelled button-ups, and, once, a pair of velvet house shoes with mink pom-poms. When I got older there were kisses in the sand dunes, bonfires at Asilomar Beach, drug-induced tree hugging, and waiting for the effects of acid to wear off in the park beside the library.

When I could drive I drove my friend the three blocks home, I drove to school, I drove along the water,

I drove to the Aquarium where I volunteered, I drove to the Pebble Beach Equestrian Center where I rode other people's horses all over the forest. I drove over the hill to Carmel where my dad and his family lived. I drove to Big Sur, I drove to Carmel Valley. I drove to Arcata for college, then I drove to Seattle for college, then I flew to Europe, the Far East, Australia, the Mediterranean, Turkey, the Middle East, and the town, my town, my Pacific Grove, had its houses bought up and torn down, Irma's AstroTurf plowed under so pampas grass landscaping could soften the edges of a void, lot-filling structure some people call a house but not, I imagine, a home.

But now there's a farmers market, and chickens in the backyard, and families again, and it is my mother and her friends who have become the old-timers, though instead of drinking and fighting they are more prone to ride bikes, sail boats, hike up and down bluffs crusted with poison oak; they do not confiscate each other's kittens. And though there is no longer a place for me in my own home town, though perhaps it does not even exist apart from my chemistry with it, my experience of it, when I step off the plane /every time/, the first blast of sea air hits me and I'm home, my ocean, my forest, my town, Pacific Grove.

P.G. Freedom Riding
Dawn Armstrong

In 1955 PG, a bicycle was freedom. Noisily, with playing cards pinned to the spokes, or quietly. we cruised Pine Street and Sinex Avenue, standing up and pumping hard so the wind felt like we were going really fast. We rode anywhere we wanted to go.

We rode to the David Avenue End O' the Lane Stables for horseback riding lessons. I wasn't very good at that. The horse always knew I was scared. For my last lesson, I had a choice of English or Western saddle. I chose Western on that day and it was a good thing. The only horse available was the owner's daughter's horse. He was way too much for me to handle. When my best friend and I turned back from the Del Monte Forest trail, my horse took off with me clutching the saddle horn.

As we approached the barn I realized I had a life or death decision to make: stay on and risk decapitation or let loose and risk flying off into something that would hurt. I flew off, hitting the side of the barn and sliding down to the ground. I was sure I was in pieces and chose not to open my eyes or to move. The people who came running thought I was seriously hurt.

They had me get back on a different horse as soon as it was determined I was shaken but not broken. I bravely but miserably rode around the corral twice. Except for one elderly steed, my later equine experiences were no better. My friend went on to ride in the Salinas Rodeo Parade every year on her own beloved horse. Sixty-two years later, I made an offer on a house where the End O' the Lane corral once was. It crossed my mind that there might be horses buried under the cul de sac.

Another regular adventure was a ride to Ice Cream Mountain. We packed lunches and put the paper bags into our bicycle baskets. My friend and I rode to the bottom of the widest and tallest dune, near where Spanish Bay is now. It was an effort to climb, sliding back a bit each time we stepped up and forward. At the top we could see everything - Pebble Beach, Del Monte Forest, Asilomar to the Point Pinos dunes. Our private mountain retreat was a special, secret place. We talked about stuff we didn't share with anyone else. Sometimes we didn't talk at all.

The railroad track ended at the dunes where sand was loaded into train cars and delivered to fill sand boxes like the one I had before we moved to Pacific Grove. We were told that children all over the world played in our soft white sand. The first time I returned to Pacific Grove I wondered where all the dunes were. Was it all used up in play or did kids no longer have sand boxes?

SECTION 6
THE SUPERNATURAL

MIRACLES, MAGIC AND FAIRY TALES

I Got the Fairytale
Kathy Cuen-Ashby
happily married and retired Nana

After arriving here five-and-a-half years ago, I often wondered if I hadn't died and just didn't remember, because certainly I must be in heaven! I really did, and I still do every now and then. Pacific Grove is paradise. January of 2012, with "Mary Jane's Last Dance" blasting at full volume, I merged onto I-8W and said goodbye to the sizzling hot desert of southwestern Arizona that had been my home for 40-plus years. It was time.

I was off for a new adventure for the second half of my life. Funny to think that just six months prior, I had no idea that I would be doing that, no idea that my life would soon be unrecognizable to me. But, on a fluke in mid-June, I met and starting "talking" with a man online. We connected immediately and spoke freely and often with each other. In September, he traveled to Arizona to meet me, and we had three wonderful days together.

He returned home to Pacific Grove, and soon after, I was putting a "for sale" in my front yard and packing boxes. When I eventually made it to Pacific Grove, the first few days were a whirlwind of sightseeing and exploring the Peninsula. It was too much to take in! Beauty galore! I also spent a lot of time walking Lighthouse Avenue, looking at the fun shops and talking with people I met on the way.

Such friendly, nice folks! (I have since concluded that people are happier here because we don't have the stress of the extreme heat and the blazing sun beating down on us all day. Day-to-day living is easier here for that reason alone.) While out exploring, there were a few times I would just stop and look around and think, "OMG! I get to LIVE here!" and be so tickled and blown away that I'd burst out laughing.

The day before leaving for the Esalen Yoga Festival of 2012, the idea that we might have an impromptu wedding while there arose. I went downtown "wedding dress" shopping and within a few minutes, was taking the outfit from a mannequin in the windows of Marita's Boutique on Lighthouse Avenue. Just another sign that I was right where I was supposed to be!

Another thing that impressed me early on was reading the "cop log" in the *Cedar Street Times*. It's like 1950s *Mayberry RFD*! I didn't think places like this still existed. I'm glad they do. And the Post Office! I never would have imagined I would ever enjoy going to the Post Office, but I do in Pacific Grove! I enjoy seeing the great people who work there, and trust me, they go out of their way to provide good service. How they have deciphered some of my grandchildren's attempts to address an envelope and actually get it to my house is nothing short of a miracle.

Every once in a while, I'll miss the hum of an air conditioner and the Arizona sunsets, but that's OK; I've definitely "traded up." This exquisite, wondrous, magical place called Pacific Grove is my home! So if you ever see a woman laughing uncontrollably while out and about, go ahead and say, "hi." It's probably me.

August 22, 1992
Kathy Apodaca
descendant of 1890 P.G. Methodist ministers

August 22nd, 1992. That's when I first came to live in Pacific Grove. Living in Pacific Grove truly was a miracle in my life. My new home was a haven provided by my Aunt Patricia Hamilton and my Great Aunt Charlotte Berry. We were all living in my Great-Grandpa Harry Murray's beautiful Victorian home on the corner of Park Place and Grand Avenue just across from Jewell Park near the P.G. Public Library. Harry had left lifetime use of the house to Charlotte, who was in her 80s, and Patricia had come to live there to help Charlotte. I enjoyed my chance to get to know Charlotte better, as she was my Grandma Charline's triplet sister. Charline and brother Charles had died before I had a chance to know them and thus I had an insight to what my Grandma may have been like. Charlotte was a strong, kind, and interesting person.

Getting to know and love Pacific Grove was a blessing, too. The "Last Hometown," I was told, was a real community-oriented town. With events like Good Old Days, Feast of Lanterns, the Butterfly Parade, Victorian Home Tours, and Stillwell's Snow in the Park, there was always something to do. There were also the many open art gallery evenings. Grove Homescapes comes to mind as I was blessed to have worked there. The beautiful building at 472 Lighthouse Avenue was the old Grove Laundry, transformed by two brothers, Thompson Lange and Beau Finklang, into a design showroom of art, home furnishings, and orchids, including a beautiful sweeping staircase leading to the balcony showroom upstairs. The open art gallery evenings and other festive parties were held on a regular basis and much to be admired. Memories of visiting with friends and enjoying the ambiance still ring in my head to this day.

Nature

Jewell Park had many musical events and sitting on the grass in sunshine listening to music was magical. Moonlit nights swimming in the ocean with a friend who had seaweed glistening around his neck comes to mind, along with all the other trips to Point Lobos for hikes and to China Cove for swims. I was a real nature-minded girl. But the most memorable thing that comes to mind these days is something else. The other side to nature, and a miracle-maker.

Father Edge

There was a café in downtown that held poetry nights. And that is where I met Father Edge. He read his poetry with great enthusiasm, and I was drawn to him like a moth to a flame. He helped me to see the other side of nature with his poem that I will share with you now, just because there are two sides to every coin.

Nature by Father Edge

keep your nature walks
your back-to-the-roots consciousness
your backpacking, tent-pitching,
mosquito-net panorama
of state parks brimming with
the Neanderthal existence
our ancestors fought so hard
to climb out of
I am a child of civilization
I like the hustle and bustle
of activity-mad streets
of human-psychobabble
of industrial juggernauts
of effort and enterprise
of life, life, life, life,
LIFE!
not insect life
not foliage life
not bird life and fish life
snail life or slug life
HUMAN LIFE!!
the bumping and grinding of crowded buses
and subway cars
the heat and sweat of a happening nightclub:
condensed sex/proximity thermal
the explosive cheers at a touchdown or
the sound of a playground full of children.
we're not meant to live on lofty mountaintops
where the air is rare,
life is scarce,
and the silence
deafening
or in dark forests
where Nature's protozoan chaos is smothering

and the blind grope after the blind,
in slow mineral orgasms
Look around! we're not there anymore
it's called, evolution:
the climb out of the slime
I don't want to hear about your camp-making
tick-biting, nettle-bristling, insect-eating,
mud-mucking, granola-munching,
Gortex-bedrolling, Coleman stove-cooking
escapist mania;
puffing your chest up when you speak of it,
like taking a hike is hard—
'exercise' for the rugged:
those elite capable of
"roughing it"
It ain't rough, it ain't exciting
It's just plain BORING!
put your back into a shovel
to dig the foundation of a building,
channel a river to harness the energy,
move a mountain to create roads—
hammer, saw, carry, lift
all in the name of human enterprise—
that is "roughing it"
our race wasn't meant to sit on the side of a
    mountain
picking its nose and watching pretty sunsets
we were meant to be architects
of a technological dynasty,
blazing across the galaxy
upon the power of the human dynamo
building empires
so keep your 'return-to-nature' myopia
I don't have time for even a visit
for I am a busy human god
fulfilling my role in the multiversal script
by designing a Universe
IN MY IMAGE

A Migratory Guest
Elayne Azevedo

I was thrilled to arrive to this magical place of Pacific Grove with friendly people in a safe community surrounded by natural beauty. The year was 2011. It was time to stop moving, unload the trunk, close the door to the storage unit and settle down for a while. The question was, "Where to settle for the next phase of my life?" The answer came as clear as blue skies and white rainbows. A migratory guest, a short timer, a new resident—any label fit.

People had a genuine hospitality, warmth and friendliness about them. They were quick to share advice: valuable information about pastry shops, early bird specials at restaurants, great hikes, and free popcorn on Mondays at Lighthouse Cinemas. Passersby actually made eye contact and stopped to chat. Staff at Grove Market would give me the same friendly smiles and service with my $1 purchase of spring salad mix and peanuts as the next customer.

Kindness and caring overflowed. On my walk, I would notice odd items: a fleece glove, red sock, blue baby shoe placed on hedges, fence posts, tree trunks. It was as if someone was helping the little kittens who lost their mittens. That people actually took the time to place items off the dew and dirt was radically decent! I fancied the courteous nature of this charming hamlet.

Being able to park my car safely on the street for days at a time was great. Being able to go for night walks, listen to soothing waves and catch the full moon at Lovers Point was fabulous! The P.G. Museum of Natural History was a wonderful resource. There was a big whale there! A kind of a promontory welcome. Later I learned that it was "Sandy"—designed and created by Larry Foster. Sandy spent a decade of traveling, serving as an ambassador for save-the-whale campaigns and later retired here and became a permanent resident. The community had rallied together to purchase the statue for the children.

On a bad day, a quiet gaze across the bay would lift my mood. I remember shivering my first summer and shaking my head into the fog. The locals would just whisper, "go to the valley." One early morning at Asilomar Beach I saw a shimmering white rainbow! Luckily, I took photos to prove this effervescent moment. Later I learned it was a "fog bow." After that I stopped complaining about cold summers.

I have lived here six years now. As I head up the walkway to see Sandy. I look into her dreamy eyes and imagine a quick wink of agreement that we were both lucky and wise to stay on this migratory stopover.

Still...
Rebecca Riddell

As an old lady, I often find myself reminiscing about the Good Ol' Days of P.G. Then I immediately remind myself that even in 2017 this is a wondrous place. One of the most spectacular on earth, if I do say so myself.

There's a special kind of light here, as any artist as far back as the turn of the last century would tell you. It's that pinkish kind of light that makes everything sing. Not during the months when the fog rolls in, of course. Yet, that's its own kind of awesome. Ever walk down the street in fog so thick you couldn't see your hand? If you grew up in P.G. back in the day, you did. I think watching the tall, aging pines dance in the fog is one of the most beautiful sights to behold. You can still watch them now in June or July.

You can still sit out on your porch in the morning and hear the seals barking from the Monterey Coast Guard Pier. No matter where in P.G. you live, you can still hear the bells chime the time from City Hall and the test runs for the Feast of Lanterns Pageant from Lovers Point Beach. I still watch the school band march down my street on their way to the Good Old Days or the Butterfly Parade, just as it has always been.

You can still get a burger from the shack at the beach. While they're really not the same, I still stop by for lunch every once in a while. The glass bottom boats where I worked as a teen are gone, yet now they have kayaks and bike rentals and such.

You can still see the butterflies fluttering through town from November through March, and deer, raccoons, squirrels, and possum still navigate through my yard each day. Yes, a lot has changed and much has stayed the same.

The mayor, the butcher, the baker, they still know me by name. I still leave my front door wide open on occasion when I run to Grove Market. I have found an assortment of stray animals and even an ex-husband, yet never a thief or intruder. Foolish in today's world, I know. But, this is still P.G.

This is still a magical place to raise children, with the beaches, the parks, and the neighborly neighbors. Even with the high percentage of second homes and short-term rentals (as can only be expected in the most beautiful place on earth), I now have young children back in my neighborhood. May they share in the wonders I've experienced growing up in this unique little town by the sea.

On The Road
Four Local Boys

Jack Kerouac wrote about; it Willie Nelson sang about it; Steve Covell and Ray Byrne of Pacific Grove experienced the joy of travel in September. It was a trip to Santa Fe where they took Steve's cousin's classic Rolls Royce to a Concours. After four days, they headed back to the Peninsula. There was the consideration of which lovely town, Needles or Laughlin, to spend the night; they picked the former, as neither had been there and hope never to revisit.

The next morning they were on the road again, at least rested if not exhilarated. They arrived in Pacific Grove and Steve unpacked his truck, realizing with shock that a garment bag with over $1,000 worth of clothing was missing. "How could this be?" he despaired. Had he failed to lock the camper door? Had some miscreant lifted his favorite sports jacket, his Talbot tie (a Valentine's gift from Jan, his wife)? He called Harrah's and complained about the lack of proper parking lot surveillance, then Tom McKinney at State Farm to ascertain if his insurance policy would cover the loss. No such luck, and he began to prioritize the belongings to see what should be replaced.

Two days later there was a telephone call. "Hi, are you Steve Covell?" asked the man on the line.

"Yes, I am." Steve answered.

"Did you lose a garment bag?"

Steve couldn't believe it, as he sat down and listened in amazement to the story. The caller was a truck driver whose route took him on Interstate 5 from Bakersfield to Fresno. He had noticed a tan bag on the side of the road but didn't have time to stop. The next day he tried to remember the location of the bag, cruised slowly down the highway and, sure enough, there it was. Inside was a shirt still in the bag with a laundry tag, from Pacific Grove Cleaners, bearing Steve's name and telephone number.

The bag was mailed, Steve received it and sent the Good Samaritan a nice reward and thank you note, to which the driver responded with gratitude, as he expected nothing, it was his pleasure to help. This is one of these minor miracles and, as Steve said, "Some truck drivers are still the 'guardians of the highway.'"

There was another Pacific Grove miracle. Nancy Shammas lost her little dog, Lola, in Rancho San Carlos about the 14th of October. How it happened doesn't really matter; the dog was gone and no one could find her. Nancy, her significant other, Allen, her family and friends went up daily for over two weeks. There were sightings from time to time, so at least she was still alive in the mountains inhabited by carnivorous animals, but no one could find her. They called, they hiked, they prayed, Allen spent two nights looking.

One day Nancy saw Lola, but the traumatize pup would not go to her. It was desperation time, but no one gave up hope and the faith paid off; a few days later Allen caught her and Nancy was reunited with her beloved pet of almost ten years. Lola was glad to be home, a little thinner and, hopefully, wiser from her glorious adventure.

It shows that in big things and small, all is never lost. If there is hope and belief the impossible can happen. We will look forward to seeing Steve in his splendor and Lola with her purple collar.

Since this was written our Nancy passed away, and a few years later, Allen told us that Lola had joined her.

Polka Dot House, Ghost House
Lindley Muender

My father, a New Jersey native and World War II veteran, was driving through Pacific Grove with my mother and older brother before I was born. Dad exclaimed, "I am going to figure out how to live here! The beauty is incredible, and I never want to shovel snow again!"

Mother replied, "It is indeed lovely, but I hear it has foggy summers."

Lucky for me, my dad and mom got good jobs at the Naval Postgraduate School, and it was double luck I was born here. We settled into a nice home by Country Club Gate, next door to a colorful polka dot house. Mom said she and Dad used to drive to Monterey for wine because Pacific Grove was a "dry town."

As I grew up I made magical memories of summer days at Lovers Point Beach with my brother and me splashing around, lunches at the old Holman's Department Store eating club sandwiches and enjoying in breathtaking views, and Christmas full of lights and wonder on Candy Cane Lane. Let's not leave out teen bonfire parties at the Asilomar Beach, much to my father's chagrin.

Years later I was married at the Methodist church on Seventeen Mile Drive on a foggy September morning. Partway through the wedding the fog cleared up, and the sun shone through the butterfly stained glass window. My lovely son and daughter came from that marriage, and we moved to the Sacramento area.

Twenty-five years later after diapers, dealings with work, kids, traveling and divorce, finding a new mate and blending a family, my mom got diagnosed with cancer. My teen daughter and I moved back to Pacific Grove and landed on Congress Avenue in a historic, cute little doll house with some strange hauntings such as tappings, doors sounding like they're opening and lights going on by themselves.

I used to walk to Asilomar Beach and every day the tides and weather shifted. I even went boogie boarding. I found a job teaching art to kids with the Pacific Grove Natural History Museum and it was like stepping back in time from when I visited as a Brownie.

Although Holman's was closed, good eats were abundant at Red House Café, Toasties and the Fishwife. I reside in Carmel Valley now, but Pacific Grove will always be part of my heart.

Red and Gold Birthday Wish
Jeanie Gould
Long time resident and author

As our country was trying to make sense out of 9/11, we needed a diversion, something positive to focus on.

In October, I asked my son Brian what he would like for his upcoming 17th birthday. He thought for a moment and then matter-of-factly said, "I want to play in a championship football game on my birthday and have both sets of my grandparents there." I thought, *Yeah, right…that's going to happen.*

"That's a big order," I said. "Especially as this season has barely started."

As the season progressed, the team continued to excel. It was the buzz of the town, and the team progressed through multiple contenders to earn a spot in the championship game.

On December 1, 2001, Brian's 17th birthday, they would be playing in San Jose for the coveted CCS Championship. The stars must have been in the correct alignment for this to happen. My husband Steve's parents drove down from San Francisco and my parents jumped on a train from Oregon. As the hour of the game approached, a freak windstorm caused a tree to blow down over the tracks, delaying their train. They finally pulled in to San Jose and took a cab to the stadium, arriving like refugees with their luggage in tow as the game began.

We had all gotten to the game, mostly on time, and found the bleachers were jam-packed with P.G.'s red and gold, and with an unbridled energy buzzing throughout the crowd.

As the game started, you could see the players fueled with restless energy and determination. They started out the game strong, and throughout the first half, they dominated.

At half-time I asked the announcer if they could wish "happy birthday" to Brian on air. He wasn't sure, so he yelled up to the booth, "Hey, George, can we announce happy birthday to one of the players on the P.G. team? His name is Brian Gould." He answered back, "Well, that's cool, but I'm not sure if that's allowed."

"No problem," I said. "You can't blame a mom for trying."

The second half of the game was also dominated by P.G.. *Was this really possible,* I wondered. As the final seconds ticked away on the scorecard, I realized that Brian's obscure birthday wish was coming true – the final score: P.G. 17: Pioneer 0.

The P.G. bleachers erupted! The players were jumping up and down, hugging each other, coaches got ice water dumped on them, and the fans were screaming! The town was celebrating!

When the bus full of players got back in to town, we had them all over to our house for a huge birthday party. A few days later there was a celebration parade right through the heart of downtown to honor the champions.

Then, when we later watched the game tape, we were surprised to hear that my entire exchange about Brian's birthday with the announcer at half-time had been recorded. That really put the frosting on the cake!

The Epiphany
Amy Krupski
harpist

In August of 1969 I visited the coast of California with dreams of a place to relocate. I had recently gone through a divorce and was very motivated to get away from the suffocating Texas heat. After exploring several places between San Diego and San Francisco, I visited a friend here on the Monterey Peninsula. We stopped at The Bread Basket, now Nob Hill, for food and headed down Oceanview Boulevard looking for a place to enjoy lunch. I don't remember the exact spot, but we were near what later became The American Tin Cannery Outlets just outside Pacific Grove.

I said to my friend, "I really like this part of Monterey." He corrected me, saying, "This is Pacific Grove, not Monterey." At that very instant I had an epiphany and knew I would be right here the rest of my life, even though I had no work in the area and had never heard of Pacific Grove!

After returning to Texas, I was relieved to learn I had been accepted to work at the Health Department in Salinas and had no problem foregoing an earlier offer to work at the prestigious Menninger Clinic in Topeka, Kansas. I knew I would take a cut in salary and probably give up this singular opportunity to move forward in my career as a Clinical Social Worker, but never questioned what I knew was best for me. I met my late husband two years later, and we raised our two children right here in the last hometown.

Yes, for me to trust my epiphany was the best decision I ever made. I am thankful I listened to my heart rather than my head and followed the wisdom of that powerful phenomenon back in 1969!

The Time I Saw A Fairy in Pacific Grove
Joyce Day Meuse
astrologer, wedding minister, radio host

I've had a few experiences in my life which could be called visions and this one stands out. In the early 1980's I took a psychic development training course that taught people to read auras and chakras, talk to spirit guides, and investigate past lives. After three introductory eight week classes, those who were interested pursued a yearlong training program. We met a couple of times a week to give student readings to willing volunteers. Three of us would sit in a line of chairs and face a single person also in a chair in front of us. The teacher was observant and encouraged us and gave his perspective on the aura and past lives we were seeing. The whole course of study operated on the concept of amusement. Lots of laughter kept the energy moving and prevented us from getting bogged down in pain and problems. Everybody enjoyed it from the readers to the so called "readee." It was so much fun.

After one of these student reading sessions, I went to a music party in Pacific Grove. A friend of mine rented a two-story old house that was said to have been a speakeasy during prohibition. It was on a very large lot with lots of trees and bushes all around it. It backed up to the old railroad tracks which gave it a sense of space and privacy.

The live music was blasting away in the living room. The ever-present belly dancers were dancing. My friend was wailing away on her saxophone. There were always plenty of percussionists playing on hand drums, and guitar players and whoever else wanted to join in. I remember one fellow who played a goatskin bagpipe. That woke everybody up.

I was sitting on a chair against the wall enjoying the music when this blue fairy entered right through the wall, quickly floated through the living room and exited out to the kitchen. She was about a foot tall and looked exactly like the fairies you see in children's books. I was flabbergasted. Apparently, no one else noticed this but my jaw dropped. After the party, I tucked this experience away as a longtime favorite memory.

Eventually I started teaching psychic development classes myself. During one I mentioned my fairy experience to the group. One women who lived in that same neighborhood said that her then small son came home one day from playing in the back of their house that also bordered the trail and said, "I just saw a dead fairy down by the creek." The open-minded mom probably chalked it up to imagination until I told her my story which corroborated his. And it validated my experience. I still walk on that wonderful railroad tracks trail where I saw my P.G. blue fairy.

An Elf Land
R. M. Zurkan

Pagrovian. The name implies a citizen of a different kind of place, an elf land, perhaps, or middle earth. Well, Pacific Grove is a magical place.

I was late to discover it.

Before moving to the Monterey Peninsula, I used to meet my daughter in Carmel, halfway between her home and mine. I knew nothing about Pacific Grove except, perhaps, wasn't there a conference center, a Chappequa, called Asilomar, or haven by the sea?

A weekend wasn't long enough to explore other towns around Carmel, but, after moving to the Monterey Peninsula three years ago, I wasted no time discovering all the beauties of the region. In this, I was accompanied, always, by my best friend and constant companion— Stella, my border collie mix.

The first time we strolled down Lighthouse in Pacific Grove—where were we going, I don't remember, the excellent Grove Nutrition for vitamins, the Grove Market for any number of goodies? A stranger greeted us, bending down and addressing the delighted dog in a friendly way. Later the same afternoon, we met him again, and he greeted us again. "My new friend," he said to the dog.

I love the fact that there are so many animal help shops in Pacific Grove, each serving a different portion of the animal loving public: Animal Friends Rescue Project, Tailwaggers Animal Welfare, Peace of Mind Dog Rescue.

Fridays are our particular day to explore Pacific Grove. We drive down Lighthouse and up Forest, stopping for the newspaper, *The Cedar Street Times*, and continuing to Rip Van Winkle Park. It did not take us long to discover the park as well as the path beyond leading to the ocean and leash-free beach.

I'm not a Californian by birth, nor do any of my relatives reside here. I was born and grew up in New York. However, walking down the street in Pacific Grove I have the sensation of being someone else from anywhere else, someone more agreeable, more open to the beauty around me, beauty no less of the smiling faces than the magnificent ocean and cliffs.

What made my parents move east to New York instead of west to California? To Pacific Grove? My father was born in Minnesota to Swedish immigrants. My mother had no connection with New York either. She emigrated from Hungary, nearly the sole survivor of a family which perished in Auschwitz. Somehow, her younger brother managed to join the American Army and served as a radio operator in the Pacific. But my parents moved to New York. Why couldn't they have moved west instead?

Never mind. I'm here now. My dog and me. Is it possible for a person to reinvent herself, to let go of the detritus, the wrong turnings of the past? Yes. Here, if anywhere.

When the Spirit Moves...
Linda Iversen Johnson
resident since July 2016

A garden of words grows in my head as I think of what moved me to live in Pacific Grove. I know I was drawn by the restless peace of the sea. But perhaps my search for a retirement landing found me coasting here like a homeward bound monarch butterfly searching for the perfect grove to overwinter in.

Today sunlight spreads my eyelashes upwards as I look out on the blue ocean shore to take in the landscape: the sky itself holds a prayer meeting attended by flocks of surf boards and shiny black wetsuits like exclamation marks chasing the noisy curls, while overhead the soft cotton candy white of clouds drifts gently towards the horizon.

I hear not a choir but see a chorus line of brown pelicans skimming across the silence in the distance. Beyond, carved out by crayon-colored kayaks paddling through the bay, there's a playful sea otter in the kelp beds rolling over to splash dive into the ruffled surface.

Next my attention is drawn like a hummingbird toward the drum beat of footsteps along the sandy Recreation Trail where a runner leads a long-eared dog sniffing the salt-tinged air. Perhaps he's heading for the local farmers' market wedged in between stately Victorian homes or beyond the arches framing the proud historic library to end his parade at the leisurely paced Post Office nestled in a charming downtown filled with artwork in shops, tantalizing food stops, and anchored by the signs of real estate.

I stop to be here, part of the community festival, smile at the rambling deer, and then I pocket my image-filled camera to take in a deep breath of gratitude. My new wings have sprouted. Behind me I leave my history as a native Californian that comes uninvited again and again but is forever welcome to join my future harvest-full picnic. My years of living as a tourist in life have been uprooted. My Bay Area home 100 miles away has been sold, a permanent replacement purchased.

My treasured old friends wave me onward as I leave them behind, and like museum quality sea shells, my new friends and activities are being collected as if they represent both the familiar and the exotic. My retirement is in full bloom. I have moved beyond the dream stage, and actually been successfully transplanted. Watch out, Pagrovians. I am bubbling over. Now I'm officially a year-round happy local.

SECTION 7
A CREATIVE AND LITERATE COMMUNITY

ARTISTS AND ARTISANS OF ALL PERSUASIONS

Renaissance Man Steve Hauk

Jane Roland

Steve Hauk is a renaissance man. "Why do you say that?" you may ask, adding, "He is an art dealer." Ah, but he is much more than that. If you bear with me I will explain. In life there are certain people with whom one comes in contact at many stages. Steve Hauk has been one of those individuals in my travels through the years.

In the late 1970s we were involved with Marcia Hovick's Children's Experimental Theater; Ellen was a student and John and I co-chaired the board. We decided that to raise a little more money, we would develop a membership category. After this was completed we held a fundraiser at the barn at Mission Ranch, featuring one of Marcia's plays. The young theater critic from the *Herald* was there. I had not met him before; it was Steve.

A few years later Ellen was attending York. She and a few classmates wrote a play for the Monterey County competition and won. They were to perform one night at York, then at the Conference Center. I asked Steve to come. His response was that he didn't review student plays, nor one-night stands. The night of the production, there he was and the girls' "The Dock Brief" was featured in the *Herald* with a picture. They later went on to win the regional competition.

I am not sure Steve wrote his golf column in tandem with the play reviews, but golf guru he was and one time, challenged by Anne Germain, the society columnist, took her out on the links. The resulting story was very amusing. Steve has a divine if slightly sarcastic sense of humor and Anne a talented, angry, Dorothy Parker wit. I wish I could find that column, Just visualize a long, lanky woman being taught the game by a rather serious, quite adept teacher.

When I accepted the job of managing the SPCA Benefit Shop in 1987, Steve was opening his gallery. We had by then become friends; we shared social activities and the love of literature, the theater and art. He offered his assistance in appraising pieces that were donated, took ones to his gallery that were not appropriate for our shop and when sold took no commission. His love of animals made him a great advocate. He and Nancy were valuable contributors (and often customers} When I moved to the AFRP Treasure Shop, he was one of the first to wish us well and make a contribution in Piper's name (Piper was the beloved Cairn terrier who was a friend to all and held court at Hauk Fine Arts.)

Remember *The Accidental Tourist*? Steve was almost an accidental gallery owner.

Why This Writer Lives in P.G.
Brad Herzog

Some people arrive by chance. Not us. Our decision to settle in Pacific Grove was the product of design. And careful comparison. And a dollop of existential epiphany.

Back in December 1995, my wife and I were a couple of twenty-something newlyweds who were living in our native Chicago, taking stock of the road ahead, and wondering (amid the numbing cold of a Windy City winter), What's out there? Suddenly gripped by madness, I turned to Amy and said simply, "How'd you like to quit your job, scrape up a down payment on an RV and travel around the country for a year? And I'll try to write a book about it."

To my amazement, she replied, even more simply, "Sure."

So we hit the road, piloting a 34-foot Winnebago (we called it the Rolling Stone), trailing a Saturn behind it (the Day Tripper) and hoping to counter my inherent cynicism by embarking on a search for virtue in America. Actually, we turned it into a literal search, visiting tiny hamlets like Love (Virginia), Pride (Alabama), Wisdom (Montana) and Harmony (California). The book that came out of it was called *States of Mind*. A few years later, it very briefly rose as high as #2 on the Amazon.com bestseller list, behind only a Harry Potter tome.

Damn wizard.

But our magical journey was more than a literary quest. It became a 48-state search for a home. We had a feeling that we wanted to relocate, to escape our bubble, to dabble in the myriad possibilities. So over 314 days and some 35,000 miles, we sampled a full helping of the American Experience, visiting Disneyland and Graceland, Gettysburg and Williamsburg, the Alamo and Appomattox, Monticello and Hearst Castle, the Rose Bowl and Camden Yards, Dupont Circle and Times Square. We tasted dim sum in San Francisco, fresh guacamole in San Antonio, barbecued ribs in Kansas City, grits in Tuscumbia, crawfish po'boys in New Orleans, shrimp gumbo in Savannah, crab cakes in Baltimore, and lobster in Maine. We marveled at the White Sands of New Mexico, the Black Hills of South Dakota, the Green Mountains of Vermont, gray whales, redwoods, Yellowstone and the House of Blues.

And most important, along the way we developed criteria for what we wanted out of a place to live. We decided we wanted good weather (yup) and beautiful scenery, nice people and a family community, a walkable town that seemed exotic yet without pretension, a locale somewhat off the beaten path but not too far from a world-class city. And maybe it wouldn't hurt if it had a literary pedigree, too.

So we found a place where my favorite author and his marine scientist pal used to stare into tide pools and ponder the human condition. And maybe it wasn't a choice after all. As John Steinbeck once declared, "We do not take a trip; a trip takes us."

Wow! 1986—What a Year!
Dick Robins

The New York Mets beat the Boston Red Socks in a close, exciting seven-game World Series and *Phantom of the Opera* had its first performance as a musical in London's West End.

Also in that year, I was not only hired as the music department head at Carmel High School (after the music program underwent a five years' hiatus because of the passing of former music director Henry Avola in 1981, but I was approached and hired to direct and conduct the Monterey Community Band.

In 1986, three months into the semester at CHS, we put on our first concert, with 20 student musicians wearing tuxedos and or black formals, at Sunset Center. Our guest piano soloist, Congressman Leon Panetta, performed two Chopin compositions. David Wittrock, who was the voice for the classical radio station KBOQ, narrated "Peter and the Wolf." The house was packed and we never looked back.

Clint Eastwood, who was mayor of Carmel, sent me a congratulatory letter in 1987 and opened a jazz scholarship fund for my new jazz program for graduating students entering music colleges.

Stefanna, my wife, and I were renting an apartment in Monterey and our landlord, who was also a realtor, thought it could be more beneficial for us to buy a home rather than rent. He and Stefanna found a wonderful fixer-upper in Pacific Grove in 1989.

So began our love of P.G. and the beginning of many gigs from the P.G. Chamber of Commerce President Moe Ammar and the eventual opening of Stefanna's Crack Pot Studios, offering creative mosaic adventures.

During the time between 1986 and 2017, I have performed, conducted, composed, arranged and taught music.

I have had the pleasure of performing with church groups, concert bands, brass quintets, swing bands, 18 piece jazz ensembles, straight-ahead jazz combos, dance bands, Italian, Irish and French music and Dixieland groups.

Currently I am retired from teaching school and from conducting the Monterey Community Band after a 30-year stint. However I am having the time of my life playing my horn and arranging for small ensembles. You can normally hear me playing for First Friday and the Art Walk on Lighthouse Avenue in P.G.

Our house is nearly completed with our large backyard deck with a Jacuzzi and my wife's wonderfully creative P.G. garden with a plum tree, two apple trees, all species of flowers, butterflies, and all species of birds and squirrels who befriended Stefanna.

We can hear the ocean waves singing, smell the breeze and bathe in the joy that Pacific Grove is our home and I still say, "Wow!!"

Imagine Art
Germain Hatcher
Keith Larson

Art has always been Germain's thing. At two years old this little girl was developing sensibilities and definite opinions about art-making. One night with scissors in hand she decided the cat and the hat didn't belong with each other on the same page and extracted the cat from the book page, leaving only the hat. On June 19, 2015, Germain rented the property at 309 Forest Ave. and the Imagine Art store became a reality, opening on September 9. Always encouraged to explore the world around her, Germain follows instincts that lead to continually unfolding creative expressions. She loves the stories intuitively encountered in people's lives. Following these stories as far as she can results in the creation of many of her art pieces. Germain feels a special connection with each of her customers. Her two cats, Jude and Jordana, having established special cat-only places in the store, also place their stamp of ownership on everyone who shops at Imagine Art.

Grace Paints
Kathy and Anthony DeMers

Our five year old daughter is already an artist. Grace sits down almost every day, takes a piece of watercolor paper and creates. She has made about 75 paintings over the last eight months. Many of them are quite beautiful. Don't roll your eyes. I'm not imaging this out of some intrinsic parental bias; we're not talking smears of overworked primary color. She looks at her blank paper, picks a color, and without hesitation makes a confident mark. Within minutes the paper is overflowing with dripping paint. She has finished. Somehow she has selected just the right colors and applied them with balance and beauty. There is a sense of order while also often seeming to be free and sometime chaotic. There's something amazing about watching her just create.

Once a philosophy teacher posed the question, "Why do we value youth? What do children have to offer, when the elder can offer us wisdom and experience?" At age 19, I didn't know what to say. I wish I could go back now and give him my answer: because it's fleeting. There's a freedom, purity, and innocence that diminishes as time marches on. Once it's lost, it's lost. Once you are told to color inside the lines, you are aware of the lines for life. I am an artist myself, but it's different. I discovered my artistic talent in my late teens, after I had been taught the rules. I'm burdened with the need for a subject or object to paint. But not Grace, she is a budding master of non-objective art. However, my husband and I can't help but feel like Grace's free-flowing and natural artistic sense will suddenly come to an end. Whether it's the kindergarten class she starts up in three weeks, or the busy lives we all be leading after the summer, we can't help but think that this magical moment might just disappear.

We are hopeful, though, that Grace's natural independence will keep her resilient. She certainly has her very own style and strong imagination. She makes her choices as an artist with confidence and stubbornness. We're grateful to have a wonderful artistic community in Pacific Grove that she can grow up alongside. We have no idea what's in store for Grace, but this period in our lives has been very special.

Child Poets of P.G.
Patrice Vecchione
academic, writer, poet

Dedicated to the memory of Robert Down teacher Jen Hinton, who was a poet herself.

Shortly after I moved to the Monterey Peninsula from Santa Cruz in 1996, thanks to Judy Wills and school principals Matt Bell and later Linda Williams, as well as many topnotch teachers at Robert H. Down Elementary School, I began doing what I've done since I was 19 years old—teaching poetry to children. It was also my good fortune to bring poetry writing workshops to Forest Grove Elementary School and both the middle and high schools as well as to the Pacific Grove Public Library.

At Robert Down, however, in essence I got to sort of live there. Year after year, usually in the spring semester, I would come, not with pillow and sleeping bag, but with poem-stuffed book bag. I'd become the Robert Down Poet-in-Residence, and for many years I'd arrive at school, walk up the tall steps, enter the foyer and have the uncanny experience of being greeted by children who'd call out to me not by my actual name; instead they'd say, "It's poetry!" with such enthusiasm you'd think that bag of mine was full of candy.

Nope. Never had I any candy in that bag. This reaction to someone who would soon ask those same children to sit quietly and turn their attention first to listening to poems read aloud and then to writing their own, might be considered odd. Their abundant joy wasn't actually due to the sight of me, nor to the idea of being still, but to their previous experiences of writing poetry.

When writing poetry, children get to feel free in a way they often can't in school since they are there to learn things that require them to think in particular, organized ways. But the experience of writing a poem is different from that, and after writing a poem or two, many kids get excited by the opportunity to write another one—to be in charge of what gets written, to temporarily ignore important things like spelling and grammar that don't matter when writing first drafts, to put down on paper whatever comes to mind without regard to making sense, to be surprised by their own ideas, to be playful and inventive, and to bend or break any rule they like. "You're the boss of your poem," I tell my students.

One of my favorite things about having been the poet-in-residence at Robert Down for over ten years was that I got to work with children just as they entered kindergarten up to when they were getting ready to go to middle school at the end of 5th grade. And another favorite thing was the sense of community that is so strong in Pacific Grove—I could see it in the security the kids felt, the small town sense of camaraderie that is so strong in P.G.

At the end of each school year, we'd publish a selection of the children's poems in staple-bound anthologies. Here's a selection of those poems.

First
Suzanne Campbell
grade 3

When it was the first time I saw you
I could never ever stop seeing you.
You were on top of my mind,
the center of my eye,
the core of my heart.
And it shall always be that way
throughout life and death.
You will always be the first
memory. I will never forget you.

Isabella Reese Fontecchio
grade 4

A poem is a
code that
magnifies the
words of its
writer.

Too Fast
Brad Nielsen
grade 2

Once I lost my dog.
She ran off.
I was chasing her down
but she was too fast.
I didn't see her for a week.
Then I saw her walking
in the forest.
I found her!
I took her back home.

White Cloud
Willem Miller
grade 1

A cloud is white
because that is nature's breath.

Mexico
Elian Corona-LoMomaco
grade 3

I like Mexico: the scorching sun in the winter,
the downpours in the summer,
the mile trip by mule to the top of "El Salto,"
the milking, planting and mango picking,
the swing my uncle made in the avocado tree,
the cows, goats and dogs,
chickens running free in the rocky streets,
the nights at the plaza, soccer games before dusk,
fresh handmade tortillas,
me playing on the soccer team, "Chiva Barrio."
So much I can't explain. I love Mexico.

Shy
Tessa Merrick
grade 1

Hidden in my pencil are words
that are shy.
They will not come out.
They are hiding from us.
They will come out
on Monday.

Writing, Written, and Wrote
Kip Johnson
grade 5

The pencil is mightier than the sword. It has a graphite core,
stronger than steel, made to write through chaos and to give life to characters standing on a blank page
without feelings, dumb.
It can write peace and scribble war. In a second it can claim life
and give death and put a line through
hope and happiness. But the beauty of pencils is, they have erasers!

Artist Memories
Irene Evers Elisabeth

"The Cookie Lady," as all us kids who went to David Avenue School called her, is one of my favorite memories. We didn't know her name, but we knew where she lived—David Avenue in Del Monte Park. That neighborhood was called Del Monte Park before it was annexed to the City of Pacific Grove. A little knock on the door after school and we would be greeted by a smiling old lady with a plate of cookies in her hand. This was normal and we accepted it as part of life. This was in the 1950s; life was good. I still smile thinking of the "Cookie Lady" with a plate of animal cookies in her hand—thank you Cookie Lady!

Another favorite memory is "Franks" and his big red truck, who would sell hotdogs and paintings around the beach, also in the 50s.

I, too, try to give back some smiles and contribute to a better world with my craft of mosaic stepping stones. The stones have inspirational messages to help lift the spirits, such as my logo of "Art in the Ark," and they give me a sense of mission and healing. My work is carried at Butterfly Cottage, a botanicals and local garden gift shop. The most popular message on my stepping stones is: "Carmel by the Sea, Monterey by the Bay, and Pacific Grove by God." Indeed, thank you, God.

Paintings by Janet Bohrman: Kenny fishing off the rocks, and New Paint for the Carol Ann.

Passions and Hobbies
Janet Bohrman
Keith Larson

Janet Bohrman was an oil painter who did a number of beautiful coastal scenes. My cousins Ken and Chris remember their mother taking them along when she went out painting. She would always warn them to be careful of the waves so as not to get washed off the rocks.

Recently I was over at my cousin Ken's house when he told this story and showed me a painting hanging in his living room that his mother had done. It showed him out on the rocks with a wave crashing near it. He said she created this painting to illustrate her concerns for their safety. The painting, "Kenny Fishing off the Rocks," created in 1962, appears above along with "New Paint for the *Carol Ann*," painted in 1955 at the boat works.

Chestnut house sketch by Carol Bohrman, Janet's daughter.

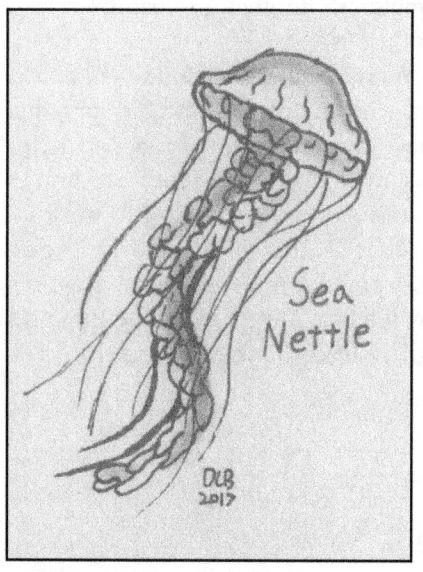

In these three drawings, Dan Bohrman, Janet's grandson, continues the tradition of drawing and painting in Pacific Grove.

202 *Life in Pacific Grove, California* STORIES OF AMERICA

Elizabeth Harer

Jeanie Harer De Tomaso

My brave, adventurous grandmother, Janet Bohrman (Hemmy), began bringing her two daughters and their cousins to Pacific Grove for the summer in the 1920s. She was a single mother and a one-room schoolhouse teacher in the Santa Cruz Mountains, so coming to the seashore for a few months was a retreat. Other aunts and uncles had settled in P.G. in 1914, so there were relatives to visit, besides forest and sea excursions. Thus began the evolution of future generations moving permanently to Pacific Grove and raising their families here.

In 1962 my parents, Rev. Ralph Harer and Elizabeth, bought a bungalow in the Retreat area, and my mother began painting in a little studio she named the Cypress Tree Studio. She painted local nautical scenes on driftwood and designed stationary, which she sold in galleries and local craft fairs. I am honored to have in my ancestry strong, creative, nature-loving women who decided it was important to live by the sea and help make the world more beautiful through their art.

Pencil drawings by Elizabeth Harer.

1009
JM
retired letter carrier, ceramic artist

To start I must explain my five year move-in. We closed on our house in 2012. My wife had six years to work and I retired later in the fall. This began an odyssey of trips to and from Sacramento. Eventually this spring I moved into our Pacific Grove house. It was after several months of long commutes that I started to envision a new art project. My hobby and passion for the last ten years has been ceramic art. This project, in which I would make ceramic sculptures of P.G. houses, would make me new acquaintances, if not friends. Let's expand this idea. I would leave the houses on their porches in the dead of night with only a note of thanks, signed with my logo, 1009. Then after I moved back permanently I could make the proper introductions. This idea was batted around among friends with no dissenting opinions so I decided to go with it.

The idea is now a reality. I called them Thank-You Houses. I thank the recipients for preserving and maintaining their historic houses. The first house was the Church Office, followed by the White Fence, the Green House, the Blue House, and finally the Forest Green House.

Occasionally I would have to check out some architectural detail and by chance would happen to run into the owner. This happened twice. The owners freely shared the stories behind the historical plaques attached to their houses. So it was for this that I thanked them. I asked friends to drive the getaway cars, and we made adventures out of it. They were all dropped off around 9:00 p.m. This gave me the cloak of darkness and I could still get to bed early.

A few notes: At the church office, I almost got caught. A door opened in the middle classroom next door. I froze in the street. The man turned away. The White Fence presented difficulties in construction. On the card of the Blue House, in my excitement, I put the address of the Green House. I had to sneak back and leave a second note. The Blue House was selected by a local artist. At house number five, I almost got caught again. A visitor arrived seconds before I did.

Much to my delight I received a thank you message. There was a picture in the Cedar Street Times (Aug 15, 2014) with a nice message underneath. My intentions all along were to reveal myself upon returning, which I have just done. One Saturday morning as I walked past White Fence, the owner was sitting on her porch. I stuck up a conversation— so now I have a friend. It works. So let's do some more!

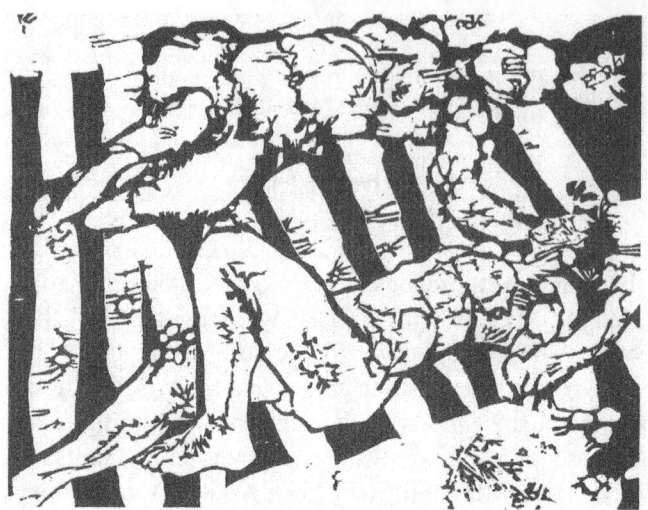

Bill Minor woodcut from his Pacific Grove book

Our Life in Pacific Grove
William Minor

Having survived teaching in Wisconsin for five brutal winters, I felt blessed when I landed a job teaching in the English department at Monterey Peninsula College. With two sons, Tim and Steve, ages thirteen and eleven, my wife Betty and I headed west by U-Haul (having fit all our earthly possessions into a fourteen-foot van). Betty went house-hunting while I unpacked the van at the college—and she came back with the good news that, solely by accident (having made a wrong turn), she had discovered a delightful town by the ocean: one that, with its Victorian residences, reminded her of San Francisco, where we'd lived when the boys were just born.

The town she'd discovered was Pacific Grove. When we found a home to rent here, it was not, by any means, Victorian, but it was a small, comfortable place on Funston Avenue, and we moved in after having camped out for thirteen days (and nights) in a tent in Carmel Valley. I commenced my educational chores at MPC; Tim went off to the middle school in P.G., and Steve attended David Avenue Elementary School. Betty would work as an aide in Extended Learning Programs at David Avenue Elementary, Lighthouse Avenue Elementary, Robert Down, and Forest Grove Elementary—continuing to work at the latter now for 43 years.

Betty, Tim, Steve, and I would picnic at Asilomar Beach, while our pet dog, Ursa Minor (The Little Bear), would frolic in the surf; the boys and I would fly kites and they would run off and play in the dunes at the sand plant that existed there before Spanish Bay usurped that land. Our second home was in Pacific Grove (we never intended to live anyplace else), on a cul-de-sac off Crocker Avenue, Oak Place. The tracks that once carried a train out to the sand plant ran directly behind our house. We rented this place at the end of a sabbatical year that Betty, Steve (a recent graduate of Pacific Grove High School), and I spent living in Greece. Tim had graduated from P.G. High and gone on to the University of Nevada-Reno, where he was a cross country All-American—having also been on Dick Chamberlain's CCS championship team at Pacific Grove High School.

Our third home in P.G. was—and remains—on Junipero Avenue, just a block and a half from spacious Washington Park, where Ursa Minor also loved to go for a daily romp with Betty. Betty also began to tend a backyard garden rich in blazing red begonia, overtly orange tiger lilies and petunias, with midget impatiens in the front yard.

Throughout our history here, I have played pianos at the Pacific Grove Art Center, The Balthazar Café, The Portofino Café, Wildberries, The Masonic Auditorium, Lattitudes, The Works, and just about every venue at Asilomar Conference Grounds that has a piano.

The boys (Tim now 59 years of age; Steve 57) have "flown the nest," working in Reno (Tim), Steve in San Francisco. Tim is married to Shannon (we have four grandkids, also no longer "kids": Emily, Blake, Megan, and Michelle), while Steve is married to Yoko. Betty and I are fortunate to be able to spend time with family fairly often, and we are enjoying our life together on a quiet street with excellent neighbors.

We shop at Safeway, Trader Joe's, Nob Hill, Lucky's, and downtown at Grove Market. When we first arrived, we bought books (they sold them there then) and writing supplies at Alpha—and we find musical scores at Marcia Stearns' Bookmarks. I have been a habitué at Juice & Java for years ("double espresso decaf" my beverage of choice). Over the years, we have enjoyed meals at International Cuisine, 17th Street Grill, Beach House at Lovers Point, Fishwife, Fandango, Passionfish, Peppers Mexicali Café, Max Grill, Favaloro's Big Night Bistro, Café Ariana, Fifi's Bistro Café, and many more fine restaurants in Pacific Grove.

We have fully enjoyed the 47 years we have spent living here.

I Stood
Ryan Hubanks–age 11
inspired by Robert Frost

I stood where I stood
They would try to get me to talk
But I did what I would
They tried to change my mood
But I stood where I stood
In my mind I knew this wasn't fair
And they would just have to believe whatever I claimed
They tried to make me happy, but that wouldn't wear
They tried to make me sad and say, "there, there"
But I stood where I stood and acted the same.
And that morning when I was in bed
They rushed in and said what they said
But I just lay there with a frown on my face, knowing his was going to be a horrible day
I thought I should leave this town, and get on my way.
But I could not help looking back and deciding I shall stay.
So I came back to town with a sigh, seeing all the couples passing by, and I knew that i should change my mood and get a better attitude, but in the end I stood where I stood.

Metamorphosis

I am just a cripple boy trying to find what way to go.
I wish I were a lovely dove flying in the sky
I started to pray to the Lord asking why I was this way.
I asked the Lord should I have love and why can I not change.
I feel like I am one big stone, hiding from other people's eyes. I felt like I was the only one, as I looked up at the sky.
I fell out of my wheelchair, I raised my arm to try to get up, but I fell thinking "what do I know?"
In my head I felt a little twitch, thinking this could be. But I am a cripple boy and on that day, God spoke to me.
Saying, you are just a cripple boy, but goals can still be achieved. I started speaking in front of crowds and they all cheered for me.
They yelled "Cripple for President" so I did what they said and I made it to the final day, November 8. I won in a flash, 270 to 55.
I thought to myself, I am just a cripple boy, but I changed that day - my heart grew in that moment and I changed my appearance to be a man.

I Feel America Dying
Nathan Hubanks–age 12
inspired by Walt Whitman

I Feel America dying, the ear-piercing screams I hear
It would be easiest to make them all disappear,
But alas, the rich must come to our aid,
Weather the farmhand, the Native, or the Maid,
All who claim they're not getting paid,
I hear The Grocer crying as his store closes,

I hear The CEO laughing as America crumbles and a small
    business loses
I hear The Steelworker crying as his home forecloses,
I hear The Stockbroker dying as the stock's market bruises,
And I know The Banker who's submerged in debt,
Thinking it might be worth taking a bullet to the head
And the crying of the infant, whose Dad's not there,
For he bled and bled after he took that bullet to the head,
Everybody is losing things except for the rich,
As they lock themselves in their fake reality in which,
All is well and America is fine,
When in reality people struggle to make a dime,
For if the rich refuse and don't pitch in,
Then they will all pay for their sin.

Maybe "I" am You

Maybe I is the Hebrew
Maybe I is an autistic
Maybe I's paycheck isn't realistic

Maybe I is women's athletics
Maybe I is the medics
Maybe I is the police
Maybe I is public school
Maybe I broke the rules

But I knows that I isn't the pharmaceuticals
And I knows that I isn't the ones who make the rules
No, I knows that I is the LGBT
And I knows that I is the ones who farm turkey
And I knows that I aren't ones who lobby
For I knows that for big companies, it's a hobby

I is all that go unheard,
Like the artist trying to save the birds,
I is all that get mistreated,
Like the child who consistently gets beated.
I is all that isn't white,
And that is just not right
I is all that are underrepresented
Like the gay man who some say is demented

Maybe I is a homeless child,
Maybe I is too fat to run a mile
Maybe I took meth
Maybe I is in debt
Maybe I am a Jew

Maybe I am you

Sam Coburn
Son Cyrus Coburn

Sam Coburn (1909-1993) was a local treasure. In his later years, he drove for Joe's Taxi, because, like so many artists, it didn't really afford a living, although in his final years his painting became very collectible. He was a traditionalist as well as modernist. One of his paintings of Carmel Valley has a simple rendition of fieldworkers on one side; on the other is a vibrant display of the same scene. He later said he should have charged twice as much for the piece. He was a fixture and beloved in Pacific Grove.

Watercolor was Sam's preferred medium. A prolific painter, he worked quickly outdoors on location, developing a style that was elegant, luminous, spontaneous, and fluid, though requiring tremendous control of the medium. Sam was one of the most colorful characters to walk the Monterey coast. His paintings are as much an evocation of the region as the writings of John Steinbeck and Robinson Jeffers, or the photography of Edward Weston and Ansel Adams.

Sam Coburn: Artist, Golfer, Teacher and Cab Driver
JD Foley

The first "real" artist I knew, I met in 1980 in Pacific Grove. He was about 70 and his look reminded me of photos I'd seen of Depression Era workers on Cannery Row.

He wore a flannel, long-sleeve shirt with a tee underneath, and belted baggy pants that needed hitching up. A trim white mustache triangulated his upper lip. He was famous for wearing a flat brimmed straw hat with a high crown that dented in on the top. His deliberate manner was unfettered by pedestrian niceties, which might be construed as gruff for those who didn't know him.

At the time, he was working as a dispatcher in Carmel for Joe's Taxi, where he had been a cab driver for years. But Sam Coburn was first a watercolorist.

He lived on Asilomar Avenue just up from Pico, across from Sand Dune Hill. The sign over his door read: Artist and Golfer. It was a funky old place, artsy, "rustic." A black stovepipe from the heater ran up to the ceiling, similar to mine. So was the whiff of mildew. There were paintings on the walls, and several that lined the perimeter of the floor of the tiny living room. A mission-style easy chair dominated the space, with art supplies within arm's reach. The light from the French doors made it a perfect studio.

Without hesitation, for ten bucks a lesson he agreed to teach me to paint. I admitted my complete lack of skill or training but it didn't concern him. Our first session was 'on location,' so off to the hills we went in his VW bus.

The smooth mountains along the Monterey-Salinas Highway were a favorite and frequent subject of his. He roughed out a sketch on a textured piece of watercolor paper taped to a wooden plank. With what looked like a house painter's brush, he washed water over the entire surface. Colors from his pallet bloomed as the pigments oozed from one side to the other. Very quickly, a suggestion of amber rolling hills emerged from the primordial mix. I hesitated at the thought of drawing anything, let alone applying paint to paper. He urged me to do it anyway.

We did still life painting in his studio after a while. One morning, yellow apples and green pears in a bowl were our subject. He quickly penciled geometric shapes, then just like before, in swirls of yellows and purples, reds and blues, the planks of color took form. He was so loose with his style at times, if I hadn't been there I might have needed a title to know what I was looking at. But it didn't matter. The very vagueness of the objects and the vibrant colors provoked interest.

I already knew he didn't believe in sponging up excess water on the paper. His advice was mostly about practice, with a few fundamental tips. "Don't scumble!" which he explained was scrubbing the paper. "Let the water do the work!" His chuffing did not scare me. I knew it was a privilege to be there.

Sam was a teacher to many amateurs like me, privately, and formally at Monterey Peninsula College. He was juried into the Carmel Art Association in the 1940s and served on the board for years. He was a well-connected member of the community, meeting often on the golf course. He published *Tales from the Taxi Cab*, and wrote a column, "Art Notes," for the *P.G. Monarch*.

Sam was the subject of many articles himself. His paintings are included in anthologies with references to abstract artists, with descriptions like "modernism" and "realism." While he was a local maverick, his work as a watercolorist is nationally known.

I received a card from him that Christmas, in familiar chunks of color painted on the back of a 'recycled' painting. His mini-sunset hangs in my living room, a reminder of this elegant, authentic, down-to-earth man (and golfer, he would insist!) "Art" he said, "makes the whole thing worthwhile." At 84 he passed on, leaving behind a prolific portfolio and easily as many friends.

On Art
Keith Larson

My dad never considered himself an artist but even he could not resist the creative energies in the area. He would sometimes look for driftwood on the beach that he could sand, stain and mount on wood as art pieces. My mother put her creative energies into quilting. I also remember her teaching me how to make an oak ball necklace by pushing a threaded needle through a string of small oak balls which are abundant in the area. We would paint them with red fingernail polish and let them dry. I would insist she wear them on Sunday to church.

My mother took me to my first art class around the age of four. I always remember how excited I'd be to get a new box of Crayola crayons. I liked the orange and blue tones best. I loved the comic pages in the newspapers and would cut out the strips and save them in a scrap book my mother gave me. my mom would also take me to the library to check out drawing books, I remember my brother Ned who was pretty good at drawing showing me how to draw my hero the Hulk. Having done a number of art classes with children I can appreciate the time my elementary school teachers put in at Forest Grove school to prepare art experiences for us. I have my family, parents, teachers, and relatives to thank for practicing and sharing their artistic abilities and creativity with me. through their examples and encouragement I grew up never thinking I couldn't draw, paint, or make something. I was never afraid of a piece of blank paper or art materials that were new to me. I have used art in many ways to make greater connections with myself and with others. From having grown up in this beautiful area with a rich heritage of creativity I have been able through my life to follow the path of art and creativity where ever it has led me.

Coming Home
Barbara Brussell

I grew up here, but then moved away and eventually married another displaced local. One day my husband declared "I have to be back on the Monterey Peninsula!" And I thought to myself "What's wrong with that? My bags are packed!" Los Angeles had been full of congestion. Sacramento, where we were living, was 108 degrees. New York was a reach too far…so since we were both from here it was a perfect fit to come breathe this fantastic air back home near the Pacific Ocean.

When I lived here before, I went to Carmel Middle School and Carmel High School, where I did dance concerts. But a car accident put an end to that path and so I went to a small music school called the Academy of Music. I studied voice, piano, composition and a myriad of other classes. I'm a lyric soprano and eventually got a BFA in music. I also studied at American Conservatory Theatre. I did eight musicals here, starting as Hodel in Fiddler on the Roof. I was Louisa in The Fantasticks at the Barnyard Theatre in the Valley and I played Anne in A Little Night Music at the Wharf Theatre. I even did Maria in West Side Story at MPC.

But I left Pacific Grove when I was twenty-six to go to New York, and I took classes with William Hickey and Uta Hagen at HB Studios. I did a new musical there that then went on tour. I ended up in L.A. for eighteen years where I did another tour, Gilbert & Sullivan this time… and that went through twenty-six states and Canada in three months. William Katt from Carrie was in it and also Broadway legend George Rose.

I did my first cabaret show in L.A. at the Gardenia Room. I'd seen Charles Aznavour when I was thirteen and I just loved the idea of being on stage the whole time, becoming a character if I chose and then coming back to myself. Picking material myself, doing a variety of songs. It was different than theatre, where you put on a character and wait backstage for other people to finish their songs. So I took a workshop and we talked about what was the dream we always wanted to do and within five weeks I made my debut as a cabaret performer. I made two CDs and I sang at the Algonquin, which was one of the highlights of my life. It's the hotel where the famous Round Table with Dorothy Parker had happened, and My Fair Lady was written upstairs.

When my husband and I came back here we got so lucky and found a P.G. apartment with a view that looks out on the Monterey Bay.

Now I have created Cabaret-by-the-Sea, where my vision is to coach others, create shows for myself to sing in, and bring other cabaret artists to this area. Eventually I want to have an annual summer camp for cabaret singers that lasts a week. So far I've produced three shows at the Cherry Center in Carmel and one at the P.G. Arts Center.

I teach voice to the students at Pacific Repertory Theatre and I also offer cabaret singing classes at the Arts Center. There's ongoing classes that are drop in on that day, or there's private sessions with or without an accompanist. They're a very safe environment where any singer can bring in any material and explore the world of their song, to make the song their own. Cabaret style encompasses singing, storytelling, acting and personal expression. Live theatre is a transformative experience and developing one's own material can be self-revealing. It's authentic and enlivening and awakening and fulfilling, a journey and an adventure.

I feel very blessed to be back home on this new adventure. I want to bring the best of what I'd learned in the world out there, performing for thirty-five years, to the Peninsula. I want to see, and be in, some great cabaret acts!

The Story Tailor: William Neish
Clarissa Bell

"You can't just mention that an affair occurred which precipitated a divorce and not explain the circumstances," I found myself being told in no uncertain terms, to which I inwardly balked but outwardly kept up a good front. After all, I knew this person to be a consummate professional with only my best interests at heart. With studied calmness I listened on as he continued to reason with me. "And furthermore, I also think you've chosen to leave someone very important in the lurch and you might want to rethink that choice. After all, its morally wrong what you've allowed to happen to her—especially someone we've all become so emotionally invested in."

So, I thought to myself while squirming slightly, just who did this person think they were, taking my own personal drama to heart and suggesting I was being morally insensitive? And yet, I must confess that I was at the same time flattered that they cared at all about, let's face it, a mere figment of my imagination. And so it was that my friendship with William Neish at Alpha Stationers blossomed when I casually asked if he knew of any typists, as I was new to Pacific Grove, and he so graciously offered his services.

William, I quickly learned, was no ordinary typist but a former story editor for International Creative Management in Los Angeles, not to mention a reader of prospective new material for the acclaimed Circle Repertory Company in New York City. I had the good fortune to meet him as he had recently returned to his home town of Pacific Grove and established himself as the Story Tailor, working with writers as they prepare their manuscripts for publication.

Prior to working with him on my manuscript we had bonded, albeit loosely, over the subject of pugs, based on the fact that I currently have one and he had two growing up. In fact, whenever I stopped by Alpha to pick up the tools of the trade, William paid, let it be said, scant attention to me but spent it lavishly on my pug, Samuel. It was therefore only natural, I suppose, that he suggested I create a pug character in my book. William's last suggestion about my heroine had actually precipitated the basis for a second book so who was I, I told myself, to cast aspersions at the idea? But still, I wondered with no small degree of skepticism … "a pug?"

The idea, as it turns out, wasn't half bad and so it was that William was beginning to establish a very decent track record. So decent that when he charmingly snuck in his next suggestion I was able to ignore my first impulse to laugh outright and give it more weighty consideration than I otherwise might have. What if, he suggested half mischievously, one of my characters (in his defense, it *was* a child) saw fairies in the garden?

Yes, fairies. And so I found myself facing a dilemma as I wondered, not unlike Niels Bohr had wondered about Werner Heisenberg, were his ideas *merely* crazy or were they crazy enough to be correct?

Once again I gave William the benefit of the doubt and as the story began to develop in previously unforeseen and insightful directions I had to admit William was very possibly a genius himself.

When I finished my first manuscript William congratulated me warmly and said he would give me the same advice he gave all his writers in New York. Rest, he said, relax and read a good book by that great American author from whom there was much we could all learn. Who would it be, I wondered with bated breath. F. Scott Fitzgerald? Henry James? Earnest Hemingway?

"Judith Krantz," he said with a knowing wave of his hand.

William Neish can be reached at thestorytailor@yahoo.com

CENTERS FOR THE VISUAL AND PERFORMING ARTS

Working in Pacific Grove: Dante Rondo and the Pacific Grove Art Center
Dorothy Vriend
teacher, journalist, photographer, poet

A painter, photographer and inveterate surfer, Dante Rondo travels too, but always comes back to his studio and his students at the Pacific Grove Art Center.

"What can you do to make the eyes look more penetrating and dimensional?" he asks a young student in a Thursday afternoon class. She is drawing a pencil portrait of a young girl from a photograph. "Think about shading and highlighting around the eyes." Dante leans over to demonstrate, picking up a pencil and shading deftly, with the practice of long experience.

Just back from spending time in Hawaii in 1987, Dante Rondo met artist Sherard Russell at a music event, and she told him about the Pacific Grove Art Center. Dante had taught art to youth at The Lyceum of Monterey County, and now this meeting marked the beginning of a new teaching experience that was to become an important part of his life. He has taught at the P.G. Art Center ever since, chalking up almost three decades on his resume.

Dante Rondo's own work as a painter ranges from impressionistic realism to figurative art and abstraction. He is a painter first, a photographer second, he says. When he travels, he takes his surfboard, camera gear and art materials with him. His travels have taken him to Hawaii and the South Pacific, to Mexico, Europe, to Bali and Costa Rica and elsewhere. He may go for a month or six months, but he always comes back to his art studio and his students.

A typical day might include a morning of surfing in Carmel, where he lives, and an afternoon of working and teaching at the Pacific Grove Art Center. Surfing can be spiritually uplifting, he says, but it can be frustrating too, if the conditions aren't right, or if there are too many people vying for the same wave.

His frustrations on the water could be a metaphor for his concerns about the future of Pacific Grove. He worries that rising real estate prices and high rents may crowd out the middle class and limit the kind of enterprise that can exist here. He often attended the Portofino Cafe that operated in Pacific Grove in the late 1980s and 1990s, bringing in live music on a regular basis. He lists the type of music he remembers listening to there: folk, Americana, jazz. "The Portofino Cafe went away; it couldn't afford to operate," Dante says. "Pacific Grove has that quaint quality. If it wants to retain that, it can't sell its soul."

Born in Los Angeles in 1951, Dante moved to Carmel in 1967, but generally spends as much of his waking day in Pacific Grove as in Carmel. He loves that once in Pacific Grove he doesn't have to get back in his car; to get from place to place he can walk or get on his bike. And his favorite thing to do here is what he does most days: work in his studio or meet with his students.

Halcyon Days in Pacific Grove
American Tin Cannery Artist
Christine Chatwell

It was a dream come true! In 2003, my spouse, May, and I bought a house in Pacific Grove. We had always wanted to live here but it wasn't until 2015 that we arranged our lives so that we could leave Mountain View and live here full-time. We love the small town ambiance, the ocean, the friendly, helpful, open-minded residents, and the temperate climate.

Being retired, I was thrilled to be able to do artwork fulltime.

My other love? Farm animals! As such, a few years ago I adopted a vegan lifestyle in order to save pigs, cows, sheep, chickens, turkeys, fish, and goats from the unimaginable cruelty to which they are subjected in the process of becoming food for humans.

Cheese was the most difficult to give up because of the addictive ingredient, casein, contained in cheese. Casein affects the same part of the brain as does morphine. After watching a video showing how, after carrying her baby for nine months, the calf is taken away from her mother the day she is born, I was able to let go of cheese. Mother and baby cry out for each other, grieving for many months.

A few months ago, an artist friend informed me of an opportunity to rent a studio space for a reasonable amount in the American Tin Cannery. I eagerly did so and feel lucky to work there with 17 other artists. We're like family—enjoying, supporting, and encouraging each other. Each first Friday of the month, we organize an exhibition for the community, which includes wine, hors d'oeuvres and live music.

I paint portraits of farm animals from an up-close perspective to allow viewers to look into the eyes of the animal and experience his/her soul. Proceeds of sales are donated to animal sanctuaries.

I can't thank Pacific Grove enough for giving me the opportunity to get up every morning and express my two loves. BeautifulSoulsArt.com

Connie Pearlstein—Be well, Be Strong
Steve Hauk

Connie Pearlstein had a presence that will keep her around forever.

For years she was the heart and soul of the Pacific Grove Art Center, guiding people through the galleries on Saturdays and holding court on Sundays in her studio overlooking Lighthouse Avenue.

There she would work on her current exquisite needlepoint, collaborating with artists such as Johnny Apodaca, Jay Hannah, Suzanne Olson, Jack Cassinetto or Caroline Kline. Artist-writer Belle Yang recently spoke of an inspiring Connie Pearlstein needlepoint gracing her bedroom wall.

Working with others excited Connie. Sometimes she reproduced a composition by one of the artists, asking permission first, of course. The artists were honored. It was something to have a painting seen in Connie's needlepoint.

Visitors who knew little about art climbing the stairs to the Art Center came down an hour or two later enthusiastic about the creative process - with Connie's directive to visit this or that gallery as a kind of homework, sometimes with an implied ``or else."

But then Connie was a natural teacher and disciplinarian. Connie taught for 22 years for the Berkeley Unified School District. Testimonials are legion. And she volunteered for 12 years at Canterbury Woods, teaching residents knitting and needlepoint.

Connie and her daughters moved to Pacific Grove in 1973. It was a move inspired by the desire to leave the stresses of Berkeley and to move closer to her dear friend Corey Miller. Corey and her family provided decades of support and kinship to Connie and her daughters.

She was able to do all this - and raise five strong daughters - despite her diagnosis of Multiple Sclerosis. In fact, she probably accomplished all she did in part because of her M.S.

She discovered early the best way to combat the disease was to keep to a schedule, ``I know every day I need to get up, get ready, and set out to do something I want to do and feel is important." Each day began with a check in phone call to her friend Lynn Stralem in which she listed the menu for that night's dinner. Then she'd put on her hat and coat and walk to and from the Art Center or the Grove Market– until recent years, when the walk back up the hill to home became too much and friends such as Mark Wiggins gave her a lift.

The image of Connie walking was so strong some artists, such as Anita Benson, painted it.

Connie was famous for frequent and brief phone calls. She'd discuss serious moments in a person's life or something happening at the Art Center, and then might exclaim that it was all beyond her. She'd usually sign off with - and there was great sincerity in it - ``Be well, be strong." (Pearlstein, Connie photo courtesy Pearlstein family collection)

I Was Connie's Favorite
Michael Kane Miller

Connie was my godmother, a role in which she took great pride as it was an honor given her by my mother, Corey, her lifelong friend and confidant whom, by the way, she adored.

My relationship with Connie was a special one. It was as informal as it was direct. Connie was the personification of independence and self-reliance. She was the first to ask for help when she needed it and just as quick to let you know if she didn't.

Anyone who knew Connie knew also she had rough edges. Outrageous, even indignant at times, Connie could rail with righteous indignation. She did not suffer fools. Connie was a relentless good sport and was not an apologist for herself or anyone else.

Last week I found myself parked in front of Connie's home. The weather-beaten fence had been stripped away, exposing for the first time in decades the beautiful painted-lady of a house she called home. I thought of Connie living behind that fence in the safety of the sanctuary she created therein. So too behind Connie's very protected façade was a truly vulnerable person.

Connie's life revolved around rituals, Easter and Christmas at Grove Acre, rice pilaf in tow; super bowl parties with hot dogs prepared to exacting specifications; art collecting; artist collecting; needlework, smoke breaks and chardonnay. Her intrepid walks to and from the art center, churning through town like a 'ubiquitous purple blur, was as much a part of P.G. as the town clock, only more predictable.

I visited Connie shortly after my mom's death. She was clearly affected by it and mentioned that she had outlived all her friends, and that she too had worn out. Connie died the same way she lived, on her terms, with dignity, without fear. In fact, Connie didn't exactly die as much as she resigned herself to stop living.

P.G. Performing Arts Center
Susan Bilich

Our favorite place is the Performing Arts Center on the campus of the Pacific Grove Middle School. Where else would one be able to enjoy such a variety of performances in P.G? This 738-seat Art Deco jewel serves both as school auditorium and a community theater.

Twenty-five years ago my husband Michael and I visited P.G. between Christmas and New Year's. We returned year after year until we realized this was a place we could live, and did so a few years later after I retired from Belmont Elementary School District as school secretary. Soon after, I became a volunteer for the Foundation for the Performing Arts Center P.G. and found myself in love with the town and the P.G. Arts Center.

The renowned California architect William H. Weeks designed the middle school building (originally the high school) in 1911, and the auditorium in 1931. By 2004, the facility was showing its age. P.G. Rotary Club members, including architect Jeanne Byrne, interior designer Michael Krokower, contractor Steve Covell, and project manager Jim Quinn began renovations to return the deteriorating theater to its former glory. When the work was finished, the Rotary Club revealed the beautifully restored venue to the school district and the community. FPAC-P.G. was formed in 2005 as a volunteer-run nonprofit corporation charged with ensuring the Center would have the resources to continue serving students and residents.

The Center has been the venue for many exciting performances over the years, by artists including the Von Trapp Family Singers, Robert Joffrey Theater Ballet, the San Francisco Opera Quartet, and Metropolitan Opera baritone Robert McFerrin. More recently, FPAC-P.G. has kicked off the holiday season with its Celtic Winter's Eve Celebrations and also brought the U.S. Navy Jazz Band (The Commodores), popular zydeco performers Tom Rigney and Flambeau, the Kingston Trio, and John Denver and Fleetwood Mac tribute bands. From 2005-17, FPAC raised money to maintain the Center and upgrade seating, lighting, and sound systems. We enhanced school arts programs by bringing professional musicians such as the Synergy Brass Quintet to provide tutorials to students. Supporting us in these efforts have been a wide variety of organizations and businesses, including the Rotary Club, P.G. Unified School District, the Heritage Society, the Chamber of Commerce, and P.G. High School Alumni Association.

Pacific Grove has a long history of interest in the performing arts. Shortly after the Retreat Association held its first summer encampment in 1875, the P.G. Chautauqua Assembly (1880-1926) was established to bring lectures, concerts, plays, and academic courses to the community. The Performing Arts Center building was dedicated on April 22, 1931. From the day the auditorium opened, it has been used for untold numbers of school, civic, and social events. The Monterey Peninsula Concert Association, founded by Elmarie Dyke, brought concert performers to P.G., many of whom placed the venue on their tour schedules. Although FPAC-P.G. has stepped down as the primary event manager for the Center, the P.G. Unified School District continues to book performances and cultural events there to delight townspeople and visitors alike.

Myself, I have been involved in the arts not only as a volunteer but as painter and sculptor for over 40 years. Currently I make hats for cancer survivors and donate and ship them to people who are going through treatments all over the country. HappiHats can be found at the American Cancer Society Discovery Shop in P.G.'s Country Club Gate shopping center.

KAZU 90.3 on the Dial
Keith Larson

It was a cold and foggy night in downtown Pacific Grove. As usual, everyone had gone home at 5:00 p.m.; this was the 1970s. A dim light shown on the second floor above the five-and-dime store; Pacific Grove's own radio station was on the air.

I walked across Lighthouse and went up the steps of the old Sprouse-Reitz building with my collection of records from the 1940s. There sat my friend Joe. We were both in high school at that time and Joe was interested in radio and broadcasting. Joe had invited me to be on his show so I could play my records that I had collected in different Goodwills and thrift shops in the area. Al Jolson sings again, along with many other hits from the World War II era.

While the records played, we wondered if anyone were listening; the signal might have been able to reach clear around the block at that time. The proof that someone was indeed out there in radio-land came in the form of a VW bug with a couple of girls in the seat waving to us. We could see them from the second floor window of the KAZU studios as they rolled down Lighthouse, soon disappearing into the fog. We went back to playing hits from the 40s, proud of ourselves that at least we had a couple of listeners.

Hometown Radio KAZU
Joyce Meuse
local, hometown woman

One of the most rewarding times of my life in Pacific Grove was being a volunteer programmer at KAZU radio. KAZU began as a small 10-watt radio station broadcast built from discarded equipment and a limited budget by Don Mussell, a radio tower engineer involved with helping to create many radio stations in the area. The first broadcast was in 1977. The station grew into an interesting mix of musical genres and spoken word shows that lasted for many years. Over the years, it increased its wattage and was heard far and wide in central California.

Mae Brussell was one of the first conspiracy theorists I was aware of. She did a show called "Dialogue: Conspiracy" which was later changed to "World Watchers International." She was focused mainly on the assassination of John F. Kennedy and the history of fascism. She had uncovered many threads of malicious intrigue involving the American government. It was a

great loss for many of us when she died in 1988.

There was blues, folk music, classical, rock, Celtic and jazz. Even the opera was represented. Something for every musical taste. The early morning hours were devoted to New Age music. The spoken word was on every day at noon and included my call in psychic show that I got to host every other Wednesday, sharing the show with Adolphine Caroll.

I especially enjoyed JT Mason's shows, one of which was "My Sister's House." This introduced me to the women's music genre and many beloved artists. Another favorite show was the "Green Witch," a gardening show that encouraged us to grow things in any containers even those big black trash bags.

There were many people involved in the station from the board of directors to volunteers and eventually a paid staff and the subscribers. I was even on staff for awhile as the Traffic Director helping to schedule public service announcements and the hourly required announcement: KAZU, 90.3, Monterey Bay Public Radio. Fundraising was a big part of our job. Twice a year we went on air and asked for community support. There was lots of camaraderie, characters and lifelong friendships that began at the station.

Once the station started getting federal funds from the Center for Public Broadcasting it was required to hire five full time staff positions. Things changed. I remember one programming director who said she wanted to take all of the power away from the volunteers. She did. Maybe it was the paid professional staff, many from out of our area, maybe it was a combination of other factors, but things went downhill.

The station still exists now on the air as a part of the local California State University. It is all talk radio all the time with most of the shows coming off of the satellite and some local news. A far cry from its origins as a beloved, grass roots, local, people and community powered public radio station.

A Boy From the Bronx
Steve Kane
Mimi Sheridan

Can a boy from the Bronx find happiness in a small town like Pacific Grove? According to Steve Kane, the answer is an enthusiastic "yes"! Steve is known around Pacific Grove for his extraordinary knowledge of music and his eagerness to share it. He credits his parents with cultivating this avocation. Steve's father traveled to Harlem to pick up the latest jazz records, and he and his wife went to clubs and hosted "listening parties" for friends and neighbors (Stan Getz had grown up in the neighborhood). As a cab driver, he met many jazz luminaries, often regaling Steve with tales of his experiences in Harlem and Greenwich Village.

Already under the influence of music, Steve became seriously ill when he was 8 years old. He, spent months in the hospital, with radio as his main companion. He fell under the spell of radio theater, enjoying shows such as "The Lone Ranger" and "Sergeant Preston of the Yukon."

Steve, who has been visually impaired since childhood, has always been adventurous. After his first job helping out at Warner Brothers in New York, he moved on to Pittsburgh where he did stand-up comedy at coffee houses and campuses. He even did some local TV. He came west in the 1970s, settling in San Jose, where he found his calling in radio. He excelled at advertising sales, a very useful talent that opened many doors for him.

He ended up with his own interview show at KFAT, a very eclectic "hippy" station, where he explored a wide range of topics with community folks. At the same time, he broadened his musical contacts by emceeing concerts at Paul Masson Winery in Saratoga—often introducing people he had always admired.

Steve arrived in Pacific Grove in 1986 to work at KRML, which was then a jazz station. He began by selling ads, but soon was a DJ with his own show. He sometimes emceed at an influential P.G. institution—the Portofino Café. In the 1980s, owner Barbara Murphy booked all types of music, providing a gathering place for people of all backgrounds.

But Steve's major radio gig was at Pacific Grove's own very eclectic community station, KAZU. Back in those days, the station was operated mostly by volunteers, who developed their own playlists with every kind of music. Interview and talk shows focused on local concerns and issues. From 1986 until 2002 Steve was a DJ at KAZU. He began with a Saturday morning show known as "Chicken McMusic," a very popular compilation of jazz, rock, blues, country, swing—whatever he was moved to play. He also became "Dr. Feelgood," hosting the "Rock n' Roll Hospital" to bring the "healing and soothing power of rock and roll" to a local audience. For something different, he developed a morning show, "Joyful Noise," with comedy, jazz and inspirational music. All his shows showcased his intense love, and knowledge, of all music genres as well as his quirky sense of humor and willingness to interact with the audience.

Tragically, a fire at the station in 1997 destroyed all of Steve's personal record collection, which he had stored there so he could compile his shows more easily. The fire forced the station to move to a new studio, with higher rent. Although the station was popular, donations could not keep up with the increasing costs. After several years of struggle, the board sought a non-profit partner to turn the station over to. They selected California State University Monterey Bay (CSUMB) to operate the station as an NPR affiliate. In 2002, it ceased being a volunteer-run community station and, in 2008, relocated to the campus of CSUMB in Marina.

Without a regular radio gig, Steve turned to another of his early loves, radio theater. He joined a company that brought the magic of radio drama, featuring original scripts and realistic sound effects, to community centers and senior facilities.

He also honed his talent for improvisational comedy with the Mirthomatics, an improv group performing in coffee houses and community centers. Most recently, he has presented a series of shows at the Sally Griffin Senior Center. Each one is planned out in style of an old-time radio show, combining music and stories, with a specific focus such as the rarely-heard songs of Elvis Presley, the works of Nat King Cole's piano trio, and celebrations of the 100th birthdays of Frank Sinatra and Ella Fitzgerald. Steve always finds way to share his love of music and stories with others.

BOOKWORKS AND LOCAL WRITERS

The Bookworks
Nell Flattery Carlson
owner

Every once in a while, when I walk into the dark bookstore early in the morning before the smell of coffee has filled the air, I am hit by the familiar smell of the old Bookworks. It is the smell of paper and dust. A smell that reminds me of my time spent while growing up in Pacific Grove perusing the aisles of Bookworks or when I was just fresh out of college and I had joined the Bookworks staff as a cashier.

The Bookworks has been here as long as I can remember. Originally started in the late 1970s, it began at the Country Club Gate shopping center and was brought down to the center of town around 1979. My mother and co-owner, Margot Wells Tegtmeier, worked at the store when I was in middle school. She helped start the coffee bar when it was just a counter in the back room. Then she became a receiving clerk. I used to walk downtown after school and hang out with her while she received books in the back. At that time, it was owned by Gene and Kathy Palermo.

The store underwent a major remodel in 2006. After changing hands a few times in rapid succession, it was bought by Robert and Lila Marcum. They boldly moved the coffee bar to the front room and the books just filled the back of the store, leaving plenty of space for their music events. It was during this time that the independent bookstore was hit hard by the emergence of Amazon and big box stores like Barnes & Noble.

In many ways, by downsizing the book inventory, the Marcums may have saved the Bookworks for the long term. Today, a large portion of the book industry belongs to Amazon and will continue to do so. However, independent bookstores offer that intimate book shopping experience, one where you can still hold a book, read its back cover and flip through its pages. Listening to the booksellers or customers gush about their favorite books is a unique experience you just can't get from browsing online.

Today, as the owner of this beloved local bookstore, I am so thankful that I get to provide a place for people, young and old, to come and browse the aisles and grab a cup of coffee. The magic of a book to lift us up, move us, educate us and teach us compassion is unsurpassed. We need bookstores to help us find that book we never knew we needed to read, but somehow found us anyway.

The independent bookstore and the physical book is surely not dead. Just swing by the bookstore on a Saturday or Sunday morning to see the children reading in the aisles. The magic of reading for young people is a passion that drives me every day. I am amazed by the number of young adults who love books and want to read the classics and poetry. It fills me with joy and gives me hope for the future.

Back to the Bookworks
Danielle Cumberland
Fall 2005

I was running around downtown P.G. when I noticed a Help Wanted sign in the window of our local independent bookstore. Without really thinking about it, I went in and applied, had an interview with Bill Buckhout, and was hired within 20 minutes for a job selling books. It all happened so fast. Five-and-a-half years later, I had sold hundreds of books, learned a lot about retail sales, and had been a manager of Bookworks for two years. I worked with the best crew and had so much fun during my time at Bookworks. There was laughter, tears, appreciation, friendship and bonds that are still intact today, 15 years later. Adina, Roxy, Colleen, Maria, Shell, Kelly, and a few others made my time at Bookworks a wonderful experience.

Until the day Bill and Linda Buckhout came to me with the news I didn't really want to get. They were selling the bookstore. I began thinking about what I was going to do. I applied at the Monterey Bay Aquarium, thanks to a musician who had played at the store often. (Thank you, Jack, for getting the ball rolling on that one. I had a successful 11 years with the fish!)

After nearly 11 years at the Aquarium, I was getting antsy for something new, so I left and applied at different places in Pacific Grove.

Fall 2016

Little did I know that 15 years later, I'd be back at Bookworks for my second stint as a bookseller. I returned and everything was different. The Bookstore wasn't in the front of the building anymore. There was a café, with tables, coffee-making machines and people I didn't know behind a counter I had never seen. I walked through the unfamiliar territory to the back, where the remodeled bookstore now existed. I stopped at the counter in the back, obtained an application, left my résumé and went home to fill out the application to return as soon as possible. I wanted the owner, Nell Carlson, to know how interested in a job I was. Thirty minutes later, I had the application back in her hands. She remarked, "Your résumé is beautiful." A good sign, I thought. We made an appointment for an interview. I was so nervous because everything was different. The interview went fine, even though I felt nervous. I was sweating waterfalls the whole time. I got a call from Nell a few months later. She offered me a job. Yes!! I have always loved books and I was so excited to be back in my element doing what I really love.

It's been almost seven months this time around and I can honestly say I love this job. Nell and Margot are awesome to work for.

I have gotten to know other people at the bookstore and in the café. I am thankful to Perry for being patient when she trained me my first few weeks. Trent was there my very first day. We worked on taking inventory. I wasn't great at it. Coral was there to answer any questions I had regarding the program we used to sell books and other things.

I didn't meet the baristas at the café right away. I was pretty shy in the beginning and was quiet with everyone. Thanks to Natalie, Eric, Giossi, Brittany, Danielle, Megan and Kiana, I had caffeine to keep me perky and energetic when helping customers.

Even though things will never go back to the way they were from 2000-2005, I love the "new" Bookworks and I couldn't be happier to be surrounded by my passion of reading. I am so thankful to Nell and Margot for bringing me on board and taking me into their family atmosphere.

Come check out the books, puppets, candles and cards! Visit me and I'll tell you some stories from both times I was blessed to work at Bookworks.

Here, There and Everywhere
Diane Tyrrel

It was late September the first time I came to Pacific Grove, and there I met the man who would become my second husband. We had been corresponding on eHarmony for several weeks and decided to meet at the Bookworks.

He lived in Salinas and I lived in Santa Cruz. He had suggested Pacific Grove because he loved it and wanted to share it with me. I agreed because it seemed like a good neutral zone. It was eight years since the death of my first husband, and I had my guard up.

Driving down Lighthouse Avenue, I saw Jon's truck, just as he'd described it: a black Dodge with no chrome, parked across from the coffeehouse. I was excited and nervous about meeting this stranger. I'd never even heard his voice—we'd moved straight from talking online to a meeting without a phone call in between. But I held my expectations firmly in check. My grown daughters, more knowledgeable about such things, had warned me that I must be prepared to kiss a few frogs.

My marriage to their dad had been a good marriage, though somewhat scattershot and improvisational from the beginning. Our hastily planned outdoor wedding got rained out so we'd moved the ceremony to a mountaintop fire station. I arrived late and disorganized. My new brother-in-law had practiced the Beatles song "Here, There and Everywhere" to play on his guitar when I walked down the aisle.

But our timing was off for some reason and when I came in with my father, there was only silence. So my girlfriend Charlene started humming "Here Comes the Bride," and everyone joined in. Twenty-five years later, at my husband's memorial, his brother and sisters stood up and surprised me with an incredibly touching guitar and vocal rendition of "Here, There and Everywhere."

I walked into the Works, smelling the coffee, scanning the room, and I heard my name. His voice was deep and resonate with a hint of Kentucky. He had been waiting for me by the door. I turned and we were embracing awkwardly.

A strange thing happened at that moment, and lasted all afternoon and into the evening until we parted. Although I was aware of the others around us, the friendly welcome from the café workers, the people sitting at the tables with their cups and their computers—it was like I was viewing the world through the wrong end of a telescope. Everything and everyone but this man sitting across the table from me—he was the only one in focus. We were talking and it was like a few moments had passed but suddenly almost two hours had gone by.

At last we got up and wandered through the passage into the little bookshop. Soft music was playing, an instrumental version of a familiar tune. It took me a moment to realize it was "Here, There and Everywhere."

It wasn't quite sunset when we left the Works, and Jon said he knew a great place for a walk. He took me to Asilomar and we were graced with the sight of whales spouting—a pair of humpbacks near the shore, side by side, traveling south. (I teased him later that although I enjoyed our date very much, the whales were a bit over the top!) Not ready for it to end, we kept things going with beer and lobster ravioli at the Fishwife. When we finally said goodbye that night, we both knew we would see each other again.

I kept thinking about the strange coincidence of hearing "Here, There and Everywhere" in the Bookworks. Several years later, after we were engaged, I would tell Jon about the meaning of that song for me, and how I had heard it on our first date in Pacific Grove.

Jon and I were married last November and we needed to find a home that would welcome our blended family, which included a German shepherd and a total of three (!) cats. We searched the Monterey Bay from Santa Cruz to Carmel, and finally a retired veterinarian said to us, "That's my niche—I rent to people with animals!" We moved into a charming cottage with views of the ocean off Asilomar Beach.

We've come full circle, back to Pacific Grove.

Thank you, Nathan
Jonathan Oser

Taking a new job challenge, I moved to the coast from Fresno in 2010 and rented a house in Pebble Beach.

While in Fresno, I had purchased a 1974 MG Midget and restored it just enough to have fun in it while adding the final touches to bring it to perfection. My greatest pleasure was driving it around Pacific Grove, Pebble Beach, and down to Big Sur.

When off work, I spent most of my time in P.G. at the Works Coffee & Bookshop or at the coast.

I moved to Salinas in 2012 but I always returned to my favorite city, P.G., on weekends.

My youngest son Nathan came to visit from Japan in August of 2012. While he was here, I took him to all the usual spots I frequented. I will never forget when we were sitting at a bistro table on the sidewalk on Lighthouse Avenue one afternoon as the fog was creeping silently in with a light sea breeze. He took a deep breath, looked around and said, "I love it here. I hope to live in a place like this if I return to the States."

What I realized is that you see things you like in a more pronounced way when you see them through the eyes of the person you are introducing them to.

In March 2017 I returned to live in P.G. with my new wife, Diane.

One Half Mile Radius
Jan Roehl and Robert Huitt

When we were looking for a place to live in P.G.—way back when—we drove by Bookworks and Robert proclaimed, "Any house we buy in Pacific Grove has to be within a one-half mile radius of this bookstore!"

Chai Tea Latte
Evelyn Helminen
website and graphic designer

I was on a temporary restricted diet, and wasn't allowed to have, among other things, sugar or coffee. The sugar prohibition wasn't too bad most of the time, but my one cup of coffee per day habit was a hard one to give up. There's just something about a robust cup of coffee in the morning that has no replacement.

I suffered through for a while with tea, trying a variety of flavors to find one that gave me the coffee feeling I was so craving. In general, I like tea. But when all I wanted was a café latte, tea tasted like grass-flavored water.

Besides drinking coffee on a regular basis, I often make the drive from where I live in Monterey to Pacific Grove. I like bouncing between the unique P.G. coffeehouses while blogging and working on website projects for clients. During my restricted diet phase, coffeehouse time became less enticing. All pastries were off-limits. The smell of coffee was torture, so close yet unattainable. And tea, the one thing I could have, just didn't do it for me. It was bland, watery, thin, and I had to choke it down without the aid of any sweeteners.

I arrived at BookWorks in P.G. one day at the height of my tea-coffee frustration. I was conflicted in my desire to both work at a coffee shop and be as far away from forbidden coffee and disgusting tea as I could.

My iron will was starting to bend. What was one small coffee? What difference would a spoonful of honey make? A normally stoic Finn, I couldn't hold in my feelings any longer. I poured my heart out to the barista, and she suggested something that I had never considered.

What about a tea latte? She could make me a brewed Masala Chai Tea Latte, which had no sweetener because it didn't come pre-mixed, and would be robust like the café lattes I was used to and craving so badly.

My savior.

Only problem was, I would have to wait a bit because she had to brew the tea before making the latte. I would have gladly waited ten times as long.

That Masala Chai Tea Latte was the best thing I had ever tasted in my life. Flavorful, foamy, hot, satisfying. That day as I sat by the window and blogged, the words flowed like never before, and I was so happy.

I learned a few things that day. One, there is a decent replacement for coffee. Two, there's something to be said for opening up to a complete stranger about your troubles. And three, Pacific Grove is always the answer.

Life in Pacific Grove
Phyllis Edwards
author, editor

Following my career as an educator and later as an editor for National Geographic's textbook division, I settled on the Monterey Bay more than 20 years ago. The longer I enjoyed the area, however, the more I realized that when I retired I would want to live in Pacific Grove to avoid driving my car most days. I envisioned my older self whiling away my days toddling to the water, toddling to the library, toddling to the market, and toddling to the pharmacy. So, a few years ago I relocated to "America's Last Hometown" and nestled into my ideal life here.

When I met Patricia and she invited me to contribute to a book called Life in Pacific Grove, I wondered, at first, what the experience would be like for me because I did not feel that I had yet unearthed any of the deep flavor of the town. In short, I felt unworthy to the task. However, I was also very excited about the idea of people of the town sharing our stories and contributing to the coffers of the public library in some way. After ruminating for a while about what I had discovered during my regular walks throughout the quiet little town and its lovely neighborhoods, one particular detail captured my attention: the plethora of Little Free Libraries scattered among the various sections of town, which appear as the last chapter in this book.

Inspired by Patricia's encouragement, I took courage in hand and soon began to appreciate unanticipated benefits granted to me through my participation in the book project.

First, since elaboration on my topic requires walking

all over town to garner details, I pay more attention to my surroundings than when I have been less keenly focused.

Next, because my writing is about the contents of the town, rather than my experience of it, I harvest a new understanding of the layout of the town and the various moods, charms, and idiosyncrasies of its neighborhoods.

And finally, I have encountered a fascinating array of interesting people who contribute to my writing and enrich my personal life as well.

The great satisfaction I derived from writing for the book produced an unexpected desire to be involved in other aspects of the project as well. Patricia's fertile imagination, of course, readily devised a few tasks I could undertake to support her work, such as promoting participation among local businesses and editing essays submitted by a few of the local participants in the project. These small contributions engendered in me a vision of the companionship that awaits discovery through shared stories in communities anywhere in the world. In sum, writing for *Life in Pacific Grove* is developing within me a sense of real kinship with my hometown.

Life in Pacific Grove Enriches My Artistic Life
Keith Larson
illustrator, painter, writer

When I was in my early 20s I realized there was a part of myself that needed looking at which didn't appear in a mirror. At that time I wouldn't have been able to even form a thought like this, let alone write it down. It took blind faith and a faint inner knowing to start down a forest path which later I found out had many definitions and labels such as inner work, Hero's Journey, 12 step, self-realization, art therapy and the presence process.

As I hiked on, I realized my inner landscape was being reflected in my moment-to-moment life experience just like a mirror and automatically adjusted as I continued hiking on this path. I now had tools such as meditation, journal writing, art and connected breathing to look inside, which had been the reason to start this journey.

Adjusting my life experience with these tools also became a possibility. I started to search for a personal meaning, something that would put it all together. The fog rolled in but when it lifted, the word connections came into my thoughts.

Working on *Life in Pacific Grove* to me was about connections, and I became involved with the project because I could see the potential ripple effects of a community of people sharing their stories with each other. This book is now an example of what can be accomplished. We've worked together to create something that closes the distance between us on many levels. Personally it was important for me to make some connections with my past, having grown up in the Grove—to tell some stories of those times and to be in that space of being a little kid again.

Like many of you, I had some doubts about my writing abilities, but we decided to put our fears aside and show up anyway on the pages of this book. It also felt personally rewarding to reconnect with other family members and record and acknowledge our heritage in the area, which dates back to 1914.

It is satisfying to think that my family and grandchildren, Mattias and Kaia, will someday be reading something about our lives here in the Grove and looking at sketches I had done on these pages. I was excited to be asked by the publisher, Patricia Hamilton, to do the illustrations for this book. I had worked as a freelance magazine cartoonist for many years but also enjoyed sketching and painting in Pacific Grove.

My favorite teacher was Carmel artist Nancy Johnson, who taught at the Sunset Center in Carmel. I had mentioned to her that I wanted to be a cartoonist and she said it would also be more exciting for me if I learned to draw. I've taken many types of art classes and have learned something from each one of the creative teachers and artists that I've had the pleasure to work with. One of those individuals was Bill Bates, who drew the wonderful cartoons in the *Carmel Pine Cone*. I knew him when he had a studio at the Sunset Center and offered a class for us aspiring cartoonists. Bill used gray felt pens for his cartoons and was very proud of the finished look that these pens created.

The pens have evolved into brushes, and for many of the illustrations in this book I used them to create a graduated tonal effect. When it came to the seascapes I felt I needed a little more tonal variation, so I experimented with watercolor pencils over the tonal pictures made with the gray brush pens. Most of my sketches were done on the spot since. Over the years I have felt more comfortable being outside making art rather than being in a studio. In Pacific Grove that means I was in the fog, wind and, yes, sunshine when it came. I talked with all kinds of people visiting us from France, India, and other parts of the world who were interested in seeing what I was doing. Some would ask me to draw a picture of their child. Others would just want to talk about the points of interests in the area. This was very enjoyable and a new experience for me.

Before I go any further, I want to mention that I bought all my art supplies at Imagine Art Store on Forest Avenue across from the City Hall, where you can go in to play with the cats a little while if they are not napping.

Life in Pacific Grove is, has been, and will be, an unfolding gift in my life. I hope what I have contributed through my writing and art is a gift to community as well, not only beautiful Pacific Grove but, in a larger sense, to other cities, individuals and groups that decide to make bridges to each other using story-writing and art as the building materials that create greater connections and paths to the common themes we all share.

Blessings, Keith

The Missing Woman
Marlene Perfecto Huckelbery
excerpt from her writings

The woman sat in her rocking chair working on another quilt piece, the second of a set of floral patterns. This time she used the standing hoop with a magnifying glass attached to it. She was emotional and felt physically tired. What had she really done in her life? She thought about it and was disappointed.

At age 63, Estelle was thinking about herself and what she had accomplished in life. She had many dreams and desires that had not been fulfilled. She thought back over her life to remember what she had done that determined her accomplishments, and found that she had more memories of wishes for what she wanted to do rather than wishes she wanted to do that had been done.

Her life had been normal where she completed school, was employed in an occupation to earn a living, married, gave birth to two children, took care of her husband, and was looking forward to retirement. She read good books, saw a few plays and fewer movies, and she quilted. Most of their vacations had been at home or at a place nearby. In between the accomplishments of a normal life, she thought she did not have enough exciting events occur where she could say, 'I did that.'

Her chest began to heave into crying. She bowed her head and covered her forehead with her hand to endure the emotions welling up. Something else was happening to her. Lately she had been emotional to tears and irritable. Was this old age? She asked herself, realizing she did not know what happens to a person when they grow older into their sixties.

Estelle did not want to have resentments about her life. Her husband was a fine mate. She loved him. Their children had grown up without problems and were living successful lives. Yet her soul wanted something. It wanted to regain what she had lost as a woman. What all women let go of when they marry.

Estelle sat longer in her place in the house for sewing to finish embroidering a rose. She sat and just looked at everything, her mind still in a slump of tiredness. She loved their home in Pacific Grove, their Victorian house and how they decorated it, where they had lived their life and raised their children. She felt good in every room; each was a sanctuary from the confusion of the world outside. Their garden was quiet in green this year. Every year her husband changed the theme of the garden to floral or vegetables that brought its bounty into the house that changed the energy and life in it.

Estelle decided to arouse out of her thoughtfulness. Her attention focused on how she was breathing, so she took a few deep purposeful breaths, then thought about lunch. She decided to go out for lunch and walk around the town. She was already dressed well enough to go to a good restaurant. Estelle wore a skirt and a light pullover sweater that tied at her neck. She took her single handled purse.

CENTRAL COAST WRITERS CLUB—CHAPTER OF CALIFORNIA WRITERS CLUB

President's Message
Joyce Krieg
California Writers Club President

The beauty of Pacific Grove and its surrounding communities has always been an irresistible lure for literary artists of all stripes, from Richard Henry Dana and his description of the original Californios in *Two Years Before the Mast* to Robert Louis Stevenson, Robinson Jeffers, and John Steinbeck. Today's storytellers, bloggers and poets have found a home with Central Coast Writers (CCW) and its friendly, informative monthly meetings at P.G.'s Point Pinos Grill.

CCW is a branch of California Writers Club, founded in 1909 from the outdoor literary salons at the home of Oakland poet Joaquin Miller, gatherings that sometimes included Jack London of *Call of the Wild* fame. California Writers Club now has some 1800 members in 22 branches ranging from Mendocino to Orange County.

The Central Coast branch sprouted in the summer of 2002 out of a critique group that met at the old (and greatly missed) Thunderbird Bookshop at the Barnyard in Carmel. These writers were joined by other local authors who were aware of California Writers Club through a conference at Asilomar that the club sponsored in the 1990s, and who were weary of the long drive to San Jose to attend meetings at the nearest branch. In the spirit of "let's put on a show," these wordsmiths banded together with a common goal of forming their own branch of California Writers Club right here on the peninsula. Several Pagrovians were key figures in the early days of the club, including Ken Jones, Anita Alan, Laura Emerson, Kerry Wood, and our own Patricia Hamilton.

Central Coast Writers bounced around from a variety of locations—the Barnyard, two Monterey hotels (Casa Munras and the Bay Park), and a now-defunct barbecue restaurant in North Monterey—until the club finally found the perfect home at P.G.'s Point Pinos Grill. The beautiful locale, with the view of the sea, the cypress, and the setting sun, the hip, trendy décor, and the friendly, accommodating staff make it the ideal venue for a gathering of creative folk.

Today Central Coast Writers boasts 164 members and then some, ranging from authors with multi-book contracts with major New York houses to newcomers who just "always wanted to write." The monthly meetings feature a guest speaker on a specific topic relating to the craft of writing or the publishing industry, as well as opportunities for networking and fellowship. In addition to the monthly meetings, the club sponsors a booth at Good Old Days, encourages young writers with a high school short story contest, and hosts social events just for members.

Meetings take place on the third Tuesday of the month, except for August and December, at Point Pinos Grill at the Pacific Grove Municipal Golf Course. Join us for dinner (ordered off the menu and paid for individually) from 5:30 to 6:30 p.m., or come just for the meeting and speaker, starting at 6:30 p.m. Admission is free for members and non-members alike. For the latest details about upcoming speakers, as well as information on membership, go to centralcoastwriters.org.

The world of book publishing has come a long way from the days of Jack London, what with the global dominance of e-readers and Amazon, but humankind will never outlive the need for a good story. As long as there are lovers of the written word who are drawn to Pacific Grove, Central Coast Writers will be extending a warm welcome.

My Personal Story

I like to tell people I ended up in Pacific Grove because I won a Westinghouse Scholarship, but the truth is a bit more involved than that. After a long career working in print and broadcast journalism, spending many years at the big news/talk radio station in Sacramento, in 1994 I suddenly found myself without a job, a victim of one of those big corporate upheavals with massive layoffs that were just starting to hit the radio industry in the mid-1990s. The old owner of the station happened to be Westinghouse, at the time one of those benevolent, old-school companies that believed in doing good by their employees. The result is that good old "Group W" offered me a very generous severance package. If I'd been thinking rationally, I would have stayed in Sacramento, gotten a gig as a Public Information Officer with a state agency, like so many of my other broadcast colleagues had done, and been set for life. But the Central Coast, where I spent almost all of my vacation time, had been tugging at my heartstrings for many years. So I took the money and ran—right here to Pacific Grove.

Favorite Hang-out for Writers

We have several very special, independent coffeehouses here in P.G.—Juice n' Java, Carmel Roasting Company, Bookworks, among others—but I have to admit to a special fondness for Crema. This sweet Victorian cottage at the corner of 13th and Lighthouse is a writer's dream:

lots of nooks and crannies in which to hide, free WiFi, plentiful caffeine, a hip, artsy vibe, and a friendly staff that tolerates customers who hang out for hours at a time. I belong to two writers' groups that regularly meet at Crema and engage in the aforementioned "hanging out." Both of these groups have become such an important bookmark in my life that I've found myself scheduling appointments and out-of-town trips around these standing commitments—and a large part of their appeal and sense of urgency in my life is due to the very special atmosphere at Crema.

Lifetime of Reading and Writing

I grew up in San Jose "before it became Silicon Valley." I was always an odd, bookish kid, far too smart in an era when girls were supposed to be merely quiet and decorative. As a voracious reader, I'd always harbored a dream of someday writing a book or two of my own and becoming rich and famous like my idols, Sue Grafton and Janet Evanovich. Well, the "rich and famous" part of the plan hasn't happened yet, but I did manage to get three of my mysteries published by one of the big New York houses. I'm currently president of California Writers Club, active in my local branch, Central Coast Writers, and am working on my bucket list project, a historical suspense novel about the birth of Silicon Valley in the early 1960s. My obsessions include Abyssinian cats, hiking at Point Lobos, dark chocolate, and 1960s British Invasion teen idol Peter "Herman" Noone.

A sampling of Central Coast Writer's stories follow. More CCW member stories appear throughout the book.

Poetry
Patrick Flanagan

The coastline of Monterey County prompted my wife and me to move to Pacific Grove. We have not been disappointed. The calm and sometimes violent beauty of the ocean invites contemplation. Sitting quietly on the edge of a continent can lead to pleasure, passion, and poetry.

The Coast

Nervous little birds
dart across the face
of a seaside cliff.
Endless waves
roll and foam
rattling the rocks below.
A black cat with no tail
stretches in the sunlit
garden above.
Life moves and sings
out of the great silence
all around.

Surviving the Storm

How do they do it?
How do dolphins and great whales
survive through night long storms
when white capped waves
cover the ocean from horizon to horizon,
when spray fills the air,
when rain pours down in solid sheets?
How do they suck air
into their huge lungs without drowning
in the water all around them?
They must know the secrets that we know.
They must know the secrets that help us
smile and breathe and survive
without drowning in the sorrow all around us.
They must be able to
see the beauty of a raindrop,
hear the song of the wind,
feel their belonging to the universe.

Layers

Scientists call it sedimentary rock,
the result of patient settling
onto the ocean floor
where time and pressure
push silt and particles together
until they let go of their individuality
and become part of vast sheets of stone
layered one on top of the other.
Here at the foot of a cliff
on the edge of a continent,
those multihued layers
do not rest horizontally
as they were formed.
They point straight up
toward the heavens
as if in prayer or meditation
trying to forget
the rage and wrath
that wrenched them
from the sleepy ocean bed.
I sit on a water worn boulder,
too full of doubt to pray,
too restless to meditate,
trying to remember
the songs my mother sang
when I was a child.

The Secret Life of Walter Mitty
Suzanne Stormon
response to ccw writing challenge

In Walter Mitty, the author James Thurber has created an Everyman. Henpecked by his wife and beaten down by life, Mitty is a middle-aged man trying to navigate the challenges of ordinary life with little success. Nagged constantly by his wife and mocked by others he encounters in the course of his mundane existence, Mitty retreats into a fantasy world of extraordinary events.

In his imagination, Mitty becomes a daring combat pilot, a uniquely skilled surgeon called in to consult on a puzzling medical case, and a brilliant lawyer whose eloquence saves the day in a tense courtroom drama. In all of these fantasies, Mitty is the hero, a sharp contrast to the little failures of his real life. Indeed, it is exactly that contrast that gives Mitty relief from the humiliation of his day-to-day existence.

The Secret Life of Suzanne Stormon
Aka – Ms. Mitty

Suzanne moved to the Central Coast in 2012 with a small pension and big dreams. As the car pulled into Monterey County, her mind started to arrange the possibilities. Now was the time to become a famous writer, maybe the next John Steinbeck, with stories and poems about all the ocean's creatures and the quirky people on the shore.

As she settled in, her dream grew bigger and she met another woman with an even bigger personality who led her to the Central Coast Writers meetings near the golf course in Pacific Grove, the little town on the peninsula that seemed to be stuck in the mid-twentieth century.

On her way to her first meeting, she drove down the rocky coast road and stopped to watch the pounding surf at Lovers Point. Maybe, just maybe, she could qualify for a "60-and-over" surf team. She was sure they had one. She saw herself standing on the beach, ready to accept her medal for first in her class. Even though she hadn't surfed for 50 years, all her old surfing friends would gather around to watch the ceremony, then lift her onto their shoulders to take her to a beach bonfire celebration in her honor. The party would go on late into the evening, the fire lighting up the night sky, but she would slip away into the shadows of the rocks with a marvelous young lover.

A car door slammed behind her and she turned to face the noise. But the sound and the smell of the ocean drew her attention back to the shore, where a fisherman cast his line into the surf. Maybe, just maybe, Suzanne would buy one of those heavy-duty surf rods and begin catching the biggest halibut on the coast. People would watch her as she hauled her catch onto the shore. Soon they would want to learn her tricks and she would set up a surf fishing school that Hollywood celebrities would flock to like the seagulls on the beach. She'd have to fend them off just to have a few minutes of fishing to herself. Life is so busy when you're the best, she thought.

Just then the phone in Suzanne's pocket rang.

"Hey Suzanne, where are you?" her friend asked.

"On my way." Suzanne said and jumped back into her car.

She turned up from the coast onto Asilomar Avenue, passing a doe and her fawns grazing on the tender grass of the Pacific Grove Golf Links, then turned in to the parking lot of the Point Pinos Grill, the home of the CCW monthly meetings.

As Suzanne met her fellow Central Coast Writers for the first time, her mind floated back to her dream of being the next John Steinbeck. That is, if she wasn't too busy surfing or fishing to write the novel of the century.

Suzanne Stormon finds many commonalities between aspects of her life and the "Secret Life of Walter Mitty," although she is actually much more humble. She is a writer/writer's helper who moved to the Central Coast in 2011. She is the founder of Nevada Narratives *(www.NevadaNarratives.com), an online magazine featuring stories, poems, and pictures that explore that state.*

Ms. Toad's Wild Ride to Pacific Grove
Patricia Hamilton
response to ccw writing challenge

Once upon a time … a little girl was enchanted by a book called "The Wind in the Willows" by Kenneth Grahame … which became a Disney animated feature called "Mr. Toad's Wild Ride" … which became a popular attraction at the Disney theme parks … and now presenting …

Patricia Hamilton's Classic Everywoman's Tale comes to life in this outrageous tragio-comedic saga filled with danger, high-spirited antics and adventure! Bring the whole family along on MS. PATRICIA'S WILD RIDE, a live-action faux-fantasy adapted from the pages of her classic THE CALIFORNIA WOMAN, and commemorating the unforgettable encounters with Ancestors and Family, Friends and Teachers, Husbands and Children, Bosses, Mentors and Clients.

How It All Began

"The hour has come!" said the Badger with great solemnity. "What hour?" asked the Rat, uneasily looking around. Mole busied himself with travel preparations. "Why, Ms. Toad's hour! The hour of Toad! We'll teach her to be a sensible Toad, to drive her powerful Limousine of Life, set to begin in Surprise Valley this very day, March 30, 1946!"

They reached the lane to Toad Hall in Cedarville, California, to find, as Badger had anticipated, a shiny new life, known hereafter as Ms. Patricia Hamilton. She received her own unique genetic nature from 23 pre-Revolutionary ancestral families, and was being nurtured by well-meaning parents who really hadn't a clue. Ms. Patricia came carried down the steps, sucking on her tiny thumb, and before they could counsel anyone, she was whisked away in a Hudson Hornet, off on her uncharted road of a life less traveled!

Trapped in the Ancestral Family Car

The Ancestral Family car proved powerful beyond belief! Farmer Father was at the wheel, Genteel Mother by his side, seven children hanging on for dear life. Father's genetic code sped them wildly along country roads, stopping briefly in small towns up and down the West Coast, seeing sights, making friends. Careening with Mother's literary genes, they crashed into libraries, showering Ms. Patricia with a love of books and a curiosity for all things.

With no real supervision, the car repeatedly spun out of control—she fell out of one speeding car; Father ran over her with farm machinery; she nearly drowned in a water reservoir. Narrowly avoiding preachers of hellfire and damnation at every turn—and in order to survive AND to hope to thrive—she retreated into her own confused, yet determined and powerful inner world, with her genetic bent for happiness intact.

Taking the Wheel

Bailing out of the Family car, Ms. Patricia boarded a Greyhound bus to California, right back where she started from. Now at the wheel of her new Toyota Celica, taking a left turn, she flew at high speeds past bosses, crashed through all glass ceilings, and rolled over every husband. Life was going too fast, and during a powerful tsunami, she lost the grasp of her daughter's tiny hand and the car began to dangerously drift sideways.

Safe Harbor at Last!

Awakened by recent events, she made a sharp right turn and took off in a new and quite different direction. Ms. Patricia headed for an ancestral safe harbor and created a new family of friends in Pacific Grove, a seaside paradise. Ms. Toad's Wild Ride came to an end and her sensible life began at last.

Ms. Patricia shed that erratic car and took to walking the Recreation Trail. Life experiences were examined, lessons were learned, college degrees earned, and travel to Ice Age ancestral sites undertaken. Transcendental meditation, mentors and sea air enlivened her and refreshed her spirit. She established her own book publishing company and welcomed her daughter, son-in-law and two glorious grandchildren to share in her good fortune. And she always followed the advice of her good friend Leonard Epstein to "Give thanks and expect more!"

She Lived Happily Ever After

"Very well, then, Ms. Patricia," said the Badger firmly, Rat and Mole looking on. "You've learned to be a sensible Toad, to nurture your nature and to confidently drive your powerful Limousine of Life. We knew you would!"

Grandma Happily Interrupted

It was 1998 and I'd just returned to Pacific Grove after two years living in Europe. My Gale/Griswold/Murray family home on Park Place had been sold and I'd rented a room in a house on Junipero Street. Thompson and Beau Lange had recently created the Grove Homescapes business and upstairs apartments for themselves out of the old Grove Laundry building on Lighthouse Avenue. I'd helped them open the doors for business, and was managing the office while I contemplated my next move.

"There's a studio apartment for rent upstairs in our Victorian home," said Yvette, a Homescapes customer. "Would you move in and be my health advocate?" She was over 80 and seemed healthy, but she was concerned about dying alone.

"Well, I do need a place of my own—and I'd like to see what's available—but my cat Chu-Chu needs access to the outdoors."

"I'll take the upstairs apartment then," Yvette offered, "and you can move into mine, which opens out upon a spacious garden with a hundred-year-old rubber tree. You can meditate under its branches."

I intended it to be a temporary move, as I intended to live abroad. I had become entranced with the idea while on a visit to a half-timbered manor house in Solihull, England, built in the 1500s. Now in the British Trust, it had been home to my Griswold ancestors. It was inside that house that I experienced "blood memory" for the first time. I held in my hands centuries' old pewter mugs with my family crest and emblematic greyhound handle, and realized ancestors had actually used the mugs five hundred years prior.

The layout of the studio mirrored that of my space in Grandpa Murray's home on Park Place. Only the floor plan was flipped, with the front door where the back door had been, etc. And it opened onto Garden Lane in the back, which is a two-block continuation of Park Place to the west.

A new friend, Diana Dennett, a ninth-generation Montereyan, asked me to publish her memoirs, *Tell Me More Ancestor Stories, Grandma*. I opened Park Place Publications with an office in the Giles Building. Other requests followed and I've been here since, working with local writers such as playwright Morgan Stock, former Mayor Dan Cort, jazz musician Bill Minor, columnist Phil Bowhay, and others, to produce more than 100 books to date.

The idea of moving vanished in August 1999 when my grandson, Zachary Andrew McCoy, was born in Sacramento. I took one look at this pink, squirmy little fellow and said to myself, "I'm not going anywhere until he's old enough to go with me."

Grace Erin McCoy followed three years later. My little apartment and big backyard in Pacific Grove has been the perfect venue for my life as a grandmother. For 18 years now the three of us have cuddled and slept together in one room—one big slumber party. We've shared secrets and made plans for adventures: walking to the Aquarium, taking the trolley to Fisherman's Wharf—their favorite is sampling all of the clam chowders and always choosing the one from Abalonetti's. We would buy a quart and three sourdough rolls, and eat under the oaks by the Custom House. Here's a video Zack made of a 2011 visit: https://www.youtube.com/watch?v=1Nz7BfmNJJk

Our strolls around Pacific Grove take us shopping at Charlie's Grove Market for ingredients to make special meals; to movies at Lighthouse Cinemas, where the manager hands out posters for their bedroom walls; to taking Clara Torres, the 90-something resident of my home for 50-plus years to Peppers Mexican Restaurant on Forest Avenue for tacos, enchiladas and quesadillas; to seashore tide pools (Grace's favorite). Zack and Grace meet my friends and clients and have become a part of my Pacific Grove life.

Grace, now 14, still heads for the backyard to turn over rocks, hoping to spot a skinny lizard—when she was five it was to find rollie-pollies (sow bugs) and worms. She's taking art lessons and when she saw this drawing by Keith Larson, intends to draw one of the backyard too.

Zack, now 18, no longer swings from the rubber tree's branches, but helps me in the house with meals and cleaning up. He's an excellent cook. We made and posted two cooking videos on YouTube. Here's a link to a 2009 video about making butter from heavy cream: https://www.youtube.com/watch?v=WVTEVrwzAyo.

Recently the three of us perched on the back steps were planning a garden party for house residents. Grace, idly tossing nuts to Peanut, our backyard squirrel, said, "Grandma, I just love your place. I love that it's near the ocean. I love all the things we do and the places you've taken us. And I love this town—it's so much fun to be here. Don't ever move from this house or this town."

I wouldn't dream of it!

The Surprise
Nancy Jacobs

Toby the cat and Sammie the Siamese were busy playing between periods of sunning themselves on this rare sunny, warm Pacific Grove Saturday afternoon when there was a knock on the door. I was not expecting anyone so I was surprised by the door knock. I opened the door and there was our friend Eldon Dedini with a package.

I said, "Please come in." I then called my husband Don who came right away and was equally surprised to see Eldon at the door. Don invited Eldon to sit down and I brought a bottle of Chianti, cheese, grapes and biscotti.

I stayed close by because their conversations were always beyond interesting. This time they chose to talk about Hieronymus Bosch, the 16th century artist who is hard to define with his fantastic images of everyday life, including the devastating illnesses of the period.

As I was listening I noticed that they often dressed alike, a casual jacket with either jeans or casual slacks, every now and then a colorful sweater. Today was one of their more talkative days. They were talking about early airplanes that were made of paper and cloth, from what I could hear. And they would sketch something in their sketch books every now and then. I loved watching them sketch because that pen or pencil became alive on paper. Dedini was famous for his cartoons for Playboy magazine, my husband not so famous, but their talent was equal. They both loved art. We did have a bit of excitement when Sammie the Siamese decided to jump on Eldon's lap, causing Eldon to almost spill his wine.

It was almost 6 o'clock and Eldon had to go home and eat dinner, so he called my name and I went closer to the coffee table where they were sitting. He opened the package and there was a poster he had done for the Concours d' Elegance. He said the image of the dark-haired girl on the poster was me. I was literally stunned. He handed the framed poster to me. My husband loved it. I still have it, such a precious memory. All I could say was thank you! He was so generous. My husband and I both asked him to come again. I was so lucky to have known Eldon and all of the other cartoonists.

West Virginian
Nancy Swing

How did a girl from West Virginia end up in Pacific Grove? Via Kazakhstan. And Guyana, Tanzania and Laos. And lots of other countries. After spending most of our adult lives working in the Third World, my husband, Russell Sunshine, and I've retired and returned to the States.

But it wasn't a straight shot. In the late nineties, we bought and renovated an old farmhouse in Italy, expecting to retire and die there. But I developed an extreme sensitivity to sunlight, with doctors recommending we leave Umbria and find a cloudy, foggy climate.

We began our search in Portland and drove south, rejecting each potential nest. Finally we reached Pacific Grove, and it just felt right. We'd appreciated the small-town atmosphere of our Italian community, and we found it again in P.G. Strangers saying hello as they passed. Locally-owned shops downtown, with welcoming, friendly staff. Ditto the restaurants, and the food was really good! Interesting architecture, lovingly preserved.

Yet we wanted to be sure. After all, this was a big move, from Central Italy to Central California, not just in distance, but in ambiance. And we only knew one family in the area, from long-ago days when we'd all lived in Sacramento.

We decided to try an experiment. We took turns living here in a rented, furnished apartment for three months. Meanwhile the other one remained in Italy, caring for house, dog, two cats and an olive grove.

I remember walking around the Asilomar neighborhood and thinking, "How perfect this is." Close to shore; close to town; lots of places to amble, from the old railway right-of-way through streets of quaint cottages to the natural forest of George Washington Park. And I felt healthy, freed from the almost daily migraines that had been crippling my life in Italy.

Those short-term stays sealed the deal. We packed up and moved within a matter of weeks, never looking back. There were more delights to come. The longer we've lived here, the more we've realized that P.G. has much more to offer than we'd first appreciated.

Yes, there're the cloudy and foggy days I need. But we also get sparkling days of sun when the light bounces off the seafoam and fills the air with glittering effervescence. Those times when the fog drifts across the dunes and slips through the trees bring a bonus -- hair and skin agleam with unexpected vitality.

So many more gifts: Neighbors who truly treat us like family. Celebrations of heritage, from annual renovation awards to Good Old Days every April. Fourth of July in Caledonia Park, sharing food and dancing to live music. The family of deer living in our backyard, bringing forth fawns every spring. The Monarch Sanctuary in winter, when rising sun caresses sleeping butterflies, and thousands of orange-and-black wings lift into the sky. Early morning walks on Asilomar Beach, dogs scampering in the surf while their humans stop to pass the time of day with strangers.

In fact, we're not strangers. Not even from the first day. After wandering the world, we've come home. — Nancy Swing is the author of *Malice on the Mekong*, a mystery set in Laos, and *Child's Play*, the first in a mystery trilogy set in West Virginia. nancyswing.com

Rock Solid*
Russell Sunshine

One of the special pleasures of living in our Asilomar neighborhood is the stream of pedestrian surprises. Some of these treats jump out at you, noticeable because they weren't in place the last time you passed. Others are permanent but more difficult to spot.

I stepped over the curb into a sea of tall grasses. A dozen paces along a narrow deer path, I literally bumped into a prehistoric marvel. Topping an inconspicuous formation of granite boulders were a dozen grinding bowls gouged into the rock surface by Native Americans, probably within the past thousand years. Our neighborhood's ancient heritage, hiding in plain sight.

The freestanding cluster of boulders measured 15 yards by 10. The four largest bowls or "bedrock mortars" were a yard off the ground, about six inches in diameter and four or five inches deep. Smaller indentations, some just above ground level, averaged two inches across and one deep. Archaeologists tell us that Rumsien-Ohlone tribespeople hollowed out the larger receptacles to grind acorn kernels, pine nuts and edible seeds with stone pestles. In her basketry exhibit at the P.G. Natural History Museum, tribal descendent Linda Yamane has illustrated how woven collars were glued around the rock-bowl rims to keep the produced flour from blowing away. The smaller craters may have been used for pulverizing medicinal herbs and body paint.

This might sound like elementary technology. But it transformed an entire culture. Hunter-gatherers had previously kept on the move, stalking game and harvesting ripening plants for seasonal sustenance. Mortar-and-pestle knowhow, probably imported onto the Central Coast from adjacent areas, changed not only diet but also social organization. Acorns were rich sources of protein, fat and carbohydrates, dramatically boosting calorie intake. When ground into flour, leached with water to dissolve bitter tannins, and cooked into porridge and bread, they permitted a sedentary lifestyle with stored nuts as a year-round insurance policy.

It didn't take great imagination to animate this communal kitchen. I flashed on women and girls working, laughing and gossiping together, their menfolk two hundred yards down a gentle slope, hunting marine mammals and waterfowl, abalone and mussels in bay shallows.

At least five major shell mounds have been identified within sight of these mortars. Tools, arrowheads and even human bones have been found beneath Lovers Point and Cannery Row, a short hike to the east. But for me, this waist-high food-processing workstation made it easiest to visualize and connect with our local precursors' daily routines.

As I write this appreciation, paleontologists at the San Diego Museum of Natural History have just claimed dates of 130,000 years ago for splintered mastodon bones and adjacent chipped stones accidently unearthed during a freeway on-ramp upgrade. The analysts' interpretation is that the stones were adapted by early humans as hammers to extract nutritious marrow from the bones. The estimated dates have won considerable scientific support, but the inference of human tool use is not yet accepted by most California archaeologists. If this connection is confirmed by further research, it will blow the lid off of the prior scientific consensus about humans' arrival in the Western Hemisphere.

Whether hammers or mortars, ancient artifacts communicate powerfully with us across the ages. As with all fragmentary messages, these relics raise as many questions as they answer.

For example, if modern man (Homo sapiens) didn't walk out of Africa until 60,000 years ago, which human species could have been feasting on San Diego bone marrow 70,000 years earlier? The discoverers' candidates include Neanderthals, Denisovans or some third since-extinct species. And if modern humans migrating from the north occupied Southern California's Channel Islands 13,000 years ago, wouldn't geography and common sense suggest they must also have settled our own bountiful Central Coast at least that early, even though the oldest remains found thus far on the Monterey Peninsula date back only 9,400 years?

Far from comprehending our region's entire prehistoric saga, we're still near the beginning of our learning curve. And since a relative handful of isolated sites and identified remains hold the keys to that quest, their preservation and protection are crucial. In the case of the San Diego remains, bones and stones excavated in 1992 had to be carefully preserved by their scientific discoverers for 25 years before uranium-dating technology had sufficiently advanced to yield a broadly convincing time measurement.

Proactive protection of our Central Coast bedrock mortars is equally necessary. At the Asilomar site, several boulders have already been dislodged and damaged. Benign neglect isn't working. Mindful stewardship can serve a constellation of complementary interests: scholarly research and childhood education, to be sure, but also respect for the traditions and sensibilities of surviving Native American descendants.

Our P.G. community is privileged to share this rich cultural inheritance. We should join hands, cherish and celebrate our resilient legacy.

*With thanks for expert advice from historian Dennis Copeland and archaeologist Gary Breschini.

Russell Sunshine's memoir, FAR & AWAY: True Tales from an International Life, is available in paperback and e-book editions. www.amazon.com/dp/1943887195 .

CCW and My Love of Writing
Sharon Tucker
author, copywriter

I began writing at a very early age. One day while my sister and I were outside playing, my mother called us into the house. She was having a discussion with a friend as to how to encourage kids to write. At that point, she handed each of us a pad of paper and a pencil and told us to go back outside and write a poem.

About 20 minutes later she called us in to read what we had written. I remember my mother's reaction to my poem. She and her friend said they were amazed and thought it beautiful. They liked my sister's poem as well and told us we both had talent. That was a very significant moment for me and from that day forward I began writing. I wrote poems, short stories and plays. In my senior year for my final in social studies class, I wrote a play about the Ku Klux Klan. I got an A. When my husband passed away, I wrote about the experience of grieving in "The Mourning After."

I have written off-and-on for most of my adult life, sometimes for work and sometimes for pleasure. But joining Central Coast Writers has been one of the most positive things I could have done for myself as a writer. Every month we meet at Point Pinos Grill in Pacific Grove for dinner and friendship. I've made some amazing friends, learned a lot from the guest speakers and workshops, and enjoy the camaraderie of sharing and supporting other writers. Just recently I began writing a novel in the first person based on a true story. I was struggling with how to make myself interesting. Someone suggested I try writing from my husband's viewpoint. Voila! It worked.

Each month I come away inspired to continue my efforts and a renewed dedication to do the obvious… write. Who knows! Maybe I'll write another poem.

Pull of the Central Coast
Lana Bryan
retired technical writer

The rental was a shotgun house. Living room, kitchen, bedroom, bath. Bam.

On a quiet street near the Pacific Grove Post Office, it hunkered down in a nondescript way with other small houses. When I was nearing retirement, Bob asked, "What do you want to do right after your last day at work?" My answer was immediate: "I want to stay in Pacific Grove for two weeks and pretend we live there."

Pacific Grove is only 60 miles from San Jose, but a world away. Big city vibe to small town vibe. I loved it. That fall, the October temperatures hit the 80s. I didn't know then that fall is the warmest and sunniest time on the Central Coast, so I had plenty of jackets and long sleeves and no summer-weight clothing. That made for some hot, sweaty walks—and for some shopping.

Our rule was to go to the beach every day and to get in the car only rarely. We walked from Lovers Point to Holly's Lighthouse Cafe., from Bookworks to Victorian Corner. Up and down Lighthouse Avenue looking for interesting shops and good restaurants; never disappointed. When we did get in the car, we went to Asilomar, Point Lobos, and Cannery Row, where Bob did his first scuba dives in the 1970s.

After dinner out in one of the fabulous restaurants on the peninsula (Fifi's Bistro Café remains our favorite), we watched a whole season of *Battlestar Galactica*. To this day, the Universal Television music takes me straight to that little house. You know it: "Ta DA ta-ta-ta DA ¼"

I read all of Steinbeck's books. On a road trip, I read aloud to Bob the appendix to *The Log from the Sea of Cortez*. It was an homage by Steinbeck to Ed Ricketts, after his death following the train hitting his stalled car. We both sobbed. On another afternoon, we found Edward Flanders Ricketts' columbarium in the El Encinal Cemetery.

We toured Cannery Row with Michael Hemp, author of *Cannery Row: The History of John Steinbeck's Old Ocean View Avenue*. Hemp took us into Doc's Lab and then introduced us to Kalisa Moore at her restaurant across from the aquarium. She snatched his book out of his hand and looked herself up. Thrusting it back, she said, "Only a few lies."

Every time we came back to Monterey Bay, we made new discoveries: all of the places where Steinbeck lived and wrote; the Gravity Garden past Point Lobos; the Coast Guard pier, its end covered with seals. Then one day, the seals were down to a very few at the end of the pier and the cormorants were nesting in their place.

A few years later, who knew that I would not only live in Monterey, but also be a member of Central Coast Writers (we found their booth at Good Old Days), the Historic Garden League, and the American Association of University Women.

It is often cold here, but the warmth of the people makes up for it. And I'm still exploring.

Great Happenings!
Elaine R. La Fleur
aspiring poet, book/ocean lover

My husband Curtis and I began visiting the Pacific Grove area in the early 2000s, staying at hotels and bed and breakfasts and enjoying the coastal attractions. Then Curtis attended the 2012 Monterey Jazz Festival and took time to explore Pacific Grove's unique neighborhoods, including the lovely late 1800s homes displaying plaques of original owner names. Spotting an Open House sign on an attractive old two story home, he went in and met realtor Maureen Mason, who asked him whether we were planning to relocate. Curtis said we'd like to because we loved the area and had always hoped to live near the ocean, but couldn't do so now as he was still working. Maureen took our email address and agreed to send us possibilities in our price range as they came available.

When Curtis returned to tell me about discovering Pacific Grove's historic areas and the home he had visited, of course I wanted to see for myself and we subsequently made a number of trips to the town, checking out homes that looked inviting and that might be suitable.

Fast forward to 2015 and things had changed! Curtis had retired AND the Bay Area housing market had heated up. We looked at a home in Pacific Grove that was a ten minute walk to the ocean and fell in love with it: a new home built atop a 1950s garage, formerly one part of a three-building motel. We were able to sell our Bay Area home for a good deal more than we'd paid for it 20 years earlier and could make an offer on our dream house in Pacific Grove. We finally made our long hoped for move to our new home on June 10, 2015.

Then the next wonderful event occurred. Moving to a new area after many years I was eager to meet new people and began attending the Pacific Grove monthly book group at The Bookworks, along with local yoga classes. In July, reading the *Cedar Street Times*, I saw a small notice about a group called Poetry in the Grove meeting in the Little House in Jewell Park on Saturday, August 1st. I was thrilled because I had written poetry since the 1970s, attending poetry writing workshops and a small weekly poetry writing group in nearby Palo Alto.

In August I went to my first Poetry in the Grove meeting, discussing the poetry of Linda Paston, and while there discovered other members of my clan: people who loved and read poetry aloud together, enjoyed both discovering new and older poets as well as discussing their books and how their poetry changed across time. I have been happily attending monthly Poetry in the Grove meetings ever since and recruiting new members. Wonderful things happen in Pacific Grove!

Noisy Neighbors
Patricia Watson

The exhaustive work of Silicon Valley takes a heavy toll on its workers. Years ago, friends recommended Pacific Grove as a respite from the noisy neighbors, long hours and ceaseless demands of work. It sounded like a perfect getaway. We booked a historic P.G. inn perched on a hill over the water and settled in for a well earned, quiet weekend. Around sunrise on that first morning, construction sounds woke me.

Tap, tap, tap, tap, tap. I checked the clock. Five-fifty in the morning and someone was using a hammer! I dragged the bedclothes over my ears and tried to ignore that workman. Tap, tap, tap, tap, tap.

I tried not to wake my husband. I went to the window

to see if I could locate the thoughtless carpenters outside. The hammering was louder with the window open. Tap, tap, tap, TAP! No workers in sight. I could see birds and some kind of dark animal floating on the bay. I picked up the inn's binoculars to get a closer look at that wildlife and search for those workmen.

The creature I'd spotted was an otter floating on its back. I got so excited the hammering didn't matter anymore. That otter had something that looked like a rock balanced on its belly. Clasped in his two front paws, I could see a shell. I watched the hungry otter bang his shell over and over against his rock. Tap, tap, tap, tap. I'd found the carpenter.

After every few slams on the rock, he checked if it had broken enough to provide breakfast. I couldn't stop watching. He used those cute little paws like human hands turning the shell, examining every angle. When the otter finished off its contents, he rolled and dived underwater.

I waited but my otter come didn't up again. I thought I'd had a once-in-a-lifetime experience. I put down the glasses and ran to the bed to shake my husband awake.

"What's wrong?" He didn't want to wake up.

"You won't believe what I just saw outside." I couldn't contain my excitement.

"Somebody dead out there? If there's no murder, I'm going back to sleep." He buried his head in the pillows.

Tap, tap, tap, tap, tap.

"Wake up, honey, you hear that? You'll never believe what that sound is."

"What?, Just tell me and let me get some rest."

"It's an otter in the bay breaking shells on a rock!"

I had his attention now. "You're kidding."

Tap, tap, tap, tap.

"Come on, you have to look."

My husband rolled out of bed, threw on his robe and grabbed the binoculars by the window.

"Oh my gosh, look at that! I didn't think they came this close to land!"

We took turns watching the otter feeding until he swam out of view.

That hungry otter sealed our love for the Monterey bay. Every vacation we managed was in Pacific Grove. Now we live here and we never tire of our noisy neighbors.

What the Deer Said
Ned Huston

While we were packing our bags, getting reading to check out of the Gosby House, I said to my wife, "We ought to come back to P.G."

She gave me one of those looks. Sidewise. "You didn't." One of those looks where she turns toward you, the reader, with lowered eyebrows. Only, you weren't there, so she turned to me.

"You're not one of the locals. You don't get to call it P.G."

We took our bags and left the room.

"The deer said it's okay."

She eyed me sidewise again. "The deer don't talk. This isn't Disneyland. Just because deer inhabit downtown doesn't make them supernatural."

We checked out and headed to the car. "When I took that picture of myself at Lovers Point with the clouds and the ocean behind me, one of the cloud people came down from the sky and whispered in my ear, 'You can call it P.G.'"

My wife gave me one of those looks again. "They're called Sylphs, not Selfies. You can't dignify the practice of taking vanity pictures of yourself by conflating it with European mythology. This isn't Ireland. They don't have a mythological creature living under every rock."

"The locals call them Selfies," I told her on the way to the car. "Sylphs, Selfies, same thing."

We loaded our luggage into the trunk then drove down Forest on our way out of town.

"I have proof," I told my wife, handing her my phone. "I have pictures of the Selfies."

"Sylphs are invisible," she declared.

"That doesn't mean they aren't in my pictures."

She rolled her eyes as she thumbed through my shots. "The only thing I see in these photos is *you*."

I got a pained expression on my face. "The only way you can get a picture of them is when they sneak up behind you. These aren't pictures of me. They're—"

I paused a few beats so she could catch up.

"Selfies," she said.

Exactly.

Day Spa for the Mind
Sarah E. Pruitt

Getting from Salinas to Pacific Grove takes thirty minutes but seems like going back in time to a different era. Even the air feels different. Disney could have designed it. Walt would have made it into one of those rides popular with the very old or very young. A ride where you sit in a boat or a train and glide past elegant gardens, Victorian houses and, at night, trees lit by fairy lights.

Coming into town on Lighthouse, slow down as you pass Crema and take a moment inhale the smell of its bacon biscuits. Check out the windows of Spirals for a new-to-you outfit. A block further, you are surrounded by dozens of little stores with everything you'll ever need: groceries, shoes, clothes, books, antiques and even a laundry mat. Near the end of the business district is Juice n' Java. One of the few coffee places where I can find ginger cookies

During World War II, my father, Nero Pruitt, ended up in Pacific Grove courtesy of the U.S. Navy. For several months preceding a trip to the South Pacific, he served on a small ship that patrolled the coast between Big Sur and Moss Landing. When he was off duty, he lived in a rented room in Pacific Grove. One of the other sailors grew up on a nearby dairy farm. Despite a large army presence in the area, Dad and his fellow sailors never lacked for milk.

I was born in Oakland and grew up in the San Francisco Bay Area. My visits to Pacific Gove began shortly after I moved to Salinas to teach. Soon, I was lunching at Aliotti's Victorian Corner, having tea at the café on top of Holman's Department Store (both alas gone) and dinner at Fandango. Back Porch Fabrics became my main source for quilting supplies. As a retiree, I visit for the leisurely lifestyle, the walks past some of the Peninsula's most beautiful gardens and the city's mission-style Carnegie Library where the friendly staff always manages to find just the right book.

Cold Irony
Donnolo Beren
Anonymous CCW Member

Sleight is for the sophist—reason for the wise—
Strictures for the pedant, dotting j's and i's.
"Good," said the skeptic, sitting in his hall,
"But irony – cold irony – is master of them all!"

So he flung sarcasms against received belief,
Mocked reputed miracles and ridiculed their Chief.
"Folly," said the sacerdote. "You'll learn at trump's last call
That irony – cold irony – is master of us all!"

Still the skeptic plied his doubts, scouted Heaven's hosts,
As "superstitious nonsense" dismissed eternal ghosts.
Doctrine is to faithful as slavery to thrall,
Its irony – cold irony – seeks mastery of all!

But illness laid the skeptic low, fortune played the bawd.
Kindred came to him and said, "Make your peace with God,
Else your doom is sure. Before you looms a fall,
For irony – cold irony – is master of men all!"

"Never!" said the skeptic. "I, traduce my creed?
Why should I abase myself, to kneel as though in need?
That were shameful treason. I'll stand and front the wall,
Lest irony – cold irony – prove master after all!"

Yet believers strove in turn, citing moral debt,
Named precédent cónverts, touted Pascal's bet .
"Nay!" said the skeptic, "mock not at my fall,
Till irony – cold irony – is master of men all!"

"Tears are for the craven, prayers are for the clown—
Halters for the supple neck that willingly bows down.
As my fate is grievous, so my fear is small,
For irony – cold irony – is master once for all!"

Like the beasts that perish, like a cresset's flame
Doused, he dimmed away, returned to whence he came:
Nothingness reclaimed him. Thus it will befall
That irony – cold irony – is master of men all.
The irony of ironies is mustering them all!

CAVEAT: This isn't about my, D.B., experiences (yet); it's about my beliefs, which are rather antithetical to Kipling's "Cold Iron."

Companions of the Heart
Illia Thompson

I turn off Highway One north, toward Pacific Grove. A welcoming feeling arrives. I recall the year our family of three lived in Pacific Grove. We had just returned from Kona, Hawaii, after finding out fishing provided more sport than sustenance, and the pull of the Monterey Peninsula became stronger than the lure of the sea. With naiveté, and a sense of adventure, we sold many of our belongings to travel west, only to find that we fared better on the mainland than on an island.

Pacific Grove offered us haven. A small house and a combination of jobs for my husband kept us afloat. We discovered the beauty of the coastline, the offerings of culture and recreation, until a full-time job took us back to Carmel Valley, the place we had called home before our Hawaiian departure.

Yet, Pacific Grove still called to us. My husband built the first hot tub that warmed the divers at the Monterey Bay Aquarium when it opened. He would come home with stories of the joys going "backstage" to view the beginning of this marvelous addition to the community.

Later, through my work at Monterey Peninsula College, I taught memoir writing at the Sally Griffin Senior Center and Canterbury Woods, as well as visiting local nursing homes to share stories. Almost weekly, I drive to Pacific Grove, gather with friends, and write.

Today, companions of the heart live in Pacific Grove, on streets with names that intrigue: Weldon, Shafter, Lighthouse, Willow, Junipero, Seaview, Crocker, and streets with numbers that add up to the charm of a small town, continually vital in its offerings.

Using the Printed Word to Bring People Together
Alana Myles

This article originally appeared in the Keepers of Our Culture column in the *Cedar Street Times*, September 4, 2015

Alana Myles, a member of the board of trustees of the Monterey Peninsula Unified School District. She is a retired elementary school teacher and the author of *The Way It Was*, available on Amazon. In this essay, Ms. Myles reminds us of the importance of preserving memories so that future generations may connect in a personal way with the struggles of the civil rights movement.

The sun filtered through the window, flooding the room with what should have been a soft, calming light, but I remained more than a little excited. I sat in Park Place Publications with owner Patricia Hamilton, discussing the printing and marketing of my middle grade book, *Monterey Bay Mystery and Mischief.*

Concluding our business, Patricia asked what inspired me to pen my children's mystery. I responded that I write for the children in my family and this mystery was written for my grandchildren, my niece and nephews. I want them to have "a fun read" and I want them to get psyched about this amazing place we call the Peninsula and all there is to do here.

Our discussion segued into a conversation about preserving family history, traditions, and cultures, and using the printed word to bring people together: breaking down racial barriers, correcting misconceptions, celebrating our differences and honoring and recognizing our sameness.

I mentioned I had published a memoir, *The Way It Was,* a brief autobiographical sketch, the retelling of my family experience on a trip to the East Coast, to Columbia, South Carolina. Patricia wanted to know more. I told her I had taught a third grade English as a Second Language class in Salinas and how, one February, the class was engaged in various activities in recognition of Black History Month. We watched a short video about young Martin Luther King, Jr. and another video about Rosa Parks, the African-American woman who refused to give up her seat on the public bus to a white man and consequently was arrested and jailed for her defiance.

Helping Her Students Connect with the Past

Despite the class discussions and activities, I was not satisfied and I struggled with the feeling that I had not succeeded in getting the students to connect in a personal way with the struggle for civil rights.

I wanted them to understand how racism demeans us all and keeps our country from becoming the great nation it could be. When sharing my frustration with my mother, it occurred to me that there was a way I might expand my students' understanding.

What would it be like to suddenly find oneself living under an openly repressive racist system? I had lived through such an experience as a child and it was that experience I would write about.

In the summer of 1957, my parents, Lawrence and Elizabeth Hagood, received word from "back home" that my mother's mother was critically ill. They immediately set about making arrangements to head cross country to Columbia, South Carolina. The Packard was loaded with all we would need to make the trip. It was as though we would be going on an extended camping trip. We had sleeping bags, cooking utensils, clothing for all types of weather, and some food items.

So off we went, Dad, Mom, four brothers ranging from ages two to eight, and me, the oldest, age nine. Shortly after we left the comfort of the more liberal West Coast, (racism on the Monterey Peninsula, then and now, is of a subtle, hidden nature) we encountered the type of discrimination most think only existed in the Deep South. But, in fact, it was in Barstow, California, that my family (we are African-American) was refused service at a restaurant and directed to go to a different part of town.

Reality in the Deep South

Days later, once we passed the Mason Dixon Line, I learned firsthand what I had only heard my parents and relatives talk about when they referred to the plight of "colored folk" living in the South. I saw the signs posted above doors and drinking fountains that read either "whites only" or "colored."

The family had to use side entrances to buildings or had to wait until all the white customers' needs had been met. I recall how disappointed my brothers and I were when we were turned away from a movie theater where a new John Wayne cowboy movie was playing. The theater did not have a "colored" section.

We slept in parks along the way where we could lay out our sleeping bags and set up a propane gas stove or cook our meals on an outdoor grill. It wasn't a matter of my father not having the money to stay in a hotel, but rather, we were not welcome or allowed to stay in nice travelodges. They were reserved for whites only.

On occasion, if we found a fair-size town, my father would stop and ask a black person where we could find decent, safe lodging for an evening. Most often we would be directed to a home that had been set up as a boarding house in the colored area.

Not all whites were demeaning, indifferent or unhelpful. Many were cordial and friendly. One white man went out of his way to assist my father in finding help when our car broke down.

And, yes, I do have many fond memories of that trip. Ones that speak to the hospitality of family members, the feeling of mutual respect, unity, and looking out for one's brethren. I remember bountiful meals featuring good, down-home cooking and evenings listening to family history, tall tales included. I remember falling in love with fried okra and Texas-style chili con carne. And I remember warm evenings sitting on a screened porch listening to the songs of insects and the wondrous display of the flashing lights of fireflies in the night sky.

Raising the Consciousness of Our Community

The writing of *The Way It Was* provided a means to educate others about a deplorable state of affairs that is an unfortunate part of our nation's history. It is meant to present a balanced picture of my personal experience. It is meant to inform, not to inflame. It is an effort to help raise the conscience of our community. And it is meant to help spur action for continued amicable advancement in our dealings with one another in the fight for civil rights and the elimination of racism in all its forms.

I see my involvement in education and community service as a way to help make a difference in bringing about a better world. I encourage others to find their personal connections and join in the movement for equality and social justice. We have come a long way in the struggle, but so much more work must be done before we all are truly free.

Short Hot Flashes
David Rasch, PhD.

My first, ultra-short, flash fiction story was an entry in a contest sponsored by the Central Coast branch of the California Writer's Club, which meets in Pacific Grove. That story, "Fruit Fly" (a tale of professional jealousy, and desperate revenge among scientists) was declared the winner and I discovered a new passion.

I decided soon thereafter to challenge myself to write one hundred and one stories of one hundred and one words within one year. I ended up writing a couple hundred stories and then selected my favorites to create a book, *Short Hot Flashes*, which includes illustrations by Jason Cirimele and was published in 2015 by Park Place Publications in Pacific Grove. It was challenging to generate so many story ideas in such a short time frame, and the unrelenting need for new material forced me to venture into the unexplored backwaters of my psyche. For better or worse, the inspirations I found were less than conventional in nature, as is evident in many of the stories. "The Process" is one of them.

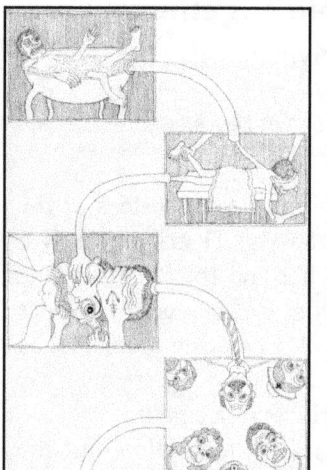

The Process. Because I still have issues, I stupidly agreed to do *The Process*™ again, forgetting what it was like. First, I had to get completely naked and float in a tub of hot water in total darkness. Then a team of sadistic masseuses began squeezing my body to the point of suffocation. After a miserable hour of that, I was tortured mercilessly with two more hours of excruciating cranial-sacral therapy. When they yanked me out of the water, I wailed with relief that The Process™ was finally over. The light was blinding and someone was shouting, "It's a boy, it's a boy!"

People jump off bridges for many reasons. I believe it was press reports about a man who parachuted off the Bixby Creek Bridge in 2011 that first got me wondering what it would be like to leap off that majestic span. It would probably be terrifying, and possibly glorious, if I picked a sunny day and my nylon wings successfully delivered me, condor-like, onto the pristine beach below. It might also be that I would be less lucky negotiating the perils that gravity poses. Perhaps each new life is another adventurous soul leaping into space, hoping the sea winds will greet and sustain them until their thrilling

descent concludes in the sand, and the ocean whispers its congratulations. Here's my story.

Bixby Creek Bridge. At the Bixby Creek Bridge, something with a ten-foot wingspan briefly eclipsed the sun and cast an eerie shadow on the mourners. The word "condor" was whispered, and one by one we squinted upward and tried to see the massive carrion-eater, but the sun was too bright. I found myself imagining that Martin had magnificent angel wings, and that when his feet left the rail he had soared like a majestic condor on the thermals rising out of the gorge. When the pastor finished praying, two enormous winged creatures were waiting on the bridge. Condors and angels both welcome the dead.

Riding Through Euthinium
Wanda Sue Parrott

Chapter 1

Reminiscing about Pacific Grove means recalling the Dwight D. Eisenhower decade through my pomegranate-loving poet's sweet-sour seeds of sentiment. If memory is accurate, my P.G. pilgrimage started as Sue Childress, 17, graduate of Monrovia-Arcadia-Duarte High School's class of 1952.

That summer, I suffered my first cracked-egg heart and nearly ruined my reputation-minded father's impeccable accountant's image. Why? My first love rode a Harley Davidson like a Hell's Angel. He was busted for marijuana and thrown in jail.

Ed was 19. Despite looking like Marlon Brando in *The Wild One*, Ed played sweet jazz piano, danced the jitterbug in pre-Elvis blue suede shoes, and never went beyond kissing my cheek.

The things that scared my parents were that Ed introduced me to sexy saxophone music, bump-and-grind dancing, and smoking. I sneaked Lucky Strikes from their packs.

After Ed's arrest, I discovered poet Ben Burroughs, who helped me survive the heart-wrenching grief. His poem appeared in the conservative *Los Angeles Herald-Express* and taught me that forgiveness is vital to survival.

Mistakes by Ben Burroughs
Most everybody makes mistakes, some big and others small,
And, therefore, we should not be hard on those who slip and fall.
Instead, we should extend our hand and help to rectify
Those oversights and undersights they may have let pass by.
Sometimes it's hard to overlook a blunder made in haste,
Especially if that error caused a lot of grief and waste.
So that is why I say "think twice," and show a kindly sign,
For to err is human, but forgiveness is divine.

I forgave my parents for their dislike of Ed, forgave Ed for using me to hide his secret life as a drug dealer, forgave myself for wanting to see Ed behind bars. I never heard from him again.

"Mistakes" helped me enter a state of healing grace I named Euthinium. It's the threshold between symbolic death and rebirth where we all land as we travel our personal evolutionary paths through Life. Euthinium is where we gain Wisdom of Experience by learning the pain of right-mindedness for ourselves.

Before graduation from high school, we seniors took aptitude tests that indicated our potential career paths. I scored highest as a future airplane mechanic. No way!

No one asked me my opinion. I started my freshman year at Citrus Junior College in September 1952, where my conservative, well-meaning father enrolled me in business classes. He hoped I'd become something "decent" like a file clerk. Mother hoped I'd meet Prince Charming.

My parents' visions tried to turn me into images of their own aspirations for success. They failed.

Counselors in the liberal arts junior college saw my potential and nominated me for student council, where I would have to learn to think and make decisions. We could smoke in class!

As electives, I chose parliamentary procedure, art and the weekly student newspaper, which published my gossip column doggerel.

In 1953 I discovered Asilomar while representing Citrus Junior College at a California Student Government Convention. Side tours included 17-Mile Drive, Cannery Row and Fisherman's Wharf.

I fell in love again. Not with a man. With Monterey. Or, as Marlon Brando said in *The Wild One*:

"Once upon a time, in the land of Ooh Papa Dow…"

I named it "Euthinium" and promised to come again.

Chapter 2

My return to Pacific Grove was delayed until 1962. After graduating from Citrus Junior College in 1954, I had moved to Hollywood and returned to college as a theater arts/creative writing student at the old UCLA-Los Angeles City College Evening Adult College on Vermont Avenue. To be an actress or a writer?

Writing chose me after my Humpty Dumpty Heartbreak, meaning second disastrous failure in love. At 23, I fell for my leading man and nearly died afterward.

My muse surprised me by pointing me north with this life-changing spiritual injection:

Travelers
Do you feel the sweet call of the long open road,
Do you sense the new life in your soul?
Do you hear the soft song the whole universe sings?
Do you feel your heart suddenly sprouting new wings?
What a glorious feeling—this farewell to home—
As you lift up your pack and you set out to roam.
The world is the playground of peasant and king,
Where each traveler goes at the coming of spring.

Retiring from Hollywood in March 1962, I hit the long open road as an aspiring writer. With John Steinbeck as my newly chosen literary role model, I worked my way north through places he immortalized.

In *The Grapes of Wrath* setting of Kern County, I was offered a police job as juvenile officer. I chose to carry a pen, not a gun, and became a budding poet in Big Sur at a pen pal's home.

Artist Emil White let me sleep in a lean-to at his house on Highway 1. He was domiciled with an attractive young hitchhiker half his age who smoked a clay pipe full of unknown substance.

"When you hitch rides, wear baggy unattractive clothes to make yourself look unattractive," she advised.

She was beautiful, like folk singer Joan Baez, who lived nearby. Joan had hip-length, raven-colored hair, wore jeans and boots, and drove around in an open Jeep with a big black dog.

Emil was a liberal who served carrots from his garden and sold postcards of his paintings to tourists. He used wood from orange crates to build his place.

Steinbeck wasn't mentioned, but Emil regaled us with stories of his friendship with former Big Sur author Henry Miller, whose literary sex sizzlers held international notoriety. I slept on a cot under a Milleresque picture of a nude man over whose private parts a fig leaf was tacked. With a slight finger flick, the leaf unveiled a man imitating the statue of David.

"Henry married mail order brides," Emil said. "They rode the train from San Francisco. I ended up with his women. They left him because he couldn't satisfy them."

"What was wrong?" I asked.

"He made love like a rabbit."

My Education in Euthinium continued after I left Emil's place in September 1962 and arrived in Pacific Grove during the Monterey Jazz Festival. There were no available rooms in P.G., so I rented a fisherman's shack on Van Buren Street in Monterey and became the opposite of what my parents hoped I'd be: the first "Untouchable" hired by Dick O'Kane for his new Cannery Row speakeasy, Al Capone's Warehouse.

As a "hostess" I wore a tight, red, off-the-shoulder fringed dress and spike heels. I served pizza and beer to soldiers from Fort Ord, officers from Naval Postgraduate School and students from the Defense Language Institute. I also played with the honky-tonk band, shimmying to the rattle of my tambourine and playing "Oh Susanna" on a harmonica in the key of C.

My mouth harp attracted attention from a gentleman who played "John Brown's Body Lies A-Mold'ring in the Grave" on his harmonica. Like me, he claimed to be an aspiring writer. We became inseparable and my poetry took a less-structured turn as it flowed into free-loving verse:

New Euthinium
Oh, to feel your flesh,
A cluster of wild grapes,
A taste of summer honey …

We sailed to the three-mile limit aboard the 70-foot staysail schooner *Tamarit* and exchanged wedding vows. The former Sue Childress became Wanda Sue Parrott who, in 1965, was named runner up Poet Laureate of the Monterey Peninsula in a contest sponsored by the *Monterey Peninsula Herald*.

To Youth (excerpt)
Sweet youth, take heed
Or else your golden flower
Will turn to seed,
And in its wake an empty hollow pod
Will shrivel and await the call of God.

That same year, my husband, young son and I left the peninsula. In 1972 my heart broke a third time when our perfect marriage ended in divorce. I went on to co-found the National Annual Senior Poets Laureate Poetry Competition for American poets age 50 and older, a role I played for 21 years.

Writing, smoking and food were substitutes for love.

Chapter 3

I didn't return to New Euthinium until 2009, when I joined the Central Coast branch of the California Writers Club. One weekend in 2012, a writer friend and I toured the Henry Miller Library in Big Sur. I exclaimed, "Sue Childress slept here fifty years ago!"

As an octogenarian in Euthinium, I now perform as a dancer with the Tap Bananas troupe sponsored by the Monterey Recreation Department, and am actively involved in social-justice issues through the Unitarian Universalist Church of the Monterey Peninsula.

I've still never actually lived in Pacific Grove, but am getting closer. My weekly column "Homeless in Paradise" has been running in the *Cedar Street Times*, P.G.'s hometown newspaper, since 2014.

As to smoking: I exchanged cigarettes for little cherry-tipped cigars in 1999 and finally kicked tobacco by going cold turkey on New Year's Day 2009. Is it coincidental that my first love appeared in a dream after I took my final puff? He had exchanged his black-leather jacket for a tuxedo and bow tie.

In November 2016, Californians voted to approve recreational marijuana. Think I'll hitch my first ride on a motorcycle, wheel through Asilomar, have a final smoke, and tell Ed goodbye.

A Doughnut Caper
Jonathan Shoemaker

You won't believe this story! This guy comes out of a local grocery store eating a doughnut and I ask him if he wants to buy some candy for the football team.

He says, "I'll give you a dollar."

Steve, the quarterback, says, "It's a five dollar donation and you get to pick anything you want." We had a lot of stuff for people to choose from.

He says, "I don't want the candy. I'm just making a donation to the P.G. football team." So, he sticks the doughnut in his mouth, takes out a dollar and gives it to Steve.

Steve says, "Hey, didn't you used to coach the Junior Varsity team? I think you were my brother's coach."

The guy says, "Yes, but I can't stay to talk. I'm in a hurry."

So, right then this kid comes out of the store and says, "Hey mister, you have to pay for that doughnut!"

The guy says, "Yes, I will—tomorrow, when I do my shopping. Right now I'm in a big hurry to get dinner home."

The kid says, "No you won't." He's wearing an apron and name tag and all. "You're not in a hurry. You're just standing talking to them. And you're stealing a doughnut!"

"No, I'm not!" he says. "I just told you I'll pay for it tomorrow." And he takes another bite.

The kid watches him bite the doughnut. Then he looks like he's getting mad and he gets in the guy's face. He says, "You're coming inside. We called the cops and you're gonna pay, or else." And he pushes the guy's shoulder.

Now, I think that Coach could have handled the kid, but he doesn't get mad. He laughs. Yeah, he laughs. He says, "Don't touch me, young man!" And the kid gets even madder. He's got fire in his eyes.

And then another clerk comes out of the store and says, "What's going on here?"

They're both talking at the same time, and the kid is saying, "He stole a doughnut!" And Coach is saying, "Henry, get this boy away from me. He's out of control." And he takes another bite. The kid is like shaking and staring at the doughnut.

Henry tells the guy not to leave. He takes the kid into the store and they stand in front of the doughnut counter, talking.

So, Coach goes in and pays at the self-serve checkout. Then he stands there and waits for Henry.

While he's standing there—hey, you know I *had* to go in and see what was going down—a little girl walks up to him and says, "Hey mister, can you lend me sixteen cents? I don't have enough."

Well, he reaches into his pocket. He's shaking his head while he looks at his coins. He says, "No, I don't lend money to people I don't know. Here, I've got a quarter I can give you." And he turns to Henry who's coming over. Henry is looking back and forth between me and Coach. I guess he thinks we're friends. I just *had* to hear this!

He tells Henry that he was gonna pay for the doughnut when he checked out, but they were out of pork ribs, so he'd pay it tomorrow when he did his Saturday shopping.

He says, "You know I always pay for what I eat, Henry." And he walks out.

While he's on his way out, two policemen come in and head straight for Henry. I couldn't stand it. I had to hear what would happen next. They talked real quiet and I moved closer. Then one cop said, loud enough to hear it all over the store, "You called us in over a 69-cent doughnut?"

Steve told me that he gave Coach a high five when he left the store and asked if he was gonna press charges for assault. Coach just said, "Nah. Do you know where I can get barbecued ribs this time of day? The barbecue guy across from Trader Joe's is closed and this place sure doesn't have any."

Motherly Instincts
Marlene Martin
retired teacher, mother

It was 1971. I was a young teacher at Pacific Grove High School. And I was pregnant. I have often been told that in that era there were prohibitions on teaching in that condition. In Pacific Grove, no one seemed to notice my incipient motherhood. I had been married for a couple years to a young Hopkins Marine Station prof, and we wanted to have a family—in a year or so. But way had led onto way, and there I was in the office of P.G. High Principal Rex Dunipace in June. "The baby is due January 10," I told him.

"That's fine," he said.

He had escaped the trauma of forcing one of my very reluctant English teacher colleagues to move to social science because I had volunteered for the move, so the social science teaching worry was a problem of his past. Pregnancies did not make his worry list. My English department colleague had been adamant about not teaching in a department populated by retired military men. In Vietnam, a controversial war raged.

When I showed up to teach in September the military guys had a big bouquet on my desk along with a welcome sign. They were solicitous and they were all dads—should I need any help with speedy delivery issues perhaps they could help. Their welcome did not waver all that semester while I grew rounder and rounder. Also not wavering was Mr. Dunipace's lack of concern about his pregnant teacher. I showed up in his office every couple of weeks to plead to have a replacement identified. His only reaction was to nod.

I finished my Childbirth Education class with another Pacific Grove teacher—Sandra Jordan. Sandy taught me to relax about the challenge of childbirth, but together we felt anxiety about delivering a baby at Pacific Grove High. I needed to find a replacement. I looked around and found an eager candidate in a middle school substitute. Mr. Dunipace was still unmoved.

During Christmas break, my doctor, Alf Rydel, announced that the January 10 was no longer the target. "Much sooner," he said. He did not think I would be able to return to Pacific Grove High after the holidays.

Then came a dinner party. Among the eight guests was our long-time Congressman, Burt Talcott. He stayed by my side all evening talking politics and assuring me that teachers were all too liberal to invite him to class. Each week during the semester, I had invited a guest speaker— everyone from the John Birch Society to the Sierra Club. I invited our Congressman to speak. I would keep that baby inside for a couple more weeks. I created a plan. Dr. Rydel expressed doubt.

January 3: Mr. Dunipace helped me set up an assembly for the junior and senior classes.

January 4: I prepared my students.

January 5: The Congressman spoke.

January 6: I led the class in a debriefing discussion.

Pacific Grove High students have a reputation for politeness today. In January 1972, they were Polite. With his shock of red hair and his Eagle Scout manners, Student Body President Rusty Cureton looked like the model for a Norman Rockwell painting of a small town American young gentleman. At the end of the Congressman's talk, Rusty asked a courteous question about the war. Apparently offended, the Congressman grabbed Rusty by the shirt. Although it would be almost 48 more hours before I would become a mother, my maternal instincts were in place. I interrupted and thanked the Congressman. Everyone escaped physically unscathed and better informed.

January 8: Ian Cameron Martin, nearly eight pounds, arrived at Community Hospital.

The next fall, I began my 41-year teaching career at Monterey Peninsula College. Pacific Grove came with me. This time, P.G. High colleague Ellen Coulter was in place to teach my classes for my weeks of maternity leave, and Morrie Fisher was a student during the semester when my next son was born.

Vanessa Smith
Remembering a CCW Friend Who Left Far Too Soon
"Keepers of Our Culture," Cedar Street Times Dec. 2015

Few events are as profound as the sudden, unexpected loss of a friend or family member, a stern reminder of the fragility and impermanence of life. We often hear the instructions to "get your affairs in order" when someone is confronted with a terminal illness or the end-of-life issues surrounding advanced aging. But the fact is, life is a terminal illness, and our last act is always but a heartbeat away. Thus the importance of putting our thoughts in writing, not just directions on how we want our estate divided, or the music to be played at our memorial service, but also a written record of our life and times, the events we've experienced, the people we've encountered, the lessons we've learned. In short, a legacy for our children and grandchildren, and their children and grandchildren, as well as for historians of the future.

Those of us in the local literary community have had to face this sad reality with the passing last week of Dr. Vanessa Smith, a Pacific Grove resident and past president of Central Coast Writers. As writers, we naturally turned to pen and paper to share our memories and to begin healing our sorrow.

Helping a Fellow Writer Get the Details Right

I met Vanessa the Saturday morning I attended my first Central Coast Writers Executive Committee meeting, held at her parents' home on Ocean View Boulevard in October, 2012. From her comments and questions that day, my initial impression was that she was a very smart person. Boy, did I under-calculate her intelligence!

I gradually got to know Vanessa better through general meetings and work on Scribbles, the club newsletter. Eventually, I asked her for help with some scenes from my novel that will come out in February, 2016. I wanted a character to be shot at close range with a pistol. She would survive, but lose most of the hearing in her right ear.

Vanessa spent over an hour working me through the shooting scene, the hospital sequence, the damage and treatments, permanent damages, etc. I tapped away at my laptop as she slowly dictated what she would say to the patient and to her husband and family members. In the following days, I'd email Vanessa scenes and she'd write back with corrections, clarifications, etc., until we had it all just right.

Once I worked out exactly how things would happen, what the doctor would say and how the story would progress, the scenes really came to life. I think they're some of the best in the novel. I only wish I'd been able to give Vanessa a copy of the final book so she could see my thanks to her in the acknowledgements.

—Leslie Patiño

Sharing a Love of Literary Crime Fiction

Books, always books—that is how I will remember Vanessa. She and I shared a love of literary crime novels, detective stories and who-dun-its that made you think and touched your heart in a profound way, the kind of books that the critics like to say "transcend the genre." We both admired—and probably secretly lusted after—Michael Connolly's fictional LAPD detective Harry Bosch. We were both reading Dennis Lehane's Live by Night at the same time and had to be very careful not to drop any spoilers to each other.

One special memory I have of Vanessa relates to the Central Coast Writers annual member potluck in December 2013, the year she was president of the club. We are always very careful to promote these parties as generic "holiday" events, but despite our best intentions at multi-cultural inclusion, they usually end up being pretty darn Christmassy—everyone in their Christmas sweaters, a Christmas tree in the picture window at our host's home, loads of Christmas cookies. And then through the door sails Vanessa, wearing a headdress worthy of Carmen Miranda, featuring a dreidel, a menorah, and a Star of David. She made a statement that was both fun and in-your-face ... which pretty much was the very essence of Vanessa.

L'chaim, Vanessa, with hopes that wherever you are, they have plenty of good books.

—Joyce Krieg

A Beautiful Soul Who Spiritualized Surgery

I first met Vanessa on a Sunday afternoon at Bookworks in Pacific Grove, where a small group of us came together to try out Harold E. Grice's idea for a memoir-writing critique circle. People who wanted to create personal works in the form of poetry, anecdotes, collections of letters and other family or personal history met only a few times.

It must have been around four years ago, because Harold was trying out the idea of publishing his now-series of California Country Boy (Park Place Publications) books about growing up in rural California during the 1930s.

A woman sea captain read about her life at sea. A retired music teacher read her attempt at poetry about life in Big Sur. An author from Iceland read letters from home during her first months in the United States.

And then there was Vanessa!

This medical doctor, who read her spellbinding short piece about life-and-death surgery on a suffocating child, took me on a listener's journey through the microscope of a surgeon as soulful as a guardian angel.

The dexterity of the surgeon's hand combined with the scalpel-sharp decision-making that saved the patient's life made me breathe more than a sigh of relief when the patient lived following tracheotomy.

I breathed gratitude for such a caring and beautiful

soul who spiritualized surgery as if she were divinity incarnate, one to whom each second counted as a life or death sentence for the patient, whose throat was occluded. Turn left or right? How best should the surgeon work her way through the mass that was cutting off the airway?

I nearly suffocated from holding my own breath as Vanessa read her brilliantly crafted memoir.

Later, when I learned that Vanessa Smith was no longer practicing medicine because she had a "problem," I chose to remember her as the bright and brilliant spirit she truly was, one who, after joining Central Coast Writers, saved its life by serving as a bridge over which members walked when we were temporarily without a president. I never saw her as less than perfect and still see her that way.

Beautiful, Vanessa. Your light now shines among the literary angels whose perfection far outshines human frailty. Thank you for lighting my path.

—*Love, Wanda Sue Parrott*

As "Keepers of Our Culture," we remind our readers that the time is now, whether it's putting your own story in writing, or in letting the special people in our lives know how much they mean to us. Patricia Hamilton is using the loss of her friend Vanessa Smith as impetus to prepare end-of-life instructions and to commission her own eulogy, which will appear in a future issue of Cedar Street Times. *Check out our website/blog, keepersofourculture.com, for more stories, including those from past* Cedar Street Times *columns. For assistance with writing your life story or a tribute to a loved one, or in creating a book out of your writings, contact Patricia at 831/649-6640, publishingbiz@sbcglobal.net, parkplacepublications.com*

A memorial service for Dr. Vanessa Smith is planned for this Saturday, December 12, in Pacific Grove. For details, contact Patricia Hamilton at publishingbiz@sbcglobal.net.

King Tide
Dorothy Vriend

The tide is out
sea anemones soft flesh pulsing
in rock-hewn pools
hundreds of small tentacles
reaching out

I tread carefully
toward the expanse of the sea
amongst unfamiliar life forms
I can almost touch what it is I long for

The tide is in
water dragons curl and churl
spraying sand and water
in a sun drenched dance

I meet the water's fury head-on
sea breath on my skin

ESL AT P.G. ADULT EDUCATION – JANET THAYER, program specialist

English as a Second Language Program

In creating this book, Patricia Hamilton produces "a tapestry woven of the many threads that make up our community." We at Pacific Grove Adult Education (PGAE) are delighted that one of the threads in Patricia's own life led her to our school. PGAE in itself represents a tapestry woven of adults of all ages engaging in lifelong learning in so many areas: fitness, dance, drawing and painting, photography, foreign languages, computer skills, parent education, high school diploma and equivalency, English literature and writing, English as a second language (ESL) and United States citizenship.

Having visited some of our ESL classes, Patricia wanted to devote a section of this book to our amazing students, and with good reason. They come from a vast array of cultures, representing 43 countries this year alone, and are also members of our Pacific Grove community. They inspire us teachers daily with their courage, compassion and determination to understand our language and our culture so that they can participate actively in the life of Pacific Grove and the United States.

Pacific Grove hosts a mini-United Nations here. Students from Iraq and Iran dance together at a potluck lunch. A Bulgarian helps a Korean learn to use the verb "to be." A Paraguayan helps a young Oaxacan feel welcome and more comfortable joining the class. A Thai from the advanced class walks down the hall to the beginning class to meet and greet Salvadorans, Brazilians and an Uzbeki. Grandmothers from China, Afghanistan and Ukraine share photos of their grandchildren with smiles and laughter that transcend differences. People who were homemakers, architects, truck drivers, economists, farmers, engineers, shop owners, day laborers and university students in their native countries gather together to join in the great task of learning American English, culture and skills for success in our society. While doing so, they become friends of our dedicated faculty and staff here at PGAE. The mutual regard, and yes, even love is palpable. And you can be sure that when these students communicate with their families and friends back in their native countries, they are telling them about the interesting and caring people they have met here in Pacific Grove, and the friends they have made, to their own surprise, with people from "unfriendly" countries. Pacific Grove's ESL program is an incubator of world peace!

I myself was unaware of these wonderful members of our community until five years ago, when I began to teach ESL here. Please allow me to introduce some of these ambitious and admirable adults, and then you can read some delightful pieces written by students in our higher-level ESL classes.

I would love for you to know the story behind each student, where they have come from and why they are here with us. Some eventually reveal a bit of this information, but most of them come from cultures in which "putting oneself forward" and revealing the details of their private lives is not considered polite or respectful of one's family. Also, some students are not yet fluent enough in English to write for this book. Therefore, I offer a few thumbnail sketches of some of our students.

❧ **An Afghani woman** speaks her native Pashto but never learned to read and write it. In fact, she never attended school in Afghanistan. Now, she is learning to speak, read and write English. She has even learned the computer skills to use our online program, Burlington English. She is humble when praised but clearly pleased with her accomplishments and her increasing ability to function in American society. Her school-age children also appear pleased that their mother is stepping into their multicultural world in P.G..

❧ **A pharmacist from Nepal** is excited to participate in a pharmacy role-play as he offers the correct medicine to a customer who has come in with a cough and cold.

❧ **A woman from Mexico**, who has worked here as a housekeeper for years, attends our ESL evening class. I have helped her register at Monterey Peninsula College and enroll in a career-training program that will help her fulfill her dream of becoming a pastry chef. She promises to bring some of her creations for us to sample as she continues in our ESL class, giving us more than one reason to be happy for her success in following her career pathway!

❧ **A young man and his sister have made the trek from Central America,** bringing with them his young daughter. They worry about the violence back home that threatens their family members daily and are grateful to live here in peace. They both attend ESL classes when they can. Like many immigrants, he is holding down two jobs. He is happy that his daughter will begin preschool in the fall and that he knows enough English now to help her learn it.

❧ **Two young women, a Christian from Egypt and a Muslim from Jordan,** practice an English dialogue together and then laugh after exchanging a few comments in Arabic.

❧ **A team of students from Syria, Mexico, Thailand, Brazil, and Russia** create a business, a job description, résumés and interview questions. They conduct mock job interviews, playing HR director, department head and candidates. After much discussion, they select a candidate, who gladly accepts the job!

❧ **A university student in mathematics from El Salvador** came to us after his freshman year with no English at all. He progressed rapidly in our program and in his work as well, moving from dishwasher to cook. With his two jobs, he pays his living expenses and also helps his sister back home attend university. We hope that someday he can further his own education here and contribute to our country with the skills we know he is capable of achieving.

❧ **Iranian women** come to stay for months with an adult child in the United States and then return to Iran. Some of them seem to be on the "six months plan," alternating countries and cultures regularly. They are joyful women who laugh freely, and often at themselves. What flexibility to step in and out of our culture. They are members of our extensive team of ambassadors!

❧ **A server at a local restaurant** is coached after class by his teacher, who helps him with his pronunciation and with phrases used by servers. He wants to be given more hours of work in order to better support his family.

❧ **A number of women** walk from their apartments to Forest Grove Elementary School to drop off their children. Then they walk the distance to our school and at noon walk "up the mountain" home to eat lunch and do chores. Then they walk back to Forest Grove to pick up their children and walk home again. Some also attend our Parent Education ESL class (ELAC) at Forest Grove two afternoons a week. There they learn both English and academic skills in order to help their children with reading and other homework. Also, they can be better parents in America when they understand our school system and culture. Children see that mom and dad are still relevant, even though some may speak, dress, and eat differently than the parents of the children's schoolmates.

❧ **Two artists, men from Paraguay and Cuba,** run a joint studio and gallery in Pacific Grove. They are also building websites to showcase and sell their art online. Their growing English skills are helping them grow their businesses.

❧ **A Pakistani woman** walks all the way from New Monterey, escorted by her husband, to our school. She learned some British English in Pakistan and giggles at our American pronunciation.

❧ **A student from Iraq and one from Syria** have become United States citizens! We are glad once again to offer a class in United States Citizenship Preparation.

And now, here are some impressions of life in Pacific Grove, written in the words of another PGAE teacher and of our students themselves....

THE MOST WONDERFUL STUDENTS — BARBARA KRAUS, teacher

I'm a really lucky person. I have good health and good friends. I suppose I have to add that I also have good genes! But all of those assets stand in the shadow of the main reason that I am lucky and healthy at my advanced age. I HAVE THE MOST WONDERFUL STUDENTS IN THE WORLD!

Every day I learn from my ESL students at Pacific Grove Adult Education. Every day they teach me about acceptance and good humor and patience and respect and love. They even teach me about the English language: words I never learned, grammar I never studied, and idioms that I had forgotten.

Do you know that our students come from all over the world and speak many languages, some that I had never heard of before? And this diverse group of individuals quickly finds itself joining and blending into a whole, helping each other, listening to each other, speaking for each other, studying with each other, producing projects with each other, and looking out for each other. All of this is accomplished in ENGLISH! It couldn't be any other way. How else could a Korean, a Thai, a Japanese, a Mexican, an Iranian, and a Turk work together? English is the answer.

When my students ask me what I am, I answer that I am an American. I was born in Salinas and have always lived in California. I am fourth or fifth generation American, but that is not what they want to know.

They want to know who my ancestors were and why they came to this country. They want to know if my family is the same as theirs in that we all are immigrants. The fact that they understand this shows me that they already know what has made our country so unusual, so unique in the world. Yes, we are all the same.

Many of our students attend our school in order to improve their chances of getting a better job or to prepare themselves for Monterey Peninsula College or California State University at Monterey Bay. Others want to learn more in order to help their children with their schoolwork. They are serious about these goals and pursue them even while working at jobs and taking care of young children. Some have cars, others ride the bus and there are a few who ride bicycles from as far away as Monterey. You have to be determined about your goals in life to attend school in the morning and then work all afternoon and evening at your job. You have to be determined to walk for an hour to get to school. You have to be determined to drive from Toro Park to Pacific Grove every morning in the traffic to be a student in our school. These are the people who are our students.

We also have students who are here in Pacific Grove for short visits and want to use the little time they have with us to improve their English. They are welcomed in our classes and become a part of the group quickly. I believe that when they return to their countries they become ambassadors from the United States. Their experiences in our ESL classes help increase the positive relationships between our countries. So, in a small way Pacific Grove Adult Education is bringing the people of the world closer together. At least, that's my belief.

Yes, I'm lucky, I have good friends, I'm healthy and I have good genes. But, the most important part of my good fortune is the fact that I have the most wonderful students in the world.

Happy Life
Maha from Syria

Many things in Pacific Grove give me a happy life. Ever since I came to Pacific Grove I have walked on the beach enjoying myself. After that I walk to Lighthouse Avenue to have lunch because there are a lot of restaurants and coffee shops. I know more than 15 of them. I think none of them are cheap and good at the same time. Also, I wish to enjoy one close to the beach but Pacific Grove doesn't have any. The best thing that makes me happy in Pacific Grove is my school and my friends. I live in Carmel. I've been here for six years. I came here as a visitor but I'll stay here because my country has a war. I have my American citizenship now!!

Natural Pacific Grove
Priscilla from Korea

The first time I came to Pacific Grove was two years ago. I came because I had a class for my son in Parents' Place. I liked to come to the class and to see lots of natural beauty like the smell of the trees, fresh air, flowers, and butterflies. Also, some of the animals do not run away from people. The people who live in this town care about animals, too. When I come to Pacific Grove I always feel relaxed in the natural environment.

For a few years now I have come to Pacific Grove every day for school. I still feel the same as before. I meet lots of people who live in Pacific Grove. They all say they like to live here because it is very quiet and people are very friendly and nice. They like to walk with their dogs and exercise. It has a lot of parks where kids can play.

This town is close to the ocean and mountains where my family can do a lot of activities.

I moved here nine years ago. I live in Toro Park. I came to the United States to study more about my major but now I'm married and am a housewife.

So Many Good Things
Yeni from Mexico

I think the school in Pacific Grove offers good education. It has good teachers and they help our kids, especially when the kids came from other countries and don't speak English. They can help the parents, too. They use high technology in school. The teachers always are teaching them about responsibility. The kids learn the good use of technology. The school has different activities; sometimes the kids go out of the school; they go to the aquarium, museum, farm, and other places. The education is excellent and also free.

I have been living in Pacific Grove for nine years. I came here because my husband is working here. I love Pacific Grove.

Teachers are Very Kind
Maryam from Iran

ESL English helps me to communicate with other people. Working with the Burlington English Program helps me to get better in speaking and spelling. I also like the environment at school. I have met many people from other countries. Our teachers are very kind and care about students.

I live in Monterey on David Avenue, but my house is close to Pacific Grove and every day I can take the bus to school. After all, I am very happy that I have this opportunity to come to adult education in Pacific Grove.

I have been in America for 13 years. I came to the United States because of my children, but now I feel like I want to live here more years or forever. The reason I like to live here is that I am close to my children and maybe because it is the 13 years that I have lived here. I am getting used to everything. Especially learning English helps me to live here better. Next week I will go to my country for one month. I hope when I come back I will have no problem and I will live in the United States again.

Education for Our Minds and Bodies
Chie from Japan

There is good education in Pacific Grove. My son studies at Pacific Grove Middle School, which is where we wanted him to go. He goes to the ELD class that is for students who need to learn English. Teachers give students assignments every day, which vary: online, worksheets, or watching movies. Parents can check the scores and see if they finish their assignments every day in every class. He has a Physical Education class every day that is good for his health. That's why I think education in Pacific Grove is good.

I live in Pacific Grove. My husband works in Carmel and we wanted our son to learn in a good school, so we decided to live here. I've been here for seven months.

Raccoons
Kyung from Korea

When I moved to Pacific Grove my neighbor told me, "Raccoons are very dangerous. You need to be careful about them." She said that they are very dirty because they live underground so they have a lot of germs. When they bite people, people will get sick. So when I saw raccoons, I ran away to another place. That's why I am afraid of raccoons.

I have been in Pacific Grove for five years. I live here because my husband works here and my son studies here.

Victorian Houses
Megumi from Japan

When I came to Pacific Grove for the first time, I was surprised at the Victorian houses. They caught my eyes. I thought how cute and colorful they are. When I was a kid, I used to read a lot of fairy tales. These Victorian houses reminded me of fairy tales like Cinderella, Snow White, and Sleeping Beauty. I felt I was in the fairy tales. I'm from Japan and there are no Victorians there. When I was a kid, I used to want to go abroad and live in a cute house like the Victorian houses in Pacific Grove because princesses in the fairy tales live in beautiful palaces like Victorian houses. Many years later, my dream came true! I live in Monterey, but my condo is not Victorian. I got my next dream. It was to enter these cute houses. It didn't take a long time to come true. My relatives came to visit us last November. They borrowed a vacation house, and it was a Victorian house in Pacific Grove. I was excited to visit them, although they came to visit us. Then that time came! There was my dreamy house in front of me. It was literally the Victorian house, which means it was colorful, beautiful, cute, and like a palace of fairy tales. I can't forget that moment when I opened the door. It was the same as the excitement I felt when I saw snow for the first time. My excitement didn't last after I opened the door. I don't know what I was imagining and expecting. But something was over in my heart. The inside of the house was very normal. The house's exterior was Victorian, but inside was modern. But I'm sure I felt like I was a princess before opening the door. I come to Pacific Grove to study English on weekdays. Whenever I see the Victorian houses, I remember that exciting moment.

Megumi is not a princess name and we don't have a princess culture in Japan. But Victorian houses in Pacific Grove make me a princess. I've lived in Monterey for one year and a half. The reason to be here is that my husband goes to graduate school. I'm very happy to get a chance to live here.

Beaches
Lin from Thailand

The beaches in Pacific Grove are amazing. One of the beaches in Pacific Grove is Asilomar. I usually walk to the beach to see the sunrise and the sunset that show the different colors. There are many sandpipers, bull kelps, rocks, colorful flowers, California gulls, and dead fish. Many people take their dogs to run on the beach. Many activities are going on at the beach, such as walking and jogging. Some people do diving and surfing that sound like fun even in the cold water. Sometimes the big waves come from Hawaii and hit the shore like a storm, but that cannot stop people from going where they can get the beautiful view and fresh air. Would you like to go there?

I live on Congress Avenue in Pacific Grove. I came to visit my friend who lives in Pacific Grove I came here on December 3, 2016. I will go back to Thailand on April 2, 2017. Just thinking of the day I'm going back upsets me.

People in Pacific Grove
Emiko from Japan

There are so many wonderful people in Pacific Grove. When I walk on the street in Pacific Grove, people smile at me even though I don't know them, and they make me happy. My English is not good yet, but many people listen to me carefully at the store, at school, and anywhere. So, I'm relieved to live here with my English. Also, I think people in Pacific Grove love singing and dancing because I can see them sometimes. It's wonderful that they enjoy being happy by themselves. When I moved here from Huntington Beach, I thought they were so friendly and kind. I have been here for eight years and I haven't changed this thought at all. I love the people in Pacific Grove so much.

I live in Monterey and go to school and work in Pacific Grove. I've been here for eight years. My husband and I moved here because he went to Middlebury Institute of International Studies at Monterey.

Deserted Town
Lisa from Belgium

When I walk in Pacific Grove I feel alone. I never see anybody on the street and it makes me sad because I love to meet people and see people. Moreover, I would like to do something in Pacific Grove but

I never know what to do except go to the beach. There are not pretty boutiques like in Carmel and also in Pacific Grove the ambience is not good for me. I'm not feeling at home here. In Carmel I'm feeling at home. I have to say that I'm 19 years old, so I guess that my feeling is surely not the same for an adult person. Actually, I'm living in Carmel Valley and I go to school in Pacific Grove I have been here for two months. I'm in California for my *au pair* adventure.

Family Life in P.G.
Eleuteria from Mexico

Pacific Grove is a nice place to live with family. I have lived here for nine years with my family. It is a great city and my kids love to live here. Pacific Grove has a good school for our kids for their education. What I like the most in Pacific Grove are the nice people. Also, Pacific Grove has an adult school for us. Pacific Grove celebrates Good Old Days every April and it has the Monarch Sanctuary for butterflies. I think life here is great for my family.

I came here from Mexico with my mom to get a better life. Here I got together with my husband and I had my two girls.

The Best Town
Rosa from Venezuela

Pacific Grove is the best town to live in. It's a small town on the coastline of California with beautiful surroundings of nature and sea life. The weather is perfect for everyone; it's neither cold nor warm. In winter the lowest temperature is 39 degrees and in summer the highest is 75 degrees. People in Pacific Grove are so friendly that it makes one feel at home. It's a safe and quiet place to live. For a family with children, it's a town that I highly recommend. Education in Pacific Grove is of the highest quality. Pacific Grove is a sanctuary for butterflies. You can watch them in October when they migrate from the north. It's something that's wonderful to watch. Come and visit Pacific Grove and I'm sure you'll fall in love with this town.

I live in Pacific Grove with my cousin and her family. I come to the adult school every day where I enjoy mornings taking class and talking with my classmates.

Two Days in P.G.
Veronica from Brazil

I have been in Pacific Grove for two days, so I don't know much about it. I heard about Pacific Grove when I was looking for a school, so I came here to study. I have never been in Pacific Grove downtown but while I was driving to school, I saw the city has a beautiful view of the ocean. It's possible to see the ocean from many places. I realized that in Pacific Grove you can have contact with nature. There are trees and places where it's possible to sit down and feel the nature environment. Pacific Grove also has large avenues and very organized traffic. In Pacific Grove I found a good school to study and to improve my English, and in this school there are friendly people. I was well received in Pacific Grove.

I have been here for two months. I have been living in Carmel-by-the-Sea for two months, working as an *au pair*. I'm here in the United States to learn more about the culture and improve my English. I'm in Pacific Grove because I found a good school to study, meet people, and improve my English.

Two Lives
Juliet from Korea

I've lived two lives. My second life started in Pacific Grove. My husband and I married at the Defense Language Institute church. Then we lived in a cozy nest in a Pacific Grove apartment. My first life was with my parents in Korea. My second life was with my husband and daughter. We lived on the third floor in the apartment. It had a very good view. I miss it. Then we moved to a different city. Part of my second life was

coming to the adult school in Pacific Grove and my English is getting better now. Fortunately, Pacific Grove Adult School is a great helper. Thank you to all teachers.

Now I live in Pebble Beach because we needed more bedrooms and space for our daughter in a house. My husband worked at D.L.I. for 30 years, so our family lives here.

Mature and Wiser
Beritha from Sweden

Moving to Pacific Grove made me realize that it was the first step into adulthood. Leaving my family in Sweden to come to America was a bit hard. That was the very first step into adulthood for me. Saying goodbye to my mother and sister was when I realized that I am on my own and need to look out for myself. Being alone the first three months in Pacific Grove gave me the chance and time to think about what type of person I want to be or become. The purpose of my trip was to go out in the world and see what the world has to offer but also to grow on my own as a better person. When I first came to Pacific Grove I thought that it was a boring, calm place where nothing really happened, but it grew on me. Not everything can be all crazy or energetic; it is also good with a calm atmosphere. As a conclusion, Pacific Grove is the best place to come to if you want to calm yourself down and grow mature or just simply find yourself because of the beautiful nature.

I'm 19 years old. I came to Pacific Grove as an *au pair* to travel and grow as a person and to try to become more mature and wiser than before I left Sweden.

I Enjoy My Life Here
Musaab Kamil from Iraq

I came from Iraq to the United States of America in 2008. My father was killed in Iraq in 2006. My brother and his family and I went to Jordan for one year. We came to the United States of America in 2008. I am so happy that my mother is now also here with us in the United States of America.

I love Pacific Grove. I moved to Pacific Grove City three years ago from Monterey. In 2011 I went to Pacific Grove Adult School to learn English language. I got my citizenship on March 20, 2015. I always walk on the beach in Pacific Grove. I see the ocean, museum, stores, and the Lighthouse Cinema. Every year I go with my sister and brother to the Pacific Grove Good Old Days festival. Some people are buying food, juice, and jewelry, and listening to the music and singing songs. The kids are riding the Ferris wheel. I like to take pictures when I walk to the beach and the park. Sometimes I study in George Washington Park.

I enjoy my life with friends and family here in Pacific Grove Adult School, a student since 2011.

Wonderful People
Gina Juntaradarapun from Thailand

I love the wonderful people in Pacific Grove. They are very friendly. When I moved into my cozy, white house on Wood Street, my neighbor warmly welcomed my family with colorful flowers from her back yard. That impressed me and filled me full of confidence to start, my new life in this town. I am from Thailand and I have a strong foreign accent; my pronunciation is especially difficult to understand. When I talk to someone in Pacific Grove, they try to speak slowly and sometimes tell me the correct word. That is very helpful.

Another reason I love the people in Pacific Grove is that I enjoy shopping here because the businesses are locally owned. The owners love their community, and they support each other. Parents buy stationery from Alpha Stationery, and Alpha's owner buys food from Grove Market, and once I saw the market owner walking into ACE Hardware. It is very impressive.

Furthermore, people always gather together to create events for the community. Kids and adults show up on the street to participate in these amazing events.

These are the reasons that Pacific Grove makes such an important impact on me. I adore the wonderful and friendly people in this unique little town of Pacific Grove.

Being a tropical country, Thailand has four seasons, and the tropical heat can soar beyond 105 degrees F in the central part. Fortunately, I live in Chiang Mai, where the weather is similar to Pacific Grove. Ninety percent of Thais are Buddhists. The important things that Thais have in our souls are happiness, honesty, and respectfulness. Please don't be surprised if you see an Asian woman who smiles to you with her happy face; it might be me. I moved to Pacific Grove eight years ago. Now, I study as an ESL student at Pacific Grove Adult Education.

Excited and Grateful
Gitee from Iran

I lived with my husband and my family in Iran until 2001. I have four children: three daughters and one son. My husband was a pharmacist and he had a pharmacy in Iran. After the revolution, we left the country because we had a lot of problems with the new regime.

Now, two of my daughters and I are living here and two of my other children are still living in Iran. My husband passed away four years ago. Now I live by myself in Monterey, but I am not all alone. My oldest daughter lives in San Diego and the youngest daughter lives in Carmel.

I am so happy to be here with my two daughters although I miss my other children all the time.

I am excited about learning English in the Adult School and grateful to have such teachers.

Surprises
Bertha from Peru and Japan

Life gives us many surprises and challenges us with new opportunities. My new life in the United States of America started October 23, 2016. My family and I got to enjoy and experience a new life in Pacific Grove. Pacific Grove is a unique and incomparable city. We can enjoy the sea and the breeze. We feel very healthy breathing the pure air of the ocean, and we like to watch the sunset. Sometimes we go fishing on the weekends. My family and I often lose track of time because we enjoy and share much more now than we did in other times. In everyday life here, there is no monotony. On waking up every new day, we feel the renewed energy that helps us face the challenges of work or study. And the people of Pacific Grove are friendly and unique. I like them.

I like to see the goals of my family fulfilled. It makes me happy. Living in Pacific Grove is a dream come true.

A Beautiful City
Jila Amiri from Iran

Pacific Grove is a beautiful city and has nice weather. The weather always surprises me because it changes frequently. There are many different restaurants from different countries and a lot of shopping centers in Pacific Grove In summer time many tourists visit the city and they walk or ride a bike by the ocean. I go to Pacific Grove Adult School. I really like this school because I feel I'm learning English and at the same time I have found so many good friends from America and Iran.

It's been four years that I'm living in the U.S. I came from Iran to live here with my family and help my daughter come here and join us. In February she came and now my whole family is together here.

Recharging Batteries Sanctuary
Otavio Serino Castro from Brazil

Finding a way to relax after a tough and busy week is a challenge to many people, at least for the ones who have never visited Pacific Grove. The first time I rode along Pacific Grove's coastal bicycle lane was amazing, and the most impressive thing is that this feeling is still present today no matter how many times I repeat it. The natural contrast designed by the sea, rocks, colorful vegetation, and bright sand creates a unique atmosphere. On top of that, you will be able to contemplate the Pacific Ocean breeze and animals like marine birds, deer, squirrels, and even seals animating the landscape. If by any chance you felt tired, there will be plenty of spots available for you to sit and relax; one of my favorites is the lawn of Lover's Point.

In the same place you can find picnic tables and barbecue grills to stop for a snack. However, when I go for a ride in Pacific Grove I carry with me only water because paying a visit to one of the many outstanding gastronomical places there is compulsory for me. From traditional American breakfast to exotic Thai cuisine is what you will be able to enjoy. Further, in the restaurants there will be really nice opportunities to meet and interact with the friendly and amazing people who live there. There is no way to not feel energized after spending some time in Pacific Grove.

I moved to Monterey with my wife to work in the United States. We are professionals from the agribusiness sector and she was relocated to work in the Salinas Valley for a vegetable seed company. I am 31 years old and graduated in Animal Husbandry with a Master's Degree in Marine Sciences and an MBA in marketing. My favorite hobbies are outdoor activities, such as hiking and going to the beach, sports like skateboarding and Brazilian jiu-jitsu, playing guitar and going out with friends to enjoy music, cinema, food, and drinks.

This Magical Country
Galina from Russia

I came to the United States on May 4th. Now I have the opportunity to study English in Pacific Grove Adult School. Moreover, I can walk every morning to school and from school to home. After school I can relax sometimes.

I like California. The nature here is very different and beautiful. There are many mountains and forests; the air is fresh and magically foggy. I was surprised when I saw deer in the park and seals on the beach. When I go back to Russia for a visit, I will tell about this magical country.

Pacific Grove is Harmonious
Jae Woon (James) Jeong from South Korea

I live in Pacific Grove where the people and the environment are naturally and perfectly harmonious, friendly, and peaceful; it is the heart of Monterey County.

First of all, you go to any place in Pacific Grove, you can meet such friendly people who say, "Hi, good morning," or "How are you? It is a gorgeous day!" to you with warm smiles. Wherever you go, that is to the downtown or the fabulous rocky seashore or the pristine Asilomar Beach, you can listen to their friendly greetings. Their faces are so peaceful and sweet that you can feel their warm-hearted souls.

Second, Pacific Grove has an awesome ocean with the fantastically curvaceous seashore and a lot of characteristic trees; houses and streets that are wonderfully harmonious with the ocean and mountains. Inside this small area, people and animals like deer, raccoons, squirrels, birds, butterflies, and dogs are living all together with peace and harmony. What a great place where the people and the nature are perfectly sociable. Living in Pacific Grove is a great gift and blessing from God. That's the reason I live in this place. I am living a peaceful and friendly life in Pacific Grove, like a heavenly life, since 2015.

My family and I immigrated to the States in 2015 because my lovely son loves to study in the States.

A Volunteer
Chungwei Shen from Taiwan

I am like a monarch butterfly that migrated from Taiwan to beautiful Pacific Grove. Since I have to return to Taiwan to take care of my elderly mother for five months, I move back and forth between Taiwan and the United States. I have been living in Pacific Grove for ten years.

When I stayed in Pacific Grove, I served as a volunteer for the Monterey Bay Chinese Association and a volunteer for the Pacific Grove Adult School where I am a student. As a volunteer for the Monterey Bay Chinese Association, I helped set up for the Chinese Lunar New Year Party every year to promote cultural exchanges between China and the United States. Furthermore, I have participated in "The Language Capital of the World Cultural Festival" in Monterey. We teamed up with the city of Monterey to ensure that cultural festivals run smoothly. I helped organize the Chinese and Taiwanese cultural exhibitions.

I started volunteering at the Pacific Grove Adult School when I learned that three students from China struggled to learn English in the ESL class. During the class, I had to be a simultaneous interpreter. When they started responding to the teacher's questions, they felt satisfied and confident. Besides the Chinese students, I have also helped students from South Korea, Iran and Afghanistan to learn English. Besides teaching English, I have also helped Chinese students to adapt to life here. For example, I reminded a Chinese student to set the time forward on the day Daylight Saving Time began when she was going back to China. She said that if I hadn't reminded her she might have missed her flight. I also told her how to locate a family doctor and find out if the doctor is covered by her health plan. I found that volunteer experience is unique and rewarding. Volunteers have the power to make a difference. Confucius once said, "He who teaches, learns." When I tutor English, I benefit from learning something new and keep away from getting dementia.

I was director and professor of Graduate Institute of Educational Technology at National Pingtung University in Taiwan. After I retired, I joined my family in Pacific Grove because my wife is an instructor teaching Mandarin Chinese at the Defense Language Institute.

Diversity in People Here
Yuki from Japan

I am really glad to live here in Pacific Grove because I can communicate with a lot of great people. First of all, I should mention how friendly and moderate people are in this town. Every time I pass someone on the street or park, we exchange smiles with each other. Everybody looks very calm and peaceful. I especially enjoy small talks at the stores. It is literally about small things, like weather, food, or fashions; however, these conversations give me a warm feeling.

A diversity of people is one of the interesting things about this area. As an ESL student, I have met many people from all over the world. I like to know about their culture, so I have learned not only about America and English but also about the world from living in Pacific Grove. Since I moved here, I have noticed that people who live here love our town more than people who live in other places. Many people try to be involved in the community; they enjoy volunteering, participating to local events, and talking about Pacific Grove. Most people say to me that they like this town.

In my daily life, I have several great neighbors who can share fun times. We always talk when we see each other around our apartment; we have dinner or parties together sometimes. Now, I know even their friends and they know my friends. It did not happen in my previous apartment in another city. Since I moved here, I have connected to other people more than before. My English skills have also been improving!

My husband got a job in this area, so we moved to Pacific Grove.

Travel the World
Berna from Turkey

Pacific Grove has different weather from Turkey's weather. It's a beautiful place and it has beautiful nature, but I prefer hot weather. Pacific Grove is colder than my country. Also, there is a big difference between the daytime and nighttime temperatures here. There is the possibility that at the same time we can feel cold and hot. That's why I really don't know what I need to wear. But I love Pacific Grove.

I am from the south of Turkey near the Mediterranean Sea. I have been here visiting friends for two months. I like traveling. I want to see the whole world. It may be impossible but I really want that.

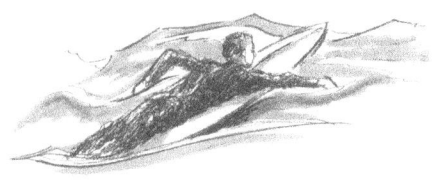

I Love the Beach
Maysoun from Jordan

I like Pacific Grove. I have lived here one month. I have an American passport. I feel better for everything in Pacific Grove. My daughter got residence last week and we are so happy about it. My husband works in the Defense Language Institute. We have everything we need. I like the weather. I'm always so happy to speak and learn English in school. I walk one hour every day near the beach.

Many Good Experiences
Mona from Iran

I think Pacific Grove is one of the best places for having good experiences. There are many beautiful places to visit in Pacific Grove. For example, there is a beach where you can rent a bike and ride by the ocean. There is a church named San Carlos; it is designed beautifully and it's a very calm place. There are a lot of markets in Pacific Grove; for example, there is a market called Farmers Market, which opens every Monday and is located on Central Avenue.

People in Pacific Grove are kind and always smile at each other. They also are ready to help you any time you need. I think the houses are really beautiful in Pacific Grove and they build them perfectly. Most of the people don't live in apartments and they have a garden and yard at their houses. Pacific Grove has mild weather. It's sometimes rainy and sometimes sunny. I like the weather here very much. Food is also very delicious in Pacific Grove

There is an English school for adult students in Pacific Grove. I decided to go to the English class in Pacific Grove with my mother to practice and improve my English more. This school is really helpful. You have the opportunity to meet new people from other countries and talk to them about different things. You also may find very good friends. Teachers in my school are kind and patient. They always have time for you if you need help. I also love their way of teaching. They make you talk in the class, which helps you to improve your English.

We also work on a program at school and away from school. The program is called Burlington English. I love Burlington English because it has a lot of parts and you can practice listening, writing, reading, and getting better in English. Unfortunately, I have just a little more time to come to school and practice Burlington because I'm not staying here for a long time, but I'm trying to practice with Burlington as hard as I can.

I recommend that you visit Pacific Grove at least once because you will enjoy visiting beautiful places and meeting wonderful people, like I did.

I'm living in Pacific Grove temporarily because I'm going to join my sister in Portland soon. I'm here to be with my mother and spend time with her because we were far from each other for a long time. After our New Year's holiday, I will go to Portland to work and live, but I'm worried about the future because I don't know anything about living in the United States.

A Safe Little Town!
Lien Pham from Vietnam

Pacific Grove is a safe little town where I feel like I'm at home with security 24/7. I have lived in many cities in different countries, but never have I felt so safe when wandering around like I do here in Pacific Grove. I often walk to many places in town by myself without feeling harmed or attacked.

I enjoy the quiet and peaceful surroundings at night in Pacific Grove that makes me appreciate more about this beautiful world. I also like the fact that there are many police officers driving around the town to ensure everything is safe and sound. Knowing how crazy and violent the world is out there, and being blessed enough to live in such a protected place, that makes me so grateful and thankful for what I have.

Thank you, my little town, Pacific Grove!

I moved to the United States to be with my husband who happens to live in Pacific Grove.

Pacific Grove's Fascinating Natural Environment
Natalie from China

The fascinating natural environment in Pacific Grove made me fall in love with her unconditionally. Surrounded by the Pacific Ocean, Pacific Grove is like an artless girl in the sapphire blue dress with white lace. Walking along the coast of Pacific Grove to enjoy the endless blue and dulcet sound of the waves is the best way to start my brand new day. With your exploring eyes, you can find various kinds of sea creatures living here peacefully as your neighbors. Harbor seals either bask in the sunshine on the beach or swim delightfully in the sea; sea otters float along wrapped in kelp with food on their stomach; whales travel with their families using their tails and spray to say hi to us. Not to mention my favorite sandy beach, Asilomar. Sitting on its soft white sand to enjoy the sunset and waiting until both the ocean and the beach become golden is the most romantic thing I can come up with.

Let's come to the "mainland" of Pacific Grove. Deer appear everywhere just like your neighbors' dogs. They may go into your backyard to have some snacks or have a family picnic outside on the lawn of your school. Their adorable appearance symbolizes the friendly environment in Pacific Grove.

As we know, Butterfly Town is the nickname of Pacific Grove. Monarchs fly a long way to the Pacific Grove Sanctuary to gain nutrition and spend their winter here. They not only have a good rest but also give us a great opportunity to lift the veil of Mother Nature. All kinds of these beauties that Pacific Grove owns make her captivating and irresistible. I am willing to be a lapdog of Pacific Grove, who is the artless girl in the sapphire blue dress with white lace, and live with her till the seas run dry and the rocks crumble.

Canton is located in the southern part of China. One of the nicknames of Canton is the Flower City, as there are different kinds of flowers and green trees all year around because of its humid weather. For me, Canton is like a sweet and warmhearted sister who always welcomes people with her open arms. I have lived in Canton for over twenty years until I came with my husband to Monterey a year ago. I go to Pacific Grove Adult Education for ESL class every week. This is the reason why I can get to know the charm of Pacific Grove.

For me, Pacific Grove Adult School is just like the butterfly sanctuary. We all come from different places but we all "re-energize" here. Maybe for some of us, now is like winter in our life, and it's too cold for us to fly free and high as we used to. Fortunately, we find Pacific Grove Adult School as our sanctuary. We stay together so that we do not feel lonely; we encourage each other so that we stay positive; we study together so that we get more preparation for our next journey.

So once again, thank you all, my dear friends! These days are precious. I wish you all well, too! And for the ones who are sometimes confused or depressed, "If winter comes, can spring be far behind?"

Student responses to Natalie's essay:

Gina

Every day is my wonderful day because I am studying at Pacific Grove Adult School. It is the one place in Pacific Grove where I feel safe and comfortable. I learn many interesting things in this place. My teacher teaches me how to be an educated student. She said we have to use standard English because we are English as a Second Language students. I'm learning new things every day. Furthermore, I meet new friends from many countries who are really friendly. There is a friendship through education. It's fantastic! I have good days and good times with my global friends. How time flies! From 2008 to 2017 I'm still studying here. Some of my friends asked why I didn't move to another school or finish my English class. The only answer I explain to them is I feel safe and comfortable with my teachers, my friends, and my place. So, I am happy to say that every day is my wonderful day in Pacific Grove Adult School.

Karen

It has been a rich experience to study at Pacific Grove Adult School. Although our journeys together are not extensive, I feel grateful to be there and to learn through our teachers and our classmates who are from different countries. This quiet place is surrounded by warm people that smile gently and help me to improve this language in a friendly and supportive environment. I always will be thankful to everyone and I'll keep this experience with love forever.

Nuch

A lot of people that I know asked me the same question, "Why are you taking an ESL class at Pacific Grove Adult School?" I told them that I used to take an ESL class at Pacific Grove Adult School a long time ago. I always liked the school and the teachers. Also, I feel safe here.

Yuki

There are many people who know my name and call me by my name in the ESL class, and I am encouraged by them. It is very important that someone knows your name and calls your name in your life. I realized it here in Pacific Grove.

I have been enjoying living in the United States, and Pacific Grove is a particularly great place to live. However, I have fear and anxiety all the time. Because of living far away from my country, Japan, I always face many things that I cannot do. It makes me less confident and weak. In such a tough life, I get energy when someone calls my name. I feel that this place accepts me. Needless to say, the ESL class provides me a great education with great teachers, but also mental stability.

When I moved to Pacific Grove, I knew nobody. Then nobody knew me. After eight months, now I have many people who I can talk and smile with. I am so grateful to attend the ESL class.

Jasmine

I knew about Pacific Grove Adult School three years ago. I really wanted to come to school to improve my English but I couldn't do it because I had to work. I worked at a sandwich store, "Goodies," and took care of my baby. Then, I came back to Monterey and could come to school. I'm still awkward and nervous in class, but I think I will adapt. I pass by downtown Pacific Grove on my way to school. I like that. Soon the class will feel comfortable and fun like my home and the playground.

Gina

My name is Gina Juntaradarapun. I am from Thailand, located in the heart of Southeast Asia. Being a tropical country, Thailand has four seasons, and the tropical heat can soar beyond 105 degrees F in the central part. Fortunately, I live in Chiang Mai, where the weather is similar to Pacific Grove. Ninety percent of Thais are Buddhists. The important things that Thais have in our souls are happiness, honesty, and respectfulness. Please don't be surprised if you see an Asian woman who smiles to you with her happy face; it might be me. I moved to Pacific Grove eight years ago. Now, I study as an ESL student at Pacific Grove Adult Education.

Megumi

As Natalie said, Pacific Grove Adult School is like a sanctuary. Every student has their own individual reasons to attend the ESL class, but I think we have the same aim, which is that we want to improve our English skills. I can be a student in class and I don't need to think about house stuff. I feel like I am a "person" not a mother and a wife. And teachers teach me not only English but also American history and support me when I have trouble with something. Students also encourage me to study English and to live in America. I'm very lucky to get a chance to attend the Adult Education Pacific Grove ESL class.

Lien Pham

I think Pacific Grove Adult School has been a great place for me to meet new friends and to learn new things. I have made friends with many people in my ESL class. We not only share knowledge but also life experiences. Barbara and Brooks are the two very nice and genuine teachers who have provided us a lot of useful information about life in Pacific Grove. I'm so thankful and grateful for having had the chance to know all of these beautiful people at Pacific Grove Adult School.

2017 MONARCH AWARDS FOR TWO EXCEPTIONAL STUDENTS

Monarch Award for Emiko Case

Imaginative, Generous, Steadfast

Emiko Case is an outstanding English student. She came to our school eight years ago and joined the B class. Later she came to the C class. She was determined to learn our language so she could develop her calligraphy business. She was serious about her schoolwork and always asked her teachers questions so she could understand better. While in our classes she has always given generously of her artistic talents by helping to decorate for parties, making signs, and fashioning beautiful cards for her teachers and classmates. Her message has always been the same: peace and love.

At the beginning of this year the students in the C class were asked to choose a goal that they wanted to achieve by the end of the year. Emiko's goal was to learn enough English so that she could become independent. She also wanted to be able to teach her calligraphy classes without having to depend on someone to speak for her. She wanted to be able to display and sell her calligraphy work without depending on someone to speak for her. She wanted to speak for herself. That goal was chosen in the fall of 2016. It is now the spring of 2017 and Emiko has reached her goal. She teaches three calligraphy classes and sells her work at many art fairs and all without anyone speaking for her. She alone was the tour guide and translator for a group of Americans who traveled to Japan.

Emiko will move to the D class this summer to continue her mastery of English. In the meantime, her husband can retire. He doesn't have to be with her all the time in order to speak for her. She's an independent woman.

Monarch Award for Jila Amiri

Dedicated, Responsible, Inquisitive, Welcoming

We are extremely pleased to present this Monarch Award to Jila Amiri who has been in our ESL program for two years. In that time she has dedicated herself to welcoming and supporting new students to the class.

She has helped us by being responsible for collecting money, buying snacks, making coffee, and cleaning up. Whatever we ask her to do, she does willingly.

She is inquisitive and always asks questions and has her hand up to answer. She has a great sense of humor and often offers comical stories to the class.

Jila has dedicated herself to becoming a citizen of the world by improving her English and taking citizenship classes. She hopes to become a U.S. citizen in the near future.

Jila Amiri, you more than deserve the Monarch Award.

INTERNATIONAL RECIPES FROM STUDENTS

Mango with Sweet Sticky Rice by Gina Juntaradarapun

Ingredients:
1 ½ cups glutinous (sticky) rice
½ cup coconut milk
3 Tbsp fine sugar (add more if needed)
¼ tsp. salt
2 ripe mangoes (champagne mangoes)

Instructions:
Soak the rice in a bowl of water for at least 3 hours, then rinse and drain.
Put the rice in a cheesecloth and steam in a steamer or rice cooker for 30 – 35 minutes.
Put the coconut milk, sugar, and salt in a small pan over low-medium heat and set it aside. Reserve about 5 Tbsp. for the topping.
Mix the cooked sticky rice with sweet coconut milk and let stand for 10 minutes.
Top with sesame and serve with mango slices.

Bulgogi by Jasmine Kim

Ingredients:
2 pounds of tenderloin beef
½ cup soy sauce
¼ cup sugar
1 Tbsp. honey
12 cloves of garlic, minced
Small Asian pear, crushed
Medium onion, crushed
Sesame oil and toasted seeds
½ cup water or wine

Instructions:
Make marinade sauce for beef by mixing the following in a food processor:
soy sauce, sugar, garlic, onion, Asian pear, water or wine, and honey.
Pour the marinade sauce into a large stainless steel bowl.
Slice the beef thinly against the grain to make it tender.
Place the sliced beef into the marinade and add 1 or 2 Tbsp. of sesame oil and the toasted sesame seeds.
After 3 hours, you can grill the meat on a charcoal barbeque, broil it in an oven or grill it in a pan.

Stewed Chicken by Karen Castro

Ingredients:
6 drumsticks
1 carrot
1 onion, chopped
2 green onions, chopped
4 red tomatoes, chopped
1 – 2 bay leaves
Parsley
Oregano
Salt
Black pepper
Olive Oil
Peeled potatoes
Garlic and red pepper (optional)

Instructions:
Put the drumsticks without the skin in a bowl.
Add a spoonful of olive oil and mix with the parsley, oregano, salt, and ground black pepper.
Cover and keep refrigerated for about an hour.
Brown the onions and green onions in a tablespoon of olive oil in a saucepan.
Put the marinated chicken into the saucepan with the onions. Add the tomatoes, carrot, and bay leaves.
Add a medium cup of water and let cook, covered, about 40 minutes.
Meanwhile, mix and taste to see if you need more salt or black pepper.
When the stewed chicken is close to ready, add the peeled potatoes and turn over.
After 40 minutes or after the stewed chicken is fully cooked, turn down the temperature, remove the lid and let it sit for about 10 minutes.
Transfer the stewed chicken to a serving plate. It is ready to eat.

INTERNATIONAL RECIPES FROM STUDENTS

Asian Ground Beef Pasta by Yuki Takenaka

Ingredients:
200g pasta (spaghetti, penne, etc.)
1/3 lbs. ground beef
1 eggplant, diced
1 Tbsp. minced ginger
1 Tbsp. minced garlic
1 Tbsp. red pepper flakes
1 Tbsp. soy sauce
1 Tbsp. fish sauce
1 Tbsp. white wine
2 tsp. sesame oil
lettuce
bean sprouts
cilantro
green onion
vegetable oil

Instructions:
In a skillet, sauté minced ginger and garlic with vegetable oil.
Add the ground beef and the red pepper flakes.
When beef turns brown, add the eggplant, soy sauce, fish sauce and white wine.
Cover the lid and simmer about 5 minutes. Stir occasionally.
Cook the pasta until *al dente*. Drain water and sprinkle sesame oil on the pasta. Mix well.
Dish up the lettuce and the bean sprouts on the pasta.
Add the ground beef sauce, the cilantro, and green onion to taste and garnish.
*When you eat it, mix the whole thing well!!

KimChi by Jasmine Kim

Ingredients:
1 or 2 medium heads of Napa cabbage
1 cup plus 1 Tbsp. sea salt
Water
1 garlic with cloves peeled and cut
1 grated radish
1 tsp. ginger
1 tsp. sugar
2 to 3 Tbsp. seafood flavored water or fish sauce
¼ cup Korean salted shrimp
3 to 4 Tbsp. red pepper or hot pepper flakes
¼ cup Korean radish, peeled and cut into matchsticks
4 scallions cut into 1-inch pieces

Instructions:
Cut the cabbage into quarters and remove the cores. Cut each quarter into 2-inch strips.
Put the cabbage and salt in a large bowl. Massage the salt into the cabbage until it gets soft. Add water to the cabbage. Put a plate or any type of cover on top of the bowl and wait for 1 to 2 hours.
Rinse the cabbage 3 to 4 times under cold water and drain in a colander for about 20 minutes. Wash and dry the bowl and set it aside.
Put garlic, ginger, sugar, seafood flavor and 3 Tbsp. water in a small bowl and stir altogether until they are completely mixed and become a paste.
Put the cabbage in a large bowl with scallions, radish, red pepper powder and seasoning paste.
Gently massage altogether until they are completely mixed.
Pack the kimchi into a jar and press it down until the brine rises to cover the kimchi. Leave 1 to 2 inches of headspace in the jar. Seal the jar with a lid.
Keep the jar with kimchi in it at room temperature for 3 to 4 days to ferment. Check it on a daily basis and you might see bubbles inside the jar.
Taste a little and when you think it is ripe enough, place the jar in the refrigerator. Maybe you will want to eat it immediately, but it's better after another week or so.

INTERNATIONAL RECIPES FROM STUDENTS

China Pan-Fried Chicken with Ginger and Onion
Natalie Zhu

Ingredients:
3 boneless chicken thighs with skin
Half of a chopped red onion
Some shredded ginger and scallions
1 Tbsp. cooking wine
1 ½ Tbsp. soy sauce
1 tsp. cornstarch
2 tsp. sugar
¼ tsp. salt
¼ tsp. pepper

Instructions:
Make the marinating sauce: wine, soy sauce, cornstarch, sugar, salt, and pepper.
Chop the chicken thighs and marinate them for at least 1 hour.
Heat up the pan and fry the chicken (skin on the bottom) with medium fire until the skins become golden. Do not stir.
Tip: use less oil than usual as the skins will bring out some chicken oil.
Turn over every piece of chicken and put the red onion and ginger into the pan evenly.
Sprinkle a small amount of salt on the red onion and ginger; cover with lid for 3 to 5 minutes.
Put the scallions into the pan and stir-fry them for 30 seconds or so.

Kuku Sabzi–Persian Frittata and Fresh Herbs
Maryam Khatapoosh

Ingredients:
5 eggs
1 cup fresh parsley, packed
1 cup fresh cilantro, packed
1 cup dill, packed
1 cup chopped chives or tareh
1/3 cup walnuts
1 – 2 Tbsp. zereshk (barberries) washed and drained
1 tsp. baking powder

Instructions:
Toast the walnuts for a few minutes.
Place the eggs in a bowl.
Add baking powder, salt and pepper. Mix well.
Remove stems from all herbs.
Rough chop the herbs
Add herbs, walnuts, and zereshk to the eggs. Mix well until all nicely incorporated.
Warm up a non-stick pan with some oil. Add the egg and herbs mixture. Cover and cook for about 20 minutes on medium-low heat.
Cut the kuku into four pieces and carefully flip each piece. Cover and cook for another 20 minutes or until kuku is cooked through.
Cut kuku into 8 wedges and place on a serving platter.

Potato Korokke (croquette) Chie Saito
Natalie Zhu

Ingredients:
1 lb. potatoes
1 tsp. oil
½ lb. ground beef
½ onion, minced
¼ – ½ tsp. salt
pepper
flour
eggs, beaten
Panko (bread crumbs)
oil for deep-frying
Tonkatsu sauce or soy sauce

Instructions:
Peel the potatoes and cut them into 4 pieces each. Cook in boiling water until soft. In a big bowl, mash potatoes well.
Heat oil in a pan and start cooking the onion.
Add ground beef and cook until browned and cooked through.
Season with salt and pepper.
Mix potatoes and meat mixture, add more salt and pepper to taste, and let it cool.
Divide potato mixture into 8 pieces, make oval patties, and refrigerate them for an hour.
Coat with flour, then eggs, and finally Panko (break crumbs).
Heat deep frying oil to 350-375 degrees F for 3-4 minutes on each side.

INTERNATIONAL RECIPES FROM STUDENTS

Recipes and Calligraphy by Emiko Case

Tofu Ice Cream — Emiko Case

- 300 g   tofu (silken)
- 200 cc   milk
- 6 tbsp. sugar or honey
- 1 tsp.   vanilla extract

1. Put all ingredients in a blender.
2. Put 1. in a resealable plastic bag, and make smooth, and freeze.
3. After freezing, knead and unstiffen by hand.
4. Add 3. in a blender again.

Green Beans with Sesame Seasoning — Emiko Case

- 0.5 lbs. green beans
- 3 tbsp.   sesame seed
- 1 tbsp.   soy sauce
- 2 tsp.   sugar
- 2 tsp.   mirin

1. Boil green beans with 1/2 tsp. salt for 3-5 minutes.
2. After boiling green beans, put in cold water, drain off, and cut into approximately 1 inch pieces.
3. Grind sesame seed with mortar, add soy sauce, sugar, mirin, and mix up
4. Toss 1 and 3.

❖ Mirin is an essential seasoning for Japanese food.

WELCOME TO THE PACIFIC GROVE PUBLIC LIBRARY—JOYCE KRIEG

I was always one of those kids who had her nose in a book and remained a life-long reader, so when the opportunity arose in my mid-40s to choose a new place to live, a decent library was one of the big items on my priority list.

Number one on the list was a mild climate. After enduring the scorching summers in the Central Valley for 20-plus years, I was beyond eager to escape the heat. Also on the list: low crime, animal-friendly, no major traffic issues, Macy's, Trader Joe's, Jazzercise, a fabulous bookstore—and the library.

My first step into the Pacific Grove Public Library and I knew that yes, this "town that time forgot" could work for me. Sacramento, where I was living at the time, had just slashed its library budget to the bone, resulting in many branches open only a few hours in the middle of the weekday, and hardly any new acquisitions. Imagine my delight here in Pacific Grove to discover a library open seven days a week, including several evenings, shelves bursting with the latest releases, as well as a healthy supply of magazines, books on tape, and VCR movies. For a town of only around 15,000, I was impressed.

Further searching revealed most of the other "must-haves" on my list: Macy's at Del Monte Shopping Center, Jazzercise at Chautauqua Hall, and a little slice of heaven for us bookish types, the Thunderbird Bookshop in Carmel's Barnyard. No Trader Joe's, though—I would have to make do with a weekly trip with my cooler to the nearest TJ's in Capitola. But still, the P.G. library sealed the deal.

That was nearly 25 years ago and, inevitably, much has changed. Traffic on most weekends is now as unbearable as what I used to slog through on my commute in Sacramento. Our beloved Thunderbird Bookshop is no more. Now that I'm no longer dressing for success, Macy's and high-end shopping in general has fallen off the priority list. But we got our own TJ's a year or so after I arrived, and I'm still going to those Jazzercise classes at Chautauqua Hall.

As to the library, the Sunday hours fell victim to budget issues, the materials on tape are now on CD and DVD, and computers have replaced the card catalogue. But this wonderful community resource not only endures but flourishes, ready to serve the latest generation of little girls and boys with their noses constantly in a book.

What follows are a set of stories about the Pacific Grove library, some by staff, some by patrons. Learn more about the artwork that graces the library's walls, the fate of the original library windows, and – my favorite!—the tale of the little boy who accidentally got locked in the library after hours.

A MESSAGE FROM THE DIRECTOR

Scott Bauer
Director of the P.G. Public Library

Having been the Director of the Pacific Grove Public Library for all of two weeks as I write this (I started on Monday, August 21, 2017) it seems strange—and a bit presumptuous, perhaps—to be writing about the Library that has long been central to the lives of people in Pacific Grove and that many of you know so much better than I. So while I will happily bend your ears talking about all the great programs, materials and services you can find at the Library, let me put that off to another time and start instead by telling you a little bit about myself.

I am one of those increasingly "rare" folks born-and-bred in California, bouncing up-and-down the state the first 10 years of my life until my parents finally settled in Concord in the eastern part of the San Francisco Bay Area. It was during this time that I started amassing a fairly large collection of science Fiction and Comic books, some of which, despite selling many of them to help pay for college, I still own to this day.

I graduated from Ygnacio Valley High School in Concord, then majored in English at San Francisco State University. It was around this time that I started working in libraries, shelving books at the Contra Costa County Library's Pleasant Hill branch. I spent nearly 15-years working for the Library there, during which time I met my wife Sallie and obtained my Masters in Library and Information Studies for the University of California in Berkeley. In addition to the Contra Costa County LIbrary I also worked for libraries in Redwood City and Marin County before coming to Pacific Grove.

A major reason I wanted to be the Library Director here—setting aside the physical beauty of this area, that is impossible to do—is the support and love that people in Pacific Grove have for their library. Already I can see this, from the number of people who volunteer for the Library, the Friends of the Library and the Foundation to the incredible number of books, movies and other materials that Library patrons check out (in the top 25 per capita in the state of California). The great staff of dedicated people working for the library is icing on the cake!

The Library is looking forward to starting a revitalization project that will restore much of the the original Carnegie building at the core of the Library. While how people use libraries has changed immensely from 1906 when the building was opened, the reasons why people continue to use the Library remain much as they were over a hundred years ago—as a place for information, for education, for the exchange of ideas and as a meeting place for the community. In honoring our past we are also preparing for the future and keeping the Library in the heart—and hearts—of the Pacific Grove community.

I hope to see all of you at the Library soon!

Stefanie Tylor, CSUMB Intern for Park Place Publications, spent some time writing and interviewing at the library, then went on to pursue her literary career. We wish her well.
—Patricia and Joyce

LISTENING TO MY ELDERS – A SHELLEY NEMETH PHOTO ESSAY

After my retirement from a 20-year career in education in 2007, I began volunteering at the Pacific Grove Library—shelving books in a place that has always been close to my heart. As a child, I loved my local library and spent many hours there. As a young adult, I wished to eventually find myself employed in a library, but life had already taken me off in other directions. So, finally, I was satisfying that yearning in my retirement years. To my delight, a few years later, I was offered the opportunity to become a part-time employee, working at the circulation desk. It was the perfect way for me to become more involved in my community and to further enjoy the many resources available in the Library.

Five years later, as I had become better acquainted with many individual library patrons and enjoyed sharing the delights of life in Pacific Grove with them, I focused especially on Saul. Saul was (and still is) a daily visitor at the library and each day, as he approached me at the front desk to complete his varietal checkouts, he gave me the most beautiful, heartfelt greeting and smile I've ever received. I looked forward to seeing this bright, joyful 97-year-old each day. As a photography hobbyist, I began to wish I had a photograph of Saul's smiling face to capture that magic.

Inspired by Saul, I realized that there are many other delightful patrons of advanced age who use the library regularly, stopping at the front desk to chat and share their lives. So I decided to develop my project, capturing 15 of them in portraits to share with the community. Each individual has found the library to be an integral part of their lives, not only as a pleasant haven, but also as a vibrant connection to the community and to the world.

They have shown me how to keep growing as I age, to be continually engaged in life as it changes, and to have the curiosity and courage to meet each new day with spirit, even if it becomes a challenge. I am deeply grateful to each of them for agreeing to be a part of my project. One aspect of working in the Library that I treasure most is seeing and getting to know our regular patrons. It is clear that the library is an important part of this community and I decided to acknowledge the patronage of our elder visitors in particular with this special exhibit to honor and represent an important segment of our regular customers.

Photography

When I was in my twenties, I found myself moving forward to a career in advertising and public relations, which I enjoyed and where I learned many skills. At the same time, whenever I passed a library or a bookstore, it tweaked my soul and called to me as an alternate career. I grew up with books and libraries as a primary source of curiosity, knowledge, and peace. But as my professional life took its own direction, I continued to picture myself working in a library as a fallback, even though there was never a good time to switch paths.

As I traversed the steps of life—career, marriage, parenthood, and eventually, retirement—I finally found myself volunteering at the Pacific Grove Library and then, a couple of years later, being hired as a part-time employee here. Now, at age 68, my time at the library continues to satisfy some basic, primal need within me. I am honored to spend time each day in what I see to be the heart-center of the community, and even more gratified to meet and know so many wonderful citizens. When I'm not at work, however, I enjoy exploring our community and beyond with my keen interest in photography. This project has given me the unique opportunity to combine two of my greatest passions.

Amy

At age 81, Amy is a loyal library user in addition to her regular volunteer work around the community. At Sally Griffin Senior Center, she prepares meals provided to recipients of "Meals on Wheels" and pursues a variety of other local interests and causes. At the library, she enjoys perusing periodicals, which give her inexpensive access to useful sources, and broadens her connection to the world with a breadth of information both useful and enjoyable. Amy grew up in Honolulu, then to Illinois for college, and relocated to California, where she was a teacher. She has lived in Pacific Grove for over 46 years.

Anne

Anne grew up in the Midwest, where she began as a library patron at the age of nine. She is now 83 and makes regular use of the library, reading at least two books a week. She enjoys the fact that, whatever her interests, she can count on the library to find sources for her. She also spends time regularly volunteering at Sally Griffin Senior Center.

Bob

Bob is the 'young whipper-snapper' of our group, at just 78, well on his way to a lively future with involvement in a variety of community and creative pursuits. He is a photographer himself, and enjoys adding creative twists to his images. In fact, his work can be seen at local venues like Juice & Java, along with his friend and co-participant in this show, Jerry. He was born in Watsonville and grew up in the local library, since his mother was a librarian. To this day he considers the library as a place of refuge. He's also a history buff, having lived all over the world, with several years in Germany, which impacted his life view in many ways.

Chubbs

"Chubbs" enjoys many things about the library, but especially the friendly, helpful staff members and fellow patrons she encounters. She is 81 years old, and especially values the personal touch she experiences here, where librarians respond to her inquiries of all varieties, encompassing entertainment, social information, news, education, day-to-day resources, and just plain friendship. She likes to include a visit to the library in her daily routine, and has been frequenting the library for around 33 years. She feels that a library is "a must" in every town, providing a connection with the community to its citizens.

Doris

Doris is a beautiful 85-year-old who is a regular reader, and especially appreciates our large-type collection. She says she is "never without a book." She lived for a while in Saudi Arabia, and arrived in Pacific Grove in 1968 with her husband, a Naval officer. She has been using the library ever since. Among her other interests and pursuits are Ikebana flower arranging and a weekly golf game.

Dorothy

Following a long career as a junior high school teacher in the Bay Area, Dorothy retired to Pacific Grove with her husband in 1991 and has become another contented resident. She is now 90 years old and uses our Library - her "favorite" - frequently. She loves the environment here, and enjoys the considerable DVD collection, but also frequents the children's area, checking out books and making use of pictures in them.

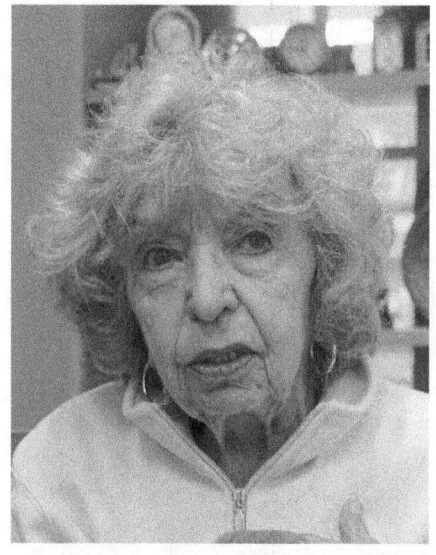  

Dušanka

Dušanka is not one to share her age, but she keeps herself young by being actively involved in life. She feels that the library is an integral part of life, and that we should all spend more time reading than watching television. She immigrated from Hungary as a teenager, joining her mother in New York and learning English in order to work for a wealthy family as a housekeeper. She is happy that life's events brought her to Pacific Grove.

Gordon

Gordon is now 93 and has been a loyal volunteer at the Pacific Grove Library for more years than he can recall, shelving books weekly and with care. He is known and loved by the library staff for his dependability and careful work. He loves being a part of the library, both as a patron and a volunteer. He retired from Monterey Peninsula College in 1989 after many years of teaching chemistry there.

Jerry

At the ripe old age of 90, Jerry passed away a few months after this photo was taken, in November of 2016. He was proud to share his age and remained very much a vital, involved member of the community. He was a life-long learner who had a special gift as an artist, with periodic shows of his work in local venues such as Juice & Java, and Monterey County Fair entries (and winners!). He said he could not imagine a life without books or libraries, and was seen in our library almost every day.

Ken

Ken, age 89, has been a regular library visitor and reads lots of books, to which the circulation desk staff members can attest. He loves the mystery section especially, and is always looking for something new there. He has been married for 60 years and was known locally as the owner of Scotch Bakery, in addition to running a gas station and, later, a photo lab in Carmel. He is a World War II veteran, serving in the U.S. Navy in the Pacific Rim.

Michelle

Michelle is 85 years old and lives conveniently right across the street from the library, which she has been actively making use of for over 30 years. She especially appreciates our extensive collection of audio-books, which she says have changed her life, giving her access to literature, entertainment, and information that her eyes no longer serve well. She listens to audio-books about five hours daily.

Rusty

Rusty, at 90 years old, is an active, friendly, and stylish woman who enjoys getting out and about in the community and makes the library a regular stop. She says she grew up near a library and learned early in life to make reading a constant pastime. It remains a very pleasant and vital part of her life.

Saul

At age 98, Saul is our senior-most participant in this exhibit, and the original inspiration for the project. He delights the entire library staff with his unflappable good cheer, beautiful smiles, and positive outlook during his daily visits. He enjoys checking out books and movies, which he makes good use of within the library collection, and often he just enjoys sitting in the rotunda and reading the newspaper. About the library, Saul says, "The library just makes life better!"

Ted

Ted is 86 years old and retired from a successful career as a local architect. He grew up in the Chicago area, where he was also a pilot. He is impressed during his library visits that there are "So many books!" - with always something new to keep him reading. He usually chooses one from a known author and one unknown, with particular focus in the mystery section.

John

John is a tall gentleman who always greets the library staff with a sweet smile. He's 84 years old and has lived locally since 1956. What he enjoys most about this library is the quiet peacefulness, enabling him to read the paper here, as well as find books to take home. He also, however, values the importance of the library to the community, especially to the young people, and appreciates that the library continues to serve all ages. He hopes it's "here to stay!"

LIBRARY STAFF AND PATRONS

Chubbs Lavalier
Peggy Langford

When I was young, a family reunion meant lots of great uncles and aunts—all bespectacled, white-haired and full of stories, WWII or otherwise.

I started working at the library in 2015 and had only been working at the reference desk a few months when a feisty, brilliantly blue-eyed older woman plunked herself down in the chair by mine and asked if I had any biographies of Elvis Presley. We talked at length about famous singers and their interesting lives. Before she left, she introduced herself as Chubbs Lavalier, and I always looked forward to her frequent reference questions. She would remind me every time she loved her P.G. library.

A coworker of mine, Shelley Nemeth, interviewed and photographed a baker's dozen of our senior patrons. My new friend was among them. Every time I visited the gallery, it brought back memories of my great uncles and aunts who were so full of life, stories, and laughter.

Working at the PGPL is a reminder of the importance of family, community, and sharing the love of reading and learning. Thank you, Chubbs Lavalier! You are the very reason I continue to work in a library. (See Shelley Nemeth's photograph and story for Chubbs in the following section.)

Stranded Book Drop
Indika Karunasiri

One day, when it was my turn to deal with the book drop, I went out with an empty cart, retrieved another cart full of books, brought it back to the library, and started the check-in process. In the meantime, one of our staff member's husband happened to drive by and saw the empty book drop all by itself at the corner of Grand and Central, and informed us of it. I ran outside to put it where it belonged. To my surprise, no one had put anything in from the slot to the ground. If it had been a windy day it would have become a runaway book drop. I did not know what I was thinking. To this day I do not let my mind wander when I am getting the book drop.

The Time I was Locked in the Library
William Neish

I was born at Ford Ord, and grew up in Pacific Grove. At age ten I made the papers for being locked by mistake in the Pacific Grove Public Library.

I spent endless hours in the P.G. library when I was little. I loved books and stories, which probably began because my mother would tell us opera, movie and Shakespeare plots as bedtime stories. A lot of fairy tales are very violent, like *The Robber Bridegroom*, in which a girl's finger is cut off with an axe and then found floating in a glass of wine. (In *Cinderella*, the stepmother is put into a pair of "red hot iron shoes" and "made to dance until she was dead.") Our copy of *Grimm's Fairy Tales* had half the stories marked with babysitter warnings in big black pen: "RATED X – PLEASE DO NOT READ TO MY CHILDREN."

Maybe that's why my mother eventually switched over to telling us *Romeo & Juliet, Carmen Jones* and *Gone with the Wind*. Some people might have died in them, but the death scenes were no match for the spectacular bloodbaths dripping across the pages of Grimm.

At any rate, once I learned to read for myself I loved getting stacks of storybooks from the library, and could spend hours reading them there or at home. Or in the car. Or during recess at school. So on this fateful day in 1975 when my mother brought me with her to the library to return some books, I told her I would be in the Children's Room, looking for more.

In retrospect, I think the key factor that proved my undoing was being too short to be seen above the checkout counter. My mother, who planned on being there for a while, knew I was toddling off deeper into the library, but the librarian on duty, who must have known the building was in the process of closing up for the day, did not. So no one stopped me.

It was the perfect storytime storm.

I selected a bunch of books and plunked myself down in an oversized bean bag chair that pretty much swallowed me up. (This also might have contributed to my going undetected.) All I know is, about a half hour later I was having trouble reading the pages of *A is for Annabelle* because the building had grown increasingly dim. And very quiet.

Wondering where my mother was, I wandered back to the checkout counter . . . only to find the building completely empty and as quiet as *Romeo & Juliet's* tomb! I WAS ABANDONED!

My storybooks dropped to the floor.

Over the years I have asked my mother how this could have happened, and she *claims* she thought I got tired of waiting and had just walked home. So (and this is where her role becomes a bit sketchy, from a social worker's point of view) she simply headed off for her modern dance class at MPC . . . which is how young divorcees kept in shape before the days of everyone having a gym membership.

(I will leave aside the fact that my mother was a preschool teacher by trade, and therefore a person you would expect to be adept at looking after children.) (I'm not bitter.)

But back to 1975.

With slowly percolating panic, I examined every door and found none would yield. It's possible a window would have opened, but that would have meant leaving it unlocked post-escape . . . and *clearly* the library was supposed to be locked up after hours. Who was I to challenge the system??

I found a side door with an old fashioned, brass push bar that could be depressed, yet there was a chain with a clasp (almost like a dog leash) wrapped around it. There were also intimidating electrical wires all about this doorframe, while a big red sign any 10-year-old could make out announced an ALARM WOULD SOUND if it were opened. For some reason, I imagined a SWAT team would arrive *immediately* if such an alarm went off and I would be hauled off who-knows-where.

It was now getting *quite* dark in my picturesque prison, and it occurred to me I could call my mother from the front desk. I felt bad going behind it, as another sign warned me this area was STAFF ONLY. But this had all sadly spiraled into a *Mission Impossible* type situation. No immediate help was forthcoming, however, for when my brother and sister answered the phone, they said our mom was out.

Though the light was quickly dying, I could make out a list of emergency phone numbers taped to the counter by the phone, and decided the time had come to call the police.

I should mention that throughout this ordeal, various residents were dropping returns through the book slot and could see me through the big glass doors. One lady asked me if I lived in there. Strangely, no one offered to wait with me until I was sprung (!)

When I did reach the police, they at first thought I was a prank caller. After I insisted that I was in fact a real child locked in the library, they (grudgingly, it sounded to me) said they'd send someone over. It seemed to take awhile ... with people continuing to drop off books and stare at me. 1975 Pacific Grove was simply not ready for this!

When two policemen arrived, they explained through the glass that they were unsure how to help me. Calls were being made to City Hall and I don't know where else as we spoke, yet obviously those buildings were now closed, as well, so no one was answering. It seems a need for a key to the library after hours had never arisen before, and no one knew where to find one.

Yes, it can happen here.

Finally I explained to them that I had in fact spied a side door I might get open, if they would first explain to the Police Department that the alarm would go off and I was not to be blamed. After staring at me for a minute, they told me this was a good idea.

I got the chain off the side door, it opened, and I was free. FREE FREE FREE! Bliss was short-lived, however, as one of the officers proceeded to question me with obvious suspicion. He frankly stated he believed I had slid into the library through the book deposit slot (I am not making this up) but then could not get back out. I can still see him today, with his crew cut hair and hateful burly face, ordering me over to the book slot to measure my head against it. The indignity!

It was eventually decided my head, though petite, was in fact too large to fit through the book slot, and this same officer gave me a ride home. We did not speak.

And so ended my night of terror. Fresh horrors arose the next day on Bentley Street, however, when my mother saw the local paper had identified me as Billy. "Billy? BILLY?" she said incredulously. *"Have they ever heard of a BILLY SHAKESPEARE??"*

(It seems petty to point out the article also mistakenly gave credit to the police for masterminding my escape, when in fact it was I myself who alerted them to the vulnerable side exit. Now the truth can be told.)

I am happy to report that this experience just about sums up my complete police record. It is true that decades later I was ticketed for eating a snack-sized bag of 7-11 brand Oriental Cracker Mix on public transport (beneath a sign clearly reading NO FOOD OR BEVERAGES.) And yet, let the jury note I could probably get that expunged from the system, as the police mistakenly claimed on my ticket that I was seen eating "trail mix" when it was, in fact, Oriental Cracker Mix.

I have the receipt, yet it is not my habit to challenge the police. Ever since they held my head up to a book drop, and called me Billy.

Our Path From the Library
Jacquelin LaVine Jones

My sister Sally and I spent a lot of time at the Pacific Grove Library. As I look back, walking home was always an adventure. At that time over 75 years ago, there was a roque court at the park across the street from the museum and we would stop and watch the old guys play. We would then walk a couple of blocks further on Central Ave. past the hotel.

One of these days, we were probably 8 and 10 years old, we came upon an older lady who was dressed in black from head to toe. Her manner of dress probably made her look even older. She was on the steps of the Centrella Hotel and having a hard time getting to the top. As any little girls would do, we went to help her. She pushed us away and said "Leave me alone." The sweet little old lady was drunk. So much for our good deed of the day.

Two blocks further on our way home, we would probably stop at Caledonia Park and swing or teeter-totter for a while.

We would then walk across the street to the empty lot where now stands the Masonic Hall. Next to that, lived a woman named Irma who lived in a little house which is now the ice cream store. Her baby was usually outside in his playpen and we would spend a few minutes playing with him.

We would then walk up Lighthouse Ave., past the Carmel Pinecone business which was then my Uncle Jack Irwins' house.

The end of our journey was in sight when we reached the corner of Lighthouse and Pacific Street, where we now have a bench honoring our mother. We would then cross Lighthouse to 210 Granite. There, we were met by our precious mother, and were the happiest, luckiest children in the world.

Our lovely old Victorian home was later sold by my older sister. There are now two apartment buildings on the property. Progress in some ways is very sad.

Caper at the Library
Jane Foley

My sister came to live with me in Pacific Grove during her high school years in the mid-1980s. This was the dawn of the in-home entertainment age, when people rented VCR machines along with their video cassettes. You had to leave a deposit of three hundred dollars, either on a credit card or in cash. I didn't "do" credit cards at the time and any spare cash would have gone living expenses. *9 ½ Weeks*, a steamy film with Mickey Rourke, had come out that year. Barbara and I wanted to see it but how to get a VCR? The wait list for our movie was about three weeks long.

I got the devilish idea to watch *9 ½ Weeks* at the Pacific Grove Public Library! We were hesitant with good reason. Sexual content was an integral part of the movie. I knew the alcove where the library's VCR was housed was somewhat isolated. It might just work in our favor. The call finally came: Mickey and Kim (Basinger) were waiting for us at the video store.

We walked our celluloid contraband up the street. The librarian was extremely helpful finding a second chair and another set of headphones. The TV and VCR were next to a tall rack of music cassettes that spun around like a sunglasses stand. No one else was there: the coast was clear. In went the film and down into darkness we were drawn: these two "beautiful people" have successful careers, but their personal relationships are lacking. *9 ½ Weeks* explores the boundaries of new romance. The viewers quickly become voyeurs at the edge of this sensual, erotic affair. But! Back to the library.

The machine is put on pause several times as patrons wander too close for comfort. An older man, mid-70s, has been looking at the cassettes for an unusually long time. He has on baggy pants and a parka unzipped half way. He ducks behind the rack of music cassettes whenever we make eye contact. Off goes the VCR, waiting for this Peeping Tom to go away. *He reminds me of someone familiar but I can't quite place him.*

The plot intensifies: he has been manipulating her. She breaks things off but her heart is still invested. *Barb and I are 'still invested'* but the fear of getting caught hovers like the afternoon fog. And! The old man is back. I won't resume our movie until it's safe. After a few more pauses, he leaves us alone.

It hits me. I *know* where I've seen our library guy:

Sitting alone on a park bench, in a modest dress, thick stockings and hairnet, Ruth Buzzy clutches her purse to her chest. Along comes Arte Johnson in baggy pants and a dark overcoat. Sitting next to her, "Uh... Wanna bite of my Walnettos?" the old guy croaks. Outraged, she bops him with her purse.

Oh! *The Walnettos guy* from *Laugh-In* I explain to Barb, as we make our way back to 19th Street.

The Art of the Library
Linnet Harlan

While libraries mean many things to many people, "art" may not be the first idea that comes to mind when someone thinks of the Pacific Grove Public Library. But the library is the repository of a plethora of art in many forms.

The most accessible art is the copies of paintings available to check out. Cassatt, Klee, Vermeer, Van Gough, Picasso, Seurat, and Monet are all represented by admittedly worn copies of their best paintings. But don't scoff at the impact copies, even poor ones, can have. More than once I have gone out of my way to see or been delighted by an unexpected encounter with the original of a library-lent copy of artwork my mother checked out of our local library during my childhood. I felt I was greeting an old friend. Art that is part of one's daily existence helps inform the eye and create the desire to experience more art.

Perhaps you prefer to engage with the original art in the library. If so, stroll around the building. Slow down. Allow the art to engage you.

Several paintings represent the library itself. One, by Howard W. Brod, is of the building's Grand Avenue side. Another, by Joseph Normann, is of the rotunda at the rear of the building. A third, a watercolor, was created for McDougall Brothers architectural firm in San Francisco and depicts the original Carnegie library while a fourth is a pencil sketch created for the Robert R. Jones architectural firm of Carmel and shows proposed alterations to the library in 1949.

Seeing the partial views allows the viewer to focus on the geometry of the building while the full-on representations help the viewer to understand how the library or plans for it have changed through the years.

Personal favorites of mine include the Harold C. Landaker paintings scattered throughout the library. "Red Sunset (Cypress Point)" and the mural in the children's section are two of the most obvious. The mural's seven panels depict scenes from children's books, including a boy who leans against a tree reading while a clipper ship sails by (*Two Years Before the Mast,* set in part California during the Mexican colonial era),a girl wearing ruby slippers accompanied by a smiling scarecrow and a Cheshire cat, and a peg-legged pirate chortling over a treasure chest crammed with gold. One former librarian admits to craving Landaker's untitled piece, now in the children's section, showing an elephant assisting in taking down a circus tent. Some might argue the tent is going up. Look carefully at the mood of the painting, and see what you think.

I also enjoy the four watercolors by Louise McCaslin commissioned by realtor John Reynolds to illustrate properties he was selling. Though as far as I can tell, all the buildings represented in the paintings have now been replaced, these simple watercolors convey a real sense of Pacific Grove to me. Note that the painting of the gas station specifically provides contact information for Mr. Reynolds in case a viewer from another era was moved by the painting to explore a purchase. No phone number appears, which perhaps provides a hint as to when the paintings were created.

Watercolors of the "Pryor House" on Ocean View Boulevard and the Seven Gables house by Marie Russell and a watercolor of the Centrella Inn by "Tarin" provide images from the past of buildings you can still see today on a stroll around town.

A handsome "Library Quilt" by Gail Abeloe, Sue Broenkow and Erica Howe, an untitled plaster bronze-faced sculpture of a sleeping boy holding a book, and a glazed ceramic sand dollar are all evidence that the library's art isn't confined to paintings. An untitled abstract of greens and blues with yellow and red by Joan Savo demonstrates not all the paintings are representational.

Another personal favorite is the cheery "Push Me, Pull Me" bronze statue by Gary White; it's sure to induce a smile. Appearing on the pedestal for the sculpture, the biography of the artist may make you gasp.

Perhaps the most Pagrovian piece of art is Lester Zucchini's 1980 poster photograph of City Hall, painted white as it was for so many years. Evening has fallen; the glow from a streetlight creates a half-light accentuating the mist and shadow shrouding the corner of the building. Looking at the poster, I inhale cool salt air and feel P.G. in my bones.

* The library's holdings of artwork are so rich, I've only mentioned a small portion. I've also omitted mention of some of the more "important" works to allow you to discover them for yourself. When you explore the library for its art treasures, be sure to stop at the library's Nancy and Steve Hauk Gallery to see what's new or what's been rehung so it can be seen in a new light.

My Self-guided Tour
Lois Carroll

It felt like a warm sweater wrapped around me the first time I walked into that library: comfortable, relaxed, navigable, and pleasant. The green speckled rug on the floor muffled the sound, but the library hummed busily with human voices both young and old. There was no cold and lonely silence.

Start with a quick self-guided tour, I thought. I can see the division of fiction and non-fiction on the left and right sides of the main walkway. I pass by the computers on the left, where several people intently search the Internet. I enter a bright room with cozy padded seats surrounded by a wall of windows facing out in the direction of the Monterey Bay. The magazines are spread out logically in alphabetical order on metal shelves with the older issues hidden comfortably underneath like eggs inside a shell. I observe some very old wooden chairs and wooden tables. Sit on these chairs for more than an hour and your body begins to ache and protest. But this furniture lasts forever.

I examine the old clocks and timepieces sitting like retired soldiers on the upper shelves and in glass cabinets, aware that there must be an interesting story behind this collection that I would love to know. Across the way there's the new art gallery with a bunch of large, expensive library art books sitting just outside the entrance to enhance the enjoyment of the art hanging inside. My heart warms at the sight of the old card catalog and I lovingly open one of the drawers just for the sensual pleasure of seeing all those yellowing cards typed up on old manual typewriters in perfect order. I discover they contain a catalog of old Pacific Grove newspaper articles. It's a perfect spot to dig into the history of the town's origins and development.

Ok, now get a library card. There's a friendly face behind the circulation desk to help me register. I listen to the instructions for connecting online. Now I see the reference librarian at a small desk just outside the children's room. I walk into the enchanting children's library with the small chairs and tables, the display of books for the upcoming holiday, the posters and artwork on the glass wall separating the children's room from the rest of the library. I recognize the corner for story hours with the special rug in front of the storyteller's chair, the display board for telling the stories visually and the stuffed animals and puppets. I know I'll return soon to this area with my preschool-aged grandson.

But first I want to take something home with me now that I have that precious card. Feeling like a kid in a candy shop and marveling at the sight of all those materials free for checkout, I get that giddy feeling of finding tantalizing books, DVDs, audio books on CDs, large print books, newspapers and materials for teens and the pure pleasure of being here. I help myself to some free donated magazines and also pick up the latest issues of the *Monterey County Weekly* and the *Cedar Street Times*. At the self-checkout station, I unload my precious selections and use my new library card at the machine. I'm happy and sit on a bench in the warm sun across the street in Jewell Park, thumbing through my selections and watching the children chase each other vigorously across the green expanse of grass. It doesn't get any better than this, I thought. Thanks Mr. Carnegie for this gift of a library established so long ago and updated for this town that fits me like a glove.

The Center of Town
Ronald Ochsner

Many years ago when attending college, my wife and I met for the first time in a library. Later on when we married, I was in the Army and stationed at Fort Ord; consequently, our first home was an apartment in Pacific Grove. I love libraries and Pacific Grove.

We enjoyed our time here in Pacific Grove, it being a small, friendly Victorian town on the coast with little traffic, beautiful flowers, a coastal forest of wind-blown pine and cypress trees, ocean-walking trails (especially Lovers Point—we were newlyweds), plus a variety of wildlife from Monarch butterflies to deer and sea otters. Everything we liked about the area was so close and easy to get to—Monterey, Carmel, Point Lobos and Big Sur.

Generally, the weather here is mild with a cool breeze bringing together a refreshing scent of pine trees and ocean. While living here in February 1962, we had a surprise from the weather—lots of snow. It actually stayed on the ground for two days, enough to build a snowman on our balcony. He lasted for three days—cool!

Following my military service, we settled in San Diego (my wife's hometown) to work and raise our family, a son and daughter. Almost every year, starting in about 1988, we would spend part of our vacation on the peninsula (Pacific Grove, Monterey or Carmel). Afterwards, we would continue on to visit family and friends in northern California.

As time went by (a lot of time), my granddaughter became the manager of 17 Mile Drive Village in Pacific Grove. This made our visits here even better. She married; they have a home here and she gave birth to a wonderful baby boy. Unfortunately, my wife of 54 years developed Alzheimer's and passed away in 2016. I sold our home in San Diego and moved into 17 Mile Drive Village.

Right after moving in, I went to the Pacific Grove Library to research the community, find out what was available and where to go. I found the staff very friendly and extremely helpful. The library is a storehouse of knowledge and information, and I go there almost every day to research subjects and catch up on current events.

The Pacific Grove Library is located in the heart of town, making it easy to move from one place to another. It's across the street from the Jewell Park and the gazebo, the Natural History Museum, and the Chamber of Commerce, just one block from Pacific Grove's unique shops, restaurants, bakeries and art galleries, and only two blocks from the ocean and the beautiful walking trail to Lovers Point.

Just a few driving minutes from the library, I have found (with the help of library materials) a variety of interesting places: Hopkins Marine Station (a seal sanctuary), the American Tin Cannery building with its shops, restaurants and artist lofts, Monterey Bay Aquarium, the Point Pinos tide pools, the Pacific Grove Lighthouse, the Monarch Habitat Sanctuary and the Asilomar State Beach and Conference Center.

My hobby is art and I enjoy the natural beauty of Pacific Grove. I've see this beauty change, not only with the seasons but also with the rising and setting of the sun and ocean tides. Another special moment is when the low fog slips in and creates a mystical, enchanted-like stillness—so cool!

I enjoy opening my door and seeing deer eating on the lawn and smelling the fresh scent of pine trees and the ocean; it's always a new day with new opportunities. I'm thankful for Pacific Grove, its wonderful people and, of course, the library.

Windows of Pacific Grove
Bobbie Morrison
Pacific Grove Library Director, retired

Since my retirement, I've been enjoying my many walks along the Recreation Trail in P.G.. I love watching for whales, otters, birthing seals; what are the birds up to this time of year? I enjoy my interactions with dog owners and my surrogate dogs.

But each time I pass the intersection of Sea Palm at Ocean View, where Mermaid Avenue ends, I think about the library before 1978. A house just around the corner has a piece of P.G. Library history: a window that used to be part of the library building. It's painted turquoise with white inner trim.

Up near the corner of Laurel Ave. and 13th Street (maybe it's 14th; the owner and their neighbors will know), you'll find another one. This window is green and has two shades of green trim, I think.

Now, the third window, I always have trouble finding; it's kind of like going on a treasure hunt. It was on a house near Hillcrest at Forest. I looked again today, but I can't find it. Has it been taken out by a remodel? Or is it hidden behind a tree that used to be a bush? Am I just blind to it? Or do I have the wrong street? It's right up there somewhere—maybe you can find it.

Another house in town has a window and two sets of doors from the old library, but I was told some years ago that they can't be seen from the street, and now I don't even know which street it is. Maybe you live there or in the neighborhood? Northrup Kirk bought the windows and installed them in his home; he told me so after I had spoken at a Rotary meeting many years ago. The window and double doors were on the wings of the library, facing the patio at the library's entrance. Now they open on to a backyard where family and friends gather.

These windows and doors, and a few more, were sold at public auction when the 1978 expansion was done. The new owners cleaned them up, installed them, repainted them, made them part of their homes. The people who live in these homes now, do they know the history? Do they ever visit the library and wonder why the windows on the back part of the library look so familiar?

This is a small piece of P.G. history. When I walk through our neighborhoods, I wonder how much more of P.G. history lives in these homes. Has any other part of the city's history been re-purposed for someone's home, their yard, their decor?

A Ride Around the Block

During the last expansion of the Pacific Grove Public Library (c. 1977), we who worked at the library thought the mural by Harold Landaker that graced the wall in the Children's Department was painted directly on the wall and we would lose this piece of history when the wing was torn down. Imagine our surprise and pleasure when the demolition crew found out the mural was painted on canvas and came peeling off very nicely!

Margaret McBride, Library Director, had seen a story in the *Herald* about a young woman living in Carmel Valley who had just returned to the area after living in Florence, Italy, for a few years while she learned art restoration techniques following the 1966 flood of the Arno River. Margaret contacted the woman, who agreed to clean and restore the mural for $250. Doesn't sound like much today, does it? However, in those days, it took the library over two years to raise $25,000 to pay for the furnishings and equipment needed in the expanded building. Two hundred fifty dollars to restore a painting was not in the budget.

As the Children's Librarian at the time, it fell to me to find the money. I came up with the idea of having a "Trike-a-Thon" with the preschool story-time groups soliciting donations based on how many laps the children rode their trikes (or Big Wheels) around a course. We were able to use the playground behind Robert H. Down School on a Saturday morning, borrowed traffic cones from Public Works, rounded up a few volunteers to keep track of the laps, provided cookies and punch, and set the children on their way. Less than an hour later, the last tired child finished his last lap on his trike. And over the next few weeks, we received about $300 in donations.

When the mural restoration was completed, it went back up on the wall, at the same orientation as the previous location. Many people thought it was the same room, just repainted. However, the young woman who did the restoration had come up with a clever solution to any future issues of saving the mural. It is now mounted on several panels, which are inside the "track" frame. If you look closely at the boy and girl sitting on either side of the tree, you will see the sections of the tree don't quite match. Originally the boy leaned against a tree at one end of the mural, the girl leaning against a tree at the other. Now they sit back-to-back, sharing the "same" tree.

For many years, people who have previously lived in P.G. and remember the mural come into the library to show it to their children, and they almost always comment on how nice it is that nothing ever changes in P.G..

Steven Silveria
Upon his retirement 2017

Library and Information Services Director at the City of Pacific Grove from March, 2013 to May 12, 2017.
This review was given by his wife at his farewell party.

Steven believes in hard work, and people who work hard. He grew up in Merced, California, swamping melons, picking peppers and bucking hay as a young teen, and being told he wasn't smart enough for college, to stick to shop class instead. Steven went on to earn a BA in Philosophy from CSU-Chico in 1980 and a full-fellowship Masters of Library and Information Science from UC Berkeley in 1982; he was the first college graduate in his family. He remembers what it feels like to be young and seen as "less than," and has always welcomed children and teens to be exactly who and how they are in every library he's managed.

Steven's path to the P.G. Library began at the movies. The Merced Theatre led to a film assistant job at Merced County Library in 1976. He brought films to library branches from Yosemite Valley to rural towns like South Dos Palos (where the projector ran from an extension cord to the grocery store next door.) After college Steven taught at Merced Community College (2/5 time librarian, 3/5 time philosophy), then was hired as a children's librarian at Prunedale branch of the Monterey County Free Libraries, where he was known for inviting a boa constrictor—a real, live, snake—to story-time! He wanted story-time to engage children through books <u>and</u> experiences.

Steven brought his respect for hard-working people and his love of community to his jobs at Monterey County Free libraries (1984), Watsonville Public Library (1998), Salinas Public Library (2008) and P.G. Library (2013)—developing adult literacy programs, supporting Spanish, Vietnamese and other language collections, and developing the first bi-lingual children's collection at P.G.. One of Steven's best hires was a woman who turned in her farmworker field hoe to become an outstanding Seaside literacy assistant. He helped develop the Watsonville city diversity training curriculum (and was its first trainer), actively seeking and welcoming diversity in staff and patrons his entire professional life. Steven never forgot to acknowledge the importance of every single person at every job, including here at P.G., he's always known the custodian by name, their families and life stories.

In his four years as P.G.'s Library Director, Steven worked with the Friends of the Library, Library Board, city government and citizens to envision a community art gallery from a back staff office, to upgrade the front and staff entrances, to clear shelving and open the library's central areas for greater use and programs. During his tenure, circulation increased by over 20 percent and programming for adults and children by 100 percent. The P.G. Library Renewal Project, now underway, will restore the heart of the original Carnegie section of the library, upgrade restroom accessibility and provide a renewed community library for the 21st century.

The P.G. Library Renewal Project is not Steven's first building project. He helped design, move, or renovate 15 libraries in his career, from a former chicken coop in Parkfield, to new libraries in Soledad, Watsonville, Buena Vista, Greenfield, to renovated or repurposed libraries in Pajaro, Aromas, Marina, Big Sur, King City, San Ardo, Freedom, Salinas (Main and Cesar Chavez), and now, P.G.. Designing facilities to meet community needs also means technology. At Seaside Library, Steven developed the first public Internet service in the tri-county area in 1994 and was recognized by Vice President Al Gore. He was the system administrator for a tri-county shared union catalog, helped develop a teen Apple Lab at Salinas, conducted technology reviews for libraries across Northern California, and spoke at statewide conferences on future technologies as a consultant.

Steven is ending his 42-year career in public libraries in Pacific Grove, the town he's lived in for 20 years, at the library he unexpectedly "fell in love with," reluctantly leaving the staff and the community who mean so much to him. How fitting that Steven's last working day was the 109th anniversary of the opening of the P.G. Public Library!

Growing Older and Wiser in Pacific Grove
Keith Larson

Pacific Grove is a story that keeps writing itself, each of us are the authors creating an individual and collective experience of our little town.

Having grown up here wherever I go there is a story memory that has already been recorded and one set in the present waiting to be told if only to myself or in a casual conversation with someone else. I met a man at one of the writing classes for this book. His name was Saul and he has lived in Pacific Grove a number of years. Saul is a man in his 90's with a big smile on his face. as he wrote a piece with one of his memories of Pacific Grove he laughed and was having a good time with the writing assignment. Without knowing the details of his life, I just knew that smile on his face was his life story. Although our stories are so different I like to also connect with the common themes that we all share so as not to feel isolated and separate, those common themes include the need to feel loved, happy and useful to others. Saul's life story is one that I'd like to aspire to, that smile on his face is the best advice one could ever give or receive. (See Shelley Nemeth's photograph and story for Saul.)

SECTION 8

DOWNTOWN AND ITS MANY PLEASURES

SOCIALIZE, DINE AND SHOP 'TIL YOU DROP!

SeaSer: A Dragon Dines in P.G.
Ajax Minor
aka Paul Sinsar, Pebble Beach

First, allow me to introduce myself. My name is SeaSer, pronounced Caesar, as in the famous Roman general. My parents conceived the name while I was *in ovo*. Since I am a winged sea serpent, it's not terribly original. But they felt it flexible if I were to have been female. They could have inverted the syllables and called me Circe, another star from Classical times. And, I should say, they were very particular about the pronunciation as they greatly admired Caesar. They had known him, you see. Dragons live a very long time.

I am fortunate to have a bit of notoriety, as a rendering of me serves as the logo for one of the local golf courses. And I do play golf. But that is another story. Sufficient to say I enjoy all, or most, things human. Especially food.

Interestingly, Pacific Grove has, bar none, one of the greatest collections of fine restaurants in the area. This is probably due to its proximity to the resorts on the Monterey Peninsula. It pains me to say this, but America, away from resorts and big cities, can be a culinary desert. So Pacific Grove is fortunate in its location.

Now I'd like to take you on a peripatetic overview of my favorite restaurants.

Soaring into P.G., as it is called by the locals, is uplifting and raises the spirits for a good meal. One gains a particularly arresting vantage, with all of the gaily-colored seaside cottages juxtaposed against the lovely blue waters of Monterey Bay. Homes are yellow with red trim, blue with green—well, the combinations boggle the mind.

Having worked up a great appetite on the flight in, I've decided to visit Passionfish first. And I do have quite an appetite! Some have called me a gourmand due to the great quantities of food I can consume; but I assure you nothing is further from the truth.

And I do have a passion for fish. In fact, the great schools of salmon and cod, following the Pacific currents, first attracted me to Monterey Bay. But of Passionfish I have two comments. First, you must sample the sturgeon. It is exceptional. And it's right here in my backyard, rather than having to swim or fly the distance to the Columbia River. Sturgeon itself is interesting. It is a prehistoric fish and looks it, with small spikes sprouting all over its surface. Horny, I'd call it. But what else would one call a species that's reproduced for 60 million years?

Sturgeon has a firm flesh and one of 'pale' flavors common to freshwater fish. And it remains firm on the fork. It is best paired with an orange wine from Jura or Slovenia, which takes its name from the color, resulting from exposure to the air and the resulting oxidation. And this is the real treasure! Passionfish has the most extensive and varied wine list on the Peninsula, so no matter what you chose for an entrée, there will be an excellent wine to accompany it.

Next, I'd like to stroll up the street to an Italian restaurant that used to be known as Joe Rombi's and is now La Mia Cucina.

Despite what you may have heard, dragons are not strictly carnivores. My recommendation would be the eggplant parmesan, delicately fried and topped with a very light sauce that is sweet rather than bitter or acidic. But the best part is a big hug by Paula, co-owner and maîtresse d'! Her enthusiasm just puts one in a great mood, which is essential for a good appetite. Oh, and I would suggest a Montepulciano, made from the eponymous grape, moderately priced, and particularly rich in monoterpenes, giving it a white pepper finish.

Next, we'll stroll across the street to Fandango. And since I've now had two meals, I do mean stroll.

The proprietors of Fandango are Pierre and his lovely wife, Marianne. You may recall that Pierre had been maître d' for Club 19 at the Pebble Beach Lodge. Club 19 is no longer extant and has been replaced by The Bench, which serves the best plates of roasted vegetables you've ever tasted. As I said, I like vegetables and, as you might expect, am proficient at roasting. But we're talking about Pacific Grove, not Pebble Beach.

Pierre will often greet you himself at the door. With his dark hair and moustache, and round, cheerful face, he looks as if he had been dropped in directly from Dijon.

At Fandango, they always give me a seat next to the wall so I can stretch out my tail. I would not want to put any of the diners or the wait staff at risk by having my tail lolling about in the middle of the floor.

The escargot are delightful, plump and juicy, and I usually have a dozen along with a baguette to sop up the garlic and butter sauce. For the main course, I would recommend the cassoulet: white beans, duck and sausage. It is especially appropriate on a cool, damp night, of which there are many in Pacific Grove! And of course, what would a French meal be without a soufflé for dessert? This particular evening I am offered both chocolate and Grand

Marnier. Since I have the room, I decide on both. Oh, and the wine list offers something for every budget: Pierre has always priced his wines modestly above his original cost so there are some real bargains!

Leaving Fandango, I stretch my wings and decide to fly over to our last stop of the evening, Jeninni. Now, you may be wondering how I fit into these establishments. Well, we dragons always possess some sort of magic or other, and I am able to scale myself down to human size. There it is.

I decide to fly to Jeninni, which is not too far, but gives me a vantage of the main street, which dips down and rolls upward, almost a reflection of the sea swells hard by the town.

At Jeninni you are greeted by Thamin, who is less effusive than Paula but equally gracious and welcoming. He is recognizable by a distinct lack of hair, which is actually quite becoming on him.

Jeninni offers a variety of dishes in the Mediterranean style: Spanish, Italian and Middle Eastern. Seasoning is the magic of the food. Exotic spices such as Za'atar, sumac and urfa are used. Personally, I like the house-made sausages: Loukaniko, a Greek pork sausage with fennel and Merguez, a North African lamb sausage. Having just had a great dish of white beans, I need to be careful, since the volatile combination of my fiery breath and a touch of flatulence present a fire hazard. But a glass of pink Prosecco settles one's stomach. And the wine list, though not as encyclopedic as Passionfish's, is varied and reasonable.

For dessert, I decide on goat flan. I love goat. Usually roasted. A technique I've perfected myself, if I may brag a bit.

At last, I emerge and lift myself, with some effort, enjoying the quaint early 20th century stores on Lighthouse and the magnificent palms on Pine. They are not called Royal, but should be. The night air is sharp and I finally land at Point Joe and fall asleep to the sound of the surf breaking on Spanish Bay.

Victorian Corner Restaurant
Domenic and Mary Aliotti
by Patricia Hamilton

Mary and Dominic Aliotti.

One of the most beautiful and historic buildings in Pacific Grove is home to Victorian Corner Restaurant, built in 1893 as one of the first commercial Victorians on Lighthouse Ave. Today Victorian Corner stands proud showing off its vivid colors, which attract attention from locals and visitors around the globe. It is regarded as one of the most photographed buildings in Pacific Grove.

Victorian Corner was established by the Aliotti family in 1977. Even as a young boy in Sicily, Paul Aliotti had a dream of someday having his own business. "It is the American dream to have your own business and I feel that I accomplished it with a vengeance," said Paul. He and his wife Sandy were very hands-on and worked hard to ensure that their business grew each year.

As the years went by, their son Domenic, who grew up working in the restaurant, made it apparent that he wanted to carry on the tradition and keep Victorian Corner alive. He started as a young boy working in the kitchen, standing on milk crates next to his dad, learning how things worked in the kitchen. Over time he learned how to cook and then manage the entire restaurant.

"To run a restaurant it is very important to understand and appreciate each job that goes into making a successful restaurant run like a well-oiled machine," Domenic has preached over the years, as he mastered how to manage a busy restaurant that serves breakfast, lunch and dinner.

Domenic met his wife Mary at Pacific Grove High School. Little did he know then when he asked the cheerleader out on a date that they would be running their own restaurant in the town they both grew up in.

"Domenic's mom called me in one night to help out;

Historical Tidbits
Elaine Hermann

There was a fire in what was the Grove Theater in the early 1950s. The weekly newspaper for that week had several photos of the fire; the photos and the story were on the front page and continued inside as well. The library had the specific week's newspaper on microfiche as of about four or five months ago.

A medical office on the corner of Lighthouse shared a wall with the theater and was damaged by smoke and water from the hoses. The two physicians, Dr. Albert Herrmann and Dr. Richard Hane were forced to relocate, moving to 702 Lighthouse once construction of that building (which also housed a dentist's office and the Masonic Temple) was complete. The fire was started by a lit cigarette left in the theater after it closed for the night.

The theater became Kidwell's Paint Store. The medical office became a furniture or housewares store, now a physical therapy office. 702 Lighthouse, which became the physicians' new office, is now Toastie's.

Toastie's dining areas were once two exam rooms, the physician's office with desk, the waiting room, and the work area for the nurse and receptionist.

In the summer of about 1955 there was a great white shark attack right at Lovers Point, below the swimming pool area. Teenagers were frolicking on the beach and in the shallow water right off the sand when a boy was attacked by a shark. Someone rushed to the office of Dr. Hane, who apparently went to the scene, but the boy died from the injuries.

I was only seventeen. Then she called me the next night to help out again," Mary said. "Before I knew it I had a fulltime job working at Victorian Corner."

Domenic and Mary continue to run Victorian Corner like that well-oiled machine, making it one of the most successful restaurants in Pacific Grove. This past year Victorian Corner celebrated 40 years in business, becoming the longest running restaurant in Pacific Grove owned and operated by one family. Victorian Corner specializes in amazing breakfasts, delicious sandwiches for lunch and homemade pasta for dinner. They have three separate menus for all times of the day, with a wide variety of options. "People taste the quality and thank me for offering such amazing food," Domenic says.

Domenic and Mary take pride in their family restaurant, hoping that one day one of their children might be interested in carrying on the Aliotti tradition. "Dom and Juliana enjoy bringing their friends to the restaurant after school to eat. Dom's favorite is a grilled cheese and french fries, and Juliana favors our homemade pastas. We enjoy seeing them with their friends so we can hear about their day and how school was," says Mary. And for now, Domenic and Mary enjoy working at the restaurant and visiting with the many regular customers, as well as meeting new people from all over the world.

Charlie and Kate at Grove Market
Charlie Higuera and daughter Kate Matuz

as told to Patricia Hamilton

Charlie is a Mutsun and Eselen native local Indian. His mother, Carrie Corona, and father, Joe "Chico" Higuera, lived in San Juan Bautista and relocated to the Monterey Peninsula 1929. The brothers, meat-cutters, used a horse-drawn wagon outfitted with a big ice box to deliver meat to Big Sur. Charlie's maternal great-grandmother, Ancension Solansarno, was a tribal shaman and the last tribe member to speak their native tongue.

Charlie was born in 1933 at home in New Monterey, and moved to Pacific Grove in 1945, where he worked several years in the meat business, with 15 years as meat-cutter and manager of the meat department at Forest Hill Market (now the site of Trader Joe's). He opened Grove Market and erected the trademark Grove Market sign in 1969 when it needed to be replaced. He bought, remodeled, then sold what is now Jerome's Carmel Valley Market.

"My whole life is family, customers and community," Charlie says. He provides the barbecue for the Breakers Club, Taste of P.G., the Police Department, Pony Baseball, P.G. Auto Rally, and the high school, among many events and venues. "The Bud Giles family (owners of the Grove Market building) has been good to us. We appreciate them very much."

Daughter Kate is married to George Matuz and has managed the market since 2000. Her motto is, "We're always there for each other. Sacrifice? You can do it." Her mother-in-law, age 90, lives in a granny unit at Kate's house. She sees her brother and sisters every day. Marge, the mother of Charlie's children (Dan, Kate, Gary, and Karen), works at Grove Market along with daughter Karen, and Karen's children John and Kristy. Son Gary retired from Granite Construction. Dan owns Beck Drywall. With 13 grandchildren and six great-grandchildren, the Higuera family has huge family reunions every Easter and many other holidays at the Carmel Valley Community Park. Charlie always provides his ever-popular barbecued meats.

Charlie was best friends with Morrie Fisher for 70 years and is adjusting to the recent loss of his friend and golfing buddy.

Welcome to Your New Home Town
Judy Obbink

happy volunteer

We decided to retire in a little quiet town by the ocean. First thing I did was go to a local bank and get a checking account, second thing I did was decide to try the little local town market with the rounded roof.

I found everything I needed and went to check out. When it was time to pay I proudly wrote my first check, number 101 to Grove Market. The checker looked at my check and called out in a loud voice 'Hey Charlie, looks like we got a new customer by the name of Obbink". Charlie dropped what he was doing behind the meat counter and came over and shook my hand saying welcome to Grove Market.

I knew right then we had truly moved to a perfect Home Town. Twenty years later I still go there.

Reflections of a Pacific Grove Local
Vanessa Bredthauer

retired school teacher

In the beginning, I never thought I'd be able to call myself a true local. But 42 years later, here I am ... a real local. We fell in love with Pacific Grove in 1975, bought a little Victorian close to town and thought we'd fix it up and move to Vermont. But after getting jobs and getting hooked on the life here, we settled in for the long haul.

But this piece isn't really about us. It's about the people and the pace of life we found in Pacific Grove. For over four decades I have come to depend on my relationships with the owners and staff who work in downtown P.G.

My husband, Ed, took our daughter every Thursday to the library and the children's librarian got to know her so well that she always had a stack of books ready for her. I could not live without the group at P.G. Hardware, who, always with smiles, continually solve every problem I bring them.

Then, of course, there is Grove Market, which I have been known to visit five times in one day. I meet friends there often, so of course we have to chat, catching up on local happenings. And if I can't find something, they often times will order it for me. I taught fourth grade to the grandchildren of the owners of P.G. Cleaners, and love to catch up with their accomplishments every time I pick up my cleaning. And by the way, they miraculously removed red wine stains on my white linen slacks … four different times (and no, it wasn't my fault!).

And when I need cheering up or a creative gift for a friend, I visit Tessuti Zoo or Fusion Confusion … two remarkable 'feel good' shops with inspired handmade textiles and glass, with owners who sparkle too. Every Thursday a group of friends and I have coffee at Joe's La Piccola Casa. I've gotten to know many of the other patrons there, too. There's always a reason to chat, sometimes in Italian.

The real beauty of Pacific Grove goes way beyond the historic architecture, the lovely beach front, and the quaint size. It revolves around the people who live here and work here, and have found that taking time to really get to know each other is the reason we all remain.

Sacred Massage—Butter Me Up
Michele Pietrantonio

My favorite place in P.G. is my place of business, my favorite people are my wonderful precious clients. My private pedicure studio is nestled in the back of Danielle's Hair Design, built and designed with love from my guy Allan Mill. It is an enchanted, special space created for my clients. My clients love their treatments, but through the years my business has become more than that. We have come to build relationships that are life-long. It's our sacred space for me and all the beautiful people who sit across from me. We have shared birth, death, despair and bliss thru nine years of business. Just blocks from the beach on 17th street I can step out and see the sea. I am a transplant from L.A. and have been a resident for 14 years in our Bay. I am also blessed to have been able to open and create my business. I can't take all the credit as I was given the opportunity by Danielle to let me be unique in creating this sacred space for all our cherished guest who enter our place of business. Someday, when I will look back I will close my eyes, smell the sea air and remember how great P.G. was to me.

Forest Hill Barber Shoppe
Cut and Rumble: A Local Barber Uses Motorcycles (and Metaphors) to Help Out Strangers
Fred Reynolds
as written by Joe Ede

Books like *Falling into Grace* by Adyashanti and *Love* by Mother Teresa aren't usually the type of literary fare one finds in a men's barbershop. But Fred Reynolds isn't your average chap with scissors and a straight-edge. Of all the books in his shop, *Generosity* by Gordon McDonald is probably the sharpest reflection of the man. As his customers know, during the last two weeks of September they either have to go without a trim or visit another barber, because Reynolds is somewhere between California and Montana with two of his good friends, on a mission of giving they refer to as Spirit Ride.

In explaining its purpose, Reynolds speaks frequently in metaphor: "It's like a dam with a causeway and the water flows more and more; the mud in the way is self-centeredness, and we are channels for generosity."

Reynolds gives fellow Spirit Rider Perry Shoulders credit for naming the annual run, coined on a solo trip through the desert of southeastern Oregon. It was there that Shoulders came across a hitchhiker and his dog, parched in the relentless heat and in need of help. It was then that Shoulders also unknowingly created the group's oft-used catchphrase, "How can I help you?" Being on a motorcycle, he couldn't offer a lift, but he could run on to the next town and bring them back water, snacks, and a sun-shielding sombrero.

He later shared his story with Reynolds and fellow rider Hugh Seagreaves, fostering an infectious enthusiasm toward philanthropy that has the men devoting time every year to motoring across the open places and towering peaks of the West, helping out their fellow humans with everything from automotive fixes to food. For one down and out family in Jensen, Utah, they sponsored a family vacation.

Reynolds calls Seagreaves, his brother-in-law, a mentor. Seagreaves takes to the skies for Angel Flight, which connects terminally ill cancer patients to pilots who offer free flights to hospitals with experimental treatment programs.

Reynolds admired this compassion, and wanted to do something too.

"I don't have a plane," he remembers thinking, "but I have a motorcycle."

He saves tips and any other extra income he can salvage, which doesn't seem like much, but he admits he is surprised by the amount of money he has been able to save in the years since the first Spirit Ride.

"The first year I only had three hundred eighty," Reynolds says, "but each year the money seemed to multiply and by the fourth year, we all had over a thousand dollars."

Faith doesn't enter the dialog until a customer asks if there is a religious side to Reynolds' charitable instincts.

"Religion is a vehicle, like a BMW or a Toyota," says Reynolds, a Seventh Day Adventist. "People get too hung up on what they're driving."

Reynolds says added inspiration came from watching the likes of Hopalong Cassidy, Roy Rogers and Gene Autry on TV—old guys, like him, out to offer a hand up. The Spirit Ride fellows feel as if they are living the life they watched other men act out as television's first action heroes.

"It's the idea of the golden rule," Reynolds says. "Treating one's neighbor as yourself is what drives us, but I'm more drawn than I am driven.

They are drawn annually to La Vida Mission south of Farmington, New Mexico. It was here in the 1950s that Shoulders' adopted mother, Vida, came across a group of Native American orphans living in old cars. The site has since been converted into a safe haven complete with a medical facility, dental clinic, and K-8 school. It's one indication that their regular mission runs deeper than buddies enjoying an adventure with a little philanthropy in the sidecar. One alum even gave up his motorcycle last year, selling it so he could move to Chile and do missionary work in a hospital full time.

The generosity tends to spread as the ride progresses, he adds. During a gas station stop they noticed a car with what Reynolds calls "maypops," tires so bald they could burst at any time. As the men spoke to the car owner and offered to buy him new tires, he seemed a little shocked. The man at the auto shop was even more surprised—and threw in a new set of shocks.

Being a former pilot in the Navy, Reynolds is a whiz with engines, keeping his Yamaha FJR 1300 in pristine condition and rehabbing stranded vehicles back into gear. His view of the world's working parts, however, places him in a more humble place. "I'm just a spark plug," he says, "in an internal combustion engine."

Charles "Fred" Reynolds—P.G. Loves You

Every person is potentially divine, all of P.G. is heavenly, and every event is thrilling and fulfilling. P.G. is like the Garden of Eden without the snake. Everybody loves P.G., but what makes P.G. different is that P.G. loves *you* back.

Mum's Place
Mimi Sheridan

At first glance, one might be surprised to see such a well-stocked quality furniture store as Mum's Place in a small town like P.G. But according to owner Mugo Tersakyan, the secret is that it's a regional business. They serve customers not only on the Monterey Peninsula but in the Bay Area and as far away Sacramento and Fresno. P.G. is relatively hard to get to, but anchor businesses such as this enhance the community and the economy by drawing people who might not come otherwise.

Mugo, of Armenian descent, originally came to Pacific Grove from his home in Paris to visit his sister. When he could not find a job in his field, electrical engineering, he rented a small store and began to establish a furniture business. He's been at the current location for 24 years, and has expanded from 6,000 square feet to 10,000 square feet. The historic building, on Forest Avenue just across from City Hall, was originally known as the City Hall Garage, providing parking and servicing of vehicles—even the fire trucks.

Hard work and a keen sense of the market has made the business grow. Mugo knows that people on the Peninsula are sophisticated and well-traveled; they want tasteful and stylish décor. He regularly attends furniture shows, going to Europe at least twice a year to keep up on the latest trends in design. The key is to be flexible as the market changes and to provide excellent customer service. This is what attracts—and keeps—customers from all over.

P.G. Motorcycle Museum Guy
Neil Jameson

Born and raised on a ranch in Aromas, a trip to Pacific Grove was a special treat. During World War II (and after), my dad was the conductor on the railroad line that ran from Watsonville to Salinas to Pacific Grove and back, transporting produce and troops.

When I was tall enough to see out the window of that huge engine, I got to "drive" the train and imagine that I was driving down to Pacific Grove to see my great-uncle Dick and have an ice cream cone.

Uncle Dick was probably better known to Pacific Grove denizens as Richard Williams, retired lighthouse-keeper. He was the lighthouse-keeper at Pt. Pinos from 1914 to 1931, and when he retired, he stayed in Pacific Grove for a number of years before moving to Willow Glen. Conveniently so for me, as I got to have private tours of the lighthouse and trips to the ice cream parlor besides having "driven" the train down here.

During the war, ice cream was an exotic treat. To this day, I remember banana ice cream at the old shop on Lighthouse. I remember, too, the roar of the empty cans going on an overhead conveyor belt from the American Tin Cannery to the sardine factories. Eventually they'd be loaded onto the train to be shipped. It was a sound I can't imitate, but will never forget.

Eventually, the family moved to Saratoga and Uncle Dick, my connection to Pacific Grove, moved to Willow Glen.

After a stint in the South China Sea with the Navy, I joined the San Jose Fire Department where I stayed for 30 years. Along the way, I met Marge Ann at a wedding and it was all downhill from there. A number of my friends got me involved in volunteering at Laguna Seca. I'd drag my Airstream down and Marge Ann and I would park it in the corporation yard at the race track.

After a number of years of this, it became an ordeal and we began to think about finding a place to stay on race weekends. We both had good memories of Pacific Grove, and began looking for a toe-hold. After searching for two years, we settled on a small single-family dwelling with a garage that had been converted into a granny unit. We moved into the granny unit for those five race weekends each year and rented out the main house full time. Five weekends grew to more, having made ourselves a rule that if it was going to be hotter than 70 degrees in Ben Lomond, then Pacific Grove was the place to be. It worked for a number of years, but the last renters left it in a state of disrepair and we had to renovate it before renting it out again. We decided to just move into it, lock, stock and barrel, and the renovation continues.

In the interim, Marge Ann started her own newspaper, having worked at another in the San Lorenzo Valley since 1982. A couple of doors down was an unsuccessful art gallery. They'd refurbished the 1930 building with beautiful floors and galvanized walls. Perfect place to store motorcycles. After a tedious process involving banks and lawyers and realtors, we bought the building and moved 27 of the motorcycles out of the living room in Ben Lomond. I remember thinking, "How will I ever fill it?" and there it is today: Jameson's Classic Motorcycle Museum, some 75 to 85 motorcycles, scooters, retired race bikes, and sidecars. Exhibits include samples from a 1913 Harley-Davidson to a Kawasaki we leased from the City of Pacific Grove's retired stock at the corporation yard.

Now and then, we take tour groups who come to visit the motorcycle museum out to the lighthouse. We go by there often on our Sunday morning rides and I still think of Uncle Dick and his handwritten displays on the walls at Pt. Pinos.

Cedar St. Times Newspaper Gal
Marge Ann Jameson

I came to Pacific Grove in stages. The first was in the early '70s when a college friend, stationed at Ft. Ord, called and asked me to transfer to Pacific Grove as he had an acquaintance who needed a roommate. What better reason to move to Paradise than to rescue the friend of a friend?

She was a teacher. I learned that a good number of the single females in Pacific Grove were teachers because there was not much other work. Teachers were in demand because of the heavy military presence of the time. She drove a Volkswagen Beetle, as did half the population, it seemed. One was either wealthy and drove a Mercedes or lived at the other end of the spectrum, was part of the military population, and drove a VW. I had a 1966 Sunbeam Alpine that I had to park at night on a slope so that I could bump start it in the mornings, as the battery was constantly at low tide.

Down by the ocean then, on a small point, there was an ugly little concrete building on the inland side of the road. Maybe you remember it, or maybe you wondered what it was. They tore it down in 2011.

Fine, and good riddance, but with it went some interesting memories for a lot of us.

Forty years ago, gasoline was cheap and I had all the time in the world. I would drive my Sunbeam to work using a different route each day, and come home to Pacific Grove with the same plan in mind. I played a game with myself, attempting to come over Highway 68 without touching the brakes. Great for the brakes, not so good for the clutch: I went through three of them in my first Pacific Grove sojourn.

Often I would drive by that squat, gray building, enjoying the play of sunlight on the surf and the seabirds wheeling in the sky. There weren't as many tourists on the pullouts then, and I could pretend it was possible to just keep driving forever. There were times I stopped and gathered beach glass on the rocks as the days faded, and I still have a mayonnaise jar full of it sitting in my window sill.

But I never drove that way on a foggy day. Or if I did, I'd sneak up on that little gray building, then hit the gas and roar by it as fast as I dared, as if it were a sea monster lying in wait for me. In a way, it was a sea monster. It was a foghorn. On damp days, it would build up a charge and then let loose with a roar I was sure would knock me and my little car right off into the rocks. On particularly dark, thick days I could picture Ray Bradbury's unfortunate, lovelorn sea monster rising up from the rocks in search of its lost mate, and squashing me in the throes of its ardor as it answered the sad hooting of the foghorn.

Home safe in my apartment, I would listen to that foghorn in the wet, dark night and know that someone was watching out for the ships at sea and all was right with the world.

Phil Bowhay, chronicler of life in the 1950s on the Monterey Peninsula, had a different memory of the foghorn, and even named a compendium of his columns from the *Monterey County Herald* after it: "When the Lord Spoke." He wrote of how young people would go "parking" near the beach and how the foghorn, with the voice of God, would blast them out of the back seat and back onto the road of righteousness.

Like the lovelorn sea monster, the foghorn outlived its usefulness and became extinct. The mournful bellow ceased. Then it came down. No, I didn't care to save it. I have my memories, in a jar with a rusty lid, sitting on my window sill.

I eventually moved back to San Jose, unable to afford the rent when my roommate moved to L.A. In San Jose, I met Neil—40 years ago—and we worked our way back to Pacific Grove in stages. I'll let him tell his story his way.

Pacific Grove Travel
International and Family Travel
Joe Shammas
owner

My family arrived in Pacific Grove in 1952. My dad, Jacob, was born in Baghdad, Iraq, and immigrated to the United States in 1947. He went to a small college in Lancaster, Pennsylvania, where he met my mother, Betty, a hometown girl.

Dad was hired at the Army Language School, as it was called then, at the Presidio of Monterey, to teach Arabic. (It is now the Defense Language Institute.) Dad was the second Arabic instructor hired! They lived in Ord Village (now the site of Seaside High School), which was housing offered by the U.S. Government for civil servants. In 1952, they purchased their home in Pacific Grove on Weldengrove Place and in 1958 moved to our home on Candy Cane Lane. I was the youngest of four children. It was great growing up there with lots of neighborhood kids to play with. Christmastime was very special and it was always the topic of discussion in November what our decorating theme would be.

Since Mom and Dad were both not from here, we had a wonderful ensemble of "aunts and uncles" from the Army Language School. These were people of all different cultures. Dad's friends became our family: people from Russia, Poland, Lebanon, Syria, Egypt, Romania, Germany, Vietnam, Korea, Japan and many more. These wonderful people were at our home often and even then, as a little kid, I was fascinated by them. Many families of different cultures found a home in Pacific Grove.

Many of the Language School instructors sent their kids to St. Angela's Catholic Grammar School. We had quite a group of kids from different backgrounds. It was like a mini United Nations and we thought nothing of it. But looking back now, what a great experience!

I attended St. Angela's School from grades 1-8. The school building is still there at the corner of Central and 9th St. It was opened in 1948 and closed in 1972. It was run by the Parish of St. Angela's and the teachers were nuns from the Dominican Order in San Rafael. Our classes were large. There was only one class per grade. Many classes had 50 kids. The Sisters worked hard to educate us and I don't remember any of them having classroom aides. I got a great education and was well prepared for high school.

Somehow, I think that my early introduction to different cultures in our family was a prelude to my interest in travel. I opened Pacific Grove Travel in 1979. We were located at 230 Fountain Avenue for 20 years, before Bud Giles invited me to rent from him in the prime spot I have now at 593 Lighthouse Avenue. We are celebrating our 38th anniversary this year. It has been a privilege to be born, reared here and able to work and live here.

An Unexpected Career
Helen Gehringer
as travel agent at P.G. Travel

At the age of 16 I left Pacific Grove to pursue a ballet career. A number of exciting years followed, performing in San Francisco and New York. However, ballet is a rigorous profession and when I developed a serious foot problem, my ballet career was over.

Devastated, I returned to the West Coast where I planned to start a business career thanks to classes I'd taken at Pacific Grove High School. But obviously that was not the career I wanted.

Many years later I came home to help aging parents move from a rural area back into town and when they bought a home with a studio apartment attached, I decided to stay if I could find a job.

For several years my family had been clients of Pacific Grove Travel and when Joe Shammas and Kay Webster learned I was looking for a job, they offered to hire and train me as a travel consultant.

Starting this new career was a wonderful experience. I loved planning travel for my clients and enjoyed doing some world travel myself.

Now, at age 80, I still work at Pacific Grove Travel on a very minimal basis and will forever be grateful to Joe and Kay for being willing to take a chance on me.

Park Place Publications
Book Services Since 1982
Patricia Hamilton

When I take a break at my office in the Giles Building, I head downstairs, push open the double doors to 591, and step out onto Lighthouse Avenue. I stretch my legs, breathe in the fresh air, and gaze around the streets of historic downtown P.G, with its Victorians, meridians of native flowers, and pedestrians strolling arm-in-arm or walking a dog. I might chit-chat with Joe or Laura at P.G. Travel, on my left, or stop in next door for a cup of coffee with Frank at Juice & Java. When I'm hungry, within one block are Mauricio's, Juice & Java, Lighthouse Café, Fandango, Peppers, and Jeninni Kitchen. I might pick up grilled salmon from Charlie at the Grove Market deli and eat by the wishing well at The Heritage Society's Ketcham's Barn on Laurel Avenue at 17th Street.

I could visit my bank, or stop in to see William at Alpha Stationers—he tells and writes such interesting P.G. stories. I can visit with Juanita at Grove Nutrition and get excellent health advice and products.

It's a few steps to Lovers Point, the library, Jewell Park, P.G. Art Center, the post office, numerous thrift stores, and dozens more shops.

If dogs and owners appear willing, I'll ask to pet every dog I meet! I love to have my grandchildren, Zack and Grace, visit—P.G. is the best place to be a grandparent.

My family in P.G. dates back to 1890 and I moved here in 1990. Other than one year on campus at UC Santa Cruz to finish my degree in Philosophy and Religious Studies, plus two years teaching, studying and traveling abroad in the UK and Spain, I've been here since.

Boomers are writing their memoirs and making that genre boom as well. To better assist, I became certified in the James Birren Guided Autobiography Method and taught classes using his sequence of reviewing our lives by writing about our experiences through various themes. In doing so, I married Joseph Campbell's "The Hero's Journey" steps from his book, *The Hero of a Thousand Faces*, to Birren themes and consistently use my new method for teaching and writing—clients find the heart of their story quickly and come away with new understanding of the overall arc of their lives.

P.G. Juice N' Java
Frank Morris, Owner
as told to Mimi Sheridan

Frank Morris opened his coffee house, P.G. Juice n' Java, in 1993 and it remains one of the most popular spots in town. Frank was an Air Force kid, moving constantly and having no idea what he wanted to do in life. He finally hit upon the idea of running a coffeehouse—after all, he liked to sit around and drink coffee. But he had no experience and no cash. He lucked out when he noticed an empty storefront on Lighthouse Avenue and approached the owner, Bud Giles. Bud agreed to give him a chance, despite his extreme skepticism that a coffeehouse would succeed. Frank proved him wrong by providing a living room-like ambiance with quality coffee, smoothies and baked goods. Ironically, Frank seldom has the time to sit around and drink coffee any more.

The Giles family built several buildings in downtown P.G., and Bud himself operated a menswear store for many years. He was very active in the Chamber of Commerce and was often thought of as "Mister P.G." However, he may have been best known as one of those who brought the Bing Crosby Pro-Am Golf Tournament (now the AT&T Pebble Beach Pro-Am) to Pebble Beach. In the 1940s, he worked tirelessly with the Crosby family and local leaders to make sure every need was met to make the tournament a success, and it remains one of the most important events on the Monterey Peninsula.

Brazilians Talk to the Natives
Andrea and Felipe Tavares

Wow! It is a small world, isn't it?

We moved with our son to Pacific Grove a year and a half ago. Of course, our hearts beat fast when we face changes and challenges while living in a foreign country. Fortunately, we decided to move to a city where people are courteous, charismatic, and compassionate. As a way to give a little bit back to this amazing community, we all decided to become volunteers. My adorable neighbors across the street, Heidi Feldman and Gary Karnes, introduced us to Patricia Hamilton, who presented an opportunity to collect stories for her remarkable project, *Life in Pacific Grove*. It was a perfect combination because I used to work in a hotel in Brazil, where my job was to offer all the hotel's services to different companies. So, it was amazing to visit more than a hundred stores in P.G., especially because we were talking about a brilliant project that will benefit the whole community. We soon found out that people are people everywhere no matter which nationality you are. We all have similar needs. For example, if you bring good energy to a place, you will definitely get good energy back. Even though most businesses were busy, they had the time to stop and listen to me with a big smile on their faces and so much love in their hearts. Thank you P.G. for giving us hope for a better world!

Rocky Coast Ice Cream
Lane Edgington
as told to Linnet Harlan

Shortly after my 15th birthday, during dinner with my parents, my mother turned to me and, out of the blue, said, "Lane, get a job."

"Mom, I'm 15. No one is going to hire a 15-yearold."

"At least start applying."

"Sure, I'll start tomorrow."

"No, now."

"In the middle of dinner?"

"Yes. Now."

I walked to Rocky Coast and went in. The owner, Dennis Faherty, was serving a customer. I asked if he was hiring. "I just hired somebody a couple of weeks ago, but you can fill out an application." The application was basic: name, social security number, age, school, and extra curricular activities. He knew this job would be your first. "We'll see how things are going in a couple of weeks. Come back then."

Two weeks later, during dinner, my mother said, "Lane, it's been two weeks; go back to Rocky Coast and ask about the job."

"Now?"

"Now."

So back I went. "You told me to come back in two weeks. Is there an opening now?"

"I said that two weeks ago?"

"Yes."

"What was your name again?"

"Lane."

He flipped through several applications and pulled out mine. He looked at it for a minute, didn't ask why I wanted the job, didn't ask any of the things, you later find are the common questions. "You're hired."

That's how I started one of the best jobs I've ever had.

Dennis, through his actions, taught me how to interact with people, how to put on a smile, greet people and make their worries go away, whether from a double scoop of cookies and cream or by having a friendly person happy to listen.

For all of us, the job was our first. We'd mess up sometimes. When we'd mess up, he would use it as a teaching moment for later in life. If you said you wanted to be a police officer and you forgot to shut a window closing the store, he'd remind you police officers need to notice such things and suggest you begin to practice.

One employee left the freezer open overnight. Over two thousand dollars' worth of ice cream melted. His first reaction wasn't to fire the employee, as some employers might have. Instead, he called the employee to the store, sat him down and said, "I'm going to give you two options: the first—I fire you. Or you take the harder path: beyond your regular job for the day, you clean every nook and cranny with a toothbrush." (Need I mention Dennis was a military man?) The employee took the harder path, did the job Dennis described, and that was the end of the issue.

Dennis wanted to teach, in ways that schools don't: how to be an employee, how to work in a professional environment, and, most of all, how to be a good human being. At least for me, I like to think he succeeded.

Hambrooks
Mimi Sheridan

Pacific Grove is fortunate to have its own full-service auction house. Hambrook's Auction Center was founded by Phil and Renate Hambrook in 1990. Today it has more than 16,000 square feet of display space right in downtown P.G.. The live auctions, held every three weeks, feature everything from fine art, furniture and jewelry to wicker baskets and toy trains. The silent auctions offer an even broader range of bargains. Office manager Sarah Elias says that most bidders are most local people buying for their own homes or collections. Others come farther, from the Bay Area or the Central Valley, seeking good deals and the excitement of discovery. Each auction brings the promise of something new and different.

Sarah, who has worked at Hambrook's since 2004, sees these as these as good days for auctions since so many people are downsizing to smaller homes or apartments. People entertain more informally, not using dining room sets or fine china, and children don't want these items. The impact of media shouldn't be underestimated, as television shows like *Antiques Roadshow* and *American Pickers* have raised the visibility of auctions. Viewers are more aware of hidden value—everyone dreams of finding an unrecognized treasure in the attic or at a garage sale.

Hambrook's also liquidates estates, which vividly shows a person's life and interests. Perhaps the most interesting item was a document signed by Abraham Lincoln, forgotten in the bottom of a box that even the estate executor didn't know about. Sarah's favorite objects are the unusual or quirky ones, such as a fine carousel horse or a primitive artwork. In the end, her work is about finding good homes for objects of all types.

Hambrook's Auction House
Susan Peick

From time to time I would visit Hambrook's Auction House to see what interesting items might be for sale. On one visit, I spotted a large wooden, antique polychrome Buddha that I really wanted. I asked the auctioneer how much it might sell for. He gave me a range of what I might expect in the auction. After re-thinking my bid upwards a bit, I decided I wanted to try for it. I registered, got my placard and then chose a special spot at the back of the room which gave me a view of all the people in the audience. I also made sure it was a spot where the auctioneer would be able to see me. My strategy was this: Why participate in a bidding frenzy, only to whip up the price with emotions? I decided to let any bidders bid against each other, while I waited to see where the final bidding might land. I didn't want to show any interest whatsoever in the bidding. The field started out with three or so bidders; after a minute the number was down to two bidders.

At last, one bidder dropped out. The price was still in my range. I was still in the game, although no one knew it except me. My heart was racing as the auctioneer started the count down for the winning bid " … .going once, going twice … " At that point I raised my placard high into the air. The auctioneer saw it and looked surprised. The guy who thought he had won the bidding whipped around to see who the mystery bidder was. He bid one more time against me, while I kept my placard firmly in the air. "Going once, going, twice, going three times…." The bid was mine. Phew. I got my Buddha. Later the auctioneer passed by me and said quietly, "That's the way to do it." I agree, but it sure is hard on the nerves.

Grove Nutrition Center
Juanita Coleman
Mimi Sheridan

Holman's Department Store on Lighthouse Avenue was once the largest independent department store between Los Angeles and San Francisco. Although the store closed long ago, the building still houses some of P.G.'s most notable stores. One is Grove Nutrition Center, widely known for its warm customer service and unique products. The store has been in business for almost 60 years—it was previously located on the south side of Lighthouse before the move into the Holman building.

Juanita has owned Grove Nutrition for 16 years. She was extremely busy during this Holman building renovation and asked that we take the comments from customers who posted to Yelp—all were glowing reports:

"The staff were extremely helpful and knowledgeable. I love the look and feel of the store and the many, many offerings. Enough options but not overwhelming."

"They made us feel welcomed and provided for with more information than we first asked for."

"They always have what I need. Everyone is knowledgeable and very helpful in finding the products for you."

"There are plenty of products, so you're not stuck buying the most outrageously priced ones. The staff is very helpful and attentive."

"They listen and care, above and beyond."

Women Rule!
Rebecca Riddell

March 8 is "The Day Without A Woman." I believe this is a terrific time to show our solidarity. The objective is to stand together for a day and make our presence known. Many of us can't take the day off work as suggested, yet we can wear red and if we must shop (please try to get gas and groceries the day before) …

Shop Only at Women Owned Businesses

Pacific Grove is loaded with businesses owned and operated by women—here's a partial list: Adrianne Michele Jonson's Artisana Gallery, Alpha Stationers, Nell Flattery Carlson's Bookworks, Butterfly Cottage Botanicals, Rosemary's Carried Away Boutique, Evolution Studios, Germain Hatcher's Imagine Art Supply, Marina Patina, P.G. Antiques, Renata Hambrook's Auction House, Patricia Hamilton's Park Place Publications, Babs Du Pont Hanneman's Habitat, Chatterbox Children's Shop, Marita's Boutiques, Nest Boutique, Juanita's Grove Nutrition, Nancy's Attic, Emily's Tessuti Zoo, Tides Gifts.

Grand Avenue Flooring and Interiors
Michael Krokower
by Mimi Sheridan

In 1990, Michael Krokower was seeking an escape from Los Angeles when he discovered Pacific Grove. He jumped at the chance to be a partner in a carpet store, and within a few years had his own thriving carpet and interiors store, working with local contractors and property managers. But a primary interest has always been community service, promoting and improving his adopted city.

From the beginning, he has been involved with the local Rotary Club. Many activities focus on P.G. students, such as supporting an annual track meet and refurbishing the Performing Arts Center at the middle school. Other projects benefit the entire city, such as working on the P.G. Auto Rally, raising funds for public sculptures and upgrading structures in Jewell Park.

He has also been a leader of the Chamber of Commerce, promoting business and tourism. He is currently the Chairman of the Board of the Pacific Grove Chamber of Commerce. He has seen changes over the decades, with the city becoming more encouraging and open to new ideas. The numerous events and activities that are the framework of P.G.'s year—from Good Old Days in the spring to year-end holiday events—continue to nurture a thriving tourism industry. New restaurants have joined the old standbys and motels have been upgraded. But the chamber is now focused on a new challenge—promoting the identity of Pacific Grove to make sure that people know that they are in indeed in Pacific Grove, not one of the better-known nearby cities. This enhanced image will hopefully lead to even greater prosperity.

Life and Work in P.G.
Jody Hutchinson
massage therapist and educator

I first moved to Pacific Grove over 30 years ago. I shared an apartment near Lovers Point and worked at the Tinnery. After quite some time I returned to P.G. I rented a small office on 17th Street. Eleven years later, I moved my office onto Lighthouse Avenue. I enjoy working here as I can walk to the beach, post office, bank, Grove Market, and other businesses.

I really enjoy the slower pace and quiet streets, and you can't beat a sunny day here in P.G.

I like the parades, the Christmas lights, and the many stores where people are friendly and helpful.

The beach at Lovers Point is a wonderful place to sit and watch the world go by. I have contemplated moving to Monterey and have decided to stay in P.G.; it has many positive things to offer.

I have been practicing massage therapy almost 30 years. I am married and have two dogs.

Dreamcasters Voyage
Kevin Kenoyer
by Mimi Sheridan

Tourism is a vital aspect of Pacific Grove's success. A new company, DreamCasters Voyage, aims to give visitors an authentic experience of the Monterey Peninsula, tailored to their interests. Using small buses that can go nearly everywhere, they drive down to Big Sur and to Carmel Valley wineries, but the most popular excursion is the historical/scenic tour featuring Monterey, Pacific Grove, Carmel and 17-Mile Drive.

According to guide Kevin Kenoyer, most tour-goers come from the Midwest, the Southeast or Texas; about 20 percent are from out of the country. They learn about Monterey's long history and enjoy the beauty of the coastline and Carmel's uniqueness. And they are entranced by Pacific Grove—a little jewel that most were completely unaware of. Guides entertain with anecdotes and tales of P.G.'s quirky history as a Methodist retreat and a long-time dry town. The Victorian houses, Lovers Point and the lighthouse are featured, but the festivals, the monarch butterflies (and the fog!) are not forgotten. It's an excellent means to introduce unsuspecting newcomers to the charms of P.G.

Taste Restaurant
Home Away From Home
Bill and Sue Karaki
owners/chefs, parents

For us, home was always Beirut, Lebanon, up until the year 1988. With my wife's hand in mine, we came to the beautiful town of Pacific Grove. Knowing nobody, we quickly came to realize the importance that this small town holds: from the history, to the serene nature, and most importantly the friendliest people.

Flash forward to the year 2017: my wife and I have owned Taste Cafe & Bistro since 1997 where our four beautiful kids help us. All of them attended schools in Pacific Grove and we couldn't ask for a better place for our kids to get their education. My family and I have found the most welcoming home away from home here in the delightful town of Pacific Grove.

Liberty Tax Service
A Childhood Spent Two Doors from the Beach
Charlene and Desiree Smith, owners
by CSUMB intern Stefanie Tyler

The story of Charlene and Desiree Smith was very touching as I listened to them talk about their lives in Pacific Grove. Charlene and Desiree are mother and daughter, and are owners of the Liberty Tax Service franchise in Pacific Grove. It was heartwarming to hear about the family relationship, and how it all seemed to tie together around P.G.. Pacific Grove wasn't always their home, but they visited frequently over the years, and they're now living in their grandmother's house. "She lived here for over 50 years, and now that she's gone it's ours," Charlene said.

Charlene shared reminiscences of visiting her grandmother in Pacific Grove. "I used to come and spend the weekend with my grandmother almost every weekend. And we'd go to the beach because she lived two spaces from the beach there." Desiree added, "Both of us as children went over there, and walked to town with her. So we grew up coming to visit Pacific Grove."

One of their stories stood out to me because of how simple it was. Desiree spoke as if the memory was still fresh in her mind. "I had a tree. I would play in the tree ... the tree was a playground."

According to Charlene, "There was a stretch of grass," where the tree stood. Desiree picked this tree because of how it overlooked the ocean and Lovers Point beach, for it also stood right beside the bike trail. Growing up, it was her favorite place to be. The conversation kept circling back to the tree. "For me it's that tree." Desiree said.

Asking for a personal glimpse into their lives that had led Desiree to that moment in time when she was still a child ready to climb that tree and sit on its branches to watch a lazy day go by, or a special event taking place on the waterfront, I could only imagine how it must have felt like having a front row seat at one of P.G.'s many gatherings. Desiree told me she felt the same way.

Desiree pointed out to me that "P.G. used to have a boat parade during the Feast of the Lanterns." Both Desiree and Charlene took turns describing the event to me. Charlene said, "They'd put lights on their boats, and you could see them from Lovers Point or the ocean down there."

Desiree said that the boats would "come every year for the fireworks." However, over the years, interest in the boat parade dwindled, but one thing that never changed was the fireworks show. That is, Charlene said, "The only place they still do the fireworks is over the ocean ... we'd go down by the ocean there so that we could see Lovers Point and they'd shoot off the fireworks." On Desiree's face showed a smile and said, "That was fun! I'd sit in my tree, and just watch the fireworks over the ocean."

Tessuti Zoo Art Gallery and Gifts
Emily Owens
owner

P.G. has so many wonderful places: Asilomar Beach, Feast of Lanterns, Grove Market, P.G. Hardware, Marita's Boutique, Red House Cafe, Alpha Stationers, Holly's Lighthouse Cafe, The P.G. Art Center, Max's Grill, Peppers Mexicali Cafe, Sprout Boutique, the P.G. Post Office, the colorful ice plant, all of the lovely inns, Lovers Point. Too many places and things to mention!

I moved to the peninsula in 1980 from Topanga Canyon, and loved Pacific Grove from the start. We purchased our small P.G. home in 1985, raised our two girls and have lived here ever since.

Thirty-seven years ago, when my husband Tom and I first took winding Holman Highway down into little foggy Pacific Grove, I knew I was home. The quiet, quaint town was the perfect place to start a family and create a life by the sea. Opening the doors at Tessuti Zoo for the past 21 years has been pure joy. Creating my one-of-a-kind dolls and creatures daily with buttons, bobbins and beads has been wild, wonderful, and whimsical! With twirling bolts of colorful fabric, neon threads, bright paints and imagination, I especially enjoy transforming found furniture into colorful artistic statements: that's pretty normal around here. I almost always end my day at The Zoo by going to neighborhood Grove Market. It's so pleasant being able to do my daily shopping here with the wonderful staff and visiting with fellow Pagrovians. From food, to clothing to hardware, I am blessed to call Pacific Grove home!

Juliette "Jette" Ferguson
realtor, as told to Margie McCurry

I celebrated being married 14 years to my love, Kurt Kurt Ferguson. We met in Pacific Grove in February 2002 and were married in 2003. Thank you God for this life with Kurt. Life is fragile. We are blessed to have grown together in faith and love.

I had moved to Pacific Grove and lived at 140 Forest. He lived at 136 First. The neighbors at 138 Forest introduced us over the garbage cans, and that's how it all started!

We married in Pacific Grove at my mom and dad's house, with photos at Lovers Point! We bought our home in Seaside and closed escrow a few weeks before the wedding.

He has put up with my freakish love of all animals, including hens in the house. I often say, if it weren't for Kurt, I'd live in a barn with fifty animals. It wouldn't be pretty.

Kurt really supported me (literally and figuratively) to go back to school for my MBA and to go full-time into real estate when I had doubts about 100% commission business. He has walked me through challenges and fears and helped me grow up... I'm still working on that part. I hope I support him equally.

I know how lucky I am to be fully loved and accepted as I am. Thank you, Pacific Grove, and you Kurt Ferguson for changing my life forever!

J.R. Rouse
realtor, as told to Margie McCurry

"I truly enjoy being a part of this town I adopted many years ago," he says. J.R. and his real estate team support and sponsor local events like the Feast of Lanterns fireworks, Good Old Days and other annual events.

J.R. Rouse has lived and worked as a realtor on the Monterey Peninsula for more than 16 years—and he says he LOVES Pacific Grove, because he lives here—and for lots of other reasons!

His mantra is, "What you can believe, you can achieve" and it obviously works for him. J.R. was awarded the 2016 Individual Contributor Top Producer award for Sotheby's International Realty Carmel. His passion is working for his clients—whether it's finding the perfect home for a new P.G. resident, or selling a P.G. home to the perfect buyers.

Whenever J.R. sees clients, people at a cafe or others waiting in line at a P.G. grocery store, he has a smile that captures anyone—his gratefulness for life is infectious.

And watch out … J.R is a hugger! He says that's the way he was raised. Always with a hug available for those who need it—for comfort or simply for good feelings,

J.R. is the walking embodiment of all that's cherished about this special haven of Pacific Grove and the Monterey Peninsula.

My Pearl on the Peninsula
Susan Carol Smith
owner Butterfly Cottage Botanicals

The scent of rosemary focaccia bread in Fournier's oven penerates the fog billowing like damp dust over Lighthouse Avenue.

CoCo, leashed, tugs me toward caffeine brewing in the coffee shop. Wearing Ugg boots and a scarf twice wrapped around my neck is typical of Pacific Grove's average 57 degree temperature.

Peering toward the bay for whales as sea gulls squeal, I see the hawk-walker. The shoulder-perched sentinel hawk flies to a pine tree shrouded in gray-green moss that dangles from its branches like ancient men's beards.

Swooshing brooms dust the storefront walks. No noisy gas blowers permitted in our quiet city. Delivery trucks caravan, snail-crawling within our 15 mile-per-hour speed limit, bringing fresh ingredients as our chefs await.

I make my way to Ms. Flora Conover's historically marked 1897 cottage where I rent space for my garden gift shop here in Butterfly Town, USA. Towering oaks canopy as I wonder if Miss Conover realized these five once saplings, would become the graceful legacy of beauty bequeathed to this place when she planted them 120 years ago.

My shop is filled with monarch merchandise, plants and local art. Reminiscing customers tell me they, or their children, or grandchildren wore monarch wings and marched right out front in the Butterfly Parade.

I think back to my daughter.

She loved my jewelry, rubbed her tiny fingers over sparkling stones; pearls. One evening I asked her, "Should I wear the pearls or the gold chains?"

"The pearls, Mommy." Pinching her brow together, she asked, "Where do pearls come from?"

"Oysters," I said, wondering if that could satisfy the curiosity of my inquisitive child who knew nothing of the depth of the sea or the mystery of an oyster's nacreous layers.

I fumbled with the clasp; the strand broke and pearls scattered onto the floor. I scooped as many as possible, leaving errant ones rolling into the angular recesses of the bedroom.

Months later, my daughter, with beams of light bouncing from her blue eyes, a grin of awe, stood with her hand behind her back.

"Mommy, I *know* where pearls come from."

"You do?"

"Pearls aren't from oysters," she said as she brought her hand from its hiding place, opening her fist to expose a pearl in a wadded clump of dust. "Pearls come from dusty corners."

In that moment I saw in my daughter a revelation; we can limit or expand ourselves simply with perspective. Through the darkest moments of life, I have found pearls. In those moments wisdom emanates from the dusty corners of our minds.

Here in Pacific Grove—our quaint city—I treasure living my dream, cherish this quiet place whereby my daughter took passage from here into eternity, am at peace each new dawn, to hold the gift of being given another day of life in this perfect place … may it always be between "*Carmel by the Sea and Monterey by the Smell*" and remain "*Pacific Grove by God!*" The pearl of the Peninsula.

My Work as an Interior Designer
Denise Holland

My fascination with creating environments began at age six, when with my Mom's kitchen shears, I embarked on cutting an elaborate pattern in the grass. My fingers failed before my vision became a reality but over the years the passion to create didn't fade. So my career as a designer that began in Toronto, Canada, has followed me back to Houston, L.A., and places in between. While working with an architectural firm in Walnut Creek, I started a project for the Navy in Monterey.

That was when I first fell in love with Pacific Grove. I found an upstairs flat in a remodeled Victorian and moved within six weeks. I quickly fell into step with P.G. life. Besides morning walks with spectacular ocean views,

I loved that I could shop, have dinner, a gelato and walk to a movie.

Beginning work with a local design firm, I was delighted that my first project was not only in P.G., but at the end of the street where I lived. It was such a thrill to watch the changes take place using the client's list of requirements while paying homage to the style of the home. I was able to use both traditional and contemporary pieces including a custom-built sofa to fit the scale of the room. I still smile when I drive past that home.

After starting my own firm, I've had the pleasure of working on various styles of homes in Pacific Grove, from 'tent lot' homes with single wall construction to mid-century and the Craftsman influenced cottages that are so beloved.

Regardless of architectural style, what is most important is my client's image of "home." Starting with drawings and color palettes and finishing with furniture, rugs and accessories, each project unravels into its own discovery process that ultimately transforms that image into reality.

The most gratifying discovery for me is that over the years, I have made friends and become part of families. I have been allowed to influence lives and as a result, my life has been touched in lovely and unexpected ways.

Opening P.G. Hardware
Richard Stillwell
Linnet Harlan

I'd been involved with M&S Building Supply (I was "S") for some time. Then we sold it, but after a while I decided I'd still like to have a hardware store, without the lumber. But this time I wanted to be on my own.

In the early 1970s, Walt Matteson was renting the location P.G. Hardware now stands on. He had a service station there. He and his wife Connie were up at Bass Lake with me and my wife Bev when he got a call from the landlord, Bob Emmons, saying he wanted to sell the property. Connie was worried and started crying. I said, "Don't worry; I'll buy it."

I talked to Emmons about buying the property, but it probably took four years before he gave me a final answer. Once he did, I said, "Okay, let's get in the truck and go sign the papers."

I'd known for a while I wanted to have another hardware store, but I wasn't sure where I wanted to put it. I'd even dreamed about the store and what the layout would be (and, for the most part, what it is today). But, in my dreams, whenever I'd walk over to the windows and try to look out to see where the store was, I'd wake up.

Vernon Herd was the manager at Holman's Department Store. He kept telling me to go ahead and start my hardware store. Holman's was carrying hardware in the basement, but he wanted to use the space for something else.

Walt suggested I tear out the service station and put in a garage with three or four service bays. Once I started looking into that possibility and we started drawing plans, I realized I could have a hardware store too. Then the architect said to do two stories so we even got some office space.

I wanted a store that offered service, where the employees knew what they were talking about and could give service. I worked at the store for a while, but I decided I didn't like to work inside; I liked being outside and building. So the service aspect of the store wasn't just something I wanted. It's something my son-in-law, Bill Derowski, made a reality.

My Hardware Hero
Bill Derowski
John Bridges

Our first home in Pacific Grove was a small house in the middle of town on a quaint, one block long street called Rosemont. As a first time homeowner, I made more mistakes than I could count, or wanted to remember. The house had been recently updated so there wasn't much to do inside, but outside was a different story. After completing the backyard landscaping (a small grassy area for the kids and a vegetable garden plot), I turned to the front yard. Located near the front door was an old, decrepit water softening unit that had long since been abandoned. It was an unsightly piece of odd and rusty plumbing equipment, so I determined to remove it. I mean, how hard could that be? Because it was connected to the water main, I dutifully turned off the main. Good thinking and well done, I told myself. Next I went to disconnect the equipment. Of course, after God only knows how many years of sitting there unused, the fittings wouldn't budge. So, I got in the car and drove downtown to the local hardware store, where I met the owner, Bill. I calmly relayed my plight, and he explained how I could overcome the problem. It all sounded simple enough, so I returned home with the correct tool in hand and removed the fittings. But then I realized I had forgotten to get a new pipe to bridge the gap in the line where the equipment had been. Two more trips back and forth to see Bill netted me a hopelessly unresolved problem.

It was getting dark, and the water main was still off. My wife was getting a bit edgy as she wanted to bathe the children and fix dinner. I arrived at P.G. Hardware (for the fourth time) about five minutes after the store had closed for the day. Bill saw me standing at the door looking tired and worn. Taking pity on me, he unlocked the door and invited me in. He grabbed a bag and walked around the store tossing every possible pipe and pipe fitting into the bag and then said, "Come on, let's go fix this." So, on a Sunday night, after hours, the local hardware store owner came to my house and, while I held a flash light, he taught me a few of the finer points of plumbing and fixed my pipes. It was an unprecedented house call from the hardware guy. Bill refused my offer to pay him for his above and beyond service, and said, "That's just what we do here in P.G.; we help each other." Needless to say Bill became one of my heroes that day, and I think I have since single-handedly sent more than 100 customers to him by retelling this story. You've just got to love Pacific Grove.

The White Hart
Jim and Kathy Turley
proprietors

It looked so lonely without us.

We'd lived in P.G. for years, and like most of our neighbors, we'd walked around the downtown shops, restaurants, apartments, Post Office, and other buildings a thousand times. "Oh, look, that shop is having a sale." Or, "Hey, that business just changed hands." Or, on a day ten years ago, "When did the old Hart Mansion go up for sale? Didn't that used to be a restaurant?"

And for another two years after that, we'd pass by the tall Queen Anne Victorian, painted all in white, on the corner of Lighthouse and 19th Street, wondering when someone would move in. Surely, it must be in escrow by now. We probably just missed the notice in the paper, right? But still the house looked vacant.

Finally, we couldn't stand it any longer. We cajoled our real estate agent into letting us inside. "We're probably wasting your time," we told her. "We're perfectly happy where we are. Maybe just a little peek …."

Fifteen minutes later we'd decided to buy it and move down the street. This is too lovely a home to waste. It needed a family in it. Someone to turn on the lights, keep it warm, and fill it with footsteps and laughter. Since nobody else seemed willing to step up, we took the plunge.

They say old houses are a money pit, but Dr. Hart's home/office from 1893 was in remarkably sound condition. "It's the finest construction I've seen," said the structural engineer. "Promise me you won't screw it up."

I hope we haven't. We replaced every inch of the vintage plumbing (some of which was clay pipe that crumbled to the touch), but did it all without tearing out walls or damaging the hand-laid plaster and lath. We upgraded the electrical wiring, again without ripping up walls or floors. We've hung period-correct wallpapers, reproduced the original redwood trim, polished the old brass hinges, and a thousand other chores we can't even remember. (It's all documented at http://hartsurgery.blogspot.com.) And we've had the outside painted. Can you guess how many colors are on there now?

After five years of living, working, sweating, and swearing we decided the house was finished enough to start sharing it with others. We didn't want to be dogs in a manger, just the two of us living in this big house, with only the occasional visitor or our skeptical kids. But how best to share it? Another restaurant? A retail shop? A professional office? Limited by what we actually know how to do, and by the desire to protect all the restoration work we'd just done, we decided on a limited-use event center. "Let's rent the ground floor to people for their parties, weddings, dinners, or whatever." But what about folks who aren't planning a wedding or going-away party? How to we accommodate them?

"Let's open a tea house!" It's perfect and age-appropriate for the house, it's something P.G. doesn't already have, and it's within our limited skillset to manage. So now we bake, cook, clean, and fuss over our tea guests four days per month. We serve on our grandmothers' china and silverware, using recipes we've gleaned from friends and family. Our tea guests have become the life of the house. They're the warmth we wanted to put back into the Hart Mansion. Thanks, everyone, for coming.

Our Family Laundromat in 1960
Peter Melville
translator English to Dutch, the Netherlands

I was eight years old when my father bought a laundromat. Our family lived in Carmel by-the-Sea, but this was around 1960 and there were no laundromats in Carmel. So my father bought one in Pacific Grove.

My father had never owned or ran a laundromat before. He thought they were unattractive and decided to cheer his up. He commissioned an artist to paint the walls with murals, and on the opening ceremony he poured cocktails, which he mixed in one of the machines.

I was too young to be involved with managing the business. Occasionally I would accompany my father if some trouble called him to Pacific Grove, and I remember us driving down a winding road to the strip mall where our laundromat was situated. Mostly we had to refill the vending machines that dispensed packages of soap, and to empty the machines of the dimes they had collected. Back home we splashed the dimes onto the dining-room table, where all four members of our family scrutinized the minting dates, hoping to find one that was rare and valuable.

My father passed away in 1962. My mother sold the laundromat, and the house and the car, and took my brother and me with her to her native Holland. I have been back to California several times, but never to Pacific Grove. Not, that is, until this May, when I visited Monterey Peninsula. Highway 1 has changed; traffic is heavier. But when I took the exit I found myself driving down the familiar winding road, through the woods and onto the road that leads past the strip mall. On my left I spotted a laundromat—that hadn't changed. But I forgot to stop and see whether the walls were still decorated with murals.

P.G. Grows on You
Alex Bokde
Edward Jones financial advisor

I love to take the eight-minute walk to Lovers Point and glance up the coastline and admire the amazing natural scenery and all the color. I've always loved the ocean and the movements of the waves and the color of the water.

Once on lunch break, I took a chicken wrap to Lovers Point to enjoy it under a tree and breathe in the fresh air. A gull approached to say hello and see what I was doing. As I watched him get closer and closer I didn't suspect what he was really there for: in an instant, the gull grabbed my wrap and flung it several feet onto the ground whereby a flock of gulls suddenly descended upon my lunch to devour it.

Pacific Grove grows on you and what I've come to love are the Lighthouse Cinemas, the restaurants where one can linger, the way the town seems to come to life around ten in the morning every day, the alternating blue and gray skies, the Holman building where John Steinbeck's roller skater tried to break the Guinness record for rooftop roller skating, and the town's diversity. It all becomes home and makes me feel better each time I experience them.

Insurance Man

Tom McKinney

state farm agent

My favorite P.G. person is Dick Trotter, deceased December 2015. A true legend, retired Army Air Corps, veteran of WWII, past president of Rotary Club of Pacific Grove, great golfer, friend to all.

I am originally from Independence, Missouri. Joined the U.S. Navy in 1965, then came to California. I stayed here to attend college and moved to Pacific Grove in 1988.

I married Janice 1981, and we have one son, Matthew I'm an ardent golfer and traveler and a past president of the Rotary Club of Pacific Grove.

Charlie Higuera

'I Have to Take Care of My People'

Richard T. Oehrle

retired linguistics professor and data analyst

My wife and I moved from Berkeley to Pacific Grove (P.G.) in 2003 so that she could assume the position of Provost at the Defense Language Institute (DLI). Among the many pleasures of living in Berkeley is being able to shop daily (parking permitting) at the Berkeley Bowl (B.B.), where many exotic products are available. (Our son worked as a checker there in the early 2000s and he had to memorize all the product codes—including about 20 for different types of garlic alone.) Naturally, one of our top priorities when we moved to P.G. was to find the B.B. of the Monterey Peninsula (if there was one).

It doesn't take long for transplants to P.G. to find themselves at the Grove Market (G.M.). It's located in a distinctive building built in 1951 as a Purity Store (a grocery chain in California and neighboring states) in the heart of P.G.'s downtown business district. The building itself is basically a masonry Quonset hut, consisting of a masonry-block rectangle surrounding about 6,000 square feet of floor space, with the long axis parallel to Lighthouse and perpendicular to Forest, and the short axis parallel to Forest and perpendicular to Lighthouse. Geometrically, the roof consists of a long arch connecting the two long axes of the basic rectangle. Since 1969, the G.M. has been leased and operated by the Higuera family and managed by the family patriarch, Charlie Higuera.

The entrance to the G.M. leads directly to an aisle parallel to Forest, with prepared foods and the butcher counter on the left and three checkout lanes on the right.

On the walls are mounted certificates from the *Monterey County Weekly*, asserting that the G.M. has been voted by its readers to be the 'Best Butcher' and the 'Best Local Market,' countywide, year after year, in both cases. The G.M. also contains a large display of sports memorabilia, focusing on golf tournaments at Pebble Beach and on G.M.-sponsored youth teams. At the opposite end of the G.M. from the customer entrance, there is a storage room and a receiving door for incoming goods. Between the checkout lanes and the storage room, the G.M. is divided into five aisles.

The G.M. doesn't have either the size or the customer base of the B.B. and can't possibly offer the range and diversity of products found there. But the G.M. does have advantages over the B.B. with regard, first, to its relations with its suppliers and, second, to its relations with its customers.

On the supply side, consider the case of asparagus. Asparagus grown locally is seasonally available at the G.M., sourced from a local field whose yield is dedicated to the G.M. Local asparagus is typically ready to harvest in late March. As soon as the harvest begins, crates of fresh, local, organic asparagus appear prominently displayed in the G.M. produce section. Every year, in the days and weeks leading up to this event, asparagus-loving G.M. customers eagerly, anxiously, even impatiently, pester the G.M. staff (as politely as possible, of course) about the exact timing of the arrival of the asparagus. And as soon as it arrives, the mood of both customers and staff noticeably improves. Similar annual cycles are linked to English snap peas, apples and berries, and no doubt others that I am not so attuned to.

On the customer-relation side, the G.M. offers many special services: charge accounts, home delivery, special butcher orders (duck, goose, prime rib). For some customers, one or another of these services might be critical: walking into town last week, I stopped to compliment one of my neighbors—a woman in her eighties—on her beautiful garden, and when I let it slip that I was headed to the G.M., she immediately mentioned how important the G.M. home delivery service is to her, especially in the rainy season.

This leads to two interrelated questions: was my neighbor just the lucky beneficiary of a G.M. service? Or was the home delivery service offering part of a larger strategy of customer outreach to create as large, loyal, and satisfied a customer base as possible? I don't have direct evidence in favor of a positive answer to either question. But I do have indirect evidence suggesting that the answer to the second is 'yes,' implying that the answer to the first is 'no.' This indirect evidence takes the form of an anecdote about Charlie Higuera.

After a rainstorm had knocked out the town's electricity for over 12 hours, I happened to be in downtown P.G. around lunchtime. With two exceptions, all the businesses on Forest between Lighthouse and Pine were powerless and closed. The first exception was the Police Department. The second was the Grove Market, where Charlie and his staff had set up in the parking lot a portable barbeque, whose grill was full of a variety of meat and sausages, destined to be the main attraction of sandwiches to be sold to hungry members of the quickly forming crowd. Charlie presided over the event, talking softly with one of the town's dignitaries. One member of the hungry crowd caught a small part of their dialogue.

Dignitary: (rough paraphrase) "Why are you going to all this trouble, Charlie?"

Charlie: (as I remember it) "I have to take care of my people."

My Neighborhood Grocery Store
Rebecca Riddell

I've been shopping at Grove Market for over 50 years. It's the place you will find fresh produce, local wines, and the best meat this side of Texas. Yet, that's not why I shop there. Grove Market has been run by the Higuera family since I can remember. Charlie Higuera, a California Indian native, is a legend in these parts. He's the man you see if you need those special tomatoes for your spaghetti sauce, that beautiful baked turkey for the holiday, and to find out what's going on in town. Charlie knows everybody and everything in and about P.G. and he especially keeps tabs on which local ladies are single at the moment. They don't pass the butcher department without being called back behind the counter for a quick kiss.

Grove Market has been such a big part of my life I sometimes pop in just to check on Charlie. He must be 150 by now. Or close anyway, judging by my age.

In the good old days, I'd run into Charlie barefoot and wet from the beach and he'd hand me a couple of freshly cut pieces of salami to snack on and ask about my day. He'd ask about the family and tell his latest big fish tale. All the kids loved Charlie. He was never far from our minds as we'd no sooner get home from his store and start making prank calls to him. "Hi Guara (we thought we were so smart with the pun on his last name), is your refrigerator running?" Of course, he recognized our voices and would use the opportunity to tell us another fish story.

Back inmy day, you didn't even have to have money to shop at Grove Market! Everyone was on a tab and Charlie kept fairly loose records. I'd call it more of an honor system tab, and some of us kids were less honorable than others, running up the family bill on treats. But, it always worked out, one way or another, at the end of the month. I was the subject of a few talking-tos.

As we grew older, his daughters and friends from school began working at Grove and, for most, it was their first real job. What's so wonderful about that is many are still there today, along with their children, and even grandchildren, carrying on the P.G. tradition. Most importantly, Charlie is still running tabs and cutting the meat. I ordered my Thanksgiving turkey from Charlie again this year. At 8:00 a.m. on Thanksgiving morning, I hear a honking from the street. It's Charlie, looking a lot like Santa Claus, in a beat up old truck loaded to the brim with hot turkeys!

Just as it has always been, I make almost daily stops at Grove Market. It's a part of what I love best about Pacific Grove. I find an excuse, whether it's to grab some of those local, organic tomatoes, a couple hot chicken pot pies from their awesome deli, or simply a kiss from my favorite butcher.

Life in a Perfect Town
Paul Miller
publisher of *The Carmel Pine Cone*, 30-year P.G. resident

After a career chasing news stories in at least 25 countries around the world for CBS and NBC, I was fortunate enough to be able to move to Pacific Grove in 1987, and I've been in love with the city ever since. It has a unique small-town feel, plus scenery that's more beautiful than anything in the Louvre. My three children all grew up here, and I'm certain that I'll never live anywhere else.

Meanwhile, I have also always loved the news business, and I was extremely lucky, in 1997, to be able to become the owner of *The Carmel Pine Cone*, which is one of the Monterey Peninsula's most important and respected sources of local news. In 2005, when the lease on *The Pine Cone's* rental space in downtown Carmel was up, I set my sights on buying a suitably historic building that would become the newspaper's permanent home.

I very much preferred to keep *The Pine Cone* in Carmel, and my first choice was a small inn at the corner of Junipero and Ocean, but when that city's zoning zealots refused to let me convert the inn to office space, I was forced to look elsewhere. Nothing else was available in Carmel, but it so happened that a perfect building was for sale on Lighthouse Avenue in downtown Pacific Grove—a building that has now been *The Pine Cone's* home for 12 years.

And that's my life in a nutshell: I live in the perfect town, work just one mile away in a perfect building, and have a wonderful staff and a successful business. I'm sure I don't deserve any of it, and every day I remind myself to be grateful for *The Pine Cone*, and for wonderful Pacific Grove.

Houston Transplant
Peggy Hansen
development director

Five days after I moved to the Monterey Peninsula from Houston in 1980, I started working in Pacific Grove. The office was in the small yellow house on 17th Street, next door to Fandango, then the home of Planned Parenthood of Monterey County. My position was being their first Development Director. It turned out to be my favorite job; I was working for a cause I believed in with a superior group of people.

Many years later, I found myself in the same room that had been my office there, for a very different reason. By then, the building was the home of a legal firm, and my divorce mediation took place in the exact same space where I had worked!

Following my divorce, I needed a new place to live. I knew I wanted to stay on the Peninsula, but had no idea where. So I decided to rent. I looked at apartments, condos, and town houses near where I had lived for seventeen years in Carmel Valley. Finally, I followed up on a newspaper ad for a house in Pacific Grove. I hadn't considered a house or Pacific Grove. I had only associated P.G. with work, and for some reason, maybe because I had only rented apartments in my single days, it had never occurred to me that one could actually rent a house.

I walked in and my mouth went dry. I knew this was it, and I hadn't even seen all the rooms yet! It reminded me of an earlier house I had lived in in happier times. This ranch-style house was fresh and spacious and light, with a front door that opened right onto the living room, and a white painted brick fireplace. I had always liked those classic English novels where a widow lived in a seaside village, and when I left this house that day, driving downhill, I suddenly realized how close it was to downtown and the ocean!

By a stroke of good luck, I was able to rent the house and loved it. After two years I realized I wanted to stay in Pacific Grove, and asked the owners if they ever decided to sell if they would give me first option to buy. Finally, that worked out as well, and I have been here for twenty years, the longest I've ever lived in one place.

Hearing seals barking, being able to walk to do errands, passing folks who all offer a greeting with smiles on their faces, seeing the ocean every day, knowing shopkeepers by name, the mild climate, annual parades a half block away from my house . . . there are so many things I love about this peaceful, small town life. I think my favorite thing to do here is to breathe. Sea air heals everything.

Ms. Trawick's and PGPD
Lucky to Be in P.G.
Roxane Viray
co-owner/officer

One of my favorite things to do is take part in the traditional events of the Butterfly Parade, the Feast of Lanterns and Evenings by the Bay. When I speak with visitors and see how much they enjoy them, it makes me so proud of my hometown. Pacific Grove is a special place that we shouldn't take for granted. Tradition is what makes it special.

My family moved here in the 1970s to give us a better education and upbringing. I'm so happy to call Pacific Grove my home. To be able to live, work, and own a business—Miss Trawick's Home and Garden Shop—in your hometown is pretty special. As a co-owner of the business and a full-time city employee, I meet a lot of people. I enjoy conversations with them and love seeing them enjoy our beautiful area.

I have lived in Pacific Grove since the '70s and attended Lighthouse Elementary, P.G. Middle School and P.G. High School. I studied criminology at CSU Fresno. I was hired with the Pacific Grove Police Department in 1999, and I am presently a patrol sergeant. I was able to purchase a home in 1997 and was lucky enough to start a business with my best friend in 2014.

Danielle's Hair Design
Danielle Coelho
owner

On Butterfly Parade morning, it has been a tradition that my clients and I go outside and watch the parade. So many of the teachers, parents, and children in the parade are friends and clients. It's wonderful to say hi and wave as they go by.

In January 1985, I moved from New Jersey to Monterey. As a young girl not really knowing how to use a map, I promptly got lost and wound up on Lighthouse Avenue in downtown Pacific Grove. I instantly fell in love with the town and asked someone, "Where am I?" I knew right then that Pacific Grove is where I would make my roots, and I did.

I was looking for a slower pace and a small town. Within the first year, I purchased a darling Victorian home and opened my hair salon. My family visits me here in Pacific Grove quite often and feels like it's their second home. Besides being a cosmetologist, wife, and mother, I am also a pilot. I am an aviation enthusiast and currently am on the P.M.L. Aviation Association Board of Directors.

I enjoy seeing the beauty in nature whether it's from the air or land. I feel fortunate that my chihuahua, Oscar, and I can walk down the street and stroll along our beautiful coastline walking path or enjoy walking through our downtown with great restaurants, fun shops, and local friendly businesses.

Paul's Mortuary
David Domedy, owner
Jane Roland

How does one become a mortician? Ask David Domedy and he will share his history. He was born in Mason City, Iowa. In 1944 his family moved to Los Angeles. He grew up in Eagle Rock which is between Glendale and Pasadena, and attended Eagle Rock High School, Los Angeles City College and California College of Mortuary Science. He was drafted into the army after which he started looking for work, applying with Forest Lawn Mortuary and Cemetery in Glendale where he was offered a job in their service department helping set up and run funerals.

David worked in the area for a few years. He married Patti in 1964, and in 1969 had an opportunity to become associated with the Paul Mortuary where he subsequently became a partner. He became senior partner and CEO in 1980 and retired in 1999. They have two children, daughter Tracy, son Derek and two grandsons, Dane, 16, and Jack, 14.

"I guess being a mortician wasn't a grave undertaking after all," David Domedy says.

Mando's Mexican-American
Mando Cruz, owner
Jane Roland

We have our favorite restaurants, and one of our choices for Mexican food is Mando's at 162 Fountain. Mando Cruz was born in Barcelona. When he was six his family moved to Fresno where he lived until he moved to the Monterey Peninsula in 2009 and opened the Pacific Grove eatery. He has never been married and attracts the young (and older) women with his friendly demeanor and ready smile. He truly gives to the community in every way. Most of the time he is cooking, and the restaurant offers every kind of food, not just Mexican. His breakfasts are famous, while his hamburgers are rated by food critic Mike Hale about the best in town. For six years Mando has given a Christmas tamale dinner to his customers and anyone else who chooses to come to have a "free" meal. His waiter, Antonio Lopez, is also a favorite and both love their customers, many of whom drop in daily for a meal or, at least, a cup of coffee.

Fandango
Brenda Taylor

There is a special restaurant here in Pacific Grove. I partied there on my 24th birthday when I first moved to California. My husband and I dined there to celebrate our sixth month anniversary of dating. Now that we are married we go there for a night out, our anniversary, or a romantic lunch date. We take friends from out of town there because it is close, inviting and delicious and I don't have to cook! We have celebrated many special occasions in its intimate corners.

Which restaurant would this be? Why Fandango, of course! It is both a visit to the past and a Mediterranean escape in the middle of a parking lot. When the door opens, you are greeted with French music from days of long ago and warm lighting, beautiful, abundant floral arrangements, delicious aromas from the kitchen, an attentive maître d, courteous wait staff and luscious food from the south of Europe. It is always cozy and romantic. I love the quiet little intimate rooms and always linger looking at the huge map of southern France on the wall. They have delicious black olives and wonderful ciabatta bread and butter. They make all the difficult food that I don't even want to attempt to cook at home.

I bought the book that celebrates the story of the restaurant and includes a few choice recipes. One day at lunch the owner signed our book with a personal note and a flourished signature. Someday our son will probably take a girl there on a date and eventually our family will be enhanced with more treasured celebrations. Our son first learned to love chocolate mousse there with Daddy. I appreciate Fandango for offering a perfect place for all of those times in life.

Healing Powers of P.G.
Tides on Forest Avenue
B.J. Deane
owner

My arrival story begins with two quiet kids—a fisherman surfer whose grandfather was born in Tahiti, and a sand-seeker swimmer girl.

It was the end of summer 1970. Being a teenager, the surfer enlisted into the Army in the middle of the biggest draft dodging in history.

Four years, Vietnam, and some countries later, the surf rider came back with a resolve to live—not in Marin County—but just up the street from sleepy Pagrovian beaches. I said Yes!

We know now the life of a returning veteran is a tough one. The healing salt water and fog brought us a long way. We have been lucky and tenacious to keep our roots here, blessed with a beautiful son who turns out to have the highest IQ of us all—or anyone we know.

He too has been taught the way of waves, the names of fishes and seabirds who enthrall us with their flight.

My own father retired as a Navy Admiral. His draw to sea is in us. Along with the skills of working hard, staying true, "toeing the line," living lives of simplicity, to support the land we love.

Message received. Lessons learned. Gratitude to Pacific Grove.

Welcome to Tillie Gort's Café
Joyce Meuse

Local Favorite Since 1969… Old Gort would like to express his appreciation toward each and every one of the astonishing variety of our customers. The young, the wise, people of the business world, followers of the spirit, family folk and loners, grandmothers, musicians, carpenters, students and teachers, working folk, those just passing through, and the perennial "regulars", whose loyalty keeps us alive during the slow times … We all share one thing in common … The love of good food and good company in a comfortable atmosphere. — *Rosie 1976, tilliegortscafe.com*

After I had my second child in Pacific Grove it was time for me to get a job. I had been to Tillie Gort's Café at 111 Central Avenue. All the folks who worked there seemed so cool to me. I went back a number of times to beg for a waitress job from Steve, one of the owners. He finally relented and I got the job, which lasted for nine years.

Each shift crew consisted of the cook, the backup—who did dishes as well as food prep—and two wait staff. Our customers were mostly locals who came in regularly for lunches and dinners. Some folks came in daily for a cup of coffee and small talk. I remember when the people who began the Monterey Bay Aquarium would often come in for lunch, as well as the people from across the street who worked at Digital Research, an early computer company. Our opinionated cook had nothing but disdain for the computer geeks.

Eventually I became one of the soup-makers and bakers who could earn extra money aside from our wait shifts. We had a special vegetarian soup made fresh every day. The daily special was a half sandwich with a cup of soup. There were a number of us who got paid to make the huge pot of soup, then put up a colorful sign on a paper plate and post it for our customers. A few of us also made Black Bottom Cupcakes, Jager Pie, No-Meat Loaf, and the wonderful Annie Laurie's Shortbread. I loved the homemade cheesecakes that Arlis would make.

There were many characters who worked there and many became lifelong friends. We had daily fights over what music would be played in both the dining rooms and kitchen. Usually, the cook had his or her way. After work at night when we did cleanup and put the restaurant to bed we played upbeat and pretty loud music. All of the crew would join together in a trash can train the night before pick-up.

The owners had made a list of duties for the wait staff on poster board in the kitchen. You would go down the list of things to do before opening, and after closing. The staff was free to trade shifts as long as our days were covered. We had wonderful Christmas parties hosted by the owners—who gave each a Christmas bonus. A local photographer and sometimes employee, John McCleary, would take an annual photo in front of the restaurant. Many of the photos are still displayed on the walls at Tillie's.

Those of us who worked and came to eat at Tillie's made a wonderful heart connection that has continued into the present. Many of us still gather on Thanksgiving Day for an annual get-together. We all still feel like an extended family.

Looking back on my life, working at Tillie's was the best job I ever had.

Centrella Inn
Amrish Patel, Owner
Mimi Sheridan

Amrish Patel, who has owned the Centrella Inn since 2004, sees it as a community, a place where people can visit time after time, always finding a warm and personal welcome. Guests arrive from all over the United States and Canada, as well as from Europe and Asia. Most of them are well traveled and are seeking a place with personality, rather than a typical chain hotel—a refuge where they can interact personally and get to know the staff and other guests.

The Centrella is unusual among P.G. inns as it was built originally as a boarding house, not a family home. It opened in 1889 to accommodate participants in the Chautauqua lectures. It continued to operate as a boarding house, including meal service, into the 1950s, when it became a simple rooming house. A massive restoration in 1981-82 transformed it into the elegant bed and breakfast inn that it is today.

With this long history, the inn has created a strong following. Visitors often drop in to say that a relative got married here or they remember coming as children. It often hosts family reunions and becomes virtually a part of the family. One guest has come regularly since 1982, initially with his employees and, later, with his family. They enjoyed Pacific Grove so much that they considered buying a house here. But they realized that they had already had the best home—the Centrella, where they always feel welcome. The children who began visiting in the 1980s now continue the tradition with their own children.

The Martine Inn
Tammy Neal

On a beautiful sunny afternoon in the heart of Pacific Grove at a romantic villa, the Martine Inn. White puffy clouds abound upon a sky-blue back drop with the sound of waves crashing against the rocky coastline, a courtyard filled with love, an array of roses in addition to coastal breezes and "Rhapsody on a Theme of Paganini" wafting in the air. These elements together created an exhilarating, romantic ambiance for our wedding day July 30, 2005.

On the eve of our special day upon arrival at the Martine Inn, we were greeted with fresh baked cookies by a very accommodating and cheerful hostess named Anne. We were then escorted to our room, "The Parke," which was oozing with charm and timeless elegance. An 1860 American Chippendale four-poster king bedroom set filled the room, along with an 1880 Chippendale mahogany arm chair which was perfectly placed in front of the charming window to view the stunning ocean views. The 1890s mahogany and tile fireplace beckoned to warm after a cool evening on the beach and a claw foot tub/shower welcomed upon entering the bathroom through the elegant French doors. We were in awe.

We chose the Martine Inn as our destination for our special day while we were visiting Pacific Grove one November weekend. We just loved everything about this luxurious Mediterranean-inspired 1890s Victorian villa. Don Martine has created a fantastic gem of charm in every room, all tucked along the scenic California coastline of Pacific Grove.

Continuing on the eve of our wedding day we ventured through the lovely town of Pacific Grove in search of some last minute touches for our special day and came across a quaint little flower shop around the corner which allowed us to pick up bouquets of gardenias splashed with speckled bits of baby breath accenting the bold dark foliage to complete our decor. The shop's owner was ever so friendly and helpful. We returned back to the Inn just in time for an evening of wine, cheese and fruit, served right in the courtyard, which was a perfect way to end a busy day.

Our wedding day began with a superb chef-plated breakfast by Chef Ismael Vizcaya Diaz, served on their fine china of silver, crystal and lace in the beautiful Victorian dining room overlooking the coastal tides.

Next, it was off to our room to get ready for our big moment. The hostess Anne and her staff made our day so special they were unparalleled in terms of their professionalism, excellence, guidance, passion and enthusiasm. No request was too big or too small for Anne and her team. Every concern was addressed without hesitation and every detail was executed flawlessly.

We had an intimate ceremony performed by Rev Francis Duda of Pacific Grove and we took our nuptials in front of 30 of our closest family and friends. The day was blessed with beauty, romance, love, laughter and fun. A day we will never forget.

Reincarnation Vintage Clothing
Nancy Holland
owner

I love so much about this town! I have been in business here since 1986—one of the longest running small businesses here. So just walking around town, I see so many friends. I was born in New Jersey, spent a couple of years in West Vancouver, BC, Canada, in my early teens, and have lived here since 1975. I've always loved fashion and when the opportunity arose I was lucky enough to be able to buy my store, Reincarnation Vintage Clothing, which was my favorite place to shop while I was in high school.

I volunteer at the Animal Friends Rescue Project on Lighthouse Avenue and often foster their dogs. I love to take my dogs to the far end of Asilomar where they can run off-leash, then head over to Goodies for a sandwich—the best way to spend an afternoon.

I'm quite proud of the fact that I've been able to keep my shop thriving so long. I think people in this town like individuality and the fact that almost all businesses in town are small, owner-operated. Nothing cookie cutter about Pacific Grove!

17th Street must have been a blast in the 70s! I have met many people over the years who come in the shop, point to a corner, and say, "I slept in that corner over there." I guess it must have been a hippie flophouse of some kind.

Another thing I love about this town is how many people from around the world come here for a visit. This month alone I've met customers from Denmark, China, Italy, Germany, Holland, and Mexico. They tend to love the image of Elvis and 1950s rockabilly and fashion.

My parents came here on vacation in the mid-70s and decided to move here. My sisters moved away after high school, but I stayed put. Couldn't imagine a better place to live!

Catching Up With Friends
Marilyn (Marly) Wheeler

I love catching up with friends over a great cup of coffee, especially at Crema in Pacific Grove. My favorite sitting room is on the second floor where, if you're lucky, you'll get the two high back comfy chairs with a large window for a delightful view of life passing by.

This day I was excited. Patricia Hamilton, author of this book as well as publisher of my book, *Lost and Found in Macedonia*, was joining me for an hour or two. I never know what will be shared: a recent experience, a great book discovery or perhaps life in general. Patricia and I both being, shall I say, more than halfway done in life, began talking about aging.

We both agreed that to ignore the process was useless. Familiar things we've done for years were becoming more difficult like yoga (bad shoulder), running (that's a no for me) and then there's that surprise photo on Facebook. Ouch! OK, so we agreed there's nostalgia every so often and sometimes the feeling of being invisible. However, I'd become aware of something else and I was anxious to see if Patricia might be feeling the same. Something I never expected or even thought about. A feeling of peace, of acceptance and almost a quizzical sense of being. This didn't happen overnight but rather because of an experience—joining the Senior Center.

With this new endeavor, life changed. The center is sort of like high school where everyone is in an age range that has similar experiences and issues. I signed up for the Monday exercise class … goodbye, gym jock.

Monday is also the food delivery for those in need. "In need" doesn't mean homeless. A wage of $15 an hour cannot support a family! The variety of people opened my eyes. I talked to a lovely Hispanic woman who cares for four grandchildren. She shared their story along with all her great ideas for extending the food she was getting. Then an attractive younger woman, on a new life path. She prefers healthy eating and tries to expand her small income by the free greens and fruit. I can't leave out the eccentric woman, very alive, dressed in disarray and obviously entertaining.

Sharing with Patricia made me become even more aware that these experiences were changing me. I've been surprised, intrigued and always left with an open heart. Once I heard two women speaking Macedonian, or so I thought. I knew some of the language from living there, but they were actually from Croatia and spoke a similar language. My attempts to converse with them were met with much laughter!

As Patricia and I were winding down, we both agreed that looking at the outside of someone can separate who we think we are or better yet, who we think they are. The happier we are with these changes, comfortable moving into this chapter, we realize life is about listening, connecting, caring and love. The less we try to be who we were, and love who we are, the more peace we experience.

Central Coast Silkscreen
Len Chodosh

Our family business was originally founded by Alex and Cheryl Rodriquez, and Ted and Jean Trendt in 1976. My wife and I have owned the business for the past 25 years. Known affectionately by locals as "the T-Shirt Shop", it is one of the oldest active screenprint shops left in Central California. We have done screenprinting and embroidery for NFL coaches, famous race car drivers, as well as thousands of businesses, schools, teams, and individuals. We feel very fortunate to have worked0o23 with two generations of Monterey Peninsula families and are proud to call Pacific Grove our home.

Our Lady of the Parking Lot
Barbara Moody

The parking lot is at Country Club Center in Pacific Grove. It is where I go to shop for groceries at Lucky, get my prescriptions at Rite Aid, and of course, check out my favorite store, the Discovery Shop.

Every time I park there I encounter "Our Lady of the Parking Lot." She is not young. Gray streaks her dark hair. She wears worn sneakers, faded blue jeans and tops. She is always smiling and never fails to give a cheery "Hello!" She spends her days rounding up stray shopping carts left carelessly around the parking lot and returning them to their proper places.

If a dog confined to a car barks at her she goes to that car and with kind words tries to comfort it.

She picks up trash. It is as if the parking lot is hers and she feels responsible for keeping it neat and tidy and for welcoming every parker.

If she goes in a shop she walks around with her hands clasped behind her back as if she has been told, "You may look but don't touch." And that is what she does.

I guess you might say she is a local character, a sweet gentle soul, bringing order to her area of the world, working without reward, "Our Lady of the Parking Lot."

Lighthouse Cinemas
Jose Gonzales, Manager
as told to Jane Roland

The Lighthouse Cinemas on the corner of Lighthouse and Fountain is small and welcoming, with ample parking and great amenities. The theater was built in 1987 by the Anea family. It was shut down a couple of times. About ten years ago it was a church in the morning and after mass it would go back to being a movie theater. SR Entertainment Group took it over in 2008 did some remodeling and opened in May of that year.

The General Manager is Jose Gonzalez, whom I have known for years. He started at SR in 2005 in Southern California (his first job). He moved to Monterey in 2009 to finish school at CSU Monterey Bay and transferred to Lighthouse Cinemas. He has been there ever since, and became General Manager in 2011. Jose has done a really great job. He has been a volunteer guide mentor at the Aquarium for eight years, loves all wildlife and nature, has two dogs, a black collie/lab and a little brown chihuahua mix, both rescue dogs he adopted. If you see him thank him for giving us such pleasure with his lovely, clean, friendly little theater.

Saturday Matinee at the Grove Theater
Richard A. Chatham
retired teacher, P.G. lover

Pacific Grove in 1940 at the ripe old age of 4. Dad had a new job at Safeway in New Monterey. A few years later, after I had entered Pacific Grove Elementary School, I discovered that the kids in P.G. went to the Grove Theater on Saturday afternoons. For twenty-five cents a kid go to the movie, buy a coke, popcorn, and bubble gum. with snacks in hand, one could settle into a seat as close to the front as possible and be surrounded by one's friends. For the next few hours we were treated to a comedy movie such as The Three Stooges, a Warner Brothers cartoon, a cowboy movie, and a serialized mystery which usually continued for the next three or four Saturdays.

There was another treat that could be purchased for twenty-five cents in those days. At the drug store fountain on Lighthouse Avenue, there was a concoction called a banana split. Bananas were my favorite fruit, and there was no sweet treat better looking than a banana split. However, I had never been able to try a banana split. My family was not poor, but they were wise with their money. This meant that the few times we ever ate out, I was never allowed to waste money on a banana split.

One Saturday afternoon on my way to downtown to join all my friends at the movie, I got an urge to try one of those wonderful banana concoctions I had seen at the drug store. Temptation got the better of me, and I walked right past the theater and headed for the drug store.

The banana split was all that I dreamed it would be... delicious. About twenty minutes later, reality hit me. I now had no money, since my parents never gave me more than I needed for the movie, and all my friends were comfortably ensconced in the theater. I couldn't go home and have my mother find out what a wastrel I had been, and I couldn't meet up with any of my friends. For a ten-year-old, two hours with nothing to do but wander around town seemed like an eternity. I don't remember how long it was before I ever got another banana split, but I do think I learned a little bit about managing my money after that.

Looking back now, I realize that Pacific Grove is really a pretty neat place to have two hours or more in which to have free time to "wander around."

Exploring Pacific Grove with Omi
Heidi Feldman

My granddaughter Vivien was the reason why her parents moved back to Pacific Grove. My daughter and her husband had been living abroad in Germany and were planning to stay there for a few years, to get to know my home country and spend time near our family there. But when they expected their first child, they decided it was time to return home, and "home" meant Pacific Grove, where Julia had grown up, and where I was living in a historic Victorian cottage in the Retreat neighborhood near downtown. They found a sweet small house on a quiet street nearby, and this is where little baby Vivien Claire began her magical Pacific Grove life. As her "Omi", the German name for grandma, I was delighted to help her explore the many special kids' places in our home town. After a few months, the family moved to a larger home on Ocean View Blvd., where Vivien would get a front row look at the big ocean, and the many cars and people passing by. When she was almost three years old, Vivien became a big sister to little baby Romy, and the family moved once again to an updated Victorian on the quiet street where they had lived before, this time with a nice garden to fit their growing family's needs.

I had been a happy resident in Pacific Grove for many years, but being a steady presence in my young grandchildren's life gave me a brand new perspective on this special town. Vivien and I began to explore our hometown together when she was still a wee little infant. I wheeled her along the recreation trail in her stroller, or took her for a walk into town for a coffee or shopping excursion.

The real kiddy fun started when Vivien reached toddler stage. She could now sit in the baby swing at Caledonia Park playground, always a favorite even now that she's a big girl of three! And very soon she was old enough for her first visits to the Monterey Bay Aquarium, easily reached with a 15-minute stroll along the scenic rec trail. With our family membership, we could go to "see the fishies" often, just stay for a couple of hours before she got tired from running from one exhibit to another and was ready for a nap on the walk home.

Other fun activities for young children have also been plentiful in Pacific Grove. The Public Library offers the weekly popular children's hour. Afterwards, it's time to spend some active time next door in Jewell Park, climb around the gazebo, have a picnic lunch and run around on the grassy lawn. The park's small community building and outside area proved to be a perfect place for Vivien's second birthday party, with many of her little friends having fun in a splash pool, games and art on a warm September afternoon. Her first birthday was celebrated at Caledonia playground, under the pleasant shade of the park's tall trees.

Just across the library and Jewell Park, our other favorite spot is the Pacific Grove Museum of Natural History. Free to local residents, we can wander in for a leisurely visit to the main hall with the big bears and other exhibits, next to the bird hall where Vivien has learned to identify the many different local winged species, make bird foot prints in the sand, and admire different sized eggs from various birds. She also loves going outside to check out the museum's native plant garden, usually a quiet place for her to explore natural plant areas, playing with the gravel near the big rocks, and cuddling in the giant cozy nest.

On warmer days, the beach, pool and grassy park at Lovers Point are perfect places for a family with small children to spend a few leisurely hours and eat an alfresco lunch at the Beach Grill, where Vivien loves to munch on the french fries that come with Omi's calamari burger! And on the way back from Lovers Point, we never miss a visit to the "17th St. chickens," a mini farm experience right here in the city.

Lunch and dinner outings in Pacific Grove can be fun with young children. Restaurants here are family friendly and greet Vivien and Romy by their names. Among our favorites are Mando's Mexican place, Victorian Corner, Red House Cafe and the International Restaurant.

Vivien's latest stage of Pacific Grove life has just begun, with enrollment at the Robert Down coop preschool, another of our town's beloved institutions where many local adults recall happy childhood days. Walking to the school and back has become a new family favorite, passing through town past the stores on Forest Ave., or along quiet residential streets with their quaint Victorian houses.

Soon, little Romy will be able to join our special outings. With Omi's and her parents help, her big sister will help her discover the many fun things to do in Pacific Grove. And maybe one day a few years from now, Vivien and Romy will create their own lives here, strolling down to Lovers Point with their little children and showing them the magic they found with their Omi in their very special home town.

My Dream Come True
Charlotte Redstone
massage therapist

I love the overall small town and friendly feeling in P.G. Wherever I go in P.G., people are smiling and helpful. I love the variety of services and restaurants in the downtown area, all within walking distance from each other.

I fell in love with Pacific Grove over 40 years ago on New Year's Day when I was walking on the beach at Lovers Point. I was born and grew up in Buffalo, New York. P.G. was my dream come true! (Weather.)

I am a California Licensed Massage Therapist and I have had an office in P.G. for almost 30 years. I also teach therapeutic massage at the Monterey Institute of Touch, our local massage school of the highest quality.

Lighthouse Avenue at Dawn
Jane Haines

Lighthouse Avenue is the broad main street of Pacific Grove. All night, fog from the nearby bay circles above the deserted street, cartwheeling vertically and leaving a glistening trail of dampness shimmering on the avenue's surface between light cones descended from dim street lamps. A bacchanal of fog droplets spin uninhibited.

But as the first light appears on the horizon, the fog droplets tense, constrict like runners before a race, bend over, prepare to spring forward toward the bay from whence they came, just as day slowly rises. Night turns into day.

At this moment when light first appears, I sometimes drive my car onto Lighthouse Avenue, arriving from Congress Avenue, turn left, head north in the direction of Monterey. The guard is changing. Night's dark sentinels are relieved of duty as gray replaces darkness.

I see in my headlights a boy riding a too-small bicycle, zig-zagging across the avenue's center line with a bag of newspapers slung across his back. A man with the collar of his jacket turned up walks swiftly in a southerly direction, led by a small dog on a leash. I reach for the knob of my radio, then withdraw my hand, unwilling to subtract or add to the moment of Lighthouse Avenue at dawn.

I know, and I have always known, Pacific Grove, even before I first arrived here 40 years ago.

Now I am on Lighthouse Avenue at dawn. Here I am—

this is home.

The Chief—1950s
Jacquelin La Vine Jones

In the 1950s, the Bank of America was in the corner building at Lighthouse and Forest Avenue, now occupied by Sotheby's. The bookkeeping room where I worked was above the main bank.

My desk overlooked Forest Avenue and Johansen's Fountain and Diner, which is now occupied by Pepper's Restaurant.

There were two attorneys who often visited Johansen's for their morning coffee or lunch. One was Reginald Foster, the city attorney, and his law partner, John Redhead, both of whom were very large men.

Mr. Redhead had a tiny Austin car, which he parked directly across from my office window. I marveled at the fact that he could actually fit into the small vehicle.

The police chief, Ernie McAnaney, was also a regular at Johansen's. He was a real jokester.

One day, I looked out the window and saw Chief McAnaney and one of his police officers. They were picking up Mr. Readhead's car and putting it on the sidewalk. One of them wrote out a ticket and put it on the windshield.

A couple of years later I was working in the city clerk's office. We shared space in the old town clock building with Judge Eldred.

Who should appear but John Redhead with a ticket he wanted the judge to expunge, written by— you guessed it—Chief McAnaney. The offense— parking on the sidewalk.

I don't know how long this went on, because I only worked there a year.

I suppose if this were to happen today, someone would get sued or fired.

It is too bad life has become so serious. Getting rid of the bad has also taken away much of the good. It seems everything must be organized. We need spontaneous fun.

BIKE, HIKE AND WALK ABOUT

On My Postal Route
Jacob Munoz

I was born in Mexico and came to the United States when I was 17. I received my citizenship five years later. I've been here 14 years and currently work for the P.G. Post Office, walking the downtown route.

One cheerful lady on my route, Patricia Hamilton, asked me for my story and this is it.

I love P.G.! It's a beautiful town, a good, small, and loving town. The people are nice. There are a lot of retired military on my route.

Robert, who was high ranking, told me stories every day when I saw him. What got me the most—he said whoever was a bad person in the army—they just shoot him and say it was from crossfire. Like in Panama—if they mistreat or rape girls—it happened. … you kill them. This was hard for me to take.

My good story is taking lunch at Lovers Point—my nice wife comes for lunch and my oldest daughter plays in the park—she really loves that park. My youngest was just born. The tattoos on my forearms are my daughters' names and their hospital footprints—so beautiful, and won't upset anyone to see those tattoos!

I like to listen to people. I'm always with music, whistle all along my route. Cheers up people. I like Spanish rock and metallic, Rolling Stones, Doors.

I'm the youngest of 12. My closest brother is a coach. I play soccer with the Salinas Soccer League.

City Hall Clock Tower Bells
Brenda Taylor

One of the most special things about our hometown is the chimes from the clock tower. The clock is always on time. I can hear the chimes every quarter of the hour and the number of chimes on the hour. It is centered in the middle of town, so you can see it from several vistas. It is an old-fashioned custom that we can appreciate. At Christmastime I get a little teary eyed with sentimental joy. The clock tower chimes some well-known Christmas carols out loud and clear. When it starts getting dusk and you run in to Grove for a special delicious treat, the chimes make our hometown more friendly.

Walk Everywhere
Gina Lynn Puccinelli

I call myself a Pagrovian. I moved to Pacific Grove when I was a young woman of 13. I attended Pacific Grove Junior High School as well as Pacific Grove High School; a graduate of class of 1980. Now at age 55, after living in all of the surrounding communities of the Monterey Peninsula, I have returned to my quaint little Butterfly Town!

My perfect day in the Grove is to take my dog Buddy Om for a morning walk down to the ocean Recreation Trail. We like to breathe in the fresh ocean air, observe and take in the colorful magic carpet groundcover, and stop for a short practice of yoga looking out at the expansiveness of the sea.

Living in Pacific Grove, one can walk everywhere. We have everything: a movie theater, delicious restaurants, coffee shops, hometown grocery store and hardware store, and a feeling of a friendly Victorian community.

Often I see the monarch butterflies floating from one place to another, and the life force energy here is magnificent. This is definitely my happy place, as well as my heaven on earth!

Falcons and other birds of prey help to keep the seagulls at bay.

Walkin' the Walk, Talkin' the Talk
Howard Roland

Due to a long-standing pelvic tendon injury of mine, one of my doctors has prescribed that I undertake a daily, non-stop, one-mile walk in a flat area with no steep inclines—and do this the rest of my life, if possible. And I have been doing just this at various locations in New Monterey and Pacific Grove for the last six months or so.

My favorite walk by far has turned out to be on P.G.'s Lighthouse Avenue from Forest Avenue to the intersection with Alder Street and back—exactly one mile. Even though I am a long-time resident of New Monterey, I have always shopped in the upper area of P.G.'s Forest Avenue and consider the downtown area of Pacific Grove to be the center of my commercial life, the place where I feel most at home.

In fact, the label of Pacific Grove as being "America's Last Hometown" may be a sort of trite or hackneyed phrase by now, but as an outsider who was born in Oklahoma but then grew up mainly in New Orleans, I can attest to the fact—and to my personal feeling—that there is a great deal of truth to this.

People are almost all quite friendly, or at least civil, to me as I trudge along the residential area from Congress to Alder and back and greet other walkers, and almost invariably I run across someone between Congress and Forest with whom I can have an amusing long or brief conversation.

Kernels of Truth from Offhand Remarks

Although my body is full of stiff Anglo-Saxon blood and I could perhaps have acquired or been taught better social skills as a young man, I find that the people who live and work in downtown P.G. are amazingly easy to communicate with, and sometimes I have learned incredibly accurate kernels of wisdom from them in their offhand remarks.

A few months ago, right after the presidential election and during my daily walk, I poked my head through the open top half of the door to Phill's Barber Shop. As I looked at the men sitting along the wall waiting for their haircuts, as well as at the three barbers and their customers being worked on, I could tell that there was a fairly glum atmosphere that prevailed due to the election results. However, I decided to take the bull by the horns, so I shouted: "Well, I hope everyone's survived this election OK!!"

There was no response from the group there. There was no joking to be expressed concerning this election. But Phill, a young man who owns the shop and is fairly obviously far wiser than most of his elders anywhere, looked at me, smiled slightly, and said: "No sweat, man. Tomorrow the sun is going to rise again."

"Wow!" I thought to myself as I said good-bye to him and then walked away. "He's exactly right! America will survive! America always survives, no matter who wins an election!"

Meeting a Tall Fellow Named 'Littlejohn'

I was engaging in my weekly raid on the ATM machine at the Bank of America, where a security guard is usually stationed at the bank's entrance to discourage all Bonnie-and-Clyde types from trying to "case the joint" for a future robbery. The one mostly there nowadays is a young middle-aged man whose last name is "Littlejohn," even though he is at least 6'3" tall. He is so laid-back and popular that he is almost always surrounded by two or more local citizens who stop to chat with him.

Just a couple of days ago I noticed from a distance that the security guard Brian Littlejohn had grown older, had gray hair, and was slightly shorter. As I approached, I realized that it was definitely somebody else, and the last name on his badge was "Oliveira."

"Aha!" I said to him as I went up to him. "You have a Portuguese last name. Does it mean 'olive tree' or 'olive'?" I asked.

"It means 'olive tree,'" he answered. Then he added, "And I am Portuguese."

Noticing his slight foreign accent, I asked, "Were you born in Portugal?"

From the Azores to Angola to Pacific Grove

"No," he replied, "I was actually born in the Azores, but I mostly grew up in Africa, in Angola."

We went on to have a very interesting conversation. He told me, among other things, that although there was no apartheid policy between the Portuguese and native Africans like there used to be in South Africa between whites and blacks, the Africans in Angola did carry out a revolution and most of the white Portuguese had to flee for their lives. And he ended up in America.

"I worked here in the US as an engineer for many years," he went on, "but the company went out of business, so I got a job here as a security guard. It's a good job, and I like it because it keeps me busy, and I really love being in America. Especially here in Pacific Grove."

"Well, we love having you here," I said to him as I told him goodbye.

After talking to Mr. Oliveira, I ran into an older man, right outside the Juice and Java coffee shop, who was taking his little Shetland sheepdog for a walk.

"Ah, a Sheltie," I said to him. "I just lost my 12-year-old female Collie last year. Let me pet your dog."

"Go ahead. He's friendly. And I'm sad to hear about your loss."

"Thanks," I said. I then kept petting his dog for a little while, since I felt myself starting to cry, but didn't want to show this.

After about 15 seconds, the grief inside me started to pass, I looked up, and we continued the conversation for a bit, mainly comparing which of the breeds, Collies or Shelties, bark more than the other closely-related breed. We concluded that both dog types bark one hell of a lot, and told each other a couple of anecdotes to back this up.

Then I went back to my little house in New Monterey, got myself a shot of my favorite honey-flavored Russian Stolichnaya vodka, sat in my big easy chair, and started writing this story.

Paris in a P.G. Day
Linnet Harlan

You can do it, you know, spend a day in P.G. in the same way you'd spend a day in Paris. The two won't be precisely the same, but you can give yourself that same sense of pleasure and satisfaction if you include a particularly French idea in your perambulations and wear comfortable shoes.

For the duration of your Paris/P.G. day, you will be a *flaneur* (or *flaneuse*, if you're female). A *flaneur*, a term invented by the poet Baudelaire, is someone who strolls around without apparent purpose, who immerses himself in the crowd, taking in what greets him.

Because you're a *flaneur*, you'll ease through your day. Personally I'd start with a *croissant*, eaten at a table chosen to facilitate eavesdropping. I prefer eavesdropping when I don't understand the language being spoken. I can imagine arrangements for assignations if a couple's vibe seems appropriate or an intense debate over foreign policy if the exchanges seem more heated. Alas, when the conversation is in English too often the conversation is as mundane as a discussion of an impending root canal.

Post-*croissant*, you'll need to decide which is more important at the moment to you: art or shopping. If art appeals, rejoice that you will not face the crowds of the Louvre or the d'Orsay, even though P.G. has a wealth of art that is publically available. The life-sized whale outside the P.G. Museum of Natural History and the bronze statue of the grandfather in front of the Chamber of Commerce building are worth seeing as are "Push Me-Pull You" and the mural in the children's section of the P.G. library and many other statues and murals scattered about town. Take your time. No one will elbow you out of the way.

If shopping is your choice, explore not only the shops offering new goods, but also the plethora of resale shops. You're sure to find something that calls to you, perhaps a bit of blue and white porcelain or a knife you can sharpen back to life. Your time is your own.

"But the Seine, the bridges, the beautiful old buildings, where are they?" you might protest. "The Pacific Ocean, the Recreation Trail, and beautiful old buildings here," I'd respond. You can't see China from Lovers Point, but, on a clear day, you can see Moss Landing. You can experience the difference between the bay side of P.G. and the ferocious ocean side. Most Parisians would be happy to spend a day strolling along either.

For lunch, walk to the top of P.G.'s own *Montmartre*, Forest Hill. Or, if the weather's cooperating, grab a *baguette* and other provisions for a picnic in Berwick Park near the statues of the breaching whales and the playful otter.

At the end of the day, stroll along Lighthouse Avenue. Let the magic of the lights entwined around the trees in the median soak into you. Think to yourself, as you would in Paris, "How did I get so lucky?"

The Need to Belong
Chris Swainson
engineer, scientist and budding writer

I make my way just after 8a.m.: Sinex to Cedar, Cedar to Spruce, Spruce to 16th, 16th to Laurel and Laurel to Fountain, perhaps. There are too many ways to sample the delights of this tranquil little community on the Monterey Peninsula.

Whichever way I choose the end result is, at the same time, always the same yet always different. The sameness is the time and the goal, the differences are the people who show up. Different but all with a common fabric—their association with Pacific Grove.

We leave at 8:30, sharp! We zigzag to Grand where the vista of Monterey Bay is revealed. Sea fog or no sea fog. White caps or calm. Either way you cut the cake, this is one of the most splendid of ways I can start my days here. We hug the coast and sample the delights of living by one of the richest marine sanctuaries in the world. Maybe it is the variety of sea and land life that is echoed in the diversity of the people who join me these mornings. All walks of life are represented: doctors, engineers, lawyers, those with their own businesses, those from IT, office workers, shop owners, young and old and so the list goes on. Each smiling, each eager to see what today has to offer.

There is a phrase often uttered by my companions: "Ha, we live here." It is their way of conveying how much they appreciate the day's splendor that is being unfolded as we ride. Yes, we are cyclists.

Amongst the many wonderful and interesting people I have met since joining this community, there does appear to be a common story, one shared not just by native North Americans but by those from other countries, too. The details may be different but the thread remains the same.

"Oh, I attended a conference here 40 years ago and never went home." "We came on vacation and decided to move here." "I was offered a temporary job after college and never left." Accidental discovery leading to the need to belong. In my case, my wife and I discovered Pacific Grove while on a trip down Highway 1. We kept returning until we were able to try to make a home here.

After our brief tour of Pebble Beach, we return to town via Asilomar and Point Pinos Lighthouse. Lovers Point welcomes us back to coffee. We pass the community heart: Jewell Park, the Pacific Grove Library and the Museum of Natural History—such a rich tapestry for a city of less than 20 thousand.

Now, two-and-a-half years into this very special community, there are times I will surmount a local hill, maybe heading west in Fort Ord, from Parker Flats towards Normandy Road. Here Pacific Grove reveals itself across the bay—home to butterflies, Victorian houses, small businesses, interesting, and interested people—and I am pleased to say, "Ha, I live here."

P.G. Works Out Fine!
Ann Harmon
Tahoe visitor

Way back when, Fort Ord was exactly that: a full-fledged military base housing and training thousands of soldiers, a significant part of the U.S. readiness-for-whatever effort. My husband signed on to become an officer in the Officer Candidate School (OCS). Luckily, I was able to get a job there in Administration G-4 as a secretary which turned out to be one of life's luckiest situations. Soon after, my husband discovered he wasn't a military type after all. Too much marching? saluting? always following orders? At that point what arrived on my desk was that piece of luck: a directive stating that, if a soldier were to lose pay under newly issued regulations, he could apply for a discharge. He did and he was out— in a week!

We were Californians from Palo Alto, we loved the coast, we loved living in the apartment at El Carmelo Hotel on the main drag, we shopped at Holman's Department Store. So why leave and why not get a job at Holman's? So we didn't leave and my husband got a job selling vacuum cleaners at the store.

We stayed in the area for two years or so living at the top of the road on Huckleberry Hill in P.G. and also in Carmel, fishing, hiking, enjoying life. No crowds then! The very best fish were rock cod. Finally, it seemed time to grow up and go to college.

But there was an earlier history in the area lived by my grandparents, also from Palo Alto. They loved the Peninsula and, incidentally, Big Basin. They would drive down for a weekend to go to Pt Lobos, the Mission, to visit Robert Louis Stevenson's house, to walk the shore. No crowds then!

We now live at Lake Tahoe on the Nevada side where winter means no hiking and snow, not rain. Pacific Grove draws me to it around February every year as a warmer place to stay for a while. So, with a cousin having a house near Lovers Point, why be cold? We loved the shoreline walks, who doesn't? We were within walking distance of the Sally Griffin Center so could enjoy its classes. The Museum's lectures were not often enough, we had to enjoy movies downtown as well. And the library kept us going, away from home and otherwise book-less. A month in the town of Pacific Grove works out just fine!

MOVIE STARS … !

Michael Parks
Tracy Lee Phillips

The actor Michael Parks passed away at the age of 77. He was very nice to a little girl in 1969-70 ¼ me! He graciously gave me his autograph, and he talked to me a few times as I watched them (with Martin Sheen) filming (or shutting down), a lot. Their trailers were set up between 17th and 18th Streets off Lighthouse Avenue. It used be a vacant lot between the bus depot and movie theater at 17th, and the gas station at 18th in our little town of Pacific Grove. He could've easily ignored me, but he didn't! He was a down-to-earth kind of guy ¼ Very cool memories. RIP Michael Parks, aka James Bronson of Then Came Bronson.

Then Came Bronson Meets Local Low-Rider
Kathryn Voeykoff Payne
P.G. Native

In the 1960s Pacific Grove was a different world—kids had the freedom to explore their neighborhoods. Pacific Grove was kid-friendly. It was as if every house was filled with kids; schools were busting at the seams with students, and Pacific Grove was one big playground. We had a certain freedom kids no longer enjoy today. Our weekends weren't scheduled. Of course, there may have been the occasional family outing or scouting event, but for the most part, we were free to "hang-out" with our friends.

My ultimate freedom came in 1969 when my mom bought me a bike. Not any bike, but a blue banana, glittery seat bike with sissy bars. I dropped the seat, raised the sissy bars and off I rode with my friends, Jay, Doug, and Craig, to explore Pacific Grove. We found adventure around every corner. There was just one Mom rule—"be home for dinner."

I was a tomboy at this age, pre-teen. Playing with dolls and having tea parties didn't interest me. I wanted adventure. I loved the out-of-doors. I liked to collect autographs. I used to seek out movie stars to get their autographs, which was not as problematic as you might think—more often than not, there was filming going on in town and, of course, there was the Crosby—the Crosby was a small town thing. Among my collection that I keep to this day, tucked away in a blue box, are John Wayne and Glen Campbell's autographs, among others.

One Saturday in January 1970, my friends and I were out for a Saturday adventure on our bikes when we came upon a movie crew. The moment we saw them, we knew what they were doing, so we peddled right over to where they were set up to get a better look. As soon as we pulled

up, we saw "him." I knew it was Bronson. He was right there. They were all just standing around. I felt like it was all serendipitous, perfect timing. It was then, I don't remember how it happened, but my bike's chain came off. Bronson said, "Cool bike. Got a problem? I can fix that," and he did. I asked him for his autograph, he obliged—without the condescension often offered me when I asked a "movie star" for their autograph. He was nice; he didn't talk down to us.

I have to this day Michael Parks' autograph with his greasy thumbprint—the result of his putting my bike chain back on the sprockets. We sat on the curb for a few more minutes, watching the crew and Bronson stand around. It was boring, so we left to find our next adventure.

I was reminded of this single moment in my childhood when I heard that Bronson, Michael Parks, died this past May. I remembered how he made me feel at our chance meeting. Bronson had made me feel like we were part of the same kind of adventure, that we shared that same spirit for adventure. He had a motorcycle, I had a bicycle—but we were the same.

Postscript: Michael Parks was in town filming episode 22, "Still Waters," for the first and last season of Then Came Bronson. *It aired February 25, 1970. This episode told the story of how the editor of* The Pacific Grove Press *was publishing a series of editorials about the ecological havoc industrial pollution was having on the bay. Kismet would have it that today the location of the* The Pacific Grove Press *in the TV show is the same building that now houses Jameson's Motorcycle Museum and the* Cedar Street Times.

Turner and Hooch and Tom Hanks
Jane Roland

The year was 1989. The SPCA Shop on Forest Avenue was thriving. One day when I was working at the counter, a man came in. He told me that he represented Touchstone Pictures and they were preparing to film a movie with Tom Hanks on our street. The stores and businesses on the first block of Forest Avenue would need to close. The production company was prepared to offer an incentive not to open for a few days. I thought about it and suggested $500. This amount was agreeable and early in the week we shut the doors.

The street was changed. The police station scenes from the film were staged at what is now a Chase Bank. The Union Bank was the site of the wedding reception. In the background were iconic figures such as Sandy the Whale in front of the Pacific Grove Museum. We naturally hoped to see the stars of the movie, but were afforded only a glimpse from time to time.

Later when it opened at the Lighthouse Cinemas we attended the local premier, hoping to see the shop and, maybe a peek at one of us exiting; however, that was not to be. I was advised by a well-meaning friend that I could have asked for three times the amount. Turner and Hooch, not a great movie, but an example that Tom Hanks can work with anyone or anything: Wilson, the volleyball, and Hooch, the dog.

Viva: In Pacific Grove

A note from author William Neish: Last year, a tall lady with fantastic bone structure came into Alpha Stationers. After I drew a map to point her toward an address in P.G., she thanked me and we exchanged names. I was then inwardly agog…because Viva Hoffmann is an important figure in American culture!

Viva was part of Andy Warhol's Factory scene in the 1960's, and was photographed by Richard Avedon, Cecil Beaton, Francesco Scavullo and William Eggleston. In addition to Warhol's films, she acted for Woody Allen, Wim Wenders, John Schlesinger and French New Wave cinema legend Agnes Varda. I loved her two novels (Superstar and The Baby) and her landscape paintings of the desert in bloom and the seascapes of Malibu are in collections worldwide.

Determined to associate Viva with Pacific Grove FOREVER, I later tracked her down to get her impressions of our little town.

What brought you to Pacific Grove?

My friend Patricia Purwin. I've known her for a long time and her life dream was to live in Pacific Grove. She and her husband, Charles, went there every summer until Patricia credited her long dead guru Paramhansa Yogananda, superb author of *Autobiography of a Yogi*, with finding a house for them to buy. Then last year I was in Santa Monica where my daughter had rented me an apartment so I could be close to her while she was shooting *Transparent*, and when the rental was up I drove up to Pacific Grove to visit Patricia for a week.

How would you describe Pacific Grove to someone who had never been here?

It reminded me of Hitchcock's *The Birds*. It just had the feeling of that same atmosphere of that little town, with an abundance of flat, white light like they have in Bodega Bay. And no congestion. And the beach with the cement pier reminds me of the 1920's…like an old photo from an European town.

Is there another place in the world you might compare it to?

A place I've lived that's a little similar is Positano in Italy, where the old houses are all up steep hills and there is a pebble beach. And it also has the mountains behind, like in Pacific Grove. Though in Positano you could walk to another town up higher along a trail, with no road back then. It gave you the sense of adventure; that you could just keep going and find anything. It's similar to living on the Saint Lawrence River, where you can dream of getting in your boat and ending up in Nova Scotia. I like that feeling of being able to imagine endless voyages. With the ocean in front of you at Pacific Grove, you can imagine getting in a boat and going anywhere.

When did you live on the Saint Lawrence River?

In 1952, when I was 14, I found Swiftwater Point, a gorgeous, 1900 Adirondack-style house with English rock gardens, a huge dock, boathouse, a bay, wetland, woods… twenty-three and a half acres total. It was on Wellesley Island in the Thousand Islands, which are part USA, part Ontario, Canada, in the Saint Lawrence River. I convinced my father to buy it. The year we moved in for the summer there were nine of us. I spent my summers there and took my kids there years later, until we sold it after our father died.

So, back to Pacific Grove. What was your best time here?

The thing I liked most was the ocean…watching the seals on the beach and hoping for the sight of an otter or two. While doing that I noticed a couple who'd swum from another place and ended up in Pacific Grove. They said the only way they could do it was because they were wearing wet suits with long sleeves and long legs. It's a shame the water is so cold, but I suppose otherwise it would turn into Venice Beach.

Another thing I loved was the Grove Market, where everyone was so nice. I ordered a lamb roast and picked it up the next day. It was so sophisticated. They had all kinds of exotic vegetables and would order anything you could think of. And I loved being able to walk anywhere in town; the library, the nature museum, the coffee shops and restaurants, the market, the beach. That is so great - not having to drive. And when you do drive, you can go down that gorgeous coastline…for example to Clint Eastwood's fake ranch and watch the one black sheep grazing with the white ones.

The next time I come to Pacific Grove I'm going to convince Patricia to take me with her on a tidal pool search. She is a certified California naturalist and belongs to the LiMPETS program, which monitors changes to the sea. When I lived at Paradise Cove I used to examine the tide pools, which are the spots where the ocean comes into little rocky outcroppings, at low tide, and leaves little sea creatures: anemones, which are always pretty stationary (and actually look like the inside of an artichokes after you get all the petals off), limpets, cockles, star fish, and tiny crabs sheltering in tiny shells. Once to my utter dismay I watched a schoolteacher in charge of some kids capture a baby octopus into a water filled jar! When I reproached him he said it was going into the aquarium under the Santa Monica pier, and that anyway octopi feel nothing. In fact, they are so sensitive they turn reddish or pink when frightened! To this day I regret not snatching the jar from his hand and liberating the baby octopus.

What might the Andy Warhol factory crowd have said about Pacific Grove?

They all really hated nature so they wouldn't have come near the place. Andy couldn't wait to get back to New York any time we went anywhere. We went to Sweden for a Warhol Retrospective…or maybe it was Denmark. I don't remember which, as we only stayed one night. I only remember what the profiles of the young boys in a nightclub looked like, as they all looked exactly alike. It was the same with going on location. We went to Tucson, Arizona, and made *Lonesome Cowboys* in three days because Andy couldn't wait to get back; though he did say while watching a Mexican gardener mow the grass in front of the motel that he might like that job. We went to La Jolla to make *San Diego Surf* and stayed less than a week; Andy couldn't wait to get back to dirty old smelly New York City!

Why do you think Andy Warhol was uncomfortable outside of Manhattan?

Some artists I knew didn't like being anywhere where people didn't know exactly who they were. They had to have the adulation from people who knew they were famous. I took John Chamberlain once to a *Village Voice* staff party and he introduced himself as a famous sculptor!

Though Andy didn't have much by way of social skills, at least he had the brains not to admit - assuming it were true - that he had to leave somewhere because nobody knew he was a famous artist. My interpretation is that they were so insecure and so ignored before they became famous, once the fame hit them they couldn't stand that prop not being there. And Andy might have had that autistic thing called Asperger's Syndrome. He had all the symptoms. They need routine, they become disturbed by the slightest change. And, he was first and foremost a workaholic. Paul Morrissey thinks Andy could neither read nor write. However, he wrote me a letter I received in Rome. Each line was in a different handwriting.

Is there any chance you will come back to us in Pacific Grove?

I would move to Pacific Grove myself if I could find a really good swimming pool there. No rush, no fuss, no traffic. No big buildings…all sweet little houses. I would go whale watching and tide pool searching to my heart's content. The ocean is my love.

SECTION 9
BUILDING COMMUNITY SPIRIT

VOLUNTEERING AND THE JOYS OF GETTING TOGETHER

St. Mary's Church
Outreach Ministries Provide Good Feelings
Kit Franke

Every July, my "life in Pacific Grove" focuses on the Antiques and Collectibles Show at St. Mary's by-the-Sea Episcopal Church. As members of the "little red church that cares" since the early 1980s, my husband and I have volunteered in a number of roles: vendor contracts, furniture movers, signage, ticket sales, kitchen detail and publicity, to name just a few of the tasks that we parishioners undertake to raise money for our church outreach ministries.

I look forward to this time in our shared congregation life because it is a way for all of us, no matter what generation we represent, to interact with each other, to welcome the extraordinary vendors who decorate their booths with incredible style, and to visit with the many members of our P.G. community in a relaxed and joyful setting.

This annual fundraising event, which celebrated its 60th anniversary in 2017, is held the second weekend in July. Begun by women of St. Mary's Guild, it was originally staged at the Monterey County Fairgrounds but somewhere along the line was moved to church grounds at Twelfth Street and Central Avenue.

Grounds and Halls Transformed

Rooms in Edwards Hall and Clay Hall are transformed into 25 or more antique booths. The St. Mary's Thrift Shop becomes an amazing boutique with the addition of very special items like silver, Oriental art, china and jewelry donated to the shop throughout the year just for this weekend. The front lawn is turned into a Vintage Village of collectibles and garden décor. At one time, we had the popular blacksmithing and weaving displays on the lawn.

The show also features delicious daily lunches cooked on site and served by our youth group members to guests on the patio. The Bistro Snack Bar and the Corner Cupboard sell homemade desserts, jams, bread and cookies. Another committee tirelessly works on obtaining unique silent auction items that are displayed in exquisitely wrapped baskets.

Not to be missed are the free tours and the classical, Celtic and organ concerts inside the historic church each afternoon. Did I mention that the preparations for this event begin in January and that over one hundred parishioners volunteer their time?

Worldwide Attendees

I love the fact that every year I hear people say how much they look forward to attending the show and they wouldn't miss it for the world. I meet former parishioners who were once stationed at Fort Ord and are now visiting the Peninsula again and planned their trip so they could be here when the Antiques Show was held. I talk to couples that were married inside the beautiful redwood sanctuary and return with their children to show them the "little red church" which, by the way, is the first church building constructed in Pacific Grove, back in 1886.

Yes, July is a busy and very rewarding month for us living in Pacific Grove. And as soon as the Antiques and Collectibles Show is over, we hang our lanterns and eagerly await the Feast of Lanterns festivities. Always something fun to do in Pacific Grove!

Bringing Help for Women
Michael Reid

Outraged! That's how I felt when I came to work and discovered that a young woman said she had been raped the night before while sleeping outside on St. Mary's church steps. Men from the I-HELP program had been sleeping inside, and she claimed that at some point in the middle of the night, one of the men came out and attacked her.

For several days prior, I and others at St. Mary's had attempted to find a place for her to find shelter. She had been given (and used) several nights of hotel vouchers, telephone numbers of service provider agencies (which she had called), and nowhere was there an organization that could assist her.

She was too old for programs for youth. She did not have children, was not mentally ill, drug addicted or escaping an abusive partner. She was unemployed, evicted from her home and now relegated to living outside. So, as a last resort, she decided to sleep on church property. She said that was where she felt the safest.

I called the Pacific Grove police. A news team from KSBW arrived with cameras. She was taken to the hospital by one of our parishioners and an investigation ensued. As far as we were able to uncover later, her perpetrator was never found. In fact, there are doubts if her rape kit was ever processed. But after alleging rape, she actually qualified for emergency housing. She became a victim and was given shelter.

It took that—a rape, literally on my doorstep—another validation that beds did not exist for a growing population of women on the Monterey Peninsula and that something had to be done.

Becoming Visible: The Face of Homeless Women in Monterey County

In October of 2011, while working as the Associate Rector at St. Mary's by-the-Sea Episcopal Church, I received a letter from a person named Joyce. In her letter, Joyce stated, "… there are too many homeless women in the streets without help … When I was homeless, there was no family to help me, plus it was during the rainy season and getting cold. I had no sleeping bag or blanket, tent, nothing to protect me … no safety in the open while sleeping." Joyce went on to say, "No woman needs to wonder if she will live to see another day." She asked if I could help. And although I didn't know exactly how, I decided to try and Becoming Visible was born.

The shortage of emergency housing for women on the Monterey Peninsula was real and continued to grow. In Pacific Grove alone, the number of homeless women who came to St. Mary's by-the-Sea Episcopal Church for food, clothing and other resources had increased significantly. I looked at statistics from the first ten months of 2011 and noted that out of 330 persons who were single and homeless, 20 percent of them were women. This caused me to look further, and through conversations with other clergy and homeless service providers, I learned that the growing number of women who were homeless had outstretched already scarce community resources.

According to available data, there were over 2,500 homeless individuals in Monterey County, and approximately 39 percent were women (which represented an increase of 24 percent from the previous census). The experts agreed that the most vulnerable and underserved in our communities were homeless women, particularly older women; and those without dependent children, mental illness, domestic violence or substance abuse. I learned that for women like these, the possibility of a bed for the night was becoming more difficult to find. And if you are a woman veteran, you are four times more likely to become homeless than your male counterpart.

Although surprised and disturbed, I was certain that others would want to help, once they became aware of the need and then given the opportunity to connect with stories that would challenge preconceptions and shatter existing stereotypes.

Over the next 12 months, with the help of many partners, Buddhist priest Kathy Whilden, Carl Cherry Center Director Robert Reese and I created a photo exhibit that included the work of documentary filmmaker, now Monterey City Council member, Timothy Barrett, photographers Lina Vitel, Ken Wanderman and Margo Duvall, writer Erika Fiske, and editors Roxane Buck-Ezcuerra and Patrice Vecchione. The exhibit, called *Becoming Visible: The Face of Homeless Women in Monterey County*, documented the faces and lives of women who were homeless but chose to become visible, hoping that their personal narratives would make a difference in finding solutions for women like them now, and in generations yet to come.

This show at the Carl Cherry Center for the Arts, ran for five weeks, challenged assumptions about homelessness, and encouraged community action for change. "We don't want to be invisible, feared or blamed." Heidi said. "We are not dangerous. We only want to be safe and to be given another chance."

This was only the first step. We encouraged others to open their hearts and minds to the images they saw.

They became more aware of and sensitive to the needs of these members of our community who most have failed to see. Many became volunteers at one of the service organizations on the Peninsula, while others offered much needed financial support by giving to a newly established fund at the Community Foundation of Monterey County for homeless women—opened by my request after discovering this crisis in our midst.

We have the power to help meet this growing need and ultimately discover sustainable solutions for the countless women who live outside. These women are our sisters and mothers, daughters and friends. They have found the courage, the strength and dignity to show us who they are. It is now our turn to show them who we are as well.

Aunt Merce Provided Shelter and Hope

Somewhere around the year 1935, a doctor and his family travelled from New York to Jamaica, West Indies, for an exotic vacation. Once there, they discovered the need for someone to care for their children. I'm not sure exactly how, but they secured the services of my mother's Aunt Marcella as a nanny during their stay.

When their vacation ended and the family returned to America, they realized how attached they all had become to Aunt Merce. They arranged for her to immigrate to the US—where she ultimately came to live and work—and became the first one in my family to find shelter in America. To call it "home."

Some years later, after the war, Aunt Merce did the same for my mother, who did the same for her sister, who then (many years later) did the same for my grandmother. Over time hands had reached out and back for many others, providing shelter and hope, and making a lasting difference in the lives of my family for generations to come.

Perhaps that's why I was shocked to originally discover that there were at least 350 women who lived alone, without safety or adequate shelter, on the Monterey Peninsula each night. It disturbed me to learn that single women who are 50 years of age and older had the least available to them in terms of options for programs and services if they lost their jobs and became homeless. Women who didn't have a diagnosed mental illness, substance abuse or dependent children were especially in danger.

Women who were simply poor, were alone, frightened and fending for themselves on the beach, in the park or in drafty doorways.

I met one woman who would return to her tent at Jacks Peak every night after receiving chemotherapy infusions for cancer. Another woman spent all her resources caring for her sick and dying mother, and ultimately lost everything, including the roof over her head in Pacific Grove.

Another proudly showed me her teaching credential from San Jose State, but at the age of 77 she could no longer work in the classroom or provide care for the elderly, and after years of low-wage jobs, she had no savings and nowhere to call her own but a place under the freeway in Seaside.

When I met a woman who was 81 years old and had been living in her car for over two years because after being laid off from her job in Pebble Beach, she couldn't find employment nor any housing that was affordable; I knew that the people of this community were better than that, and that something had to be done.

But nothing is done in a vacuum or by one individual. It takes a collection of like-minded people, a community rallying around a common goal with determination and generosity, to create change.

One Starfish Safe Parking Program and the Fund for Homeless Women

So, with the help of my friends, Kathy Whilden and Marian Penn, we established the Fund for Homeless Women in 2012 as a field of interest fund at the Community Foundation for Monterey County and have raised over one million dollars to support programs and services for women living without adequate shelter.

Over the past five years, with contributions from concerned community members, we have been able to support the opening and operation of programs like:

One Starfish Safe Parking Program—providing safe parking and case management services for women living in their cars.

In collaboration with San Carlos Cathedral, we supported the open and ongoing operation of Gathering for Women—where last year over 450 women have been fed in body, mind and spirit through a weekly lunch and service delivery program.

Shelter Outreach Plus and Community Human Services received funds from us to increase their ongoing programs for women young and old.

St. Mary's by-the-Sea, Unitarian Universalist, and the Community Church of the Monterey Peninsula have all been awarded grants to help them meet the emergency needs of unsheltered women and help to keep them safe.

We tripled the amount of money we were able to award to our grantees. And in addition to ongoing support of programs we helped to initiate, we were thrilled to support the creation of 12 units of transitional housing and a day program through Community Homeless Solutions.

We granted seed money for I-HELP for Women and supported temporary housing for women who have mental Illness through Interim, Inc.

Because we live in an area of such high rents and low inventory of affordable housing, the Fund for Homeless Women partnered with Housing Resource Center to create a program called SOS—Saving our Senior Women—finding and securing permanent housing for senior women through a comprehensive approach of case management and the education and cultivation of landlords who care in our community.

This would not have been possible without the generosity of community members who want to make a difference in the lives of women who are homeless, and the partnership of Community Foundation staff who had the vision and the courage to say "Yes" when I came to them with just outrage and a dream almost five years ago.

We have a long road ahead before all women who are living without adequate shelter in Monterey County have a place to call home, or at the very least a way to come inside and out of danger, but this is just a beginning.

In addition to annual grant-making, the Fund for Homeless Women continues to build an endowment that will support in perpetuity programs for women living without adequate shelter in our community.

And fulfilling our greatest hope, donors are leaving lasting legacies by making planned gifts and naming the Fund for Homeless Women in their wills and estate plans.

With the Community Foundation, our donors and partner organizations, the Fund for Homeless Women will continue to endeavor to meet the needs of women who are homeless in Monterey County now, and for generations to come.

I think my mother's Aunt Merce would be proud.

Dedicated to shelter, safety and community, the Fund for Homeless Women is here for good. After all, we say we live in paradise. And there's certainly more than enough to go around.

Housing for Women
Jean Stallings

I was delighted to be offered a position on the board of directors of a non-profit that sponsored transitional housing for battered women and their children.

Within a year we discovered financial problems and several board members resigned for fear the problems might impact them personally. Someone told me the word "on the street" was that the organization was about to die. When the last staff person left, she showed me how to unjam the copy machine and to figure out payroll. She wished me luck as she walked out the door.

I became president and the few remaining board members voted to reduce staffing and take steps to reduce expenses. I wound up working fulltime in the administrative office. I put on the answering machine during working hours and I had to run all errands and make banks deposits, etc., between noon and 1:00 p.m. so that the phone would be covered all day.

What a thrill after six months when a long-requested grant came through and we could gradually start increasing staffing to reach the number we had reported to granting agencies.

An even greater thrill occurred when the agency returned to full staffing. It still exists and many battered women and their children have learned self-esteem and parenting skills they had not known before.

Heidi Feldman picking up Khenpo Karten Rinpoche at the airport to bring him back home to Pacific Grove.

Khenpo Karten Rinpoche
A Resident Buddhist Teacher for Pacific Grove

Heidi Feldman

"The teacher will come when the student is ready."
That traditional Buddhist saying proved to be true for two local Pacific Grove residents. Khenpo Karten Rinpoche and I met at a chance encounter in 2008, at a teaching by His Holiness the Dalai Lama in Madison, WI. Rinpoche, a Buddhist monk and teacher, had been in the U.S. for a year, after a long journey from Tibet via India, Nepal and other places around the world. In his home country of Tibet he had been the abbott of his monastery near Nanchen in the Kham Province, until the Chinese occupants made there his life too dangerous to stay and he began the difficult trek across the Himalaya to India in 1998.

I was a beginning Buddhist student and follower of the Dalai Lama, who wanted to find a local teacher who could provide Buddhist training for her and other fellow practitioners in the Monterey Bay area. Briefly after their brief first meeting, they saw each other again in Berkeley and soon I arranged a teaching for Rinpoche at the Pacific Coast Church. More than 40 people attended and many came back for another Buddhist talk he gave the next spring.

By then, Rinpoche had decided that he liked the Monterey area better than other places across the U.S. he had visited. "I really liked the ocean, the nature, the quiet, and Big Sur," he recounts. Parts of the landscape reminded him of his beloved Tibet, especially the green hills during the springtime. When some of his new students offered to bring him here as their teacher, he readily accepted. Soon, he found a temporary home where he could offer weekly Buddhist teachings, and he continued to give public talks at various places around the Peninsula. Several students provided him with a place to stay, hoping that one day he would find a permanent place to live and teach.

His first regular teaching location was a very small commercial place in the center of Pacific Grove, one side of a Victorian duplex he shared with a real estate office. The tiny room, which at most could accommodate exactly 21 people, in addition to his shrine table and his teaching chair, was cozy and allowed him to meet many local P.G. folks, as well as tourists staying in hotels nearby. Soon, everyone knew the friendly monk in his maroon robes in the little yellow house, sitting on his small porch or working in the side garden with the colorful prayer flags.

With the help of other students, Rinpoche's was able to set up his "Manjushri Dharma Center" as a nonprofit organization and to attain refugee status on his way to become a U.S. citizen. His presence in Pacific Grove was made permanent when he received a generous donation to purchase a house which would be suitable for both a Buddhist Center and his home. A very happy Rinpoche greeted his students and friends on a spring day in 2015, after a few busy weeks of group effort to renovate his new home. Since then, the center at 724 Forest Ave. (at Sinex across from P.G. Middle School) has become a highly visible center for an active Buddhist community on the Peninsula, with weekly meditation sessions, chanting practice and in-depth teaching by Rinpoche, with the help of local interpreter and Tibetan expert David Molk.

It had been many years since Pacific Grove had its own resident Buddhist teacher. What began as a wish by a student and a dream by her teacher had become a reality, for the benefit of many here and elsewhere who have come to attend Khenpo Karten Rinpoche's teachings about love and compassion, and peace around the world.

Find out more about Khenpo Karten Rinpoche and his Manjushri Dharma Center at manjushridharmacenter.org or visit him in the saffron and maroon house at 724 Forest Ave., in Pacific Grove! Tel: 831/901-3156.

THE THRESHOLD CHOIR OF PACIFIC GROVE—SUSIE JOYCE

Singing at Bedsides is Like Bringing Chicken Soup

Not music therapy and not performance, Threshold Choir's bedside singing is more like bringing chicken soup to an ailing neighbor. That is how those of us in the three-person Threshold Choir of Pacific Grove think of the service we have been providing for friends, neighbors and patients of Hospice of the Central Coast since 2010. The rewards of this practice are many, but being able to step away from the ego of performance to focus on the needs of a patient is certainly one of them. Singing with the intention of being fully present allows us to connect on a deeper level, and we are often privileged to make that connection during that tender time at the end of life.

Although we prepare a song list for each visit, we often find that the songs that best fit the needs and responses of the patient will surface at a bedside. A song like "You Are Loved" or "You Are Not Alone" sung at the right moment can be a message so welcome that it brings tears to the eyes, and "May Peace Be with You," sung over and over, may be just the medicine needed to calm an agitated patient and lull them to sleep.

At times, it is support for the struggle that is called for. One friend who succumbed to cancer at a young age was buoyed by the healing songs we sang to him. Seeing him enthusiastically nodding acknowledgment that the lyrics of songs like "Don't Give Up" spoke to his personal journey is a precious memory that won't be forgotten.

There are times, however, when our carefully honed harmonies and selection of compassionate Threshold Choir songs aren't what a patient needs. We added "Don't Fence Me In" to our songbook when a friend told me that she heard her husband singing the song while gazing out of his hospital room window. He was delighted when we showed up at his bedside singing his song, and as sick as he was, he rallied to sing with us as we repeated chorus after chorus. That sing-along was the first of many over the course of 14 months of regular visits with the plucky Pacific Grove octogenarian who pushed us to expand our songbook to include his favorite Broadway show tunes.

Even in the last hours when he was unresponsive, it was not Threshold Choir music that reached him. After singing at his bedside for over 90 minutes, it was "Swing Low Sweet Chariot" that got his toes moving to the rhythm, then his hands, and moved him to open his eyes and whisper words of affection to his wife.

The poet philosopher Kahil Gibran wrote, "Music is the language of the spirit. It opens the secret of life bringing peace, abolishing strife."

Invitation for a Song Bath

The Threshold Choir of Pacific Grove invites weary community members to receive a Song Bath, offered between 8:00 and 9:00 p.m. on the last Tuesday of each month. Song Bath is our name for an invitation to relax and get comfortable in our reclining chair placed in the middle of a choir member's living room, while three-to-four singers gather around you singing gentle songs from our repertoire of original Threshold Choir music. We sing songs like "You Are Loved" and "May Peace Be with You," softly, with the intention of providing support and comfort, much like a mother singing lullabies to her child.

We offer Song Bath Tuesdays as outreach to community members, who, for whatever reason, may wish to experience the healing effect of being soothed by music. There is no charge for the 20 minute song baths offered in Pacific Grove; we volunteer our time providing this service as a love offering to our community. We ask nothing of participants, except to receive the gift.

The Threshold Choir of Pacific Grove has been honoring the ancient tradition of singing at bedsides in our community since 2010, adding singing for Hospice patients to our service in 2012. As part of the larger Threshold Choir organization of 2,000 volunteer singers in communities around the world (www.thresholdchoir.org), we believe that music has the ability to bypass the chatter of the mind, ease our burdens, and touch us in a profound way. Although we do not sing religious music, we consider our songs to be more of a prayer, or meditation, than a performance.

Our small Pacific Grove choir is seeking new members to help us expand our service singing in homes, hospitals, convalescent homes, at memorials and at community gatherings. If you are interested in singing with us, receiving a song bath is a lovely introduction to what we do.

Due to commitments to Hospice and practice time, only three song baths can be scheduled on the last Tuesday of each month between the hours of 8:00 and 9:00 pm. Please call me if you have questions or wish to schedule a song bath. Susie Joyce, 707/815-0745.

For more information about Threshold Choir of Pacific Grove and becoming a bedside singer, visit www.thresholdchoir.org/Chapters

Maggie's Shangri-la Rock
Margaret Barlow

As a young woman I knew nothing of synchronicity—yet my life has been guided by it. While at San Jose State University, I met my husband quite by chance. We dated for a year, and then his family invited me to join them at the Grove while we were still in school. The rugged coastline, the power and serenity of the ocean, and the charm of the quaint "home town" of the Grove captured my heart.

Life has taken me many places to live, from the sunny shore of San Diego to the craggy mountain tops of the Rocky Mountains. I have had "cabin fever" twice from the extreme "white out" for days and weeks at a time. At those times my soul languished for the coastal scenery I love.

In 1964 my husband made a career move he had long awaited. If I was going to support him, it would mean another three years in the deep mountains of Idaho near Jackson Hole. My psyche was not prepared to do this again! I needed the solace of my Shangri-la, Pacific Grove. With my two little boys and a dog, I came to Pacific Grove and stayed in a cottage near Asilomar for two months.

Near Bird Rock, if it hasn't washed away, is a rock with my name on it. I sat on that rock for hours daily as I watched my boys play in the tide pools. I was in meditation, trying to find what depths of my soul I could harness to endure the mountains again. Shortly before my retreat ended, my husband joined us. He knew what a trial I was facing. As the sun was setting, we took a long walk on the beach. It was a very tender moment and he promised me that we would return to the Grove to live.

This is where synchronicity comes in. I left Pacific Grove with a personal goal to learn to be "magnanimous." Two years later, the night before Thanksgiving, news came that my husband had been killed coming home from Jackson Hole. I was 34 years old.

We returned to California where our families could help with our wounded hearts. Through synchronicity, we were drawn to rural Sebastopol. I bought a small apple ranch where I reared my boys. With grandparents in San Jose, it was easy to spend weekends in Pacific Grove.

When Fort Ord closed, I purchased a cute little house in Seaside. When the market was right, I came to Pacific Grove and have lived in Pacific Grove for 15 years. I have made good friends here and enjoyed activities at the Sally Griffin Senior Center. Our memoirs class recently compiled and published a book of memoirs. Pacific Grove has been my place to ponder difficult decisions and find renewal. It is my Shangri-la.

From the other side of existence, He kept his promise.

"I'm sorry … please forgive me … thank you … I love you."
Ho'oponopono
Joyce Meuse
longtime resident, friend to many

Among my most significant experiences in Pacific Grove was when a Hawaiian Kahuna came to town to give a workshop on Ho'oponopono which is a karma cleansing prayer. It was the mid 1980's and the workshop was held at the Pacific Grove Art Center. It was a two day event where Kahuna Morrna Nalamaku Simeona presented her resolution-forgiveness healing methods as well as other wonderful tools of consciousness.

Originally, the Ho'oponopono was a very long and involved thing that Morrna had abbreviated to make it more simple and available to everyday people. Morrna also taught the use of the pendulum to check if energy had been cleared and also to answer yes-no questions. The Ho'oponopono clears negative energy from places, people and anything else that needed cleansing. Through doing this process you could not only clear your own energy field and that of others, but also inherited karma from your ancestors and relatives.

The original one that I learned from Morrna went like this. "Divine Creator, Father, Mother, child as one, I wish to do a Ho'oponopono on me, myself (say your name), my ancestors and relatives from the beginning of creation to the present time. And (another person, or situation) their ancestors, relatives from the beginning of creation to the present time. I ask that any and all negative energy be transmuted into pure light. I ask that all aka cords be cut, severed, released and removed. I ask that any and all out of body beings be gone with no remaining negativity. We are set free. And it is done."

Morrna said to finish up with any prayer or affirmation. She also suggested to make a list of all of your relatives and friends and do a Ho'oponopono on all of them.

I copied this wording and gave it out to all my psychic students and clients. I said it when going to, being at, or leaving any highly-charged situation or place. And especially when having a conflict with a friend or relative. There is hardly any situation where this karma cleansing will not help resolve or relieve difficult conditions

In the last few years I came upon an even more shortened version of the Ho'oponopono. It is simple but still powerful. It is saying silently or out loud, "I'm sorry, please forgive me, thank you, I love you."

Try it on any difficult situation or relationship in your life. Can't hurt and likely it will help to change the energy and make a subtle difference in circumstances in your life.

History and Mission of Pacific Grove Masonic Lodge No. 331

"Make a Good Man Better"

Herschel R. Amos

Pacific Grove Masonic Lodge No. 331 has been a part of this community for more that 100 years. The Lodge was originally chartered in 1897 to provide a gathering place for local Freemasons. The current building at 680 Central Avenue was constructed in 1949 with over 2500 hours of donated labor. The building was dedicated by the Grand Master of Masons at a Masonic Cornerstone Ceremony on February 4, 1950. The actual cornerstone of the building is located in the northwest corner of the structure. During the 1800s many distinguished citizens of Pacific Grove were members of the Masonic Fraternity and were instrumental in establishing a Masonic Lodge in Pacific Grove. Freemasonry is a system of morality veiled in allegory and illustrated by symbols. It uses the tools and techniques of the stonemasons' guilds of the Middle Ages to illustrate simple moral and ethical principles. To this it adds a philosophical and spiritual framework for personal improvement, portions of which come from other philosophical schools. Freemasonry seeks to make a good man better by encouraging its members to focus on improving their relationships with others, and to practice a life of tolerance, compassion, honesty, and the pursuit of justice. It makes the world a better place by making it members better citizens of the communities in which they live. Freemasonry is not for business or other commercial advantage but for self-improvement.

A Promise Kept for 103 Years

Ken Cuneo

Cedar Street Times article, June 2, 2017

This is a story of continuing dedication and adherence to a promise made over 103 years ago in Pacific Grove. Back then, the Pacific Grove Masonic Lodge was in its infancy (1887) and met upstairs in what today is the Pacific Grove Art Center.

The first Master (President) of this Lodge was a man with the last name of Fifeld. Brother Fifeld was the spark that planted fertile roots for the Pacific Grove Masonic Lodge that enabled the Lodge to expand and flourish.

As Brother Fifeld grew older and neared his last days, he decided to bequeath a large sum to his Lodge for he had no near family left. His bequest came with a simple request that every year, members of the Pacific Grove Lodge would come once to his simple grave and place flowers on it.

On this Memorial Day current members of his Lodge honored his request as has been done for the past 103 years and will continue to be done into the future. After all, a promise made should be kept!! Those in attendance were Jason Walters, Tom Thiel, Herschel Amos and Mark Burger.

Kind and Understanding Masons

Gary Ozuna

My favorite people in Pacific Grove are the Masons and the Masonic Temple, which is about 150 years old. The people are very kind and understanding. The buildings are very well constructed. The Masons help many people with their projects and activities.

My grandmother came to Carmel from Denver in the 1940s and lived there until the mid-80s. I came to live with her as a child and went to Carmel Wood School and High School, too, then MPC. I'm an artist and musician.

I grew up in Big Sur and Carmel and started the Little Love Psychedelic Shoppe in Carmel in 1966 with friends. The hippie life was in order: surfing, wilderness living in the Los Burros Mining District. This was the last legal mine in Big Sur, jade and gold, and was open 11 years.

The Lure and Promise of Beacon House
Bob McGuire

"There it is!" Annie said with nervous excitement. "Do you see it? Right there on the corner."

"Wow," I said. "It looks like an old Victorian house."

"It is," she said. "Isn't it awesome? This is where I'm going to start my internship on Monday. I can't wait!"

As I drove our car past the Beacon House and it faded from our view, Annie's sparkling eyes looked at me and said: "Let's go 'round again."

We approached it from a different direction this time, and I slowed the car down as the towering spire and majestic multi-story house entered our vision. Annie didn't say a word. She just stared at it through the window. Once we passed it again, she turned to me and said, "One more time? Please?"

It wasn't just a therapist internship job that Annie was going to start at Beacon House on Monday. It was a complete rededication of her life. Deep in her soul, she had resolved to dedicate her life to help others survive the nightmare of addiction in a loved one. She survived that nightmare, and emerged focused, stronger and burning with purpose.

It began with our son's high school addiction to alcohol. Then the downward spiral progressed to oxycodone in college, and finally to heroin. The deep descent into the black hole of addiction warped all three of us in different ways, and we groped around in panic to grab onto anything to help us survive the insanity. Our reactions just pushed us in opposite directions: I enabled and Annie screamed. Our marriage of 30-plus years started to crack under the pressure.

We started our long climb out of the pit with 12-Step meetings, which provided tremendous help and support. But Annie needed more. She sought out the help of a therapist who specialized in addiction. From the very first moment of her first therapy visit, her life changed direction. She came home from that visit a changed person. Over the weeks of intense therapy work that followed, her steady climb towards recovery eventually led her to a burning desire: to become a therapist, to help others the way she had been helped.

She then completed her Master's Degree in Psychology, and started her internship at Beacon House. She thrived. She beamed. She helped people in their own recovery from addiction.

Annie's last day at Beacon House came in October 2015. She had worked over 2,000 hours towards her dream before terminal brain cancer eventually ripped it away from her. She would not live to see her dream come true.

But Annie's dream is not over. It lives in other people who have that same burning desire to help addicts and their families in recovery. And through Annie's story, they will receive the education and training they need to make their therapist dream come true.

Someday, a budding therapist intern is going to drive up to that beautiful home in Pacific Grove and say, "Wow, there it is! That's where I'm going to start my internship."

Breakfast for Al's Friends
Started by Al Seikert in 2014
by volunteer Michele Barat

The idea for the Breakfast was conceived by Al while attending the Beach Church at Window on the Bay, Del Monte Beach, which was started by Pastor Brian Bajari. Pastor Brian ministered to people every Sunday and passed out donuts. Al Siekert attended and the idea came to him that the hungry people gathering needed a nutritious breakfast.

Since 2015 Al and volunteers have served more than 10,000 breakfasts—every Sunday and holidays to 30-60 people, 8:30-10:00, rain or shine. Al cooks the hot, main course and volunteers make fresh green salad, roasted vegetables, and baked goods. Dave and his young daughter bring hot coffee. There is always orange juice and bottled water. Al says it's "5-Star Michelin food for the hungry."

The cost for the Breakfast is covered by donations at the MPC and Pacific Grove farmers markets, and in front of Charlie Higuera's Grove Market. Charlie and his staff support our cause and we collect donations every Saturday. Many other local businesses contribute to our success.

If I had to come up with a mission statement it would be "Serving good food to the hungry, with dignity and respect." Everyone that attends is very appreciative and we all have a really good time.

In 2016 Al Siekert was nominated for a Jefferson Award, representing Pacific Grove. He has worked tirelessly for this cause and it has grown into something we can all be proud of. Al has lived in Pacific Grove for over 30 years and Sunday Breakfast is almost solely supported by the generous and kindhearted citizens of Pacific Grove.

Serving the Community

The Bridge Restoration Ministry
Daniel Chisholm

Pacific Grove originated as a Methodist summer camp and morphed into the charming town it has become today. But there's a group of P.G. residents who struggle, every day.

Since 2006, The Bridge Restoration Ministry has ministered to men and women battling substance abuse (often just released from prison) and who want to change their lives. Two Pacific Grove residential settings provide safety, structure, discipleship and supervision for a minimum of a year to help restore them back to God, family, work, and community. A third residence is currently for male graduates and has no time limits. And the process is working!

The Bridge is operated by Mike and Michele Casey and their Board of Directors. Mike Casey says he took his first hit of heroin with the help of his father and has fought addiction most of his life. He has been a firefighter and a paramedic—but heroin always took another hold.

He lost jobs, he says, and his wife kicked him out, fearing he would never change. After living in his car in a local church parking lot, he reached rock bottom. He entered Victory Outreach's church-based men's rehabilitation center in Salinas—and then had a massive stroke. He couldn't walk, talk or feed himself. By the grace of God, he says, he recovered quicker than anyone expected, although he is still numb on one side of his body.

Casey sees the stroke as God's way of relieving him from his addictions. Since then, he has been clean, reunited with his wife, and working to help others recover.

The Pacific Grove community has been a key factor in The Bridge's success. "Something I learned early on in my recovery," Mike says, "was that for 40 years I thought only of myself. I was the center of my own universe, but by the grace of God I was delivered from addiction and began to serve others. This concept was at the top of the list when we began The Bridge restoration ministry 10 years ago. Our Bridge shirts said it all—'Serving The Community'— and that's a philosophy we hold to."

The Bridge is privately funded through donations, and does not require a fee from the resident or the county. The organization holds annual fundraising banquets and

operates Second Chance Thrift Stores in Pacific Grove and in Monterey. Bridge graduates work in the stores and are frequent volunteers for community events.

Law officials work closely with The Bridge and like it. State law Proposition 36 took effect in 2001 and offers first and second time nonviolent offenders convicted of drug possession the chance to receive substance abuse treatment instead of incarceration. Each year, more than 500 drug offenders in Monterey County qualify and about half need residential treatment—and in 2007 the county only had 27 available beds, until The Bridge began.

For more information about The Bridge Restoration Facility or to donate, go to their web page at http://www.tbrm.org/.

Finding P.G. and Rotary
Victor Johnson

It all began in 1996 when Lynda's father, Randy Morris, heard Les White speak at the Downtown Rotary Club of San Jose. Mr. White was a former city manager of San Jose and had accepted a position to lead the effort to close and define the civilian use of Fort Ord. Randy was so taken with his talk about all the good things that would happen to the area that he rented a weekend place on Belden Avenue in Monterey. The idea was to scope out the area and possibly move down from San Jose.

Randy and wife Pat would come down to Belden Avenue about once a month. Lynda and I, however, started to make the trip more often. We would drive down Friday night and start walking around town by 8:00 a.m. During one of our walks, we ventured further south and came upon Pacific Grove. You have to understand that our prior trips from San Jose to the beach involved either Santa Cruz, Capitola or Carmel. We had never heard of Pacific Grove, so our exploration extended from 8:00 a.m. to 5:00 p.m. or later. As time went on, our walks evolved to scoping out neighborhoods and open houses. One Sunday, we happened into an open house on Ocean View Boulevard and met Marilyn Vessalo, a local realtor. We exchanged business cards and were on our way.

I started working seven days a week on a software implementation so our trips to Belden Avenue diminished. In 1998, I got a call at work from Lynda. She said Marilyn had called and a house was going on the market today. I left work, picked up Lynda, and took off to Pacific Grove. We arrived about 11:00 a.m. and by noon we owned our

new home. Our San Jose house sold within a week, so we moved to P.G. in May 1998 and began our new adventure.

I retired in 2005 so no longer needed to spend time in San Jose. Lynda moved her office from San Jose to P.G. and joined P.G. Rotary and that's when our involvement in the community began. Lynda met Jeanne Byrne at Rotary and heard about the Pacific Grove Concours Auto Rally. Since I had an interest in cars and Lynda thought I needed an activity, Jeanne approached me about helping with the Auto Rally. It's one of the best things that could have happened to me. I've had the pleasure to work with many other Rotarians like Steve Covell, Lindsay Munoz and Matt Bosworth, sell ads to the local merchants like Lisa at Peppers and Moe at the Chamber, work with Patricia Hamilton on the event program, and design rally shirts with David at Federico's in Monterey. A truly wonderful experience.

P.S. As it turns out, Pat and Randy beat us to P.G., moving in 1997.

Pacific Grove Rotary Club
Jane Roland

The Pacific Grove Rotary Club grew out of the Pacific Grove Service Club in 1948. A slate of officers consisting of Roy Bancroft, Al Coons, James T. Rye, James Grand, Dr. Ralph Maxell and Dr. John Nelson were selected to serve until June 30, 1948. The Forest Hill Hotel was the weekly meeting place. There were 33 charter members. Initially Rotary was exclusively male. In 1989 women were admitted and this club boosted the first woman and first female President, Pamela Norton, in 1994-95.

The site of the lunches has changed over the years, From Forest Hill to Asilomar, to Sticks at The Inn at Spanish Bay and, currently at Pèppoli. There are 56 members. The club is famous for the Auto Rally held in August and Good Old Days Parade in April and other fundraising events over the years. Members feed homeless men and women, give scholarships to high school students, support the Rotacare Clinic started by Pam Norton, and projects such as restoration of the Little House in Jewell Park, which members initially built, and the Sunset Performing Arts Center. These projects have expanded and raise valuable funds for the community. Many of the members serve on the City Council, including the mayor. The president and executive director of the Chamber of Commerce are members of the club. The current president is Tom Greer, retired manager of the Monterey Regional Airport.

I-HELP with Rotary at St. Angela's
Joe Shammas by Jane Roland

Joe Shammas grew up in Pacific Grove and attended P.G. schools. He is the owner of P.G. Travel and belongs to the Rotary Club of Pacific Grove as did his father, Jake, and sister, Nancy, both of whom were presidents. It came naturally for Joe to assume that leadership position in 2007.

In 2007 during his presidential term, Joe saw a great need for the community to assist in the I-HELP program at St. Angela's Church, his parish. Once a month, anywhere from 20 to 25 homeless men are bused to a facility which provides dinner, breakfast and a sack lunch as well as shelter for the night. The Rotary Club agreed to take on the responsibility every other month at St. Angela's. Joe is there every time, unless he is leading a tour group. There are usually about eight Rotarians helping. John and Jane Roland have missed only twice in the ten-year period. A hearty dinner is served with vegetables, salad, rolls, dessert and assorted drinks. The men arrive around 6:00 p.m.; Rotarians purchase, prepare the meal, serve it and sit down with the men to enjoy the repast. Ted Voigt, a fellow Rotarian, and his wife, Lisa, always bring an ample sack lunch for the following day. The "guests" are responsible for cleanup and dish-washing. The Rotary Club brings clothing and has purchased pillows and mats as well as warm jackets and socks for the men. It is a warm wonderful tradition, one we hope will continue indefinitely.

Statue of the Virgin Mary
in front of St. Angela Merici Catholic Church.
St. Angela's was founded in 1928 and is
celebrating 90 years in Pacific Grove.

THE GIFT OF OUR COMMUNITY GARDEN—NANCY BENNETT

Sometimes, it's the first thing I think about in the morning and, sometimes, it's the last thing I think about at night—all the little raised beds, trim and neat, with their individual signatures of what people like to plant. Some gardeners start with seeds and they water and wait, and water and wait. Others bring their seedlings and opt for a little head-start. All-in-all, the little lettuces, bright carrots, deep purple beets, ruby-red tomatoes and such eventually reward us with earthly delights and that unique taste of something grown and tended with your own hands.

On any given day the community garden space is shared with crows, blue jays and other small birds, squirrels, butterflies, bees, and marvelous hawks (did I mention gophers?). The tall trees surrounding the garden bend and sway in the afternoon breezes and it's easy for one to feel the rhythm and heartbeat of life when beauty is all around. There is often the sound of voices sharing ideas about planting, seasons, weather and gardening techniques, with each contributing voice lost in their love of growing things. Because we are located close to schools, the small and tender voices of children can also be heard. They often visit the garden and bring their wonderful questions of *why*, and *how* and *when?* And, just as we plant our raised beds in a community with all kinds of seeds, side-by-side and row-by-row, the gardeners and visitors who pass through the welcoming gate are also a community of thoughtful, caring people who love the satisfaction of watching things grow—watching Mother Nature at her finest. The gift of our P.G. Community Garden goes beyond what is seen and reaches deep into the hearts and minds of people who love this planet, this beautiful home we call Earth, and all her creatures.

This brief history of a garden is dedicated to my beautiful mother, Ruth, who loved the earth and all living things. Ruth lived her 101 years in complete harmony with the natural world—the world that was *her* garden.

A Garden Story
Heidi Feldman

My grandfather would have been proud. He was an avid gardener who provided much of our food after the scarce postwar years in Germany. And helping him with garden chores, followed by happy, imaginative play, was one of the favorite pastimes for my brother and me, the two youngest of a brood of six siblings in our family.

Now, several decades later and living in a different place halfway around the globe, I am thinking of my "Großvater" every time I open the rustic bamboo gate and enter our thriving Pacific Grove Community Garden. Much like ours, his garden was in a separate area away from his home. He would reach it by bike, pushing it up a steep road in the morning, and riding it down in the evening at a good speed, loaded with baskets of garden bounty—vegetables and fruit to feed our hungry family. I reach the garden in 15 minutes with a brisk, slightly uphill walk, or on most days, with a lazy drive of a couple of minutes, on my way to other errands.

Much like my grandfather's garden, I consider my happy garden plot a special blessing. I first heard about a new community garden project when Karin Locke located a small, challenging space in downtown Pacific Grove, generously offered by an environmentally oriented solar power company in the dirt patches around their parking lot. Our small, determined group of urban farmers made the most of this little space and installed growing areas wherever possible, including vertical beds built creatively with wooden shipping pallets. Our persistence paid off, again with Karin's help, when we were offered a garden patch on a piece of real plant-able earth behind the P.G. Adult School. Soon we were erecting our fence and other infrastructure, only to be told that we had to relocate the garden in a rear area, a challenge at the time but a much better location in the long run.

Not having been aware how long it took my grandfather to establish what eventually became a one-acre paradise of garden beds, fruit orchards and small shed, I was amazed how quickly our garden turned into a verdant collection of raised beds, creative growing configurations, and shared public spaces. My first photos show us building our eight boxes from redwood boards, lining them with hardware cloth, and filling them with fertile soil, waiting for their new inhabitants of seedlings and seeds. My first plants in the beds were French sorrel, my grandfather's favorite herb, and lovage, my grandmother's favorite flavoring for her garden soups. Just a few months later, the garden took on its verdant, more horizontal look. Slender beans grew up on their tall poles, tomato plants spread up along their cages, and more exotic denizens came along, including spiky artichokes and towering sun chokes.

Our gardeners began to add their creative touches to their plots, building special cages to keep out hungry critters, and furnishing their garden homes with reused cabinets to hold their tools, as well as a funky collection of assorted chairs to sit and relax. Sturdy and practical water barrels, mounted to tall wooden poles, turned the various sections of the garden into a loose system of neighborhoods.

Over the years, there have been challenges to growing our precious crops, with invasions of bugs and critters. Thankfully the deer are kept away by our solid fence. And the humans in the garden have had their own challenges as well, with sickness, family needs, or other issues keeping them away from their garden chores, or forcing them to leave the garden altogether. But there's always a waiting list of eager newcomers hoping to join in, and new friendships ready to be made. Talking with each other happens easily in the garden, as we learn from and encourage each other, watering and weeding, planting and harvesting.

When I enter the garden, the day's news and problems stay behind. I greet the garden with a grateful smile, thank my grandfather once again, and head to my plot to start yet another page of the garden story.

Meyer Lemons
Joe Strang
community gardener service

Citrus, including Meyer lemons, are semi-tropical fruits, so they have no dormant period and require no chill factor (32 to 45 degrees) to leaf and flower. They do, however, need a good eight hours of sunlight. Citrus trees do not require regular pruning; however, if pruning is desired to shape the tree, it may be done at any time unless there is danger of frost. When first planting any fruit tree, be sure not to bury the root stock, the thick trunk at the base of the tree, as it will root better if the root stock is exposed.

A Meyer lemon is a cross between a "regular" lemon and a Mandarin orange, which makes it less tart than pure lemons and provides it with a more fragrant aroma. It has more juice than other popular lemons such as Eureka.

Healthy lemon trees have an abundance of deep green leaves. Citrus fertilizer is high in nitrogen, the element that provides the deep green leaves essential for fruit production. Fertilize all citrus every season but winter by sprinkling about six inches beyond the drip line as the feeder roots are just beyond the ends of the tree. If the leaves do not turn deep green a few weeks after applying a high nitrogen fertilizer (i.e. 20-10-10 or 10-5-5), try adding iron. As our soil does not accept iron by itself, use iron chelate, which is a compound that allows the soil to absorb iron.

Meyer lemons may be semi-dwarf or full size. Both produce the same size lemons, but full size trees live twice as long, up to 75 years if properly maintained. Citrus trees have a much longer life span than other fruit trees. Full-size apple trees, for example, produce for about 50 years, while other fruit trees are fruitful for about 15 years.

Be careful not to let potted lemons become root-bound. Do not over water. Watch the leaves for signs of drooping, a signal of over watering, which is the primary cause of the death of fruit trees. Water deeply but infrequently rather than sprinkling often, as deep watering helps the roots to grow downward. CalAm provides free water meters.

I have been operating as Joe's Pruning since 1982. Before that I lived on the East Coast, where I landscaped my property with trees that I earned by working for nurseries during my vacations from teaching high school English. It was an El Niño year in California and I had been laid off from teaching at a middle school in Salinas due to budget cuts. As the rains produced an abundance of vegetation, it was an ideal time to begin a gardening business. In addition to pruning fruit trees and roses, I teach free Saturday workshops on fruit tree pruning at McShane's Nursery on Highway 68 in Salinas. I also tutor homeowners on how to trim their fruit trees.

For advice or to schedule a work appointment, call 831/375-8672 or email strangjoe@yahoo.com.

My Garden Plot
Ginny Stebbins

I feel very fortunate to have a small plot in the Pacific Grove Community Garden. And even though gardening in this climate has been a challenge for me, I'm getting better at it.

I love planting, watering, trimming, weeding, collecting seeds, tasting, harvesting, and admiring so much that I'm always disappointed when I'm all done and I can't find another thing to do.

I have gotten really tired of eating chard (my best crop) so I've planted some new and interesting vegetables in my quest for variety. I found four different kinds of plants that I'd never heard of before. It's too soon to say whether they will be a success or not. Each one of them is sitting quietly in the ground patiently waiting for the sun to come out. Perhaps they will begin to grow in the fall.

Besides what grows in my own garden I am also really interested in the plants that grow wild in our area, especially the edibles and natives. I want to know all of their names. One thing that motivates me is that edible wild plants and fruits are nutritionally superior to cultivated vegetables and fruits, and so many of them have medicinal value, too. I get great satisfaction out of making a salad with miners' lettuce or tea with nettles. I delight in telling my family where I found the particular item they are eating—be it from my garden or from a field!

A few years ago I started a Facebook group called "Monterey Area Spring Water, Wild Food and Foraging." It's a place for me to share what I am learning and to learn from others. I also explain about foraging for water at Grimes Spring in Big Sur. It is the only water my family uses for drinking and cooking (that is, until the Pfeiffer Canyon Bridge collapsed). It's great fun when people stop to chat when they see us filling up. Some are locals who have been drinking from the spring their entire lives and others are travelers from around the world wanting to fill a couple of bottles. All are grateful for the clean, free, living water. And it's only a one hour drive from Pacific Grove. I invite anyone to join the group and please stop by the garden to say hello and see what we are growing!

Facebook: Monterey-Area-Spring-Water-Wild-Food-and-Foraging

SALLY GRIFFIN ACTIVE LIVING CENTER—MIMI SHERIDAN, historian

Moving from Seattle to Monterey, where I knew no one, was undoubtedly a big step. Finding the right places to do things—have coffee, get a haircut or a pedicure, go to aerobics, etc.—was a challenge. But I really scored when I found the Sally Griffin Active Living Center in Pacific Grove. The center is a focal point for a vast array of services and activities, but what sets it apart is friendliness—staff, volunteers and members all welcome newcomers enthusiastically.

A typical morning at the center can be dizzying. A quilting group stitches and chats in the back room. Tables are being rearranged for a lunchtime musical performance. A yoga class comes to an end. Women socialize while waiting for a fitness class. Others just hang out—checking e-mail on the computer, reading the newspaper, drinking coffee from a bottomless urn.

The center's most basic principle is that socializing, learning and physical activity are all vital to the quality of life. Weekly movies, workshops, musical and dramatic performances and discussion groups are all opportunities to learn and to enjoy other people's company.

Meals on Wheels

But the major activity every morning takes place in the shiny professional kitchen. The center really revolves around the Meals on Wheels program. Meals on Wheels began in Monterey in the early 1970s when Sally Judd Griffin noticed that some of her neighbors were no longer able to prepare healthy meals. She began cooking and delivering them herself, eventually working with others in church kitchens and the Carpenters' Hall in New Monterey. In 1972, Meals on Wheels of the Monterey Peninsula was established—two years before the national organization.

It operated in borrowed kitchens until the 1980s, when the City of Pacific Grove offered a beautiful piece of land on Jewell Avenue at the edge of the Pacific Grove Municipal Golf Links, only a block from Lovers Point, one of the most spectacular beaches in the country. A community-wide capital campaign raised more than $1,000,000 for a new building, which opened in 1986—and was named in honor of Sally Judd Griffin. The activities grew well beyond meals, requiring an expansion in 2004-2006.

Today, Meals on Wheels of the Monterey Peninsula offers three core programs. The best known is Meals on Wheels, which prepares and delivers meals five days a week to frail, elderly and disabled people in the area extending from Carmel Valley through Monterey and Seaside up to Marina. Another program serves hot lunches every weekday at senior centers in Marina, Seaside and Monterey as well as at Sally Griffin. The lunches are notable social occasions, particularly the holiday celebrations and monthly birthday lunches, when decorated tables overflow into the side rooms. The third core program is operating the Sally Griffin Active Living Center itself, with its numerous services and activities.

Executive Board

A board of 15 community members oversees more than a dozen food service and administrative staff. Executive Director Viveca Lohr is a veteran with the program, having worked with Sally Griffin for nearly 30 years. The center director, Andrea Fuerst, a former Peace Corps volunteer, came here after serving as the Program Director for the Girl Scouts of Monterey Bay. She's a very positive presence, often seen visiting with volunteers and program participants.

Volunteers

Like all programs of this type, the center really runs on volunteer power. The front desk is staffed by a rotating team of people eager to answer questions. Other volunteers sell luncheon tickets, staff the weekly produce market, serve meals, and give presentations or classes. In 2015-2016, 350 people volunteered nearly 28,000 hours of their time. Meals on Wheels alone has 150 volunteers who delivered nearly 185,000 meals to almost 500 homebound, mostly low-income people. More than 750 individuals in the dining program enjoyed nearly 18,000 hot lunches.

Funding and Membership

Funding is a constant challenge. Because the Monterey County organization is independent, it must raise all the funds for its programs. Membership fees (only $35 a year) and payments for meals cover only a small portion of the cost. Foundation and government grants provide additional funding. Members themselves help though activities such the regular "treasure sales," which clear out clutter and raise money.

The greater Monterey community is drawn in by donating to the Sponsorship for Independence Fund and by special fundraising events such as the annual Women Who Care luncheon and the Culinary Classique d'Elegance. This major event at the Spanish Bay resort has brought together top local chefs to produce a unique meal and auction, raising more than $1.8 million over the past 20 years.

Partnerships

Partnerships are another key to the center's success. Among the most popular programs are the fitness classes sponsored by Pacific Grove Unified School District's Adult Education. Participants continue attending for years, becoming a family looking out after each other and welcoming new members. Some of them actually took PE classes at local high schools from the same teachers, Joan and LaVerne. Yoga and tai chi are offered for those venturing beyond the simple aerobics classes. One instructor, Sherri Beck, moved to P.G. more than 30 years ago and began teaching cardio classes. She became a certified instructor and continues today, with regular Pilates and Gyrokinesis classes at the center and other P.G. locations.

Another valuable partnership is with Episcopal Senior Communities, which sponsors a weekly produce market, run by volunteers assisted by the Food Bank of Monterey County. This highly anticipated event allows people to buy small quantities of fruits and vegetables at wholesale prices.

Services for Members

Also enhancing seniors' independence are health screenings, support groups and workshops on the use of computers, smart phones and the internet, as well as assistance with income tax, health insurance, financial planning and legal services. Many of the activities foster creativity and participation. Art adorns the walls, with sales benefiting both the artist and the center. The frequent musical and dramatic programs include sing-alongs and dramatic presentations and readings by center members. Discount tickets and transportation are offered for cultural events such as the Carmel Bach Festival.

Each member uses the center in the way that works best for their needs. Some people come for a specific class, while others just come to enjoy lunch with friends. But many local seniors take advantage of a range of Sally Griffin's programs. Harriet Rosen, a dancer who moved to Pacific Grove from the St. Louis area in 2000, began by taking a yoga class. She lives nearby and often drops by to use the computers or attend discussion groups. She especially values events such as the topical film series (such as "Aging at the Movies" and "Women in the Movies") and talks on issues of importance to seniors like health insurance.

The Sally Griffin Active Living Center's services and activities, including meals, will have growing importance in the coming years as the number of senior citizens increases and more people seek to maintain their independence and quality of life in Pacific Grove.

My own story at Sally Griffin has barely begun. After becoming a devoted participant in aerobics and strengthening classes, I branched out to a tai chi class, which I enjoy tremendously. I'll soon live within walking distance of the center, and look forward to more classes and films.

ACTIVE WOMEN

Women Heroines and The Seven Stages of this Heroine's Journey
Rose Flanagan
memoir writing class challenge

Even though I had not even settled in America, I knew for certain that I would have to take my four children and leave the life I had been living as a married woman.

I was a very happy, outgoing and almost "fey" kind of person. I loved my home city and I loved the home I grew up in. I loved my mother (a widow) beyond words. I loved my two sisters and brother and felt protective toward them. I loved the fact that we always had a cat.

It was Easter 1974. My husband, Jim, was out again, and I knew he was at a bar. My fifth child, Jennifer Eileen, had been born just two months earlier (January 30th). She was very ill, premature, and the delivery was difficult. My darling baby lived for just a week before she died. Jim had been drunk during the delivery and after. I was all alone as I tried to get through the awful loss.

I had made some good friends in America. Among these friends was a dear, warm lovely person. Her name was Margaret McAnaney. I had met Margaret at an Al Anon meeting. St. Patrick's Day. Sometime after the death of Jennifer Eileen, the phone rang at 10:00 p.m. I thought it was Jim. At first, I hesitated to answer. I knew he would be drunk. However, something made me go to the phone. It was Margaret McAnaney wishing me a Happy St. Patrick's Day. She was at an airport waiting for a plane to Hawaii. I began to cry, and she hushed me and said, "Rose, leave Jim. I will help you."

Jim came home drunk as usual on that Good Friday of 1974. He was unusually agitated and even violent. I left the house with the children with a woman friend, Cathy, who had happened to drop by. The children and I stayed at her house for a few hours. She took us back home around 7:00 p.m.

Soon after we got back to the house, I turned to the children and, addressing mainly John, my oldest (12), I said, "John, you, Catherine, Liz and I have to leave and go and stay with Margaret McAnaney." John just nodded his head and set about to leave for Margaret's. At 10:00 p.m., the children and I were seated on a Greyhound bus headed to Margaret's and the town of Salinas.

It is hard for me to describe my feelings, really. I left a situation that I knew was very bad for my children (especially my children) and me. To be honest, in looking back I am amazed that I was able to leave Jim. I had loved him very much. Again, my love for the children was my driving force. Also, wonderful, caring, loving friends, even from strangers.

Despite all the harrowing and even traumatic events in my life, I always have had a core of, not strength exactly, but a strong sense of when things are wrong, action is needed. My children are amazing. They have all graduated from college and are good, decent people.

I feel that I need a lot more time to heal. Patricia Hamilton, my teacher, was great. Patricia, if only you knew how many women "heroines" I have met in America.

Woman Warrior
Mary Roberts

Stories about my life raised in P.G. and all the other little home towns around the Peninsula. Went to Catholic school all of my school years. Went to Walter Colton for a short time. P.G. High for a very short time. Seaside High a very short time. Was expelled for getting in a big fight with a big bunch of black girls—they did not know I was told by my mother that if I got in any fights that I had better win or not to come home crying, as she would beat my ass all the way back to the school. And that just wasn't an option for me, because I had already been beat by her way too many times and I had enough of that. So I became a very good fighter, enough from her. I was an only child and I didn't have siblings of any kind, as I was adopted from Hawaii and brought back here to the mainland at the age of two weeks old. Thanks for inviting me to tell you some of my stories. Thank you.

My Heroine's Journey—On Becoming a Woman
Betty Fox
memoir writing class challenge

Here's a story that tells the age-old tale of a young girl on her way to becoming a woman as she goes after her calling, but comes face-to-face with first love's touch.

Betty Fox, as a young woman starting out in college at seventeen to fulfill her purpose of becoming a nurse, had hit a detour on the path she was following when she fell in love with a "funny man," as she called him. Being so young and in love, she couldn't see the path she'd carved for herself changing in a different direction than she originally planned. Still, she became engaged to the man she fell in love with after two years of dating.

And so, the idea of going off to nursing school was demoted to the back of her mind because love happened to fog everything up except for her windshield as she drove forward anyway. First loves, while they may be the easiest to fall for, are the hardest to step away from, and just coming to the realization of that is a battle all its own.

Betty faced this challenge when she recalled, "When my fiancé wanted me to get married and stay home with the children and be a pastor's wife, I felt trapped and too young for marriage."

By that point in the relationship, she started sifting through the recesses of her mind to find the very thing she had lost sight of. When she finally recovered her life-long desire to go to nursing school again, she became faced with a choice.

However, at a moment's hesitance she wondered how she could make both choices a reality—like a fork in the road merging together to create one cohesive path. But it didn't work that way; it hardly ever does, if at all. For challenges must be met and conquered, not remedied. Betty understood this as she stood standing at the fork. A daunting feeling—a never-ending chasm filling the pit of her stomach—as she decided on either right or left. Letting go, though, she chose the path she originally started with.

Sometime after breaking up with her fiancé, Betty's sister came to the rescue and showed her an application for nursing school. Finally getting back on track, Betty found her resolve again and applied. The timing seemed off, for the class started in February, and she was in the wake of January. However, she made it in. This was the "it" moment she'd been running towards.

Though it wasn't without heartache that she chose her career over her relationship, the fact of the matter was she found more happiness there than she would have if she had stayed where she was. If Betty had not gone on to nursing school, she might not have earned her B.S. in nursing, and then she wouldn't have fallen in love with one of her classmates.

Only by knowing her own destiny, was she able to create her own path in life; her own heroine's journey.

Jayne with Don Gasperson
Andrea Tavares

Jayne Gasperson is a person everybody wants to have as a close friend. She is full of light, joy, and love! In her emails there is always a smiley face at the end :-).

When at age eight Jane moved from Los Angeles with her parents, the population of Pacific Grove was about 4,000. Jayne attended the Pine Street School where Robert Down was the principal. After graduation from eighth grade, she worked as a "soda fresh" at Christensen's Creamery and she used to go to the beach every afternoon. That was where, one summer, afternoon before she had started as a freshman at Pacific Grove High School, she met Donald Gasperson.

For Jane it was love at first sight, but she never thought about asking if it was the same for him. Jayne still remembers that Don was wearing an argyle sweater. She dated Don off and on during her freshman and sophomore years while he dated other girls as well. Don graduated in 1947 and began attending MPC. They started dating exclusively in January 1949 and became engaged and got married in June of that year.

Don liked to play golf and together they used to watch TV, travel (they took cruises to Mexico, Canada, and Alaska), visit close friends every month in Fresno, and go out to dinner with friends every Friday.

After graduating from at MPC, Don became a fulltime Pacific Grove fireman. At that time, there were only two firemen for the whole city, and they used to trade 24-hour shifts. Unfortunately, the income was not enough, so between shifts Don used to paint houses, put up television antennas, fix roofs, and so on. Don and Jayne had two adorable boys (one still lives in Pacific Grove), and four grandkids (the oldest had called her minutes before her interview, just to know if she was okay).

Jayne feels protected by having part of her family living in Pacific Grove. She is also grateful for the wonderful husband that she had. Although he was pretty busy as Fire Chief, he was a great father as well. Jayne believes that Don enjoyed being busy because even after he retired from the fire department, he became a City Council member.

What he could not do for his kids, he tried to do with his grandkids. She remembered taking them to some kind of zoo in Northern California. Unfortunately, in 2010 Don was diagnosed with cancer. The doctors gave him three days to a month to live, and he was gone after only ten days.

Jayne has a picture of Don right by the bed and she says that when she gets up every morning, she puts the picture on her heart and says, "I gotta do this again." Even though Jayne still misses Don a lot, and says that she is ready to go, she tries to keep doing something interesting in her daily life.

She has an amazing sense of humor and a meaningful smile. Recently, at a social event, she sat next to a man who was a friend of Don's. He just got there and sat next to her and said, "I'm ready to go," and she said, "You just got here," and he replied, "No, I mean leave it all," so she said, "Okay, if you find out how, please tell me."

Jayne has a lot of energy. Her gardening tools are in her car all the time. If she sees anything in the city that needs chopping, she does it. The city crew already knows her. Also, she waters all the plants at the Pacific Grove Library and she takes care of the plants at the park next to Chautauqua Hall. Don used to water with her as well.

Jayne was proud because recently her nine-year-old great-granddaughter sold hot chocolate and cookies at Candy Cane Lane and donated $70 to Meals on Wheels. Besides that, she is addicted to making the most beautiful potholders just for fun. She concluded by saying that if she needs to be here, she needs to do well.

Monday morning, three days after our last meeting, Jayne sent an email saying that she had woken up with remembrances of two more stories about P.G. This time instead of an interview at her place, we drove her around P.G. to visit some significant places. The first stop was in front of the P.G. Butterfly House (9th Street between Pine and Laurel). The themed butterfly house belongs to J and Sonja Jackson. J has been doing this artwork for his wife, who is visually impaired. Jayne is happy that her grandchildren have their names in some of the butterflies next to the Jackson's house fence.

The second stop was at 200 Asilomar Avenue to see a beautiful moose statue with monarch butterflies painted all over its body and wearing long striped socks. The house's owner brought the moose all way from Vermont. The way Jayne found to thank the owners for bringing the amazing moose to P.G. is by trimming the tree next to the moose so that everybody can admire it.

The third stop was to see one of the places listed on her bucket list. Her desire was accomplished when she climbed the green rock at Asilomar State Beach to enjoy the ocean. When asked about her bucket list, Jayne said that all the things on it had been done.

Wonder Woman?
Stefanna Murphy Robins

One morning, after Dick left for work, I realized that I really loved my life and even more my husband. Some women will understand this, as there are actually days when you do love them more, and days when, ehh, not so much ….

I determined that I was going to be Wonder Woman that day.

When his car was out of sight, I dressed in what a neighbor referred to as the anti-rape outfit. It was rather hideous, consisting of a faded oversized sweatshirt, baggy, bleach-stained sweatpants and some sort of a baseball hat to cover my unwashed and uncombed hair. Didn't even brush my teeth. Oh, yes, and there were blown-out sandals with lumberjack socks.

I went outside and immediately started to work. I raked what need to be raked, I swept, I pulled weeds, I trimmed bushes, I even washed the spots off of the windows that the spray from the hose had hit. Then I went back inside.

I vacuumed, I dusted, I washed the breakfast dishes, I waxed furniture, I cleaned the bath tub and the toilets, I was on a cleaning "high."

I knew in my soul that all these things would be done, and done well, by the incredible me. Yes, not only was the house and yard going to be in spectacular shape, but I was going to have an incredible dinner ready when he arrived home. HAH!

My plan was to do something astonishing with chicken breasts (it involved pounding them paper thin, slathering them with some concoction, rolling them and placing them in the oven). And while dinner was in the oven, I would have time to jump in the shower and transform myself into the natural beauty that I am not. I mean, full battle makeup, hair that has been blown out to look like it just happened and a lovely casual outfit for which he will never know how much I paid.

… and this is where things turned bad.

I raced into the garage where the chicken breasts were residing (second fridge in the garage) and missed the step. I went down. Hard. I heard a "tink" … and then I knew. I had broken my ankle … no doubt about it. I tried to stand … no doubt about it, standing was not going to be possible.

I crawled back into the house and knocked the phone out of the cradle and onto the floor. It never occurred to me to call 9-1-1 and I probably wouldn't have because of the way I looked … and you know how those good-looking firemen are the first ones to arrive.

I called Carmel High and asked to be connected to the music room. If he was conducting a rehearsal he might never hear the phone. I took my chances. After about five rings, thank you Lord, he answered the phone.

"Dick, I've fallen and I've broken my ankle."

"No!"

"Yes!"

"Really?"

"Yes, really."

"Well, put some ice on it."

Right about now. I loved him … ehh, not so much

"Dick, if I could stand up, I would put some ice on it."

He managed to get home in about 20 minutes and got me in the car. Please keep in mind that I was dirty, smelly, sweaty, in the anti-rape outfit and still hadn't brushed my teeth.

I was totally, unquestionably gross.

My great concern was that no one I knew would ever see me.

HAH!

I had come to know quite a few people in Pacific Grove through my work. I sold women's clothing. One of my favorite customers was Cynthia Siebe, who worked as an ER nurse at CHOMP. I had forgotten this.

When we arrived at the emergency entrance, Dick went inside to get help and a wheelchair. So far so good, only my husband had seen me smelly and ugly, and after all, it was for better or worse, you know.

I was wheeled into the emergency waiting area, and there, sure as hell, was Cynthia. I was mortified. She says, "Murphy, is that you?"

And I, not wanting to look her in the eyes, so I looked somewhere over her head, because I can't look her in the eyes and lie, replied "No, it's not me!"

Life Before Title IX
Bob Crispin

In the early 1960s, I ran track and cross country at P.G. High. There were no such options for the girls, no track or XC at all.

Even the athletic banquets were men and boys only, a father/son event. I was raised by my mom, who came to my meets most weeks, but could not be at the rewards event.

The school offered me a "stand-in," another male to be with me. I always declined, as my buddies were my mentors, not some stranger.

I was never angry, as that was the way it was. But I do thank the women's lib movement for changing the paradigm. Now I see the girls and women run, records falling. A high school girl beat my best mile last year. In 1963, they were a full minute slower than my best.

COMBINED DESTINIES — ANN JEALOUS, activist, author and retired therapist

Most P.G. residents care about our town, families, friends, country and the planet—as one interdependent entity.

After *Combined Destinies* was published and Caroline Haskell and I gave presentations and facilitated workshops based on the courageous stories in that anthology, our community's conversations about racism seemed to become more significant, more useful. Some of the contributors from Pacific Grove also seemed to increase their commitment to anti-racism work. Three of them (Fred, Sue, Caroline) were among the co-founders of *Whites for Racial Equity*. Among the others who attend their events are Patricia and Lynne. A recent email from Lynne said that WRE makes a "positive difference" in her life. When I asked her to elaborate a bit, she wrote: "WRE provides increased understanding of racism and its impact on all of our lives; opportunities for taking action; and perhaps most importantly, the hope that comes from connection with others who are actively resisting racism."

That invaluable organization, now two years old, is growing in membership and action. Whitesforracialequity.org is well worth a long look.

As I contribute all that I can toward the struggle to end oppression based on racism, it becomes more and more clear that ignorance is a huge part of the problem. That is, that people of goodwill would do a great deal more to end systemic racism if they became more knowledgeable about the universal damage it creates and if they were willing to reach across cultural lines for connection and understanding, even as they work within their own identity groups.

Separation – segregation – apartheid has such awful consequences. In order to realize how much we have in common and how easy it would be for us to love each other, we have to be able to talk to each other and to listen to each other. In order to do that, we must sometimes share the same space.

Last week, I received a sweet phone call that illustrates that reality. The call came from Alex Norton.

Alex is a neighbor who became one of our son's best friends forty-one years ago. They were both three years old and beautiful: Alex, tow-headed with fair skin that reddened in the sun; Ben, with dark hair and skin that tans easily, thanks to his African heritage.

When Alex went to work on the morning of the day he called, the windows in his house were intact. When his mom stopped by, she noticed that one of the windows was broken. She called Alex. Alex came home. When he arrived, a young African American teenager was walking out of his yard. When confronted about the broken window, he denied involvement. Alex contacted the P.G. Police Dept. who located the boy at school and then brought Alex a letter from the boy acknowledging accidentally breaking the window. Alex did not press charges because he had learned from Ben about the speed with which too many black boys travel through the justice system pipeline to prison, thus destroying far too many lives. Also, the description of the accident seemed real to Alex and the way in which the letter was written let him know that he and the boy share a learning disability. "I really was not interested in compromising this young man's future," he said.

After a phone conversation with Ben, Alex went to the boy's home, talked with his mother, and realized that assistance was badly needed. Responding to that need, he made arrangements for the boy to get a part-time job at his work place and called me to get information about The Village Project Inc., hoping that family counseling and tutoring could be arranged.

"I know I can't be a significant man in his life," Alex told me, "because I am not black."

"But, Alex," I said, "you are good. You are a good man and you care about what happens to him. That is what matters most for this boy at this time in his life. Eventually we will connect him with a good black man, for that is important. However, being black is secondary to being good."

Today, I received an email from Alex. The boy has enrolled at The Village Project, Inc. His mom feels grateful and wants her son to have time with Alex. And Alex? Alex has "a feeling that I'll take him fishing."

Because You're a Girl
Jean Hurlbert Jorgensen

"Jean! Don't RUN! It's not lady-like!" "Jean! Don't WHISTLE! It's not lady-like!" Seventy-plus years later those words from our proper aunt still reverberate in my memory.

Daddy's family, part of the conservative Methodist community that built P.G., expected us kids to behave "appropriately," especially challenging for a "tomboy" like me.

Luckily Mother had grown up a free spirit riding her pony to school in Los Gatos. Daddy had less influence on our lives, as he was away in the Navy fighting "The War."

Being a girl in the 40s and 50s was frustrating and challenging because of the things you weren't allowed to do that boys could do, such as:

Jean Hurlbert at age four.

There was an acrobatic tumbling team, now called gymnastics, that my brother was part of. It looked like such fun but it was only for boys. Imagine that!

Jerry was a paper boy, delivering newspapers in the neighborhood, but rarely were there paper girls.

I ran fast and was good at sports but girls had to wear skirts or dresses to school, which discouraged active motion. And except for PE classes, there were no sports teams for girls in P.G. schools at that time.

Jerry took a fun-looking class at P.G. High called Mechanical Drawing, now known as Graphic Design. You guessed it: Boys only. And for girls? We were *required* to take Home Ec, interested or not. I recall sewing an ugly drab-colored tweed skirt which I may have worn once.

I was a pretty good student in high school and did well in English classes under the demanding supervision of Mr. Naas, and Mr. Down in Journalism. I especially liked writing for *The Knockout*, the school newspaper, as well as working on the yearbook staff, but when I told my parents that I'd like to go to journalism school their response was, "Oh, no dear. That's a rough world. That's a man's world. No, you should get a teaching credential like the women in our family do." I didn't have the guts to stand up for my own passion, shrugged my shoulders and muttered, "OK."

In general during those times girls were expected to be a nurse, secretary, teacher, or possibly a stewardess, though the latter had to have good eyes and I was near-sighted, having worn glasses since third grade, so no chance of that. Many felt that the only reason for a girl to go to college was to meet some guy to marry.

So I did as I was told, got an elementary teaching credential and taught two very uninspired years, got married and stayed home to raise children for the next 20 years—"Because you're a girl."

I find it satisfying to have seen my own daughters pursue their passions, and now I have three granddaughters beginning their college careers. There are so many more opportunities for them than there were in P.G. for girls "back in the day."

To Jean Hurlbert
my longest, most influential friend
Inge Kessler

In August of 1963 I arrived in California with my new husband. Thomas Schultze and I had married on July 20th in my hometown of Rastatt, Germany. For our honeymoon, we sailed from Bremerhaven, Germany, to New York City on an elegant ocean liner, *The SS Bremen*.

From there, Thomas and I travelled seven days across the country to a little settlement in California named Los Olivos. We were in our Volkswagen bug with no air conditioner and no sunroof.

Thomas had been hired as a teacher and I as the auxiliary nurse on the campus of an all-boys college prep school. The headmaster, a Brit, was strict and frugal, and the campus was dusty and lacking much in the way of comfort. But instruction in the classrooms was of high standards.

I was bewildered at my new life in this environment. Fortunately, however, I met another teacher's wife, Jean Huser (née Hurlbert), who literally took me by the hand and helped me get my bearings in this very unusual new life I had embarked on.

Thomas and I lived in a tiny apartment on campus, so I was surrounded all day by the student body—boys, ranging in age from 12 to 18 years, who were highly intelligent pupils.

I came to be a constant amusement to them, with my somewhat limited understanding of the English language, which was restricted to mostly literary pursuits. Also, I still lacked the vocabulary for everyday American speech and didn't understand the boys' slang talk. But again, Jean came to my rescue. She would patiently explain a situation, such as a social faux pas I had committed, or shield me from jokes that I had no idea had a naughty note to them.

My greatest joy, however, was that she shared my

interest in hiking, and on those hikes she identified wildflowers, birds and trees for me. When she invited Thomas and me to come visit her hometown, where her parents Oxy and Wini Hurlbert lived, I fell in love with the Monterey Peninsula. Their home at 675 Mermaid Avenue in Pacific Grove became a place we would have many gatherings. There I encountered true hospitality and warmth in easy social interactions, for which I was most grateful.

Jean's greatest gift to me was her steadfast support in my beliefs. When I became a first-time mother without my own mother present to show me how to bring up a baby, she stepped in. And that bond is sacred to me: an experienced woman giving her knowing to another in an intimate setting of childbearing and feeding. Jean did that for me, and I will forever hold that in my heart in deep gratitude.

Jean moved to Jackson, Wyoming. Thomas took a position as the German teacher and administrator at the Monterey Institute of Foreign Studies (as it was called in the late 1960s). I have lived in the area ever since.

For many years Jean and I exchanged letters, postcards, and Christmas photo reports to keep up with each other's ever-expanding lives, interests, life challenges, joys, and sorrows. We also had occasional reunions at 675 Mermaid Avenue.

Now it is 2017 and our friendship has lasted more than five decades … and I am delighted that my sisterly love for Jean is being documented in this book!

In gratitude, Inge Kessler

After the Jobs Are Done—Have Fun!
Girls' Night Out (GNO)
Sally Sirocky

It was 2006 and Nadine Annand's 80th-something birthday at the Chamber of Commerce grand opening of Pelican Tavern in the American Tin Cannery building. Chamber Ambassadors and business owners, all of whom were Nadine's friends, gathered around one of the tables for cake and cards. Marlyn Andreas made the comment, "This is so much fun!" and suggested that we do this once a month, which was seconded by just about everyone.

And that was the start of GNO (Girl's Night Out) which went on for over ten years … well, we don't know for sure how long it continued, for it is still in existence at this writing. This group, ages 20-something to 90-something, continues to meet, for "girls" do need to have fun! And we have, along with food and drink and a few pranks.

Like the time we met to view the *Sex and the City* movie prior to GNO. Marlyn provided "goodie bags" which contained, among other things, condoms. One of the participants who was over 90 years of age stuck a condom in her cleavage and when asked how the evening went, pulled out the condom and with a mischievous smile announced, "We had a great time!"

The years progressed and it was Nadine's 90th. We had a strict rule: NO MEN. The Chamber of Commerce president, who was a man, wanted to come so badly that he dressed up as a woman, powdering his mustache, donning a dress, nylons, and heels, and to complete his outfit, a white feather boa—to crash the party. He will not allow photos of that evening or his name to be published.

It was brought up on more than one occasion that perhaps we should do something charitable as a group. But it was decided that no, this was just for fun. We all had our own ways of giving and volunteering to good causes.

Sixty-nine women have been involved through the years. The first meeting was ten adventurous souls pictured above. Maryln then began to add hand-picked—okay, who are we trying to kid?—she begged people to come and GNO eventually got up to about 38 in attendance on a single evening. It became so popular that women were clamoring to be invited, some even offering bribes. But we had outgrown the size of the restaurants in Pacific Grove. So, a moratorium was put on new members.

We meet at some outstanding establishments and the waiters have become a token part of our group. Matt at Lattitudes was one of our favorites. Oh, did we flirt with him!—and he gave it right back. Sadly, Lattitudes shut their doors, as Pelican Tavern had before it. So, I guess you could say we shut several restaurants down.

All in all, it gave us a chance through fun and laughter to know each other better, make new friends, and establish a community.

Girl's Night Out Charter Members. Front Row: Mary Nina Hill, Sally Sirocky. Back Row: Carla Gutman, Lonnie Huston, Ilana Enns, Maryln Andreas, Diane Garrison, Jayne Gasperson. Not pictured: Dee Boyer, Victoria Carns (photographer).

SPECIAL EVENTS—SOMETHING FOR EVERYONE

Pacific Grove is a Whole Lot of Fun
Judy Parrish
Pebble Beach

I was talking with some folks who have moved to this area recently and they commented on the fact that Pacific Grove does a lot for kids. That started me thinking because I raised my two daughters in this city.

Being a kid in Pacific Grove has a lot to be said for it … the setting, with its beaches and water sports, which includes kyacking, sailing, and surfing, and promotes a healthy lifestyle. Furthermore, it is close to Cannery Row and the Monterey Bay Aquarium.

I was reminded recently how "Good Old Days" is a special time for families and children with its parade, great food, face painting, and a carnival for small children, local bands, and dance troops. And the Big Sur Marathon's annual By-The-Bay 3K run for children and their parents that begins at Lovers Point Park raises money for schools and encourages fitness.

The Feast of Lanterns in July has been celebrated for over a hundred years with a Royal Court, a pet parade, street dance, and a pageant at Lovers Point with fireworks over Monterey Bay.

The Butterfly Parade, held in October, is when kids celebrate the return of the Monarch Butterflies to Pacific Grove. I love to see the elementary schools participate and the kindergarten children dressed up as Monarchs.

Halloween is a special time in Pacific Grove with the children being welcomed from one Victorian house to another on safe streets.

The Winterfest, sponsored by the Pacific Grove Adult School co-op preschool, has good food, local crafts, and Christmas items for sale. Then there is Candy Cane Lane with its magic during the Christmas holidays.

The Pacific Grove Museum and the Pacific Grove Library, with its large selection of children's books, are both within walking distance for families—and totally kid friendly. Lovers Point Swimming Pool is where many learn to swim. The local ice cream shop is always a hit.

There is just so much support in this community for families and children. When I think about what the City of Pacific Grove does for kids, it is a whole lot.

It was great fun putting this together and I really enjoy being able to contribute to this book.

Monarch Film Festival
Cristiana DePietro
Founder/Producer

Being able to bring together people from around the world into our own backyard to witness and celebrate their mutual passion for films is something I find deeply fulfilling. One my main objectives in hosting a gathering like this is so that both the local and international filmmakers can network with one another in a welcoming and celebratory environment. I love planning it all just so, and then being present for them throughout the festival.

We host a reception every year during the International Monarch Film Festival for all the filmmakers. I get excited every time when I see our "Local's Corner" participants engage with Hollywood and international filmmakers. We never know who we will meet—we've had Oscar nominees, Sundance alum and even professional baseball players as a part of our festival. It's all very uplifting and inspirational for everyone there.

We always ensure that everyone feels at home in America's Last Hometown, from helping international filmmakers with Aquarium tickets, restaurant choices, and hotel rooms—all their travel needs, really. Without fail, I hear from attendees that have never heard of Pacific Grove, how charming our small town is, how hospitable our Board of Directors are, and what a wonderful time they had at the International Monarch Film Festival. www.monarchfilmfestival.com

Car Week in Pacific Grove
His 'n' Her Luxury, Muscle Car Memories
Patricia Hamilton

She immediately went inside the Air BnB next to my home—I never saw her. He parked the silver one first; she left her white one, engine running, in the street, then he parked it in front of his. Rumble, rumble, varoom, varoom.

He was so particular about covering each one—first he brought out the spray bottle and cleaned the windshield and wiped off some spots here and there. Then the soft elastic black cover, custom fit over the rearview mirrors. He took at least 20 minutes to clean the cars and cover them for the night.

This morning he's out there picking bits of leaves and lint from the black cover before pulling it off and stuffing it under the front hood. A couple came by, obviously Car Week people too by their dress, and he gives them the 50-cent tour—even the music "The Horse with No Name" was celestial. That's when I heard the price, "$500,000 out the door, $350,000 from some other place.

I went out, said Hi. He was nice. I took a couple of photos and pointed to my Subaru. "That's my car."

"Your baby," he said, "pearly white."

"That's why I bought it." Big smiles all around.

I inquired about the TMGBULL personal license plate on her car. He told me Lamborghini names all their models after bulls and bullfighters—I resisted screaming in horror—briefly smiled and went back inside. Off they went to have their day at the Italian on the Black Horse Golf Course.

The varoom when they left rang melodious throughout the neighborhood—I love the sight and sound of these cars, if not the naming.

I later learned that the owners' names are Michael and Toni and that they enjoyed their stay at the P.G. Air BnB so much they're thinking about returning for Car Week next year, possibly with their nine-year-old son.

Joyce Krieg

I'm guessing I echo the feelings of a lot of Pagrovians when I say I have a love-hate relationship with Car Week.

On the one hand, love those beautiful cars! They really are rolling works of art. As I stroll down Lighthouse Avenue during the P.G. Auto Rally or The Little Car Show and admire those shiny beauties, I feel as if I'm in an open-air museum, a moveable sculpture garden. Those "cherries" from the 1950s and muscle cars from the 60s bring back a flood of childhood memories. I look around for the owner, expecting to see one of those cute Auto Shop boys from high school in their jeans and grease-stained white t-shirts. Instead, inevitably, he turns out to be a geezer (in other words, someone around my age) and I have a poignant reminder about the passage of time.

But—yikes!—the traffic. The gridlock, the barricaded streets, the sheer frustration of being held prisoner in my own home. On late Friday afternoon of Car Week, I tried to make the drive from my home on 13th Street to a Jazzercise class in downtown Monterey. It took 30 to 40 minutes both coming and going, for a trip that usually takes 15 minutes, 20 max.

We all hear about the huge amount of dollars that flow into our local economy due to Car Week. But let's face it—unless we actually own a restaurant or hotel, we residents aren't seeing any direct, in-our-pockets benefit. So, how about a little something to compensate us for putting up with the inconvenience of Car Week? A thank-you after-party? Free admission for local residents to one of those swank, high-end events, kind of like how the Aquarium does with their free week for locals in December? Shoot, I'd be happy with just a ride in a fancy, high-performance sports car—especially if it's being driven by one of those cute Auto Shop boys.

P.G. Guitar Man at the Farmers Market
Chris Bohrman

Many people know (and many more are surprised when I tell them) about Pacific Grove's "Everyone's Harvest" Farmer's Market on Monday afternoons from 3:00 to 7:00 p.m. Since 2008, this has been the place to get fresh, locally grown organic produce, tasty international meals, cool artisan crafts and to hear fresh organic local music.

I'm the P.G. Guitar Man—Chris Bohrman—and I've been bringing handcrafted, kid-shakin', street-dancin' acoustic music and general good times to the P.G. Farmer's Market since 2008. Back then the market was held on Lighthouse Avenue in front of the Bank of America between Forest Avenue and 17th Street.

I'll admit that what drew me first to the market was the monstrously delicious kettle cCorn from Coastal Kettle Corn. A few Mondays into my corn habit, I decided that, since I was going there anyway, and that as a professional musician I generally have Mondays free from travel and concert appearances, I would take my guitar and tip jar down there and see what happened.

After playing a couple of Mondays, it appeared I had developed a following of toddlers who would stop by with their folks to dance and clap to my rock 'n' roll guitar and vocalizing. So my wife Lore suggested I take some maracas and egg shakers with me for the kids to join in the music.

From that day on, my appearances there took on a whole new dimension. Instead of just me singing some of my favorite obscure cover songs and originals, we have a street party with sometimes a dozen kids joining "my band."

There's something magnetic about a group of kids moving to music that always attracts a crowd of smiling people. Jeff, the owner of Coastal Kettle Corn, frequently comes over to join me and sing his favorite Lynyrd Skynyrd song, "Curtis Low." Coastal KC has become my unofficial "corporate sponsor" and many of the other food and produce vendors gift me with goodies. Also over the years I've had many musician friends show up to join me for impromptu jam sessions.

Over the last nine years I've "graduated" numerous happy kids from my street-music academy. I find that as they reach school age most kids get "too cool" to join in, but they still remember me from when they were "little." I've made so many wonderful connections with families who visit the market every week and many kids who have carried on to take guitar and drum lessons from me as they reach school age.

"Mondays at 3, The Market is the place to be"—now on Central Avenue in front of the Museum of Natural History. Come by for a song and a good time!

Pacific Grove's Forgotten Pageant
Helen Gehringer

Current residents of Pacific Grove might be surprised to learn that those of us growing up in the 1940s had never heard of the Feast of Lanterns. The Butterfly Pageant was our big event.

Helen Gehringer, Butterfly Pageant, 1947.

The play was written by Reginald Foster, president of the Chamber of Commerce, and it was a wonderful story that included local history, the arrival of the butterflies, and a romantic plot all rolled into one. It was performed at the ball park for two evenings and one matinee, following the Butterfly Parade and Bazaar. The actors were all local with the exception of a guest artist from the San Francisco Opera who sang several selections, including "Hymn to the Sun." Also in the cast were dancers, singers and tom-tom beaters.

The pageant was presented in 1939, 1940, 1941, and, for the last time, in 1947. It could not be presented during the World War II years because outdoor lighting was prohibited due to the possibility of enemy aircraft.

In 1947, at the age of 10, I was thrilled to be chosen to perform the Dance of Grief. A new material that glowed in the dark had become available and patches were sewn on my costume so that, when lights were dimmed, it looked like an evil face!

I never found out why the pageant wasn't continued, but I do know that it was one of the most memorable events of my childhood in Pacific Grove.

Parades in Pacific Grove
Brenda Tayler

My favorite small-town thing I like about Pacific Grove are the parades! Do you realize that we are lucky enough to have four parades in our hometown!? There is the Good Old Days in April, the Feast of Lanterns Pet Parade in July, the Butterfly Parade in October and the Parade of Lights in December.

My little church makes food for Good Old Days. Both my son and I have worked the booth, and I have made countless desserts to sell. Our family enjoys the food booths, the festive parade, the music and dancers, and seeing old friends and neighbors. It's always fun to walk downtown and run into people who you usually don't see.

We always have fun at the pet parade! Our son always wants to enter our two cats and every year we have to convince him that it's a really bad idea. The Feast of Lanterns holds many fond memories. My husband and I used to watch it when we were dating. Later when we had a family we would take our son in the stroller with his stuffed animals, and now we can see the fireworks from our living room window.

The Butterfly Parade holds a special place in my heart, as our son was in all of them when he was in elementary school. Of course we have his butterfly wings in the attic. In kindergarten at the beginning of the parade, he was very nervous and started to cry, so we both held his hand and escorted him for the whole parade. I had fun finding and helping with the costumes over the years. In third grade, our son wore his fathers' Indian vest that his mom had made him when he was a child. The parade of lights is in early December. We always had to go see it even if it was pouring rain and cold enough to see our breath. It was worth it to see the "real" Santa!

Celebrating All Things with a Parade
Pamela Cain
journalist mom

As an Army brat who attended 14 schools, by the time we moved here when I was in eighth grade, I didn't really appreciate the close-knit community that I was to call my permanent home. After just a few months, I participated in my first Butterfly Parade, playing flute in the band.

Parades are a heartwarming tradition in Pacific Grove with streets being closed about every three months for a celebration of hometown charm. In October, all school children meander down the main street for the Butterfly Parade, with the kindergartners dressed in orange and black wings to welcome the monarchs to town. Other grades are jellies, cowboys, apples or frontier people, all celebrating our winged migration.

In December, Lighthouse Avenue is once again closed as we celebrate with the Holiday Parade of Lights with everyone from Girl Scouts to antique cars adorned with battery-operated lights to dazzle the crowds. Rain and chilly winds don't dampen the enthusiasm of onlookers who then wander around afterward, shopping for the holidays and visiting with Santa and Mrs. Claus.

In April, the multi-lanes of Pine Avenue are used for the Good Old Days Parade. This kicks off a two-day street fair but the parade is the highlight. Once, before insurance costs got so high, motorcycle cops from all over the state participated in the parade before a competition in front of the Police Station later in the day. But now you can watch legions of Little League players, martial arts participants, horses, floats, and of course the vintage cars ranging from British Triumphs to muscle cars.

And just one quarter later, Pacific Grove's main drag, Lighthouse Avenue, is shut down again so that four-legged residents of "The Last Hometown" can frolic down the street in the Pet Parade. This is not just a parade for children or dogs. Adults eagerly slip a leash on their canines and children can take a stuffed animal if they don't have the courage for a live one. There's been boa constrictors, birds, hamsters, a goldfish named Admiral Akbar and even a brave cat or two. Wagons, strollers, and bikes are decorated to be a part of this Feast of Lanterns' tradition, typically on the last Friday afternoon in July. Then all are invited to Caledonia Park where free ice cream is handed out by the postal workers' union.

Those are the annually scheduled parades, but Pacific Grove has been known to close the streets for impromptu parades when a Breaker team has won a CCS championship or there is something else remarkable to celebrate.

Pacific Grove is a special place and one that I'm glad to call home and raise my family in, and I'm looking forward to participating in every parade in the future.

Butterfly Parades – Back to the Future
Kay Krattli

This is my husband's story, but I am his wife and so it is my story too. My husband grew up visiting his grandfather in Pacific Grove each summer, running through the forests, playing on the beach. There was no Aquarium then, but discovering the ocean and its teeming life was a do-it-yourself experience perfect for John and his two brothers.

The boys didn't pay much attention to the fact, but their grandfather was the city attorney for Pacific Grove. His name was Reginald Foster and he loved the city. He served as the city's attorney for 26 years. During that time Reg, as he was called by his friends, helped lay the foundation for today's city of Pacific Grove. He once was quoted in the local paper saying, "Pacific Grove has been my life, and there is nothing I wouldn't do for it."

One of the events Reg helped start was the Butterfly Festival. From its small beginnings, he helped it grow into the iconic symbol of the town. He wrote the original script and directed the first production. He was a creative individual. When John's parents passed away, we found a manuscript Reg had written which was set in Pacific Grove and supposedly based on local inhabitants. It was a murder mystery. I don't remember who killed whom, but Reg must have had fun putting his friends and neighbors into the plot. Creativity ran in the family. Reg's dad, Dr. Clarendon Foster, a well-known heart specialist, had started the Feast of the Lanterns celebration in Pacific Grove.

Reg had been trained as a lawyer and was attorney for the California Council of Native Americans. At times he worked on a pro bono basis representing them in court. Many times he was paid with a Native American basket, a piece of pottery, or in one case, a deerskin cradle worn to carry a baby on the mother's back. We have some of those artifacts to cherish.

When Reg retired from city government, he was honored with a Certificate of Appreciation from the City Council. He passed away in 1970. His only child, Barbara Foster, was my husband John's mother. John lived in Southern California for many years and his mother was thrilled when he studied law at UCLA. Reg would have approved.

Jump to 2014. John and I are starting to talk about retirement. We are the grandparents of twin boys and a charming granddaughter and we want to be where they are. That means a move to Oakland. Just as we retire, our daughter Karin and her husband Eli find new jobs on the Monterey Peninsula. We are on our way, back to the future.

This is a story of coming full circle, of ending up by chance in a place you knew and loved as a boy. Where your grandchildren can play on the same beaches you did and visit their great-great-grandfather's grave knowing that he had a hand in helping make it the wonderful city it is. It is a story of how fate conspired to move us where it thought we should be. Last fall we watched our grandsons walk in the Butterfly Parade for the first time, the sun shining on their butterfly wings, their faces full of pride. We're home.

The Parade of Lights Festival
Jonathan Shoemaker

Yes, it was December 1st in Pacific Grove and already after dusk, so I knew I would have to hurry to feed and walk the dog before all of the downtown parking spaces were taken. I thought that I had left home in plenty of time to park the car and walk to our family's traditional gathering spot across from Juice n' Java for such events before the start of the parade.

I was amazed to see the number of cars parked above Pine on both sides of 17th Street barely allowing a car to pass between them. Oh, well, I'll see if there's a spot in the block by the Fire Station.

I drove down to as far as three houses from Pine Avenue when a 1953 Chevy with only one headlight turned onto 17th and blocked my way. After some waving, blinking my lights and yes, even honking my horn, he got out and came over to inform me that he can't back up so why don't I just park in the open space behind him?

I said, "It's a driveway."

"Oh good! Then back in so I can pass." And he went back to his car.

Of course, in the meantime several cars had turned in and stopped behind him before backing out and leaving.

When all was clear, I drove across Pine Avenue and found a parking spot across from the Fire Station. I checked to make sure I wasn't blocking either of the tiny driveways that I had squeezed between, and headed for Lighthouse Avenue where the parade had already started.

I was pleased to see that both sides of Lighthouse, as well as the middle parking area, were already packed with groups of friends and families who had come to watch the parade as we do each year for the Butterfly Parade, the Good Old Days celebration, the Feast of Lanterns Pet Parade and the Homecoming Parade.

I stopped to watch a Cal Fire truck pass close to me. In the open window appeared the beaming face of my middle granddaughter who waved vigorously, saying, "Happy Birthday, Grandpa!"

I guess I wasn't too late after all!

Big Sur Half Marathon
Tom Rolander

This story is taken from the transcript of an oral history of Tom Rolander, interviewed by David Laws, recorded at the Computer History Museum, Mountain View, CA, in December 2016 and is published here with permission. CHM Ref: X8018.2017 © 2016 Computer History Museum, Page 46 of 48, http://archive.computerhistory.org/resources/access/text/2017/02/102717253-05-01-acc.pdf

David Laws: Another activity you've been very determined at is long distance running.

Tom Rolander: Okay.

Laws: And you've run in every marathon, I believe, at Big Sur since day one?

Rolander: Actually, my very first running was in high school. As a freshman I ran the mile, and then as a sophomore I ran cross country, and I got a letter, and that was at I guess 17 or 16 or whatever I was at that time. I got a job, so from then on I was working and then went on to other jobs. So when I went to work with Gary Kildall he was a frequent jogger, so a couple days a week he'd go out and I quite often went out with him. He usually liked to have music on and I preferred my own thoughts. But any rate, that was a fun thing to do. When we traveled we would oftentimes get up early before a flight, and we found it was a good way to wake ourselves up and become alert, was to get out and get running, so I did a little bit of that.

In 1986 I was 38 years old and. I was over 200 pounds, and I had that one sort of moment, that epiphany when you look at the mirror and you go, oh, my God. This is not going to end well. I said, I've got to do something about this. What can I do?

And I thought about it and remembered that I'd been a runner. What I liked about running is it didn't take a team. All it took was a pair of shoes and some determination to do that, and so I decided that on January 1st, 1986, I was going to start running. I mean that first day I started to run, I literally—well, I couldn't run more than 50 yards or whatever, so what I ended up doing, I learned this technique, I would pick a mailbox and I would run all the way to that mailbox. Then I'd stop and I'd say, okay, I'm going to now walk until I get to that telephone pole. <laughs>

And by the time I got there I'd pick my next place, my next destination, and that's basically how I started running, and it was all early in the morning in the dark because I didn't want anybody to see me while I was struggling through this.

Other thing that I did that very first January in '86 is, since I was 21 roughly I'd had one or two beers at dinner every night, and I was kind of wondering, you know, what is an alcoholic? Do they have a beer every night? Am I dependent on this? I like beer. I thought I be okay with that. I said, okay, I'm going to go without beer.

So I went that month of January no beer, no alcohol, and I've done that now actually for 31 years. It's kind of my cleansing month. I still know I'm in control. I can always lose five to ten pounds during that time and so forth.

But any rate, I started running. By the end of the month I got up to about seven or eight miles. I just kept running. I enjoyed it. One of the challenges of running is most people treat it as punishment. I mean those of us that remember PE days, physical education back in our junior high and high school days, we were punished by going out and doing laps around the track. Well, it's hard to get over that stigma.

But, anyway, I got to the point where I realized I was outside, and the benefits for me as a software engineer were that I got time to do some free association. I got a chance to get away from the immediate problem I was on. I've done without question the best problem solving of my life actually getting away out alone just running and thinking about that, so got into that.

Well, coming up to that April, I learned on a Friday night there was an event in Pacific Grove, a quilt show preview party, and I was actually bartending for that that evening—helping out, pouring wine, and several of my friends came up, three of them, and they said, "Are you running Sunday?" I said, "What's Sunday?" And they said, "The Big Sur Marathon." I said, "Wow. Is that 26 miles?" I said, "How are you guys doing that? I can't imagine running that far."

And they said, "Well, we've seen you run a few times. What have you done?" I said, "Twelve miles." One of the gentlemen, Ed Bredthauer, says, "Oh, you can do a marathon. Sign up for it. Sign up tomorrow."

So that was a Friday night. so I thought about that Friday night, went in Saturday afternoon, and what Ed told me to do—he gave me the coaching—he said, "Run to every aid station," they're early on every two miles and then about every mile and even closer, and he said, "Every time you get to an aid station grab some Gatorade, some water, and walk for two minutes, then run to the next aid station." He said, "What it is it's about a dozen two-mile runs, you know, so it's not a big deal."

So I thought, okay, well, what the hell? I'll give it a try. So I went in at about ten minutes to five—they close registration at five—signed up for the Big Sur Marathon, went out the next morning. They took us by bus from Carmel down to Pfeiffer Park 26 miles south of Carmel, let us out of the bus, and at seven o'clock they fired a pistol, a gun, and we all took off running Highway 1 up and down and up and down back to Carmel.

Well, I followed my friend's advice. I did a walk/run, and I finished that on as high a high as my solo flight, just for pure personal, not relationship, wife, kids being born or whatever, just purely personal. The two in my life were my first solo flight and finishing that first marathon. I was absolutely hooked. I just said, "Oh, wow. I love this."

Since then I've run a lot of ultra-marathons. I realized shortly after that that my real goal was—I'm a goal-oriented person, as you could tell from my flying and whatever—so I decided, okay, I want to be running a marathon when I'm 80 years old, so I did a little program on my computer, which counted the number of days until I was 80.

In fact, right now on my iPhone sitting in my pocket, there's an iPhone app, which is "days until", and it's got the number of days. I think it's now 4,100-something days. I can't remember when it was, but that's my next goal, which is running the Big Sur Marathon on my 80th.

So I ran the next year. I started training right away, ran the second year, ran an hour and a half faster than I had the first year, and I have now run all 31 of the Big Sur Marathons, not missed one, and all 14 of the half-marathons.

In fact, I've run 134 total marathons. I've also been very active in the organization at Big Sur. I got recruited it'll be 20 years ago this spring to do the website, to be the webmaster for the marathon. So when they recruited me, they asked me to do IT and the website, and I said, "Well, I'll do it under one condition." It's pro bono. It's free. "I'll do it under one condition. I get to race on race day. I don't want to miss being at the race," and I said okay, so fast forward a little bit.

I've been on the board for a number of years. In the last few years I have been vice-chairman, and in the end of September this last fall, I was voted chairman of the board, so I'm now chairman of the Big Sur Marathon. It's a great volunteer organization. We're a nonprofit, $3 million a year budget, and we do a lot of good for our community. So we put on world class events that benefit our community and promote health and fitness.

Laws: You can't turn up at five o'clock on a Friday afternoon anymore and sign up. It's very selective.

Rolander: Our Big Sur Marathon, it's on what's called a bucket list. We have sold out for years and years and years. We finally had to go to a lottery system. But the chief runner at Runner's World, which is the largest running magazine in the world, made a statement some years ago, and he said, "If you only have one marathon to run in your life, Big Sur should be it." Even our half-marathon, which we had two weeks ago, had runners from 48 states and 23 countries, our marathon always has runners from all 50 states and usually 40 or sometimes 50 countries.

Laws: It's a unique experience.

Rolander: Yeah, it's a beautiful event.

Stillwell's Fun in the Park
Richard Stillwell
Linnet Harlan

In 1989, the Chamber of Commerce was trying to come up with things to do around Christmas for the kids and the city. A woman named Diane suggested putting snow in Jewell Park so the kids could play in it, but people didn't like that idea. I remembered back in '62 it snowed here in P.G. and how much fun my kids had with it. I said I'd help Diane, so the Chamber approved the plan.

I went around town the next few days and collected about five or six thousand dollars.

Next we had to deal with the permits. I went to the Police Department. They said I needed to do this and that. I said, "The Fire Department has already said it's okay." They said, "Really? Then it's okay with us." But I still had to fill out a lot of forms.

Then I needed the permission from the city manager. It was mid-November. I went to City Hall, but he was gone for the next three days. We couldn't wait three days, so I said, "Just give me the form," and signed it "Richard Stillwell." The final approval was scheduled for a City Council meeting. The mayor then was Flo Schaefer. She said to the city manager, "Did you sign this?" He said, "Apparently my assistant did."

We were going to have ponies to ride, hay rides, and a petting zoo. "Is there someone to clean up after the horses?" Flo asked. "You got me there, Flo," I said. "I'll tell you what I'll do. I'll get a broom, a shovel, and a bucket and put you in charge." She didn't have anything to say after that, and the idea was approved.

The snow was in Jewell Park the first time we held it. But we decided somewhere with a fence was better after the calf from the petting zoo ran out into the street. Since then, we've held it at Caledonia Park.

We had snow for 19 years, but every year the cost of the snow went up. And we had to spend a lot of time cleaning up afterwards. Moe Ammar of the Chamber thought he could get us a little carnival. So we went with that. The first year of no snow, one little boy about eight said he missed the snow, but he's been the only one.

The petting zoo is the best. One year, a little girl watching the chickens started screaming. Finally we realized the chicken had laid an egg. Later a little boy came up to her and said, "That chicken didn't lay that egg."

"Yes, it did," she said.

"No it didn't. Eggs don't come from chickens. They come from Safeway."

About half the kids are from out of town, but they're still having fun, and we're still doing it.

Vic Selby, Father of P.G.'s Hootenanny
Mimi Sheridan

Pagrovians come together to celebrate in many ways throughout the year. One of the more unusual gatherings is a regular 1960s-style hootenanny. I experienced my first one on May 6, joining a varied group trooping up to the second floor of the Pacific Grove Arts Center.

The event evolved organically, with a few singers and several guitarists there at the scheduled time, and others wandering in over the next hour. More instrumentalists contributed their talents; one even brought an electric keyboard. Songbooks—each 200-plus pages—were passed around, assuring that everyone had the words and music. As voices warmed up and inhibitions declined, many picked up a tambourine or a drum. Before long it was a real hootenanny, rocking with the synergy of rhythm, harmony and poetry. At the break, people introduced themselves and chatted over chocolate chip cookies.

The word "hootenanny" is from an Indiana term meaning "loose or unorganized gathering." Hootenannies are most closely connected with folk music, because Woody Guthrie began using the term in the late 1950s to describe the folk sing-alongs and jam sessions at college campuses and coffee housesthroughout the country that continued into the 1960s.

Here in Pacific Grove, however, it's not just about folk music, but is truly eclectic with blues, country, jazz, classic rock, Motown—whatever people want to sing, and have the words to.

Vic Selby, billed as the Hootenanny Coordinator, has organized Pacific Grove's hootenanny every two months since 1996. Vic experienced his first hootenanny in the 1960s, while attending the University of Colorado in Boulder. He was later inspired by seeing the master himself, Pete Seeger, get everyone in a room involved in a true community experience of song and music.

Vic came west to get a master's degree at San Jose State and was hired as a mathematics teacher at Carmel High School. Every teacher was expected to participate in extracurricular activities, so Vic started a Folk Music

Club, which proved to be very popular with the students. It was a natural interest for him, since he had played the guitar since the age of 12. He began collecting songs and coaching club members in performances. When he retired from the school district in 1996, he wanted to continue with communal singing and thus the Pacific Grove hootenanny was born.

Every two months, Vic selects a theme, puts together a set list and publicizes it to an email list of 300. Each time about 40 to 70 people come, with a combination of regulars and newcomers of all backgrounds, ages and musical talents. Donations are encouraged, but they go to the Art Center, not to the hootenanny itself; more than $16,000 has been donated over the years.

The people of Pacific Grove continue to support this unique event, coming together to have fun just as they have for more than twenty years. The next one's marked on my calendar.

Finding a Haven in Pacific Grove
Victoria Carns

In 1973 I was a newlywed, married to an Air Force officer. We had orders to Madrid, Spain. Before leaving the country for that first posting, we flew to Monterey, to visit my husband's parents. Major General Edwin Hugh Carns and Jeannette had been the commander at Fort Ord and retired to Pebble Beach.

The weekend of our visit was perfect in every way. The Carns were happy, the sea sparkled, the sky was blue, alive with cumulus clouds, the air was fresh and balmy. In that perfect moment, we decided to buy a home and found a small one in Pebble Beach.

We served overseas for seven years and more than 20 years later, retired to Pebble Beach in 1994. That very year, Mother Carns fell ill. We spent many months with her and after she passed away, my husband began commuting to work in Washington, D.C., which he continues to do in this year of 2017.

Now I was a retired military spouse, with Air Force children in foreign lands, few friends and no "life of purpose." I visited the Chamber of Commerce in Pacific Grove and interviewed with Moe Ammar. My question to him was, "what can I do to meet a lot of people, quickly."

His response, "become an ambassador," and my next move was to enthusiastically sign on the dotted line. Being an ambassador has enabled me to spend time with fellow ambassadors, know the townspeople and to be aware of what is available for all in this lovely place.

What other activities were available to join? The list expanded quickly, joining the Monterey Symphony Chorus, volunteering at the Blind and Low Vision Center in Pacific Grove, the Citizens' Police Academy in Pacific Grove, joining a **book club, and the Military Officers' Association of America (MOAA),** and being Snow Queen every December. With bits of free time, there were quilting classes at Back Porch Fabrics and Monday mornings with the sewing group at Sally Griffin Center. Now, I had friends!

Each group made my transition from a busy, moving-around-the-world lifestyle as a military spouse to rewarding, rich days in our town. Now, nearly twenty five years later, I am still involved in most of these activities. Pacific Grove has been my haven.

"The purpose of my life is a life of purpose," and I gain enormous reward in being part of our "Butterfly Town."

1940s and Forest Hill Hotel Hosts Social Dancing Classes
Virginia Fox Abplanalp
one of the 7th grade dance organizers

Once upon a time in long-ago Pacific Grove, there existed a class of seventh grade girls who could not be described as exactly shy. This was in 1944 during the war years. A group of these girls decided it was time for them to organize a dance. They prevailed upon their parents to rent the Boy Scout Hall on a Friday night and to their delight, they did. The girls rounded up a phonograph, records, bought refreshments and decorations. With their parents' help, they decorated the dingy hall. At that point they told their male classmates, "Be there!" And they showed up.

Once again, as they had done back in second grade, the boys lined up on one side of the hall (instead of the school wall) and the girls did the same on the other. When the music started, the boys raced across the room, each grabbing the girl of his choice, and they all commenced doing a mean two-step. That was the best they could do. At least the girls succeeded … they had their first dance.

The parents, observing this lack of decorum, must have formed a committee of their own because the following summer, class members of both sexes found themselves in the lobby of the Forest Hill Hotel, attending what was called a Social Dancing Class. The boys were instructed as to proper attire and the proper way to invite a girl to dance. No more running and no more grabbing. The box step was taught and good manners were demanded. I don't remember it being as much fun as that original dance we organized ourselves, but we learned how to be proper.

And the hotel management was gracious enough to let us have the experience. I have never forgotten it.

P.G. Races in the 1950s
Dawn Armstrong

My younger brother and I enjoyed different kinds of races, but they both took place in the 1950's along Sunset Drive. His drag races didn't draw crowds. At most, there might be twelve of the group of car nut kids who hung out at the auto shop across from Hayward Lumber. Around midnight at the identified quarter mile stretch the boys who had spent the night adding or adjusting this or that would test it out. There was a lookout, but it was easy to see over the dunes so the two-lane challenge was relatively safe. And it was over quickly.

On any given night, there might be a Chevy Chevelle Supersport, my brother's 1935, 5-window Plymouth Coupe de luxe, or even the Ford Falcon Ranchero that the kids were taught not to make fun of because of the effort that went into it. Cars were a big deal on the Peninsula, and not just for male teenagers.

Every September, the car dealers, which were clustered handily in downtown Monterey, held sort of a joint open house. The indoor showrooms were across and adjacent to each other. Families would eagerly await the announcement of the new year models arrival and unveiling. The year the Ford Thunderbird came out was embarrassing for my dad. As instructed, he stuck one leg into the low slung specialty car and could go any farther. He got a charlie horse. I don't recall that people sued each other so much then, but there was quite the fuss to get him right and get him out of the car.

Of course the Pebble Beach Sports Car Races were well known outside the Monterey Peninsula. The little foreign cars were driven on familiar roads, around tight corners and into Cyprus trees and other natural obstacles until one too many drivers got killed. Then the races were moved to Laguna Seca. Many of us became volunteer members of the Monterey Sports Car Club and helped get the track fencing up each year. In our family the battle of foreign sports cars vs American sports cars—the Ford Thunderbird and the Chevy Corvette—ran for quite a while.

My boyfriend had a TR-3 with seat belts. Seat belts were exotic. They proved you had a sports car. I don't know if the lap belts would have saved us if we crashed. Luckily, though we drove the PG-Carmel highway in blind fog many times, we didn't have to find out. Later, he had a Chevy Corvette. Especially because I got to drive it, my argument against the validity of that model as a sports car muted until I got my own very used and very old foreign car. Then my dad and I went back to a new argument: Porsche vs Mercedes.

My version of Sunset Drive races was the Submarine Races which I attended on a double date, infatuated with the quarterback from P.G. High. I'm sure they quietly continue.

Feast of Lanterns at Lovers Point circa 1905

KEEPING THE LANTERNS LIT—DIXIE LAYNE, historian

As much as the residents of and visitors to Pacific Grove believe the Feast of Lanterns is a unique Pacific Grove event, it is not. It is a festival with wide cultural roots. Countries around the world from China, Japan, Korea, and India to cities in the United States from New York and Indiana to California and Hawaii use a festival of lights to mark the close of their local event or celebration—each with its own traditions. These festivals are often called Feast of Lanterns.

No one knows when and where the first Feast of Lanterns celebration was held, this festival of lights, but there are many common denominators—lots of lighted lanterns, fireworks, parades, feasting, and dancing. Feast of Lanterns festivals are as diverse and beautiful as the lanterns each country uses to celebrate their events and each with its own shape and/or color. The Japanese lantern is long and slender, the Chinese red and round, a lotus blossom shape in Korea.

In 1875, the Methodist Retreat Association formed the Pacific Grove Retreat Association and initiated its three week summer camp meeting as a Sunday school teachers' training program. In 1879, this Retreat became known as the cultural center of the west when it was named the west coast headquarters for the Chautauqua Literary and Scientific Circle, a national movement for popular education. Its annual six-week summer assemblies provided public lectures, concerts, and dramatic performances. Our community was affected by the diverse cultures present in the area and those individuals that came to teach, speak, and entertain as part of the Chautauqua Assembly.

Costumed Residents c1905,
Pat Hathaway CA Views Collection

In 1905, it was the Womans Civic Club organized a closing celebration for Pacific Grove Chautauqua Assembly. It was based on what they heard about the New York Lake Chautauqua closing ceremony. The Womans Civic Club, assisted by school age boys and girls, festooned the waterfront and streets with lighted lanterns and organized a parade of gaily dressed and costumed citizens that marched through town and continued across the beach. Using the beach for its setting, the Womans Club organized entertainment and picnicking, a lighted boat parade past the Cove made up of 16 Japanese boats and 4 Chinese boats, and closed the day's activities with fireworks exploding over the Cove.

The festival was held each year as the formal closing ceremony to the Pacific Grove Chautauqua Assembly until 1917, when the United States entered the Great War in Europe. The Feast of Lanterns returned as the closing ceremony for the Chautauqua Assembly in 1920 only to be cancelled again in 1925 because the local merchants lost interest. The Chautauqua Assembly, with its multi-cultural flavor gathered each year in the Grove until the almost simultaneous national popularity of the automobile, radio, and moving pictures left people uninterested in it. The last Pacific Grove Chautauqua Assembly held in tents was in 1926.

The Feast of Lanterns was revitalized in 1935, and held each year thereafter to punctuate special events, such as the 1935 City's Open House and dedication of the Plunge (swimming pool) at Lovers Point and the dedication of the Carmel-San Simeon Highway in 1938. The festival was extended from one to three days with additional activities included: bathing beauty contests similar to those held as early as 1907, swan boats were added to the lighted boat parade, there was a bonfire on the beach, golf tournaments, yacht races, and much more. In 1941, with the United States entry into WWII, the Federal government stopped "all celebrations that were not patriotic endeavors", thus putting the Feast of Lanterns on hiatus once again.

Clyde Dyke

The Feast of Lanterns was revived in 1958 at the request of Mayor Frank Shropshire. He asked City Councilman Clyde Dyke to chair the revival of the event and like many wise men, Councilman Dyke asked his wife, Elmarie Hurlbert Hyler Dyke, for assistance. Mrs. Dyke solicited the assistance of the Mayor's wife, Helen Shropshire, and together with the help of civic employees and leaders they orchestrated the revival of the Pacific Grove Feast of Lanterns with its multi-cultural flavor, Royal Court, lighted lanterns and boat parades, music, dance, theater, teas, fashion shows, and fireworks.

1958 Meeting of Civic leaders and employees

To develop the revival, Mrs. Dyke relied heavily on her theatrical background and personal experiences as a Chautauqua Assembly attendee, in addition to all the Feast of Lanterns festivals she had attended and performed as a young woman. Her goal was to develop a multi-cultural festival that preserved the history and culture brought to Pacific Grove by its diverse population and the Chautauqua Assembly.

1913 High School production of Feast of the Little Lanterns with Elmarie Hurlbert Hyler Dyke

The introduction of a Royal Court to the Feast of Lanterns was influenced by Mrs. Shropshire and her position as executive director of the Miss Monterey County Pageant. It was from the 1958 Miss Monterey County contestants that the first Royal Court was named, Miss Pacific Grove selected, and Queen Topaz crowned—thus the reason Saturday is referred to as the "pageant". In 1962, Queen Topaz, Pamela Jean Gamble, won the title of Miss Monterey County, was crowned Miss California and went on to compete in the Miss America Pageant. After 1964, the Miss Monterey County Pageant was no longer used to select the Royal Court, and gone were the bathing suit and formal wear competition, and talent contest.

Bathing suit competition, 1958

Miss Pacific Grove and Queen Topaz, Gail Matrie 1958

Formal wear competition, Julia Kahle, Queen Topaz 1960

It was 1965 when Mrs. Dyke began personally selecting the young women who would serve on the Royal Court. Her criterion for selection was simple—the young women along with their families must be active community members and live in Pacific Grove.

With Mrs. Dyke's death in 1981, her granddaughter, Joanie Hyler, and her Feast of Lanterns assistant, Becky DeSmet-Solliceto picked up the mantle and worked as co-Executive Directors to select the Royal Court and keep the lanterns lit. The following year an all-volunteer Board of Directors was established and assumed the responsibility of continuing the traditions. The Royal Court was now selected from applicants by a panel of judges comprised of active community members. In 1987, the Royal Court Scholarship Fund was established. In 2016, Chang became an official member of the Royal Court, and in 2017 a Royal Guard comprised of young high school boys was introduced as part of the Royal Court.

Pamela Gambel, Miss California and Queen Topaz 1962

2017 Royal Court with Royal Guard, 2017

For many the Feast of Lanterns is merely a pantomime of an old fable performed on the pier by the Royal Court, which ends in a canopy of fireworks over the Cove. This is unfortunate because the Feast of Lanterns is so much more. It is Pacific Grove's heritage festival presented to the public by Queen Topaz and the Princesses. They hostess, under the direction of the Board of Directors, a diverse program of dances, songs, art shows, and stories from around the world. They serve a proper tea to the seniors at Forest Hill Manor, visit schools and teach children about the world's different lanterns, minerals and gemstones, and dance Greek, Israeli, American, and many other folk dances with young and old alike. They serve as ambassadors for Pacific Grove throughout their one-year reign.

Royal Court telling the Legend of the Blue Willow

Since its revival in 1958, the Festival has been held every year, with one exception, the last weekend in July. In 1986, it was cancelled due to increased insurance costs. The Festival has had other revenue and expense challenges that altered the festival. In 1982, the fireworks were cancelled and not reinstates for five years, and in 2010, the Pageant was forced to be moved to a less expensive indoor venue.

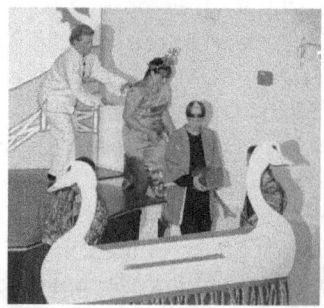

Queen Topaz and Chang escape. Performing Arts Center 2010

Queen Topaz honored at PAC 2010

Yokosan Dojo perform 2010 at PAC

The Feast of Lanterns is a celebration of Pacific Grove's heritage and traditions that has been passed down through generations of volunteers, who are dedicated to keeping the lanterns lit. For over 100 years, the Feast of Lanterns has been part of Pacific Grove's history—nterrupted by war and lack of money, but always revived by love of community.

358 *Life in Pacific Grove, California*

FIRST PERSON REMEMBRANCES

Lighting Up Lovers Point
Don Gasperson
PGFD Chief 1962-1984

I was the fire chief in 1963 when Elmarie approached me about doing something on Lovers Point for the Feast of Lanterns, "like lighting it up". Perhaps relying too heavily on my religious back-ground and 16 years in the fire department for inspiration, I put up a cross and lit it with red flares just before we started fire works show. This addition to the Pageant did not go over well with Elmarie or the residents. So the following year my fellow firemen and I built a Torri Gate on Lovers Point and lit it with red flares just before we setoff the fireworks. This time we were a success, it was well received by everyone. In 1965 we added a second Torri Gate at Berwick Park to everyone's delight. It was about this time that Roger Brown, who was a PGFD captain at the time, got his pyrotechnics license, and for many years, fire department personnel donated all their time to ensure a successful show. I remember spending many, many a cold night on the pier with Elmarie coordinating via radio with the other firemen the fireworks show and the lighting of the Torri Gates. It was a privilege working with Elmarie and our community.

The Show Must Go On
Jim Costello
Mayor of Pacific Grove, 2005

Elmarie Hurlbert Hyler Dyke

My favorite Feast of Lanterns memory had to be the last time the pageant was narrated by Elmarie Dyke. As usual, weather was a factor. Partway through the Pageant, the wind blew and the script pages scattered. Elmarie quickly gathered-up the pages and continued reading the script. Without realizing it, Elmarie began rereading a part of the script that she had just finished reading before the pages scattered. It was great fun watching the cast try to backup and repeat their actions. This led to a professional announcer being asked to takeover this responsibility. If my memory is correct, Gene Rusco, then of KIDD did the chore for one year before going off to KGO in San Francisco. After that Roger Powers, who had KOCN in town, took over.

And the Crowd Roared
Carol Bradley Lauderdale

Queen Topaz 1966

I remember that magical night in the summer of 1966 being crowned Queen Topaz in front of a crowd of what seemed like thousands, thinking all the world was watching, and feeling very special. It was a very emotional experience I have carried with me all these years. For you see, I really am a rather shy person when it comes to being the center of attention. I remember how Mrs. Dyke groomed all the gals on the RoyalCourt. She had a little "tea" for us at her townhouse and instructed us on proper etiquette-how to sit, stand, walk and be graceful. We were to strive for perfection with our hair, makeup and mannerisms, as we were representing our beloved town of Pacific Grove. To this day, her influences remain ever present in my life.

Get on Your Mark, Get Set, GO!
Elaine Dausch

Derby Races on Alder Street
Resident since 1954

In the 1960's we lived on Alder Street in Pacific Grove, and at that time one of the features of the celebration was the soap box derby race down Alder Street. Many of the youngsters of the Monterey Peninsula spent a good part of the year building their racing cars, soliciting help from Dads, big brothers and even sometimes Moms. The big prize for the winner was a trip to Indianapolis to participate in the National Soap Box Derby. Needless to say, there was strong competition. It was a very enjoyable part of the celebration we no longer enjoy.

Best Friends Forever
Gloria Newell Webster

Princess Sapphire, 1958

Thinking back to the revival of the Feast of Lanterns in 1958, I remember the strong camaraderie that developed among the princesses. At that time we were sponsored by the PG merchants and competed for the Miss Pacific Grove title. Today, I still see the same bond among the princesses as they develop a strong sense of community and contribute so much to the success of the Feast of Lanterns event.

Once Upon a Time
Garth Evans

Princess Sapphire, 1963

I remember Elmarie Dyke's ubiquitous influence on every aspect of the Festival. Weeks before the events began, the princesses met at her condominium on Lighthouse Avenue for costume fittings, hairstyling, and lessons on the etiquette of princessly walking and sitting. Then, on a misty Pacific Grove evening in July, 1963, costumed as Princess Sapphire in a bright blue Chinese silk jacket and long black skirt, I and the other Feast of Lanterns princesses waited on the lantern-festooned pier, while hundreds of festival-goers on the beach anticipated the dramatic re-enactment of P.G.'s own interpretation of the love story between the Mandarins' daughter and her peasant sweetheart, whose undying love transforms them into Monarch butterflies. The crowd watched as Miss Monterey County, Mary Gannon, was crowned Queen Topaz and the show began, with Elmarie Dyke the real queen of the festivities in her own right.

Royal Sisterhood of Pacific Grove
Alli Haylings Mayorga

Princess Garnet 2004, Aquamarine 2005, Rose Quartz 2006

Growing up in Pacific Grove meant a lot of things for me, but one sticks out—a unique tradition that continues on to this very day, Feast of Lanterns.

As a girl, I would marvel at the Pretty Princesses, as my family would take me to all the hometown events, such as the Feast of Salads, the Pet Parade and my personal favorite, the Street Dance. I would collect their cards and spread them out across my floor, choosing favorites and dreaming of which Princess I would be once I "grew up."

Once I became "of age," there was no doubt that I wanted to see my face on one of those trading cards, and take part in Pacific Grove's most quirky tradition.

One thing I have carried with me since my time on the court was the bonds that were formed, both while on the court and much later. In 2013, many years after my time on the Royal Court, I walked into a Zumba studio and saw a familiar face, Alexandra Stampher, Queen Topaz 2003. We never reigned together, but I was on the court with her younger sister, Sydney, Queen Topaz 2006. Alex and I quickly formed a bond. We danced together, we traveled together, we even led a Zumba class together on the pier for Feast of Lanterns. And while I was planning my wedding, Alex asked to officiate the ceremony. She did so, with such perfection, grace and ease it was clear to see, Alex is still very much so a Queen. I think the basis of our deep friendship is our underlying Royal Sisterhood.

After my time on the court, I went on to study writing at UC Santa Cruz. I also pursued a great love for travel, spending quite some time in Ireland, England, France, Scotland, and Whales. I returned to Pacific Grove where I enrolled in some art classes at Monterey Peninsula College. It was there where I met the love of my life and together we continued to explore, adventuring through Mexico, Greece, Spain, Austria and Northern Ireland. I currently work for the Santa Cruz Sentinel as well as write for the Cedar Street Times. In my free time, I obsessively hunt Pyrex as my kitchen hosts quite the vintage collection. My husband and I settled in none other than Pacific Grove, where we often pinch ourselves for being able to live in this perfect beach town.

It Was My Honor
Dixie Layne
FOL Board President 2009, 2010

History of the Feast of Lanterns 1905—2005 booklet

I was invited to join the Feast of Lanterns board of directors in 2004, and my first project was to create a keepsake souvenir for the 2005 centennial celebration—a booklet of stories and photographs that told the Feast of Lanterns' history. It ws an educational experience for me to share the Feast of Lanterns story—is embedded in the history of Pacific Grove. Over the years I would be involved in other projects, either by request or by design, and of all the other projects, there are three that I am particularly proud to say are now part of its history.

In the 1950s there was a Queen's sedan chair that was used to carry Queen Topaz in a parade to the town square for an evening of entertainment—I always wondered what happened to that sedan chair. When I was elected 2009 board president I wanted to give back to the Feast of Lanterns—thus the idea of a replacement chair was born. Marge Ann Jameson ran an ad in the Cedar Street Times for an artisan to craft the chair. David Brown responded. I showed him the photos of the original chair, opened an account at Hayward lumber, and the project was underway. The result of his work was an incredibly beautiful Queen's chair with hand carved illustrations inspired by the *Legend of the Blue Willow*. Marge Ann created its silk canopy.

Queen's Sedan Chair, 1958

Indoor Pageant, 2010

That same year I was approached by Lori Mannell, then executive director of the Natural History Museum, about how we might collaborate on a Feast of Lanterns project; thus the idea for an exhibit that illustrated its history resulted. I wrote the "story" on which the exhibit would be based and with lots of help from the community collected artifacts and materials that would be used to tell the story. The exhibit was the second most attended since counts were recorded by the Museum.

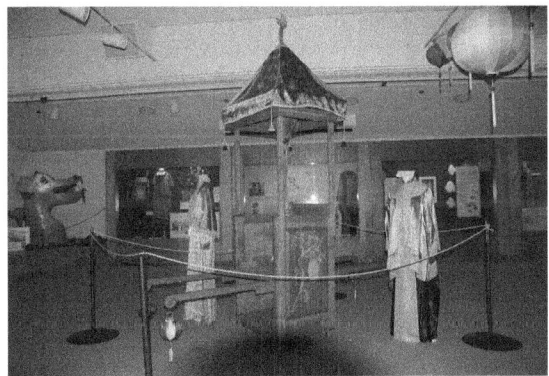

Queen's Sedan Chair 2009 at museum exhibit

It was 2010, when the economy took its toll on the Feast of Lanterns. Money was tight and our fundraising abilities were severely hampered. The Board voted to suspend the expensive outdoor Pageant and create a less expensive event. The most important thing with undertaking this endeavor was whatever we did, we must give the community an event that contained all the features and traditions they had come to expect and love. I traded my title of board president with Sue Renz for her title of treasurer and I picked up the pageant director's mantle.

We moved the "Pageant" from Lovers Point to the Performing Arts Center. Sets were built, the script adapted, electronic fireworks developed, and large butterflies mounted high above the audience. This once in a lifetime presentation received praise and we were asked might we do it again—we had achieved our goal. The best news, we were back on the pier for 2011. Adapting with such aplomb could not have happened without the support and hard work of all, but particularly Virginia and Gordon Coleman, Becky DeSmet-Solliceto, and the Royal Court families—especially Princess Pearl's (Lauren Thuesen) grandfather, Mahlon Coleman and Princess Amethysts' (Celeste Torres) brother, Pito Torres.

My time working on the Feast of Lanterns has been a labor of love, and I enthusiastically encourage everyone in Pacific Grove to participate—you'll have the best time, and the rewards are boundless.

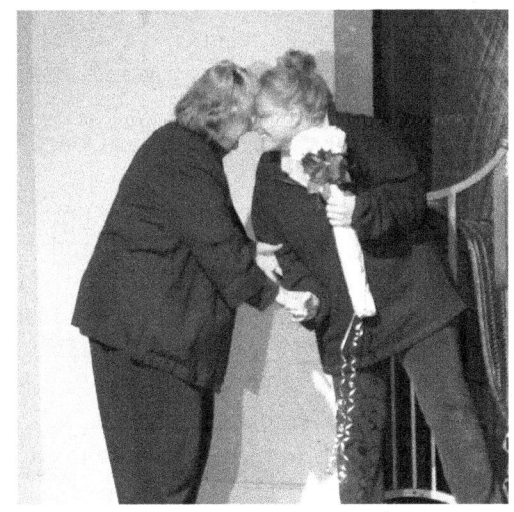

French Braids Everyone
Alexandra Stampher
Princess Sapphire 2001, Amethyst 2002, Queen Topaz 2003

My favorite memory of the Feast of Lanterns was a culmination of many moments spent

bonding with other FOL royalty. I'd spent three years as a princess, joking with the other girls, caking on makeup, and French braiding hair. When I was chosen as Queen Topaz, I knew how we'd spend our prep time. Forget gossip. We would binge watch Xena: Warrior Princess.

Throughout the summer of 2003, my dedicated court learned the warrior princess' way. We learned the power of a smile, of lipstick, and a theatrical ou8it. We learned how to serve as ambassadors of our town, role models to younger children, and sisters to each other. My princesses learned one last thing, tomy surprise and amazement. I didn't realize what they'd learned until the night of the pageant.

As Chang and I fled from my father's wrath, my sister princesses cried out. It was no ordinary wailing. They had learned the battle cry of Xena, Warrior Princess. That yodeling yell carried across the water, to my escape vessel, and beyond. I believe it was the battle cry that caught the goddess Xuannü's attention. With her help, and thanks to the shrieking princesses, we escaped, able to return every year as monarch butterflies.

Aside from the training in public speaking and smiling into the sun, I learned to French braid really well.

French braided hair was a requirement while I was on the court. During my four years as royalty, I spent well over 100 hours braiding hair.

Nowadays, I continue as if my reign as Queen Topaz never ended. As I used to rule over my

subjects in Pacific Grove, I now rule over my students at a small trade school. I still French braid my hair. I still love Xena: Warrior Princess.

If my kaleidoscope of butterflies is migrating through Pacific Grove during the festivities, we participate.

We revel in the Feast of Flavors, the Pet Parade, and the Feast of Dancing. During the big day, we'll stake out our stretch of beach early, making sure to choose a place above the high tide line. We celebrate this unique tradition.

Metamorphosis
Sydney Stampher
Queen Topaz, 2006

My favorite memory of FOL was getting ready together in the morning. I loved talking and learning make-up tips from each other, eating a yummy breakfast every time from a new princess' family, and watching every girl transform into a beautiful butterfly as we all finished up. So many things I learned at FOL still help me even today, but I think the most useful thing for me was learning the pretty pageant smile. As a freelance actress now, I really appreciate having that tool.

Note from Alli Mayorga: Sydney and I reigned on the court together for 2 years and she is still a dear friend. Sydney indeed has blossomed into a beautiful butterfly, now living in Japan with her husband Ted, she still migrates home every year for an extended visit every summer.

Photo Credits Keeping the Lanterns Lit

Feast of Lanterns at Lovers Point, 1905– Layne collection, Costumed residents - Pat Hathaway Collection , Clyde Dyke – Hyler family collection, 1958 Meeting of Civic Leaders and employees – Layne collection, 1913 High School production of Feast of the Little Lanterns with Elmarie Hurlbert Hyler Dyke – Hyler Family collection, First Miss Pacific Grove and Queen Topaz, Gail Matrie 1958, Layne collection, Pamela Gambel, Miss California and Queen Topaz 1962, - Layne collection, Bathing suit competition, 1958 - Layne collection, Julia Kahle formal wear competition, 1960: - Layne collection, 2017 Royal Court with Royal Guard, 2017 – FOL collection, Royal Court telling the legend of the Blue Willow – Layne collection, Queen Topaz and Chang escape, Pageant held at Performing Arts Center 2010 – Layne collection, Queen Topaz, Jena Hively 2010 honored by Chinese Lion Dancers – Layne collection, Yokosan Dojo perform 2010 – Layne collection

Photo Credits First Person Remembrances

Don Gasperson – Dixie Layne collection, Elmarie Hurlbert Hyler Dyke –Hyler family collection, Carol Bradley Lauderdale, Queen Topaz 1966 – Dixie Layne collection, Derby Races on Alder Street – Dixie Layne collection, Gloria Newell 1958 – courtesy Gloria Newell Webster, Garth Evans, Princess Sapphire 1963 – Dixie Layne collection, Allie Haylings Mayorga – courtesy Alli Mayorga, History of the Feast of Lanterns 1905 – 2005 – Dixie Layne collection, Queen's Sedan Chair, 1958 – Dixie Layne collection, Queens Sedan Chair 2009 at Museum Exhibit, 2009 – Dixie Layne collection, Indoor Pageant, 2010 – Dixie Layne collection, Virginia Coleman and Dixie Layne 2010 indoor pageant – Layne collection,

Permissions for publication of photos given by Dixie Layne

MORE MEMORIES OF FEAST OF LANTERNS

My Feast of Lanterns Years
Marabee Boone
Princess Turquoise

Oh, my, how do I keep this to 500 words? One of the molders of my life was Mrs. Dyke. That's right, out of respect she was never Elmarie to me, although now, in my heart, she is Elmarie Leslie Hurlburt Hyler Dyke. When Mayor Shropshire suggested, in 1958, that we "bring back" the Feast of Lanterns, Councilman Clyde Dyke was pegged to be the leader of this movement. We all know that close at hand was Mrs. Dyke, at the ready to do what she did—help get things done. Together they started gathering volunteers for every task. Being a member of the same congregation as Mrs. Dyke, I was probably one of the first to be nabbed. And I was ready. Little did I know that it would lead to a 60-year commitment. A recent Royal Court asked me what I did when I first volunteered for "The Feast." When I told them that my first job was to stuff envelopes and lick stamps, they said, "You had to lick stamps?" Oh, my.

Mrs. Shropshire was involved in the Miss Monterey County Pageant and, for a few years, the Royal Court was made up of the contestants in that program. In 1961 that's how I got on the court, as Princess Turquoise. There were Princesses from other areas of the Peninsula as well as Pacific Grove. Through the years that changed, and for a while they were chosen, I believe, for the participation of their families. When it was decided to give scholarships, the program changed again and young women applied and were interviewed to become members of the Royal Court. That is the process today and young men now have the opportunity for service and scholarships.

So, what did I do all these years? I used to say, "Whatever Mrs. Dyke asked me to do." And then she was gone and I had to grow up. I have directed the pageant, gathered Saturday afternoon entertainers, served as president, schlepped chairs, washed dishes, loaded set pieces and sound equipment, built a ticket booth, etc., (I have NOT rowed the boat) all in the name of community and fun.

Now I have stepped back from all of that. Not because I was tired of doing it but because it became time for someone else to learn how to do all of those things. I'll still be around (volunteering somewhere) but I won't be "in charge" of anything. I am now pleased to be a Board Member Emeritus. Wow. Is that a fancy way to say, "You are now free to totally enjoy the week?" My 60th Feast will be an easy, carefree, worry-free event for me.

What are the greatest things about spending all this time on this community event? Getting to know so many people. I see Feast friends every day. The families of the court members are so dedicated that it has been a joy to work with them. The greatest reward? Seeing shy young girls become confident young women through their dedication to their community and their involvement on the Royal Court.

I don't dare be specific with my "thank yous" because I would be sure to miss someone. Thank you so much to all of you who have devoted your time and talents to continuing this important community event. GOOD JOB!!!

Feast of Lanterns and First Kiss
Diana Dennis

At 20 years old, I moved to Pacific Grove from my childhood home in Modesto, in central California. It was June of 1965, and I was living in the Sunset Apartments, which my aunt and uncle managed. I had a job at Pacific Bell in Monterey, but I helped out at the apartments as needed. One day I was repainting space numbers in the apartment parking lot when I noticed a guy who looked like a younger Paul Newman entering one of the apartments. In the next few weeks, we seemed to run into each other often … maybe on purpose. His name was Mike Davis and before long we began to spend time together. He introduced me to several of his friends including Erik Johnson, who now owns the Erik's Deli Café chain. We would all go swimming in the apartment pool, go sliding on cardboard down the huge sand dunes (where Spanish Bay is now), take drives out to Carmel Valley, and watch movies at the beautiful State Theater in Monterey. Mike and I saw Cat Ballou there and laughed and laughed; by the end of the movie, we were holding hands. Soon after that, he brought me pink roses! I was dizzy with the thoughts that this handsome, smart, and self-assured guy liked me.

One afternoon in late July, Mike asked me if I wanted to go with him to the Feast of Lanterns at Lovers Point. We arrived and watched from the edge of the street above the beach, just past the train tracks where the Rec Trail is now. I didn't understand the pageant or what the Chinese story had to do with Pacific Grove, but it was fun. People of all ages held long sticks with paper lanterns on the end and candles flickering inside. A parade of boats rocked in the sea as they came in from Monterey, colored lights strung on their masts and sail edges. It was magical and matched my mood as I stood in front of Mike. The crowd seemed to sway as more people gathered and I felt myself being moved closer to Mike. As the pageant ended, he put his arms around my shoulders. Suddenly, with no introduction, the sky burst with color! I couldn't believe that such a little town could manage such a stunning fireworks display. And then Mike turned my face gently toward his and kissed me! Oh my goodness, I thought. This is true love!

I've gone to the Feast of Lanterns almost every year since and always remember that special night in 1965.

After nearly 50 years, I had a chance to talk with Mike and our Feast of Lanterns evening came up. I was surprised to hear him say that he had been very nervous about that first kiss. We hadn't known that both of us had hearts beating as loud as the booms of the fireworks. And now, I just smile about being in love in the summer near the beach with colorful twinkling lanterns all around us under a sky full of spectacular fireworks.

Feast of Lanterns Heyday
Donald Livermore

I moved to Pacific Grove in the early 70s. There were an abundance of community events and celebrations but the premier event was the annual Feast of Lanterns. A celebration honoring the city's beginning, the event was patterned loosely on the Chinese Blue Willow legend (and I mean loosely). The event is celebrated to this day the last full week of July, still wonderful hometown family fun.

The choice of theme is kind of ironic. The story was adapted from the Chinese settlement and their lighted fishing practices at night along the coastal waters. Chinatown was a thriving place in mid 1800s to around the turn of the century. It was located where Hopkins Marine Station and the renowned Monterey Bay Aquarium now sit. They were not well received by the pious locals of Pacific Grove. In fact the village was torched in 1906, many believe out of resentment of their religion and lifestyle. Lest I digress, back to the Feast.

Started in the early 1900s, I feel the heyday of it was in the 70s and 80s when a local matron, Elmarie Dyke, presided over the event. She was a key organizer of the celebration and especially the final play performed by the Princesses and their families on the pier at Lovers Point. Her overly dramatic reading of the story and her interjected comments had to be heard to be fully appreciated. For example, while dramatically reading the story, she would often give the performers cues like "Princesses, you need to move faster so you don't get burned by the torches" or, "Nursemaid, you need to get moving." She would also do scolding asides like, "We used to have a dragon in the water but eliminated it because children were throwing rocks at it and could hurt the divers." Her melodramatic presentation was priceless. You couldn't help rolling your eyes and chuckling at the wonderful hometown hokey essence of the whole event. And who could forget the spectacular closing with fireworks, illuminated American flag and a Kate Smith recording of "God Bless America." Those were the days.

Did We Move to China?
Cindy P. Gates
artist, teacher, photographer, observer

The U-Haul truck was turned in, and we surveyed the chaos of our apartment on Pacific Grove Lane. Boxes lined each room, some opened by the kids, some that would never be opened, as it turned out. The sky was blue, and the air fresh and clean, unlike our sweaty, dirty bodies.

"What's for dinner?" asked our five-year-old son, Chris.

"Dinner? Who cares?" I thought. But the kids were hungry. Sophie's eyelids were already drooping. I knew we had limited time before she began to melt.

"Let's try something downtown," my husband said. Downtown. Coming from Los Angeles, the word would have new meaning. We piled into our car and hit Lighthouse Avenue. July, 1988. A new life for us all.

Where presently Passionfish sits, there was a small restaurant, a diner, I think. The place was empty, but the kids were hungry and excited to be going out. We chose a window seat that faced the street and looked at the plastic menus.

Halfway through our meal, Chris said, "Mom, what's that?" He was pointing toward the Post Office. We looked up and our jaws dropped in unison. Even Sophie perked up.

Young girls in Chinese dresses were square-dancing in the street, surrounded by groups of people wearing similar clothing. They carried parasols and fans in beautiful blues, reds, and yellows.

"Mom, did we move to China?"

Bill and I looked at each other with the same question in mind. Where the heck HAD we moved?

Now, years later, we have learned to love the hokey celebrations, the Butterfly Parade (with two sets of monarch wings tucked safely in storage), the welcoming friends who were willing to take in Southern California Dodger fans, and the blessed years of clean air and stunning vistas. And though we still love Southern California where we were born, we call Pacific Grove home.

As we do each year, we hang our Chinese lanterns on the arbor in front of our house for the Feast of Lanterns and remember that first day in Pacific Grove when we were tired and hungry, and young girls danced happily in the streets "downtown," adorned in Chinese costumes with parasols and fans.

Gin Lung ... Pacific Grove's Dragon
Greg Aeschliman
as told to Robin Aeschliman

Probably 1967. Tom Maudlin, the instigator. I drew the plans. We made a dragon for the Feast of Lanterns ... VERY hush-hush.

Tom, his wife, Merrill; my wife, Robin, me, the kids ... we built our secret project in the Maudlin's Bishop Avenue garage. The whole thing ended up about 30 feet long—took up the entire space.

Its head was about five feet high. Tom cut a plywood dragon-head silhouette; we attached a wood framework to it. We used inner tubes and Styrofoam chunks as the base to stabilize it because when it was put in the water, the head, with its mouth open, would be top-heavy.

We wrapped it in chicken wire and sculpted it into shape. All of us worked at slathering it with torn strips of old Monterey Heralds. We covered the neck, head, jaw, and the teeth—layers and layers of flour and water papier-mâché. The wings, which hid the access to the inside of the head, were wire frames covered with orange garbage bags. We wrapped green canvas Army tarps around the base up to about two feet. If it got wet, the water wouldn't hurt it.

Two little aluminum pie tins were placed on the head as eyes. We poked a hole in the middle of each tin and fastened red Christmas tree lights, which we connected to a six-volt battery mounted in the head. We could turn the eyes on and off. We painted the head green, added gold scales; the teeth were white.

For the dragon's long body, so it would look like it was swimming through the water, we made two humps of tarp-covered inner tubes with a wooden cross-frame underneath. Molded chicken wire covered with more orange formed the humps' spikes. To control the distance and position we tied the humps to a rope connected to the head. A couple of divers would balance each hump. For the tail we covered another wood silhouette with sculpted wire, then, yes, orange plastic bags. We attached

the pointy tail to an inner tube we pinched together into a banana shape. Next time we'll attach a lantern to it. Wink. Not gonna' happen; Tom's 80, I'm 78; he's in better shape than I am.

On a platform in the mouth, we mounted a couple of CO2 tanks and affixed the nozzle of a fire extinguisher that Tom commandeered from the Fire Department. It was a guesstimate as to how successfully this thing would float. We had a trial run at Lovers Point Beach in the dark of night. Perfect. When we turned the lights on they reflected against the pie tins. Really looked neat.

No one knew about it—just the four of us, our children, and a few divers. Tom, a policeman, and leader of the Pacific Grove Marine Refuge Patrol (another story), couldn't dive that night as he had Feast of Lanterns duty. But he could stop traffic and make a path to sneak the truck carrying the dragon to the cliff at the water's edge. Tom named it Gin Lung, "... for the gin we drank building it," he laughed.

Divers and Gin Lung slipped into the water from the beach north of the pier. Launched! Quiet excitement bubbled. All exposed parts of inner tube were covered with seaweed. Divers kept to Gin Lung's far side so they wouldn't be seen from the beach. Took about ten of us to maneuver it. Eyes flashing, Gin Lung silently floated around the pier into sight. From inside the head, two of us steered—legs in the water, hands on the platform busy working lights ... passing a jug. We squeezed the handle of the fire extinguisher nozzle and a big blast of fog—looked like white smoke—roared out of the dragon's mouth.

Pacific Grove's fiery visitor either enhanced or upstaged the traditional story solemnly in progress on the pier's stage. The divers had a ball. The crowd had a ball. I think Elmarie Dyke did not.

The next year Gin Lung had a friend. Manchester, a whale. That, too, is another story.

(Notes: Greg and Robin Aeschliman, Tom Maudlin, Jim Hughes, Corky Weydeveld, Gene Dobbs, Wendell Ayers, Bob McCurdy, Don Ferrin, Joyce and Ed Seifert, Punky Kirkman, Al Schaeder ... some all the years, some not. Gin Lung was retired in 1971, another story. A couple times Jim "Doc" Hughes (Pacific Grove City Councilman, 1967 to 1986) and Tom Maudlin (Police Chief, 1985 to 1993) jumped out of a helicopter. (Another story.) Many of the divers were volunteers in the Pacific Grove Marine Refuge Patrol formed in 1963 (later called the Pacific Grove Marine Rescue Unit).

Elmarie Hurlbert Hyler Dyke was known as the "Matriarch of the Feast of Lanterns". [Sally Aberg and Betty Aickelin, eds.; Board and Batten of the Heritage Society of Pacific Grove, (Summer 2008), pg. 2. The scribe suggests that Mrs. Dyke was the Matriarch of Pacific Grove, too.] 1968 photos of Dragons courtesy of Pat Hathaway, The Pat Hathaway Collection, caviews.com

SECTION 10
NATURAL WORLD WONDERS

PACIFIC OCEAN AND MONTEREY BAY SANCTUARY

Born a Water Baby
Lois Carroll

I was born near water and if I have anything to say about it, I'll die near water.

Pacific Grove is on a small peninsula surrounded by the beauty of both the Monterey Bay and the Pacific Ocean. I now live a few blocks away from that water. In the quiet of night, at high tide, I can hear the crashing ocean waves. And during a winter storm, I can witness the drama and might of those huge waves. On a bright sunny day, I can walk along the Monterey Bay, stopping to rest on a waterfront bench and watch the birds soar about a calm sea, a blue sky and the distant hills.

It was only after retirement that I came to live here and feel within a rebirth in my mind, heart and soul. A true gift accepted with grace and thankfulness.

I was born in New Jersey and grew up gazing at the Hudson River, near the mouth of the New York Harbor, watching tug boats, ocean liners and barges crawl up the river to their docks, I'm also a child of the Jersey shore, jumping in the waves of the Atlantic Ocean in Ocean Grove during endless summer days. The water was always there and taken for granted as the way life should be.

After my marriage, we lived for a number of years both in the flat cornfields of central Illinois and the rocky peaks of Colorado. Like ocean surfers who find themselves suddenly in the middle of the Sahara Desert, we missed the intoxicating joy of living near a large body of water.

At last in 1982 we moved to the Bay Area to a place close enough to enjoy the Pacific Ocean. Our family spent weekends exploring the beaches and cliffs of San Francisco Bay, Half Moon Bay, the San Mateo coast and the cold waters of Santa Cruz. When our daughter chose to attend the University of California at Santa Cruz, I had a reason to visit her and to enjoy the Santa Cruz wharf, beach and boardwalk too. I continued to enjoy the area even after she graduated.

Five years ago, we were blessed with the birth of our grandson in San Jose. When he was still a small tot, his parents, to my complete surprise, managed to buy an old, historic 1937 house on Forest Avenue in Pacific Grove as a weekend and vacation getaway. It was a house badly in need of repair, updating and remodeling. Our son-in-law spent over two years doing most of the work himself. As part of the remodeling project he added a bedroom specifically for "grandma and grandpa." With joy and anticipation we furnished this bedroom knowing that my grandson and I could spend lots of time playing, exploring the beach and reading bedtime stories together. It has been a joy. Now when I wake up in the morning and look out the window, I rejoice that I have another magical day to live in Pacific Grave. Water, water is everywhere and neither that beautiful water nor I will ever go away.

Message in a Bottle
Laura Edeen

"Asking is the beginning of receiving. Make sure you don't go to the ocean with a teaspoon. At least take a bucket so the kids won't laugh at you." —Jim Rohn

Growing up in Pacific Grove, we were surrounded by the ocean. There were fishermen in our neighborhood who brought us salmon and dared us to eat sea urchin and octopus. My mom had an idea for those fisherman. She had my brother and me write letters to put in bottles to see if anybody would respond. My mother taught me to just put stuff out there and see what the universe offers back.

It was fun to write a letter to a mystery person and hope you could charm them into sending you a letter back in the mail. My brother liked to write like he was a pirate and then send a crayon pirate map with an X to mark the spot of where we lived (with address written on the back). I liked to pretend I was a mermaid and draw a nice picture of me as a pretty mermaid. I would put a nice shell or something in the bottle, too. After a few tries of throwing the bottles ourselves and watching them get stuck in a far-off tide pool, we got the idea to just give them to Bob, the fisherman next door. He could take them on his boat. He knew about the currents and would get our messages to Hawaii, Australia and far less exotic San Diego, California. It was like he had a magic power to talk to the sea gods.

We loved getting the reply letters, but I don't think we saved any of them. The people were always so nice and excited about the special connection they made with us. The memory of these messages stayed with me. When my boyfriend Don died, I wrote a letter to him. It made sense to put it in a bottle and throw it in the ocean. I had scattered his ashes in the ocean, so that would be the closest place for him to get a letter. It made me feel better even though I didn't get a reply.

That quotation above is true—asking or wishing is the beginning of receiving. It was a powerful personal step for me in gaining closure. I used that mindset again to ask for my little boy Hudson, who by all rights is a miracle child for us. Anything at all is possible. I must remember to keep that in mind, hold it close to my heart, and not underestimate the universe and what it can bring you. Expect great things.

In the Eye of the Beholder
A Tanka Tale
Neal Whitman, poet

Seaward ho! Hang the treasure!
It's the glory of the sea that has turned my head.
   Robert Louis Stevenson, Treasure Island
   at night
   Moon does not reflect the day
   but rises to rule
   I am a Lunatic
   whose poems arrive in dreams

It may have started with a tour of Point Lobos, a California State Nature Reserve just south of Carmel. The docent tells us that some say it was the inspiration for Robert Louis Stevenson's *Treasure Island*, "or, so the legend has it." In fact, RLS had stayed a few months in the autumn of 1879 in the French Hotel, a rooming house in nearby Monterey.

We live on the Monterey Bay side of the Peninsula in Pacific Grove. Who knows how, when, or why one of the daughters of Zeus and Mnemosyne inspires—The Muses come and go as they please. It may have been Erato whose domain is lyric poetry, or, perhaps, Thalia who wears a comic mask. No matter … that night an idea comes to me and I wake the following morning with a plan:

   on my bed stand
   I keep a pencil and pad
   up once to pee
   the Sun rises on my notes
   treasure map / treasure trove

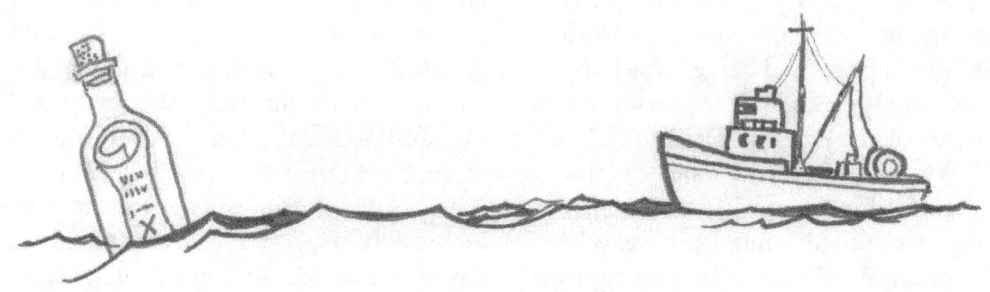

Tempted to add a jigger of dark Jamaican rum to my "crack of dawn" cup of black coffee, I choose not to dull my brain cells and draw a treasure map that will lead its finder to a tin box into which I put a used copy of *Treasure Island*.

I empty a plastic water bottle and label it with the logo of the Jolly Roger and the words, TREASURE MAP. I roll my map into the "message" bottle and, the next morning, up before sunrise, I head to the Pacific Grove portion of the Monterey Bay Coastal Recreation Trail and tie the bottle to the arm of a bench overlooking Lovers Point.

> by dawn's early light
> a black oystercatcher
> piping
> I march to my own drummer
> unseen harbor seals barking

Stepping to my own music, I head to where X marks the spot. I deposit the tin box under the replica of a 20-foot glass-bottom wooden Swan Boat that once plied the shallows around Lovers Point from the 1890s into the 1970s. None were plundered (as far as I know) by pirates! I return the next day. Message bottle? Treasure? Both gone!

Be Kind to the Tourists – They ARE Kinda Cute....
Jennifer Lee Smith

On a sunny, clear day (that's my story and I'm sticking to it), we were out for a family kayak from Lovers Point. As we paddled perhaps 20 yards to get through the seaweed field, our son Xander noticed a bottle floating in the ocean. It was an old-fashioned glass bottle with a cork—straight out of *Pirates of the Caribbean*. And it had a rolled-up note in it! A 12-year-old adventurer's dream! As we sat in our kayaks, Xander took out the cork with a pop and wriggled out the note. It read:

Hello!
We are Martin and Ethel and we hope this note finds you well! We live in Roseville, California, in the United States Of America. On a fine sunny day in February, we threw this bottle into the ocean from a place called Lovers Point in a quaint little town called Pacific Grove, in California in the United States of America. We wonder what adventures this bottle has seen!
If you find this bottle, please send us a letter telling us where you found it and we will send you a prize.
All the Best to you wherever you are in the world,
Martin and Ethel
Roseville, California
The United States of America

With a face that conveyed "eek, poor tourists," we contemplated how sad they would be to hear that their bottle traveled about 20 yards before resting on seaweed. And they would be just as sad to hear absolutely nothing. As a family, we discussed the definition (and virtue) of an occasional white lie.

We decided to write them and tell them the wonderful story of a 12-year-old boy thrilled to find a mysterious floating message in a bottle (true). And we went on to tell them how we found it floating in the ocean during a kayak trip near "Moss Landing, California, United States of America" (a little less than true). We told them we happened to live in that quaint little town of Pacific Grove they spoke of and we were very glad they visited it and chose that spot to start their bottle's journey.

Martin and Ethel, if you are reading this, we hope you appreciate the story and the 'white lie' of the successful (well, sort of successful) world journey of your message in a bottle.

The Spectacular Tide Pools of P.G.
John Pearse
retired UCSC professor

For a boy raised in the desert of southern Arizona, fresh out of college in Chicago, my first summer in the intertidal of Pacific Grove was life-changing. The slippery algal-covered rocks hid bizarre creatures, the cracks and crevices held unbelievable colors and hues of sponges, anemones, hydroids, tunicates—all mixed together, and under rocks writhing masses of brittle stars, flatworms, isopods, and crabs emerged.

Yes, I had read about them in college, but here they were! All in one place with crashing surf offshore, gloomy fog swirling around us, and the haunting foghorn of Point Pinos. My senses exploded.

That was the summer of 1959 when I took Don Abbott's invertebrate course at Stanford's Hopkins Marine Station. Early morning ventures into the intertidal were followed by donuts, coffee, and lecture and lab the rest of the day. Changed my life forever—not only by exposing me to ever-fascinating marine life, but also to a way to teach.

I returned to Hopkins in summer 1960 as a teaching assistant in an ecological physiology course, and then it was off to the Antarctic for over a year to do doctoral research.

The summer and fall of 1964 saw me back at Hopkins as a teaching assistant in Don Abbott's class and finishing my dissertation. Several years teaching and research in Egypt, and I came back in 1968 as a visiting faculty member in an innovative, student research class focusing on ocean pollution, particularly the sewage outfall at spectacular Point Pinos. That year, as only luck would have it, I met and married a finishing doctoral student at Hopkins, Vicki Buchsbaum.

We returned in 1971 when again I was a visiting faculty member teaching ecological physiology and developing the kelp forest ecology class that continues to be taught to this day.

In 1959 I lived in the upper story of 515 Granite with four other graduate students. I thoroughly enjoyed Pacific Grove as I went from our place to and from Hopkins. The summer of 1960 found me living upstairs in the Julia Morgan house on 1st and Ocean View, a short block from Hopkins.

During the more extended stay in 1964 I lived in a very small house at 314/316 2nd Street (now two tiny houses) before moving to 309 Chestnut, sequestered in the urban forest. I lived with the family of a fellow graduate student at 142 Pacific while courting Vicki in 1968; later in 1971 Vicki and I lived at 430 Evergreen and 209 Crocker. I have enjoyed many houses in this town!

While here in 1971 I accepted a faculty position at the University of California, Santa Cruz. And at the same time Vicki's father retired from his position at the University of Pittsburgh and bought a house at 183 Ocean View, across the street from Hopkins. That cemented our ties to Pacific Grove, and we made frequent visits over the next 30 years before moving into that same house in 2003—never to move again.

Photo by Ralph Buchsbaum.

P.G. and Me: A Play in Three Acts
Vicki Pearse

PROLOGUE: 1933-36. My parents, Ralph and Mildred Buchsbaum, both biologists from Chicago, came to Pacific Grove several summers to work at Hopkins Marine Station, oldest marine lab on the West Coast and still a biologist's destination. On their first visit—also their honeymoon—they roomed with Mr. and Mrs. Leslie at 519 Forest Avenue. Beautiful P.G. was heaven, and the Leslies were angels, or so went the bible stories I grew up on. In 1936, my father photographed a large Humboldt squid (held by Ed Ricketts). Humboldt squids invaded central California waters during the mid-1930s, then disappeared for decades, so the photo proved historic and is widely reproduced—now as a photo of Ed Ricketts (holding a squid).

ACT ONE: Summer 1949. On my first visit to P.G., we parked our family house-trailer outside the Leslies' home. Ricketts' death a year earlier, crossing the train track, was much talked about. This same deadly track ran by Hopkins, where I crossed, warily, each day.

As a biologist, I later learned many Latin names, but my proud first was the six-syllable Mesembryanthemum, at age six. (Sadly, this ice plant has been downgraded to four syllables, Carpobrotus). Another highlight was riding in a glass-bottomed Swan Boat at Lovers Point!

Besides the Leslies' flower garden, the Swan Boat, and the fearsome train track, my childhood memories are few. Mrs. Leslie remembered me, however, and sent me a doll in a red-and-white dress that she hand-crocheted, an example of P.G.'s warmth.

ACT TWO: 1963-71. As a senior at Stanford University, I returned to Hopkins, and P.G. felt immediately like home. For three years, I lived blissfully at 683 Ocean View Blvd., overlooking the flower garden of my nice landlords, Mr. and Mrs. Bullene, at 689.

In spring of 1968, I met my future husband at the Station, and we courted in P.G. World's most romantic place.

Drawn again to Hopkins in 1971, we lived first at 430 Evergreen (now the home of friends), then at 209 Crocker. My parents visited and, driving past Hopkins one day, they spotted a man putting a "for sale" sign in a house window opposite the Station. They stopped, inquired, and returned that very evening to buy the house at 183 Ocean View, fulfilling a lifelong dream of moving to P.G. John and I settled in Santa Cruz, and the next 30-plus years of visits only strengthened P.G.'s pull.

ACT THREE: 2003-Forever! After my parents died, John and I moved to the house on Ocean View. Again, P.G. felt like coming home. We wondered, though, how hard it might be to replace the personal connections built in three decades across the bay. Well, it was too easy. We were soon fully immersed within the community here: at Hopkins, the P.G. Museum, Sustainable P.G., the Farmers' Market, the city. Our granddaughter comes from Santa Cruz to visit, just as our son enjoyed his grandparents in this house. Many P.G. families like ours have roots over generations. We Pagrovians are the luckiest people anywhere.

The Christian Church of Pacific Grove Rec Trail Blue Theology Program
Kimberly A. Brown
retired, P.G. resident since 2004

No matter what the atmospheric conditions are in Pacific Grove, the Rec Trail offers one to experience wonder, awe, and appreciation of coastal beauty. The Christian Church of Pacific Grove's Blue Theology Mission Station offers students from middle school aged to adult, a week of learning and serving God's creation. The program is called Blue Theology. You will see us with our blue backpacks, drinking from reusable water bottles and carrying large trash bags with grabbers in our hands. Why? Because we practice what it means to take care of the gift of this Blue Planet.

When you see us, we are on a journey, a pilgrimage. We experience periods of silence at the Monterey Bay Aquarium pondering the precious gift. We also learn about the harm caused by plastics to birds and how thoughtlessly discarded plastic gathers in the ocean gyres to form huge islands of plastic. We learn that sand crabs are a signature species meaning they give scientists information about the health of our ocean. At Asilomar beach, we participate in this research in partnership with the LIMPETS program. You may see us return to Asilomar to plant and/or water native plants. When you do see us, ask yourself, "What can I do to serve in the preservation and restoration of the gift given to me?" It does not have to be big, just a small one such as picking up what you drop on the Rec Trail. It is not to late to take care of the gift.

Pacific Grove Summer 1972
Carol McCarthy

The summer of 1970 was the beginning of a new life for me. After a year of dropping out and travelling around the United States and Mexico in a red Volkswagon bus, we came to Pacific Grove for the summer. Hubby had a research grant at Hopkins Marine Station. We had already visited the Monterey Peninsula so we knew how special it was. We moved into a tiny, funky apartment on Mermaid Avenue for $75/month. The place had a wacky shared phone system, where the guys upstairs took only incoming calls and ran down the stairs for us and we all could dial out on our phone downstairs. It was a little inconvenient but it worked on our limited budget.

Mermaid Avenue then was occupied by a great mix of hippies, retirees, artists, a comedian (Chicago Steve), a motorcycle gang leader, and other interesting folks. Since living quarters were small, we tended to socialize on the narrow street or just stop by if there was a sign of a party going on. The police had longer hair with moustaches and sideburns and wore western hats and buckskin jackets.

We later moved down Mermaid to one of the original, single-wall construction missionary cottages. It seemed like a mansion to us. The side yard was filled with bamboo. We naively started to cut a path through the bamboo when our neighbors (Elmarie Dyke's brother and sister-in-law) told us it was an extension of their bird sanctuary so we left the bamboo alone. The cottage had a funky loft upstairs where we could see the bay from our bed upstairs. What a view to wake up to! Our orange-eyed, brindle German shepherd mix, Hoku, loved to climb out

the bedroom window and stare at the curious tourists walking up the street. They fondly called her the "tiger dog."

We had previously wanted to serve in the Peace Corps or some other volunteer service. So when we heard that there was a youth counseling center, Project Aquarius, starting up, we volunteered. We would bicycle to the Aquarian House from Mermaid Avenue going down Ocean View and two-way Foam Street. There was no Rec Trail, just railroad tracks. Project Aquarius still exists today as Community Human Services.

It was a unique time in my life. I sometimes walk down Mermaid Avenue and fondly remember all the characters who lived there in this my new world.

DÉJÀ VU
Linnet C. Harlan

"I've been here before," I thought, looking across the corner of Borg's Motel, Ocean View Boulevard, the swath of fuchsia ice plant, and the indigo water spraying glistening droplets from waves crashing against the rocks below. My sense was visceral and strong. I even knew where I was supposed to stand.

The only problem was, a Midwesterner newly moved to California, I knew I'd never before been south of San Jose.

On a road trip to celebrate my passing the state bar and getting a job, my husband and I had driven south from our newly-rented Menlo Park apartment for a short trip so he, a California native, could show me more of California. We'd spent the night in a Seaside motel, which led me to wonder why anyone thought the Monterey Peninsula was spectacular. Trying to see something more compelling than concrete, we'd stumbled upon a wedding on sunlit Lovers Point. Then I'd turned and seen the scene I knew I'd seen before, even though I knew I couldn't have.

For the next twenty years, the question of how I knew that particular spot so well surfaced again and again without resolution. My conviction I'd seen the spot before was deep in my bones, even though logic dictated I had not, could not have.

At one point I learned there had once been a mural of the Pacific Grove coast, with the ice plants and happy bicyclists, in New York's Pennsylvania Station. I'd passed through the station a couple of times; the mural did look familiar, but, while lovely, it didn't show "my" spot.

One day, decades after I'd first discovered the "I've been here before/I haven't been here before" mystery, as I stood in the San Francisco Galleria pushing the button for the elevator to Nordstrom, for no particular reason I realized I *knew*. I was so sure, my body shivered with the recognition. "The placemat," I thought.

When I was eight, my grandfather, grandmother, aunt and uncle had taken a road trip from Missouri to California to see one of my grandfather's sisters in Los Angeles. They'd driven up Highway 1 before heading home. During the process, they'd purchased a set of inexpensive placemats, each a single sheet of plastic with the image of an untitled California landmark. I don't remember now any of the other images, but I do remember that, charged with setting the table for dinners of the extended family, I'd shout, "I get the pink one," and claim the placemat with Borg's Motel, Ocean View Boulevard, the "pink" ice plants and the ocean.

The place I was supposed to stand? Where the photographer stood as he shot the photo.

P.G. was part of me when all I knew of it was pink ice plants, blue ocean and crashing waves. Before I even knew its name.

Vitamin O
Annette Cain
ocean lover and steward

In 2010, I moved to the Monterey Peninsula, which brought me back to one of my true loves—the ocean. I was fortunate enough to grow up by the Caribbean Sea in the tiny country of Belize. My playground was the second largest barrier reef in the world. It gave me the chance to frolic with a wonderfully diverse marine life. Some of my most memorable encounters were coming nose-to-nose with a whale shark, being followed by barracudas, and getting stung by a stingray.

Now after three decades, I am living once again by the coast, once again receiving my daily dose of Vitamin O. One of my favorite spots to soak it all in is Asilomar Beach. I love not knowing how it will be each time I come for a visit. On sunny days, the water is a brilliant turquoise, on foggy days a cocoon of gray. On windy days, the salt and sand can sting a bit, but it's worth the sight and sound of Big Blue's crashing waves. It never fails to fill me with a surge of joy!

I feel compelled to return my love to the ocean. One of the ways I do this is by volunteering with Save Our Shores. The mission of this Monterey Bay non-profit organization is caring for the marine environment through ocean awareness, advocacy, and citizen action. During one of their cleanups at Asilomar Beach, I collected the following items in less than an hour:

Over 100 pieces of plastic
Over 40 pieces of Styrofoam
36 cigarette butts
12 bottle caps
8 candy wrappers
3 straws
2 balloons
2 wooden stakes
1 little toy soldier, and
Half a pencil.

I'm always amazed at how much plastic and Styrofoam I see on the beach—little pieces mixed in with the sand and kelp. If you want to know how this affects the ocean and its marine life, check out the exhibit at the Monterey Bay Aquarium or The 5 Gyres Institute (5gyres.org). We have to end this now for the oceans' sake and our own.

I don't know about you, but Vitamin O is a necessary nutrient for me. I don't feel whole without experiencing the ocean on a regular basis, whether it's walking along the shore with my black Lab, swimming and kayaking around Lovers Point, volunteering for beach cleanups or watching the sunset. I feel so blessed that I live next to one of the most magnificent stretches of coastline. I love to just perch on the surrounding granite boulders and reflect about the ocean. How it endures with tireless power, instinctive purpose and timeless rhythm. One wavy breath after another. Gazing at the horizon reminds me of the life still before me in this beautiful place and I wonder what memorable encounters I have yet to come across here. Vitamin O might make my skin end up a bit more weathered, but it's worth it for the adventure, the awe, and the connection.

Jeweled Lights Across the Bay
Rudolph Estrada
bank executive and university professor

It was a cool, sunny February day in 1968 when I was drafted into the U.S. Army during my early years as a student at UCLA. Like thousands of other young men being drafted into the U.S. Army, the only thing certain was the immediate future was uncertain. Vietnam was in full stride and the draft program was aggressively building their ranks to support the war.

I recall the long, seven-hour bus ride from the Los Angeles Military Induction Center to our new home, Fort Ord. The silence on the bus on the ride up with the new inductees was deafening. Upon our arrival we were assigned to temporary wooden barracks and in a couple of days were assigned to our basic training units. Early in our training, which always included running in the early morning drizzle and fog, I captured my first view from the sand dunes along Highway 1 of the beautiful Monterey Bay.

Because we were restricted to our training area, the bay views were generally out of sight. It wasn't until Advanced Training that we were free to leave our barracks and I would walk to the Post Exchange adjacent to the highway and sneak a peek of the bay. In the evening, especially on a clear night, I would be drawn to the westernmost position of Fort Ord and stare across the bay, viewing the twinkle of jeweled lights from all the homes lining the coast all the way to the point.

It wasn't until after the conclusion of my formal base training and an assignment at the Defense Language Institute (DLI) that I was able to drive over to the site I had been mesmerized by for months and learned that what I had been looking at from across the bay was Pacific Grove. As a young man of 20, I remember driving along Ocean View Boulevard and fantasizing about one day living in this beautiful community. I was sightseeing with fellow soldiers as we were driving along the coast and the general sentiment was—how could anyone afford a home on this street; after all, they're selling in the $20,000-40,000.00 range?

For the past 40 or so years since my days at Fort Ord, my wife and I have been regular visitors to the Peninsula, always looking for that special home. Fast-forward to the summer of 2012, when we found a fixer-upper on Ocean View, made an offer, and were out-bid, to our total disappointment. Three weeks later we received a call from the real estate agent who informed us the buyer had fallen out of escrow and asked if we were still interested.

The rest is history and we love our second home on Ocean View. I especially enjoy being lulled to sleep with the sound of crashing waves at night and sitting outside on our bench with a glass of wine, a cigar, and just "people watching" with the beautiful Monterey Bay only feet away.

Monkey-Faced Eel
J.L. Schmidt
writer, mother, woman of strength

Albert Earl Henson, an engineer, holder of patents, and, my grandfather.

As an adult, I had the opportunity to live at my grandfather's house in the Aptos hills for a short time. As he grew older and his Parkinson's disease became more debilitating he'd rely on me to help him do some of the things he loved. One of those things was fishing. We'd often visit Lake Pinto in Watsonville, but on the days he wanted to spend significant time near the water we'd head to Pacific Grove.

I'll always remember one specific day, though I don't know why. It's perhaps the day that I choose to remember him at his best when he was physically nearing his worst. I drove my grandfather out to one of the turnouts along Ocean View, one he'd fished from before. He told me he wanted to catch "monkey-faced eel fish." I had no idea if he was pulling my leg or if that's what he was really fishing for. He enjoyed pulling my leg. It didn't matter, though; I was there to help him from the truck to his wheelchair; to bait the hook and at times cast his line into the bay when he could not control his arms and hands.

I recall sitting on a little chair next to him, both of us eating a lunch we'd picked up on the way in to town. His hair gray, his button-up, blue and white plaid shirt having seen better days, the black Dickies brand work pants he'd always favored, and the crumbs in his beard. His hands weren't as I remembered them as a child, strong and stained with grease, nails dirty from whatever work he'd done that day. Now, his skin was speckled with age spots, paper thin and delicate. Our day spent in the ocean breeze didn't provide any fish, though there were many bites. What it did provide was a wonderful memory, a picture I still have in my head. He, in his wheelchair near the edge of the rock wall, enjoying his sandwich and watching his line.

After I'd moved away, and gotten married some years later, his wife called early in the morning to tell me he'd passed away. It was around Thanksgiving. I thought, "I won't get to fish with him again," even though we hadn't done that in years. I felt that immediate loss of something small but significant.

Sometime later I'd move to Pacific Grove, that little town that held such a fond memory. Now, on occasion when driving down Ocean View I catch myself smiling as I pass the turnout where we'd fished that day. It makes me smile to think of the simple moments, most spent in silence, helping a man fish and enjoy the few activities he could. It was time well spent.

On the Beach
Susie Joyce
observer of marine life

Harbor seals pupping,
Unruly gulls grab afterbirth
Shocking onlookers

Uncomfortable

A cunning sea star
Devised an effective
Defense strategy;
It stood tall and stiff
In full 6 inch glory,
Despite the fact that it was
Trapped within the beak
Of a western gull.
The bird's yellow eyes
Wide with fear, or pain,
Fixed on my own
as I walked past
Where it stood helpless,
With beak stretched
Beyond reason.
The situation
Called for mediation
Far beyond my capabilities.
I left them there,
On the sea wall
At Lovers Point,
Knowing they needed time
To sort out the argument.

The Ocean's Throbbing Roar
Brenda Tayler

My perfect day in Pacific Grove begins by gazing at the ocean from our picture window. I hear the thundering waves calling me as the storm in churning. The roaring whitecaps invite a long, thorough run to take part in their explosive energy. I can't wait to hear the crushing and rocking of the water in my time along the path. It is a tough choice to decide between Bird Rock in Pebble Beach or along the Love Run path on Ocean View Boulevard, but today I will stay in my hometown.

I find my favorite running race shirt from my first Big Sur Half-Marathon, walk down our lovely small town and make a bee-line for Asilomar Beach.

Briskly walking past Canterbury Woods on Sinex, I liven my step and am aware of the trees, acorns, roots. At Asilomar Conference Center I take a short break, safe in the wood-filled hall and old-time allure of coffee that brings me to the Parish Hall from my youth.

Along the dunes I see sandpipers, crashing waves, surfers already finished, and step up the pace as the path opens up to me. My heart gives a little jump of joy as I turn the curve and run an invigorating beat onward. The path is tempting me to push a little more, but I walk on the boards and gaze at one of nature's best treats—the ocean. Alive and forceful, it is telling me of the storm coming soon. The raging water slaps the rocks on the shore. Sometimes I can hear the low rumble of the pebbles on the beach and the moaning water running through them.

Along the boardwalk I start running past the gazebo. The oceans' throbbing roar engulfs me as I take in the salty mist.

As I push up the hill and get ready to round the turn, my head throbs with joy. Soon I will be rewarded with the rush of a slight downhill breeze. Along the pull-outs I take in the view, and see Crespi Pond. Back on the trail I smile at the 16th hole and think of my golfing son. The salvia, sage, rosemary and fennel growing along the paths are warm and fragrant. Lovers Point is coming and the hill homeward.

At Grand Avenue I gaze at the expansive vista and continue up the street. I see our lovingly restored historic home smiling at me. I tilt back my head and drink in the puffy white clouds against the deep blue sky. Our flowers and plants are thriving in the quiet protection of the old pine and oak. On a bench in the lower yard I let out a contented sigh. It's good to live here.

A Foggy Introduction
Janet Case Beals

I was born in 1928 and to find work during the Depression, my father had to have us move many, many times in Oregon. I later married a Navy man and we moved 20 times in 24 years. The Navy sent us to Chile for three-and-a-half years, which was the longest I had ever lived in one house. My husband then received orders to the Naval Postgraduate School in Monterey.

We left three of our children with grandparents and brought Gary, our oldest son, to Pacific Grove to help look for housing. At the urging of our son, we selected a 1907 Pacific Grove house that was standing when Teddy Roosevelt's "Great White Fleet" of 16 battleships steamed past Pacific Grove into Monterey Bay on May 1, 1908.

Our other kids arrived in Pacific Grove and to show them some of the area, I drove along Ocean View Boulevard near the golf links, going towards the Great Tide Pool. Just as we came abreast of a small building on the left, a doomsday blast sounding louder than a freight train overwhelmed us. Shaking, I pulled over to the side of the road, and thus we were welcomed to the mighty foghorn of Pacific Grove.

We have now lived in that 1907 house for 40 years and almost daily my husband and I congratulate each other on our glorious good fortune. We have also purchased a plot in El Carmelo Cemetery, so our ashes will forever be in wonderful Pacific Grove.

The foghorn is no longer warning ships and scaring women and children. Forty years beats my previous record of three-and-a-half years and I guess I no longer qualify as a gypsy. And if the "Great White Fleet" or the foghorn ever appears again, those of us in El Carmelo Cemetery will be close to the action.

Our Own Wooden Bench
Andy and Karen

My wife and I really do enjoy walking around P.G. Usually about once a week we go to the Animal Rescue store and visit the thrift shops. We are blessed for finding our pet dog "Sophie" at the corner AFRP. We love the view and peacefulness of Pt. Pinos Grill, Pepper's, and the 17th Street Grill burgers! Also I have found that the International Restaurant has delicious pizza and lasagna. Karen is an avid reader so we frequent the book store. Many years ago we got on the waiting list for a wooden bench placed along the Asilomar coast and just a few

years ago our number came up and we were contacted by a city representative named Stoney. Stoney was so nice in showing us places where benches would be allowed and we were able to select a spot at a small beach on Ocean View. So, we do have a bench and warm it every few weeks when taking Sophie beach walking. Fun!

The Bench
L Bridges

Every small town has a few interesting residents with "character." Pacific Grove is no exception. For about a year, I consistently noticed while driving, walking, or riding a bike the same elderly man who was always smiling, carrying a spray bottle, scrub brush and small rag as he walked daily down by the seashore in our neighborhood. It piqued my curiosity for some time as to what he may be up to, but I dismissed it and forgot until the next time I saw him.

Then one day I happened upon him while walking my dog. After introducing myself, I casually questioned him about his scrub brush activity. He broadly smiled and said his name was Derald. He politely invited me to join him a bit further down the path to a special bay viewing bench.

The bench was in memory of his beloved wife Phyllis. Inscribed on the bench was: "Phyllis May Wade Haugh Loved by Derald E Haugh A Member of Kiwanis Club of Pacific Grove." Derald lovingly showed me the hallowed site and sprayed the bench and cleaned it while we spoke.

His routine was to come there daily to keep the bench clean and remember her. He gently spoke of his wife and caressed the wood with his aged hands. I swallowed back a few tears listening to him recall his bride.

Derald's actions spoke volumes to my heart about marital love that had grown old and precious. A love story that might have been untold had I not solved the mystery of the man with the scrub brush.

After our chat, I saw Derald off-and-on for several years and then one day I just didn't see him anymore. Hopefully Derald has since joined his sweetheart Phyllis in heaven.

Today his legacy of love still flutters my heart as I often sit and pause on that memorable bench. No worries, Derald and Phyllis, we, your neighbors, keep an eye on your bench for you.

Mrs. Noice's Bench
Richard Stillwell
as told to Linnet Harlan

My next-door neighbor, Mrs. Noice, was in the nursing home. She and her late husband had lived in P.G. forever. He was an engineer for the canneries and traveled all over the world.

She wanted to have a commemorative bench for the two of them, looking at the bay from the edge of the golf course across the street from their house near the intersection of Jewell and Cedar. She knew she wouldn't be coming home again.

I called City Hall. They said the waiting list for benches was two years. She knew she didn't have two years, so she said, "Tell them if I can have a bench, I'll donate $100,000 to use for the bike path."

I talked to the city around 10:00 in the morning. They started digging the holes for the bench later that afternoon.

Beach Bench Meditation
Lindsay Dyson
director of the TM Center of Carmel, certified teacher

I'm meditating. My eyes are closed, the warmth of the sun just enough to keep the chill of spring at bay. A tender breeze, sweet with the fragrance of flowers and salty sea, lifts the curls around my face. A murmur of easy conversation grows louder and more distinct as two women approach my bench, then passing it; their words fade quickly into the silence.

Minutes later, I stretch and open my eyes to a vast, blue ocean lit by dancing sparks of sunlight. It joins the unbounded ocean of my own inner silence and the effect is at once both breathtaking and sublime.

Pink ice plant, the rough stone of the sea wall, people riding bicycles and pushing baby strollers—all the sights and sounds along the water in Pacific Grove surround me on this blue sky day.

When I'm in Pacific Grove, after I've done my errands, I love to meditate on a bench by the ocean, or if it's chilly, in my car facing the water. One day, afterwards, inspired by the charm of P.G., I drove all over town snapping photos of the Victorians. They were among my first Facebook posts.

I live in Carmel. Before opening the Transcendental Meditation® Center at the mouth of Carmel Valley in 2014, I gave free introductory talks at the Little House in Jewell Park in P.G. (and once at the Museum of Natural History surrounded by strange specimens). Now residents of Pacific Grove come to the TM® Center in Carmel, but I still go regularly to P.G. for the unique atmosphere of the town and coastline and to visit with friends.

While on a project at the Veterans Transition Center in Marina teaching the TM technique to veterans with Post Traumatic Stress (a very moving and special experience for me), I would often unwind at the end of the day by the water with a take-out supper in "Butterfly Town" before heading home on the winding road through beautiful Del Monte Forest.

Thanks to Patricia Hamilton, herself a practitioner of TM, for encouraging me over lunch in her charming P.G. home to submit something for this book, and thanks to all the residents for keeping Pacific Grove a unique and inviting hometown.

Sea Glass
Barbara Loudon

Steinbeck called it "the hour of pearl"—that early morning gray and misty time when few beachcombers are out, the sand is clean for the first footstep and only the gentle lapping of the bay and screech of seagulls are heard.

The fog is a shroud that helps me move smoothly and glide along the water's edge in a near dream state. I bend to test the ocean's temperature with three fingers, then automatically cross myself with the primal brine. Glimpsing a spot of pale aqua in the soft wet sand, I reach for it—it is a perfect piece of sea glass, rounded and honed by sea and sand to a translucent memory of what it once was. The glass is no longer clear—it has been sanded by time, rolled in the seawater until it became opaque as if hiding the secrets of where it traveled. It is a talisman. I place it in my jacket pocket and, as though it were a natural rosary bead, finger it all the way back to the cottage, giving prayers of thanks for this precious gift from the deep.

Sometimes I feel as though we are all like pieces of sea glass. Once we were young, fresh and clear—seemingly certain of beliefs, sure of whom we were and who we wanted to be. Then we get tossed into that great sea of life—thrown about, bruised, battered, soothed, scraped, caressed—floating through currents. What a ride! Finally we make the beach again, perhaps wiser from our travels, perhaps just confused. We lie there contemplating until we are picked up and taken home.

Let's enjoy the ride—it is merely salt water, you know, that which tears and sweat are made of. It is native to us—it is where we are supposed to be, tumbling about in the glory of it all—in this precious, temporary sea of life.

This poem was written some years ago but still holds true. I have owned my little cottage here for almost 20 years and we have been here for five years and simply love it. I attend one of Illia Thompson's memoir writing classes.

A Gift from the Sea
Laura Edeen

Every year on Christmas day, my family would drive to our favorite little beach in our hometown of Pacific Grove. We would each bring with us a carefully selected shell. You might pick an exotic large one or a tiny little gem of a shell. It is important that the shell speak to you because this shell represents you in the coming year.

Early in the morning, after presents were opened, we would hop in the car with our shells. We would wander the beach with the shells hidden in pockets, looking for the perfect place to drop the shell so that somebody could easily find it. Then we would casually stroll back to the car and wait for someone to find it. People would think we were just admiring the lovely ocean scene, but we would actually be rooting for beachcombing people to find our shells. If your shell was found first, you felt like king for a day.

It is amazing to me how many people think that are looking carefully for something ... like a shell ... and are blind to the fact they are almost surrounded by them. It is a good lesson to remember when looking for the gifts in your life. Unexpected gifts are everywhere ... just waiting to be found. You only need to look carefully and love is everywhere.

Shine
Susie Joyce
poet, observer of marine life

I walk along the shore to marvel at the sights;
The shape shifting flight of pelicans,
The spectacle of backstroking otters, whales
Rising from the depths of the bay,
And to wonder at the smaller miracle
In the soil at my feet,
Where the time worn remains
Of ancient abalone shells
Shine.

Pearly fragments whisper
Stories from generations past
Where they emerge from the earth
On sandy trails in the dunes
Of Asilomar Beach, in the blackened
Midden soil that skirts the coastal trails
Of Pacific Grove, and at the water's edge,
Where waves and weather nibble at the shoreline.

Fingering the fragile jewels,
To remove the dusty veil of time
May release the sacred song
Of the Rumsen Ohlone people,
Who thrived for thousands of years
On the abundance of the Central Coast.

The rise of afternoon sea winds
May liberate the silenced story
Of ambitious Chinese immigrants
Who found the prize in the mid 1800s
And built an industry drying the meat
To ship to distant shores.

This puzzle piece of the past
May have been dropped from the precious paws
Of the multitudes of hungry sea otters
That feasted on the meaty mollusks
In these waters before Russian
And Spanish fur hunters found them easy prey.

How I love these gleaming gems
With their uniquely marbled patterns
And symphony of colors,
Constructed layer by lustrous layer
By slow growing abalone over a lifetime
That may have spanned thirty to forty years.

When tempted, as I often am,
To pocket a bit of the shell's silver lining
For personal pleasure;
When feeling the need to add this treasure
To a collection of beach glass, rocks and shells
Gathered over a lifetime of delight
In the humble gifts of the natural world;
Know that there is a price.

Removing the fragile find from the location
Where wind, waves and history have placed it
Will only result in a sprinkling of glitter
In your pocket, the dust of what was once
A shinning glimpse of the past life
Of Monterey Bay.

Our Own Private Beach
Irene Mehaffy
retired middle school teacher

It's a small beach and a relatively private one, visited by few. Located along Ocean View Boulevard at the bottom of Coral, it sits below the road, with a granite retaining wall and a few granite steps leading down to it from a narrow strip of ice plant. Too rocky for swimming, it is ideal for exploring tide pools or just enjoying time near the water. On clear days, Santa Cruz is visible across the bay.

It is less protected from winds than the much larger beach near Lovers Point, just a mile away, with its finer sand and easier access for swimming, and that makes it much less popular.

My sister and I took possession of this beach in Pacific Grove shortly after our parents bought the house on Surf Avenue, a block away. It wasn't long before we were spending hours there, wading in the always-cold water, drawing pictures in the firm sand near the water's edge, using rocks to create the outlines for imaginary houses, or poking our toes into the sea anemones to see them squirt and then close up quickly.

I often visited it alone and simply sat on the grainy sand, staring out at the bay, the rhythm of the gentle waves calming my childhood worries. Whether enshrouded in the fog that muffled the sounds of an occasional car passing by or sparkling in bright sunlight, the beach always seemed to have the same distinct, wonderful smell: a combination of fresh sea air and pungent seaweed discarded by the waves and left to dry on the sand.

I was seven and my sister four when we moved from Granite Street, and I am amazed now to think our parents allowed us full access to the beach at an early age. Undoubtedly, we were supervised at first, but I know that we spent most of our time there by ourselves. An elderly neighbor would occasionally walk by with a dog, or tourists would stop to spend a few minutes on the sand, but we always knew they wouldn't stay long. It was our beach, and it remained so until we moved away seven years later.

Each time I visit the Monterey Peninsula, I take a few minutes to drive by each of the Pacific Grove houses I lived in: my grandmother's house on Granite, where I spent the first two years of my life, the two rentals on Willow and Granite, and finally, the one on Surf Avenue. But no visit is complete until I have at least passed by our little beach. It always looks the same and is usually deserted.

Because of the many happy memories attached to it, it is one of the things I missed most when we moved inland to Sacramento in 1957, the summer I was fourteen. Now it belongs to someone else, and I must be content with being just one of those visitors who stops by for a moment to gaze down on it.

Pacific Grove is Forest Nautica
Laura Hamill

In 2004 I painted a tree that grows seashells and called it "The Gate Goddess of Forest Nautica." I knew this painting was special and would help me find my dreams.

In December 2013 I found my Forest Nautica. Pacific Grove is where I grow my dreams. I fell in love with a little corner of heaven in my sunny Junipero neighborhood.

For the first three months I lived here I found little flower buds on my doorstep. Then I joined fantastic Meet-Up groups and made friends with the community of creatives where I painted butterflies and lanterns and taught watercolor at the P.G. Art Center.

I have parked at the "Great Sunset Drive-in" along with all my neighbors (you know the place) and shared the most incredible sunsets.

I had seen days where gentle waves cut scalloped patterns in the sandy shore. I have seen behemoth waves pound against the most amazing rock structures. This place always feels new and fresh and makes my heart sing, from the moment I leave for my job in Gilroy in the morning and I see the beautiful lights of our community to when I turn onto Highway 1 and watch the golden glow on the water at the end of my day.

I have taken over 30 whale watch rides and have been so inspired by the whales I have a published fantasy novel to tell their stories!

Pacific Grove, I am a new member of our community and I care very deeply for this place where I live and dream every day.

Thank you for welcoming me home.

Love and more love.

The House Above The Sea
Sarah Kramer Fields
student, P.G. native, book-lover

My great-grandmother arrived from Chicago one foggy morning, two children in tow and one on the way. A girl would be born in the house on the hill. She would grow up running in the fields behind the houses where colonies of little green frogs would hide. She dreamed of dancing, of those beautiful pink, pointed shoes. When it was time to marry—to a fisherman just like her father—she traded in those soft bright dreams for the mewls and screams of daughters all her own. They grew up in a modest house on Spruce above the sea, in the town of P.G..

The Dragon and the Monks
Evelyn Kahan

When I was young I thought the world began with me and my parents. It didn't exist before us. Today I visit the ancient stones that disabuse me of that idea. My favorite of Pacific Grove's rocky coves is just one turnout past the pond along Ocean View Boulevard. There eternally stands the granite cluster of hooded monks praying over the Monterey Bay. A sacred spot, yes. Makes me stop and pay homage to nature for all its beauty and reminds me I am its steward. There I learned to draw and paint rocks so that even you would recognize them to be that. What a coup!, I thought. But there are still anemones to master. In the meantime, and eternally, there is the Dragon, mythical, but there nonetheless, sipping some cool ocean water, or dousing his fire. Actually I'm not sure it's a he. Hmmmmmm. I feel the Dragon too is reverent.

The monks, the Dragon and I have conversation on occasion. The Dragon tells me it's been coming down to this particular cove for years ... actually, before even the Rumsen people populated these shores. Makes me wonder if we got the plant restoration right. The Dragon would know, right?

I trudge off to the shore again, pad of paper and art box with me. A different cove today. No lack of inspiration along the P.G. shoreline. Perhaps today's a good day to visit the two kissing sea creatures. Talk about a long time courtship!

Weddings at the Beach
Joyce Meuse
long time resident, notary-minister

Back in 1990 a friend of mine worked as a wedding minister for a local service. She wanted to quit and offered me the business. I took over and eventually started A Bayside Wedding. I advertised with a web site and got inquiries from all around the state, the country and even other countries. As a notary public authorized by the county clerk, I could issue confidential marriage licenses to couples on the spot. Eventually I added photography, chairs, set-ups and musicians to the business.

Favorite spots included Lovers Point where I had gotten married. Berwick Park was also popular. Eventually the city began charging for permits at both parks. The beautiful setting is worth it. I had a secret spot in the dunes that was perfect for couples. I always preferred the smaller weddings and elopements, although I did my share of larger ones. Other spots included Asilomar Beach, Rocky Shores and the other beaches along Ocean View Boulevard and 17 Mile Drive in Pebble Beach.

Many young couples came to me from Fort Ord and also students from the Navy School and the Defense Language Institute. In 1994 Fort Ord closed its base and my military weddings declined in number, but I always had a few each month.

One military couple wed twice, once for the paperwork and again with friends at the beach. The handsome, sweet and wonderful groom tragically lost his life in the Iraq War. I cherish the picture I have of their beautiful faces.

Another couple that I married at Lovers Point had wanted to marry in Hawaii but couldn't. They married on a foggy summer day. The bride held sunflowers and they were casually dressed and barefoot. A musician sang the "Hawaiian Wedding Song." Just as he sang, "… Now that we are one, clouds won't hide the sun," the sun dropped below the fog and flooded the park in sunlight. Just at that moment a whale breached in the bay. It was amazing.

I've married couples of all ages and circumstances. I've married them in intensive care, in county jail and once in Soledad prison. One couple remarried after a divorce and an enduring lifelong friendship in his hospice room. I unknowingly married a kidnapped bride and was called to be a witness at the groom's trial. One couple married in a hot-air balloon, at dawn, moments before they took off.

One bride had broken her arm and waited until after the ceremony to have it set. On 7/7/2007 I did seven weddings in one day. At the height of my business, in the early days, I've done a wedding every hour on a Saturday. Up to ten in one day, as I recall. More than once I've been standing with my back to the ocean when the tide came in and swamped my feet.

I am retiring now but I will never forget the joy, love and happiness I have been a part of for the last 27 years.

Loma Prieta Evening
Cindy Gates
artist, teacher, photographer, observer

"Why do the birds stand on one leg?" a German visitor asked.

My shift at the Monterey Bay Aquarium had just begun. We had recently moved to Pacific Grove, and I decided that becoming a guide would help me learn about the area and, more importantly, make friends.

That Thursday in October, I volunteered for the aviary, my favorite assignment. The serene, open-air exhibit was filled with bird chirps and the gentle music of man-made waves as they lapped on the sandy shore. Sandpipers ran up and down the water line as leopard sharks swam lazily in the water.

Yes, the larger birds were standing on one leg. I was about to explain that they were conserving heat when I heard a loud noise. A generator, I thought, a rumble that grew louder and louder until it shook the building. The visitors had been looking at the black and white long-legged stilts, but now they looked at me with furrowed brows.

A Southern California native, I'd spent a lifetime

prepping for the Big One. First, survey the situation.

Aviary. Glass walls all around. Two doors out. The jerking slate floor let me know I was on the right path.

"I'm sorry, this is an earthquake, and we need to get out of here as soon as possible."

Do I take them all the way down the exhibit to the regular door or out the revolving door just behind us? I chose the latter. I didn't want us playing dodge ball with falling glass.

As I fed the couple through the circular door, the ground still shook. And then it stopped. My German visitors scuttled away as the water in the bat ray pool sloshed over the sides. We did not realize how devastating the Loma Prieta Earthquake would turn out to be.

My family had been huddled on the couch when it hit. They were watching the start of the World Series game in San Francisco. Sophie had just woken from a nap and was cuddled in Bill's arms. As the quake hit and went on and on and on, they huddled in the doorway.

When I walked into the house, the kids, excited and a bit scared, told me what had happened. The power was out but the evening was warm, so we ventured outside to the front yard. There wasn't much else to do.

Clumps of neighbors gathered in the streets. Front doors opened, and people we had never seen spilled out of their houses. We had only been in our house for a few weeks, yet we joined them. News trickled in about the damage: the Bay Bridge destruction, landslides, collapsed buildings, broken Santa Cruz roads. A boy on a bicycle said Dennis at the ice cream store was handing out free cones.

That evening, we stayed outside where the neighbors gathered, where neighbors we had never met were concerned about our children and offered food, where neighbors shared their earthquake stories and their life stories, and where our neighbors would become Pacific Grove friends.

A Drink with John Denver

October 14, 2007

Kathleen Sullivan

Approaching John Denver Beach early Sunday on a fog-freshened sunny morning, I nodded to others already gathered. On this, the tenth anniversary of John's death, quiet guitars strummed and voices crooned as fans honored and grieved a musical and environmental hero. Resting on my favorite rock, I was moved by the mixture of music with the waves, siblings of those that had embraced a beloved talent in his last moments.

Suddenly this awe-inspiring environment was shattered as if a small bomb had exploded close to us. Jumping up, I watched five gigantic Harleys swing into the gravel parking lot, spewing stones and belching acrid exhaust. Blood pressure rising, I moved toward the five thoughtless interlopers, ready to wail like an Irish banshee. All five men had long scraggly beards and wild hair as they quickly dismounted and immediately extracted items from their saddlebags.

The first traveler walked slowly to John Denver's log and carefully stabilized a small mirror in the sand. Behind him, his four friends quietly awaited their turns. Their determined, tanned and wrinkled faces bore expressions similar to the rest of us, now gathered around the log.

Soon the log became an altar reflected by the mirror: a framed photo, a large antique green glass jug, a battered Frisbee, and a ragged, multi-colored, woolen neck scarf.

The five bikers standing together began quietly singing, a capella, "County Road, Take me Home." Behind me, crying sounds soon mingled with the five beautiful voices.

Instead of clapping, the gathered offered words of thanks. A man asked if the guys would describe their treasures. "The mirror's cuz John often told us to look first at ourselves." "This is the Frisbee we messed with while we could still stand!" "That's the scarf John left saying, 'Keep it for me for next year.'" "This is that last shot of us all-together." "And this is the moonshine John loved the best."

As the local group separated, I said goodbye to the bikers by clapping shoulders and thanking each of them. Seeing that their bikes wore West Virginia tags, I realized that their noisy entrance appropriately heralded the arrival of John Denver's soul brothers.

Walking away, clear that this morning joined my category of joyful miracles, I heard gravel sounds and, "Hey, lady!" Turning, I saw one of the guys swinging the large green bottle in his hands. "You can't leave without a swig to John! Here, have at it!"

I laughed, hesitating to take the old, well-worn bottle with the nicked lip. "Thanks, but I'm off to church!" I whined.

He countered with, "Ha! The perfect place for these spirits!"

Surrendering, I took one sip, choked and blended my laughter with my West Virginia friend. I felt tears of joy and profound loss suddenly flowing as I reached for the bottle again. Looking deeply into West Virginia's weeping eyes, I slowly absorbed the essence of and gratitude for the communities created by the life of John Denver.

P.G. Sea Story
George Penley

Hanalei Bay, at the north on the Hawaiian island of Kauai, is a place of magic. Tall palm trees, stretches of warm sandy beach, and ink-blue water. Along the nearby roads, papaya trees offer fruit for the taking, and shave-ice venders sell you their cones in a rainbow of colors. For me, Hanalei Bay was the incredibly beautiful place where three different times, I spent a month at anchor on my sailboat before leaving for the Monterey Peninsula, and home.

On this particular trip I left Hanalei, as I had before, with a week left in August, sailing straight north for the 1,000 miles I needed to make in that direction, and I settled into my familiar routine—alone—on that mystic and immense blue Pacific Ocean. Solitude was out there, and the quiet rhythm of my boat and the sea.

I was looking at about a month for the 3,000 watery miles ahead—straight north first, for the wind, then a long curve east to my southeast course for Monterey Bay and the Peninsula. This is mainly a story of my arrival at Point Pinos, Pacific Grove, but as with any trip, or most any piece of time, things show up along the way and capture us.

One of my charts showed an extremely interesting feature on the ocean floor north of Kauai—an undersea range of mountains called the Musicians Seamount Trail. This underwater mountain range begins about 200 miles north of Hanalei Bay and runs northwest for 650 miles. In the range are more than 40 peaks and ridges which are named for composers. At about 240 miles my boat crossed above the Beethoven ridge; with another 170 miles I crossed the latitude of the Mozart seamount. That mountain rises about 10,000 feet above the three-and-a-half mile deep seafloor, which makes its peak just over a mile below the Pacific surface. The diameter at the mountain's base is about 15 miles—a monumental, if little-known tribute to the composer, and I was glad I had some of his music on board. My chart did not show all the names of the peaks and ridges in the range, but Google Earth does.

I had tapes of several of the well-known composers with me, and I played them mostly at sunset—tales of beauty to tell—Oscar Levant playing "Rhapsody in Blue" in the vicinity of the Gershwin Seamount, Beethoven's "Symphony No. 5," timed to start as the lower edge of the sun drops below sunset clouds onto the far Pacific horizon—fiery gold into infinite blue—and on into twilight, and darkness.

As I crossed the latitude of the last named seamount on my chart, Shostakovich, I had already started the long curve northeast, over the top of the summertime high pressure system on the Pacific. The top of my course was even with a point just south of the Oregon-California border, and about 1500 miles at sea.

For the entire trip my little boat, Windance, a 31-foot sloop, was steered by auto-pilot, which steers the boat far better than I can. That leaves me plenty of time for reading, fishing, cooking, and just watching—dolphins—they were with me often, and more than once I had dolphins from right at my boat for as far as I could see in every direction, to the horizon.

And that rare and welcome visit of an albatross, always a good-luck icon for sailors, making graceful circles high above my boat.

My goal was a hundred miles each 24 hours, and I generally made that—seldom much more than that on this trip.

There were challenges—fine-weather easy days, and wave-tossed, blow-away hard ones. Fine crystal-star nights and sinister, dead-black rough ones.

I set my course to pass about 35 miles west of the Farallon Islands. And, just like "Play it again, Sam," ("As Time Goes By ") it gets to be day 30—Sunday, my scheduled arrival day home—and fate deals a hand. Dawn was a non-happening, because morning found me and Windance in a very thick Monterey Bay fog. Joseph Conrad once described a sea condition in which "the sea and the sky were welded together without a seam." For me, on that Sunday morning, there was no sea, and no sky—just fog—and nothing else past a very few yards ahead of my boat.

I knew where I was. This was before GPS; but I had its satellite forerunner, Sat/Nav, and I had LORAN. But a pencil-line with a few position dots on a chart is one thing, and a fog-tight morning when you are moving toward a rocky coast is something quite else.

Prudence would dictate that I hold off-shore until the fog lifted, but in the steadfast courage of my ignorance, and my expectation that the fog would lift by mid-morning, I pressed on—as did the fog.

My course was still southeast towards Point Pinos, but when I got jaw-tightening close, I shifted more east with a little south. I was hoping to hear something through the fog, but Pacific Grove was keeping quietly to itself on that late Sunday morning—foghorn not operating—and I eased on toward where I thought Lovers Point should be. The rocks along that coast were much on my mind.

Joseph Conrad again: "To see! to see!—this is the craving of the sailor, as of the rest of blind humanity. To have his path made clear for him is the aspiration of every human being in our beclouded and tempestuous existence."

Then clear as a bell, the first sound I heard on that foggy 30th day—the clock on the Pacific Grove City Hall tower began to toll noon. No need to ask for whom that bell tolled.

And right on cue, the fog began to thin, and lift, and like two immense theater curtains slowly opening, brought all of the Monterey Peninsula into my happy view. Welcome home, George!

NATURAL FORESTS, PARKS AND BEACHES

The Many Parks of Pacific Grove
Brenda Taylor

When a wheel of our son's stroller fell off and broke, we figured that our strolls to all the Pacific Grove parks were over. I saved a scrap of fabric from the stroller and put it in the baby book. My husband did the math and that stroller could have gone coast-to-coast with all the mileage it chalked up. Luckily he was getting to be the age where he loved to run and explore and we could hardly keep up with him! We spent countless days at Lovers Point Park, JewelL Park, Berwick Park, and of course Caledonia Park.

Caledonia Park was where we spent the majority of playtime for a couple of years. Our son learned how to go down the slide, get into a swing, use the monkey-bars and make friends with new people. Upon arrival I told him to "go make a friend" and I would sit in the sun and catch up on my reading.

We spent many an afternoon wearing party hats and cutting cake for his or his friend's birthday parties. The kids would get a sugar high and play like crazy on the equipment, while the parents caught up on things. It was good, easy fun. The kids are all older and more independent now. I still pass by Caledonia with a somewhat wistful longing for the skinned knees, the grass stains, and the days gone by.

We cannot forget Stillwell's Snow in the Park with the mountain of snow and the community snowball fight, lots of holiday music, the Winter Queen, petting zoo and lots of friends to see. The Good Old Days hosts rides and a petting zoo, too. During the Fourth of July we enjoy the hometown BBQ and warm friendships of living in an old-fashioned area.

We strolled along Berwick Park on the Recreation Trail several times and did fundraisers or 5K races. The P.G. Pride goes along the Rec Trail and both of us did the 5K Jingle Bell Run in December.

Lovers Point Park is a wonderful family park for sitting by the beach or walking on the rocks. My family met me when I ran the Love Run 10K. After the Big Sur Half-Marathon, it's great to cool your legs and walk into the water right on the beach.

The Little House in Jewell Park is where Miss Lisa from the library hosted a pumpkin decorating contest. Poetry in the Grove meets there, as well as the writing group that is contributing to this book! The Christmas Tree Lighting is in the same park. It is nice to walk to the Farmers' Market that meets on Monday where my husband can get his favorite Indian food for dinner. Children love to climb on Sandy the Whale outside the Museum of Natural History.

Asilomar Horticulturist
Bruce Cowan

I fell in love with Pacific Grove as a ten-year-old child on a trip to California with my parents. The pine forests of the Monterey Peninsula hills reminded me of the mountains of Colorado and Utah where I grew up and attended summer camps, and the ocean here was absolutely fascinating—the flocks of birds, the creatures of the tide pools. I said, "Dad, can we move here?" It didn't happen. But 20 years later my wife Judy and I came here to stay.

My first job, from 1968 to 1974, was for the Asilomar Operating Concession as Environmental Horticulturist at Asilomar State Park, propagating and planting native trees and plants on the grounds and sand dunes, and removing invasive African ice plant.

For 35 years I had my own business, Environmental Landscape Service, drawing landscape designs, planting and maintaining landscapes, and writing botanical reports for clients needing building permits within the Coastal Zone of Monterey County. I wrote a weekly article called "Central Coast Landscapes" emphasizing native and other drought resistant plants, published in the *Monterey County Herald*.

From 1991 to about 2007, I was Project Coordinator supervising a dune restoration project of about 30 acres for the Naval Postgraduate School in Monterey. In 1990 a freeze had killed a lot of the ice plant, and the Navy wanted to restore native vegetation. We planted over 100,000 native plants grown in plastic tubes. And pulled lots of weeds. I learned that successful native plant restoration involves about 10% planting and 90% weed control.

After retiring, I continue 30 to 50 hours a month as a landscape volunteer for the Hostel on Hawthorne, the Monterey Bay Aquarium, the Pacific Grove Museum of Natural History and other Pacific Grove city landscapes, including City Hall, the fire and police stations, and recently the "Water Reclamation Garden" at the P.G. Community Center on Junipero. I initiated and still care for a native plant deer thicket where baby deer are born at El Carmelo Cemetery. I also weed, plant and maintain a greenbelt and median strip on Congress Avenue below David Avenue. I have spent a lot of time removing invasive, non-native pampas grass, acacias and genista (French broom) from Rip Van Winkle Park and Del Monte Forest property adjacent to Pacific Grove.

In April 2015, I was told that I had been given the Pacific Grove Volunteer of the Year Award at the annual Volunteer Dinner.

I hadn't received an invitation to the dinner; I didn't know when it would be and didn't attend. I wrote the city afterwards and asked, "Are there any leftovers?" Mayor Bill Kampe said no, "but you are welcome to come the City Council meeting on Wednesday and receive the award here." I was humbled and happy to be there.

I told the audience, "Most of my work is weeding. Successful weed control means getting rid of every weed before it goes to seed—each reproducing 100 more the following year. Weeds provide job security—whether for pay or not!"

Mountain Lion Alert

Just wanted to let y'all know that there might be a mountain lion prowling the Asilomar area. We saw some chewed up deer parts on the corner of Crocker and Pico while out for our evening dog walk today. Also, our dog has been obsessed with going to the edge of our yard to stare off into the darkness of the Rec Trail for the past few nights. Stay aware and maybe keep your cats and dogs inside for a bit! *(Facebook, May 25, 2017, in Crime & Safety to Pacific Grove)*

The Appeal of Beach Bonfires
Susie Joyce
facillitator

In the trunk of my car, with the spare tire, water bottles, snacks, battery cables, flashlight, and emergency first aid kit, I always carry a beach blanket, beach chair and firewood. I like to be prepared, including being ready for the possibility of a "pop up" beach bonfire at Asilomar.

There is something magical about gathering around a fire with community, the way it connects us to each other, to our ancient human family and to the wildness in the night. The attraction for me was probably sparked 55 years ago at my first Girl Scout campfire, and it has only grown since. For many years, I have gathered community together to celebrate every summer and winter solstice with a bonfire at Asilomar State Beach, where we honor the season change and the exquisite surroundings with singing, drumming and poetry. The draw is not limited to celebrations, though; any time spent together around a fire on the beach is extraordinary. I admit that I'm not above offering firewood to strangers to finagle an invitation to their beach bonfire following an evening walk at Asilomar.

Offering brilliant sunsets, unending rows of waves, minimum interference from artificial lighting and the protection offered by the dunes, there isn't a more ideal setting for a bonfire than Asilomar State Beach. I am grateful that we are still free to circle around a fire with family and friends at our hometown beach while our neighbors in Carmel, and in other communities on the coast, argue over restrictions on beach fires. It is my most sincere hope that Asilomar State Beach will continue to be available for Pagrovians and visitors to Pacific Grove, their children, their grandchildren and their grandchildren's grandchildren, to unplug for a bit and come to know the wonder and connection of coming together with a beach bonfire.

Private Citizens Save Sunsets
Robert Gumerlock
neighborly historian

Each of us probably has a favorite vantage point from which to watch the spectacular P.G. sunsets. Mine is the coast-side gazebo just below the junction where Jewell Avenue joins Sunset Avenue.

At first encounter, the structure and the land it sits on appears to be part of Asilomar State Park, a continuation of the beachfront strand heading north from Asilomar State Beach.

But adjacent to the gazebo is a Craftsman-style house and on the street stand two stone gateway pillars, mute sentinels to a grand estate that once dominated this landscape.

I would know nothing of the lineage of this parcel of land were it not for my original neighbors in Pacific Grove, Russell and Ellen Coile. Their names, together with those of other citizens and organizations, can be found carved into the railroad ties leading to the gazebo. Perhaps you have traversed this boardwalk and noticed these names, more weathered with each passing year. Ellen told me the story just as a second home was being constructed next to the Craftsman—a multi-million dollar fortress that looks as if it had been intended for Pebble Beach but lost its way and decided to settle down alongside its much more demure neighbor.

Sometime in the late 1980s the entire estate came up for sale, consisting of the Craftsman home and five other subdivided lots, one to the north of the existing house, and four to the south. Concerned residents urged the P.G. City Council to bid on the entire property, which would have prevented/eliminated all development on the riparian side of Ocean View/Sunset, from Lovers Point to Asilomar. Pleading penury, the City Council declined to act. Undeterred, private citizens formed a consortium and began to solicit donations.

At the time the parcels were sold, the consortium had collected sufficient funds to purchase the four southern lots. The northern lot was acquired by a developer and the Craftsman home ended up being purchased by a local citizen. The fortress to the north recently sold for eight million dollars.

The next time you visit the gazebo to watch the waves, the otters, or the sunset, take a moment to reflect on the fact that, but for the efforts of these intrepid citizens, there would most likely be four more stone fortresses dominating this skyline. I thank Ellen and Russell every time I visit.

Sky Fire
Diana Dennis

When the sun sets in the west
The sky and ocean look their best.
And I find I never tire
Of looking at the sky on fire.

I've finished all my work today
And now I'm at the beach to play.
I seem alone, but I'm with friends—
The surf, the sand and gentle winds.

I reach my hands toward the sky
And with the birds, I'd like to fly.
But wonder what it would require
To touch the sky and play with fire.

I breathe in smells of salt and brine
As geese fly skyward in a line.
Waves splash up and lick my hand
Erase my footprints on the sand.

One day you might come with me
When the sun sets in the sea.
Who knows? It may be your desire
To stretch your arms to touch the fire.

Swimming Lessons at Lovers Point Pool
Lenore Perez
Pacific Grove Ca. Circa Early 1960's

My five-foot-tall-and-shrinking, blonde-haired, blue-eyed Sicilian mom was born in San Francisco. My maternal grandmother was my namesake. My grandmother Leonora was in the 1906 San Francisco earthquake. My mom and her family lived on Powell Street in San Francisco. Concrete and stucco houses all scrunched together is the norm for this neighborhood. Pastel colored buildings line the streets. There was not a yard to speak of in these neighborhoods. No swings, no slides, no basketball nor volleyball courts. And no swimming pool!

My mother always had a strong desire to learn how to swim. Always remember, it's never too late to learn something new. So it was the early 1960s and my mother put her brilliant idea in motion.

The closest public pool was at Lovers Point in Pacific Grove. My mom registered herself and me in a six-week beginning swim class. Lovers Point was about two-and-a-half miles from our house on Spaghetti Hill.

So my mom and I went bathing suit shopping. She chose a black V-neck one-piece. The material was a nubby jersey type. My bathing suit was a one-piece, light blue with white flowers. Swim caps were all the rage. I think it was Esther Williams who made the swim cap a fashion statement. My mom's swim cap was white with leaf shapes around it. Hers didn't have a chin strap like my blue flowered cap did.

The class started at 9:00 a.m.. Walking to the car on those cold and foggy mornings I could smell sardines and a cool, salty breeze wafted up the hill. So my mom would back the white-finned Pontiac out of the driveway and head on down the street on Spaghetti Hill. Thick, soupy fog surrounded us as we drove. Windshield wipers were a must every morning. As I listened to the flip-flop of the windshield wipers, I realized that I was not very excited about my swimming lessons. The short ride to the pool went by quickly. I had butterflies in my stomach. When we got to the pool we had to make sure we had everything. Bathing suits on, check. Bathing caps, towels and Coppertone in hand, check. My lunch was a bologna sandwich with mustard on thin-sliced white Kilpatrick's bread, and Laura Scudder plain potato chips. We parked and I tumbled out of the car. I was cold, scared, apprehensive and excited all at the same time.

The pool seemed huge and ominous to me. It was a well noted fact that the pool was filled with salt water. My mom told me that the salt water would help me float. As we learned how to kick our feet and hold our breath underwater, something magical happened. It got sunny. The fog always burned off and a beautiful summer day ensued. To me the sun made everything better. The huge salt water pool seemed slightly bearable to me now.

The pool was intimidating all by itself, but to make matters worse for me the instructor was mean. The instructor always made me do things I did not want to do. I did not want to jump in the nine-foot deep end of the pool from the lower diving board. I cried when it was my turn. I am sure my mom felt humiliated as I cried. The instructor told me she would hold out the long pole so I could grab onto it as soon as I came up. So I jumped and when I came up the pole wasn't there. The instructor lied to me. Gulp, gulp as I swallowed huge amounts of salt water. So it was either sink or swim. I dog paddled as hard and as fast as I could. And I did it. I made it without the pole. Wow, exhilaration, that felt good.

My mom had none of the problems with swimming lessons that I had. She excelled with each new technique learned. My mom passed from the beginner class to the intermediate class. Me, not so lucky. I had to take another six-week course in the beginner class.

After lessons it came the ultimate best part of the day. We would spend the rest of the day at the beach. Summer fun, sand and swimming: those were the ingredients of my childhood summers in the 1960s. It was awesome on the beach; nothing was demanded of me at the beach. That's just how it was then; everything was simple and easy. I was free to be me. We didn't know anything about UV rays or skin cancer then. Sometimes I put on the Coppertone and sometimes I didn't.

There Once Was a Swimming Pool...
Sharon Tucker
CCW member, author, copywriter

As most residents know, the average temperature of the Monterey Peninsula is 65 degrees. The average temperature of Pacific Grove in August is 60 degrees. But on occasion the thermometer moves well above 70 degrees, especially in September and October. And on those days, moving out of childhood and becoming young teenagers, my friends and I would get our parents to drive us to meet up at the Pacific Grove Swimming Pool next to the old bathhouse. Salt water was piped in directly from the ocean and the pool was fed heavy amounts of chlorine. Parents would bring their small children to play at the shallow end; teenagers would practice their diving from the low board, and boys being boys, would hurl themselves into cannon balls expelling enough water to empty the pool, or so it seemed. Girls would preen, showing of their lovely, glowing bodies as they basked in the heat of the summer sun.

I loved to spend Saturdays at the pool. My mother would pack a lunch and cold drinks and send me off to meet my friends. We would spend hours lying around, lathering our bodies with a concoction of baby oil and iodine to enhance the sun's tanning work on our skin.

When we needed a break, we would walk down the steps to the beach below and stroll along the ocean side, picking up olive shells and bits of broken abalone shell washed ashore—leftovers from a rare, dining sea otter. When it got too hot, we would return to the swimming pool to cool off.

I looked forward to those wonderful, unusually warm days at the pool. The old bathhouse is no more, now a restaurant called the Beach House. The pool was eventually filled in (something to do with concerns about contamination, as I recall) and now serves as a volleyball court. And although there is a child's wading pool, I'll admit, it's just not the same.

Swimming Pool Blue
Lisa Coscino
executive director of a small museum

There is a shade of blue that speaks of days gone by and summers at the beach. It is bright and faded at the same time. Swimming pool blue. Lovers Point swimming pool blue.

When my kids were small we spent one glorious summer in a fog of swimming pool blue. The pool was small and shallow and only children under age seven were allowed. Each weekday morning of the summer I walked with my two small kids to the pool at Lovers Point where they took swimming lessons. They had the first lesson of the day and it was usually still foggy.

The pool deck smelt of yesterday's suntan oil and was always peppered with forgotten towels. I would leave my kids in the able hands of the lifeguards and go on a quick run, 42 minutes exactly, and as I returned I could hear the children's screams and cheers, splashes and glee. The sun would be sparkling by then, reflecting light and the promise of more summers as perfect as this one.

That summer was like magic for us all. Each day was spread before us on the beach like a banquet. It was a summer for making friends, for laughs and peanut butter sandwiches. It was summer like I remembered as a child—staying out too late, eating dinner once dark began to fall. Sticky sugar and lemonade summer, tan lines and salty water. And the swimming pool blue that sparkled each morning as I ran back to my kids.

Many summers followed but few lived up to the perfection of that one. There were foggy summers when the sun barely shone. Summers where we needed to travel for family, summers where day camps interfered in any thought of pool or beach. Maybe there is only one platonic summer in each person's life. I was glad mine was spent with my kids.

Life goes by so quickly and then so slowly all the same. Things that you wish would never end inevitably do, and everything that hurts seems to last forever. One day your kids are too big for swimming lessons at the little beach pool and you have barely noticed. You wake up one morning to go for a quick run and see the pool being filled. It sparkles in the sun, all swimming pool blue, with tattered and newly forgotten towels around the perimeter.

The moms are slathering their babies with lotion and the smell wafts up to you as you round the corner. And you remember every glorious minute you spent there with your babies, watching them, reading a book, clapping for their accomplishments, band-aiding tomato red bloodied toes and counting hermit crabs. You think of their perfect little bodies, their eager eyes, endless smiles, the perfection of the sun shining on your face and salt water left on your lips. All the years of minutes you spent watching them grow.

And you smile. What a great way to start the day.

Eco-Corps
Marilyn Beck

Every day I bike along the coast near Asilomar, walk on the boardwalk and on the beaches. I also go into the woods at the city-owned Rip Van Winkle Open Space. As I immerse myself in nature, and restore my soul, I give thanks to those people who helped preserve our dunes and woods and thereby enrich our lives. I won't be able to mention everyone here, but my gratitude goes out to all.

First, the Pacific Grove Eco-Corps. Founded by Danny and Sandy Koffman in 1991, the Eco-Corps soon set about growing Monterey pine trees from seed. The child in me marveled that we could collect pine cones, put them upside down in the oven, and soon the seeds would pop out, to be planted in small containers in the Hergott's greenhouse.

From there we planted and maintained about 2000 (!) small pine trees and also understory bushes at Washington Park, Lighthouse School, the Monarch Grove Sanctuary, and the back of Forest Grove School.

My fondest memories are of the work we did at the Monarch Grove Sanctuary. I remember dragging heavy water hoses all over the hilly sanctuary. Much credit must be given to Katy Travaille for her plans and guidance in all of our work.

The Eco-Corps helped with the restoration of the dunes at Asilomar, which was a major undertaking planned and executed by the Asilomar State Park ecologist Tom Moss. The restoration, started in 1984, was funded by the Pacific Grove Asilomar Operating Corporation, a nonprofit which was operating the conference center. At first I was unhappy because I couldn't wander all over the dunes anymore. There were trails and fences! Now I recognize the genius behind this restoration, including the controversial fences.

Soon the next hurdle presented itself: Rocky Shores. A little south of the bottom of Lighthouse Ave. and Sunset Drive was the only house in P.G. on the ocean side of the road. Next to the house were six lots. We worked for many years and were able to save five of them from development.

When you go to the gazebo there, you see the boardwalk with names inscribed on 90 planks, each one representing a donation of $1000 or more. The Monterey Peninsula Regional Park District, the State and the City of P.G., nonprofit groups, and caring individuals bought and preserved this spectacular treasure. We all worked together as a community to save our shoreline and woods, so that residents and visitors can find the peace that I find there every day. We made a difference.

Inner Dimensions of a Forest Trail
Keith Larson

At the trailhead of a forest path, a child took the hand of an old man and gave him a tour of the landscape of feelings and experiences of growing up in "the Grove." He told the old man a few stories and let him feel deeply what was in the past. They went to visit places like a favorite beach that his mother had taken him to in the summertime, a beautiful mural in the children's room at the library that sparked a five-year-old's imagination, a tree house built in 1969 that still had a few planks left in the branches of the tall Monterey pine.

Not all the feelings and experiences were comfortable to recall and the old man many times lost his footing and stumbled, but the boy was always there to help him get up and once again take his hand; being a bright child he knew they had to take this journey together. There was no way to turn back; the trail behind them disappeared as they moved forward.

Quite unexpectedly, the trail opened into a clearing. In this clearing stood a sturdy California oak tree with a brand-new treehouse in its branches. "I always wanted to have a treehouse like that one," the older man said.

"Well, now you do," said the child. "I've been building it for a long time and I knew you'd make it down the trail with me someday to find it."

"Climbing up the rope ladder to a treehouse is something I hope I will never forget how to do," the old man told the boy.

From the vista above, the man looked out and tried to see the long winding path that he and this child had traveled, but it had completely disappeared. "Look out this other window," the little boy said, "and you'll see a new one."

He looked out the other side. The fog had rolled in now and turned the forest into multi-layered shadows. Very little form could be seen. Timelessness settled over the little grove and destinations melted into imagined footholds, an elusive dreamscape constantly changing, with nothing to grasp or hold onto. Then the fog lifted as quickly as it had rolled in. There on the other side of the clearing was a new trailhead. A wooden sign marked the path with the word "Possibility."

"Are you ready to go?" said the little boy.

"I am," said the old man. "Take my hand again, will you?"

Starting down the trail, the pair moved into Possibility, like the fog, a formless energy that molds and shapes, moving in and out without warning, hiding comforts and the steps of certainty, planning and logic. A thin vale that, when removed, can frighten, delight and give hope, a creative space where anything can happen at any time. All this, but it was enough that the journey did not feel so lonely now. The sun shone through the trees, creating

shadow and light on the path as the little boy and the old man traveled on into the light of Possibility.

How I Create Forest Art

Walking down a forest trail I begin to feel peace; sitting under a tree for a time with just the sounds surrounding me in this space can sometimes produce a receptivity to receive comforting messages. Many have found nature settings to be benevolent allies helping us with emotional wounds and personal questions we have about our individual life experiences. I have always considered the forest to be my friend and this friendship has deepened with using the organic materials I find to create on-the-spot art works. I never use living materials but pick from discarded pine cones, bark, leaves, sticks and anything else I might find. My works are not preserved in any way and continue to feed the forest as they deteriorate. Designs are not complicated or hard to make over time, like the work of nature artist Andy Goldsworthy. Instead I might spend 30 minutes to an hour making them, then sit for a while with my journal to write down any personal message that might be revealed. The less complicated this process is for me, the better; these are times to visit my friend the forest and to make something from its discarded organic matter that will have value for me on many levels.

Perhaps the highest value is just having fun gathering materials and making something as a child might do. Formal art training should not be an issue in creating art works that have personal meaning and value. Perhaps the only prerequisites might be a willingness to try something new and a child's curiosity.

I'll take you through the process that I use which will enable you to have a starting point to create your own forest art. First I ask the forest for a blessing before entering, the first temples were forests. I might have a specific intent or question, other times I may just surrender all agendas and follow the art-making process wherever it wants to take me. I gather materials at random as I increasingly move into present moment awareness; intuition is at the forefront. I know what to gather and when to stop Trust also increases. I don't worry about what it will look like or any other performance type of mindset. The floor of the forest is my canvas.

I might clear a small circle in the dirt or any kind of shape in which to create a design. I might break some sticks and put them into the ground or make patterns with pine cone seeds. Something I find like a feather could become the centerpiece of the design. Crumpled leaves together make a field of color. Borders can be made of bark to create a safe space for what I'm making. There are no rules and right or wrong ways when it comes to this type of art; only you know what it is supposed to look like.

As with the gathering of the materials I also know when it's time to stop and let what has been created reveal itself. With my journal I wait patiently. Something might come to me fairly quickly and I'll start writing; however, sometimes it is best to just sit awhile with your piece. I might ask questions like, who are you? What is your message? I might write a story, see the symbolism in what I've made, as when applying interpretations of mythological stories to present-day life as in the work of Joseph Campbell. Again there is a knowing that comes and its meaning is something that only you as the creator of the piece can interpret and intuitively know.

When it is time to leave, I thank the forest for its kindness and wisdom shared. As with any beginning friendship, the deepening of the relationship builds over time. Your friendship with the forest will be the same. There is great value in cultivating a deeper connection with nature and using the varied shapes and textures of the materials provided in these sacred spaces to create this deeper connection through art works of your own.

Time-Traveling Through George Washington Park
Russell Sunshine
author and Central Coast Writer member

A misty morning in Washington Park found me musing against a massive trunk toppled across the trail. Festoons of gray-green lichen draped from oak limbs like morning-after party decorations. High above, red-capped woodpeckers swooped to latch onto bark-less pine shafts, withdrawing acorns from last season's safe-deposit boxes.

As always, I marveled at the almost palpable silence captured by the green envelope of dense vegetation. But this morning I was also restless, wondering how and when the park had been created; and how its 12 city blocks of prime open-space had resisted development pressures intensified by the surrounding neighborhood's property boom. So I put on my research hat and here's what I learned.*

Like all communities, ours has its foundation myths. P.G.'s include the conviction that Methodist visionaries took occupancy of a pristine forest primeval for their summer convocations. Washington Park replaces that legend with a more complex but richer reality. In fact, the park area's native forest had

already been logged and burned multiple times by the mid-1800s to clear land for 50 years of cattle-grazing. By the end of the 19th century, second-growth Monterey pines fertilized by those ashes had soared into maturity. The reforested site began to be used as a free tenting campground, accommodating town visitors outside the boundaries of the sequestered Methodist Retreat.

Soon the influential Retreat Association was proposing to limit the site to "recreational use only," an implicit ban on residential construction or commercial activities. By the time the city leased the site from Peninsula property baron David Jacks in 1916, the tent camp had been confined to the property's southern (Sinex) end. The lion's share of the 22-acre plot was preserved as unimproved woodland. Ten years later, Pacific Grove purchased the park for a nominal sum from what, by then, had become the Del Monte Properties Company.

Throughout the park's ensuing history, two parallel land-use conflicts flared and subsided. The first contested whether to eliminate or upgrade the two-acre campground. A Neighbors Club of prominent citizens periodically roused from hibernation to protest campers' noise, litter and hygiene.

In 1932, a brass band accompanied American Legion officials to a public ceremony renaming the park for the nation's first president. This high-visibility flag-raising in the campground center may have been a preemptive strike against encroaching "cottage courts," the precursors of motels. This was no hypothetical threat: the Seventeen Mile Drive Auto Court was the largest lodging facility of this kind between San Francisco and Los Angeles. A short hundred yards from the park, it encompassed 67 cottages, a filling station and a convenience store.

During World War II, the campground's tents-only rule was relaxed to admit trailers. In 1948, City Hall proposed boosting municipal revenues with fee-generating cement parking slots and sewer hookups. The Neighbors Club rallied to the barricades, successfully championing an ordinance to remove the trailer park entirely and limit the recreation zone to day-use only.

The second front of these conservation-vs-development wars was fought over the park's 20-acre forested component. A giant slice of this woodland was put at risk by a mayoral proposal in 1960 to expropriate all parkland south of Pine Avenue for a civic center. Mrs. W.R. Holman mobilized an irate crowd to torpedo the scheme, invoking the "virgin" forest's sacrosanct status as the last standing remnant of Pacific Grove's namesake heritage.

Since the 1970s, forest debates have focused on the park's use as an overwintering haven for migrating monarch butterflies. The sojourners' actual clustering zone measured no more than 90 x 90 feet near the intersection of Pine and Alder. But the entire park became a magnet for Butterfly Town tourism, paired after 1990 with the just-acquired Monarch Sanctuary down the hill. Unfortunately, at that precise moment, monarch numbers plummeted near zero in the park. An ambitious habitat-restoration plan arguably blurred the distinction between conservation and development. In an anxious effort to curb insect attrition, the program would have upgraded park trails, erected strategic fencing and ripped out acres of invasive grasses carpeting the forest floor. The plan was never implemented, and the migrants never reoccupied their former rest-stop.

Our mid-town sanctuary continues to evolve on its own idiosyncratic terms. In the recreation area, swings and slides, barbecue grills and picnic tables frame a popular baseball diamond. In the forest, coast live oaks are visibly displacing Monterey pines as the dominant canopy species. Rampant poison oak and spiny blackberries enforce trail discipline. Calla lilies and pink ladies take turns brightening the park perimeter.

At the end of my research rummaging, I returned to re-view the park with fresh eyes. My downed trunk still straddled the trail. The woodpecker squadrons remained hyperactive. But now I'd gained respect for 100 years of the oasis's stubborn defense. It's too easy to take for granted the amenities that make living in P.G. so special. Passions and persistence had preserved this local treasure.

Bounding Brady, a familiar but formidable gigantic black Lab, jolted me out of historical ruminations. The woods shook with his Baskerville baying before he charged into sight. Brady was legally leash-less before 9:00 a.m. But I was glad when his winded master caught up and lowered the volume.

At the trailhead where Pine Avenue bisected the park, two tentative tourists asked for directions, peering into the sylvan shadows from which I'd just emerged.

"Is this the best way to Pavel's Bakery?"

I gave them my Yoda grin. "Not the shortest, for sure. But the best? That's a different question."

*With a tip of that hat to Dennis Copeland, Research Curator of the California History Collection, Monterey Public Library; Donald Mothershead, Senior Recreation Coordinator, Pacific Grove Parks & Recreation Department; Paul Vandecarr, Collections Curator, Pacific Grove Museum of Natural History; the Reference Staff of Pacific Grove Public Library; and the *Board & Batten* team at the Pacific Grove Heritage Society.

Russell Sunshine is the author of FAR & AWAY: True Tales from an International Life, *available on amazon.com.*

"Life is Good"– The Summer of 1999
Barbara Heinzen

Monterey Bay was aglow. The brilliant summer sun cast a silver hue on the ocean as far as my eyes could see.

It was a perfect day for a family picnic at Lovers Point Park in Pacific Grove. My daughter, Jeanne, had recently bought a home in P.G. and had invited her family members for the weekend. Along for the fun were my grandchildren (ranging from toddlers to teens), their parents, and me.

We decided to eat our lunch alfresco on the little beach area adjoining the park. Uncle Mike, my oldest son, volunteered to assemble the peanut butter sandwiches along with a few simple side dishes.

Mike took his job seriously. He arranged the plates, napkins, cups, etc., into neat, colorful rows on a colorful beach towel and got to work!

Meanwhile the teens jumped into the surf, the younger grandsons got busy building sandcastles and I held the hand of our smallest toddler while she dipped her toes in the Pacific Ocean. In honor of her great-great-great-grandfather, who had arrived in California from Scotland during the Gold Rush era, the smallest toddler was named McClaren.

Finally, our chef called out, "Lunch is ready!" Suddenly, our scattered group of merry-makers headed toward the "Beach Blanket Buffet" from all directions. Lunch was ready and our clan was hungry!

Much to my surprise, McClaren let go of my trusty hand and toddled as fast as she could toward the picnic lunch! When she arrived at the lunch site, she accidentally tripped. She took a big belly-flop right into the sand. Unfortunately, most of the sand flew directly on the carefully prepared peanut butter sandwiches. What a mess!

McClaren was stunned. I gasped. I quickly looked at Mike. He calmly remained seated on the sand, and as he looked up at me he said, with a wry, gentle smile, "Life is good, Mom."

Since that moment in time, Mike's statement has become a family metaphor. When something in our lives doesn't go according to plan, we affirm our truth: "Life is good."

Note: I moved to Pacific Grove almost five years ago. I live within walking distance of Lovers Point Park. Life is good in Pacific Grove.

MONARCH TRANSFORMATIONS

A Monarch Transformation
Irene Evers Elisabeth

There will be a time when this present age fades into the days of yore and humankind's heart is troubled. The Spirit stirs and a melody in the wind, something about "what the world needs now," and those who have ears will hear. The myth is remembered that in Pacific Grove a peasant girl went to the Monterey Pop Music Festival looking for the love and peace of old. Maybe it was the herbs or something else but she was inspired by the words, "What the world needs now is love beads, sweet love beads."

It has been said, "Pacific Grove-by-God" and she believed it and set to work on her mission, inviting all to participate and add a bead to the growing love bead, praying to feel the love that will help heal a troubled heart.

"Come, let us go to this special place," they will say, "and be blessed as the rumors have it. We will follow the butterflies where they return every year and look—here are some beads to add … oh mercy … there is hope."

Life on the Butterfly Sanctuary
Steve and Mary Munsie

Nearly 30 years ago, we had the privilege to live in a cottage on what is now the Monarch Butterfly Sanctuary in Pacific Grove. We were, in fact, the last humans to live on the sanctuary, sharing it with a variety of denizens besides the butterflies—deer, raccoons, and many birds. Here are some memories of that enchanted time:

"It has been a year since we moved to Pacific Grove and four months since we moved to the butterfly park, a two-acre paradise of tall Monterey pines, cypress and eucalyptus, a truly 'pacific grove' inhabited by a small herd of itinerant deer, several raccoon families, crows, blue jays, pigeons and, of course, this time of year the monarchs, delicate mosaics of orange and black with white dots bordering the wings and body, Tiffanyesque deco masterpieces of nature."

"Last night we came home and found the front door of the cottage covered in butterflies, clinging to the glass, the trim, the plants, the stones of the fireplace, even fluttering weakly on the doorstep, rain wet and seeking shelter in the light of the house. We could look through the glass of the front door from inside and study them nose close, seeing their white dotted heads move, antennas twitching, clinging impossibly to the glass. Something magical always happens!"

"The deer here are very sweet and pleasant to talk to. The doe and her two fawns, now almost as large as her, love to sit on the hillside above the house in the mornings or evenings, so are often seen. The babies were first named Bambi and Fauna, but when they both sprouted velvety nubs on their foreheads, we realized we had two Bambis. The two Bambis love to chase each other through the trees, round and round the house, dodging tree trunks skillfully at breakneck speed. They tend to get rambunctious around sunset and twilight or first thing in the morning."

"We had another young couple we named Cinnamon and Spike, she for the color of her smooth, warm fur, and he for the lack of a second horn, lost in some first year skirmish last fall. We haven't seen them since the Fall skirmishes this year began and Spike was driven off by a buck with a bigger set of antlers. But Two Prongs was also superseded in the chase for Cinnamon by a larger buck, Three Racks, who chased off Two Prongs.

"But their skirmishing was only half-hearted as they locked racks gingerly, afraid they might lose some beautiful portion of antler in a too-sudden tug. They clacked their antlers together lightly, click, click, click, then called it a fight and Two Prongs retreated with dignity intact.

"In the meantime, Spike returned to Cinnamon's side and they were nuzzling familiarly. I don't know how this soap opera ended up but we have not seen any of the parties involved lately. Although Spike was reportedly seen in the cemetery down by the lighthouse, lurking like a shadow spookily in the tule fog among the ancient headstones ... BOO!"

"Three Racks just walked through the yard and off into the woods, antlers intact and none the worse for the wet weather today ...."

"Just had a butterfly encounter on our doorstep, literally. Went outside to sketch a monarch and saw one hanging around the door light and nearly stepped on the one huddled on the doormat, unseen. After reassuring it I did not mean to step on it, we had a lovely talk as I coaxed it to open up its wings so I could sketch it, helped it up onto my finger and watched it crawl up my arm to my shoulder where I picked it onto my finger again and it flew off. But not before I sketched it twice. Now it is hanging by the light outside and if I opened the door, I know it would fly in ...."

There were many more memories of adventures on the sanctuary, but those are for another time ....

AND Clouds of Monarchs
Rebecca Riddell

Growing up in Pacific Grove in the 1960s and 70s gave me the perfect childhood.

I will describe a few of the things that made the biggest impressions on me.

Pacific Grove was actually a "piney paradise" with Monterey pines and live oaks growing in nearly every yard, even in the middle of the street. I walked to school, to the store, to the park, through the trees. There were few fences and my route often took me through other folk's yards which were much less groomed than they are now. Pacific Grove was still shedding its wild things. Fog reigned supreme and there were days when you couldn't see your hand in front of your face but, come autumn our Indian Summer would arrive, as would the butterflies. Monarch butterflies were everywhere October through March. Just like in fairy tales, you could stand in a clearing of the forest and butterflies would surround you, dancing in the sunlight. I remember I always stopped on the way into Robert H. Down school to see all the chrysalis hanging on its stucco walls.

At the same time, we had the tallest building I had ever seen in the center of our downtown. Holman's Department Store drew people from all over to Pacific Grove. It was the largest department store between Los Angeles and San Francisco for more than 20 years. It was pretty darn spectacular, especially at Christmas. You could find everything at Holman's—from ironing boards to Girl Scout sashes to ball gowns to books. In fact, that's exactly where my mother found me the first time I ran away at the age of six, riding Holman's elevator.

On the way home from school there was always a half dozen homes with their doors open to neighborhood children. These Good News Clubs kept quite a few of us out of trouble for a couple more years. Hard to resist the nice ladies with cookies. Yet, we also had plenty of time to run free, exploring the forests, the beaches and neighborhood playhouses. When dinner time rolled around Mom would stand out on the porch and scream my name, my full name, until I returned home. By the time the message reached me it had gone through many a horn-blower. If I had jumped the train at Lovers Point for the ride to the Pebble Beach sand plant, the walk back would often make me late.

Everyone knew everyone back in that day and they

kept an eye on you as well. No chance you were staying out past curfew without your parents hearing of it, yet these same town criers were always there to lend a helping hand. Back in that day, helping hands were often needed as Pacific Grove was not a wealthy community and I credit that time for my strong instinct to share and my appreciation the little things in life.

Pacific Grove was comfortable. Nobody was putting on airs. Everyone was equal, or that's what I was taught, anyway. My best friends were Alison Joe, a descendent of Pacific Grove's long gone Chinese Village, and Lorraine Leach, the daughter of a military family. Lorraine's house was where we would play after school because her mother was an amazing cook! They were Jamaican and the flavors were like nothing I got at home. She also made ice cream, which I thought was some kind of a miracle.

By the mid-70s, the 60s had finally arrived to P.G. Downtown became a little Berkeley with hippies hanging out at "the wall," and there was a community garden in the center of town where the old Methodist church used to sit. A good number of the majestic Victorians had been transformed into boarding houses and a new generation would soon take over. My generation.

High School Sweethearts Return with the Monarchs each October
Danny Aiello and Lorelei Layne Aiello
and they lived happily ever after

It was the fall of 1957 when Lorelei moved to Pacific Grove with her family from Monterey. This coastal town was like any other small town in the 1950s: there was a soda fountain in Dyke's Drugs that served cherry cokes; car hops delivered sandwiches and root beer floats to diners in their cars at A&W; big band music gave way to rock & roll on the radio, and girls wore party dresses with petticoats and straight skirts with sweaters.

Lorelei entered Pacific Grove High School (PGHS) for her sophomore year that September. Starting a new high school can be an intimidating experience but Lorelei appeared undaunted by the occasion because her friend, Rose Souza, was also transferring to PGHS. Rose had been attending Junipero High in Monterey. Together Lorelei and Rose would be the new girls at PGHS, but it wasn't long before they started making new friends and met their new bestie, Judy Mallory. Judy had grown up in Pacific Grove and she soon had Lorelei and Rose joining school activities, attending football and basketball games, and venturing to Rec Club on Friday nights.

Danny had always played sports—all kinds of sports from the time he was a boy—and he loved football most of all. Danny was born and raised in Pacific Grove. There wasn't anyone in town he didn't know or any local business where he hadn't worked—one of his earliest jobs was washing windows at the Museum of Natural History when he was in elementary school.

It was February 1959 when PGHS student-athlete Danny Aiello and his buddy, David Nightingale (PGHS 1959), were at a basketball game. This is where Danny first noticed Lorelei and, as Danny tells it, "I was sitting in the bleachers with David, rooting for the red and gold when Lorelei and her friends walked past us. David nudged me and pointed to Lorelei, commenting, "She's cute." More than cute, Danny admits thinking, she's beautiful. After the basketball game, as after every game, the students headed for Rec Club where they would listen to music and dance until midnight with the lights turned low—all under the ever-watchful eye of Ruby Martin of P.G.'s Recreation Department.

Danny continues with their story, "I asked Lorelei to dance; we danced." With a big smile on his face, Danny quips, "Lorelei has been blessed ever since." Lorelei remembers Danny offering her and her gal pals a ride home after Rec Club, noting, "After that night, Judy and Rose had to find their own way home." Lorelei and Danny started dating, or as Lorelei explains, "He started hanging around." And that is how Danny, the PGHS and MPC football player, met Lorelei, the lovely PGHS cheerleader, and fell in love.

Danny and Lorelei were engaged when she graduated in June 1960—and married that October. They lived in Pacific Grove for almost two years—long enough for their first daughter to be born here. In 1962, Danny's work moved the young family to Utah, and two years later Debbie was born. Five years in Utah was long enough for this California family, so Danny, with his three ladies, returned to California. Today the Aiello clan boasts two married daughters, Danette (Mike) and Debbie (Greg); four grandchildren, Jamie, Michael, Nicole, and Stephanie; and three great-grandchildren, Landon, Lea, and Danniella.

Danny and Lorelei will celebrate their 57th wedding anniversary October 8th, and what better time for it than during the annual alumni reunion and Butterfly Parade weekend? Like the monarchs each October, Danny and Lorelei return "home."

J and the Butterfly House
Keith Larson

A couple living in Pacific Grove has created a love story that continues to be shared with more and more visitors each year. The P.G. Butterfly House, as it is known in the Grove, is located at 309 Ninth Street and is owned by J and Sonja Jackson, who have been married for 47 years. The house itself is an amazing piece of art, bright colors with butterflies of all different shapes and sizes.

The story behind the Butterfly House feels like a screenplay for a movie. When J got out of the army, a buddy had some advice for him: check out Pacific Grove. It was a few years before J took his friend's advice. After working at a variety of different jobs and living in Stockton, California, it was time to pack up the van and head to Pacific Grove. In those days J had a large Afro haircut, and even though it was a liberal time in California with hippies and alternative lifestyles, J was not well received at first. J was offered a job in the Monterey Peninsula Unified School District as a drug counselor and was very popular with the kids, saving many lives and keeping kids off drugs. Having grown up in the projects in New York City, J was familiar with tough street life and could relate to what the teenagers at that time were going through.

J took a leave of absence from his job and while in La Jolla, California, met his future wife, Sonja. Having read a number of books by John Steinbeck, Sonja was interested in moving to the Monterey peninsula. Married now, J and Sonja moved to Pacific Grove and bought a real fixer-upper. J did not have much experience with home remodeling, but was helped by a number of kind neighbors and contractors who were working on other homes at the time. Through the years friends like Charlie Higuera, Bill Derowski, Moe Ammar and the Stillwells have been supporters, lending their skills and talents to the Jacksons and to the creation of the P.G. Butterfly House.

At age 18 Sonja had learned she had a progressive eye disease called *Retitnitis Pigmentosa*. In her early 40s it became more difficult for her to see all but bright colors. J decided to retrieve some wood that someone was throwing away and make a big, bright colorful butterfly that Sonja could see. Not only did Sonja love the butterfly, it also made everyone on the street happy to see it. That's when J and Sonja decided to do the whole house exterior in bright colors and butterflies. It is an ongoing project. A butterfly chair sits outside the house; a neighbor had ordered it for the Jacksons just before passing away unexpectedly. There is also a mysterious neighbor who for the last ten years has been leaving ceramic bunnies in different places on the property. It would be easy to find out who it is as the property has surveillance cameras, but J and Sonja are enjoying the mystery and do not want to find out.

J and Sonja are big supporters of the Blind and Visually Impaired Center of Monterey County, Inc., located at 225 Laurel Avenue in Pacific Grove. Beautiful ceramic butterflies can be bought from them and put on a wall at the P.G. Butterfly House with the names of loved ones. All the money collected goes to the "blind center."

The lives of J and Sonja seem to be guided by a synchronicity of events that might leave one pondering the possibility of angels nearby. Tourists and visitors from all over the world come to see the beautiful colors that J has used to create their home, and if you are still and silent for a few minutes, perhaps best of all you can feel the love behind the Pacific Grove Butterfly House.

Pacific Grove, Butterfly Town
Rosemary Tintle

Monarch butterfly facts came to me during a memorial service for someone who found their natural history fascinating. I was captured by the details. During a first visit to the sanctuary, you view "clusters" of monarchs, gifts from nature that stop you in your tracks, filling you with wonder! The migration story is incredible. The journey starts with a butterfly that has never traveled the route to western North America; generations have lived and died since the last year's butterflies began their flight. They smell with their antennae, taste with their feet. A female's life span is short, with only six weeks after emerging from the chrysalis to feed, mate and lay eggs! The Natural History Museum is a fascinating place to discover all the details. Now our fall and winter guests are treated to a late afternoon sanctuary visit. The setting sun illuminates the beautifully patterned wings as they return to a cluster for warmth during the night.

After enjoying that natural display, we drive to the "P.G. Butterfly House," a man-made wonder that is testimony to a remarkable love story. En route I share the history of why the first colorful butterfly was painted. Hopefully J will write his story for this publication, as it is his to tell. Our special town is full of treasures.

a monarch haiku

Metamorphosis
egg, larva, pupa, adult
milkweed for monarchs

Butterfly Docent Shares the Magic
Lois Standley
best friend

During my 34-year tenure as a first grade teacher in Idaho, I would comb the roadsides and ditch banks looking for monarch caterpillars on milkweed. I would take the caterpillar on the milkweed stalk back to the classroom so my students could observe the metamorphosis of this remarkable insect.

As a class, we would read books, learn songs and poems, and look for articles and watch films about the monarch butterfly. We also recorded our observations of the caterpillar's behavior daily. It was always a cause for celebration when the caterpillar made a 'J' and shed its last yellow, black and white skin to reveal a jade-colored chrysalis with gold dots. MAGIC! The culmination of this unit of study was releasing the 'new' butterfly so he or she could fly to California.

I now volunteer my time as a docent at the Pacific Grove Monarch Butterfly Sanctuary. Being a docent provides an opportunity to answer questions, clear misconceptions and share the magic of the amazing life cycle of the monarchs with children and adults who are local, live in California and oftentimes with visitors from foreign lands.

The people who experience the Pacific Grove Monarch Butterfly Sanctuary often become advocates for this amazing insect's survival. Helping visitors see the clusters of butterflies hanging in the trees, or witnessing the mating ritual of the monarchs in February, is MAGIC!

Monarch Haiku
Diane Grindol

Remembering how much fun it was to create haiku verse in 5th grade, I started writing it again a decade ago. Haiku is a very old form of Japanese verse. There are only three lines in a haiku poem, and only 17 syllables. The first line has five syllables, the second line has seven syllables, and the third line contains five syllables again.

In the best haiku a moment in time in the natural world is described. Even though you're only working with 17 syllables, the very best haiku end with a twist! I have found creating haiku to be a challenge and a great brain exercise. I started writing haiku to match my experiences as a pet-sitter and pet lover.

Yes, haiku is rather addicting once you start. Case in point, you can find books of haiku I penned with friend

Ginny Tata-Phillips *Catku, Dogku, Horseku* and *Haiku is the Spice of Life* online at Amazon. My "Catku: Cat Haiku Poems" page on Facebook is pretty popular, too.

Here's a little illustrated haiku for you, in the month that monarch butterflies return to P.G.:

> Dead leaves on a branch
> cling to branches; in sun fly
> away as monarchs.

Float Like a Butterfly
Jerry Gervase
freelance writer, columnist

"I'd like to see the monarch butterflies in Pacific Grove."

It wasn't any more unusual than the requests she had been making. Especially during the past few weeks. We had driven out to Cachagua. Watched sunsets at Lovers Point. Cooked hot-dogs over a wood fire on Carmel Beach. They were all small requests. Doable. Nothing like climbing to Machu Picchu. Or sky-diving. She was way too weak for anything like that. I wasn't sure she was even strong enough to see the monarchs.

The Monarch Grove Butterfly Sanctuary draws thousands of the lovely giant butterflies to Pacific Grove every October, along with an equal number of tourists. But it was early November now. I wasn't sure if there would be any left to see. It wasn't that far from our home in Seaside. It would be a pleasant drive on this warm November day. So we went.

There were few cars parked when we arrived. Not a good sign. Probably means that there were no butterflies to see. We stayed anyway. The path to the viewing area was only about 30 yards long. Still, she had to lean on me to get there. And the butterflies were there. Not thousands. Maybe a couple hundred stragglers who weren't ready for the next leg of their journey.

We sat on a park bench that had a back shaped like butterfly wings. She let out an audible sigh when she sat. The short walk had tired her.

"How do you tell them apart?" she asked. "I mean the boys from the girls."

"They know the difference so it really doesn't matter," I said. Which made her laugh.

"How do they know if they're compatible? Is there a butterfly version of eHarmony?"

Then she asked me how they manage to fly such great distances to get here. She read somewhere that they fly as much as 3,000 miles when they migrate. Of course I didn't know the answer.

"Maybe they ride the thermals," I offered. She laughed again.

"Don't be silly. They're not hawks."

"Well, I don't know! It must takes dozens and dozens of wing beats just to move a few inches. So maybe we're witnessing a butterfly version of pumping iron. When they get here they have great pecs and washboard abs. That could be why they have such narrow waists."

She thought about that for a minute, not taking me seriously but more than willing to play the game. The way we did when we first met. Making up answers to questions or problems we didn't know anything about.

"I know. Maybe they come across with the boat people," she said. "Like from Cuba. Even Cuban butterflies must get tired of listening to four-hour speeches about how great it is to drive around Havana in a 1947 Studebaker with a tranny that never gets out of second gear."

I picked up her thread.

"They could be secret surfers. We think they are flying in from Canada when all the while thousands of butterflies are hanging ten and riding the waves at Santa Cruz."

Sometimes I wondered how we got where we are. It's like, I blinked and 50 years went by. And now here we were at a point where we knew we would be a year ago, even though we tried to live like it wasn't coming.

She was living the life cycle of a butterfly in reverse. Adult, pupa, larvae, as she deteriorated … to what. She left a week later before the last butterfly left Pacific Grove.

I went back to the monarch grove a year later. I sat on the same bench. If this were a sappy Hollywood movie a butterfly would have floated through the air beating its little butterfly wings until it perched on my broken heart, propping it up with silken threads of gossamer comfort and brush-footed love.

None of that happened, of course. I sat on the bench for almost an hour. I wondered how you tell the butterflies apart—the boys from the girls—and if they're compatible. They knew. Just like we did.

Caledonia Park Basketball Court*
Richard Stillwell
as told to Linnet Harlan

There was already a basketball court at Caledonia Park, but it was only half court and was made of asphalt. We'd churned it up unintentionally with the tractors removing snow from Snow in the Park. So I said I'd put in a new court.

John Miller, who was in charge of the Recreation Department at that time, said we needed a full court. I said okay. Then he said they needed the concrete to extend eight to ten feet beyond the baskets so kids can run under the baskets. I said okay. Then he said he wanted the concrete to be five feet wider than the court itself. I still said okay.

I went to Hayward Lumber, and they donated the wood for the cement forms. Granite Construction donated about half the concrete. Everybody wanted to help and did. We sold twenty-two commemorative benches for $500 apiece to pay for the rest of the work. That was $11,000. The total cost was about $60,000 to $70,000; apart from the donations, my wife Bev and I paid the rest.

I love to go down Central and drive by the court. One day I drove by and saw some guys I guess from the Defense Language Institute playing. There were a bunch of kids sitting on the benches, waiting their turn. I went out and stood in the middle of the court. The DLI guys said, "What's going on?"

I said, "Can you play half-court so the kids can play too?"

"Sure, sure."

So everybody got to play.

The kids also ride their trikes and skateboard on the court. To this day it feels good to have built that, to have the kids play on it. And it all started from Snow in the Park.

* *The court is dedicated to the memory of Richard and Beverly Stillwell's son, P.G. firefighter Tommy Stillwell.*

Wedding Reception on Mermaid Ave.
Melba and Jerry Kooyman
former residents, Professor Emeritus, Scripps Institution of Oceanography and wife, Professor Emeritus, Palomar College

During the summer of 1962, my fiancé was a graduate student at Hopkins Marine Station. We were married in Logan, Utah, on July 6th the take advantage of the holiday break from classes. After the wedding ceremony, we hurried back to Pacific Grove the same day so that Jerry would not miss Professor Giese's class the next morning.

Jerry had rented the little cottage at 667 Mermaid Avenue, and when I stepped into the living room, the scent of fragrant flowers filled the air. On a small table topped with a linen tablecloth I saw a full bouquet, a decorated wedding cake, and a beautifully wrapped gift.

The cake had been ordered earlier from the Scotch Bakery, and Jerry had requested that a traditional bride and groom figure be placed on top. The baker looked through all the decorations, but every bride and groom figure in the collection featured a blonde bride. I am a brunette. Somehow a brunette bride was located, and the cake was delivered earlier in the day before we arrived.

We believe we had the smallest wedding reception ever—just the two of us. It was the perfect beginning for our married life. We thought Lovers Point was there just for us.

Keepers of Greenwood Park
Patti Monahan
a happy resident

We live on 13th Street across from Greenwood Park, and it is so much about this park. Before we lived here, my husband and I often visited, taking long walks in the Retreat area which led us to decide we would buy a home here.

In the summer of 1999, my husband asked to drive by a home that seemed too small and impractical for our needs. When we arrived on 13th Street and saw that familiar open space, we knew this was going to be home.

We later learned it had a name—Greenwood Park—and its creek appeared on survey maps dating back to 1875. That creek still runs through it. I won't go into how the park was almost paved over in the 1960s for the sake of development or how a few years ago it almost became a set of treatment ponds. Instead, I will wax poetic about our little park.

Right now, it is spring with green grass, calla lilies and oxalis in bloom. The oak trees have their bright green new foliage and the eucalyptus stand tall and fragrant. Deer wander down to feed in this park—sometimes one, sometimes several. In the late spring, a doe will give birth in the park and then begins the work of protecting both passersby and deer—we have seen a doe chase a dog and its owner who unknowingly got too close to her fawns. There are also those who ignore our warnings, approach the deer and we hold our breaths, not wanting the deer to suffer for human failing. The red-shouldered hawk who calls this park home nests every summer and then teams with her mate to feed her fledglings. We hear their calls and then the distinctly different call of a fledgling as it learns to spread its wings and fly.

In the late summer and fall, the green grass will turn golden, the nasturtiums will bloom and the naked ladies will pop up with their giant pink blooms. And in the winter, egrets roost in the tip-tops of the eucalyptus, their brilliant white standing out against the gray-green leaves.

There is neighbor history in this park. A departed neighbor planted those naked ladies with a childhood friend back in the 1960s. I think of her always when I see those naked ladies bloom.

There is a bridge in the park that crosses the ravine. It is not the original bridge; a late 1800s photograph shows it constructed with tree branches, but it is a bridge built by a neighbor's son as an Eagle Scout project many years ago and it still stands sturdy and proud.

I realize that unlike a building structure, one cannot register a park as a historical asset but I fervently hope that long after we are gone, Greenwood Park will continue to be treasured as a special place. We are indeed the keepers for all those who come after us.

Donald Mothershead
Head of the P.G. Recreation Department
Jane Roland

Donald Mothershead moved to Pacific Grove at the age of four, when his father retired as a major after serving on three continents with the U.S. Army. Earl and Olga Mothershead operated the Pacific Grove Beach Stand, located at Lovers Point from 1958 to 1981 and were famous for the "best burgers on the Peninsula." Donald grew up with the swimming pool and glass-bottom boats, and helped out at the family business.

Don attended Pacific Grove schools (grades K-12), Monterey Peninsula College, then transferred to California Polytechnic State University at San Luis Obispo, obtaining a B.S. in Physical Education in 1976, and his California teaching credential (grades k-adult) in 1977.

While still a student at MPC, Don met the love of his life, Rosemarie, in 1972. After a long courtship, the couple married in 1976 and celebrated their 40th wedding anniversary last spring. They have three wonderful adult children, Heather, Crystal, and John, and three grandchildren.

After college, Donald returned home and taught for four years with the Pacific Grove Unified School District before accepting a job with the City of Pacific Grove in 1981. In addition to his more than three decades with the Recreation Department, Don has been involved in many segments of the community. He says that he cherishes the many amazing opportunities and special community friends that he has made.

Don says his favorite place in town is Lovers Point and his favorite event is Feast of Lanterns.

Rip Van Winkle Park
Joe Shammas

You know Lauren and Lucy and Asia and Essie.
You know Dudley and Farley and Bruno and Nick.
The funny thing is, you've known these dog's names long before you knew their owners' names!

Every day, there are the early risers, the noon time gang and the after work gang, all getting a little exercise and letting their dogs run free among the many trails of the Rip Van Winkle Park in Pacific Grove.

Many friendships (both canine and human) have begun and are nurtured in the "dog park." Begin your walk alone with your pup and soon you will be greeted with a friendly "Hello! beautiful day," by a fellow walker.

Dogs and owners all have a great time in the fresh forest air in our little patch of paradise!

PACIFIC GROVE GOLF LINKS—ALL FORE ONE

Pearls in the Mist
King Grossman
journalist, actor/interviewer

If you are just a bit lucky, the fog rolls in like puffs of dragon's breath, though holding coolness, haunted with some kind of invitation, and then, after a while, the sky's blue dome gives way entirely to what can rightly be called silver air. Engulfed in such magic made quite this way by Monterey Peninsula's subarctic-marine-current seaside micro climate, you stand on the tee box while a golf goddess somewhere across the links coruscates puckishly through the haze. Should you ever be pressed on the exactitude of her nexus, admitting such wiles emanate from pulses of the continuously illuminated beacon at Point Pinos Lighthouse. It is said that for certain old salts of Pacific Grove Golf Links these glimmers—which emerge with a kind of shyness and grace into fullness before retreating until there is only coquettish blankness, as if from the repetitious opening and closing of a rather humongous seashell—proffer a soundless metronome put to the purpose of timing swing rhythm: when syncopated properly, the golf ball comes off the club face true and straight and long, manifestly disappearing into grayness, for moments later, upon the golfer's approach at the green, revealing itself nestled beside the hole, a pearl slipped from an oyster like none other.

If you hear the goddess's call in the slightest, then, dear reader, by all means, leave her, for the moment, where she resides on the seaside back nine among the sand dunes. She has family on the front nine clothed as majestic cypress trees and eucalyptus trees, Nature's brothers and sisters, whom look out after the goddess, offering protection from lesser golfers, those too often ignoring the sculpted beauty of a reasonable forest left intact alongside fairways and greens.

If most all a golfer sees are obstacles to be avoided in these trees, beware of particularly careening bounces off their massive and immovable trunks, your ball inevitably coming to rest behind another trunk and in a dead stymie with the pin. If your game and the trees eventually reduce you to serial cursing, perhaps, tossing a club in anger, or, God forbid, snapping, say, a 9-iron in two across your knee, things will get worse for this golfer. Twisted branches begin reaching out to grab your ball, and, if you happen not to be worthy of forgiveness, they keep it snared in bunched feathery pine needles or thickets of green leaves. It's true, just come to the course after a windstorm or heavy rains and see for yourself all the golf balls fallen to the ground at the base of trees. The inland nine will send you home before you experience the magic the goddess has in store for you on the back nine, unless you recognize the trees as nothing less than pestiferous majesty, ecology's sculptures and, all the same, ironic sergeants at arms. If you can honestly laugh at the trees, at least most of the time they come into play, then they will grant you access to the back nine along the ocean. You will not be one of those who go to their car shaking their heads after getting to the turn but not making it. Or one of the others who ask only to play the back nine because it is semi-famous for ocean views. Even if the friendly folks who work in the pro shop grant you such a pass, the goddess will not be there for you. All you will see is some blinkered light from some obsolescent lighthouse set a bit too far off the coastline anyway.

Yes, I boldly put forward there is a special breed that gravitates to these grounds, those who naturally look for deeper truths beneath appearances. If in any way it appeals to imagine meandering your way to the course, rather than dashing along a busy thoroughfare in hot pursuit of not missing a tee time, then these eighteen holes where new myths can be made gives call. They can be kept secret if you prefer, those inner reasons without words for coming to such a place to play golf. But come you must if you are called. There is the young assistant pro working in the golf shop who takes drives along Lighthouse Blvd. right beside the ocean to get to work, enjoying no small number of his lunches seaside, too. There is the electrician from Salinas, California who is bringing on as much work as he can in Pacific Grove and Monterey to be nearer the ocean. He also drives the coastal road to the course rather than taking the more direct route through the edge of town. I know these things about these guys because I volunteered my own seafaring proclivity to them. Another fellow who works in the pro shop is a published fiction writer, my regular playing partner is an opera singer, and, as for the first two fellows I met on the first tee at the start of my first round here, one was a poet and the other a golf writer.

Some call this delightful complex "The poor person's Pebble Beach," but for golfers who really get this place, those frequenting this course with deer roaming freely, the longest uninterrupted operating lighthouse in California on the grounds' highest plateau, whale sightings as common occurrence out off holes on the back nine which hug the ocean close, and not to give pause without saluting the cypress and eucalyptus lined fairways on the inland front nine, I say, this is "The rich golfer's paradise," wealthy in artfulness, that is. And if golf is anything, it is athleticism and poetry in motion. After all, the great Arnold Palmer, may he RIP, once said, "There's nothing more poetic than hitting a really good drive."

New Golf Clubhouse Drama
Bruce Obbink
Lee Yarborough, *P.G. Bulletin*

On April 13, 2006, an open house was held for the Pacific Grove Municipal Golf Clubhouse and Point Pinos Grill with on-again off-again ribbon cutting declared by the powers-that-be. Nothing that has been said by opponents of the project, or critics of those who fought so hard to bring the golf course clubhouse into reality, will ever be considered credible by visitors who enter the wonderful new facility.

It is without doubt a great new asset for the city. All who enter its spaces, who enjoy the new pro shop and cart storage, and who look upon the magnificent vista opened to view by golfers and diners alike must give thanks to Bruce Obbink for the way he stayed the course throughout the furious flack over the golf clubhouse controversy.

Today the clubhouse stands as beautiful vindication in testimony to the righteous efforts of the Golf Committee, which Bruce chaired. Only golfers pay to retire the bond funding that made the building possible, yet all the revenue from the new clubhouse goes directly to the city's General Fund. Even the furniture in the fine structure is paid for by golfers.

Now, after the opening of the new clubhouse, it is appropriate that you all get to really know the person who has, through his dedicated efforts, brought this fine improvement to our community.

The current powers-that-be may not have allowed a ribbon-cutting to celebrate the opening of the new golf clubhouse, but the absence of such ceremony did not lessen in the least the great significance and benefit that the facility brings to the community, and the huge economic stimulus it may deliver to the city as a whole. The lack of a proper dedication only emphasized the fact that recognition for those who brought about the fine facility is strongly warranted.

To that end *The Pacific Grove Hometown Bulletin* acknowledges the support given to Bruce Obbink and the members of his Golf Course Advisory Committee by former Mayor Morrie Fisher, former Vice-mayor Don Gasperson, former Councilmembers John Stidham, Sue Renz, and Ron Schenk, as well as current Mayor Jim Costello, and the entire City Council of former Mayor Sandy Koffman.

The Bulletin acknowledges the splendid efforts of the individual members of the Golf Course Advisory Committee who pursued careful study and evolution of project development to its fruitful conclusion: Dorothy Owen, Robert Sanchez, Pete Houser, Joe Ameel, Rick Pieper and Jim Manuian.

Twice Bruce ran for election to the City Council. It was his misfortune to twice face defeat. He lost badly the second time in the aftermath of great controversy over the open space measure, major public frustration over the previous council's throwing out of a petition, and controversy about a golden parachute given to the previous city manager (that turned out to mean nothing to the administrator who chose instead to escape the harsh rhetoric of the newly elected council majority.) Competing candidates stormed about, complaining of wrongful termination and imagined planning procedure abuses with Forest Hill Manor. Since then, many have come to regret Bruce's loss in the last election for council and have come to realize that he would have served the city well with his experience and know-how.

Pacific Grove politics has a reputation for being a little bizarre. From the opposition Bruce was characterized as a "Koffman insider." (Which should be taken as a compliment.) More recently he has been called a "good old boy." (Many have, without success, tried to identify the Good Old Boys Society ever since then so that they might join.) They also called Bruce a "union-buster" because of his successful 27-year career as president of the California Table Grape Commission. He managed a $13 million annual budget and all advertising, communications, community service, merchandising, research and marketing campaigns in 20-plus countries ranging from the United States to Asia, Europe and South America. He was responsible for an enormous increase in the production of grapes to the very great benefit of the economy of our nation. *www.pggolflinks.com*

Once Upon a Golf Course
Jonathan Shoemaker
golfer, writer

On the first tee

"Hi. I'm Jonathan."

"Pleased to meet you. I'm Neil. Have you played here before?"

"Oh, yes. I'm one of the golf-marshals here."

"Good! Then you'll be able to guide me around the golf course."

"My pleasure."

"It'll be fun, Just the two of us."

I selected my seven iron. "Yes. My son and I enjoy playing the course as a twosome."

On the tenth tee

He almost ran to catch up with us. "Do you fellas mind if I play through? I'm kinda in a hurry today."

"It's my first time on this course, so I'd like to relax and enjoy it. Please, go ahead!"

His mouth dropped open as he stared at Neil. "Nah. You're right. Don't need to rush it. I'll just join you if it's okay with you guys."

I laughed. "Do you mind, Neil?"

"Fine, but we won't be rushing our shots, sir. And you can play on ahead of us anytime if you change your mind."

"Ha! That's a deal! Wow, this is great!"

As Neil stepped forward to take the tee, the stranger approached me and spoke in a low voice. "Jeez, this is so cool! Neil Armstrong! I didn't even know he played golf. How do you know him?"

"We met today."

"Dude, how exciting."

The nervous newcomer seemed to have changed his mind after a couple of holes of casual, golf-related conversation. "Hey, guys, I really do need to play faster to finish in time. You really don't mind if I play on ahead?"

Neil smiled. "Not at all, sir."

"Fine with me!"
"Wow, thanks a lot! Oh! Kin you autograph my cap?"
At the AT&T putting green:
"Jonathan!"
"Hi, Neil. I saw your name on the roster."

He came to the fence to shake my hand. "I've wanted you to know how much I appreciated the fact that you treated me like just one of the guys when we played. I rarely get that."

The Sun Also Rises

It's pleasant golfing on the links on dusky afternoons.
No one in front to slow you down.
No one behind who'd have to wait
if you decide to stop
and watch the colors change
in clouds
and sky,
And stop to watch the pine bark glowing red in
    sunset rays,
Or see the short grass glowing yellow-green
like oak leaves
when they first emerge from swollen buds
in Spring.
I saw the mother fox approach my ball
to see if possibly an egg
had somehow found its way
to rest upon this unprotected field
of close clipped grass.
She stopped, in sudden crouch
and, sniffing, watched a doe
Who, licking, nudging with her nose,
probed at the head and body
of her fawn.
The listless fawn, with legs outstretched,
responded to her gentle touch.
It raised its head, and bent its leg,
But then went limp
with heavy final breath.
The doe, with final lick upon the eye
and fruitless motion of her nose
to prod the lifeless form,
walked on
to nurse the other twin.
The fox, with backward glance at doe,
took the carcass, more than half her size, in tow.
Lifted and dragged, then paused
and dragged again. She took the meal home
to her kits, who waited at the den.
Five tiny tumbling balls of fur,
nipping at each other's ears,
advanced toward her.
Then, with scent of newfound meat,
the kits retreated toward the den.
She slipped into the thicket,
surrounded by her scrambling young,
Leaving not a trace of twitching branch
nor sound of sumptuous feast.
Then, as I moved on toward my ball
across green velvet rolling hills
which reached down to the sand and rocks,
I gazed out past the foaming surf,
along the orange and silver path,
to watch the setting sun.
Clouds, in muted colors, edged with gray
folded against the pale blue sky.
Still others, closer to the mushroom sun,
glowed apricot and gold.
Then, sinking, shrinking, seemed to push
a dent into the ocean's edge,
the sun became a line,
a dot,
And fading
to a pale green glow,
left nothing but a thin black line beneath an amber
    sky.
The deer had found a tender patch of grass,
gave nourishment to her remaining fawn,
And gave example how to graze
and where to lie to wait the dawn.
I slowly swung, and saw my ball float up
to etch a steep descending arc,
And stepped out at a good brisk pace
to finish before dark.

Transistor
Lillian Griffiths

My dad, Dave Griffiths, would go to work early. He had to be on the P.G. golf links before the early-rising golfing groups arrived. Often, he would start his patrols in the dark to see what needed to be done that day or that week on the course. Elmarie Dyke, known as Mrs. Pacific Grove (or "Granny Grove" by some), did a daily news broadcast about Pacific Grove early each morning from Golden West Pancake House across from Lugo's gas station. One day when she saw my dad at City Hall she asked if he had heard her broadcast that morning. Dad said he was sorry but he was out on the course when her program was on so he seldom had a chance to hear her news. Two days later a transistor radio arrived for my dad from Elmarie with a note saying that now he could listen regardless of where he was. That's the kind of town Pacific Grove is.

LIGHTHOUSE LOGBOOK
William Neish

"None of us really see things as they are; we see things as <u>we</u> are." Liane Moriarty, *Big Little Lies*

July 22, 2017 *Mood: Bright and clear.*

Final contributions to *Life in Pacific Grove* are in and being edited by staff. I ask publisher Patricia what's missing from the book, and she says a piece on the lighthouse. This landmark will appear on the book's cover so it really has to be represented inside. For some reason, I volunteer to take on the challenge.

July 30 *Mood: Groggy, resentful.*

Having procrastinated for a week, I decide it is indeed time to get out from under my bed, dust myself off and visit the Point Pinos Lighthouse…which I have never actually seen, despite being born and raised here. (It wasn't as publicized as a museum back when I was little. And as someone who sunburns easily, I avoid beaches in general.)

The lighthouse surprises me, as it is both big and small at the same time. At 43 feet it's a tallish building, so the light atop it is visible above the horizon, about 17 miles out to sea. But it also has modest sized rooms—two downstairs and two in the attic—connected by teeny tiny hallways and a narrow spiral staircase.

I fall in love with a small "bonus room" upstairs. Here a long bank of windows shows the everchanging blue-gray-green sea, and a wide windowsill serves as a sort of built in desk. This is the Watch Room, originally a closet for tools used to repair the all-important light that's just a few steps away, up on the next level. I want to lock myself in this room forever with a box of crackers and not turn in my piece.

August 2: *Mood: Harsh winds of anxiety in from the east.*

I've got books from the library and scoured the Internet, and am officially overwhelmed. QUESTION: *How can I research and write the history of a 163-year-old building and its many obscure residents in just a few weeks?* ANSWER: *I CANNOT.* But perhaps I can focus on one inhabitant. The obvious candidate is diligent Emily Fish, who worked as the keeper from 1893-1914. A widowed Oakland socialite, she came to the lighthouse at age 50, carting along a French poodle, fine furnishings, paintings, books and silver flatware. She could change the main lamp's glass chimney in two minutes when it had taken her predecessor seven. She also installed a fountain outside. I am impressed.

August 10 *Mood: Irritated, with flashes of anger.*

I discover that Mrs. Fish's husband was named Melancthon. WHO WOULD DO THAT TO A CHILD? Could this be a typo? Melancthon is the name of a rural farming town in Ontario. With an additional 'h', it's the name of a professor Martin Luther befriended at Wittenberg. Whatever the spelling, I hope Emily was at least able to call him Mel.

August 3: *Mood: A bit more hopeful.*

The P.G. library has a 1937 Works Progress Administration item that catches my eye: *Historical Survey of the Monterey Peninsula.* Unfortunately, on closer inspection it's just a typed version of an old newspaper clipping, from the scrapbook of one Vinnie Bickford.

The original journalist notes, *"Instead of being built on a barren rock, the Point Pinos light is located on the edge of a forest of pines and cypress. It is quite a distance back from the beach."* (The lighthouse probably isn't closer to the water because the granite used to build its walls was quarried from where the building stands now.) The article continues, *"Monterey, four miles away, is the official post office of Point Pinos, and there the lighthouse steamer Madrona carries supplies and orders once a month."*

Apparently, this location was quite isolated in 1893. *A Piney Paradise* (a memoir by P.G. resident Lucy Neely McLane) says that just ten years before, search parties were still being sent out to find lost visitors in the dense Pacific Grove woods. The Widow Fish left no correspondence behind, but she did entertain writers, artists and passing Naval officers at the lighthouse for company. She also had a faithful Chinese servant on hand (named either Que or Lew Kew, depending on the source) and often the help of a hired laborer or two, who lived in an outbuilding.

August:4: *Mood: Rejuvenated, with marked spring in step.*
I meet Rick Steres from the P.G. Historical Society, who shows me early pictures of the lighthouse. It is built in a style called the New England Plan, which means the light tower rises up through a cottage. Earlier lighthouses were separate from the keeper's quarters, but this created problems during storms when s/he had to get to and up the tower. With the New England Plan, the light source is just a few steps away from a bedroom.

Rick also provides the original floorplan. Interestingly, it labels the large, south room on the ground floor "the kitchen." (This is now a reception room.) Some time before 1910 the kitchen was moved to a shed roofed lean-to extension off the back, where it remains today. At least THIS is something I know a bit about. Having a kitchen extension like that, or even one in its own separate building, reduced the risk of the whole house burning down if there was ever a grease fire, or a hot coal fell out of the stove. It also helped keep the rest of the house cool in summer in the days before air conditioning.

Emily's parents were born in England, where Victorians were very keen on having different rooms for different activities. Having a separate dining room was a sign of status. I wonder if it was Emily who moved the kitchen to the back, to free up that south room for dinner parties.

August 11: Nate King, the collections registrar at the P.G. Museum of Natural History, has pulled some transcribed versions of Emily's lighthouse logs from the archives. They rarely touch on local events, let alone her own life, but I spot a few dramatic entries.

> March 12, 1898 – *Clear, gale…Seven Japanese capsized from boats locked together chasing a shark. They clung to capsized boat, but no one seeing them, all tried to swim ashore; four reported drowned.*

> January 6, 1899 – *A man supposed to be a tramp was found near the RR track east of station, sitting against a wall, quite dead, by some young Stanford men. He was removed to the Grove and his death was pronounced pneumonia. He had not been on this station.*

> November 16, 1904 – *A stranger came to the station for assistance – had been on a bicycle on the path, and jumping over a gate became faint. Assistance was given, and he was taken in the Keeper's buggy to his home in the Grove. He rallied with medical aide but died suddenly about 4:00 p.m. of angina pectoris.*

These entries remind me how much more common death was in everyday life at the turn of the century.

The museum also has two fat albums of press clippings and photographs detailing the refurbishment of the lighthouse interior by the National Questers Adobe Chapter in 1994-95. They illuminate a few things. For instance, if you want the Point Pinos Look, use Benjamin Moore HC-36 (Hepplewhite Ivory) on walls and ceiling, and HC-35 (Powell Buff) on the baseboard and doors. And while one keeper's 3-year-old, Erma Luce, died in the lighthouse of spinal meningitis in 1894, the building's unofficial ghost is Jiggs the cat, who has a small concrete mausoleum in the garden. (He belonged to the Henderson family and actually died when they tended the lighthouse at Point Sur. But they brought Jiggs' crypt with them in 1938 when they took over our lighthouse, and there he rests to this day.)

Sadly, I am still having trouble getting a clear impression of who Emily Fish was, at heart. She gave her daughter a gold bracelet and a traveling bag on her wedding day. I would love to theorize these were a reminder to value both 19th century refinement and bold adventure, yet there's no record as to *what* inspired choosing those items. For all we know, her daughter requested them.

August 13: *Mood: Somewhat validated.*
I'm bothered that our fabled fifth lighthouse keeper remains something of a shadowy figure to me. But a docent from the lighthouse staff makes me feel a bit better when she answers an email of mine that pleaded for info.

After clearing up a couple of points, she writes, "*There is much hearsay, speculation, and make-believe about Emily Fish. We have records of her log books but she and her friends aren't around anymore to get the straight facts. Things written are not always accurate according to the information we have, but once read it seems to become reality…*"

I think how fragile all our histories become. Facts get blurred over time, depending on who's telling the story. For instance, Emily's daughter wasn't her biological child, but rather a niece from a deceased sister. Some sources acknowledge this, some don't. It depends on where you look.

We might never learn why the teenaged Emily Fish married her sister's widow, a man twice her age. We might never know why she took a potentially lonely government job on an isolated beach after he died. Unless someone who knows us very well writes about us, generations later we are reduced to just a few documented facts.

And "facts" can change. A decade ago, as a favor to my mother I struggled to piece together the history that preceded her 1938 adoption. She was always told she was French, which is also stated in old records from the Boston courts. Yet earlier files from Virginia and Washington DC identify her birth mother as German. It was only after finally meeting up with fellow descendants of the Moess family that I learned our bloodline flows from Alsace-Lorraine … which swung from being a French to a German territory, and then back again, for centuries. So, was this woman who surrendered my mother for adoption in 1938 French, or German? It turns out she was both. None of the official records are correct, or incorrect. We are Alsatian.

There are variables of a certain event known to those who experienced it, but these can be blurred to those of us looking backwards. Colors change depending on the light, just like the ocean you see from the lighthouse Watch Room, under the eaves on the second floor at Point Pinos.

WELCOME TO THE PACIFIC GROVE MUSEUM OF NATURAL HISTORY

Jeanette Kihs, Executive Director

The Pacific Grove Museum of Natural History is an iconic part of the Pacific Grove story. Having been here since 1883, this educational resource has been a staple of the community since before Lighthouse Avenue was paved. With the sparkling waves of Monterey Bay in the background and the green grass of Jewell Park as our neighbor, not to mention the Pacific Grove Library across the street, the Museum has been a part of our childhood, and the childhood of our own children. I am sure it will be a part of their children's lives as well. Whether it's the P.G. Museum or PGMNH, we strive to be a part of the community.

Sandy the Whale greets visitors at the corner of Forest and Central Avenues every day, rain or shine. Those of us lucky enough to have grown up on the Central Coast probably have at least one photo of themselves sitting on Sandy's back. But it's not just those who've grown up here. Our visitors take these photos home with them, share them on social media and treasure their visit with Sandy just as much as we do.

Our exhibits highlight the natural history of the Central Coast; this includes stories of the people, the birds and the four-legged creatures that can be found here—not to mention the flora, shells, rocks, and fauna that make living on the coast such a magical experience. Visitors enjoy our Chinese Fishing Village exhibit, our Sands of the World display, the Native Californians basketry display, and much more. Our expansive collection also extends deep underneath the Museum with our basement collection. This wealth of history is not often on display (though we do rotate various items each year), and it is available with basement tours offered by our curator. These tours are given to our members and volunteers on special occasions and by special request. If you've never taken a tour, I highly recommend it. There you'll find everything from coins and jewelry to art and weapons. Noted collectors and scientists, such as Harold Heath and Ed Ricketts, have contributed to this collection.

Children throughout Monterey County visit the Museum with their families and friends, but they also visit on school field trips. Class trips can be scheduled on our website at pgmuseum.org. During the school year, students arrive from as far away as Greenfield and as close as Robert Down Elementary School to learn about their part in the natural world. We love being a part of their journey and try as hard as we can to connect them with their environment. Here at the Museum we're in a perfect position to do just that. We also connect with visitors to the Pacific Grove Monarch Sanctuary during monarch season, as you will see in the stories shared by our wonderful staff.

The people who work and volunteer, as well as our many members, work hard every day to ensure that our mission to inspire discovery, wonder, and stewardship of our natural world isn't just a talking point, but a way to celebrate the diversity of our fantastic ecosystem. Their passion for history and science serves as my daily inspiration.

The City of Pacific Grove makes it possible for Monterey County residents to see our wonderful Museum free of charge by paying their admission fees. We're honored to preserve and curate their amazing collection. Our members receive free entry, no matter where they live, and are gifted free guest passes for out-of-town visitors as a benefit of joining.

I hope you enjoy these personal Museum stories and we'll see you at the corner of Forest and Central!

From the Front Desk
Estrella Theoni
Guest Services

I have a fulltime position manning the front desk for the P.G. Museum and as a result, I'm the main face most people see when they walk in. Whether they're guests, students, or volunteers, they usually say "hello" before continuing inside.

Sometimes they arrive carrying something. Sometimes it could be a shopping bag, but often they've got something they'd like identified, or they have something they'd like to donate to the collection.

One afternoon, a guest carrying such a package arrived.

My first thought was, "Oh, another dead bird." We have many dead birds, mostly donations.

He asks if the Museum would like it. I ask him what it is. Between his accent and my deafness, I think he's saying it's a bug or a beetle of some kind.

I think, "Well, we could probably take a beetle, let's have a look."

I take a look.

It's not a bug.

It is, inside a clear container, a live, little brown bat (myotis lucifugus).

I politely tell him that we do not accept live animals and, if he found it injured, the SPCA would have been a better option. I ask him why he thought to bring it here and he replies, "Oh, about ten years ago I brought a snake and you guys took that."

Okay.

Patiently, he waits while I call down to the education staff. We do not, of course, accept the bat in our collection, but our garden has a bat box. After cooing over how adorable and squeaky it is, we made our way to the Native Plant Garden and attempted to put it in the box. It resisted our efforts and settled in a tree instead. Soon it was gone.

I sure hope that little bat's doing all right these days.

Inspired by Words
Stephanie Stock
Education Programs Assistant

I didn't expect to cry during a lecture about seaweed identification. Nobody does, really. But it happened anyhow.

Kathy Ann Miller is a warm, humorous, and passionate person, all on top of being exceedingly knowledgeable about seaweeds. She was the evening's lecturer at the Pacific Grove Museum of Natural History, giving a brief introduction to identifying species native to the Monterey Bay in advance of a tide pooling expedition the following morning.

The bird room was full of people excited to hear her thoughts, a fact I especially appreciated since it was Friday night. This city is overflowing with lifelong learners and educators, and meeting and learning from so many experts in marine biology has been my favorite aspect of working in Pacific Grove.

Dr. Miller shared her opinion of the lasting value of collected specimens for scientific study and brought several examples from the University of California's herbarium, seaweeds carefully selected and mounted by the intrepid female citizen scientists of the late 1800s right here in Pacific Grove.

As wonderful as it was to see those beautifully displayed specimens, that wasn't the part of the lecture that really got to me. Nor was it the various species she showed and enthusiastically described, though that was interesting and informative.

Wrapping up her talk, Kathy Ann touched on what I love most about this part of Monterey Bay: the focus on understanding and conserving the natural world through the education of children.

She said, and I fully agree, that in the face of a rapidly changing world, education is the best way forward. Thinking of how many times I've seen a child's eyes light up with wonder through the various educational programs I work with at the Museum, and how that might impact their actions and attitudes in the future, is what caused me to choke up a little. With programs for field trip groups, summer camps, outreach in schools, Science Saturdays, and the LiMPETS intertidal monitoring program, we are sowing into the future a love for the environment which sustains us and of which we must be good stewards.

Pacific Grove has a great legacy of community involvement and we are so lucky at the Museum to have so many members, volunteers, and partners in our work of inspiring love of the natural world. I'm proud to have been a part of this mission and earnestly hope it will continue for a long time to come.

Volunteering for the Pacific Grove Museum of Natural History
Mary Dainton
Museum Docent

Back in 1987, Gertrude Chappel and Fred and Marjorie Capen opened a gift shop in the main hall of the Museum. They advertised for help at the April Wildflower Show. I applied and started volunteering on May 17th. Since that time, I have continued to staff the gift store. The location and types of merchandise have changed many times over the years, but that's what keeps life interesting.

There have been many amusing moments, but the one I remember most occurred when we had an exhibit of Alaskan artist Ray Troll's work. I was sitting in the store when a young male high school teacher from the Central Valley came in and asked where the Troll exhibit was. I directed him to the large exhibit room.

"Oh," he said. "I have been in there and it's nothing but a load of pictures of fish!"

"That's the Ray Troll exhibit," I said. "He draws fish."

"Oh, dear," the teacher said. "I have a busload of kids outside expecting to see trolls."

We both laughed and I still get a kick out of the memory.

Another strange happening was when a man wearing a horsehead mask visited the Monarch Sanctuary. He walked around, listened to a talk and never took the mask off. The monarchs didn't seem to mind, but the other visitors were amused. We never knew the reason why he came dressed that way.

Meeting Monarch Mankind
Nick Stong
Education Programs Manager

As Education Programs Manager for the Pacific Grove Museum of Natural History, I get to wear a few different hats, so to speak. In addition to leading field trips at the Museum, planning the monthly Science Saturday series, and teaching our summer camps, I also have the privilege of getting to talk to people about the monarch butterfly migration.

Between the months of November and February, monarchs fly to the California coast by the hundreds of thousands, seeking a special microclimate in which to spend the winter. At the same time, a human migration is taking place, as hundreds of thousands of people flock to "over-wintering sites" to witness the phenomenon of monarch migration first-hand. One of California's nearly 400 over-wintering sites (the Pacific Grove Monarch Butterfly Sanctuary) is just one mile from the Pacific Grove Museum of Natural History. This past season, the Butterfly Sanctuary in Pacific Grove saw more than 30,000 human visitors (11,000 in November, alone!), many greeted by Museum-trained docents equipped with high-tech spotting scopes.

It was extremely rewarding to be able to talk to some of these folks, many of whom were fulfilling a lifelong dream of visiting the over-wintering monarchs.

Some of these visitors came from other states, countries, and continents to peer up into the trees at as many as 17,000 clustering monarch butterflies, and marvel at the fact that such a small insect can make such a Herculean journey. The lucky visitors may have witnessed a "burst," when a cluster of thousands of monarchs seems to take off all at once. Others may have even had one flutter down and land on their outstretched hand. However, most of these far-from-home travelers seemed content to simply tilt their heads and gaze at one of the greatest spectacles in the natural world. I am fortunate to live in a place as special as Pacific Grove, and I am grateful for the opportunity to share my experiences in this place with visitors to our Museum and to the Monarch Sanctuary.

Day of the Gynandromorph
Patrick Whitehurst
Communications and Marketing Coordinator

My eyes aren't the best, so I had to lean in close to examine the monarch butterfly. It flitted around, happy as can be, after waking up from its chrysalis transformation. The butterfly stretched its tangerine wings for the first time and made its way to a spot where the sun shone warmly through the windows of the Pacific Grove Museum of Natural History. I watched it closely. It wasn't my eyes. The monarch was a gynandromorph.

Only I had no idea what the heck a gynandromorph was at the time. What I did know was this insect had a black spot on one hindwing, but not on the other. In fact, the inky lines on the wings, common to all monarch butterflies, looked thicker on the wing without the black spot. This is a common trait for female monarchs. The black spot is a common trait for males. So, which one was it? Male or female?

As it turned out, this was both.

The monarchs born in the Museum's chrysalis chamber aren't released into the wild due to genetic differences and the risk of introducing disease to the native western monarch population. "Farmed" monarchs are kept for display in the Museum's lobby and when this monarch eventually died, we took it upstairs for further study—one that included the help of a professional entomologist.

In entomology, a gynandromorph refers to an insect with both male and female characteristics. While rare in and of itself, finding a gynandromorph monarch butterfly is rarer still, the entomologist told us, which made the revelation in our own Museum pretty exciting. I followed its progress, from our curator to our collections staff, and watched the rare monarch become a permanent part of the Museum's collection. Our collections staff took great care to preserve the specimen before mounting its small body to a base. The creation of an interpretive panel followed, one that described the amazing find for the public. Within a week, the gynandromorph became an official part of the Museum's astounding collection and was soon on display with the rest of the Monarch exhibit.

I show it to everyone.

This is, of course, just one of so many amazing collections items. A short list of these items can be found on our website at pgmuseum.org/collections/.

Taking my Mom to the Sanctuary
Andrea Lawson
Administrative Assistant

Before working here, I rarely ventured into Pacific Grove, much less the Museum. Once I started to familiarize myself with everything the Museum did, I couldn't believe I never noticed it before. I started working here at the beginning of fall, the start of the monarch season. I also had no idea about the monarchs that migrate to Pacific Grove. Part of my job required me to visit the Monarch Sanctuary. The first time (and every time after that) I saw the butterflies flying in the eucalyptus trees, I was speechless. "Magical" is the best word for it I think. I had never seen so many in one place, flying in and out of the spotlight of the sun. I loved going there.

At the time, I only worked a few hours, so I brought my mother along with me one day, a day I happened to need to go to the Sanctuary. My mother was born in Mexico and lived there for 28 years, and she had also never seen the monarchs, even though she lived close to their migrating destination. When she saw the butterflies, her eyes lit up. I watched her watch them, mesmerized by the fact that, even though she was no longer in her home country, she could see and be connected to part of it through the butterflies. I know people from all over the world come to see the monarchs all up and down the coast, but in this case the butterflies came to see my mother. I love being able to provide her with experiences like that, to thank her for everything she did and does for me. She is afraid of driving (although she knows how) so it's a treat for her when we go places together.

The Sanctuary is only able to be maintained by donations from visitors and donor contributions. I am so glad and appreciative for all the people who see how important it is to contribute to places like this. It is important to think about the creatures themselves, but we often overlook the impact these little butterflies have in the lives of people. I hope the Sanctuary continues to be a hospitable place for the butterflies to over-winter, and a place where families can create fond memories.

The Museum offers a wonderful guide to the monarchs at pgmuseum.org/monarch-citizen-science. I encourage everyone to visit.

Loving the Town
Mary Martha Waltz
Advancement Coordinator

Several years ago, I lived in Pacific Grove for four years. I grew to love the Grove Market, and now, even though I live in Carmel Valley, I drive over to the market for the least, little thing! The Pacific Grove Cleaners has also been my cleaners for many years. AND, the parades! Oh! The parades! I knew I had arrived in an exceptional home town, an original place.

Now that I've returned, my "Life in Pacific Grove" revolves around the Pacific Grove Museum of Natural History. And, when I think of the Museum, the extraordinary staff immediately comes to mind. I have never worked with a more generous and caring group who enjoy sharing their knowledge and love for our natural world.

And, most recently, I've covered for Jane Thompson, who is our Volunteer Coordinator and who took a four-month maternity leave of absence. I enjoy getting to know and work with our dedicated and big-hearted volunteers. Many have multiple positions at the Museum, for which they dedicate their time and energy. We are most grateful to each one!

The Museum has long been recognized as the "field guide to the Central Coast," showcasing local plants, animals, geology, and cultural history. However, staff and volunteers are working to transform the Museum into a place without walls where "services flow rather than just a place where people go."

We are so proud when a visitor comments the Museum is a "little gem." One out-of-town visitor even commented the Museum was better than the big museum in the town in which she lived!

"Life in Pacific Grove" keeps expanding in the most welcome way! Of course, I would be remiss not to mention how fabulous our volunteers are. We're always seeking new volunteers, too. If you're interested, visit us at pgmuseum.org/volunteer/.

Sand Crabbing
Emily Gottlieb
LiMPETS Coordinator

I overheard one student say to another, "If you think this is gross, wait until we dissect a frog in high school!"

She stared queasily at her sand crab specimen, preparing for the first step of the dissection—cutting off the sand crab's telson (tail). She took a deep breath, then bravely made the incision, before she coolly replied, "Yeah, but we will be way more mature by then."

It is dissection day for the sixth graders in Cesar Chavez Middle School's summer program. Each student hovered over a sand crab, inspecting the tiny decapod to see what it had eaten. Sand crabs live in the "swash zone" at the beach, where the waves wash up on the sand. They are important prey species for a variety of shore birds, shallow water fish, and marine mammals, including sea otters. Sand crabs filter feed by waving their feather duster-like antennae through the water to catch plankton. As they feed, sand crabs often ingest parasite eggs and microplastics, which may be harmful to the sand crabs' predators. Students use dissection tools and microscopes to identify parasite eggs and microplastic fibers in the guts of the sand crab specimens. As they cut and probe, students record data and observations in their lab notebooks. The notebooks are also filled with students' colorful diagrams and notes describing sand crab anatomy, life cycles, and feeding behavior, which they have learned about over the past three weeks to prepare for the day's dissection.

The Pacific Grove Museum's LiMPETS (Long-Term Monitoring Program and Experiential Training For Students) brings students to the beach or sand crabs into the classroom, where students become citizen scientists, collecting real data that will be entered in a statewide database. For most of these summer school students, this is their first dissection and their first time using a microscope.

"Check it out! I think I found a parasite egg!" said one dissector. "This is so cool!"

Donations provide the backbone to the Museum's LiMPETS program, allowing us to get into more classrooms and bring more students to the coast! Find out more at pgmuseum.org/limpets-citizen-science/.

Memories of the 'Kissing Booth'
Jessica Faddis
Events and Membership Coordinator

I have always had a love of nature and history, but had never felt the responsibility to further my efforts in the conservation of our natural world until I began working here. I began with the Museum in August 2016 as the Events and Membership Coordinator, as well as the Store Manager. Not having been to the Museum since I was in elementary school, I had very little knowledge of how much outreach and stewardship our Museum has done and continues to do for Monterey County. It didn't take long for me to feel attached and enthusiastic for the new community of volunteers, staff, and museum guests I was becoming a part of.

On the day of my interview for this job, the old Light Up Gem and Mineral Case had an electrical fire. When I shared the news of my new job, that old "kissing booth" was the only memory my father had of this place, other than it was filled with taxidermy. Months later, on a Sunday afternoon, the case was replaced—thanks to the help of Carmel Valley Gem and Mineral Society—with a motion-sensor wall case. The original case was very unforgiving, built similarly to a photo booth, limiting who could see how the rocks glowed under black light. Minutes after installation, a seven-year-old wheelchair-bound girl with a love for rocks entered the Museum. It was in those following ten minutes I saw why our Museum mattered. Her face gleamed as she watched the lights come on. A fun, memorable exhibit piece now had new life and had already built new memories. Even though our Museum was first opened over 100 years ago, new knowledge is still discovered and shared within these walls.

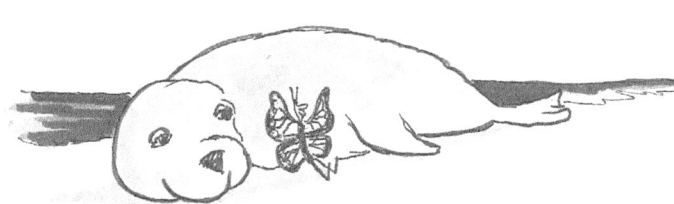

The Cultural Connection
Nate King
Collections Registrar

I hail from about as different an environment from Pacific Grove as one could imagine: the tiny town of Borrego Springs, Callifornia, nestled in the heart of the sprawling Anza Borrego Desert State Park. Being surrounded by wilderness, and having parents that valued it, I was outside from as early as I can remember, scrambling over boulders in foothill canyons and speculating whether deep holes in the dunes were coyote or badger dens. My mom taught me to keep my eyes on the ground: potsherds, arrowheads, beads, manos and metates were constantly being exposed by the shifting sand, and there was always the chance of stumbling upon rock art gracing an unassuming rock face.

Something about coming in contact with the people of the past in this way, without interpretive panels or docents as middlemen, affected me deeply. So naturally I was drawn to museums. I wanted to expand my knowledge of the incredible diversity of the human experience. I wanted to be a part of these places and just maybe pass that profound realization on to someone else.

That said, my arrival at the Pacific Grove Museum of Natural History was pure serendipity. I had been living in the area for a few years, working as a school librarian, but I didn't feel like I was making an impact or fully utilizing my skills in that capacity.

It just so happened that an old family friend from Borrego was visiting, the director of the Anza Borrego Desert Natural History Association, and had decided to visit PGMNH. In a coincidence I am eternally grateful for, she struck up a conversation with our director here and mentioned that I had an interest in museum collections. It wasn't long after that I assumed my post as collections registrar and now have the privilege of working with our Museum's amazingly diverse collection. We have the unique opportunity here to communicate to our guests, and the world at large, the connections we share with the natural world and cultures around the globe through these objects that found their way to Pacific Grove.

Editor's Note: In the next few pages Nate presents photographs and commentaries on a sampling of the collection of rare—and many priceless—artifacts that for years have been gifted to the Museum, and mysteriously referred to by the public as the "Treasure Trove in the Basement."

THE "TREASURE TROVE" IN THE BASEMENT—NATE KING, COLLECTIONS REGISTRAR

Gold, silver, velvet and rhinoceros hide Abyssinian shield by Emperor Haile Selassie on the occasion of the latter's coronation in 1930. The shield came to our museum as part of the collection of Mrs. Lou Henry Hoover which also includes a wide variety of anthropological materials from China and Australia, where the Hoovers lived while Herbert worked in the mining industry.

A pair of Malaysian Kris (daggers) that came to the museum from the collection of Naval Surgeon Henry Edward Odell. Kris were generally never intended to be used and instead served as a status symbol or talisman, thought to be endowed with supernatural powers and sometimes forged with inclusions of meteoritic iron. Odell served in the South Pacific in the early 20th century and brought home a large and diverse collection of anthropological materials from many different cultures in the region.

Blackware olla by the master potter Maria Martinez of San Ildefonso Pueblo, New Mexico. The black coloration is achieved through temperature control during the firing process and the reflective gunmetal finish is typical of the irreplicable works of her late career.

A Zuni Pueblo pot from the collection of, and an interpretive drawing of the same by Pedro deLemos. Though best known for his depictions of the central coast, deLemos also had a keen interest in Native American arts and traveled the southwest collecting and studying the work of potters in particular. He donated several of his acquisitions to our museum.

Haida chest acquired by Dr. Harold Heath in British Columbia's Queen Charlotte (now Haida Gwaii) Islands. Heath was instrumental in establishing our museum's early collections and exhibits in the 1920's and 30's. At the time the world's foremost expert on invertebrate embryology, he was also an avid collector of anthropological materials.

Mounted Golden Eagle specimen collected by Dr. C.E. Marshall. As large and comprehensive as our bird exhibit is, we have many more specimens that have yet to be seen by the public.

Western Apache coiled basket donated to the museum by Mrs. V.G. Larsen. Our museum has a large collection of Native American basketry from across the western states.

Inuit raincoat of seal gut, trimmed with seal fur. We have a significant collection of anthropological material from Northern Alaska, a product of a several significant artic researchers who retired in our community.

A Skate specimen collected and prepared by Dr. Harold Heath. Heath designed and fabricated many displays during his time at the museum, some of which are still on exhibit today.

Mesolithic tools from Northern Europe. This particular collection was donated to the museum in the 1950's. Our mission statement today guides us to acquire only objects related to the natural and cultural history of the central coast, but for much of our history our acquisitions were somewhat more eclectic.

*All photographs by Nate King.

424   *Life in Pacific Grove, California*

SECTION 11
WALKING TOUR OF
OUR LITTLE FREE LIBRARIES

Pick up free Pacific Grove street maps at the
Chamber office located at the corner of
Central and Forest Avenues,
and at the Tourist Information Center
on Central and Eardley Avenues.

"TAKE ONE – LEAVE ONE" — PHYLLIS EDWARDS

WELCOME, Readers, to one of the great pleasures of living in a small town in an area that enjoys pleasant weather virtually year-round! While every nook and cranny of Pacific Grove bears its own delights, as an avid walker, I usually avoid strolling through the bustle and noise of Pacific Grove's commercial zone, frequenting instead areas not as well known by those without my penchant for rambling several miles a day. One of the most pleasant surprises revealed by my recent wanderings was the discovery of the many Little Free Libraries that grace the streets of our little town. I was first introduced to the concept of the Little Free Libraries on a San Francisco walk with my friend, Disa Lindquist, who haunts the offerings in her great city and neighborhoods. That introduction inspired my quest to locate and document all the Little Free Libraries that currently exist in America's Last Hometown.

While I don't pretend to have located every Little Free Library in Pacific Grove, I have walked a high percentage of its streets and used some online resources to find others I had not encountered on my own. In the process of collecting information around town, I have discovered a few brand-new Little Free Libraries that did not exist during my previous walks and were not noted at the websites I used. My goal is that the following may serve as a tour guide to at least those in existence today with a hope that you may find others that have been contributed to our collection since this chapter was written. Please bear in mind that all references to cardinal directions for these tours are approximate to indicate that the main boulevards of Pacific Grove run roughly east-to-west while crossroads run roughly north-to-south.

What is a Little Free Library?

According to the Little Free Library website (https://**littlefreelibrary**.org/), "A Little Free Library is a 'take a book, return a book' free book exchange. The libraries come in many shapes and sizes, but the most common version is a small wooden box of books. Anyone may take a book or bring a book to share."

While most of Pacific Grove's Little Free Libraries appear to be members of the Little Free Library online organization, boasting Charter membership numbers and its traditional note "Take a Book Return a Book," a few seem to have been created independently and bear neither Charter number nor other evidence of affiliation. Many, but not all, of the library boxes seem to have been constructed from kits from the Little Free Library online organization that also offers signs that indicate the library's affiliation with the organization. You will see more details about the signs in the descriptions of appropriate libraries mentioned throughout our tour.

Each Little Free Library I found in Pacific Grove, with one exception (#14925 at Pacific Grove Middle School), is located on or at the edge of a private property, has been lovingly styled, and is managed by the owner as an expression of his or her love of books.

The Pacific Grove Public Library

We would be seriously remiss if we didn't start our tour of the libraries in Pacific Grove with a visit to the grand old Pacific Grove Public Library located at the very center of town at 550 Central Avenue between Grove and Forest Avenues, with Jewell Park at its left and kitty-corner from the Pacific Grove Museum of Natural History. One of many partially funded Carnegie Libraries of California, the Pacific Grove Public Library was constructed in 1908 in the Mission style so suitable for our area and later enlarged in several styles until modified in 1981 to boast a steep gable roof that unifies the whole.

The Pacific Grove Public Library contains a collection of approximately 99,000 volumes, including more than 25,000 books for children and young adults and 3,500 large-type books, as well many helpful services to meet the needs of its patrons.

The Little Free Libraries of Pacific Grove

The remainder of this chapter describes 31 Little Free Libraries located, for the most part, in and within walking distance of each other in five areas of town, starting with those closest to the Pacific Grove Public Library and then progressing to other areas of town in a sequence that I hope will assist readers in exploring the Little Free Libraries around town in an organized fashion. Each of five section labels provides a brief description of the area's location identified in part by the City of Pacific Grove Neighborhood Planning Map and some pointers to aid readers in locating each Little Free Library within the area.

DOWNTOWN RETREAT, AND SECOND ADDITION AREAS

109 FOREST AVENUE

SERENDIPITOUSLY, the very first Little Free Library I encountered in Pacific Grove appears first in our tour. Walking down Forest Avenue from the Pacific Grove Public Library northward toward the Recreation Trail that runs along Ocean View Boulevard, you will come to 109 Forest Avenue and its Little Free Library that displays the typical white sign indicating the Charter number #12499 with an image of a park bench beside a Little Free Library and the usual top note, "Take a Book Return a Book." The library box itself, however, does not appear to have been constructed from a kit such as those available via the Little Free Library online organization; it is rather small and is topped with an asphalt-tiled shed roof. An unusual exterior feature found at only three Little Free Libraries in Pacific Grove is attached by a wire to the side of this box: a paper note that explains "How This Library Works" and, in this case, is plastic-covered and has gotten a little tattered due to weather.

The builder of this Little Free Library devoted considerable attention to expressing an artistic flair via the marine blue exterior and white roof that match the color scheme of the house beside which it stands, the rather eccentric door handle on the library that is constructed of four el-sections of steel piping clasped together to form an image that resembles a Celtic cross and painted dark copper color, and the ocean shell decorations of the varnished wooden window frame, many of which have fallen or been taken off so the pattern of the shells is a challenge to discern.

The interior of the box contains one shelf created by the bottom of the box and an additional white shelf that extends about 2/3 of the distance across the interior of the box. When I visited this library last, books that stood across the bottom shelf or lay on top of the 2/3 shelf in two deep layers offered such literary treats as the following: several Janet Evanovich mysteries, all titled with numbers: *One for the Money, Two for the Dough*, etc., *Dead or Alive* by Tom Clancy, a couple of John Grisham books, a Mary Higgins Clark, and some nature books.

After discovering the sweet treasure at 109 Forest Avenue, I became intrigued about the possibility of other Little Free Libraries lurking around town and began to include searches for more in my meanderings around Pacific Grove. While the first library is located at a distance of several blocks westward from the downtown area of town, I soon found that many more could be perused within a few blocks in a more southerly direction.

To reach the next Little Free Library on our tour, return along Forest Avenue to the main thoroughfare of Pacific Grove, Lighthouse Avenue, and turn right. After proceeding several blocks westward through the commercial part of town, turn left onto Lobos Avenue where a more residential section of town begins and the next Little Free Library on our tour appears.

231 LOBOS AVENUE

At 231 Lobos Avenue you will discover a pleasant surprise. An especially attractive feature of this library is its special location at its site. The owner of this library clearly wants visitors to feel welcome, not only to the library but also to the home. To enjoy the library, you must open a gate, step inside the front yard of the home, walk down a little stone walkway amidst drought-tolerant plantings, and open the large, un-windowed door by means of a hook latch at the side of the box.

The exterior of this Little Free Library boasts a nice, natural wood finish with a plain, unvarnished or painted plywood open gable roof decorated by a cute little metal multi-colored heart screwed to the front of the roof ridge. This Little Free Library is clearly homemade, not from a kit such as those offered by the Little Free Library online organization; it is obviously made from scrap wood that probably did not cost a penny nor require chopping down any trees. The box is taller than most, nicely proportioned, and contains two shelves, one of which in the center of the box is constructed of very thin plywood. This library is, however, a member of the Little Free Library Charter, as evidenced by a two-part version of the usual Charter sign attached to the front of the box that displays the Charter number #6056, the Little Free Library online organization's URL, images of a park bench and a Little Free Library, a statement similar to one seen at the Little Free Library at 330 Gibson Avenue: "CELEBRATING HEALTHIER NEIGHBORHOODS," as well as the usual reminder to "Take a Book Return a Book."

Other unique features of this Little Free Library include a plastic sleeve tacked inside the door that contains a copy of the instructions "How This Library Works" that is also found at a few other Little Free Libraries in town, and a little greeting card that exhibits the quotation attributed to Cicero that also appears on the Little Free Library at 310 Locust Street: "If you have a garden and a library, you have everything you need."

Inside this Little Free Library, you might find such treasures as: *The Chalice and the Blade* by Riane Eisler, a Judy Blume book, a Webster's dictionary (very small version), one James Patterson, something called *Little Boy Blue* by Kim Cavin, a Nora Roberts, and *Singing in the Shrouds* by Ngaio Marsh.

Little Library Bonanza!

To reach the incomparable treasure in Pacific Grove that I call The Little Free Library BONANZA!, return northward and downhill along Lobos Avenue less than one block until it meets Short Street. Turn left on Short Street and proceed to its intersection with Granite Street where you will encounter a collection of no less than seven Little Free Libraries (or similar structures) which offer a plethora of unique construction styles all dedicated to the sharing of reading material to any visitor to the area.

As you begin your exploration of the BONANZA!, however, you might find of interest the following backstory about the explosion of Little Free Libraries here. I encountered Don Livermore and his neighbor Bill chatting in the middle of Short Street one weekend day and a fellow book-lover can only imagine my delight at the opportunity this meeting presented. When I introduced myself and explained my interest in how the Little Free Libraries that graced their neighborhood came about, the two men responded, in unison with, "Collaboration."

The two men promptly introduced themselves as scavengers who enjoy using their ample collections of accumulated materials to add various structures and ornamentations to their properties. The duo then proceeded to gleefully recount the origin of the Little Free Library at the corner of 232 Granite Street as a prime example of such a project. As I would soon discover, however, the history of any project undertaken by these handymen, along with another neighbor, Lorna, is contingent upon their boundless curiosity and the exuberant creativity their adventures inspire in them. Before the germ of a Little Free Library had begun to crystalize in the fertile minds of Don and Bill and Bill's wife Betty, news about a Pacific Grove Heritage Society award to local architect Robert Gunn reached them. When the three attended the awards ceremony, they noticed that there were birdhouses and the like on display, but not one Little Free Library; such a unique structure evidently required a special award. In response to such inspiration the three creators agreed that they could gleefully build Little Free Libraries that they call book boxes and thus the project was conceived.

This tale of ingenuity continues below as part of the introduction to each of the components of the BONANZA!

232 GRANITE STREET

The original concept for the Little Free Library at 232 Granite was to mirror the form of the beautiful home in which Bill and Betty lived, but such a design failed to adequately stimulate Betty's fecund imagination. "What about the cupola?" she proposed, referring to a 100-year-old cupola from the dome of an ancient barn she and Bill had discovered somewhere in the Santa Clara Valley on one of their invigorating excursions. As thought is often father to action, the first Little Free Library enterprise for the BONANZA! was launched.

While the cupola was in terrible repair at the start of the project, Bill knew that he could apply his carpentry skills and those of his neighbor, Don, to salvage the flavor of the old tower's charming crown. First, they lined the interior of the box to prevent rain and fog moisture, formerly admitted through the sturdy louvers on each side of the cupola that originally performed the function of ventilation for the old building's interior, from damaging the books that would soon reside inside. An old sheet of Plexiglas was utilized to serve as windows, a fence beam became the support for the book box, and shelf-holders and other surplus lumber and paint perfected the presentation. With the exception of one hinge that had to be purchased from the local hardware store and the decorative sign Betty designed and ordered online, the entire project was manufactured from 100% recycled materials, a great source of pride to the builders and their neighbors.

The Little Free Library at 232 Granite Street sits kitty-corner with Short Street. Due to its pretty little oval sign that resembles those offered at the Little Free Library online organization website, this Little Free Library gives the impression that it is a member of the Charter. On closer inspection and as verified by Bill, however, its independence from the Charter can be discerned in that it is smaller in overall size than most libraries built from kits offered at the Little Free Library online organization and the invitation issued on its sign explains to the visitor: FREE LIBRARY TAKE ONE – LEAVE ONE.

The rather elaborate exterior finish style of this Little Free Library presents an earthy green body bordered with a maroon hip roof and doorframe, golden hinges on its door, monarch butterfly decals beside its welcoming sign, and a shiny golden sphere with a tall spire atop the steeply-sloped box cable roof.

While this Little Free Library contains only one very small shelf inside, books are actually stacked in two layers, one row in back and another in front, thereby housing more books than one might expect at first glance. While this arrangement requires a bit of digging to explore all the literary delights offered inside, on my last visit I encountered several hardback books and the following: *Madeline's Kitchen* by Madeline Kamman with introduction by James Beard that probably contains a lot of good recipes, *The Last Picture Show* by Larry McMurtry, one of the Camel Club books by David Baldacci, *In the Company of Liars* by David Ellis, *I Hate Everyone, Starting with Me* by Joan Rivers, and *A Hundred Years of Adventure and Discovery* by National Geographic.

231 GRANITE STREET

As soon as Bill and Betty's neighbor across Granite Street laid eyes on the Little Free Library at 232, they knew they must have a similar structure at 231, perhaps in the form of a birdhouse. Their son won the day, however, by insisting that the form of their Little Free Library must resemble the lighthouse at nearby Point Pinos. Thus inspired, Don and Bill immediately got to work, using scrap wood for the principal shape of the box, a piece of plastic for the roof, and Bill's handcrafted window frames for the door and sides of the structure. The crowning glory of the whole emerged when Don found a little outdoor light powered by a solar feed panel that he located at the very top of the roof and devised an apparatus to spin the light merrily as it shines its warm welcome throughout the night. The only hitch in the process resulted when the tiny light proved to shed far too much light for neighbors to sleep at night, so Bill had to obscure the beam by painting half of the bulb black, to the relief of slumberers in the nearby homes.

The Little Free Library at 231 Granite Street displays a small, very clean white box with a model of a lighthouse sitting at the ridge of its black asphalt-finished box gable roof. The designer of this Little Free Library, while apparently preferring a simple, clean style of finish in some ways, nonetheless incorporated details that distinguish this library from others: black, imitation four-mullioned windows on all sides of the box with two sets of real, black-framed mullioned windows offering views into the interior via the front door.

While this Little Free Library does not resemble those constructed from kits offered by the Little Free Library online organization in dimension and size, it does display its own version of a Little Free Library welcome: "FREE LIBRARY TAKE ONE, LEAVE ONE" and its single interior shelf proudly accommodates a confident collection of hardback books. When I visited this Little Free Library last, I found the following literary gems: one Reader's Digest Condensed book, *The Simple Truth* by David Baldachi, *Lords of the Sky: Fighter Pilots from the Red Baron to the F-16* by Dan Hampton, and *Miller's Valley* by Anna Quindlen.

The next stop on our tour of the BONANZA! is the Little Free Library located across the street and a few steps northward down Granite Street.

226 GRANITE STREET

For his own corner of the BONANZA! at 226 Granite Street, next door to (and across Short Street from) Bill and Betty's, Don decided to repurpose a birdhouse he had previously designed. Using scrap lumber, leftover paint, an extra hunk of 4x4 lumber for support, and other decorative oddments for charm, the exquisite styling of the resulting Little Free Library provides only a brief glimpse into Don's and his neighbor Bill's creative flair.

Clearly not made from a kit such as those offered at the Little Free Library online organization, this library is taller than most and its structure bears a sharply-peaked steeply-sloped box gable roof with a copper face and decorated by an imitation lantern hanging from its ridge over the front door. The marine blue exterior with white trim is decorated with red decals and an arched mullioned window in the front door. Typical of Don, this Little Free Library sits next to another decorative structure, in this case a grotto and bench that were constructed apparently long before the libraries caught Don's fancy.

The ample height of this Little Free Library allows for two tall white shelves that, on the day of my last visit, housed such tomes as *Awaken the Giant Within* by Anthony Robbins, *The Children's Book* by A.S. Byatt, a book about Lyndon Johnson entitled *Master of the Senate* by Robert A. Caro, *American Cooking*, part of a Time/Life cookbook set, and *The Idiot's Guide to Italian*.

While Don's talent at embellishment and personal expression has been evident from the Little Free Library located in front of his home, just around the corner on the un-numbered Short Street, you will find three Little Free Libraries that outshine even Don's initial contributions to the abundant array of the Little Free Libraries of Pacific Grove.

Once Don and Bill were on a roll with their small structures, it proceeds, as night follows day, that their minds would quickly concoct new fabrication adventures. As a former school librarian, Don could not resist the urge to expand the offerings of Little Free Libraries to serve the needs of the youth in his neighborhood. Hence, across from Bill and Betty's home on Short Street, separated by a toy railroad track encircling a village of fantastic creatures, serenaded by a rock fountain and pond, appears Don's fantastic Children's Little Free Library. The process of rebuilding the railroad that Don had constructed several years earlier led to the notion of building a comical ticket booth to house books and labeling it the "Reading Railroad Ticket Booth." What else?!

SHORT STREET BONANZA!

Not surprisingly, what first caught my eye about the Reading Railroad Ticket Booth was the whimsical decorations and size of the structure. Clearly not constructed from any kit from the Little Free Library online organization or any blueprint other than that in Don's mind, the unusually tall, wide, bright yellow ticket booth boasts an extreme sharply peaked hip-and-valley style roof finished with white, irregularly placed shingled wooden slats, bordered with vivid turquoise ridges. A dramatic orange-mullioned window, offering an enticing ticket slot at child's hand-height, accompanies the Cheshire cat-handled door to the interior and matches faux windows on the other two "wings" of the booth. Above the face of the attic level of the booth, along a turquoise bordering path sits a small red locomotive replica to draw the visitor's attention toward the railroad track reproduction that runs at the right of the booth. As a final, climactic touch, one imitation lantern hangs jauntily from the end of the turquoise bordering path while another sprouts from the upper face of the roof attic level, providing a crowning glory to the most colorful and playful Little Free Library in town.

Inside the Reading Railroad Ticket Booth, obviously designed to attract the eyes and minds of passing youngsters, a single white shelf consisting of the bottom of the library's box offered a small collection of appropriately-aged literature the last time I visited, including: *Snappy Little Snow Time* by Derek Matthews, *Over the River and Through the Wood*, *First Look and Find*, *I Can Do It!*, *Alice's Adventures in Wonderland*, and several read-alouds, one about volcanoes, as well as several others that kids can read on their own.

Just a few steps to the right along Short Street, Don placed another of the two Little Free Libraries dedicated to offering reading material for the under-adult set.

SHORT STREET BONANZA!

The Reading Railroad Ticket Booth's popularity with the town's children and young adults soon proved inadequate to store and offer enough books for both sets of clients. To address this pressing need, the ever-industrious Don once again explored his yard sale finds and unearthed the partly assembled mechanism for a grandfather clock that he knew he could transform into a Little Free Library for young adults. After repairing the door, constructing an upper portion to house clock workings found among his stash, inserting new batteries, adorning the structure with a color scheme that corresponds to that of the Reading Railroad Ticket Booth, and installing a chime inside the clock to sound on the hour as the train passes, Don declared the youthful segment of his Little Free Library complete.

The Young People's Little Free Library is obviously one-of-a-kind, clearly not built from a kit such as those offered by the Little Free Library online organization. Its very tall, narrow structure resembles a bright yellow grandfather clock with blue trim and includes a functioning clock face above the door and beneath the split-pediment or swan's neck top. This grandiose construction, decorated in bright colors and detailed borders, houses three narrow shelves visible through the long window of the front entrance door where, when I last visited the site, I found several works that might appeal to a young teenager, including: *Love Must be Tough* by Dr. James Dobson and *Methuselah's Children* by Robert A. Heinlein.

Another few steps to the right along Short Street, perhaps the most unique Little Free Library in town appears. I remember walking by one day some time after I had examined the Reading Railroad Ticket Booth and the Young People's Little Free Library and exclaiming internally with surprise, "There's another one!" as no doubt many other Pagrovians

did at the sight of yet another concoction sprouting up on this modest street.

SHORT STREET BONANZA!

Despite Bill's belief that Don must be related to Mrs. Winchester of the Winchester Mystery House in San Jose and his attempts to curtail his friend's incessant inventiveness, Don deemed the Little Free Library Wagon next on his agenda, justifying his plans with the comment, "We had so many paperbacks." While the structure of the low, flat 1800s Amish wagon Don bought in Moss Landing years ago was convenient for paperback storage, Don declared that the structure was unfinished at the time the writing of this chapter began and undertook several modifications and embellishments: Because "older people" complained that it was too hard to get the paperbacks out of the small drawer, a "nice slider" was installed "so oldies can get their books easily." To complete the appearance of the structure as an old-fashioned sales wagon, atop the current structure Don installed brightly colored crates to house CDs and DVDs and a market umbrella to shelter the entire assemblage.

The wide, low trailer that houses this Little Free Library Wagon, boasting a hand-lettered and carved black-outlined red sign that advertises, "PAPER BACKS," could be towed by a car or truck and one can imagine it serving well as a portable library to supply the temporary reading needs of a bookish road warrior. Its bright red exterior with big, white Conestoga-type wheels and flat copper top, has a front flop-down windowed door affording access to the treasures housed in one very shallow drawer inside that pulls out to contain about a dozen paperback volumes in one or two inch deep layers.

Finally, the magazine box at Lorna's 227 Granite Street house appears directly across from Don's home and concludes our tour of the Little Free Library BONANZA!

227 GRANITE STREET

In response to Lorna's enthusiastic reaction to the book boxes on the other corners of the intersection and along the branch of Short Street that runs between Don's and Bill's homes, the final fabrication would continue the neighborhood tradition of themed constructions by taking the form of a British phone booth. Bill immediately suggested using panels he found in his materials assortment that he could reconstruct into the tall, multi-windowed, bright red structure that you see today. In response to her comment, "I like to read books but also like entertainment reading such as magazines and all kinds of different stuff," Lorna's Little Free Library would actually be a Little Free Magazine Library that would also house catalogs and other non-book reading materials.

The athenaeum located at 227 Granite Street warrants the expected label Little Free Library only in that it contains reading material. In other ways, this surprising depository should be more accurately identified according to the characterization it displays on the sign it bears: "MAGAZINES FREE LIBRARY."

While this exclusive Little Free Library is located across the street from Don's residence rather than on his property, it strongly resembles the creative flair he and Bill apply to all their creations. The very tall, bright red structure, with three large, wide clear windows down its front and each side and a monarch butterfly decal with "Pacific Grove" written on its wings on the center front window, and topped with a curved metal, bright red bonnet roof, is flanked by two large potted succulent plants. The three ample red shelves inside this library contain a hodge-podge of magazines and catalogs representing an assortment of publishers and likely to appeal to patrons with a variety of tastes.

One final note: When I asked Don, Bill, and Lorna why none of the Little Free Libraries in the BONANZA! was built from a kit available at the Little Free Library online organization website and none were Charter members, their united response was, "We're not joiners." "Everything we make is recycled," Lorna emphasized. Don summarized the trio's philosophy and explained their visionary gifts to Pacific Grove with, "We do this for the city, the love of books, and to increase reading."

From the intimate proximity of the BONANZA! Little Free Libraries of Granite and Short Streets, to return to the narrower world of solo Little Free Libraries holding court individually over their isolated locations, proceed westward up Short Street and turn left at its junction with Locust Street. Then continue a block and a half southward up the hill and away from the downtown section of town.

310 LOCUST STREET

As you approach 310 Locust Street, your attention will be drawn to the brightly colored hand-painted image, mostly in blues and greens, of a large mermaid lounging amidst seaweed with a variety of sea life surrounding her and completely covering the garage door of the home. The Little Free Library that stands next to the garage, clearly homemade and thus distinguishable from the many that appear elsewhere in town that are made from kits available at the Little Free Library online organization's website, bears more hand-painted close-up views of some of the details featured on the garage door, crowned by a sharply-pointed gable roof bordered in blue. Above the door of this small library is a hand-written quotation attributed to Cicero and sure to touch the heart of any gardening booklover, "If you have a garden and a library, you have everything you need." This Little Free Library lacks a sign that would attribute its Charter membership number or other affiliation with the Little Free Library online organization. Instead, above and below its door is the simple inscription: "Please Take a Book; Little Library."

The interior of the library, which cannot be seen through the solid wooden door, contains only one small shelf whereon dwelt, last time I visited, a variety of books mostly appealing to the adult palate, but presenting a rather broad range of tastes. There was a Danielle Steel, a David Wroblewski, a children's thesaurus, and one volume about how to write good résumés.

If you continue uphill along Locust Street, cross Pine Avenue, and turn left, you will, after five blocks, arrive at the intersection with Cypress Avenue and the next stop on our Little Free Library tour.

UP THE HILL FROM TOWN TO THE THIRD AND FIFTH ADDITIONS

725 PINE AVENUE

The Little Free Library at 725 Pine Avenue is a very tidy little Library that, by its size and general structure appears to have been constructed using a kit such as those available from the Little Free Library online organization. Its location, however, distinguishes it from most of the libraries in Pacific Grove in that it sits at an angle across the corner of Pine and Cypress Avenues instead of directly in front of the domicile where the owner resides, as if to invite visitors from both Pine and Cypress Avenues to stop and browse. The front exterior of the box is painted a very light gray to match the picket fence that surrounds the house; the sides are yellow to match the walls of the home; the windowed doors to the interior sport a light, refreshing green to match the window trim of the home, while black screws accentuate the structure of the doors as well as ornate brass hinges, spherical doorknobs, and a cheerful red adorns the asphalt-tiled open gable roof. At the time of my last visit to this library, the entire structure was festooned with white holiday lights perhaps in celebration of the winter season.

Like many of the Little Free Libraries in Pacific Grove, this one displays the typical Little Free Library online organization sign with the usual label, "Little Free Library" and its URL, plus the less common appellation, "We all do better when we all read better" below the main label, and the less common note, "Support Your Non Profit." At the end of the sign sit images of a tree shading a park bench that contains a couple of books and a Little Free Library at the end of the bench, below which the Charter number #28643 is displayed.

The two shelves inside this Library contained an interesting collection of books when I last checked, including a couple of Robert Louis Stevenson classics, *Kidnapped* and *Treasure Island*, a parenting guide: *What to Expect the First Year*, *Uncommon Fruits Worthy of Attention, A Gardener's Guide*, a student's dictionary, and almost two dozen children's/teen's books.

For the next stop in our tour of Little Free Libraries of Pacific Grove, travel westward along Pine Avenue until you reach Walnut Street, turn left and proceed uphill southward a couple of blocks until you arrive at the intersection with Junipero Avenue. There you will encounter the Little Free Library established by the owners of the home at number 850.

850 JUNIPERO AVENUE

Much like the Little Free Library at 725 Pine Avenue, the location of the one at 850 Junipero Avenue can be somewhat confusing to the first-time visitor because it actually sits on the Walnut Street side of the house, rather than on the Junipero Avenue side. The box of the library appears to dangle from a rough wooden fence that encloses the side yard on Walnut Street and hangs over a white prop that supports the structure at an angle.

While this Little Free Library's shallow size argues that it was not constructed from a kit offered at the Little Free Library online organization, a stainless steel sign sits at a jaunty side position and displays the URL, the usual "Take a Book Return a Book" note, the Charter number #30502, and images of a tree shading a park bench that offers a couple of books and a Little Free Library beside it. The exterior of this Little Free Library is painted white, its single mullioned window trimmed in dark marine blue, and its dark gray asphalt-tiled open gable roof offer a pleasingly simple, tidy presentation.

Despite its otherwise modest appearance, this Little Free Library housed two wide but shallow shelves of interesting literature, at the time of my last visit: one by Donna Liere, Tom Brokaw's *The Greatest Generation*, a Danielle Steel, *Killing Lincoln* by Dan O'Reilly, *Last Bus to Wisdom* by one of my favorite American authors, Ivan Doig (his last before he died in 2015), *Take Me With You* by Katherine Ryan Hyde, and several children's books.

For the next stop on our Little Free Libraries tour, proceed eastward along Junipero Avenue until you reach its intersection with Park Street. Turn left and continue northward about a half block until you reach number 514 on the west side of the street. Keep a sharp eye open because this Little Free Library is easy to miss.

514 PARK STREET

You may have to search a bit to locate this home's darling Little Free Library because it is almost completely hidden in the branches of a huge holly tree with its prickly leaves and bright red berries and snuggled tightly against the wooden fence of the neighboring yard. This very small Little Free Library sports a brown stained wooden exterior with pretty little flower decals on one side partially hidden in the branches of the holly tree.

While the box for this library is smaller than any I've seen in town with the possible exception of the one at 109 Forest Avenue, it does display a Little Free Library online organization sign with its URL, images of a tree beside a park bench bearing a few books and next to a Little Free Library, the number #26969, the typical "Take a Book Return a Book" note, as well as one reminding us that "We all do better when we all read better" and another to "Support our Non Profit." Tacked to the fence is a note, apparently from the Charter and like those I have seen at a handful of libraries in town, that explains how a Little Free Library works.

This Little Free Library derives a rather playful appearance from its slanted flat roof and off-kilter shelves inside. The top shelf is considerably taller than the lower shelf, which is so short that regular-sized paperbacks cannot stand and must be stacked or tipped to the side to fit. At my last visit, the two shelves contained more hardbacks than I have usually found in Little Free Libraries, among them *Hide and Seek* by James Patterson, and *By a Spider's Thread* by Laura Lippman. Among the paperbacks, I saw *Gun Games* by Faye Kellerman and *A Hovering of Vultures* by Robert Barnard.

While it may seem redundant, to reach our next stop you will need to retrace your steps by returning southward up Park Street, turning westward along Junipero Avenue, and continuing about three blocks until you reach Lobos Avenue, at which point you will turn right and walk uphill southward a few steps to number 616 on the western side of the street.

616 LOBOS AVENUE

At 616 Lobos Avenue, another Little Free Library that bears no indication of affiliation with the Little Free Library online organization sits partly on the usual waist-high post and partly on the property fence next to the home of the owner of the library. This small, yet uniquely structured library sports bright lavender double doors surrounded by an earth-green frame topped by a flat roof bearing tidy wooden tiles of the same color as the frame and decorated by miniscule black bird figurines perched along the ridge line.

Inside this library you will encounter a tall lower shelf and a shorter upper shelf made of smoothly finished wood that matches the color of neither the exterior walls nor doors of the box but that, at my last visit, contained a smattering of interesting literature, including: *The Re-enrichment of Everyday Life*, *Watership Down*, *The No. 1 Ladies' Detective Agency*, and an autographed copy of *The Immigration Debate: Remaking America* by John Isbister, published in 1996.

Continuing southward a block and a half up Lobos Avenue will bring you to Sinex Avenue, one of the several wide, graceful thoroughfares that run east-west to transect the central part of Pacific Grove. About four blocks after you cross and then turn right onto Sinex will bring you to the next Little Free Library on the south side of the avenue near its intersection with Locust Street.

847 SINEX AVENUE

The charmingly primitive Little Free Library at 847 Sinex Avenue boasts neither a Charter number nor its usually accompanying sign telling visitors to "Take a Book Return a Book." Instead, a roughly painted slab of wood is tied by coarse strands of rope to the plain, unvarnished wooden fence above and behind the Little Free Library and bears the crude, handwritten note "FREE BOOKS," while the library box itself stands a bit askew on three rocky chunks of concrete that lift the whole just a few inches above the grassy, uncultivated berm outside the fence.

This Little Free Library, obviously not constructed from a kit such as those offered at the Little Free Library online organization website, is exceptionally tall and bears a graceful, arched green-copper mullioned window with a cream-colored border that serves as the entry door to the interior that provides ample space for free books on its three tall shelves. The rough wooden frame of the exterior is crowned by a simple, unshingled open gable roof.

The interesting selection of literature I found upon my last visit to this Little Free Library included *Next* by Michael Crichton, *The Help* by Kathryn Stockett (source of the film adaptation of same name), *The Other Barack, The Bold and Reckless Life of President Obama's Father* by Sally Jacobs, a James Patterson novel, *The Lord of the Rings*, and *Julie of the Wolves*.

For our next stop, continue less than a block to the west along the south side of Sinex Avenue to find 895 Sinex Avenue just a few steps past the intersection with Alder Street that runs along the eastern border of George Washington Park.

895 SINEX AVENUE

Evidence indicating that the Little Free Library at this site is a member of the Little Free Library online organization includes a typical white sign telling visitors to "Take a Book Return a Book" and the display of the Charter number #24617, the URL of the website, and images of a park bench holding a stack of books and a Little Free Library.

The anatomy of the library itself, however, does not indicate that a kit was employed for its construction. While very tiny, the pleasant little box is color-coordinated with the home of its owner by means of a heavy, broad, white-painted unshingled lean-to roof sheltering an olive green exterior with a wide white-and-red framed window in the door to the interior, lending the box a light-hearted, rather rakish appearance.

Due to its modest stature, this Little Free Library contains only one shelf, using the bottom of the box itself to exhibit a diverse collection of books. Those available at my last visit to this site included: *The Soldier's Wife* by Joanna Trollope, a couple of Belva Plain books, *The Guernsey Literary and Potato Peel Pie Society* by Annie Barrows and Mary Ann Shaffer, a *Publication Manual for the American Psychology Association*, a book about modern China, an obviously well-used book entitled *America Through Foreign Eyes 1827—1842: Source Material for Freshman Research Papers*, and a tiny paperback called *Bible Teach*.

The next stop on our Little Free Library tour continues through the western residential section of town that is called Pacific Grove Acres. A pleasant route to this area is a refreshing walk through George Washington Park via one of several north-south running pathways that start at the corner of Alder Street and Sinex Avenue, cross Pine Avenue, and continue to the northern border of the park at Short Street. Westward about two blocks from the intersection of Alder and Short Streets a turn right onto Bentley Street takes you to our next stop.

PACIFIC GROVE ACRES

234 BENTLEY STREEET

Nestled at the corner of 234 Bentley Street is a cute Little Free Library whose exterior in pale green is crowned with a tidy varnished lean-to roof that matches the frame of the door, which bears a large, single-paned window. While the creator of this Little Free Library revealed a bit of artistic flair through its butterfly decal decorations, otherwise the box bears no resemblance to the décor of the home upon whose site it resides.

This library, constructed from a plan offered at the Little Free Library online organization website, is a member of the Little Free Library Charter as evidenced by the typical white sign bearing its Charter number #33134, the usual reminder to "Take a Book Return a Book," and images of a Little Free Library next to a park bench offering a few books and sheltered by a friendly tree. The resemblance of this sign with those displayed at most of the other Little Free Libraries in town ends, however, with the following mysterious appellation, not found elsewhere in Pacific Grove, across its top: Altrusa International of the Monterey Peninsula.

To solve the mystery of the Altrusa reference, about which I found very little information online, I stopped by the Little Free Library at 234 Bentley Street an extra time to see if I could learn more about the organization and its connection with the library. What a pleasure it was to meet both George and his mother, Mona, and chat with them for a few minutes! Apparently the book box is mainly Mom's project, although the delightful irony of a blind woman displaying a library in her front yard is not lost on George, who clearly contributes to her enterprise in many ways.

According to Mona, Altrusa International is a women's group focused on literacy and, "Our Altrusa is Altrusa International of the Monterey Peninsula." The organization keeps a record of Altrusa owners of Little Free Libraries to provide information about the libraries to its members. An Altrusa member or her husband made three or four Little Free Libraries in the Monterey area, George added, and provide a unique service to the collection. "They come around every couple of weeks and they take books that haven't moved and put other ones back. Or if there are boxes that are empty, they'll put more in." To Mona's delight, however, she has observed that, while a quarter of the books in her library come from Altrusa members, "the other ones are from people who just come and put them in there." Sounds like a pretty typical, well-functioning Little Free Library operation to me.

The interior of this Little Free Library contains two shelves that offer a rather exemplary miscellany of books, including a tattered copy of *Jane Eyre*, but distinguished by the unusual inclusion of cassette recordings of familiar classical music, one of which offers *Sleeping Beauty* and *Swan Lake* ballets by Tchaikovsky and another that features selections by Pachelbel, Albinoni, and Mozart.

◉ ◉ ◉

To reach the next stop on our Little Free Library tour, you must return to Short Street and continue westward, across 17-Mile Drive, and downhill until Short Street intersects with Ridge Road. After you turn right onto Ridge Road and proceed uphill the equivalent of two or three blocks, you will arrive at our next stop on the left, just before the entrance to the Monarch Grove Sanctuary.

202 RIDGE ROAD

The Little Free Library at 202 Ridge Road is the newest library in town that appeared just in time for inclusion in this chapter and bore no sign nor Charter number that would indicate membership in the Little Free Library online organization at the time of this writing. While this library is mounted on a tall fence that partially conceals a row of three houses whose entrances face the fence that marks the pathway to the Monarch Grove Sanctuary, it appears to have been constructed by the owners of number 202.

Walking along Ridge Road one day, I happened to encounter Michael, the owner of this new Little Free Library, and took advantage of the moment to ask him about his beautiful construction. He promptly explained that, as a recently retired science teacher who knew that his library needed some pruning and ascertaining that much of his trove of materials would be fine contributions to the Little Free Library collection in his little town, he determined that building a book box on the fence outside his neighborhood wall would serve his purpose. An old door from Michael's materials at hand would serve nicely as the front of his library. The addition of simple box sides, roof, floor, and interior shelves completed the arrangement and resulted in a new member of the Little Free Libraries of Pacific Grove.

This large, handsome Little Free Library is at least three feet tall, approximately 18 inches wide, and presents an all-varnished exterior that displays a large Craftsman-style mullioned window that encompasses the entire front of the box. The ample interior of this Little Free Library accommodates three nicely spaced shelves that contained, upon my last visit there, an interesting collection of literature including: *People of the Lie* by M. Scott Peck, *Painted House* by John Grisham, *Gravity's Rainbow* by Thomas Pynchon, *Vision of the Future* by Adler, *The Armies of Britain 1485-1980*, and, the only science "book," a large Scholastic magazine for students entitled *This is a Star*.

To the right of the Little Free Library at 202 Ridge Road, turn left at a sign that marks the entrance to the Monarch Grove Sanctuary and, after a leisurely stroll downhill along the meandering trail through the Sanctuary, you will arrive at Grove Acre Avenue. A left turn onto this beautiful, tree-shaded street brings you to the next Little Free Library less than a block ahead on the left side of the street.

277 GROVE ACRE

The Little Free Library at 277 Grove Acre Avenue crowned by an asphalt-tiled box gable roof, is brightly colored with ocean-wave aqua and neon green exterior and its surroundings are wildly festooned with giant, hand-painted, multi-petaled flowers nestled in the tree that shades the whole edifice. The particularly large size of this structure and its cheerful color scheme betokens a sunny-dispositioned builder who preferred to assemble and decorate a Little Free Library by hand rather than using a kit such as those offered at the Little Free Library online organization's website.

Because Grove Acre Avenue runs along the foot of the hill that incorporates the Monarch Grove Sanctuary, this Little Free Library sits several steps above street level so the builder furnished wide, boxed, loose-stone treads that lead up to two large boulders which provide a footing for the post that supports the whole and facilitate easy access to the delights offered inside the box.

This Little Free Library does boast membership with the Little Free Library Charter as evidenced by the usual white sign bearing an unusual heading, "Wellness with Toula.com," the customary "Take a Book Return a Book" instruction, the Charter number #38115, images of a cozy park bench offering a few books and sheltered by a shady tree next to a Little Free Library and, across the bottom of the sign, the bold inspiration, "Making the world a better place through empowerment and books."

The interior of this Little Free Library, admitted by means of two large doors, contains three wide neon green shelves. Upon my several visits to this library I was disappointed to see a very sparse collection of literature, a situation caused by either scant stock provided by the owner originally or lack of commerce by guests at its out-of-the-way location or a combination of the two circumstances. Upon one of my sojourns at this site, in addition to a pair of earbuds that dangled from one of the door handles, I appreciated the inclusion of several magazines, catalogs for toys, a huge coffee-table book of Claude Monet paintings, one edition of *Western Garden*, several paperbacks (some classic, some not), as well as *Photographing the Landscape*, a *Bible* with red lettered words of Jesus, *Power for Living*, a guidebook for traveling in Tanzania, a couple of Dean Koontz books, and a hefty tome about how to learn Spanish grammar.

Reaching the next stop in our tour involves a refreshing, tree-shaded stroll of about a half mile northward along Grove Acre Avenue to Dennett Street, at which intersection you turn right until you reach Evergreen Road. About a half-block along Evergreen on the right you will find the next Little Free Library in this section of Pacific Grove.

547 EVERGREEN ROAD

While it's easy to tell that the Little Free Library at 547 Evergreen Road is a member of the Charter related to the Little Free Library online organization as evidenced by its little white sign bearing images of a little park bench holding a few books next to a Little Free Library and sheltering the Charter number #16961, the URL, and the customary "Take a Book Return a Book" note, the structure itself is just as obviously atypical of Little Free Libraries created from the kinds of kits offered at the organization website.

Perhaps the most striking trait of this Little Free Library's design is the little scalloped front of its roof displaying the unique red-lettered admonition: "KEEP CALM and READ ON." The exterior of the tall, narrow unfinished wood box is crowned by a gable roof consisting of tidy rough-hewn shingles. Despite its narrow dimensions, the extremity of this Little Free Library's height allows for four shelves to house an unparalleled offering. The top two shelves, upon my last stop, housed several items of non-perishable foodstuffs and a random assemblage of useful household items. The rest of the box accommodated a small literature collection, including a couple of John Grisham thrillers and Tracy Kidder's Pulitzer Prize winner, *Home Town*.

The next section of Little Free Libraries in Pacific Grove is located clear across town in an area that borders on New Monterey. To navigate to that part of town, you will need to retrace your steps along Evergreen Road to Dennett Street and turn right to travel southward to Sinex Avenue. Turning left and proceeding about a mile westward along Sinex brings you to Forest Avenue where a surprise awaits you. After you cross to the eastern side of Forest and start southward up the hill, you will find yourself at the campus of Pacific Grove Middle School which houses the only Little Free Library in town that resides on a public property rather than on the border of a private home.

FIRST, THIRD, AND FOURTH ADDITIONS TOWARD NEW MONTEREY

835 FOREST AVENUE

This Little Free Library is another that is easy for casual visitors to miss, since it sits under a shady tree next to one wall of Pacific Grove Middle School, a perfect location for easy access by students as well as passersby. While it boasts a Charter number #14925 on its typical white Little Free Library online organization's sign that includes its URL, the usual "Take a Book Return a Book" note, as well as images of a park bench holding a small stack of books next to a Little Free Library, the structure itself does not appear to have been constructed from a kit such as those available at the Little Free Library online organization's website.

The designers of this Little Free Library expressed their artistic flair by incorporating a light gray, mullioned and wave-shaped window and dark blue trim to represent the water and waves so characteristic of the ocean that surrounds the town. The unusually large box is topped with a blue-bordered, asphalt-tiled roof sitting at a rather nonchalant angle, and brandishes ample double doors to its interior that, upon my last visit, contained a large collection of young adult literature as well as a few classics, including: *Roll of Thunder, Hear My Cry* by Mildred Taylor, a few volumes from a series about famous Americans, *Old Yeller*, a Kahlil Gibran book for children, and *Tales from Shakespeare* by Charles and Mary Lamb.

The next section of our Little Free Library tour of Pacific Grove requires traveling eastward from Forest Avenue, starting at a point downhill and northward from Pacific Grove Middle School and, after a distance equivalent to about two blocks, turning right onto Gibson Avenue.

Gibson Avenue, one of the long east-west streets in Pacific Grove that run parallel to Lighthouse, Pine, and Sinex Avenues, boasts two Little Free Libraries a few blocks from its intersection with Eardley Avenue. While these two libraries are a bit out-of-the-way, they are definitely worth the trip, in part because they sit only a few blocks from one another along the same graceful, quiet avenue.

430 GIBSON AVENUE

The charming Little Free Library at 430 on the north side of Gibson Avenue bears several traits of a homemade box rather than one constructed from a kit such as those offered through the Little Free Library online organization website. For example, the box is unusually shallow and its window/door to the interior is smaller than most. Its more typical features include a steeply-pitched asphalt shingled roof and the Little Free Library sign that provides the Charter number #21098, the URL, the typical top note "Take a Book Return a Book," as well as images of a park bench shaded by a leafy tree and offering a small stack of books next to a Little Free Library.

This Little Free Library clearly exhibits the owner's taste and interest in personal expression. The light blue exterior and pale lavender door color scheme of this tiny library matches that of the owner's home with its light blue walls, a lavender door and gate to the back yard, and lavender and blue planter pots on a very nicely maintained lot. The owner further embellished its charm by wallpapering the interior of the box in a pattern that complements the color scheme of the exterior and the home.

On my last visit to this Little Free Library I found a nice collection of literature on two full-width shelves inside the box: Don Clinton's *Giving*, *Mortals* by Norman Rush, *Intuitive Art: Its Traditions and Styles*, *Bridges of Madison County*, *The Bean Trees* by Barbara Kingsolver, some Kellerman mysteries, and a few romance novels.

◉ ◉ ◉

The other Gibson Avenue Little Library appears on the same side of the street, just a few blocks to the east. So, continue eastward...

330 GIBSON AVENUE

The Little Free Library at 330 Gibson Avenue, bearing Charter number #5572 and located just a block and a half from Eardley Avenue, which marks the transition from Pacific Grove to New Monterey, is a simple, unvarnished wooden box topped by a gently-pitched, copper pipe-constructed hip roof and displays several unique features that speak to the owners' personal bent and loving care of the library.

The builder of this box finished the exterior with a board-and-batten style that corresponds with that of its host house and is considered a classic Pacific Grove finish. While a typical Little Free Library online organization sign conveying its URL, the "Take a Book Return a Book" note, and the Little Free Library label with an image of a wooden bench with a Little Free Library next to it hangs from the bottom of the box, the builder gave the sign a redwood stain to correspond with the rough wooden flavor of the whole structure. Another unique feature of the sign is the all-caps note at the top: "CELEBRATING HEALTHIER NEIGHBORHOODS."

The inside of this Little Free Library offers only one shelf, the bottom of the box, but at the time of my last visit, contained an interesting collection of literature, including *Angela's Ashes* by Frank McCourt, Annie Proulx's *Postcards*, a big hardback Harry Potter book, and a thin spiral-bound volume entitled *Introspective: Contemporary Art by Brazilians of African Descent*.

On one visit to this lovely Little Free Library on a perfect spring afternoon, I encountered two excited dogs outside the open door of 330 Gibson Avenue from which soon emerged a charming woman who introduced herself as Karen Shepherd, the owner, along with her husband, Andrew, of the book box that sits in front of their home. In response to only slight probing, Karen freely agreed to share with me the history of their Little Free Library.

The first step toward the birth of the Little Free Library at 330 Gibson Avenue emerged from an article several years ago about such structures in a special edition of the Sunday paper that immediately inspired Karen to have one of her own. After noticing a few book boxes around town for a few years and knowing that her street is "full of walkers," Karen determined that a Little Free Library would be a perfect addition to her home. So, she registered her idea with the Little Free Library online organization's website, obtained a charter number and a few years later, the construction of the box became a reality. As he worked on the library, Andrew's creativity flourished and he applied his plumbing expertise to good use for the creation of the unparalleled copper roofing that adds such a distinctive flair to the small edifice.

As for the contents of the box, Karen found that the stock of literature seemed to dwindle after a while. She attributed this phenomenon to a probable lack of understanding about how a Little Free Library works, resulting in visitors simply taking books away but never returning any or filling the thus empty space with another offering. To amend this situation, she added a simple explanation to the front window of the box, "LITTLE FREE LIBRARY—TAKE A BOOK —RETURN A BOOK—DONATE A BOOK," which, she was happy to report, succeeded in keeping the book supply at a reasonable level.

◉ ◉ ◉

After your visit at the Shepherd home, to reach the next Little Free Library on our tour, retrace your steps westward along Gibson Avenue, turn right northward onto 9th Street and proceed about three-and-a-half blocks to discover 511 9th Street.

511 9TH STREET

This Little Free Library, on one of the quiet, narrow numbered streets in what is called the Third Addition of Pacific Grove, distinguishes itself from its modest environment by its somewhat formal, tailored presentation. Its heavily painted tones of dark forest green and light terracotta trim match the color scheme of the home that offers it, while the structure of the very wide, shallow box, clearly not derived from a kit offered by the Little Free Library online organization's website, exhibits an original design with a broad asphalt-shingled open gable roof and two small individually windowed doors to the interior. The Library does, however, display the usual white sign from the website with its "Take a Book Return a Book" exhortation, the URL, an image of a park bench next to a Little Free Library, and Charter membership number #23432.

Opening one of the doors reveals a single row of books along the unfinished wooden floor of the structure offering, at my last visit, such literary treasures as a James Patterson, a couple of Harlan Coben thrillers, one a *New York Times* best seller, a Tom Clancy, and a few children's books.

For our next Little Free Library tour destination, we proceed about three blocks northward along 9th Street (the last longer than the first two) to meet Spruce Avenue. After we turn right and continue approximately four blocks eastward along Spruce (again, the last longer than the first few) we will reach 4th Street, at the corner of which you will find our next stop.

261 SPRUCE AVENUE

This Little Free Library is so small and unadorned that, on first glance from its rear, I mistook it for a postal mailbox at the corner of 4th Street. On closer inspection, however, I determined that this library faces the same direction as the home on whose lot it sits, number 261 Spruce Avenue.

This Little Free Library appears to have been constructed from one of the kits found at the Little Free Library online organization website, and also boasts membership with the Little Free Library Charter as evidenced by its Charter number #23682 on the familiar white sign that also bears the URL, an image of a park bench next to a Little Free Library, and the usual "Take a Book Return a Book" reminder. The subdued color scheme of the exterior of this Little Free Library of very pale gray and bright, blue-bordered front door window blends well with that of the home of the library's owner. Otherwise, the box is completely bare of adornments of any kind. The simple shed roof is covered with plain, unvarnished wooden shingles, adding to the overall impression of an unpretentious, almost Quaker-ish, presentation of the whole.

Inside this Little Free Library, a variety of books were stored in two layers on the floor of the box at the time of my last visit, including several children's books and a large number of paperbacks for adults, such as: *The Magic Carousel* by Dorothy Levenson, *The Practical Princess* by Jay Williams, *The Principal's New Clothes* by Stephanie Calmenson, a very old, well-used tome entitled *An Anthology of Greek Drama* edited by Robinson and published in 1959, and *Die Broke, a Radical Four-Part Financial Plan* by Steven M. Pollan.

For the next stop on this part of our Little Free Library tour, walk eastward on Spruce Avenue until you reach 2nd Street. Turn left and walk about a block-and-a-half to reach number 402 on the corner lot that accommodates a large American Foursquare home, one of those that I call "grand houses" because I think of them as of early vintage in Pacific Grove, although this one sits in what is labeled "Fourth Addition" on the Pacific Grove Neighborhood Planning Map.

402 2nd STREET

833 MAPLE STREET

At 402 2nd Street you will find a rather spacious Little Free Library with white exterior and a beautifully stained, wooden-shingled, open gable roof. Bearing the number #30985, one of the more elaborate Charter signs admonishes us that "We all do better when we all read better," displays the usual URL, images of a park bench under a tree with a Little Free Library next to it, and the frequently encountered instructions: "Take a Book Return a Book." As an additional assistance to the new Little Free Library visitor perhaps, the owner has displayed in the window of its entrance door a paper sign, found at only a handful of libraries in Pacific Grove, that explains how the library works.

Pretty little pewter mermaids serve as door handles that open to a rather surprising interior of this box containing a shelf-and-a-half instead of the more common one- or two-shelf arrangement. One shelf goes halfway across the left half of the center of the box, while the shelf across the bottom is full-width, of course. In contrast to the rather formal exterior appearance of the box, the second half-shelf consists of unfinished chunks of wood, a one-inch thick plank across and a 2X4 piece to support its halfway end.

On the day of my last visit to this Little Free Library, I found a few children's books grouped in two places within the box, such as the Golden Book, *Baby Farm Animals*, and a copy of *Where the Wild Things Are* by Maurice Sendak standing on the half-shelf, and some taller children's books standing on the bottom shelf and leaning against the end of the upper half-shelf. The other half of the bottom shelf of this library displayed Scott Turow's *Limitations,* an Oprah recommendation, and *Middlesex*, a big seller and Pulitzer Prize-winner by Jeffrey Eugenides.

The last stop on this segment of our Little Free Library tour requires returning to Sinex Avenue by following 2nd Street's rather circuitous route southward, proceeding eastward along Sinex, crossing Forest Avenue, and locating its intersection with Cedar Street. After you turn left southward onto Cedar Street, you follow its gentle uphill curve to its junction with Maple Street. Turning onto Maple Street will take you the equivalent of about two blocks to find a very large and colorful Little Free Library in front of a tall hedge that shields the home at 833 Maple Street.

There are many indications that the Little Free Library at 833 Maple Street is an independent undertaking: It bears no Charter number or sign representing the Little Free Library online organization. It is not called a Little Free Library, but is labeled instead simply "FREE LIBRARY." The overall construction looks tidily homemade and bears little resemblance to the kits offered at the Little Free Library online organization's website.

The library box itself is very large and boasts a lightheartedly striking color combination of Pepto-Bismol pink doors framed with spring green. The spring green lettering on the Pepto-Bismol pink sign that sits below the box is bordered in purple and braided blue. Perhaps the most intriguing feature of this free library is that the interior is lighted with a string of clear lights powered by a solar device that is mounted on the western edge of the dark, asphalt-shingled shed roof.

The three interior shelves of this Little Free Library, whose neighborhood is full of walkers most days, were quite full of alluring literature upon my last visit, including: *Prodigal Summer* by Barbara Kingsolver, *Night Over Water* by Ken Follett, a Danielle Steel, *Love and Louis XIV, The Women and Life of the Sun King* by Antonio Fraser, *Cold Mountain* by Charles Frazier, *Lives of the Poets* by E.L. Doctorow, and *The Witness* by Sandra Brown.

◉ ◉ ◉

The next section of our tour introduces Little Free Libraries that are scattered across two areas of Pacific Grove where streets do not follow traditional right-angled intersections and require rather ambitious hiking or driving. Whether by foot, automobile, or bicycle, you can proceed eastward along Maple Street to its intersection with Cedar Street at which point you need to turn right and follow its curving roadway to its termination at Sunset Drive. After turning left onto Sunset Drive, travel up the hill along the northern side of the street to find a solitary Little Free Library across the street from the parking lot for Pacific Grove High School.

SUNSET DRIVE AND FOREST HILL AREAS

706 SUNSET DRIVE

It is easy to miss the Little Free Library at 706 Sunset Drive due to its unique location: not only is it fairly distant from other Little Free Libraries around town, but it is also positioned in a unique way. Like the Little Free Library at 231 Lobos Street, the owner of this library clearly welcomes visitors not only to its Library but also into its yard that is protected by a chest-high, orangey-salmon concrete wall.

The color scheme of the exterior of this Little Free Library, with its shiny red painted wooden gable roof, cheerfully harmonizes with the more subdued rosy tones adorning the home behind it. Atop this bright library sits the usual white sign from the Little Free Library online organization that displays the typical note "Take a Book Return a Book," the URL of the website, and an image of a park bench offering a small stack of books next to a Little Free Library. On the uphill side of this library is yet another white Little Free Library online organization sign from an apparently earlier vintage and bearing the exhortation, "A Literacy Friendly Neighborhood," followed by "We all do better when we all read better," and the website URL in all capitals beside an image of a Little Free Library next to a park bench shaded by a leafy tree.

At my last sojourn there, books arranged inside this small box in two layers on a single shelf that consists of the bottom of the box included: a couple of Dean Koontz thrillers, *Angels and Demons* by Dan Brown, a Beverly Cleary, some children's books, *Three Cups of Tea: One Man's Mission to Promote Peace, One School at a Time* by Greg Mortenson and David Oliver Relin, a Phillip Roth, and one entitled *How To Raise a Healthy Child*.

I found it so refreshing to encounter the last Little Free Libraries of our tour located fairly far from the main part of town and therefore the beneficiary of less foot traffic than the many located closer to each other. I can assure you, however, that each of these Little Free Libraries is rewarding in its own way and well worth your effort in visiting them.

To reach the Forest Hill area where the last three Little Free Libraries of our tour reside, continue westward along Sunset Drive until you turn right onto Forest Avenue. Less than a block southward along Forest Avenue, you will turn right again onto David Avenue. When David intersects with Patterson Lane, turn left and continue until its junction with Benito Court. On the very corner of Benito Court sits our next stop.

999 BENITO COURT

The modest Little Free Library located at 999 Benito Court, while not giving the appearance of construction from a kit such as those offered at the Little Free Library online organization's website, does bear evidence of membership in the Charter by presenting, on its right side, the typical white sign that reminds visitors to "Take a Book Return a Book" and presents the URL of the Little Free Library online organization, an image of a park bench offering a few books and standing next to a Little Free Library, and the Charter number #18467.

The tall, shallow exterior of this tidy Little Free Library box is handmade of plywood and other bits of lumber, the sides of which are painted a rich grassy green that blends well with the forest environment of the home beside which it stands, and sheltered by a steep open gable roof that is finished with hardy asphalt tile shingles. An unvarnished wooden door with a large, wide window to reveal the literary offerings inside graces the entrance to the interior of the library.

The only shelf inside this Little Free Library consists of the bottom of the box that is painted bright spring green, complementary to the darker green exterior, and displays a rather jumbled double layer of mostly paperback books with the bottom layer standing upright, while the top layer and several stacks in front of the standing books sit on their sides. Upon my last visit to this Little Free Library, this motley assortment offered an impressive collection of literature, including: a couple of J.R.R. Tolkiens, *The Naked Ape*, a couple of kids' Hardy Boys books, a bunch of C.S. Lewis books, *The Dreams of Women* by Lucy Goodison about interpreting women's dreams, *Tess of the D'Urbervilles* by Thomas Hardy, some Dean Koontz thrillers, *Bridge Across Forever* by Richard Bach, and *Sula* by Toni Morrison.

After visiting 999 Benito Court, continue roughly south-westward along Patterson Lane until it ends and intersects with Funston Avenue. Turn right onto Funston and continue the equivalent of several blocks to reach 1207 Funston Avenue, the next and penultimate stop of our Little Free Library tour.

1207 FUNSTON AVENUE

Although the Little Free Library at 1207 Funston Avenue bears the usual white sign with its reminder to "Take a Book Return a Book," its images above the Charter number #30879 of a park bench shaded by a leafy tree and offering a small stack of books next to a Little Free Library, and indicating the Little Free Library online organization's URL, it also displays two somewhat unique reminders: "We all do better when we all read better" and "Support Your Non Profit."

This Little Free Library is probably the cutest I've ever seen. The structure of the library itself is clearly made with a lot of help and fun from children and not from a kit such as those available through the Little Free Library online organization's website. Because the box sits directly on the ground instead of at adult eye-view, the visitor's eye is drawn to the flat, wide roof of the box, lovingly decorated with shells, sea glass, and other scraps of detritus, and to four large stones that level the structure in front of the beautiful home. The exterior of the box is constructed with used or left-over unvarnished wooden materials, both sides of which are embellished with children's hand drawings, while a small, two-door entrance portrays rather formal-looking wooden pillars bearing a white, hand-painted and much less formal inducement: "PLEASE READ."

The interior of this Little Free Library offers a rather deep space with one shelf that, due to its very short vertical space, displays two layers of books, one at the front, one at the rear. At the time of my last visit to 1207 Funston Avenue, some large children's books were piled atop the two layers of other books and included *The Coroner's Lunch* by Colin Cotterill, *Warriors* by Ted Bell, and *The Painter from Shanghai* by Jennifer Cody Epstein.

To reach the final stop on our Little Free Libraries of Pacific Grove tour, continue a few blocks along Funston Avenue until you reach its intersection with Montecito Avenue. After turning right onto Montecito, continue roughly north-westward for about three blocks to find the junction of Montecito and Miles Avenue. After you turn left onto Miles, you will reach number 1327 to see the last, and in several ways, the most intriguing of all the Little Free Libraries in town.

1327 MILES AVENUE

Not only does the Little Free Library at 1327 Miles Avenue bear the distinction of being the last to appear on our tour, it is also the only two-story Little Free Library in town, consisting of two separate library boxes, separated by a three-dimensional pillar of red brick that resembles a residence-topping chimney stack and resides next to an inviting park bench perfect for browsing through the literature in the library. Not one, but two white signs from the Little Free Library online organization adorn the two floors and indicate membership of the structure as Charter #32372 and display other individualized reminders at each level. The structure of the whole is clearly not assembled from a kit such as those offered at the Little Free Library online organization's website, but is fashioned instead from an assortment of materials creatively drawn from a variety of sources and displaying various indications of a child's artistic expression.

The top story of this Little Free Library is crowned with a crude, rippled open gable roof that shelters a white sign bearing the reminder that "We all do better when we all read better" as well as the usual "Take a Book Return a Book" note, the URL of the Little Free Library online organization, along with images of a tree-shaded park bench offering a few books next to a Little Free Library and a small suggestion to "Support Your Non Profit." The exterior of the box is composed of unvarnished but nicely stained wood in Pacific Grove's board-and-batten siding style and presents a large, single-paned window view of the interior.

Opening the door of the second floor box surprises the visitor with a whimsical interior decoration consisting of strips of print fabric pasted to the frame of the window and boasts one very deep shelf containing two layers of literature that offered, at my last visit, the following: *Life of Pi* by Yann Martel, *The American Heiress* by Daisy Goodwin, *The Birth of Venus* by Sarah Dunant, *Revenge of a Middle-Aged Woman* by Elizabeth Buchan, *The Girl Who Kicked the Hornet's Nest* by Stieg Larsson, *The Merchant of Venice* by Shakespeare, *Of Love and Shadows* by Isabel Allende, and one Tony Hillerman mystery.

The lower story of this Little Free Library bears a second white sign from the Little Free Library online organization that displays a note seen at only one other Little Free Library in Pacific Grove: "A Literacy Friendly Neighborhood," but otherwise presents the more commonly found note that "We all do better when we all read better," as well as the Little Free Library online organization's URL and the images also seen on the sign at the second floor.

This level of the Little Free Library sits atop two large, crude cinderblocks but otherwise presents the charming appearance of a small piece of furniture, a shallow cupboard perhaps, offering a very wide, but less than one-inch-deep drawer below two doors that give the appearance of gazing through windows of a library case by exhibiting beautiful oil-style paintings of a shelf of ancient hardback books as well as an open volume and a few sheets of letter paper anchored by an old inkwell.

The interior of the bottom story offers a very small, shallow shelf that, upon my last visit, displayed mostly children's or young adults' literature, including: *Monsters on the Move*, *The Biggest and Baddest Trucks*, a souvenir yearbook of *Monster Jam*, a Guinness World Record book for 2001, *Treasure Island* by Robert Louis Stevenson, and *The Count of Monte Cristo* by Alexandre Dumas.

CONGRATULATIONS, Readers! You have completed the grand tour of the Little Free Libraries of Pacific Grove. It is my earnest hope that you have enjoyed our excursion through America's Last Hometown as much as I have delighted in sharing with you the plethora of literary treasures offered here.

—*Phyllis Edwards*
2017

SECTION 12
ACKNOWLEDGMENTS

ACKNOWLEDGMENTS

Publisher Patricia Hamilton

Many thanks to all residents and visitors who contributed their own and others' personal stories, and to the many who helped me to organize, type, edit, publicize and otherwise get the job done. Special thanks to the McCoy family for their continued support, and to Lois Standley, my friend who opened her "Irving B&B" for relaxing Wednesday gourmet dinners and a movie. I needed that!

I would not have set this project in motion were it not for Keith Larson, and versatile artist who most generously offered to do the delightful illustrations. We worked well together. Thank you, Keith.

To continue your own writing efforts, I've included my Worksheet for the Hero/ine's Journey Memoir Class—used with much success to inspire some of our stories—may be found on pages 462-463.

Special thanks to local writers and historians who made collecting stories their goal as well: Heidi Feldman, Gary Karnes, William Neish, Jane Roland, Linnet Harlan, Phyllis Edwards, Dorothy Vriend, Jane Foley, Dixie Layne, Russell Sunshine and Nancy Swing, Robin Aeschlimen, Rebecca Riddell, Alex Hulanicki, Joyce Day Meuse, and to Marge Ann Jameson for our "Keeper of Our Culture" column in her *Cedar Street Times*, our local newspaper. And the inveterate Margie McCurry who has lots of good contacts, ideas and energy. Those who donated their professional services are listed separately and I recommend their services to you.

My rewards for doing this book arrive almost daily in the stories participants relate about how the book has enriched their lives by bringing their families closer and by learning things about themselves, their children and the town that they did not know. Enough to fill a book!

Profits from sales will be used for the procurement and preservation of historical documents, artifacts and memorabilia, to benefit the Pacific Grove Library. We all made this possible. Well done, everyone!

Illustrator Keith Larson

One of the blessings that I get to experience on these pages is being able to thank and acknowledge some of those I've met along the forest path over time who, through their kindness and interest, helped me to a place in life where I could also give something back to them and to the larger community through my work in this book.

Publisher Patricia Hamilton, for encouraging us to write and having the vision to see the value in gathering our stories into this collected work of unfolding possibility. Also for her dedication and generosity that leaves the community of Pacific Grove with the gift of greater connection we now have with each other through the sharing of our stories.

My parents Ed and Margaret Larson—thank you for choosing to raise your family in Pacific Grove, making it possible for each of us to form a love of nature through the surrounding beauty of this area.

My brothers—Ned Larson for his goodness and adventurous spirit, and Eric Larson and sister in-law Heidi for their generosity to me.

The Bohrmans, Ken and Cheryl, Chris and Lore, Dave and Terry and Jeanie Harer De Tomaso. Also others in our dedicated family line who keep the family history records of our heritage in this area dating back to 1914.

My loving son Wesley, always a good boy, and his dear wife Kristen, for their support and encouragement. Mattias and Kaia, my two special grandchildren, who are monarch butterflies in the making.

Karen Lindvall-Larson, for always loving her family and for being a wonderful grandmother, and my longtime friends, Jim, Pam, Olivia, and Carolyn Cain. Thank you for having always treated me like family.

Denise Turley, for the loving care she gave my mother.

My friend Dr. Rick Plant, who kept us healthy all those years.

Dan Shafer—thank you for those cosmic conversations we had; I will miss your loving spirit.

Brother Anilananda, for all your prayers and encouragement and for helping me learn to drive a farm tractor so long ago.

Ellen Speert, who has encouraged my creativity for over 20 years and has helped me to follow my art wherever it leads

Nancy Johnson, for those first lessons in drawing and painting that continue to be the foundation for a continually unfolding art experience.

Mrs. Phillips, my second grade teacher—thank you for those afternoons when you brought the clay out for us kids, and we made things and talked with each other at Forest Grove School; the feelings of those times are priceless.

Gerry and Harris Monosoff, my first forest guides down the trail of self-awareness and possibility.

Mike and April Dangerfield, who laugh at my cartoons and share their generous spirits to all who cross their path.

Laurie Burke, who will need a lot of flashlight batteries to finish this book.

I would also like to thank the spiritual communities of Self-Realization Fellowship, Quest Haven, Unity Church of Monterey Bay and Manjushri Dharma Center for their spiritual support in my life.

Thank you to all those who made contributions in this book in some way helping to break down isolation and separateness through the sharing of experiences close to our hearts—deciding to participate in something experimental and fun in spite of doubts and fears.

Thank you all again, blessings on your way.

Phyllis Edwards
writer, editor, educator, singer, and actor

Phyllis Edwards contributed the walking tour of our Little Free Libraries. Phyllis holds degrees from Boston University (M.Ed.) and Wheaton College (B.A.). Serving as a teacher, a school principal, and a district curriculum director in the Monterey and Santa Cruz county school districts and teaching teachers in the Chapman University teacher credential program occupied more than 30 years of her professional life. She wrote and edited textbooks for National Geographic Learning for another ten years. Singing and acting has filled her "leisure time" with the Carmel Bach Festival Chorus for 12 years, Cantori di Carmel and VOCI a cappella ensemble for more than 25 years, as well as performances in stage shows at the Carmel Forest Theater and Monterey Peninsula College Theater.

ABOUT OUR PROFESSIONAL TEAM

Joyce Krieg
writer and editor

Like fabled TV anchorman Ron Burgundy, Joyce Krieg is "kind of a big deal."

In her fantasy life, she has been best friends with Laura Ingalls and Jo March, an Olympic figure skater, a secret agent, a Pulitzer Prize-winning investigative reporter, a contestant on the *Jeopardy!* Tournament of Champions, a rock star's girlfriend, a perfect size seven, and a best-selling author.

In her real life, Joyce is the president of California Writers Club, a 501-c-3 nonprofit with nearly 2,000 members in 22 branches ranging from Mendocino to Orange County. P.G.'s own Central Coast Writers is a branch of California Writers Club.

Joyce's career included stints as a print and broadcast journalist in the Sacramento area, where she was part of the management team that discovered Rush Limbaugh and launched his career. She calls that her "greatest claim to fame and shame." During her years in newspapers and broadcast news, Joyce gained two skills that have played a crucial role in whatever success she has been able to achieve in later life: the ability to produce readable prose on short order and on deadline, and a keen eye for catching misspellings, typos, and grammatical errors.

Relocating to Pacific Grove in 1994, Joyce turned to one of her fantasies—becoming a published author—and immersed herself in a self-taught crash course on writing a novel that other people might actually want to read. Through countless conferences, workshops, and "how to write" books, Joyce got pretty good at analyzing fiction and narrative nonfiction, identifying the elements that make a story "work," that keeps readers up all night to finish a book—and eager to read the author's next release. Her industriousness finally paid off when her mystery novel, *Murder Off Mike,* won the St. Martin's Press "Best First Traditional Mystery" contest, leading to a three-book contract with a major New York publishing house, as well as an invitation to teach a course on mystery writing through the UC-Santa Cruz Extension.

Today, Joyce combines all of these elements in her background in the services she offers through Park Place Publications. Whether you need someone to read your first draft and offer suggestions for shoring up weak spots, filling plot holes, and fleshing out characters, or if you simply require a final set of proofreader's eyes before going to press, Joyce can help.

Life in Pacific Grove

Joyce provided a final edit for many of the stories that appear in this volume. Because the stories are so individual and unique, she was careful not to make major changes, instead seeking to preserve the author's voice. She thus confined her editing to spelling errors, typos, and errors in fact. She says, "What really struck me after reading these stories is how much everyone really and truly loves Pacific Grove. It helped me to see the town through fresh eyes and to appreciate it all over again."

These days, she continues dip into her fantasy world from time-to-time, even though her "bucket list" contains just one item—becoming a best-selling author—well, maybe also fitting into that perfect size seven ☐

Joyce may be reached through Park Place Publications, or through her website, joycek.com.

Mimi Sheridan
historian

Mimi Sheridan is a newcomer to P.G., and has found her work on this book an excellent introduction to the workings of the town. Mimi, originally from California, moved to Seattle after graduating from the University of California, Santa Barbara. She worked in community involvement and, for many years, as an architectural historian. Eventually, Seattle (home of Amazon, among others) just seemed too crowded (and cold and wet). It took a long time to decide where to move to, but she finally settled on the Monterey area for its deep history, beautiful oceanfront location and mild weather. She's now settled in P.G. and eager to learn more about the area.

Nina Solomita
playwright, editor and writing coach

It has been a pleasure to work on this book and to read stories from people who have lived in and love Pacific Grove. Together they form a beautiful tapestry woven from memories, reminiscences, and tales of hope, love, good times, and hard times.

Life in Pacific Grove is a gift for those who love this beautiful coastal town, those who want to learn about it, and future generations who will discover its colorful characters and unique attributes.

Writing a memoir—the story only you can tell—is a unique gift for future generations. You never know the impact your story can have on others. By writing your memoir, you may encourage your children to write theirs or to create something unique—a poem, a play, a talk, a novel.

As a writing coach and editor for over 25 years I have assisted numerous authors at all stages of their projects to bring their individual stories to fruition. Each project is unique as are the individual needs of each client. I tailor my assistance to those needs.

If you are at the beginning of a project, I can offer guidance and suggestions. If you've written some of your story but are at a standstill, I can assist you in recommitting to the work and creating with you a plan and timeline for its completion. If you don't want to write your story, but simply want to tell it and have someone else write it, we can record your experiences, and I can then maintain your voice while transforming your words into prose. I also offer all editing services and suggestions for ways to publish your work.

Typically, my process begins by asking a client to think of whom they are writing the memoir for and what messages they want to pass on to their readers. Some people are interested in reviewing and recording the important events of their lives; others are inspired to share the lessons they've learned from life or want to focus on a specific time, incident, adventure, or person.

I work to stimulate the imagination, encourage exploration and expression, and discourage the harsh voice of the inner critic. To get your creative and memory gears going, I suggest collecting objects that have played a significant part in your life—cards, letters, journals, books, awards, important documents, and photographs—to see what stories they evoke. One of my clients found that an old Bible with her mother's name in it prompted a flood of memories.

Another helpful technique is to review the major news and cultural events that have occurred in your lifetime, recall where you were at the time, and reflect on the impact the event had on your life. Many of my clients are from the "Greatest Generation," with vivid memories of World War II and remember exactly where they were when they heard the news about Pearl Harbor. Everybody of a certain age remembers the ice man bringing a block of ice to the house.

For some, just one printed copy is all they desire. Others choose to publish their memoir to be presented to family and friends, or offered for sale in bookstores and online.

Nina Solomita has an M.F.A. degree in writing. In addition to assisting nonfiction and fiction writers on their projects, she has developed and taught numerous courses on creative writing as well as formal courses about writers and their work in many venues, including OLLI programs at Berkeley University, Dominican University and CSUEB. For more information, please go to ninasolomita.com.

Diane Tyrrel
editor

Diane Tyrrel is a multi-published novelist and editor of over thirty books of fiction, non-fiction, and memoir. As well as editing and ghostwriting projects for private clients, she has written suspense novels for Berkley (Penguin Group) and romantic fantasy with Avon/HarperCollins.

Writing & Editing Services

Tailored to the individual needs of the project, whether it's concept or copyediting, developmental editing or producing a complete book-length manuscript, Diane's specialties include: popular fiction, memoir and autobiography, spirituality, and holistic living.

Diane's clients are fiction authors, educational and business leaders, Olympic champions, physicians, law enforcement, clergy, artists, filmmakers, and more. Each author has fulfilled a dream of writing a book; some have sold to major publishers, received prestigious awards, and achieved bestseller status.

Experienced in a variety of literary styles, POVs, and genres, from edgy political thrillers and sweeping historical novels to books on parenting, business, and dating, Diane combines technical skill with an intuitive understanding of the creative process.

"As an editor and ghostwriter, I approach each project as creative collaboration, one that is ultimately designed to bring out my client's unique style, voice, and message. My aim is to enhance what's best and most compelling about your book, while helping shape it to meet the highest professional standards that agents, editors, and readers are looking for."

Prices are based upon level of service desired and word count of manuscript.

A partial list of genres and topics of books ghostwritten and edited by Diane Tyrrel: suspense fiction, historical drama, horror, mystery, romance, young adult, LGBT, fantasy, sci-fi, crime fiction. Non-fiction titles in business, self-help, social media, true crime, the arts, new age, biography, memoir, and popular psychology.

Contact Diane Tyrrel by email at dtyrrel@sbcglobal.net and by phone or text at (831) 239-8337.

Evelyn Helminin
Internet services

I'm sure many of you can relate: I was supposed to meet someone at an address on Lighthouse Ave. I biked like crazy to make it there on time, flying down the bike path and apologizing over my shoulder to the tourists whose peaceful strolls I was interrupting. I arrived in Pacific Grove, completely out of breath, but with one minute to spare. I looked at the building numbers and was dumbfounded to find that the address I needed was an empty lot. I called the party I was to meet and learned that they were located at that address on Lighthouse Avenue in Pacific Grove, not where I was in Monterey.

Small details are everything.

I'm usually more careful than that. My parents own a print shop in Michigan, and I grew up working for them. One of my jobs was to proofread brochures before they went to press. I needed to catch any mistakes before hundreds or thousands were printed, to prevent a massive waste of paper, ink, and time.

After college, my work transitioned to websites, where I learned that one tiny pixel could throw off an entire website design. I now have significant experience in graphic design, website design, writing, blogging, and online marketing.

My Contribution to *Life in Pacific Grove*

I designed the website, lifeinpacificgrove.com, which was used to solicit contributions to the book, as well as keep everyone informed about the book progress. I also set up and designed the e-newsletter that shared sneak previews and kept everyone up to date about what was happening next with the project.

My name is Evelyn Helminen. I grew up in a tiny town in Michigan with my fourteen brothers and sisters. That's right, I'm the third oldest of fifteen kids—not something you hear too much about anymore. Perhaps to escape the din, I became a voracious reader and escaped to the worlds inside the pages.

That's one reason I was so excited to help work on this book project. How many worlds do we get to experience through the stories that everyone has contributed? Hundreds, all between these pages. What a fascinating look into Life in Pacific Grove.

Another reason I enjoyed being a part of this process was because this book helps describe what makes PG different from any other place in the world. I have tried my entire life to differentiate myself from my 14 siblings. I had to join the Peace Corps, move to California, pierce my ears, and learn to play the mandolin in order to separate myself from the crowd.

I passionately believe everyone is unique. It is my goal to help authors, artists, and small businesses share their unique message with the world and differentiate themselves online.

You may know how you're different, but might not know how to express it to others. It may be especially confusing when you throw technology into it. It's not easy to make sure all the right things get done when you don't have enough time or background knowledge.

Would you love a completely personalized website with custom graphics that doesn't look like anyone else's? How about a weekly or monthly blogging strategy that helps you share your personal message on a regular basis? Or maybe to send a custom e-newsletter to your audience to remind them of the value that only you can offer?

I am here to help. I can either teach you how to do it yourself, or do it all for you. I know I can help you differentiate yourself as you build your professional online presence. Send me an email at evelynhelminen@gmail.com, or fill out the special contact form, just for readers of *Life in Pacific Grove*, on my website at evelynhelminen.com/lipg for a free consultation.

It's Content + Design

By Dixie Layne

I read an article some years ago that said if you know what you want to do when you grow up, that is your favored destiny, your life's passion. As a child and into my teens, there were three things I enjoyed more than all others; writing, reading, and listening to my grandmother's stories.

On any number of occasions I was told I was a good writer but never thought much about how that translated into anything at all beyond expanding my already too active imagination, not anything practical anyway. I loved to read as so many young people do. My reading list was filled with historical fiction and biographies – from stories of European ruling classes of centuries past and America's own colorful, fast paced history to biographies of Charles II to Thomas Jefferson. And I loved Nancy Drew, a smart, imaginative young woman who could figure anything out, solve any mystery. Then there was my paternal Grandmother – the only one of my grandparents I met. She would tell me her stories – how she traveled from Texas to Tennessee in a covered wagon; how she met the Senator (she always referred to her long deceased husband as the Senator or Mr. Layne) and how he courted her, and stories of our ancestors … her family and the Senators. I could listen to her for hours.

It was only after spending a decades' long career in banking – product development and management, and segment management, and then taking a detour into architectural design that by happenstance did I find my interest in writing and history rekindled. I was recruited to join the Feast of Lanterns board, and my first project was to research and write a small book on the story of the Feast of Lanterns for its centennial celebration. This project reawakened my passion for writing and brought to my attention two mediums that brought these stories to life – photography and graphic design.

While working on the Feast of Lanterns stories I became acquainted with Pat Hathaway and his extraordinary collection of photos, as well as his talent as a photographer. Hathaway has an enormous collection of historical California photographs and was able to share with me the stories behind the images. He has also documented history in the making during his lifetime, using his own photographic skills. His photographs are a beautiful companion to my stories. His vintage photos are also available to the public – visit his website for a preview and a walk back in-time.

Over the past decade and a half, I have been writing for newspapers, magazines, individuals, and organizations.

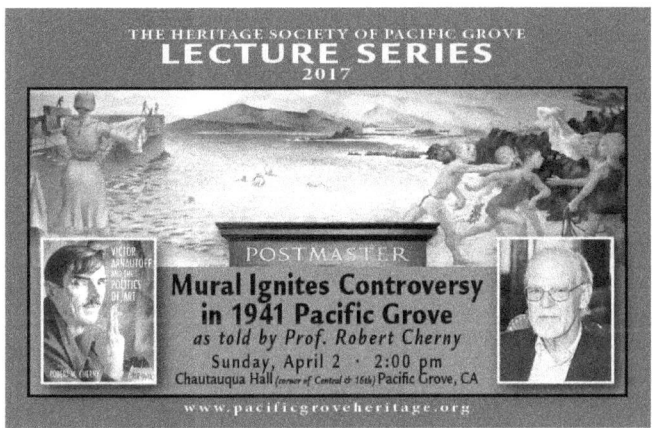

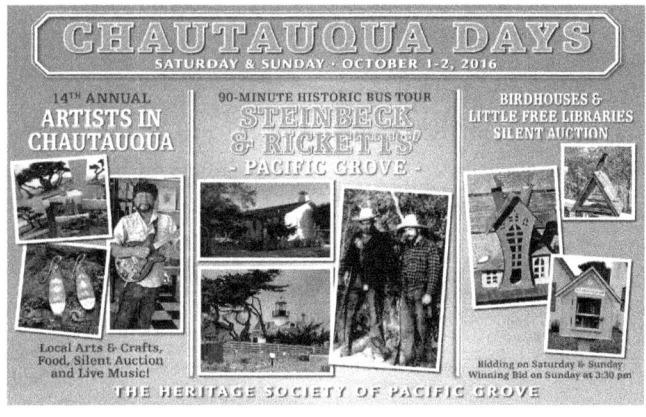

After working with a graphic designer who dressed up my Feast of Lanterns stories in a beautifully, appropriately designed book, I realized that even with books, packaging makes a difference.

As I engaged in writing stories for various publications, I met a graphic designer that possessed a very wide range of graphic design skills. Like myself, she didn't start out in her working-life in her chosen profession … it was by happenstance that she came to be a designer. It was a lesson in, "when life throws you a curve ball, catch it".

Sarah Davis was introduced to graphic design and layout when she "worked" on her high school newspaper and yearbook, which is where she found out she had a natural ability for it. While still in high school she took some night classes at Hartnell with her sisters for kicks – her career goal was to become a police officer; this design stuff was just for fun. Then life threw her that curve ball, and her dream to become a police officer evaporated, and so she continued at Hartnell taking classes in design and photography. One thing led to another and she started working in a print shop where she built a solid foundation on what it took to get from things to work in print. Then over the next many years she worked at a variety of different newspapers honing a wide range of skills and it wasn't long before she started taking on some freelance work.

Davis was working at one of our local newspapers when I met her, and with her formal training and the wide breath of experience she had built quite a portfolio, from branding to communications and the list goes on. Her talents meshed well with mine.

Teaming up with Davis over this past decade has been a good thing. We have worked together on so many projects to build organizations' brands and communications strategies, create and organize events, and tell stories. We are particularly proud of the work we have done that tells the story of Pacific Grove. That is what it is all about for me. To tells stories of our history. I love history. I love the stories history can tell. I love the lessons it can teach. And I love my hometown – Pacific Grove.

THE HERO/INE'S JOURNEY WORKSHEET page 1

"LIFE IN PACIFIC GROVE"—Session 5—You are Your Own Hero(ine) pg 1

Patricia Hamilton, Park Place Publications, presenter and co-sponsor, with the Pacific Grove Public Library.

Stories have power—to enchant, to inspire, to entertain, to define our lives, to bring us together. And the most powerful stories of all are the ones we tell about our own lives and share with others.

Each short story you tell about your life has a before, a during, and an afterward. Today we will work through the steps you take when meeting an unexpected challenge—that make you a hero! Before, you are who you are, doing what you do. A conflict within this ordinary life occurs and propels you into a troublesome period. ***By facing a variety of challenges and overcoming obstacles you come out victorious and, in the end, share insights and rewards with others.***

Using the stages of *The Hero's Journey*, let's deconstruct and reframe one such story today.

The 7 Stages of the Every Hero's Journey Through Life

PART 1—DESCRIBE A DIFFICULT CHALLENGE THAT YOU FACED SUCCESSFULLY

_____

_____

PART 2

1. ORDINARY WORLD

This is who you are before your present challenge began, oblivious of the adventures to come - your safe place. Your true nature, capabilities and outlook on life. **DESCRIBE WHO YOU WERE BEFORE THE CHALLENGE:**

_____

_____

_____

_____

2. CHALLENGE ARISES: YOUR CALL TO ADVENTURE OR ACTION

Then you receive a call to action, perhaps a threat to your family, your way of life, or to the peace of the community where you live. It may be a dramatic call, such as being fired, or a phone call or conversation that ultimately disrupts your comfort zone to present a challenge. *LIST WHO, WHAT, WHERE, AND WHEN:*

_____

_____

_____

_____

3. INITIAL REACTION AND RISING TO THE OCCASION

Although you may be eager to solve your problem, you may have fears that need overcoming. Doubts about whether or not you are up to the challenge. You may remain for a time in your comfort zone. At this point, you have some insight, meet someone, or learn something that gives you the confidence, dispels your doubts and fears, and propels you into committing to take action. *LIST YOUR DOUBTS AND FEARS, AND WHAT HAPPENED TO PROPEL YOU TO TAKE ACTION:* _____

_____

_____

_____

The Hero's Journey was first published in "The Hero With a Thousand Faces," by Joseph Campbell, who lived in P.G. and was John Steinbeck's friend.

THE HERO/INE'S JOURNEY WORKSHEET page 2

4. CHALLENGES

Now you investigate and begin to experience all aspects of your challenge: facts you need to know; skills you may need to, if not master, have a working knowledge of; understand the people involved, helpers or opponents, are on your way to conquering your challenge. Tension can build, and major obstacles may bring up old doubts. *DESCRIBE HOW YOU APPROACHED AND GATHERED WHAT YOU NEEDED TO SUCCEED:*

___

5. TURNING POINTS

At one point you reach the defining moment, the high point of your journey and your story. It may be facing your greatest fear or foe. Perhaps only an "aha!" moment or an epiphany will give you the greater power and insight to draw upon all your skills and experiences to set your world right—or fail. *DESCRIBE THE "HIGH POINT" MOMENT WHEN YOU KNEW IF YOU PERSEVERED YOU WOULD WIN:*

___

6. REWARD AND RELIEF

After overcoming your challenge, you enter a new state of awareness, emerging as a stronger person, perhaps with a prize. It may be an object of great importance or power, a secret, greater knowledge or insight, or even reconciliation with a loved one or ally. *DESCRIBE YOUR FEELINGS WHEN THE CHALLENGE WAS MET. WHAT WAS IT THAT YOU LEARNED ABOUT YOURSELF AND YOUR ABILITIES TO OVERCOME IT?*

___

7. RETURNING TO "NORMAL LIFE"

This is the final stage of YOU, the Hero(ine)'s Journey in which you return to your Ordinary World a changed person. You have grown as a person, learned things, faced many challenges and look forward to the start of a new life. You may bring fresh hope to family and friends, a direct solution to their problems—or perhaps a new perspective for everyone to consider. Your final reward may be a cause for celebration, self-realization or an end to strife, but whatever it is it represents three things: change, success and proof of your journey. Ultimately you, the Hero(ine) will return to where you started but things will clearly never be the same again. *WRITE DOWN THINGS THAT HAPPENED IN YOUR NEW "ORDINARY WORLD." DESCRIBE HOW YOUR LIFE CHANGED:*

___

What is one thing you learned about yourself through this writing exercise?

___

Use your Worksheet notes as an outline for a more detailed story of your journey: show don't tell; how feelings change over time; add dialogue—and humor if you can. *This worksheet may be used with all genres.*

NAME INDEX TO PROFILES AND PERSONAL STORIES

Abplanalp, Virginia 164, 179, 353
Adamson, Erik 58
Aeschliman, Greg 367
Aiello, Danny and Lorelei Layne 401
Albano, Tony 73
Ammar, Moe 57
Amos, Herschel R. 328
Andreas, Maryln 344
Andy and Karen 380
Annand, Nadine 21
Anton, Jean 22
Apodaca, Kathy 188
Arlson, Sue 53
Armstrong, Dawn 169, 177, 184, 354
Austin, Jan 154
Avila, Judy 81
Azevedo, Elayne 189
Baldwin, Margaret 109
Barat, Michele 329
Barlow, Margaret 327
Beacon House 329
Beals, Janet Case 380
Beck, Marilyn 394
Bedwell, Barry and Kim 92
Bell, Clarissa 209
Bennett, Lori 52
Bennett, Nancy 333
Beren, Donnolo 232
Beritha from Sweden 248
Berna from Turkey 251
Bertha from Peru and Japan 249
Berwick, Edward 42
Biersteker, Kathleen 106
Biery, Bud 78
Bilich, Susan 213
Blume, Harriet 96

Bohrman, Chris 148, 347
Bohrman, Dan 202
Bohrman, Janet 202
Bohrman, Ken 146
Bokde, Alex 298
Boone, Marabee 365
Bowhay, Phil 167
Bredthauer, Vanessa 283
Bridges, John 296
Bridges, L. 381
Brown, Karen 104
Brown, Kimberly A. 103, 376
Brussell, Barbara 208
Bryan, Dennis R. 171
Bryan, Lana 229
Bui-Burton, Kim Ly 111
Butterfly Children and Butterfly Dog 120
Butterfly Cottage Botanicals 295
Butterfly House 402
Byrne, Jeanne and Ray 149
Cain, Annette 377
Cain, Pamela 348
Campbell, R. Wright 8
Campbell, Suzanne 200
Carlson, Nell Flattery 216
Carns, Victoria 353
Carroll, Lois 273, 371
Cartier, Francis 97
Castro, Otavio Serino from Brazil 249
Cavallini, Ed 67
Cedar Street Times 287
Central Coast Silkscreen 306
Centrella Inn 304
Chatham, Richard A. 307
Chatwell, Christine 211
Cheng, Chungte 20
Chie from Japan 245

Chisholm, Daniel 330
Chodosh, Len 306
Chrislock, Pamela Furman 160
Chungwei Shen from Taiwan 250
Coburn, Sam 206
Coelho, Danielle 302
Coleman, Juanita 291
Corby, Yolanda Zena 153
Corona-LoMomaco, Elian 201
Corona, Ella Magsalay 150
Coscino, Lisa 394
Costello, Jim 359
Courtney, John 151
Cowan, Bruce 391
Crispin, Bob 9, 138, 341
Cruz, Mando 302
Cuen-Ashby, Kathy 187
Cumberland, Danielle 217
Cuneo, Ken 65, 328
Dainton, Mary 418
Danielle's Hair Design 302
Dausch, Elaine 360
David, Tim and Marie 152
Davis, Patricia A. 9
Deane, B.J. 303
DeMers, Kathy and Anthony 199
Dennis, Diana 366, 392
DePietro, Cristiana 345
Derowski, Bill 296
Devol, Shirley and Sharon 96
Doerr, Ann 15
Domedy, David 302
Downey, Robert J. 153
Dreamcasters Voyage 292
Dyke, Elmarie Hurlbert Hyler 37
Dyson, Lindsay 382
Edeen, Laura 372, 382
Edgington, Duane 105
Edgington, Lane 290

NAME INDEX TO PROFILES AND PERSONAL STORIES

Edward Jones 299
Edwards, Phyllis xvii, 219, 456
Eleuteria from Mexico 247
Elisabeth, Irene Evers 201, 399
Emiko from Japan 246
Englander, Alice 98, 175
Englander, Bill 100
Estrada, Rudolph 378
Evans, Garth 361
Faddis, Jessica 421
Fandango 303
Feldman, Heidi 71, 105, 308, 325, 333
Fields, Sarah Kramer 385
Fischer, Joy Ann 76
Fischer, Rudy and Kathleen 64
Fish, Emily 35, 413
Fisher, Bob 51
Fisher, Elizabeth 42
Flanagan, Patrick 223
Flanagan, Rose 338
Flury, Jane 9, 87
Foley, Jane 124, 271
Foley, JD 206
Fontecchio, Isabella Reese 200
Forest Hill Barber Shop 284
Forinash, Jintanan 55
Forno, Karen 75
Four Local Boys 190
Fowler, Dorothy 37
Fox, Betty 339
Franke, Kit 321
Freud, Margot 80
Gale, Jane Elizabeth (Cloyd) 10
Gale, Sylvanus Gale 10
Galina from Russia 250
Gamble, Richard W. 170
Garcia, Carmelita 36
Gasperson, Don 359
Gasperson, Jayne 34
Gates, Cindy 367, 386
Gehringer, Helen 167, 288, 348
Gehringer, Millie 21
Gervase, Jerry 404
Gina Juntaradarapun from Thailand 249
Gitee from Iran 249
Gonzales, Jose 307
Gottlieb, Emily 420
Gough, Nina 178
Gould, Jeanie 191
Grand Avenue Flooring 292
Grannis, Nina 58
Griffith, Madeleine 29
Griffiths, David 45
Griffiths, Lillian 61, 411
Grindol, Diane 403
Griswold, Charles Dr. 10
Griswold, Charlotte Cloyd (Gale) 10
Grossman, King 407
Grove Nutrition 291
Guerrero, Diana L. 77
Gumerlock, Robert 392
Guthrie, Cynthia 74
Haines, Jane 309
Hambrooks Auction 291
Hamill, Laura 384
Hamilton, Charline Edith (Murray) 11
Hamilton, Claude Fisher 11
Hamilton, Patricia 10, 21, 103, 104, 117, 225, 289, 346, 455
Hanks, Tom 315
Hansen, Peggy 301
Harer De Tomaso, Jeanie 203
Harlan, Linnet C. 89, 272, 312, 377
Harmon, Ann 313
Hatcher, Germain 199
Hauk, Nancy 33
Hauk, Steve 27, 197, 212
Hauswirth, Sheri Stillwell 156
Courtney, John 151
Headley, Laura Courtney 151
Heinzen, Barbara 398
Helminen, Evelyn 219, 459
Hermann, Elaine 282
Herzog, Brad 198
Higgins, Sally 21
Higuera, Charlie 283
Holland, Denise 295
Holland, Nancy 305
Hollander, Simone 183
Holman, W. R. 173
Holman, Zena G. 35, 176
Howe, Wendy Salisbury 150
Hubanks, Nathan 205
Hubanks, Ryan 205
Hubley, Georgia A. 53
Huckelbery, Marlene Perfecto 221
Huitt, Jan Roehl and Robert 219
Iulanicki, Alex 14, 91, 155
Hummel, Virginia 20
Huston, Ned 231
Hutchinson, Jody 292
Hyler, Joanie 137
Iman, Sandra Thompson 62, 107
Iverson, Dick and Becky 17
J and Sonja 402
J M 204
Jacobs, Linda A. 16
Jacobs, Nancy 227
Jacobson, Joe 61
Jameson, Marge Ann 38, 287
Jameson, Neil 286

NAME INDEX TO PROFILES AND PERSONAL STORIES

Jealous, Ann 342
Jeong, Jae Woon (James) 250
Jila Amiri from Iran 249
Johnson, Kip 201
Johnson, Linda Iversen 194
Johnson, Victor 331
Jones, Berta 21
Jones, Jacquelin La Vine 152, 177, 271, 309
Jorgensen, Jean Hurlbert, 162, 183, 343
Joyce, Susie 326, 379, 383, 391
Juliet from Korea 247
Kahan, Evelyn 385
Kampe, Mayor Bill vii
Kane, Steve 215
Karaki, Bill and Sue 293
Karnes, Gary 120
Karunasiri, Indika 269
Kenoyer, Kevin 292
Krattli, Kay 349
Kessler, Inge 116, 343
Khenpo Karten Rinpoche 325
Kihs, Jeanette 66, 415
King, Nate 421
Kooyman, Melba and Jerry 405
Krasa, Kyle A. 149
Krasa, Peter 110
Kraus, Barbara 244
Krieg, Joyce 222, 346, 457
Krokower, Michael 292
Krupski, Amy 192
Kyung from Korea 246
La Fleur, Elaine R. 230
Langford, Peggy 269
Larson, Keith 16, 86, 102, 111, 122, 144, 181, 207, 214, 220, 277, 395, 402, 455
Lauderdale, Carol Bradley 360

Laws, David A. 12
Lawson, Andrea 419
Layne, Dixie 24, 140, 355, 362
Lazare, Heather 176
Lehmann, Hans 54
Lesch-Gonzalez, Kelly 161
Liberty Tax Service 293
Lien Pham from Vietnam 252
Lighthouse Cinemas 307
Lin from Thailand 246
Lisa from Belgium 246
Livermore, Donald 110, 366
Lojkovic, Antoinette 126
Loudon, Barbara 382
Lubeck, Gayle 43
Maha from Syria 245
Maliszewski, Judy 14
Maliszewski, Stan 14
Mando's Mexican American 302
Manjushri Dharma Center 325
Marino, Jeanne 62, 89
Marquart, Carol 90
Marshall, Barry 109
Martin, Marlene 238
Maryam from Iran 245
Masonic Lodge 328
Maturanga, Carol Anne 151
Matuz, Kate 283
Mayorga, Allison Haylings 142, 362
Maysoun from Jordan 251
McCarthy, Carol 376
McClung, Ruth 33
McCoy, Grace Erin 11, 115
McCoy, Jack Ross 11
McCoy, Melanie Marie (Sawyer) 11
McCoy, Zachary Andrew 11, 53
McCurry, Margie 294

McDonald, Katy 171
McGuire, Bob 329
McHugh, Margaret 72
McKinney, Tom 299
McNeil, Jean Justice 95
Megumi from Japan 246
Mehaffy, Irene 384
Melville, Peter 298
Merrick, Tessa 201
Meuse, Joyce Day 54, 192, 214, 303, 327, 386
Meyer, Bill 54
Miller, Michael Kane 212
Miller, Paul 300
Miller, Willem 201
Minor, Ajax 281
Minor, William 204
Mona from Iran 252
Monahan, Patti 405
Monning, Senator Bill xii
Montanez, Summer 58
Mrs. "Z" 82
Moody, Barbara 306
Moon, Sandra 82
Morris, Frank 289
Morrison, Bobbie 274
Morse, S.F.B 20
Mothershead, Donald 406
Motorcycle Museum 286
Mountrey, Barbara 93
Ms. Trawick's
Muender, Lindley 191
Mullany, Jim 80
Mums Place 285
Munoz, Jacob 310
Munsie, Steve and Mary 399
Murray, Alice Elizabeth (Griswold) 11
Murray, Harry Johnson 11

NAME INDEX TO PROFILES AND PERSONAL STORIES

Musaab Kamil from Iraq 248
Myers, David 66
Myles, Alana 233
Natalie from China 253
Neal, Tammy 305
Neish, Mary Joanna 178
Neish, William 83, 269, 413
Nemeth, Shelley 263
Neutra, Richard 95
Newton, Constance 118
Nielsen, Brad 200
Obbink, Bruce 408
Obbink, Judy 283
Ochsner, Ronald 274
Oehrle, Richard T. 299
Olin, Jeanne 88
Osborne, Charles 20
Oser, Jonathan 218
Owens, Emily 294
Ozuna, Gary 328
P.G. Hardware 296
P.G. Juice N' Java
Pacific Grove Travel 288
Pagnella, Linda 178
Park Place Publications 289
Parks, Michael 314
Parks-McKay, Jane 45, 46
Parrish, Judy 345
Parrott, Wanda Sue 235
Patel, Amrish 304
Paul's Mortuary 45, 302
Payne, Kathryn Voeykoff 314
Peake, Bill 64
Pearlstein, Connie 212
Pearse, John 374
Pearse, Vicki 375
Peick, Susan 291
Penley, George 388
Perez, Lenore 393

Petersen, Marion 28
Phillips, Mrs. 16
Phillips, Tracy Lee 314
Pierce, Frank D. 68
Pietrantoni, Michele 284
Platt, Julia 39
Porras, Ralph Dr. 66
Powell, Betty 94, 96
Powell, David C. 97
Priscilla from Korea 245
Pruitt, Sarah E. 232
Puccinelli, Gina Lynn 310
Purwin, Patricia 78
Randall, Sharon 143
Rasch, David PhD. 235
Redstone, Charlotte 309
Reid, Michael 322
Reincarnation Vintage Clothing 305
Reinstedt, Randall A. 3, 8
Reynolds, Fred 284
Ricketts, Edward "Doc" 30
Ricketts, Nancy 30
Riddell, Rebecca 190, 292, 300, 400
Roberts, Mary 339
Robins, Dick 198
Robins, Stefanna Murphy 340
Rockefeller, Lois 79
Roland, Howard 311
Roland, Jane 17, 19, 45, 120, 125, 179, 197, 315, 331, 406
Roland, John 84
Rolander, Tom 350
Rondo, Dante 210
Rosa from Venezuela 247
Rotary International 331-2
Rouse, J. R. Realtor 294
Sanders, John 52

Sawyer, Larry Dean 11
Schmidt, J.L. 379
Seikert, Al 329
Selby, Vic 352
Shammas, Joe 288, 332, 406
Sheridan, Mimi 457
Shield, Blanca 56, 115
Shoemaker, Jonathan 237, 350, 409
Shropshire, Helen 34
Shuler, Barbara Rose 60
Silveria, Steven 276
Sinsar, Paul 281
Sirocky, Sally 102, 344
Skidmore, Gail 125
Slate, Denise Mellinger 160
Smith, Charlene and Desiree 293
Smith, Jennifer Lee 373
Smith, Susan Carol 295
Smith, Vanessa 238
Solomita, Nina 457
St. Mary's Church 311
Stallings, Jean 324
Stampher, Alexandra 364
Stampher, Sydney 364
Standley, Lois 403
State Farm Insurance 299
Stebbins, Ginny 335
Steele, Susan 124
Steinbeck, Beth 28
Steinbeck, Carol Henning 25, 36
Steinbeck, Elaine 26
Steinbeck, Gwendolyn 26
Steinbeck, John 24
Steinbeck, Thomas 26
Stewart, LeeAnn 112
Stillwell, Richard 107, 296, 352, 381, 405

NAME INDEX TO PROFILES AND PERSONAL STORIES

Stock, Stephanie 417
Stone, Virginia 19
Stong, Nick 418
Storey, Beth 95
Stormon, Suzanne 224
Strang, Joe 334
Sullivan, Kathleen 387
Sunshine, Russell 101, 228, 396
Swainson, Chris 313
Swing, Nancy 227
Taste Restaurant 293
Tavares, Andrea and Felipe 290
Taylor, Brenda 303, 310, 348, 380, 390
Thayer, Janet 242
The Bridge Restoration Ministry 330
The Martine Inn 305
The White Hart 297
Theoni, Estrella 417
Thompson, Alyce 85
Thompson, Illia 233
Tides on Forest Avenue 303
Tillie Gort's Café 303
Tintle, Rosemary 403
Torres, Clara 103, 104
Tubman, Michele DeVaughn 141
Tucker, Sharon 229, 393
Turley, Denise 116
Turley, Jim and Kathy 297
Tussuti Zoo 294
Tyrrel, Diane 218, 458
Vaughn, Diana Dennett 151
Vecchione, Patrice 200
Veronica from Brazil 247
Villela, Maria & Kids 108
Viray, Roxane 301
Viva 316
Verwold, Walter "Wally" 104
Vriend, Dorothy 210, 239
Wall, William 117
Waltz, Mary Martha 420
Waterhouse, Lavinia 42
Watson, Patricia 230
Weber, Sarah 18
Webster, Gloria Newell 361
Wheeler, Marilyn (Marly) 306
Whitehurst, Patrick 419
Whitman, Neal 372
Whitmore, Jeffrey 59
Wilcox, Martha 122
Williams, Gary R. 159
Wills, Judy 86
Wylly, Phillips 13
Yeni from Mexico 245
Yuki from Japan 251
Zurkan, R. M. 193

Trimmer Hill, the first mayor's house

www.ingramcontent.com/pod-product-compliance
Lightning Source LLC
Chambersburg PA
CBHW060501240426
43661CB00006B/874